To Philippa Strum,
   for making this book possible,
and Elizabeth M. Cox,
   for making it better

Contents

A Room at a Time

How Women Entered Party Politics

Jo Freeman

ROWMAN & LITTLEFIELD PUBLISHERS, INC.
Lanham • Boulder • New York • Oxford

ROWMAN & LITTLEFIELD PUBLISHERS, INC.

Published in the United States of America
by Rowman & Littlefield Publishers, Inc.
4720 Boston Way, Lanham, Maryland 20706
www.rowmanlittlefield.com

12 Hid's Copse Road, Cumnor Hill, Oxford OX2 9JJ, England

Copyright © 2000 by Jo Freeman
First paperback edition 2002.

British Library Cataloging in Publication Information Available

The hardback edition of this book was catalogued by the Library of Congress as follows:

Freeman, Jo.
    A room at a time : How women entered party politics / Jo Freeman.
        p. cm.
    Includes bibliographical references and index.
    1. Women in politics—United States—History. 2. Political parties—United States—History. 3. United States—Politics and government—19th century. 4. United States—Politics and government—20th century. I. Title.
HQ1236.5.U6F74   1999
305.42'0973—dc21   99-30542
                                                              CIP

ISBN 0-8476-9804-1 (cloth. : alk. paper)
ISBN 0-8476-9805-X (paper : alk. paper)

Printed in the United States of America

∞ ™ The paper used in this publication meets the minimum requirements of American National Standard for Information Sciences—Permanence of Paper for Printed Library Materials, ANSI/NISO Z39.48-1992.

Preface and Acknowledgments

In the spring of 1986 I began a book on women and American politics for a nonacademic audience. That book died on November 28, 1988; this is its daughter. Writing it has been a voyage of discovery rather than a synthesis of things already known. My original focus was on the years since the mid-sixties, when the feminist movement rewrote the script to give women more opportunities and better roles. But, I thought, there has been so much new historiography since I began my graduate studies in 1968, why don't I write an introductory history chapter? A decade later, that chapter grew into this book.

I started in 1920, mistakenly assuming that women worked first for equal suffrage and then went into politics. As I explored more and more sources—new books, trailblazing articles, microfilmed collections of original papers, manuscript collections, newspaper morgues and the rich six volume History of Woman Suffrage—I learned that women were in politics well before most could vote.

From 1920, I took a journey back in time. A draft of Jackie Braitman's dissertation alerted me to the crucial election of 1916. Melanie Gustafson's and Maureen Flanagan's work taught me the importance of the Progressive era. Reading old newspapers highlighted the election of 1912 and women's work in municipal reform in the 1890s. Rebecca Edwards sent me a disk of her 1995 dissertation on gender and party politics from the 1860s through the 1880s. Her rich detail convinced me to spend more time in the nineteenth century. Whenever I thought I had found a starting point for women's public participation in elections, another scholar identified an earlier origin. I finally gave up looking for the moment of birth.

Delving into history revealed how thoroughly the political roots of feminism are in the Republican Party and its predecessors. The major parties have divided on gender issues since the Republic began, but not the same way. Until 1970 the Republican Party was more supportive than the Democratic Party of women party workers, more successful in organizing and educating women about politics and more likely to promote the feminist position on issues when there was one. It was also the major beneficiary of woman suffrage.

I had known for some time that parties switched sides between 1970 and 1973 and have since gone in opposite directions, but until I wrote this book I did not know the depth of the Republican roots. Since I am a Democrat, as are most of the people I speak to, the idea that our party's feminist leanings are relatively recent is intriguing. When the Republican Party embraced antifeminism in the 1980s, it threw away its heritage. Why the Democratic Party is now the feminist party and the Republican Party is the home of antifeminism will not be answered here; that requires another book.

Although this book emphasizes national politics, that is not where most political activity occurs. Politics is local. Political parties are mostly concerned with state and local elections; committees exist at every level; clubs are organized around local units; workers spend most of their time in their communities. And most public policy, particularly that affecting women more than men, is made by state legislatures. Consequently, the study of women and politics is the study of grassroots political activity.

Women's political history is scattered and buried in many places. The women who did it rarely left records in library archives, and the few that survived are scattered in personal papers. Nor were political parties much concerned with recording their history, and when they did, women's contributions were usually slighted. Researching this book was like panning for gold; brilliant nuggets hidden in lots of mud. Fortunately newspapers, in the days when they were numerous and news was also local, did a decent job of reporting the public aspects of political work. I used newspaper morgues and partial indexes to learn what women did in New York City. None of what I found is mentioned in the standard texts on New York politics and only some of it is in this book. For other cities I relied on the limited secondary sources and some newspapers. I found more on women in Chicago than for any place else.

This book is just an introduction, an invitation to explore the field of women's work in mainstream politics. Only after many local studies have been written will the building blocks exist to construct a solid edifice. Even though I tapped only a sample of the possible sources, I still had twice as much material as I could reasonably expect a publisher to put between the covers of a book. After thirteen years of research and six years of writing it was time to put it out for public view. The fact that gold exists in places I did not get to leaves much for other scholars to mine.

Help in excavation came from friends and colleagues who believe in my work. Their many years of in-kind contributions to my scholarly endeavors I've collectively dubbed the Friends of Jo Freeman (a typical name for campaign committees). In addition to Philippa Strum and Elizabeth M. Cox, charter members include Nancy Henley in Los Angeles and Ruth Shinn and Norma Zane Chaplain in Washington, D.C., who have regularly been my hosts while I visited libraries in their cities, often for several days at a time.

My work with Elizabeth Cox on her bibliography on Women in Modern American Politics revealed hundreds of obscure publications. She told me about forgotten works that she found, informed me of new sources, fed me reams of useful material from her own research at the Library of Congress and trips to Colorado, Texas and other states, and corrected some errors in the book. Her contributions made this a much richer book, as well as more fun to write.

Among the Friends are other hosts and many who have sent me items which I could not get myself, sometimes on request and sometimes on their own. They include those who have read portions of the manuscript, sent me material from files or libraries and drafts of their own work before publication. This book has taken so long that I cannot remember all of my benefactors. But my notes, letters, and imperfect memory disclose at least the following in addition to those mentioned above: Cynthia Harrison, Martin Gruberg, Anna Harvey, Charles Hadley, George Chambers, David Weakliem, Kira Sanbonmatsu, Ruth Mandel, Rob Persons, Mary Hawkesworth, Patricia Kolb, Terri Susan Fine, Susan Ware, Carol Nackenoff, Kristi Andersen, Kristie Miller, Doug McAdam, Maxine Chenault, Diane Monk, Elaine Stocker, Kim Nielsen, Ruth Rosen, Rebecca Edwards, Jacqueline Braitman, the children of Louise Young, Denise Baer, Maureen Flanagan, Melanie Gustafson, Rosemarie Zagarri, Kathleen Frankovic, Heather Booth, Jim Reichley, Genevieve McBride, Beverly Goldberg, Amy Hackett, Stoney McMurray, Edith Mayo, Sherry Warman, Jennifer Knerr, Brenda Hadenfeldt, Lynn Gemmell, Willa Baum, Marshall Levin, Harry Rubenstein, Tom Bourke, and Alice Dowd.

Deserving special mention are Jewell Fenzi and Sandra Bieri of the Women's National Democratic Club, and Lila Prounis and Georgianna Mardirossian of the Women's National Republican Club who provided help, hospitality, and access to material at their clubhouses.

As is true of every scholar, I have many debts to libraries and their seldom-sung heroes, the librarians. The latter are too many to mention. In rough order of the amount of time I spent in the libraries are Brooklyn College, Library of Congress (Manuscript Division and Periodical Division), Columbia University (Oral History and Microfilm Collections), New York Public Library (Research Division), Brooklyn Public Library (Brooklyn Collection and Microfilm Division), District of Columbia Public Library (Washingtoniana Collection), Franklin Delano Roosevelt Presidential Library, New York University (Tamiment), New York State Library, UCLA Special Collections, Huntington Library, Chicago Historical Society, Northwestern University, WNDC Archives, Swarthmore College (Peace Collection), University of California at Berkeley (Bancroft Library), Albany Public Library, Syracuse University, University of Rochester, the National Archives and the Political Collection of the Division of Social History in the Smithsonian Institution, Howard University, Moorland-Springarn Research Center.

To my assessment of party women, their successes, and failures, I bring not only my years of research and judgment as a scholar, but my own extensive political work. I was raised in the Democratic Party and although I left it for twenty years to organize outside of any party, eventually I returned. I've paid my dues as a pretty good precinct captain, a not-so-good party hack (independence is not a virtue in party hacks), and an occasional unsuccessful candidate. I've been a paid staff worker in two Presidential campaigns and an unpaid worker in dozens of state and local races. These experiences exposed me to the different politics of many states and shaped my judgment of what it was possible for women to do. And what was possible must always be the measure of success and failure. Assessing what was done and not done requires an understanding of what could be done in a particular time and place. Such is the nature of politics.

A Note on Nomenclature

In writing history it is always difficult to decide whether to use the terms proper for their day or more contemporary forms, particularly when the words are loaded with ideological meanings. Although some historical forms grate on my ears, I concluded that it was better to use them to maintain consistency with quotes and to convey the flavor of the era. Words such as Great War, reformer, and chairman are at least somewhat neutral. Others are not.

During most of the period I cover, Mrs. Hisname Husband was the proper title for a married woman; Mrs. Ownname Husband for a widow or divorcee, and Miss for the never married. After World War II it became more common to address a married woman as Mrs. Ownname Husband—a pattern I found in reports by Afro-American women well before the war. A few women kept their maiden names when married (Miss Frances Perkins) or used their own variations (Mrs. Florence Kelley). Again, I have followed convention or personal choice, except that I include a woman's given name when I could find it. Too many women have been lost to history or confused with others because they used only their husband's name, and these changed when they changed husbands.

In the interest of verbal efficiency, I include in the term "state" the District of Columbia, Puerto Rico, territories, and other political divisions under U.S. suzerainty that are represented on each party's national committee or can send delegates to their national conventions.

A few other terms readers will encounter have an archaic ring to them. They were in common use in their day, and I felt their retention helped to understand how people thought when their vocabulary was different than it is today.

· *Introduction* ·

Feminists, Reformers, and Party Women

> I have often talked with Mrs. Emily Newell Blair, the very
> able and charming resident member of the Democratic
> National Committee in Washington, about the way men
> dreaded a change in politics when the women came in, and
> yet were disappointed when the change didn't come. . . .
>
> "What the men expected, I suppose," she said to me, "was a
> terrible old-fashioned house-cleaning, in the kind of a rum-
> pus their mothers used to make in the spring just about the
> time the first robin came—carpets up, dust in every room, all
> the family in flight. I clean house with a vacuum cleaner, don't
> you? My husband hardly knows the cleaning's going on. But
> it is. That's the way it seems to me women are breaking into
> politics. A room at a time."
>
> *Florence (Daisy) Harriman, Democratic National*
> *Committeewoman from the District of Columbia, 1923*[1]

MYTH AS HISTORY

Historians as well as men were disappointed when, after gaining universal suffrage, women did not go into politics with sabers drawn and banners flying.
Many lamented the "failure" of feminism to use women's votes to reform the
political system and radically alter public policy.[2] Marjorie Wheeler summarized
the accepted argument of "political analysts and historians":

> despite suffragists' claims that women would transform politics, many failed
> to vote, and those who voted did not vote as a "bloc." As a result, politicians
> quickly lost their new-found respect for women voters, and women were
> relegated to a minor role in party politics. Furthermore, the massive and
> cohesive women's movement, having lost—by winning—the issue that held
> it together, disintegrated, with many former suffragists becoming politically
> apathetic and the few that remained active locked in bitter combat with one

1

another over the Equal Rights Amendment introduced in 1923. Such theories imply that woman suffrage was a failure, or, at best, a great victory that led (ironically) to a decline in women's political activism.[3]

Although feminist historians have long since discredited this interpretation, its longevity exhibits a problem scholars do not always understand: sometimes myth becomes history.

Political history is particularly susceptible to this phenomenon because many of its sources are politicians, and many of its documents were created for political purposes. Part of a politician's job is the creation of myths, colloquially referred to as "smoke and mirrors." Even those who do not create myths out of thin air put their own "spin" on the facts. Politicians create myths about themselves, their ideas, their policies, their achievements, and in particular about anything they don't like. They create myths in order to get other people to do what they want: elect them to office, vote for their proposals, persecute their enemies, ignore their competitors, or defeat their opponents. Once these goals are achieved, or finally defeated, most political myths fade so that few remember exactly why they did what they did.

The "women's voting bloc" was a political myth. No political analyst who paid the slightest attention to the lengthy record of voting women (and men) believed that women would vote as a bloc.[4] By 1920 there was some evidence that some women voted differently than some men some of the time. There was a lot of evidence that most women voted like most men most of the time. Those who expressed fear or hope about what women might do with the vote did so for political reasons, without regard for the facts.

Sometimes myths created for political purposes take on a life of their own. *Political myths can become historical myths.*

The historical myth is not merely a misinterpretation (or a different interpretation) of something that happened in the past. It is the acceptance as fact for which belief is strong and evidence is skimpy. Myths don't just happen. They are created to serve a purpose, usually the legitimation of one's actions or the delegitimation of opponents. When they live on long after they have served (or failed to serve) their original purpose it is because they "fit" people's expectations or values. An axiom of social psychology is that people believe what they want to believe and see what they want to see. Myths survive because their exponents want to believe them. They are repeated ad infinitum until they become part of "common knowledge," accepted and uncontested even by well-trained historians. And when evidence is presented that undermines an ingrained myth, it is ignored.

The "failure of feminism" is a classic historical myth. Before women had even got the "habit of voting," woman suffrage was dismissed as a dud. "Have Women Failed As Citizens?" *Collier's* asked in 1923. "Woman Suffrage Declared a Failure" said the respectable *Literary Digest* in 1924. Other mass magazines such as *Century, Good Housekeeping,* and the *Ladies Home Journal* were quick to assess "Where Women in Politics Fail."[5] Despite many testaments by former suffragists that woman suffrage had achieved what they wanted—made women full citizens with the right to vote as they chose—and frequent lists of bills passed and women elected, the cacophony of negative evaluations continued.[6] And of course this "failure" was attributed to female ineptness and not male resistance, to suffragists and not to politicians or political institutions. After men got over their fear that suffragists might actually organize women voters, they told women that their vote was meaningless because they had not done this. Men said that woman suffrage had "promised almost everything and accomplished almost nothing" when neither of these was true.[7]

The myth that feminism failed after 1920 because feminists did not organize women into a major political force obscured what was really going on. The Nineteenth Amendment which brought universal suffrage was one step in an incremental process whose roots lay deep in the nineteenth century. Multiple social, economic, and political changes were simultaneously expanding women's sphere, expanding the role of government, erasing the demarkation between male and female realms, and redefining politics.[8] Women were part of this process; they contributed to it as well as benefited from it, as did men. One can see these changes and their interconnections best from a distance; up close they blend too much.

Indeed, from an institutional perspective woman suffrage was a rousing success. Vastly expanding the electorate did not disrupt the political system. The few changes to accommodate women—such as reducing rowdyism and moving polling places from saloons to schools—were salutary ones. It was much harder for the political system to digest more men in the nineteenth century than to absorb women voters in the twentieth. Adding more men to the electorate brought increased corruption; adding more women brought increased civility. So easily were women accommodated that the question should be asked, what were the men afraid of? Were they so out of touch with political reality that they really thought voting women would bring about a revolution, or was this just propaganda with which they fooled themselves?

One cannot assume that it was women in politics that men feared, rather than suffrage alone. By 1920, women were already in politics and had been for quite some time. Women got suffrage *after* they proved themselves to be an important political force. Suffrage was a consequence as well as a cause of the movement of women into politics. Indeed the news stories and magazine articles before 1920 make it clear that while woman suffrage was viewed as radical, women in politics was not. However, the women who went into politics were rarely the same as those who campaigned for suffrage. Instead, the movement of women into politics and the movement for woman suffrage were parallel movements. While one body of women demanded the right to vote, another tried to influence the men who could vote. And still a third focused their energies on shaping government polices toward women and issues of special concern to women.

POLITICAL WOMEN

As the twentieth century began, there were three major types of female political activists: feminists, reformers, and party women. For several decades they wove together like a somewhat frazzled braid. Their activities were often intertwined and sometimes indistinguishable. Their relative strengths varied. At times they worked together, and at other times they unraveled. Within each strand there were major fights and generational gulfs. By the 1960s, they largely went their separate ways. Reformers appeared early in the nineteenth century. Feminists—then known as suffragists—soon followed, but were few until the 1890s when their numbers burgeoned. Party women began to appear in numbers worthy of note in the 1880s and 1890s; by 1900 they were becoming a distinct type, at least in some states.[9]

Political women specialized for two reasons. One was that greater numbers made it feasible. Until there was a critical mass of activists in a given community, politically concerned women had to do everything or it didn't get done. The political passions of the 1890s were a magnet for women, who then gravitated to one of the three strands as their primary center of activity. Reformers, suffragists, and party women might share some concerns (or not), but as more women became involved, individual women chose a single arena for action. The second reason was that each strand demanded absolute loyalty. Suffrage leaders told women to work only for suffrage. Party men preached party loyalty to those who would be party women. Reformers had their own priorities, which they put before suffrage or partisanship.

The final drive for the Suffrage Amendment in the second decade of the twentieth century wove these three strands together into a common cause. Reformers came to see suffrage as necessary to achieve their policy goals and party women to chafe at a system that allowed them to work for candidates but not to vote for them. However, this coalition was unstable because the motives and goals of these women were different. The ranks of suffragists were swollen by women whose major interests lay elsewhere. After 1920 they specialized once again.

Soon after the Nineteenth Amendment was ratified, reformers and feminists split into antagonistic camps. Party women were in both camps, and some continued to be active in their post suffrage activities, but most returned to their partisan homes. Some suffragists entered the party ranks who had not been there before, but they were disappointed because it was an alien environment, whose denizens had different motivations and different views of the purpose of politics. While some party men initially welcomed suffragists into the parties, they soon learned that these women could not be controlled and replaced them with women they could count on.

Suffragists didn't tell the new woman voter to organize around a woman's agenda. They told her to go into the political parties. And that is exactly what those with an interest in politics did. It was party women, not feminists or reformers, who undertook the task of mobilizing women to vote. It was party women who had the resources, and the reason, to do this. And it was the ranks of party women who were augmented by the increased interest in politics by women who had not been involved in anything political prior to 1920. While feminist and reform women's organizations struggled to survive, the political parties recruited, organized, absorbed, and co-opted large numbers of politically inclined women.

The parties did this by constructing a special place for women. The national committees of the major parties created women's divisions to educate and mobilize the woman voter, and most state parties did as well. Party leaders appointed women to organize women into separate party clubs and gave them representation on party committees. At the same time they publicly denounced the idea of "sex solidarity" and insisted that party women do the same. Above all, they demanded party loyalty. Although party women echoed the call of the men that women should not join together to work for the interests of women, within their own parties party women thought women were a distinct group and used their identity as women to stake out their turf. On the one hand, party women exclaimed that women should not be elected or appointed to positions *as women*. Women were citizens, and a given woman should be favored only if she was the most qualified candidate available. "Better men, but only the best women" was what they asked. On the other hand, party women frequently insisted that women were needed in politics because they saw things differently than men and because the woman voter would favor the party that favored women. They acknowledged that women were "shackled by sex" while insisting that they be treated as individuals.[10]

While the feminist strand survived after 1920, it did not thrive. The generation which led the Suffrage Movement to victory shifted their interests to other arenas or retired to their private lives. Although they urged women to go into the political parties, few of them did so themselves. Of the 128 women identified as suffragists in *Notable American Women,* only ten were or became party activists, and only three others were elected to office.[11] Some of the younger generation of suffragists, who had only become active during the peak years of the second decade, hoisted the banner of feminism and looked for new battles, finally choosing passage of another constitutional amendment, the Equal Rights Amendment (ERA), as their primary goal. But the idea that women should work together for women was systematically stigmatized by mainstream politicians and by reformers. In this hostile atmosphere its legitimacy was undermined and "feminism" became a dirty word.

The great women's organizations of the reform era also declined. Some died, and some changed their agenda. Few of the women who made their reputations as reformers shifted their energies to the major political parties.[12] The new generation of women reformers largely worked with men in quite different organizations: some for traditional reform goals such as the protection of women in industry, and some for new ones, such as civil liberties and civil rights. Reformers and feminists fought each other for five decades, while both strands weakened. Not until the 1960s would a new generation form new organizations, both feminist and reform, which, unlike their predecessors, would see the world through the same lens and work for many of the same goals.

During these years only party women thrived. Their numbers exploded in the 1920s, but rose and fell in subsequent decades in patterns that varied enormously by region, party, and year. Party women were not radicals and they were not trying to change the world. They weren't even trying to change their parties. What they mostly wanted was inclusion, with equal rewards for equal service. To their repeated requests, party men responded with chivalry and promises. When they threatened revolt, they were clubbed with the demand for party loyalty, or replaced with more compliant women. Some party women were also feminists and a few were also reformers, but most were only party loyalists. Their mission was to get women to vote for their party and its candidates, not for a woman's agenda. Nonetheless, they identified certain causes as women's issues and educated women, as women, to participate more in politics. From their parties they demanded more jobs, responsibilities and appointments for women, using the elusive "women's vote" as the bait to back up their demands.

Party women had their own style of action. Whereas feminists had assaulted the citadel, and reformers had banged on the door, party women infiltrated the basement of politics. But while their actions were incremental and only occasionally attracted notice, their numbers expanded and they helped bring about significant changes in the parties. They also built a base of well-informed women with years of party service who were quick to take advantage of the opportunities created by the new feminist movement that arose in the late 1960s.

On the stage of women's political history all three types of political women played important roles. But they do not all get equal time in this book. Feminists and reformers only get honorable mentions because their work has been covered by others. Party women have been neglected. Here they are on center stage.

POLITICAL PARTIES

Political parties are not mentioned in the U.S. Constitution, and were disparaged by our founding fathers. However, in practice they have proven to be the connective tissue of democratic government, providing the links between citizens and the state, and even between many organized interests. As political scientist Denise Baer noted only a few years ago, political parties are "The Missing Variable in Women and Politics Research."[13] In the nineteenth century, political parties constructed the framework in which politics was, and is, conducted. It was a male preserve. The very places where men congregated for political purposes—the polling place, the barber shop, and the saloon—were closed to women, or at least respectable women. The personal networks through which information flowed and within which decisions were made were male networks. With suffrage, women could enter the polls, but voting was just the foyer to the political house, not the living room where candidates were chosen, nor the dining room where the spoils were divvied up, nor the kitchen where the deals were made. To enter these rooms women had to pass through several doors; the doorkeepers were the major political parties.

This book is the story of how women slowly filtered into some of the main rooms of the political house and took over the basement. By and large they did not do so as a group; instead individuals slipped past the doorkeepers, some widening the opening and encouraging other women to follow, and some not. Nor did they rearrange the furniture they found there. But, one room at a time, women moved into all our political institutions—the legislative bodies, the administrative bodies, the judiciary, and the political parties. The slow pace of infiltration was given a great boost by the new feminist movement that emerged in the 1960s. Yet, if there had not already been many women inside all of our political institutions, this movement would have faced the same closed doors that women discovered in the 1920s. It took the concerted effort of both insiders and outsiders to hoist women's political participation beyond the level of tokenism. This volume stops in the mid-sixties, as the new feminist movement begins. What happened next is another story, requiring another book. This book describes how women slipped inside the political house in the half century between the two waves of women's political activism, and the barriers that women had to overcome in that time to lay the foundation for the accelerated progress of the 1970s and 1980s.

· One ·

Social Movements and Party Systems: Where Do Women Fit?

𝒫olitical history is not a smoothly flowing river; there are periods of great calm punctuated by times of rushing rapids. These changes in topography are not erratic. Their patterns have been studied and dissected by political historians and social scientists. Two of the most important patterns—episodic social movements and periodic party systems—have generated vast bibliographies of literature, but have rarely been looked at together.

It was also rare for scholars to look at women's participation in these patterns of activity, though it is becoming less so. Political historians ignored women's political work because women could not vote for most of our history, and even when they could, were seen as auxiliaries to political life, playing only minor, supporting roles. Social movements scholars usually acknowledged the importance of women's movements, but treated them as phenomena apart from those run by men, sideshows rather than part of the main event. Those who write women's history of course put women up front. But the spotlight is sometimes so narrowly focused that one can't see the theater in which the drama is taking place or understand that the lines spoken by women are usually part of a dialogue with men.

Context is crucial to political history. It is impossible to understand what people say or do in the political arena without knowing the influences upon them and those whom they are trying to influence. Otherwise one runs the risk of seeing the past through the eyes of the present, and distorting both. To understand the history of women's entry into political parties, one must first look at the context in which this occurred. This requires an understanding of social movements and party systems.

SOCIAL MOVEMENTS

Social movements come in clusters. There have been periods in our history in which entire regions or sectors of society have been repeatedly convulsed with waves of social movements. One movement stimulates another, which in turn stimulates another ad infinitum. The different movements attack different social problems but are not completely independent from each other because ideas, values, and even people move between them. Social movements also prompt countermovements by people who oppose the changes sought, and these in turn stimulate other movements, some of which are countermovements and some of which are not. A cluster of movements and a cluster of countermovements carry competing social values. Thus one can identify major themes or mindsets typical of a cluster. Movement participants work through the political system and outside of it to change institutions, laws, practices, and above all attitudes to bring them into accord with their values.

Since our country's founding there have been three great clusters of social movements which have transformed institutions and values in a variety of ways, and there was a previous wave which led to our Revolution. Each has lasted roughly twenty to thirty years, though individual movements are usually shorter in duration. The movements within these clusters resound like waves throughout our society. They ripple and rebound. Some are contained; some spread everywhere. Movements and countermovements battle for public support on the values most appropriate for each time and place.

If one were to chart the spread of activity and impact of a given social movement it would resemble the classic bell-shaped curve. An indefinite beginning, a sharp upturn of activity, a peak, followed by a decrease of activity and finally a long decline. These bell-curves are not identical; some are long and low, others short and sharp, and not all are symmetrical. But they are all curves. While it is hard to pinpoint exactly when a cluster or a single movement begins and ends, the periods of peak activity are easy to discern and the take-off and fall-off points aren't hard to see when viewed from an historical distance. The first and third clusters are essentially outside the scope of this book, so they will be only briefly mentioned.

The first social movement cluster after our Revolution was in the 1830s and 1840s. Its main theme was moral reform. Movements to abolish slavery, encourage temperance, oppose sin, and relieve want looked first to individuals to act properly, and then to the state to enforce morality on those who did not do so voluntarily. These movements were heavily motivated by a sense of Christian duty, and often separated the godly and deserving from the ungodly and undeserving.

The second great cluster is known as the Populist/Progressive Movement. It had two crests. Beginning in the 1880s and peaking in the 1890s, producers in Midwestern, Rocky Mountain, and Southern states sought to recapture government for the people and to curb the economic power of corporations. At the same time elites in major cities organized municipal reform movements to purify politics and remove city government from the hands of party bosses. The Populist Movement quickly coalesced into a political party (the People's Party) and elected some men to public office. The municipal reform movement also elected city officials, but emphasized non-partisanship, arguing that cities should be run like a business, without concern for party loyalty. Much more widespread and diffuse than the 1890s movements, the Progressive Movement expanded on their ideas. To the goals of eliminating corruption in politics and using government to curb corporate exploitation were added relief for workers and concern with the problems caused by industrialization and urbanization. Progressivism was strongest and most successful in the Western states, particularly those in which Populism had made inroads, and weakest in the Southern states, even those which had had strong Populist Movements. While the Progressive Movement peaked between 1910 and 1914, its ideas lived on and eventually became staples of the New Deal.

The third great wave of social movements is known as the Sixties, although it began in the 1950s and eddies were still present well into the 1980s. Its themes were greater social and economic equality, preservation and redistribution of resources, and opposition to war.

The backlash begins before a cluster ends. Inevitably, countermovements germinate in response to early movements, and grow as they grow, shifting terrain to meet each new demand. By the time later movements arise in a cluster, the countermovements may be quite strong, providing instant opposition. Women's movements have never been the initial movement in a major cluster. They always come later. Thus they always face significant opposition almost from their inception—opposition that links the demands by women with those of the earlier movements from which they sprang.

In between social movement clusters are more quiescent periods. There is no such thing as a permanent social movement. They always decline, whether they succeed or fail or both, but not always in the same way. Some cease completely. Some institutionalize, becoming part of the mainstream they once challenged and fighting their battles through institutional channels. Some succeed so well that they capture the very institutions they were trying to change. Some encapsulate, creating social movement communities that survive but have little impact outside their own boundaries. Even during lulls there are sporadic new social movements—the political pot is always boiling—but they are isolated, affecting only a small geographic or demographic area. While such movements may see some successes, they don't result in major transformations of how people act or how they see the world. The troughs between clusters are times of consolidation and retrenchment, in which some changes are absorbed into the social fabric and become part of the general consensus, and others are resisted and undermined.

PARTY SYSTEMS

In our two hundred–year history many different political parties have been active in one or more of the United States. But, with only temporary exceptions, there has always been a national two party system, which reflects "a natural division between competing ideological traditions." Political scientist Jim Reichley calls them the party of equality and the party of order. The former, tracing its origins from the anti-federalists and Jeffersonian Democratic-Republicans, favors "economic and social equality," while the latter, stretching from the Federalists, National Republicans, and Whigs to the modern Republicans, prioritizes "public order and economic growth."[1]

These traditions have fostered different political cultures. What I wrote in 1986 about the Democratic and Republican parties of the late twentieth century applies to the nineteenth century versions as well: "Essentially, the Democratic Party is pluralistic and polycentric. It has multiple power centers that compete for membership support in order to make demands on, as well as determine, the leaders. The Republicans have a unitary party in which great deference is paid to the leadership, activists are expected to be 'good soldiers', and competing loyalties are frowned upon." Factions and fights in the Republican Party are usually over ideology. In the Democratic Party they are more likely to be over spoils—the distribution of tangible and intangible rewards. Because of these cultural differences the style of governance, as well as the content of policies, changes with a change in party control.[2]

Party control of Congress or the Presidency, or the ruling bodies in each state, only requires a simple majority. Thus there can be a major shift in power with only a slight shift in voting patterns. Nonetheless, the pattern of party control is normally stable. The periods when there is a durable distribution of partisan power are called party systems. Every few decades, the pattern shifts and a new party system emerges. In the nineteenth century there were three national party systems, and in the twentieth century there have been at least two. Political historians have identified the breaking points between them as roughly: 1828–36, 1856–60, 1894–1900, and 1928–36.

Transitions between national party systems, when voting patterns realign along new axes leading to new majorities, proceed rapidly through a few "critical elections." These critical elections have often been analogized to earthquakes, because the political landscape changes significantly. However, a sharper image is conveyed by comparing what happens to island building. By looking beneath the surface, one can see change come slowly, over many years, just as a land mass grows underneath the sea. Since a change in a few votes is all that is necessary to create a new majority party, at some point power shifts, just as at some time a new island appears above the surface of the ocean. Party systems, like new islands, are only *relatively* stable. Storms wash over these islands, sometimes obliterating the changes in surface topography. But unlike islands, these mid-system storms also have a pattern. In the middle of most party systems there has been a crisis, often accompanied by a shift in voting patterns leading to a different distribution of partisan power for a few years. These are called deviating elections.[3]

The underlying cause of new party systems is alterations in the composition and size of the electorate and the effect this has on the social base of each party. These changes happen gradually—just like the growth of an island. They come from (in order of importance): 1) *differential accretion* to each party's pool of voters, largely from foreign immigration and naturalization, but also from uneven birth rates in different population segments; 2) *internal immigration* of large populations who bring their culture, values, and party preferences with them; 3) *mobilization* of normal nonvoters into the active electorate; 4) *demobilization* from the active electorate of normal voters; 5) *conversion* in party preferences of identifiable population segments, a transition usually aided by temporary support for a third party or not voting; and 6) *generational falloff* as children inherit their party preferences but not with the same commitment or reliability, until a critical election creates new or reinforces old loyalties. Such changes in the voting population are necessary but not sufficient causes of critical elections. Crucial is a crisis of some sort—social, economic, or political—which galvanizes people to vote, or to not vote, or to vote differently than before. Unlike deviating elections, voting patterns do not return to "normal" once the crisis is over. A brief history of the first five party systems will illuminate these processes

The First Party System began with the "revolution of 1800."[4] However, the parties were more like factions among elites than a true *party* system. Participation in the meetings and caucuses that selected candidates was limited to "respectable" men. "Party" meant devotion to special interests in contrast to public spiritedness. By 1820 the Federalists had declined as a national party, leaving Thomas Jefferson's Democratic Republicans as the dominant—sometimes the sole—party outside of New England.[5] In the first three decades the electorate rapidly expanded as the American population almost trebled, western settlement increased the number of states to twenty-four and property qualifications for white male voters were removed in all but six states. These changes created the foundation for the Second Party System.

After the election of Andrew Jackson in 1828, his opponents in Congress allied against him. Calling themselves Whigs, they ran several candidates against his successor, all of which lost, as well as candidates in state and local elections, many of which won. By 1840, the Whigs had elected governors in a majority of the states, and united behind William Henry Harrison to win both the Presidency and the Congress with 80 percent of the electorate casting ballots. There was a viable two party system in all regions for the next sixteen years. During the Second Party System voters were organized into party bodies at all levels. The first national party convention was held in 1831; the first national party chairman was installed in 1844 and the first national committee created in 1848. The parties selected their candidates at conventions, from the bottom up. Conventions were first held on the local level where delegates were selected to successively higher levels at which the party's candidates would be selected.[6]

The Second Party System was shattered by the slavery issue, specifically whether to extend slavery to the Western territories, and the Fugitive Slave Law. Population changes also contributed to a new pattern of sentiments. By 1860 half the voters lived west of the Appalachians; most of these settlers came from New England and the Middle Atlantic. The total population had almost trebled to over thirty-one million people living in thirty-three states and the territories. New immigrants came largely from Catholic countries, especially Ireland, and often replaced native-born Protestant workers in the industrializing Northeast. While only 11 percent of the population, the newcomers were a quarter of the free, white males that composed the actual and potential electorate; in the North they were over a third. This stimulated enormous xenophobia by native-born Americans who experienced loss of jobs and feared loss of political control.[7]

During the 1850s minor parties formed and reformed, some of which were ardently anti-Catholic. The two major parties fractured and reorganized. In 1854, those who could stomach neither slavery nor secession founded the Republican Party. Four-fifths of the new Republicans were former Whigs, but some came from the anti-Catholic and anti-immigrant parties. That year the nativist American (Know-Nothing) party won several seats in Congress and control of the Pennsylvania and Massachusetts governments. When it fell apart, most of its adherents joined the Republican Party. The Republicans ran their first national ticket in 1856 and elected their first president in 1860.[8] Almost 82 percent of the electorate voted, the highest turnout at any election before or since.

The Second Party System collapsed into the Civil War; the Third Party System was built upon the ruins. For the rest of the century party loyalty ran high and turnout for Presidential elections was over 70 percent. On the national level the major issue was the tariff: Republicans favored protection while the Democrats wanted free trade. But underneath, the primary cleavages were region, race, and religion. For a few years after the Civil War blacks were a majority of voters in five Deep South states and the Republican Party ruled. Once former Confederates regained the right to vote, they made the Democratic Party into the Party of White Supremacy, dedicated to disfranchising the freed slaves and eliminating the Republican Party. By the end of the Third Party System the South was solidly Democratic. The rest of the country had a slight Republican majority but it was not evenly spread throughout, so competition could be fierce. In three New England and four Midwest states the Republican Party dominated; in the rest statewide elections were closely contested with wide variations within each state.[9]

The primary cleavage outside the South was religion; Catholics were Democrats, most Protestants were Republicans. Religion usually trumped ethnicity when it did not coincide. Among the Irish, Catholics voted Democratic, Protestants voted Republican. But among the Germans, the Democratic party was favored by both Catholics and Lutherans, though less so among the latter. Local conflicts over schools, "blue" laws, and liquor control usually divided along religious lines. The northern branches of most Protestant denominations that had favored the Democrats before the Civil War became staunchly Republican. The new immigrants were heavily Catholic, and when they could vote, joined their ethnic cohorts in the Democratic Party. Protestant northern Democrats were usually foreign born or the children of foreign born. Blacks, where they could vote, were Republican, as were the few Jews.[10]

At the end of the nineteenth century, in 1896, there was another critical election. By then the frontier had closed, the population was over sixty million in forty-five states, and immigration was escalating after a lull during Reconstruction. Industry needed workers, and millions came, particularly from southern and central Europe, with different traditions and more conservative concepts about women. They flooded the cities, making the urban population two-thirds of the rural one. This critical election was preceded by several years of economic and political turmoil.

In the 1880s, minor parties bubbled up in the rural Rockies and Midwest. Several farmer's alliances, calling themselves the People's Party (Populist), elected candidates to Congress and state legislatures. In 1892 they joined with Southern rebels behind a national ticket and won 9 percent of the Presidential vote, while capturing the state governments of Colorado and Kansas. The economic crash of 1893, when the Democrats controlled the Presidency and both houses of Congress for the first time since the 1850s, led to that party's seizure by proponents of the free coinage of silver. Their program appealed to the Populists. Both parties nominated William Jennings Bryan for President in 1896, resulting in the Populist Party's absorption by the Democrats. Bryan was a fundamentalist Protestant. His agrarian radicalism and "free silver" campaign drove the urban Democratic voters into the arms of the Republican Party or out of the ranks of normal voters altogether. Although Bryan tried to draw a new fault-line between the "monied interests" and the "common people," industrial workers did not identify their economic needs with those of agricultural producers. Even New York City voted Republican for the first time. The votes the Democrats gained in the sparsely populated West were more than offset by the losses in the urban centers of the East and Midwest.[11] With McKinley's election prosperity returned. This may have been coincidental, but it ensured that Democratic electoral gains were temporary, while their losses were permanent. In some areas outside the South the Democratic Party almost ceased to exist.

The Fourth Party System saw growing one-party dominance everywhere and Republican party dominance nationally. Sectionalism flourished, involving "the virtual destruction of the Republicans as an organized political force in the ex-Confederate states and a parallel and almost as complete a destruction of the Democrats throughout large areas of the North and West." States that had been evenly divided and those that had seen occasional Democratic victories became Republican bastions. By 1904 only one-seventh of the population lived in states with real party competition; by 1920 only one-ninth did so. While the Democratic Party survived, in only a few places was there a viable two-party system, and this was usually maintained by ticket splitting. State and local Democratic parties held onto some power by disassociating themselves from a national party infected with "Bryanism." Voter turnout declined. The Presidential vote dropped from 79.3 percent in 1896 to 58.8 percent in 1912, to 48.9 percent in 1924. There was an enormous variation in turnout, by region and election, but there was a consistent pattern of decline reflecting to subtle changes in the electorate.[12]

A major deviating election occurred in 1912 when progressives demanded that the Republican Party replace incumbent President Taft with former President Theodore Roosevelt. After the party refused to do so, its progressive wing held its own convention where it nominated and ran Roosevelt on the Progressive Party ticket. The split elected the first Democrat in twenty years, but with only 41 percent of the popular vote, and a Democratic Congress. Roosevelt came in second with 27 percent; Taft was third with 23 percent. In 1916 the Eastern Progressives reluctantly rejoined the Republican Party. However, Westerners were more independent. Even with a larger overall turnout the Republican candidate got only 46 percent, and the Democrat, 49 percent of the total vote.

The Fourth Party System was marked by urban/rural conflict, as the cities bulged with new immigrants from rural areas and foreign countries. The first decade of the century saw the largest wave of immigration ever known; by 1928 most had become citizens and their children had reached voting age. When Congress restricted immigration in 1921, industry recruited African Americans from the South to replenish the low wage workforce. The consequence of high foreign immigration and high birth rates before the Great War and rapid internal immigration afterwards was that the American population shifted from one living on farms to one living in small towns and large cities. Economic elites were also located in the cities. Rural regions were dominated by native-born stock and the descendants of earlier waves of immigration who worked the land and ran the small towns. Cultural conflicts over Prohibition and woman suffrage coincided with the economic divisions of town and country.

In 1928, these conflicts were personified in the candidacies of Catholic Al Smith, who opposed Prohibition, and Quaker Herbert Hoover, who supported it. The national voting rate increased to 56.9 percent, as city-dwelling ethnics and Southern supporters of Prohibition flocked to the polls. In the industrial Northeast, voter mobilization portended future Democratic victories. But in the South, temporary conversion made 1928 only a deviating election. In 1932 it returned to the Democratic column, even though Roosevelt also opposed Prohibition.

The Fourth Party System ended as it began—with a crash. The 1929 drop in the stock market and the Great Depression caused voters to turn on the ruling Republican Party in 1932 has they had turned on the Democrats almost thirty years before. But voter turnout remained at 56.9 percent. Only in the Western states, especially those with a populist and/or progressive tradition, were large numbers of new voters mobilized. Turnout in the Southern states and industrial Northern states fell or stayed the same. While there weren't enough progressive voters in Western states to elect a Republican Roosevelt in 1912, they could elect a Democratic Roosevelt in 1932, by joining with the "Solid South" and ethnics in the North who had been mobilized by Smith. It was not until 1936, when 61 percent of the voting-age population went to the polls but the Republicans won only Vermont and Maine, that the Fifth Party System was firmly in place.[13]

The dominant cleavage of the Fifth Party System was class. Region, race, and religion did not disappear as important indicia of party preference; class was superimposed on top of them, creating some strange political bedfellows. As expressed by Lubell: "Put crudely, the hatred of bankers among the native American workers had become greater than their hatred of the Pope or even of the Negro." Indeed, once blacks saw that New Deal programs benefited them, they shifted their votes from solidly Republican to mostly Democratic. FDR saw his mandate as the use of federal power to curb the consequences of industrial capitalism—a goal of progressive Republicans twenty years before. The major policy clashes were over federal regulation of business practices, the protection of labor unions and the right to organize, and the creation of and payment for various welfare programs. With Roosevelt's encouragement, labor unions increased their influence every decade and class consciousness "suppressed racial and religious antagonisms."[14]

The shift in voting patterns began nationally and worked its way down. Well into the 1940s and even the 1950s, voters, especially in the Western states where Republicans had solid progressive roots, stayed with that party in state and local elections while voting Democratic for national offices. However, over time the Republican Party became more conservative and the Democratic Party more liberal. The influence of progressive Republicans declined as some jumped ship to the Democrats, many died, and others became more conservative with age. One sign of the shift from the Fourth to the Fifth Party System was that the fight over the growth of the federal government took place between the parties rather than inside each of them, and nationally at least, the Democratic and Republican parties had switched the positions they held in the Third Party System. Outside the South, it was the Republican Party rather than the Democrats that flew the banner of states rights and the Democratic Party that saw progress in the growth of the federal government. Indeed the Democratic party almost split in 1948 over the issue of civil rights, a subject on which it had traditionally deferred to Southern views. A States Rights Party put its candidates on the ballot as the Democratic ticket and won in four Southern states.[15]

By the mid-1960s the Fifth Party System was in decline. But there was no critical election, and no abrupt realignment. The "New Deal Coalition" was clearly disintegrating, but no one knew what would replace it, or how. What ensued were a couple of decades of debate over whether realignment would occur, had occurred, or was even relevant. Some political scientists argued that dealignment was what was happening, and others that there was a rolling realignment. My own reading of the tea leaves is that there was an elite realignment, beginning in Congress, seeping into the national conventions of the Republican and Democratic parties, and slowly working its way into state legislatures, party activists, and the habits of voters. It began in 1958 when progressive Republicans in Congress were replaced by liberal Democrats and accelerated in 1964 with a Democratic landslide that defeated many progressive, and some conservative, Republican office holders. By the late 1960s and early 1970s, grassroots party activists were reforming the Democratic party. As liberals captured the Democratic Party, the conservatives within it, especially Southern conservatives, gradually left. They joined the Republican Party, adding to the conservatives' strength and eventually driving out the few remaining progressives.[16]

By the 1990s it was clear that the distribution of partisan power was quite different from what it had been in the 1950s, but this realignment had not happened in the usual one or two elections and had substantial regional variations. Indeed, the most obvious realignment was in the South, which had resisted realignment for the previous three party systems. The South ceased to be solidly Democratic; its voting patterns more and more resembled those in the North, with blacks still voting Democratic while white Protestants shifted to the Republican Party. Religion also underwent a change. The religious cleavage changed from one between Protestants and Catholics to one between those who held orthodox religious views and those who were more liberal or completely secular. Attitudes about religion, rather than religion per se, distinguished the parties, with conservatives and traditionalists becoming Republicans and liberals and seculars voting Democratic.

The driving force behind these changes was not immigration but education. Prior to 1960 there was a correlation between education, income, and party. The GI Bill, federal support of education, and expansion of state universities vastly increased the number of people getting a higher education. Most of these had Democratic parents, from whom they inherited their party preferences, but even Republican children became more liberal from a "liberal education." As a result, a curvilinear relationship emerged between education and party preference, with the Democrats commanding the votes of those at the bottom and the top of the educational ladder and the Republicans the votes of those in between. It was the educated Democrats who became party reformers. Essentially, the Democratic party changed because the children of the working class went to college. With education came changes in attitudes toward race and issues related to race. As a result the Sixth Party System was one in which race, or more accurately, attitudes about race, was superimposed over class as the dominant cleavage, while region faded from importance and a new type of religious cleavage emerged.

The results of this realignment creeped in. The Republicans controlled both the Presidency and the Senate for the first six years of the 1980s, and both Houses but not the Presidency for the last six years of the 1990s. Democratic hold on state and local offices receded more slowly as party regulars whose preferences were formed in the Fifth Party System were slowly replaced by their children who were more independent. Weak party loyalties and split tickets were the hallmarks of the Sixth Party System. Divided government was the result.

There is a relationship between periodic party systems and social movement clusters, but it is not a simple one. The first wave took place largely within the Second Party System, but shaped the politics of the Third. The moral reform movements of the 1830s and '40s eventually took on political form, through the creation of multiple third parties to bring the authority of the state behind various prescriptions for proper behavior. These movements and parties became tributaries to the new Republican Party. Inheriting the mantel of moral reform, the Republican Party counted correct moral order as well as economic order among its goals. Thus when the Prohibition Party was founded in 1872, it drew its voters from Republican ranks, and when that party receded in strength, its voters returned to the Republican fold.

The Populist Movement contributed considerably to the realignment from the Third to the Fourth Party Systems. It drew from the ranks of Democrats in the South and Republicans in the Midwest and Rocky Mountain states. However, in the South the Democrats co-opted and absorbed the Populists while in the Midwest the Populists frequently coalesced with the weak Democratic Party to produce some of the few two-party states in the Fourth Party System. There were Progressives in both major parties, but they were stronger in the Republican Party with its long reform tradition. When the movement took partisan shape, it split the Republican Party and put the Democrats into power. However, Republican Progressives met the same fate as Southern Populists. Progressivism, which had been very successful in many states, did not succeed on the national level until it was adopted by the Democrats in the Fifth Party System.

The Sixties cluster began in the 1950s with the Southern Civil Rights Movement, which eventually realigned the region. Blacks and those with liberal attitudes on race stayed in the Democratic Party, while Southerners with more traditional attitudes became Republicans. But there were changes in the North as well. The demands of the Civil Rights Movement were an issue in the Presidential election of 1964, where the contrasting attitudes of the Republican and Democratic candidates prompted most of the remaining black Republicans to shift parties. Over the next few decades some Northern whites followed Southern whites into the Republican party, particularly conservative Catholics and orthodox Jews who had voted Democratic. Many who shifted parties, North and South, claimed it was because the Democratic Party had been captured by the Sixties movements and no longer expressed their values.

The Civil Rights Movement had many children; movements formed around issues of "sex" took on partisan colors. The new feminist movement, the movement to repeal abortion restrictions, and the movement for social acceptance of homosexuals polarized the parties throughout the Sixth Party System. A gender gap emerged in which women were more likely to vote Democratic while men leaned toward Republicans. As the twentieth century ended, perspectives on race remained the dominant cleavage, but the seeds of a Seventh Party System were being sowed by attitudes toward gender, sex, and sexuality.

WHERE DO WOMEN FIT?

Women have participated in social movements throughout our history. There have also been separate movements of women in every cluster. Some of these movements have organized women to improve society generally, to aid children, to help less fortunate women, or to change men. And some have focused specifically on increasing women's rights. In the nineteenth century both types were part of the larger woman movement. Here, the former will be generically referred to as reform movements and the latter as feminist movements, even though "feminism" was not commonly used until 1910.

In the moral reform movements women had to organize separately from men because the social mores of the day saw mixed activities as promiscuous. Indeed it was the exclusion of women from abolition and temperance meetings that led them to organize on their own behalf and not just for the welfare of others—that made feminists out of reformers. Throughout the nineteenth century women worked to increase the rights of women, particularly the rights of married women to gain some independence from their husbands and the right of all women to an education. While some women advocated suffrage as early as 1848, and two major suffrage organizations were founded in 1869, the demand for suffrage did not take on the dimensions of a social movement until the Populist/Progressive period.

Women in the Populist movement usually worked with men in the same organizations, largely because they were in rural areas where families acted together. But in the municipal reform movements, women organized separately even though they worked with the men's organizations to elect reform candidates. Separate organizations for men and women were also common in small towns and urban areas. The Progressive movement combined both approaches; women worked in their own organizations and they also worked with men. Since the Populists formed their own party, and the municipal reformers espoused nonpartisanship, women in each movement had different attitudes toward parties. Populist women fused social movement and party activity, while municipal reformers separated it. They also had different attitudes toward Suffrage. The Populist Movement prompted major state campaigns for woman suffrage, two of which were successful. Women in municipal reform movements avoided Suffrage, in part because among their most prominent supporters were avowed anti-suffragists.[17] As the Progressive movement peaked in 1912, woman suffrage became part of its agenda.

During this time the labor movement was struggling to organize and sometimes it made common cause with Progressives. By and large labor preferred to organize itself and bargain with corporations over working conditions and wages rather than rely on government, which was the Progressive solution. But when it came to women both agreed that the government should protect women workers by limiting their hours and regulating their working conditions. Women in industry, when they could speak for themselves, often, but not always, agreed. Protective labor legislation for women joined the Progressive agenda very early and then was adopted by the Democratic and Republican Parties.

In their analyses of the social bases of party systems, historians have paid little attention to gender as a factor in partisanship. Voting patterns were the main source of data; since few women could vote in the first three party systems and those that could in the next two voted much like equivalent men, sex did not appear to be an important variable. There was an agreement among pollsters and election analysts that woman suffrage had helped the Republican Party more than the Democrats, largely due to higher turnout among Republican women, but no one looked much further. Yet if one shifts perspective slightly, and looks for displays of partisanship beyond voting, sex emerges into bold relief.

Throughout the nineteenth century women became more and more involved in party activities. Even though they could not usually vote, there was an assumption that women could influence the men who did vote. The only issue was whether such influence should be exercised solely in private, or also in public. Before the Civil War women gave speeches and wrote political tracts in support of their candidates and their party. They joined in the rallies and camp meetings, partially as participants and partially as cooks and cleaners. After the war women organized partisan meetings with women speakers, some for both sexes and some for women only. They sometimes stood vigil at the polls in order to increase decorum and to remind male voters of their duty to vote right. In the 1890s, women in several states took on major responsibilities for delivering male voters. They canvassed their homes, speaking both to voters and their wives. They were counted among the orators and "spellbinders" at organized meetings and street rallies. They wrote and distributed literature. Often they formed women's political clubs. Sometimes they were delegates to state party conventions.

These activities were not uniformly engaged in by women of all parties. There was a partisan pattern. Women labored initially on behalf of minor parties—Prohibition, Populist, Labor. They were convention delegates, speakers, committee members, and even candidates of these parties well before they were accepted by the major parties, indeed well before they could vote. But of the two major parties, the party of order attended to women long before the party of equality. Whether using the name of Federalist, Whig, or Republican, the party of order acknowledged women's presence, utilized their talents, and recognized their contributions a good ten to twenty years before the Democrats in most every area. The few instances where Democratic women were on a par with Republican women were ones in which minor parties were in fact major ones. In Colorado for example, a strong Populist Party fused with a weak Democratic Party and Populist women changed party labels.

This pattern is superimposed over a regional one. Women's overt partisanship was not geographically uniform. The South was significantly behind the rest of the country in the acceptance of women in political roles. The West was ahead. In the Midwest and East, local conditions shaped the political environment. Several midwestern states produced women political leaders in the nineteenth century; in others there is little evidence of female partisan activity. New York City was a greenhouse for Republican women in the 1890s; New Jersey was not. Even in the four states where women got full suffrage in the nineteenth century, women's participation varied. Colorado and Utah had an abundance of party women, including Democratic women; Idaho and Wyoming did not. As the Third Party System shifted into the Fourth, elections became less an act of male solidarity and more of a civic duty, the Progressive Movement legitimated political work as an expansion of women's duty to maintain the home, and women moved into political life in areas where they had only occasionally been seen before. That process continued after 1920 as women became normal voters and party workers at different rates in different states. There was also a generational effect. Younger women voted and worked in the parties in greater rates than their mothers. The right to vote did not divide political from nonpolitical women nearly as much as did region and party—and after 1920, age.

The class and religious bases of the major parties provide one explanation of their different receptivity toward women and women's rights. Region provides another. Different religions had different attitudes toward women and their proper roles. If one looks at how men voted in suffrage referenda, Catholics were more likely to be opposed than Protestants, at least outside the South. Catholics and Southerners were Democrats; their conservative attitudes toward women shaped those of the entire party. If one looks at the leadership of the major social movements in which women were active, they are virtually all Protestant but in different denominations. Temperance leaders were heavily Methodist, followed by Baptists and Presbyterians, while the suffragists tended to be Quakers, Universalists, Unitarians, and Congregationalists with some

Episcopalians. Of course, the anti-suffrage leaders were also Protestant—mostly Presbyterian and Episcopalian. These were all Republican denominations.[18] As for class, in the first five party systems, the Democratic Party was the party of the working man while the Republican Party was the party of the growing middle class. Middle-class women had more leisure for politics, and more education, than the wives and daughters of the working man. Partisan differences in class, education, and religion created a much bigger pool of women available to the Republican Party than to the Democrats and also a larger number who saw politics as a natural outlet for their social concerns.[19]

To this must be added the fact that the Republican party began as the party of reform; even when it became dominated by a business elite, it still viewed itself as the party of progress. Moral order was as important as economic order. Except in the South, whose social system ossified after the Civil War, women's place along with it, Democrats were much more likely to be foreign born or the children of foreign-born, urban, Catholic and to have less education. The Democratic Party was composed of marginal peoples striving to become part of American society, not to change it.

The impact of race on women's overt partisanship is not as obvious as that of region and religion. In the nineteenth century, the party of order was more receptive to African Americans as well as to women. This was reciprocated. Until the 1930s, most African Americans were loyal Republicans, regardless of sex. However, there is some evidence that black women, like white, were more loyal, longer, to the Republican Party than their men. Writing in 1892, Southerner Anna Julia Cooper observed that to "the black woman . . . a Democratic Negro is a traitor. . . ." This attitude faded when African Americans moved north, but it took a long time. In 1895, New Yorker Mary Hall commented that "the colored man who is a democrat is despicable to me." In Boston, and probably elsewhere, black men increased their registration in the Democratic Party gradually throughout the 1920s; black women waited until 1936.[20]

Despite repeated rhetoric about "the women's vote," political analysts have always known that women and men of the same race, region, religion, and class voted alike. But below this surface similarity there are some distinctions of importance, ones that determine the composition of the active electorate and thus the shape of party systems. First, women did not vote at the same rate as men until the 1980s, yet sometimes they outvoted men. Women were particularly responsive to specific issues and special organizing efforts to bring to the polls those who were not normal voters. Second, women were less likely to commit themselves to a party when they registered to vote. Where registration data exist by sex for the 1920s through 1940s, more women declare they are "independents." However, surveys from the 1950s and 1960s show more men affirming their "independence." Third, until the end of the Fifth Party System, the Republican Party had a slight edge in getting women's votes.

The "gender gap" has two components: turnout and preference. Different groups vote at different rates. Women of the higher socio-economic strata (SES), particularly those who were white, Protestant, and native born of native-born parents, became normal voters more quickly and at higher rates than women from other strata. Until the end of the Fifth Party System more of them voted Republican. The difference in turnout between high SES men and women was smaller and closed more rapidly than in the rest of the electorate. Because of this turnout effect, woman suffrage benefited Republican candidates more than Democrats well into the 1960s. A preference effect, indicating that women voters favored one party more than equivalent men, is harder to document before scientific sampling (and varies with the definition of "equivalent"). Nonetheless, there is evidence to support a preference effect in *some* elections. Here, too, women were more likely to vote Republican. But when a preference effect appears in primaries or nonpartisan elections, women favored the progressive Republican candidates more than the conservatives, and independents more than those associated with party machines. These will be mentioned in the chapters that follow, although voting analysis is not a major concern of this book.[21]

There are variations with time and place. Sometimes turnout and preference effects favor the Democrats, or are more pronounced among lower SES women. Most of these can be accounted for by differences in local political culture, or by special efforts to mobilize women. When electoral outcomes are uncertain, both parties look for new sources of strength and often find them in women, whether as voters or workers. But throughout the Fourth and Fifth Party Systems there wasn't a lot of party competition in local elections, so special efforts were rare. Since Republican women were better organized than Democratic women, absent special circumstances Republican women voters were more likely to be pushed to the polls, reinforcing the normal tendency of higher SES women to vote more frequently and to vote Republican.

Among women, all of these things—turnout, preference, and organization—meant more female votes for the Republican Party. And, despite a few variations, until the 1970s the Republican Party and its predecessors generally provided a much warmer reception to women, and in particular those women actively working to promote women's rights, than did the Democratic Party. On issues of woman's rights as well as ways to bring women into politics, the Democrats usually lagged. When they did take the lead, it was usually temporary. By the mid-1960s, partisan distinctions were slight, but they were still there. In the 1970s, they faded. It was the 1980s before the Democrats took the lead in promoting women's rights.

This book ends in the 1960s because the emergence of a new feminist movement brought a sea change in the relationship between the major parties and women. As a result, the parties switched sides, with the Democratic Party becoming the home of feminist activists and the Republican Party welcoming the anti-feminists. This sea change was one aspect of the realignment from the Fifth to the Sixth Party System. Its story will require another volume. The story of how women entered party politics during the first five party systems is long enough.

· Two ·

Cracking Open the Door:
Women and Partisanship
in the Nineteenth Century

At the beginning of the nineteenth century, there was only the bare framework of a political house and women were merely observers. By the end of the century the house was built. Women were still outside, but they had cracked open the door. Political parties were the masons that built the political house. They created institutions for identifying and running candidates for public office, organized the voters to elect them, and translated public concerns into public policy. The parties were male domains. Before the Civil War, while the house was still under construction, women knocked on the door and asked to help. After the war, some women pounded on the door, demanding entry, while others began quietly helping men finish the house. The women who demanded entry were stigmatized as radicals. The women who helped the men were quietly welcomed when they proved to be good workers. By the end of the century political parties were no longer closed to women, but their place was circumscribed. Party men accepted women's contributions to the political house, while still denying them much say in how it was constructed and none on what went on inside.

Just as women's work moved out of the home and into the factory and the office, so did women's political activities. At the beginning of the century women's influence was exercised out of the public eye, through letters or quiet conversations. It was deemed unseemly for a woman to speak in public. Attending meetings with the other sex present was scandalous. Voting was restricted to property owning white men. The New Jersey constitution of 1776 permitted some property owning women to vote, but this was changed in 1807.[1] By the end of the century women listened to speeches and attended political events with men, were highly regarded as campaign orators, were eagerly employed by the parties to canvass their voters, and had their own political clubs and party organizations in some states. Women had equal suffrage with men in only four states, but could vote for school offices and on tax and bond issues in twenty-five states and for municipal offices in Kansas. While women had little power within the parties, neither were they complete outsiders.[2]

Most party women came from two sources: reform movements and political families. While reform efforts initially focused on changing individual behavior, the growth of the state pulled women into the political arena despite the fact that it was assigned to men. As reform shifted to the passage of laws, women first circulated petitions, then lobbied and spoke to legislative committees, then worked for candidates they thought would support their programs. Once women reformers removed the stigma of political participation, women from political families picked up the banner and joined the party parades. Their success eased the way for other women, though this varied enormously by locale. By the 1890s women partisans were welcomed in many states, even where women could not vote, because party men thought they could shape public opinion and influence male voters. But they were welcomed only when they kept their place. Party men wanted them as workers, not as makers of public policy or recipients of patronage.

As women became active in the parties, they recruited new women to their ranks who lacked their history in reform or suffrage work. Whereas previously a politically inclined woman might work with equal fervor for suffrage, reform, and her party, in the 1890s the strands of activity were becoming distinct, drawing into them different women altogether. Political women began to specialize. Those who chose to work primarily through the dominant parties carved out a niche for themselves, taking on many mundane tasks previously done by men. By the end of the nineteenth century party women had become accepted if not always rewarded. Women were not inside the political house, but they had cracked open the door.

FEMALE REFORM

Women's route to politics lay through moral reform. When the first Female Anti-Slavery Society was founded in Boston in 1833 it "almost cost the reputation of every one who joined it, so strong was the prejudice against any public action on the part of women." By 1837 there were seventy-seven such societies.[3] Despite public obloquy, women agitated for the abolition of slavery, temperance, poor relief, and many other moral reform causes. This led them to speak in public in order to persuade thousands of men and women to sign petitions to legislators asking support for their goals and financing for their projects. Mass petitioning began in the 1820s; women took it up in the 1830s and after a series of lectures by the Grimké sisters in 1837–38, it surged. "The right of petitioning," wrote abolitionist Angelina Grimké in 1837, "is the only political right that women have." Canvassing for petitions led women "casually into organizing for legislative action," including speaking before legislative bodies and lobbying officials. Some women denied that what they were doing was political, since that was outside women's sphere. Others admitted it, but distinguished it from partisan activity, which was "sacrificing principles to power or interest."[4]

With the spread of universal white male suffrage and the decline of moral fervor, reform shifted from moral suasion to electoral politics. This had two effects on women reformers. One was to limit their participation. Male reformers argued that petitions should only be signed by voters, and sometimes discouraged women from attending meetings and speeches to leave room for the men who could vote. The other was to expand women's interest in legislation and politics. In 1851 Maine prohibited the manufacture and sale of distilled spirits; its law became a model for other states. Reformers began to look to the state to control individual behavior.[5]

The Civil War "unleashed the energies of American women." Before it ended they acquired skills in organization, fundraising, and bureaucratic maneuvering, through their work as nurses, on the Sanitary Commission, and in general relief. Women also moved into new occupations, especially teaching, government, and clerical work, that became available due to the loss of so many young men. Barriers of custom and prejudice, as well as to jobs, crumbled under the assault of need and opportunity. Women lecturing to mixed audiences before the war were still somewhat scandalous; during the war it became almost ordinary. Government assumed a new importance. "By their active labors all through the great conflict, women learned that they had many interests outside the home. In the camp and hospital, and the vacant places at their firesides, they saw how intimately the interests of the State and the home were intertwined; that as war and all its concomitants were subject of legislation, it was only through a voice in the laws that their efforts for peace could command consideration."[6]

After the Civil War, women used their organizational skills to found many associations and expand their concerns. The largest and most prominent of the female reform associations was the Women's Christian Temperance Union (WCTU). Founded in 1874, on the heels of "the Woman's Crusade" against saloons, it soon became "the first mass movement of American women," a "national voice through which women expressed their views on social and political issues," and "the first sizable organization controlled exclusively by women."[7]

Alcohol abuse had been a particular concern of women for many decades. Alcoholism was rampant; many a man spent his pay in the saloon and then beat his wife when she complained. Since women lacked economic alternatives to marriage they attacked what they saw as the cause of their family problems, the easy availability of hard liquor. WCTU members pledged to "abstain" and to "discourage the use of and traffic in" alcoholic beverages. One tactic was to "assemble outside the polls and sing hymns at the voters," when a prohibition measure was on the ballot. After Frances E. Willard became president in 1879, her "do everything" policy inspired the WCTU to pursue a broad welfare program. Under the rubric of "Home Protection," Willard encouraged women to involve themselves in numerous public issues despite the prevailing sentiment that women's place was in the home. As many as thirty-nine WCTU departments let women work on kindergartens, prisons, prostitution, peace, mothering, health, and hygiene. On all these issues the WCTU distributed five million pieces of literature each year.[8]

The WCTU built the bridge to wider political activity by connecting women's socially acceptable concern with the home to issues subject to legislative action and from there to the election of the men who made these decisions. As a result, wrote Susan B. Anthony and Ida Husted Harper in 1902:

> This organization has largely influenced the change in public sentiment in regard to social drinking, equal suffrage, equal purity for both sexes, equal remuneration for work equally well done, equal educational, professional and industrial opportunities for women. It has been a chief factor in state campaigns for statutory prohibition, constitutional amendment, reform laws in general and those for the protection of women and children in particular, and in securing anti-gambling and anti-cigarette laws.[9]

The person most responsible for this was Frances Willard, WCTU president from 1879 to 1898. Committed to the advancement of women on all fronts, she understood the necessity for suffrage and sought to lead women to the same realization through small steps. Suffragists were stigmatized as radicals. Temperance was wrapped in the shawl of organized religion and home protection was every woman's responsibility. The WCTU made suffrage, and politics, respectable for women.[10]

In 1868 women formed the first societies "purely for their own recreation and improvement—all others had been for the purpose of reforming the weak and sinful or assisting the needy and unfortunate—and they met with a storm of derision and protest." Nonetheless, the idea that women should do something for themselves flourished. By the end of the nineteenth century women's clubs existed in almost every town. "Every village which is big enough for a church contains also a woman's club and they exist in many country neighborhoods. In the largest cities single societies have from 500 to 1,000 members, and a number of handsome club houses have been built and furnished." In the 1880s these coalesced into national organizations, including the Association of Collegiate Alumnae in 1882 (becoming the American Association of University Women in 1921), the Young Women's Christian Association (YWCA) in 1891, the National Council of Women (NCW) in 1888, the National Council of Jewish Women (NCJW) in 1893, and the National Congress of Mothers (later called the Parent-Teachers Association) in 1897. The leader and largest organization in the club movement was the General Federation of Women's Clubs (GFWC), founded in 1890.[11]

The National Association of Colored Women (NACW) was organized in 1896 under the leadership of Mary Church Terrell. She had "observed from attending the Woman Suffrage meetings how much may be accomplished through organization [and thus] entered enthusiastically into club work among the women of my own group." Terrell had organized the Colored Women's League in Washington, D.C. In July of 1895 Josephine St. Pierre Ruffin of Boston and Margaret Murray Washington of Alabama held a Conference of Colored Women to found a Federation of Afro American Women. The two groups united into NACW with Terrell as its president. By 1900 NACW had 125 branches in 26 states with 8,000 members. The parent body had twenty major departments.[12]

While these associations were not expressly political, they created a network of women trained in organization upon which more politically active groups could draw. Political parties as well as the woman suffrage movement discovered that women with organizational skills could use them anywhere.

WOMAN'S RIGHTS

The Woman Movement, as it was then called, had two phases. The first phase attacked women's numerous legal disabilities. Most states followed the English common law under which a woman lost her legal identity upon marriage; it merged into that of her husband. Her property, her earnings, her children, all belonged to him. A married woman could not sue, make contracts, or engage in business on her own. The states and territories colonized by France and Spain viewed all property acquired during the marriage as community property, and thus owned by both husband and wife. However, the husband was the head of the family and as such could sell or otherwise encumber it without his wife's consent. Guardianship of their children was also vested in the husband.

When the Declaration of Sentiments was drafted in July of 1848 in Seneca Falls, New York, the movement to give married women the right to control their own property and earnings was well under way. Mississippi had passed the first Married Woman's Property Act in 1839; New York had done so only in April of 1848. In the meetings and conventions before the Civil War, suffrage was only one issue, and not one for which there was much support. It was not until after the war, when "male" was added to the Constitution with the Fourteenth Amendment, and the Fifteenth extended suffrage only to male African Americans, that it became the paramount issue.[13]

Debate over whether or not to support the Fourteenth Amendment split the American Equal Rights Association, founded in 1866 to agitate for universal suffrage. Lucy Stone and her husband, Henry Blackwell, along with Frederick Douglass and other abolitionists accepted the admonition that "this is the Negro's hour" and the argument that women would gain suffrage eventually by working within the Republican Party. Elizabeth Cady Stanton and Susan B. Anthony did not; they wanted all reformers to unite behind universal suffrage. In 1869 they formed the National Woman Suffrage Association (NWSA) which limited its membership to women and its goals to suffrage, particularly through a Constitutional amendment. Stone and Blackwell formed the American Woman Suffrage Association (AWSA), open to both sexes, and, despite its name, with a much broader program.[14] While the broader Woman Movement pushed for greater participation of women in all spheres of life, the National and the American Woman Suffrage Associations agitated for the ballot. In 1890 they merged into the National American Woman Suffrage Association, forever known as NAWSA.

Suffrage was the second phase. Victories were few and far between. The territorial legislatures of Wyoming and Utah voted to give women the vote in 1869 and 1870,[15] so women had full suffrage when they became states in 1890 and 1896 respectively. In 1883 Washington's territorial legislature extended suffrage to women, who voted until the territory's Supreme Court declared this action illegal in 1888.[16] In 1893 and 1896, "[e]ngulfed in the rising tide of populism which swept through the West in the early nineties, Colorado, . . . and Idaho gave the ballot to women,"[17] but despite fifteen campaigns in ten states between 1867 and 1900, voters in other states resisted.[18] The years from 1896 to 1910 were known to suffragists as "the doldrums."[19]

Many of these campaigns were led, or substantially aided, by the WCTU, which established a Suffrage Division in 1881. Since the WCTU was organized in over ten thousand cities and towns in every state and territory, and had as many as three hundred thousand members, it could field more suffrage workers than the woman suffrage organizations. The WCTU also provided a respectable rationale for suffrage and thus made it socially acceptable to many women who found "equal rights" too radical. But since the WCTU's presence prompted apprehension about woman suffrage by the powerful "liquor interests," suffrage leaders both praised and feared its participation in their cause. In 1889 suffragist May Wright Sewall "tried to unseat Helen [Gougar] as president of the Indiana Equal Suffrage Association because of her Prohibition leanings." By the 1890s, NAWSA was urging suffragists to keep the issues separate, even though its most active members were often local WCTU officers. Although Willard and Anthony were friends, and co-ordinated their efforts, the WCTU emphasized state and local suffrage while Anthony urged a sixteenth amendment to the Constitution. The latter remained wishful thinking. Bills for suffrage amendments were introduced into Congress from 1868 through 1896, then ceased until 1913. The Senate voted on this once, in 1887, defeating the suffrage amendment by 34 to 16 with 26 absent.[20]

PARTISANSHIP

In the early republic, Federalists much more than Democratic-Republicans acknowledged that women had political influence, even if only indirectly through their men. Federalist speeches paid tribute to women, while those of

the "party of equality" ignored "the fair sex." Reports of Federalist rallies, meetings, and other events show women attended while those of the other party are
much less likely to mention a female presence. Historian Rosemarie Zagarri
found that "Democratic-Republicans . . . made very little room for women,
either in their organizations or their rhetoric." Federalists were largely responsible for the provision in the 1776 New Jersey Constitution that permitted
women with sufficient property to vote, and those that did vote "overwhelmingly preferred the Federalist party." In 1801 the Jeffersonian party became dominant, and in 1807 it passed a law limiting the franchise to "free white male
citizens."[21]

Women were loyal and active partisans long before they could vote. Like
their men, they caught the party spirit that blossomed in the Second Party
System before the Civil War. By and large "the ladies" were Whigs. In the 1840
campaign the Whigs triumphed with a new campaign style, resembling that of
religious revival meetings, that emphasized marching, singing, speechifying, and
general enthusiasm. From Lowell, Massachusetts, mill girls to Tennessee belles,
"party leaders sought to get women involved, encouraging them to march in
parades, organize picnics and cheer at rallies" along with men. Lucy Kenney
wrote a pamphlet, and "[o]ther women even more daring conducted political
meetings and made speeches." Democratic efforts to mobilize women were
more limited. Although the Whigs saw themselves as the more conservative
party, "throughout the decade of the 1840s, the Whigs proved more successful
in enlisting women's support than the Democrats." The first women's campaign
clubs were created to promote the election of Whig Presidential candidate
Henry Clay in 1844.[22]

As women became more politically active, so did the debate over what
actions were within women's sphere. In the 1850s many men and women wrote
articles arguing whether or not female participation in campaigns was proper,
let alone voting. An anonymous one in the *Democratic Review* of April 1852
lamented the appearance of "Female Politicians" in the 1840 Harrison campaign. "Under that wild infatuation of party enthusiasm, ladies forsook their
home paths, and appeared in public, presenting banners, making speeches, joining in hard-cider, log-cabin and Tippecanoe processions and choruses, until the
common pursuits of duty and pleasure seemed quite dull and inane." That same
year Whig editor Sarah Hale wrote in *Godey's Lady's Book* that "women should
vote, [only] by influencing rightly the votes of men." While women could not
vote, it was accepted that they could influence the men who did; the question
was whether this should be done in public as well as in private.[23]

In the 1856 Presidential campaign a new source of political women came
to the fore: political wives. While wives had no doubt helped their husbands in
many campaigns, social mores kept them behind the scenes. In 1856 Jessie
Benton Frémont, the daughter of a U.S. Senator, was a public, and popular, presence in her husband's campaign as the first Republican Party candidate for

President. In addition to wives, daughters and friends of political men also spoke out or put pen to paper on their behalf. One of the best known was Anna Ella Carroll, daughter of a former Maryland governor, who published tracts in support of former President Millard Fillmore when he ran again in 1856 at the head of the American (Know-Nothing) Party. Maryland was the only state he carried. Once the ground of women's entry into politics was broken by women reformers, women from political families followed suit, without the qualms about partisanship that clouded the reformers' commitment. Even Southern women began to write about politics, and sometimes to speak in public.[24]

During the Civil War both Northern and Southern women became more politicized. In the South, they wrote tracts, letters, and newspaper columns. In the North, they also spoke and campaigned. Some of Anna Carroll's pamphlets on issues raised by the war were important enough to be reprinted by the federal government. Another Anna achieved celebrity as an orator. Anna Dickinson's speeches for the Republican Party in 1862 were deemed so essential to its electoral success in New Hampshire, Connecticut, New York, and Pennsylvania that she was invited to address Congress in January of 1864 and, at the age of twenty-two, was heralded as America's Joan of Arc. After the war, she became one of the country's foremost orators, earning her living as a traveling lecturer and occasional playwright. In several campaigns she was paid handsomely by candidates to speak on their behalf.[25]

Party activity by women grew slowly after the war, then flowered in the 1880s. During the 1880 contest between Garfield and Hancock, a correspondent wrote that in New York, "the men who hold the highest positions are those who treat women's political convictions with the greatest respect." She identified several important women, one of whom had organized a Democratic political club among Italian immigrants. In 1882 Indiana temperance worker Helen Gougar wrote that "the recent campaign found women more forward and active in political matters." Women's presence was especially strong in the many third parties as a continuation of their involvement in reform activities. Women served as delegates and on committees at Prohibition Party conventions from its founding in 1869. Its first platform in 1872 declared for woman suffrage, reflecting the importance of women to that party and its expectation that women would vote for prohibition if they could. Gougar was one of many temperance workers who left the Republican Party for the Prohibition Party, encouraged by the WCTU. In the 1880s Frances Willard made the WCTU a major force within that party. She was on its executive committee, four WCTU members became paid party lecturers, and "[a]t national conventions, the percentage of female delegates often exceeded 30 percent." Raised as a Republican, in 1880 Willard openly supported Republican James Garfield for President, believing that he would support both prohibition and woman suffrage. When he failed to do so, she organized the Home Protection Party in 1881, which merged with the Prohibition Party in 1882. Willard later wrote that "then and there . . . American womanhood . . . 'entered politics' for the sake of home protection and when they came they came to stay." For the next ten years WCTU ladies learned to make speeches, canvass voters, and work the polls. By 1888 even the suffragist *Woman's Journal* was amazed at the number of "women in the whirl of campaign politics," observing that the number of marching clubs, speakers, and candidates would have been unimaginable only five years earlier.[26]

In 1884 the Prohibition candidate, a former Kansas Governor, won two percent of the vote for President and the Republican candidate lost to Grover Cleveland by 0.2 percent. Republicans blamed the Prohibition Party for costing it the White House.[27] Awakened by defeat, and unsure how much influence women had on male Prohibitionists, the Republican Party decided to organize women to support Republican candidates. Campaign clubs had proliferated during elections, those of women usually named for the wife of the Republican Presidential nominee. In the 1880s young Republican men began to form permanent clubs. James S. Clarkson, National Committeeman from Iowa, brought them to a convention in New York City in December of 1887 to found the National League of Republican Clubs. In July of 1888, his close friend, Iowa lawyer J. Ellen Foster, met with the Republican National Committee (RNC) and agreed to undertake a "thorough and comprehensive organization of Republican women." She started the Women's National Republican Association (WNRA), which she headed until her death in 1910. The WNRA was not a membership association. It operated as the women's committee of the RNC during campaigns, and as an advisory body in between. Women in many states started their own Republican organizations without affiliation. For the next twenty years the WNRA distributed hundreds of thousands of pieces of literature and sent speakers all over the country to campaign for the Republican ticket.[28]

Foster's loyalty to the Republican party frequently brought her into conflict with reformers and suffragists. After gaining renown in Iowa for her temperance work, in 1884 she put her considerable oratorical skills to the service of the Republican Party's candidate, James G. Blaine. At one time an active WCTU member and admirer of Willard, during the mid-1880s she vociferously opposed Willard's efforts to mobilize the WCTU for the Prohibition Party, arguing that nonpartisanship was the right road for moral reform. In 1889 she and a few hundred of her supporters seceded, forming a Nonpartisan WCTU. In the election of 1888, Helen Gougar followed J. Ellen Foster and Anna Dickinson around Indiana, countering their Republican speeches with hers for the Prohibition Party. After the Kansas Republican Party declined to support suffrage in the referendum of 1894, Foster declared that "I care more for the dominant principles of the Republican Party than I do for woman suffrage." While she remained committed to temperance and suffrage, her devotion to and work on behalf of the Republican Party were criticized by reformers and suffragists, particularly since her husband held patronage jobs in the federal government after 1889.[29]

There was no Democratic equivalent to J. Ellen Foster, or systematic effort to organize women by the Democratic Party for several decades. While Democratic women did form campaign clubs, there is limited evidence of any that survived between elections. One of the few was in Warren County, Illinois. After President Grover Cleveland lost the election of 1888, women founded a Frances Cleveland Club which was still in existence fifty years later. They raised their own funds by running a kitchen at the annual county fair and elected "one of our members as County Superintendent of Schools—no small achievement in a county of two thousand Republican majority." The club sponsored meetings with prominent politicians, paying all their travel expenses and sharing the podium with them. In 1892, they "sent one hundred dollars to the Democratic State Committee Headquarters in Chicago," and were told that "it was the first money ever given to a political campaign by a body of women."[30]

In the summer of 1892, Mary Frost Ormsby tried to organize her friends into a "Frances Cleveland Influence Club No. 1" in New York City. Grover Cleveland himself wrote her not to use his wife's name. In September, she obtained funds from Don Dickinson, a wealthy New York Cleveland man, and hired Margaret J. Hoey to help her persuade women to influence men by mailing out circulars. Renamed the National Democratic Influence Club, after the election Ormsby wanted to turn it into a Democratic version of Foster's WNRA, but the New York group was quickly divided by a slew of charges including misuse of funds. Ormsby moved to Washington, D.C., early in 1893 where she obtained a charter for her club, but both "clubs" disappeared off the political map after a barrage of mutual recriminations.[31]

Women were particularly active in the shorter-lived People's (Populist) Party until it merged with the Democrats in 1896. Although the 1892 national platform did not endorse woman suffrage because Southern populists were afraid that black women might vote, women were conspicuous in the party. Kansas lawyer and orator Mary Elizabeth Lease was the most renowned, but she was not alone. Wrote the authors of the *History of Woman Suffrage*: Women "sat as delegates in its national and State conventions and served on National and State Committees; they were employed as political speakers and organizers; and they were elected and appointed to official positions. Various State and county conventions declared in favor of enfranchising women, the majority of the legislators advocated it, and there is reason to believe that in those States where an amendment to secure it was submitted, individual Populists very largely voted for it." The Labor, Greenback, and various Socialist parties also "have made unequivocal declarations for woman suffrage and welcomed women as delegates."[32]

In the critical election of 1896 partisan fervor was pronounced. Women's participation soared. Women in all parties marched, canvassed, and monitored the polls on election day. Though only the Democratic women of Warren, Illinois, sponsored a meeting for Bryan, many stumped for him, including erstwhile Republican and Prohibition Party candidate Helen Gougar. While women campaigned avidly for Bryan, they organized for McKinley. As head of the Women's National Republican Campaign Committee, J. Ellen Foster "issued hundreds of thousands of circulars saying: 'Never were there more powerful and obvious motives for persistent and united effort among women than now.'" She traveled the country speaking for the Republican Party, where she was heard by vast crowds. In New York, Republican women opened a campaign head-quarters in August and organized house to house canvasses with tracts in "German, Bohemian and English." Within a week, 1,500 women had literature and instructions on how to canvass. The anti-suffrage argument that women did not need to vote because they could influence men was used to justify organized campaigns by women to do just that. Why settle for one vote, women argued, when an energetic woman was worth at least twenty?[33]

WOMEN IN POLITICS

In 1892, J. Ellen Foster stood before the Republican National Convention at Minneapolis. "We are here to help you," she told the assembled men. "And we have come to stay." By 1894 the *Woman's Journal* matter-of-factly reported on women candidates for public office in thirteen states. Women were particularly visible in states where the Prohibition and Populist parties brought them directly into party politics because reform and party coincided. These were Colorado, Kansas, Illinois, Iowa, Missouri, Minnesota, Nebraska, North Dakota, and California. These parties competed with the Republican Party for votes from native-born Protestants, motivating it to mobilize women. Women were also quite active in major urban centers, particularly those with municipal reform movements.[34]

Of course the four full suffrage states fostered political women. Colorado women ran for many public offices as party candidates; in 1894 three were elected to the state legislature, one as State Superintendent of Public Instruction and others to municipal positions. Minnie J. Reynolds described how she "stumped . . . the mountainous western half" in the fall of 1894 for Governor Waite, where she "was sure of two things—a full house and an enthusiastic audience." In Utah, the 1896 Republican State Central Committee asked women to be vice-chairman and secretary. The Democrats responded by electing three women to the state legislature and several to local offices. In Idaho, women voted for the first time in 1898, helping to elect three women to the state legislature and one as State Superintendent of Public Instruction. Even sparsely settled Wyoming elected Estelle Reel as State Superintendent of Public Instruction in 1894. By the decade's end, sixteen women had been elected to the legislatures of three states.[35]

California saw many women work in politics, but its political culture was less partisan than the suffrage states. Both the Democratic and Republican parties employed California women as speakers in campaigns during the 1880s, but only the minor parties chose them as delegates to their state conventions or ran them for various offices. California women organized a Women's Republican State Central Committee in 1894. By 1900, the committee had "a membership of several hundred, and applications are continually being received from women all over the state." In the 1890s the Republican and Populist parties endorsed suffrage, while the Democrats gave "little hope for endorsement." The 1896 suffrage referendum lost in the Bay Area counties where the Democrats dominated and won in the less populous Republican areas of Southern California. Even though they could not vote, women ran for several offices in the 1880s and '90s, mostly on the Populist, Prohibition, and Labor Party tickets. They lost in San Francisco, but two women became school board members in Los Angeles in 1886 and 1892. In these efforts, California women generally had Republican support, though not always enthusiastically, but rarely that of the Democrats.[36]

The Midwest nurtured some of the best-known women political orators, including Foster (Iowa), Gougar (Indiana), Lease (Kansas), Sarah Elizabeth Emery (Michigan), and Ida B. Wells (Illinois). North Dakota elected Democrat Laura Eisenhuth as State Superintendent of Public Instruction in 1892 and Republican Emma F. Bates in 1894. Kansas women had obtained municipal suffrage in 1887 and elected the country's first woman mayor soon thereafter. Among the leaders of the Kansas Equal Suffrage Association were important party women, such as Populist Annie Diggs and Republican Laura Johns. As each campaigned for her party's endorsement in 1894, they maintained a united front even though their parties were virtually at war with each other. But after the election, in which both the Populists and the suffrage referendum lost, acrimony rent the suffrage ranks, leading to a fifteen year decline. Women continued to work in the parties and quite a few women were elected to municipal and county offices—including fifteen women mayors—throughout the 1890s, but full suffrage didn't come until 1912.[37]

In Illinois women could vote for university trustees by 1894. Organized women convinced three parties to include a woman on their slates, and the women of each party threw "themselves into the cause heart and soul." Republican women organized their own State Central Committee, with representatives from each Congressional district, and sent African American journalist Ida B. Wells throughout the state to urge a straight party vote. In 1896 they asked her to travel again, this time for McKinley. Since she was then married with a new baby, the Republican women arranged for a nurse to meet her at each stop to care for it while she made political speeches.[38] Throughout the Midwest and Rocky Mountain states women won or were appointed as county superintendents of schools, often with the help of minor parties, but rarely with the help of Democrats.[39]

The South was the only region where politics was still outside women's sphere and where support of any party but the Democrats bordered on treason. Of course African Americans were fervent Republicans, but their party loyalty was one reason Southern whites wanted to eliminate them from the electorate. For a few years after the Civil War, blacks had helped Republicans—black and white—win office, and women spoke at and voted in the mass meetings which nominated Republican candidates. After 1870, nominating conventions were limited to male voters, and by 1890 black men were systematically disenfranchised. Even for strictly Republican events, black men soon adopted white standards. They urged black women to stay home, or at least to stay silent.[40]

White women had never been so bold. An 1880 article on "Women in Politics" in a New Orleans newspaper identified several women supporting the Democratic candidate for President. Although the author wrote about women in New York, she used a pen name rather than incur public disapproval for this breach of womanly decorum. Populism "softened some men's ideas about women," but not enough to make public speaking or voting acceptable. Even in the border state of Tennessee "many people believed that female participation in politics was a worse evil than the saloon" and denounced women's public efforts to persuade men to vote for prohibition in 1887. Cosmopolitan New Orleans was more receptive. In 1891, women organized to prevent renewal of the charter of the state lottery. In 1898 limited suffrage was given to tax-paying women who then voted in a special assessment for an improved sewage system. In other Southern states there were a few outstanding women who had strong opinions that they did not hide. Most notable was Rebecca Latimer Felton (1835–1930) who used every available avenue to have an impact on Georgia politics. She began by managing her husband's campaigns for Congress from 1874 to 1880, but kept her hand, and her pen, in after he returned to their farm. Felton's articles in local newspapers giving her opinions of public officials and candidates made her a recognized personage throughout the state, as did her ardent speeches for temperance and suffrage. In 1922 she was appointed as the first woman to sit in the U.S. Senate, though she only served for a day.[41]

In the burgeoning cities, a growing movement for municipal reform invited women to help clean up the mess. "One man, one vote; one woman, one throat," they declared. Many women worked through nonpartisan good government groups. In 1897, Denver's Civic Federation held a convention composed entirely of women to "put a ticket before the people." In Chicago, Jane Addams and the Hull House residents worked with the Municipal Voters League to remove a local ward boss. In 1890 a Ladies Committee aided the People's Municipal League of New York City to run a slate of "good government" candidates. In 1893 the Brooklyn Woman's Health Protective Association helped elect Charles Schieren mayor of that city and in 1894 the Women's Municipal League (WML) helped to trounce (temporarily) Tammany Hall, Manhattan's Democratic machine.[42]

The WML was founded by Josephine Shaw Lowell, a wealthy and respected charity worker, in October of 1894, at the request of the Rev. Charles H. Parkhurst, a prominent preacher in New York City's social elite. An outspoken anti-suffragist, he invited "the wives, mothers, sisters, and daughters of our city" to help defeat Tammany. "There is no politics in the matter," he said. "It is a question of right against wrong, of righteousness against trickery." Quickly organized, the WML was lauded for arousing interest among voters previously indifferent to reformers' pleas. In the municipal elections of 1894, 1897, 1901, and 1903, the WML organized women to work for reform candidates for city office. In 1894, the nonpartisan women were substantially aided by the WNRA and held meetings in the Republican-owned Lincoln Hall. Indeed, the prospect of taming the Tammany tiger prompted many women to become active Republicans. Explained Kate Bostwick, a self described "rabid Republican": "The fever of reform was coursing through the veins of these women, and they formed the first regular Republican club . . . of college women and others of ability and executive knowledge."[43]

That club was the West End Women's Republican Association (WEA), founded by Helen Varick Boswell in December of 1894. Born in Baltimore in 1869 into a Democratic household where discussion of woman's rights was taboo, Boswell met Foster in New York and became her protégée. She became the consummate party woman, subordinating everything to loyalty to the Republican Party. During the 1892 campaign the RNC set aside several rooms in its New York City headquarters for the WNRA, and Foster put Boswell in charge of the women workers. In 1894 Boswell took charge of women's work for the Congressional campaigns. She hired women speakers for "the political mass meetings at which women are becoming so interested," and focused her efforts on "the wage earning women, the girls in the factories, shops and large stores, holding meetings among them during the noon hour, to enlist their interest as rapidly as possible." After attending meetings of the WML, Boswell asked permission of the Republican Party leader to organize Republican women's clubs. Soon she was the acknowledged leader of New York State Republican women.[44]

Boswell organized numerous clubs, including ones for black women, business women, working women, and various "neighborhood influence clubs" of twelve to twenty women. These were permanent clubs, not just temporary campaign clubs. Out of campaign season they held regular meetings to hear papers and discuss current issues. During campaigns they received instructions on how to mark ballots and to get men to register and to vote. One meeting discussed whether it was acceptable for women to give soup and coffee to Democrats as well as to Republicans waiting in the cold. New York Republicans selected Boswell as the only woman among 149 state delegates to the 1895 convention of the National League of Republican Clubs. In 1897, Boswell was employed by the New York County Republican Committee to organize Republican

Women. Until 1917, she was the most important woman in the New York State Republican Party.[45]

By 1897, women were recognized as a valuable political asset. "In the approaching municipal campaign in New York," the *New York Herald* observed, "women politicians are to play an important part. About 1,000 of them, representing the Women's Republican organizations of New York, are already sharpening their scalping knives and preparing to work havoc in the ranks of the Tammanyites." Their loyalty was tested in this election when the reformers and the regular Republicans parted company. The reformers ran Seth Low, former mayor of Brooklyn and president of Columbia University, to be the first mayor of Greater New York City. Women were so active on his behalf that he was dubbed "the Ladies' Mayor." The Brooklyn Women's Health Protective Association brought 3,000 women to hear him speak. At another meeting both pro- and anti-suffrage women sat side by side on the stage. When asked what they were doing at a campaign rally, the antis replied, "Oh, but this is for Mr. Low." Republican women were divided when Thomas Platt's regular Republican machine ran one of its own. The West End Republican women debated what to do. The Woman's Republican Union League of Brooklyn, founded by Kate Bostwick in 1896, split so badly that they were fighting over the remains in court two years later. J. Ellen Foster was dispatched to hold Republican women in line. Despite some defections most stayed in the fold. Boss Platt had already assured them that he "favors any plan tending to widen their opportunities and add to their influence."[46]

Despite women's prominent role in the effort to depose Tammany Hall, the Democratic Party displayed little interest in soliciting their support. In 1897 the *New York Times* reported a meeting of the Women's Tammany Club, to listen to speeches by men. "[O]f the four hundred persons present, only about fifteen were women." By 1901, the *History of Woman Suffrage* reported that New York City had "seven or eight Women's Republican Clubs . . . [and] a flourishing Ladies' Democratic Club."[47] The same was true of Colorado in 1894, where Republican and Populist women were numerous and active while the "Democratic woman doesn't amount to much politically."[48]

Throughout the nineteenth century, the Democratic Party trailed the minor parties and the Republican Party in bringing women into campaigns and party activities, and when it did so their participation was often more symbolic than substantive. Women were specifically invited to Whig events from the 1840 campaign onwards while the Democrats disparaged their presence well into the 1850s. Women were present at the founding of the Republican Party in 1854, attended party gatherings with their families, campaigned for its candidates, and spoke at public meetings. In 1892 two women attended the Republican National Convention as alternates. Women were not invited to attend the Democratic convention, even as observers, until 1868 and none had an official role until 1900. While both parties had paid women speakers in the

1880s and 1890s, the RNC aided in the organization of women, while the Democratic National Committee did little. As a result, by century's end permanent women's Republican clubs were flourishing in several states, while women's Democratic clubs were few and far between. Not until the 1900 campaign did the Democrats acknowledge their error. Wrote the *New York Tribune*: "The Democratic party, hitherto conservative in its utilization of woman's voice and influence, has had a change of heart, and now seeks feminine supporters the length and breadth of the land."[49]

The pattern was the same on the more radical issue of suffrage. In every contest where partisanship can be ascertained, Republicans were more likely to be favorable than Democrats. In the 1874 Ohio Constitutional Convention three-fourths of the Republican delegates favored woman suffrage compared to only one-third of the Democrats. In 1894, "woman suffrage planks are in the Republican State platforms of three States and one Territory; in the Democratic platform of one Territory, and in the Populist and Prohibition platforms of nearly every northern State." In 1900 *Harper's Weekly* wrote about Colorado: "Female suffrage owes its establishment to the Populist party, assisted in a lesser degree by the Republican party. As a rule the straight Democrats have been opposed to allowing the women to vote." Where women could vote, the Democrats were less likely to bring their women to the polls than were the Republicans. In 1894, when Illinois first allowed women to vote on educational matters, Republican women registered more of their own than did the Democrats, and "they cast three ballots to every one cast by Democratic women." In the 1896 California referendum, the Republican Party was mildly favorable; the Democratic Party was opposed.[50]

As the nineteenth century drew to a close, the movement of women into politics was gaining steam. But it was a movement divided by partisanship, and one in which Republican women were one to three steps ahead of Democratic women.

PARTISANSHIP AND SUFFRAGE

The suffrage organizations were officially nonpartisan, even anti-partisan, but in the nineteenth century most active suffragists were Republicans as were the former abolitionists, prohibitionists, and other reformers. Among the one hundred signers of the 1848 Declaration of Sentiments, Whigs and minor partisans abound; there were no Democrats. After the Civil War antipathy toward the Democrats was strong. Suffragists "hailed Republican leaders as agents of progress and castigated Democrats as the reactionary party of slavery and the white South." The Republican Party's mantle of reform contributed to the sense of betrayal Susan B. Anthony, Elizabeth Cady Stanton, and their supporters felt when it refused to enfranchise women after the Civil War.[51]

Some suffragists were more partisan than others. Lucy Stone and Henry Blackwell were devoted to the party that freed the slaves and endorsed

Republican candidates in their paper, the *Woman's Journal*. Susan B. Anthony and Elizabeth Cady Stanton wavered when they were particularly angry at the Republicans for avoiding woman suffrage, but generally felt that the party that enfranchised the former slaves would eventually enfranchise women. NWSA pleaded for a woman suffrage plank at all party conventions from 1868 on, but when Anthony personally spoke to the Republican Party platform committee in 1892, she did so as a long-time party loyalist.[52]

The Republican Party did hold out more hope than the Democratic Party, whose "national platform [n]ever has recognized so much as the existence of women," but only when it wanted their support. In 1872 it put a "splinter" of support into its platform after both the Democrats and Liberal Republicans had rejected any mention of women, let alone suffrage. NWSA responded by publishing a ringing call for support of the Republican party, which the Congressional Republican Committee distributed widely. The party called Anthony to Washington and gave her $1,000 to organize meetings on behalf of Republican candidates; these were held in eight states with many women speakers. In 1876 the Republican Party adopted another plank, patting itself on the back for "the substantial advance recently made toward the establishment of equal rights for women ... effected by the Republican Legislatures." This time NWSA responded only with surprise. Women were "wholly disregarded" for another twenty years. In 1896 the Republican Party, seeking to regain the White House and stem the Populist hemorrhage of formerly Republican voters, put another splinter into its platform, "mindful of the rights and interests of women." And in 1900 J. Ellen Foster achieved appreciation for women's "faithful co-operation in all works of education and industry" after suffragists had "met with a polite but chilly reception."[53]

Although Stanton and Anthony put women before party, their party loyalty survived many disappointments. Anthony wrote to Blackwell in July of 1872 that "I belong to neither party and approve of one or the other only as it shall speak and work for the enfranchisement of women," but she nonetheless campaigned actively for Grant, believing him to be "friendly" to women's aims and his running mate, Henry Wilson, to be in favor of woman suffrage while his opponent, Horace Greeley, was outspoken against it. On November 5, 1872, after voting illegally, she ecstatically wrote Stanton that she had just "positively voted the Republican ticket—straight."[54]

In the 1880s first the Prohibitionist and then the People's Party took voters from the Republican Party in Northern states. Many women worked in these parties both because they supported their goals and because they thought them the best hope for state suffrage. In 1884 Stanton and Anthony sought to fend off the appeals of new parties—particularly the Prohibition Party which endorsed woman suffrage and the Equal Rights Party whose candidate was D.C. attorney Belva Ann Lockwood—by issuing "a manifesto urging women to stand by the Republican Party." Henry Blackwell was particularly concerned to stop the Prohibition Party. In 1889 he wrote Frances Willard urging her not to "antagonize the Republican Party in Kansas or in Wyoming" because "woman suffrage exists as a Republican measure" and would be lost "by a premature and suicidal third party agitation."[55]

Although Anthony acknowledged that third parties were more supportive of suffrage than the Republicans, she didn't see much reason for suffragists to support them. In the 1902 "Introduction" to the fourth volume of the *History of Woman Suffrage* she and co-editor Ida Husted Harper wrote that:

> Of late years every new or "third" party which is organized declares for woman suffrage. This is partly because such parties come into existence to carry out reforms in which they believe women can help, and partly because in their weak state they are ready to grasp at straws. While giving them full credit for such recognition, whatever may be its inspiring motive, it is clearly evident that the franchise must come to women through the dominant parties.[56]

Yet even women's work in the two major parties evoked mixed emotions from suffragists. At the NWSA's convention of 1889, "Mrs. May Wright Sewall (Ind.) spoke on Women in the Recent Campaign." She said that: "All of the parties placed women on their platforms to speak in behalf of the candidates. . . . In all parts of the country Republican and Democratic women organized clubs and marched in processions; but . . . these methods are not advocated by the suffrage societies so long as women remain disfranchised."[57] At the 1890 founding (i.e., merger) convention of NAWSA the "most exciting" meeting was on "Our Attitude Toward Political Parties," where "[w]ithout exception the sentiment was in favor of keeping strictly aloof from all political alliances."

> [R]epeatedly the promises made by politicians were violated and the planks in the platforms ignored; it was shown that the suffrage can be gained only through the assistance of men in all parties; and it was proved beyond doubt that in the past, where members had allied themselves with a political party it had injured the cause of woman suffrage.[58]

Anthony was greatly disturbed by the effect of partisanship on women's suffrage loyalties. Once again Anthony wrote Henry Blackwell that "you . . . are a Republican per se. . . . I have been a Republican only in so far . . . [as it is] friendly to the principles of woman suffrage." In 1897 she criticized New York women for working in the municipal elections without first getting a party commitment to woman suffrage.[59] By 1900 she was counseling women to stay out of political parties and work only to enfranchise themselves. She noted that "the old Abolitionists were perfectly willing to have women share their obloquy and ostracism, but when they became a strong political party refused to divide their power with women," that the Populists dropped woman suffrage from even their state platforms when they fused with the Democrats in 1896, that the Prohibition Party dropped it in 1896, and that even the Republican Party had abolished the Women's Bureau for the current presidential campaign. Stanton trod the same path to non- or, more accurately, anti-partisanship. In 1894 she wrote approvingly to Lowell of women's work for municipal reform, even though none of the men running for mayor supported woman suffrage. In 1900 she wrote that "It is not of the slightest consequence to me whether McKinley or Bryan is elected . . . [because it] will not make the least difference in the present position of women."[60]

By the end of the nineteenth century the two major political parties had built the political house, effectively keeping minor parties outside except for an occasional break-in. But the parties occupied different rooms; with the advent of the Fourth Party System one-party dominance was the rule in most localities. A few states with strong Populist movements remained competitive, but elsewhere competition in the general election declined. Suffrage had been extended to all male citizens, and some non-citizens, but to women only in a few places. While politics was still a man's world, it was not exclusively so. Even without suffrage women had added some decorative touches to the campaigns that built the house and had carried bricks and mortar for some turrets. Women had cracked open the door. Some were repulsed by the dirt they saw through that crack; some were not. Others wanted in, but only with mops and brooms. Wrote Ellis Meredith about Colorado in 1894:

> Many women have read and heard about corruption in politics, . . . [W]e went in with our dust brushes, and we have come out with the knowledge gained that we need mops and soapsuds and boiling lye, and scrubbing brushes and chloride of lime and a host of disinfectants. . . . We have our choice: we can supinely "lie down and die and be buried in dirt," or we can organize for governmental house-cleaning; and though no one will aver that house-cleaning is pleasant, all will agree that it is desirable to have a clean political house in which to live.[61]

· *Three* ·

Assaulting the Citadel:
Woman Suffrage and the Political Parties

*I*t was in the Fourth Party System that women opened the door of the political house and entered the foyer. They did not do so by themselves but with the aid of the Progressive Movement. A political as well as a social movement, it wanted to eliminate corruption in politics, use government to control corporations, relieve the distress caused by industrialization and urbanization, improve wages and working conditions, and acculturate immigrants. To do this, Progressives thought it necessary to remodel the political house. Woman suffrage became part of the package of political reforms that would bring more democracy and less corruption.

Most reformers believed in woman suffrage, and most suffragists favored progressive reforms, but their priorities were different. Suffragists subsumed everything to their cause. Reformers saw suffrage as a way to empower women to improve their working and living conditions. In the second decade the interests of progressive men, women reformers, suffragists, and even some party bosses merged, creating sufficient momentum to add the Nineteenth Amendment to the U.S. Constitution. At the same time suffrage ranks were rent by a generational conflict which initially manifested itself as a strategic dispute. The younger generation was more militant than its elders and motivated by feminism, a world view that saw suffrage as just a step in the liberation of women from traditional attitudes about woman's proper sphere. Both generations agreed on at least one thing: the major political parties stood in their way.

WOMAN SUFFRAGE AND THE PROGRESSIVE MOVEMENT

After decades of petitioning for the vote, woman suffragists finally found men willing to listen in the Progressive Movement that swept the country in the early twentieth century.[1] Not so much an organized movement as a collective impulse to reform government, regulate business, and restore concern for the ordinary person, Progressives particularly wanted to remove politics from control of the bosses and the special interests and restore it to "the people." The Progressive view of the nineteenth-century political party was articulated by historians Charles and Mary Beard:

> A political party was a private association of gentlemen and others who had leisure for public affairs; its functional purpose was to get possession of the government in the name of patriotism and public welfare as a matter of course and to distribute the spoils of office among the commanders, the army, and its camp followers. How the party managed its caucuses, conventions, and committees was none of the general public's business; if leaders sometimes bought voters and marched them to the polls, they were only engaged in doing unto others what they expected others to do to them.[2]

Progressives changed the rules of the political game in many states in their effort to curb the power of political parties and bosses. They advocated the initiative, recall and referendum, direct election of U.S. Senators, primary elections, the Australian single ballot, voter registration to eliminate multiple voting, and state regulation of political parties. Progressives believed in democracy, but they were concerned that illiterate and ignorant people sold their votes, or at best cast them without concern for the consequences. They wanted to return government to "the people," but looked for ways to encourage "the better class" to vote, to discourage "the baser class" and to make "voting . . . less of a social act expressing partisanship and more of a civic duty associated with good citizenship."[3]

States passed laws to reform election practices for over twenty years before woman suffrage was taken seriously. Once the Progressive movement was nearing its peak and the militant suffragists of England were grabbing headlines, Progressives "[re]defined the people so as to include the women as well as the men." The redefinition followed naturally from the fact that Progressive men had been working with women for twenty years in various reform movements. Women had proven themselves to be effective campaigners and astute politicians; they could do everything the men could do to elect good candidates except vote. In this context, adding women to the voting population, particularly educated women who shared their values, took on a logic it had not previously had.[4]

According to Rheta Childe Dorr, journalist and active suffragist, "Woman suffrage in America began to wake up from its long lethargy in 1907–08, [i]nspired by the Pankhursts who by this time had made 'Votes for Women' a live question in England." In 1907 two wealthy New York women donated funds for a national headquarters, and in 1909 it was moved from Harriet Taylor Upton's home in Warren, Ohio, where it had rested since 1903. This "received an immense amount of space in the . . . papers . . . ; mass meetings and parades followed and thousands of women entered the suffrage ranks." In 1909 Carrie Chapman Catt organized New York City suffrage clubs into the Woman Suffrage Party. "[M]odeled after . . . the two dominant parties," its members were organized by Assembly Districts, with captains for each election district. Catt copied the parties in order to bring pressure on New York City's political machines.[5]

When the Progressive Movement began its final surge, woman suffrage was on its agenda. Between 1910 and 1914 Progressivism swept the West and Midwest and made inroads into the East; Progressive candidates won in Republican party primaries and even Democrats won in districts where they had not previously prevailed. The male voters in one Midwestern and five Western states enfranchised women, while also adopting the initiative, referendum, and recall about the same time. In four other states universal suffrage was voted in several years after the other progressive reform measures. Of the four early suffrage states, two added these measures at this time.[6]

	Suffrage	Initiative	Referendum	Recall
Wyoming	1869/90			
Utah	1870/96	1900	1900	
Colorado	1893	1910	1910	1912
Idaho	1896	1912	1912	1912
Washington	1910	1912	1912	1912
California	1911	1911	1911	1911
Oregon	1912	1902	1902	1908
Arizona	1912	1911	1911	1912
Kansas	1912			1914
Nevada	1914	1904	1912	1912
Montana	1914	1906	1906	
South Dakota	1918	1898	1898	
Oklahoma	1918	1907	1907	
Michigan	1918	1908	1908	1913

Source: Dates for initiative, referendum, and recall from Faulkner 1931, 85–86. Dates for woman suffrage from NAWSA 1940, Appendix 4.

Three of these states voted for suffrage in 1912, while legislators were ratifying the Seventeenth Amendment providing for direct election of U.S. Senators and Theodore Roosevelt was running for President on the Progressive Party's pro-suffrage platform. The Congress (1914–15) that met after its ratification was the first in which the federal suffrage amendment was voted on by both houses.[7] In June of 1913, the Illinois legislature adopted Presidential and municipal suffrage for women, when the Illinois Progressive Party held the balance of power after significant victories in the 1912 state legislative races. In 1917 New York became the first state (in the twentieth century) to give women full suffrage that did not also have one of the popular participation measures.[8] In the second decade the Progressive Movement amended the U.S. Constitution four times. That granting equal suffrage to women was the last and most difficult to achieve.

OPPOSITION TO WOMAN SUFFRAGE

The reluctance of men to allow women to participate in democratic decision-making stemmed from many sources, not all of which were consistent. One of the biggest deterrents was the importance of race in American politics, especially in the South. According to Southern historian Anne Firor Scott, "Because many of the early suffragists were abolitionists, the idea of woman's rights was anathema in the South." Ten years after Susan B. Anthony died in 1906, she and more contemporary colleagues were still being denounced for their "Southern-hating, negro-loving propensities."[9] Southerners remained implacable foes of women suffrage in any form by any means. Were suffrage granted, one prominent Georgia Senator told Congress in 1887 as the suffrage bill came before the Senate for the first time, "the more ignorant and less refined portions of the female population . . . would rush to the polls, . . . while the refined and educated, . . . would remain at home."[10] The antis fed the flames, insisting that women suffrage would undermine white supremacy and lead to racial equality. Thirty years later Southern Congressmen were still sounding the same theme in Congressional floor debates: Votes for women meant votes for black women.[11]

Decades of restricting black suffrage did not still their fears: a grant of school suffrage to women in three Kentucky cities in 1894 was withdrawn in 1902 because "more colored than white women voted in . . . the Spring election." Southern fears held back Northern support as well. In 1914, Senator William E. Borah, a Progressive Republican from Idaho, told a suffrage lobbyist that "I do not believe the suffragists realize what they are doing to the women of the South if they force upon them universal suffrage before they are ready for it. The race question is one of the most serious before the country today and the women must help solve it before they can take on greater responsibilities." To obtain the supermajorities necessary to amend the U.S. Constitution, the Suffrage Movement distanced itself from Southern efforts to disenfranchise African Americans. Yet even when Southern women finally organized a major suffrage campaign, which excluded black women in order to prove their loyalty to Southern mores, their impact was minimal. To the end, the largest block of Congressional "no" votes for the Nineteenth Amendment were Southern, and only five border states—Texas, Missouri, Arkansas, Kentucky, and Tennessee—ratified it at the time.[12]

In 1983, an African American historian pointed out:

> . . . white southern apprehensions of a viable black female electorate were
> not illusionary. "Colored women voter's leagues" were growing throughout
> the South, where the task of the leagues was to give black women seeking

to qualify to vote instructions for countering white opposition. Leagues could be found in Alabama, Georgia, Tennessee, and Texas. These groups were feared also by white supremacists because the women sought to qualify black men as voters as well.

Whites widely believed that black women wanted the ballot more than white women in the south. Black women were expected to register and to vote in larger numbers than white women. If this happened, the ballot would soon be returned to black men. Black suffrage, it was believed, would also result in the return of the two-party system in the South because blacks would consistently vote Republican.[13]

Another major source of opposition was the association of suffrage with prohibition by the "liquor interests." Women predominated in the temperance movement and it was widely believed that women would vote for prohibition more readily than men. This belief, too, was not unfounded.[14] During the many campaigns for state suffrage, opponents claimed that if women could vote, prohibition would come. In fact it came anyway, largely through the votes of men. Universal suffrage took longer than universal prohibition even though suffrage and prohibition leaders took pains to keep their distance from each other.[15] Regression analyses of the votes on prohibition and suffrage referenda in non-Southern states indicate that, like race, the negative effects of prohibition on woman suffrage were more powerful than the positive ones—i.e., those men opposing prohibition were more likely to vote against suffrage than those supporting it were likely to vote for. Suffrage did particularly poorly in referenda when prohibition was on the same ballot.[16]

In the Northeast there were some prominent politicians who opposed woman suffrage out of fear of foreign-born voters,[17] but opposition was more often based on the claim that women neither needed nor wanted the vote, and should not have this unreasonable burden imposed on them.[18] In 1905 former President Grover Cleveland pontificated in the *Ladies Home Journal* that allowing "woman the right to vote and otherwise participate in public affairs" would have a "dangerous undermining effect on the characters of the wives and mothers of our land."[19] Four years later the (male) editor of that *Journal* explained to the *New York Times* (which also opposed suffrage): "American women . . . are absolutely indifferent to it . . . [b]ecause the average American woman is too busy . . . with things of a vital nature that are distinctly woman's own questions."[20]

Outside the South, urban voters were less favorable to woman suffrage than those in small towns and more rural areas, largely due to ethno-cultural factors. Protestants and northern Europeans, who were more supportive of woman suffrage, immigrated west as the Eastern and Midwestern metropolises were flooded with new immigrants from Southern and Eastern Europe with a Catholic faith and more traditional values. The exceptions to this pattern were the Germans and Dutch, who generally opposed suffrage (and prohibition) even when Protestant, and the Italians, who were less opposed than other Catholic immigrants. The referenda analyses confirm contemporary claims that the strongest support for suffrage was found among the descendants of the early Puritans, especially native-born members of Congregational churches, many of whom settled in the Rocky Mountain states which first gave women the vote.[21] Catholics, even native-born, were more likely to object. While the Church never officially opposed woman suffrage, prominent Church officials spoke against it and the "antis" aimed some of their campaigns at Catholic voters.[22] The most consistent finding from referenda voting patterns was that men in areas with higher levels of education were more likely to vote for woman suffrage. These are also the men who were most likely to support the goals of the Progressive Movement.[23]

The women who led the antisuffragists had very different class and ethnic backgrounds from the men who voted against suffrage, being "for the most part, urban, wealthy, native born, Republican, and Protestant—members of established families either by birth or marriage, or both." Antis were activated by suffrage victories in the 1880s and 1890s, and contributed to the decade of suffrage doldrums in the 1900s. While suffrage sentiment was strongest in the rural West, "the core of remonstrant activity took place in the populous, urbanized, industrialized, East." Massachusetts was their center of operations; other strong chapters were in the urban areas of New York, New Jersey, Pennsylvania, Connecticut, and Ohio. As members of the urban elites, anti- women could exercise influence through their personal associations with important men; they didn't need to vote. Like their male colleagues, they saw universal suffrage as a threat to their social position and class interests. After women won suffrage in California in 1911, eight state anti-associations met in New York to found the National Association Opposed to Woman Suffrage (NAOWS) at the Park Avenue apartment of Mrs. Arthur M. Dodge. A wealthy widow, she became its first president and editor of *The Woman's Protest*. When the suffrage struggle shifted to Congress in 1917, NAOWS moved to Washington, D.C., and Alice Hay Wadsworth, daughter of former Secretary of State John Hay and wife of the leading suffrage opponent in the Senate, James W. Wadsworth Jr. of New York, became president. During the ratification struggle, Mary Kilbreth, also from New York, took over the leadership. Having access to the pockets of rich men and corporations, NAOWS depended on financial contributions rather than membership dues. Male antis organized separately from women, though they were also respectable representatives of the privileged classes. Not until the final drive in Congress and for ratification did the men take over leadership from the women.[24]

In 1916 Carrie Chapman Catt assumed the presidency of NAWSA and proposed a "winning plan," combining a national lobby and state campaigns. In 1917 the men of New York enfranchised the women. And in January of 1918, President Wilson finally declared his support for a federal amendment for woman suffrage. That year the Republican Party recaptured both houses, removing the Southern Democrats from Congressional leadership posts. Passage of the Suffrage Amendment was at the top of its agenda when the new Congress convened in May and on June 4, 1919, the Nineteenth Amendment was sent to the states, without many votes to spare.[25] On August 26, 1920, the United States became the twenty-seventh nation to allow women to vote equally with men.

Carrie Chapman Catt calculated that it took:

72 years of campaigning,
56 referenda to male voters,
480 efforts to get state legislatures to submit suffrage amendments,
277 campaigns to get state party conventions to include women's suffrage planks,
47 campaigns to get state constitutional conventions to write women's suffrage into state constitutions,
30 campaigns to get presidential party conventions to adopt women's suffrage planks into party platforms,
19 successive campaigns with 19 successive Congresses.[26]

Among the costs of the final campaign were the arrests of roughly five hundred women, of whom 168 spent some time in jail.[27]

FEMALE REFORM ORGANIZATIONS

Organized womanhood, as it was called, flourished during the Progressive era. Many women found reform an attractive outlet for their energies, especially educated women with college degrees. Living in a society that frowned upon women working for pay who did not have to, and finding few outlets for their energy and ideas, these middle and upper class women founded settlement houses "to provide a center for a higher civic and social life" for the poor, engaged in "social uplift" and organized charities. While the settlements generally stayed away from political parties, some realized that new laws were necessary to make lasting changes in the neighborhoods in which they worked. Women joined with male Progressives to lobby for legislation to improve factory conditions, inspect food and drugs, set standards for housing and sanitation, and reduce the incidence of disease. To gain acceptance for their activities they defined them as well within women's traditional concerns, a form of "municipal housekeeping."[28]

Hull House in Chicago, founded by Jane Addams in 1889, was a training ground for many women who would have an impact on public policy. One of these was Florence Kelley, who joined the settlement in December 1891. A Quaker, she graduated from Cornell in 1882 and received a law degree from Northwestern University in 1895. In 1899 she united Consumers Leagues in several cities into a National Consumers' League (NCL) with the goal of organizing middle class (female) consumers to bring pressure on retail merchants to improve wages and working conditions for largely female clerks by publishing a "white list" of stores that met certain standards. The daughter of an influential Republican Congressman, and an avowed socialist who corresponded with Friedrich Engels, Kelley turned the NCL into a multi-state lobby for protective labor legislation for women and children. The NCL was officially a mixed-sex organization, and always headed by a prominent man, but as its permanent General Secretary, Kelley set its tone, determined its goals, and organized most of its activities. Within a few years she had organized ninety local leagues, twenty state leagues, thirty-five auxiliary leagues, and numerous college branches. For the rest of her life she fought for laws restricting the number of hours women could work, the amount of weight they could lift, special benefits such as rest periods, and sometimes prohibitions on their working in certain occupations or at night.[29]

The National Women's Trade Union League (WTUL) was "founded in 1903 by an assortment of socialists, social workers, reformers, and a few trade unionists gathered for the annual convention of the American Federation of Labor." It evolved into a coalition of working class women and middle class "allies," who urged "women in industry" to join unions and nagged the AFL to admit women over its objections that they didn't earn enough to pay full dues. Margaret Dreier Robins and her sister Mary Dreier led it most of the time, but they encouraged working women such as Rose Schneiderman and Pauline Newman to speak out and stand up for their sisters, despite the hostile attitude of organized labor. These women and others like them on the WTUL payroll made many "speeches to working-class women on the need for woman suffrage."[30]

Women started many other organizations that concerned themselves with a variety of reforms. In major urban centers they founded women's city clubs, women's municipal leagues, and women's health protective associations which educated their members about important urban issues and lobbied on such problems as sanitation, schools, and crime. The clubs were explicitly Progressive in their approach to urban problems, looking to government for solutions. However, they often had different agendas than equivalent men's clubs even when their members lived in the same families. The city clubs were a way for women to carve out a place for themselves and "to influence political decision making" in a world where politics was still a male domain.[31]

As more and more women joined clubs, organized womanhood, which had begun with reform and moved to culture and self-improvement, came full circle. Its attention shifted to community betterment, first locally, then more widely. As early as 1900 the GFWC resolved to work for legislation benefiting women and children. In 1902, Jane Addams convinced the GFWC to add child labor laws to its agenda. Florence Kelley and the NCL pushed it to support protective labor legislation for women and children. By 1904, the GFWC urged "the formation of legislative committees in every department club, ... to keep

the clubs informed as to bills pending in municipal, state, and national legislatures. . . . Marriage and divorce, child protection, child labor, pure food, forestry
and libraries, are subjects which the clubs are asked to follow." By 1909 virtually all the state federations had legislative committees to identify existing laws
affecting women and propose new ones. By 1913 six hundred women's clubs
were involved in legislative work. At every biennial convention, the GFWC
increased its commitment to "social service," adding committees on civil service reform, pure food, industrial and child labor legislation, and even on lobbying state legislatures. Although these clubs were largely composed of
"respectable" women, they were not always well received by "respectable" men.
In two 1905 articles, Cleveland denounced women's clubs for their "unfavorable effect . . . on American womanhood" because the "club habit" is "apt to
pave the way to the reception of woman-suffrage radicalism." Cleveland was
right. Officially, "the doings of women's clubs" drifted to legislative action while
avoiding suffrage. Unofficially, lobbying convinced club women that suffrage
was necessary.[32]

Long after the GFWC leadership supported progressive programs, most of
the membership remained conservative. The national Biennial didn't even
endorse "political equality regardless of sex" until 1914. For its first decade, the
policy was to avoid all discussion of religion and politics; it would not allow
suffrage organizations to join to avoid the taint of radicalism.[33] On the touchy
issue of race it walked a fine line between Southern women who would not
join any organization that allowed African Americans to participate and reformers who objected to racial exclusion. While the GFWC never officially excluded
black members it did discourage their participation. In 1900 the executive committee voted to admit a Boston club of black women, only to be repudiated at
the next convention. The GFWC's Southern affiliates only wanted to admit
clubs of white women. Wells's *History* of the federation explained that when the
"race issue came before the convention" in 1900, "[t]here was a strong majority, but the minority in the South was recognized and we preferred to keep
them with us. We wanted to work with the South. . . ." Objecting, some clubs
withdrew from the GFWC. The suffragist *Woman's Journal* protested the
GFWC's "step backward."[34]

By 1910, with 800,000 members, women's clubs were a powerful force.
Those that took up social issues could be very influential. In Colorado, after
women's literary societies added civic and educational reform to their agendas
the "annual meeting of the State Federation of Women's Clubs became a political council." In Los Angeles, where "women began developing a reformist political culture through women's clubs" in the 1880s, the Friday Morning Club
evolved "from an organization devoted to cultural and philanthropic affairs to
'the most powerful civic body in Los Angeles.'" Some of its leaders, such as
Mary Simons Gibson and Katherine Phillips Edson, worked actively in the campaigns of Progressive candidates. Governor Hiram Johnson appointed both

women to state commissions in his administration, from 1911 through 1916. During the successful suffrage campaign of 1911, "[w]omen's clubs . . . provided the core of the coalition that waged the campaign. Their federation . . . had nearly tripled its membership to twenty thousand."[35]

The National Association of Colored Women (NACW) combined self culture and community improvement from its inception, both educating its members and creating a network of social service projects. Under the motto "Lifting as we climb," it had fifty thousand members in a thousand clubs in twenty-eight states by 1914. As was true for white women, the clubs trained black women in leadership and organization. While some black women worked for suffrage in the nineteenth century, a few joined NAWSA, and some were paid speakers who appealed to black men in state referenda campaigns, most came late to suffrage. Ida B. Wells-Barnett "tried for many years to interest the Colored Women's Clubs in suffrage, but they were in some instances unwilling to take up the work, and in some cases they showed little or no interest." Massachusetts had an antisuffrage organization of colored women. Apathy was partly due to community resistance. Analyses of nineteenth-century black newspapers show that woman suffrage was seldom discussed, and usually opposed when it was. Black women canvassing for a black candidate in the 1914 Chicago city council races encountered fierce hostility from black men. Reynolds's regression analysis of the 1915 New Jersey suffrage referendum showed that native-born whites of native-born parents were the most likely to vote to enfranchise women, and black men were the least likely, with foreign-born whites and their children in between. To combat this, *The Crisis* ran "A Woman Suffrage Symposium" in September 1912. Once suffrage was won, black men and women took greater interest in what women could do with the ballot. In 1913, Wells-Barnett and Belle Squires were finally able to organize Chicago's Alpha Suffrage Club so Negro women "could help put a colored man in the city council."[36]

The WCTU ceased being the largest or most important women's organization in the Twentieth Century. After Willard died in 1898 the WCTU narrowed its focus, and its membership gradually became both older and more conservative. Although numbers and activity did not decline until the 1930s, young women found the newer organizations more attractive. "After 1900 the Anti-Saloon League took over as prime mover of the temperance cause, the NAWSA became the main force in the women's movement, and the General Federation of Women's Clubs eclipsed the WCTU in size of membership, although it was never to rival it in political force."[37]

As the Progressive Movement crested, local party ward heelers in the cities joined forces with the "genteel reformers" to promote what were called welfare bills. Low wages, unsafe working conditions, inadequate housing, child labor, excessive hours, and unsanitary food were just some of the social problems for which legislative remedies were sought. As they worked on these issues they slowly realized that with the vote women could do more for themselves and legislators would pay more attention to the problems of women and children. Jane Addams made this argument in a widely reprinted 1910 *Ladies Home Journal* article on "Why Women Should Vote." Addams, along with such reformers as Sophonisba Preston Breckinridge and Florence Kelley in Chicago, joined the NAWSA and other suffrage organizations. Some reformers, such as Frances Perkins and Belle and Henry Moskowitz of New York City, involved themselves in local political campaigns. The former linked Progressives with Suffragists. The latter became bridges between the suffrage movement and the anti-suffrage big city politicians, such as Al Smith, sheriff of New York County and a leader of Tammany Hall. Urban reformers persuaded some of these urban politicians that giving women the vote might aid the welfare bills that would help their poorer constituents. As these men switched from con to neutral and sometime to pro, suffrage referenda in the Eastern states were more successful.[38]

FEMINISM

Feminism as a term did not come into vogue until the 1910s. Until then, most people spoke of the Woman Movement to identify the collective impulse to improve the status of women, or the Suffrage Movement to identify those working for equal suffrage. The new term reflected a new fervor—in reality a new movement—among women. It was a British import, but one for which there was a ready audience among a new generation of American women who thought the old "suffrage movement was completely in a rut." Among those who brought these views across the ocean was Harriet Stanton Blatch, daughter of Elizabeth Cady Stanton. When she returned to New York after twenty years in Great Britain, she immersed herself in the Women's Trade Union League. Impressed by the spirit of wage-earning women, in 1907 she formed the Equality League of Self Supporting Women where wage-earning and professional women could work together for suffrage. The very name of this organization reflected the growing importance of wage earners in an industrial, capitalistic economy. Rather than concern for the plight of women who *had* to work, feminism stressed the importance of autonomy; suffrage was a sign of independence from men, as was self-support. These ideas planted the seeds for future disagreement. They anticipated a paradigmatic shift in the economic role of women, but one that had not yet matured and become socially acceptable.[39]

The Equality League abjured the polite educational campaigns of the contemporary suffrage movement in favor of the more militant tactics of the labor movement and the British suffragettes. In order to garner publicity and affect public opinion, Blatch initiated the use of outdoor rallies, demonstrations, and publicity stunts that she had learned from the Women's Social and Political Union organized by Emmeline and Christabel Pankhurst. When Mrs. Pankhurst herself lectured throughout the United States in 1909, she found women were already organizing numerous new suffrage associations on the local level.

American newspapers featured stories about the WSPU's militant tactics, and her speeches inspired the American suffragists to further action.[40]

What most attracted American feminists to the WSPU's militancy was its "attitude of complete defiance, their determination to *force* the government to act on women's rights. . . . [They] did not stress women's different, gentler nature. The Pankhurst revolution sought to smash the rigid Victorian stereotypical image of separate male and female spheres and prove to the world that women were every bit as tough as men, and infinitely their moral superiors." Or, as one admirer of the Pankhursts' described them, "These English women were fighting for their cause like soldiers, not pleading like suppliants."[41]

Feminism was not a mass movement. Feminism attracted young college graduates, and in 1910 these were just 1.9 percent of women over age 25 in the U.S. population; in 1920 they were 2.4 percent.[42] Solidly middle-class—the wealthy did not send their daughters to college—these women aspired to better positions than wage slaves. Since most did not *have* to work, the "principle of freedom to choose one's work regardless of sex and regardless of marriage was a central tenet." A younger generation than the leaders of the major reform organizations, they often fused political and personal liberation, breaking the bounds of traditional morality through their freer lifestyles and rejection of traditional values about marriage and family. Socialists, "sex radicals," free thinkers, and many other cultural rebels swam in the stream of intellectual currents of which feminism was a part. Not all were active suffrage workers, though all certainly believed in woman suffrage.[43]

Among those who did work for suffrage, Alice Paul, Lucy Burns, and Anne Martin served an apprenticeship in the WSPU at different times between 1906 and 1912.[44] In 1912 Paul and Burns persuaded NAWSA to let them revive its Congressional Committee and pursue a federal amendment, provided they raise their own funds. They quickly mobilized both money and people, organizing five thousand people to parade for suffrage on March 3, 1913, the day before Woodrow Wilson's inauguration, and again in July. In April, Paul and Burns formed their own organization, the Congressional Union (CU), with its own newsletter, which lobbied Congress and the President with a persistence that NAWSA officers thought would alienate the male politicians they had been carefully cultivating for years. When Paul refused to relent, NAWSA replaced her with Ruth Hanna McCormick, who, as the daughter of Senator Mark Hanna and the wife of an Illinois legislator whose family published the *Chicago Tribune*, was well connected.[45]

Among the many differences behind the split was a strong disagreement over strategy. Paul wanted to mobilize women in the suffrage states to vote against *all* Democratic Party candidates, regardless of their personal opinion on woman suffrage. She adopted the British approach of holding the party in power responsible for the government's failure to pass a federal amendment. Wilson was a Democrat as were a majority of the members of both houses; therefore all Democrats should be opposed at the polls. NAWSA objected that this would not work in the different and decentralized American political system. However, the Democrats did seem vulnerable because Wilson had won in 1912 with only 42 percent of the popular vote and the President's party usually loses seats in the midterm election. In 1914 the CU sent organizers to the Western states where women could vote; it claimed victory because the Democrats only won in twenty of the forty-three Congressional districts in which they had candidates.[46]

In 1916 the CU called upon its members in the suffrage states to form a National Woman's Party (NWP) in order to "make Suffrage an issue." By then, women could vote for President in a quarter of the states, which made up one-fourth of the electoral college and one-third of the votes necessary to elect a President. Meeting in Chicago in June, a week before the Republican convention, the NWP elected Anne Martin of Nevada as chairman. After a highly publicized strategy conference in Colorado Springs in August, it sent organizers, speakers, and campaign literature to women in the twelve Presidential suffrage states, urging them to cast their ballots for anyone but Wilson, and any party but the Democrats. Women Democrats promptly organized Women's Woodrow Wilson leagues and denounced the NWP. Although Wilson won all of these states except Oregon and Illinois, the NWP nonetheless claimed that he received many fewer votes than he would have otherwise. It cited the results in Illinois, where women's votes for President were counted separately, as showing that "over seventy thousand more women voted against Mr. Wilson than for him." By 1918 President Wilson and the House of Representatives supported a federal suffrage amendment, so the NWP directed its energies toward the Senate. In the West it campaigned against the Democrats, as the responsible party, but in two open seats in the East it singled out Republican anti-suffragists opposed by Democratic suffrage supporters. The Democratic suffragists were defeated, along with enough other Democrats to allow the Republicans to resume control of Congress.[47]

NAWSA AND NONPARTISANSHIP

In 1912 a writer for the *New York Times*, in an article on "Women as a Factor in the Political Campaign," observed:

> There are a large body of suffragists who frown upon the idea of their sisters allying themselves with any political party whatever, on the ground that a non-partisan attitude will accomplish much more for the cause. These are the conservatives. The radicals or progressives are the women who have gone right into the Republican, Democratic or Bull Moose organizations and are fighting hard to elect their respective candidates to the Presidency, believing that each candidate, in his own way, will bring to a realization the good they are fighting for.[48]

The 1912 Presidential campaign shook NAWSA's "unwritten but care-fully observed law" of nonpartisanship. Jane Addams became NAWSA's First Vice President in 1911. In 1912 her vigorous, highly publicized campaigning for Theodore Roosevelt created controversy inside the organization through-out the year, even though he was the only major candidate who had endorsed woman suffrage. At the NAWSA convention held right after the election, several women proposed a resolution declaring that officers must remain nonpartisan. It was soundly defeated. Instead NAWSA reaffirmed that it was "an absolutely non-partisan, non-sectarian body." In 1914, when the Congressional Union revealed its strategy to campaign against all Democrats, NAWSA paraded its nonpartisanship; Addams left the board. Partisan neutral-ity was so important that when the women of Illinois faced their first vote in 1914, several suffrage leaders urged them not to vote in the primaries because doing so required enrollment in a political party. In the election of 1916 a mem-ber of the Wilson administration warned NAWSA to stay nonpartisan in order to avoid opposition that would delay suffrage even longer. NAWSA didn't need to be told. It emphasized that "no officer of the NAWSA took any public part in [the election of 1916], although . . . woman suffrage was a leading issue." It was not until 1919 that NAWSA finally resolved that "any member or officer of this association [may] join or serve the party of her choice in any capacity whatsoever as an individual."[49]

NAWSA's nonpartisanship was not merely strategic, but reflected the bit-terness long-time suffragists held toward the major political parties. This bit-terness would not fade when the Nineteenth Amendment was finally added to the U.S. Constitution. It would keep most of the experienced national suf-frage leaders away from the parties, and with an occasional exception, out of electoral politics. Alienation shines through the official description of "Woman Suffrage in the National Presidential Conventions," which reported that "dis-tinguished women were received with an indifference that was insulting until far into the 20th century." As it did every four years, NAWSA sent delegates to the Democratic and Republican conventions of 1904, 1908, and 1912 where they were permitted to address the Resolutions Committee, but suffrage was left out of the platforms. Only the Progressive Party was receptive, and "[f]rom this time woman suffrage was one of the dominant political issues throughout the country."[50]

Despite this dominance, in 1916 the Republican and Democratic parties still waffled. Even though women were active supporters of the Progressive ticket, which beat the Republicans significantly in 1912, and most Roosevelt Progressives rejoined the Republican Party, the party was reluctant to support woman suffrage. When the Resolutions subcommittee met in Chicago prior to the national nominating convention, it voted 5 to 4 to have no suffrage plank as thousands of women marched outside in a drenching June rain. The next day, the full committee agreed on a compromise by a vote of 35 to 11 after a long and acrimonious debate. On August 1, Republican candidate Charles Evans Hughes came out for a federal amendment. He supported suffrage not because it was just, but because it was inevitable. He wanted to end the struggle "promptly" so it would not "increase in bitterness." A "distinctly feminist move-ment" had organized "to the subversion of normal political issues." The Democrats might have left suffrage out of their platform altogether had not President Wilson dictated otherwise. Although the Resolutions Committee defeated unqualified endorsement by 24 to 20, and adopted Wilson's states rights proposal by 25 to 20, there was still a rancorous floor fight from suffrage oppo-nents. Even as the suffrage star was rising, there was significant opposition from the major political parties.[51]

The steady resistance to admit women to political equality did not endear the parties to suffragists. As Carrie Chapman Catt, the "general" of the final drive, wrote in the 1920s:

> During this long stretch of time, the dominant political parties, pitted against each other since 1860, used their enormous organized power to block every move on behalf of woman suffrage. The seeming exceptions were rare and invariably caused by breaks or threatened breaks in party ranks. Strong men in both parties and in all States championed the woman's cause in Legislatures and in political conventions, and eventually the number of these became too large to be ignored. But it was not until public opinion, far in advance of party leaders, indicated that a choice between woman suffrage and party disruption must be made that organized party help was given, and even then it was neither united nor whole-hearted.
>
> Between the adoption of the Fifteenth Amendment (March 30, 1870), which completed the enfranchisement of the Negro, and 1910, lie forty years during which women watched, prayed and worked without ceasing for the woman's hour that never came. The party whips had cracked to drive the nation to enfranchise the Negro. They cracked, and cracked again, to prevent the enfranchisement of women. Whenever there was an exception and the parties stood by woman suffrage in a referendum, success came to the woman's cause. Most victories were won, however in spite of party opposition.[52]

· *Four* ·

Learning the Ropes:
Emergence of the Party Woman

*A*t the beginning of the twentieth century party women were just emerging as a distinct strand of political activist. Although reform organizations and political families were still major sources of party women, some women were taking up party work on their own. By the time full suffrage came with the Nineteenth Amendment, party women were more numerous, but were still intertwined with suffragists and reformers. Most commonly found in the full suffrage states, particularly in Colorado, they were also active in many other states that had strong parties. In major urban areas, particularly New York and Chicago, party women did virtually everything necessary to elect candidates that party men did except vote. They did not have the power, influence, or patronage of party men, but they organized as women and did the work.

Entering politics without prior involvement in the suffrage movement or in reform organizations, the new party woman did not face the conflicts of those who began by working for a cause. Her primary loyalty was to her party, right or wrong. J. Ellen Foster, who began as a temperance worker but who made her mark as an organizer and campaigner for the Republican Party, understood what party men wanted as the price of admission to their home. She told the 1892 Republican National Convention: "We do not seek recognition in the party in the interest of any one of the various reforms, in which, as individuals, we are interested. . . . Gentlemen, . . . we are for service." In 1894 she told Republican women of Colorado to vote for the candidates chosen by the "party machinery" and not to insist on having a say on who these men were. A year later, the Colorado Woman's Democratic Club split when reformers within it refused to support candidates merely because of party label. When the Republican Party created a Women's National Executive Committee in 1919, its first chair, Ruth Hanna McCormick, also understood what party men wanted. She told the Republican National Committee that "Women . . . shall work not independently, but in association with men and under the leaders of the party." Party women would continue to tell party men that they were there to selflessly serve the party even while they complained that they were only allowed to serve.[1]

A specialized type of party woman was the political wife. Usually married to an elected official, her primary interest in politics was her husband's career, even though she might work on others' campaigns. As a wife, her status within her party rose and fell with his. Of course, a political wife could be a party woman in her own right, just as she could be a reformer or suffragist, but her husband's job more than her own work usually determined her standing within the party. The typical political wife left politics when her husband did. In politics as in the rest of society, what a woman's husband did had a greater impact on her fate, and her status, than what she did. Some political wives became political widows. Such women combined the advantages of her husband's prior status, name, and goodwill with the independence to forge her own path. Political widows were more successful in finding a place for themselves in the political house than most other women who worked in politics.

The new political style that became dominant in the Fourth Party System eased women's way into politics. In the Third Party System political campaigns had featured mass participation, with large revival-like rallies, parades, costumes, campaign clubs, and raucous debates. Campaigns were ritualized warfare. In the latter part of the nineteenth century, an educated class, usually employed in the professions, promoted a campaign style that emphasized education on public issues and persuasion through advertisement of candidates' positions.[2] The parties published Campaign Text Books of several hundred pages, which included copies of their platforms, candidates' views, attacks on the opposition, and anything else thought to be persuasive. Although both Campaign Text Books and rallies were common at the end of the nineteenth century, mass mobilization declined in the twentieth. Mass meetings were still addressed by campaign orators, but most campaigning was done through circulars, newspapers, parlor parties, and one-on-one canvassing. These required skills at which women were quite proficient and did not demand presenting oneself to the public in ways that many women still felt were incompatible with womanly decorum. The change in political style from symbolic war to education created opportunities for women who shied away from making speeches and marching in parades. This made it easier for women who were not active in suffrage or reform to find suitable work in political parties.

There was also a shift in *where* politics took place. Apart from mass meetings and parades, political life in the nineteenth century dwelled in places where few women entered, such as saloons and barber shops. After the Civil War saloons increased to one for every 250 persons by 1900, even while actual liquor consumption declined. Not only political discussion, but political clubs, conventions, and even polling places were located there. Theodore Roosevelt observed that, of the 1,007 primaries and party conventions held in New York City for the election of 1884, 633 were in saloons. As the Progressive Movement battled party bosses, politics moved to "domesticated space, where middle-class men and women together enjoyed refined and sober entertainments." Tea parties and socials were added to the repertoire of campaign events, and voting migrated from saloons to schools and churches.[3]

The continued growth of women's clubs also pulled women into politics. The typical literary, social, or civic club did not become a political club, but it did provide experience and contacts that were easily transferable to political work. The growth of a middle class, in which a leisured wife was a symbol of family status, created a class of educated women with time and social skills suitable for a style of politics emphasizing education and persuasion. These women provided a volunteer pool for campaigns. Sometimes, as in the 1911 race for mayor of Philadelphia, clubwomen elected reform candidates who had no other organization.[4] When additional states enfranchised women in the second decade, and the Nineteenth Amendment enfranchised all women equally after 1920, a large cadre of women, particularly white, Protestant, educated, middle-class women, was ready and eager to go into politics, as well as being experienced in club organization. Indeed, many were already in politics.

THE NEW PARTY WOMAN

Party women organized most easily in Colorado and Utah because they were full suffrage states with cities. One such woman was Mrs. William Henry Jones, a wealthy clubwoman and president of the Woman's Republican Club of Salt Lake City, who attended the 1900 Republican National Convention as an alternate. Another was "Mrs. [Elizabeth] Cohen, an alternate from Utah to the Democratic convention, [to whom] was given the honor of being the first voting delegate in either of the two great party conventions. A vacancy having occurred in the regular delegation, she was promptly elected to it," and seconded the nomination of William Jennings Bryan. Neither woman had been a suffragist or a reformer.[5] Colorado sent another two women to the Republican convention as alternates in 1904, one of whom was described as "extremely conservative." While Mrs. J.B. (Susan Henderson) West, an alternate to the Republican convention from Idaho in both 1900 and 1904, was a suffragist, by then politics and partisanship were spreading to new types of women.[6]

Women were more than occasional delegates. Several became "bosses," who, like equivalent men, traded favors and promises for votes and were given jobs in return. In 1902 *The Denver Times* profiled Alma Beswick, who "Controls Votes of Women for Democrats," and described several other women who commanded voting blocs.[7] Another was Anna Scott, designated by a national magazine in 1908 as the "Woman Boss of Denver." She went into politics as soon as Colorado gave women suffrage, without a prior history in suffrage or reform; nor did her husband have any interest in politics. Holding no office other than president of the Women's State Republican Club, she ran her district and decided which men would represent it. "She is a pioneer," *Harper's Weekly* said, "of a type of women in politics which . . . must eventually become numerous if women hope to deal on an equality with men." To elect her man, Scott relied on women. "I hired only women workers," she reported after a recent election. "I believe them to be more effective than men. It cost me just $400 to carry my ward," compared to $2,000 to $3,000 using party men. Male bosses must have learned from her experience; Sumner reported in 1909 that "Where the size of the community justifies canvassing in any systematic way, women are employed in somewhat larger numbers than men."[8]

Only a few years after suffrage, many Colorado women had learned the basics of political organization and were touting their skills. "A Colorado Woman" described what women did in an 1899 Denver election.

> A district Committee Woman . . . must find from eight to fifteen women who will take charge of their precincts . . . [some of which have] over 400 voters. . . . [These women] must get out every vote that belongs to her party, in her precinct. . . .
>
> The canvassing that precedes every election is done by women almost exclusively in Denver. They have proved more successful in getting the names, and learning the politics, than men. . . .
>
> When the canvasser's book is done, it should show the name and address of every voter in that precinct, together with his or her politics. At the end of the book the totals are set down, so many Democrats, Republicans, Populists, and so on, and in many of them, the number of "Doubtfuls" led all the rest.
>
> Armed with this book, the committee woman knows just who can be approached, and she calls on as many Democratic or Republican women as she can, or sends them an invitation to a meeting to be held at some convenient time and place. There she puts before them the necessity for concerted action, urges them to talk with their neighbors, to attend the caucus, the primaries and the convention, and the meetings that may be held thereafter. Sometimes she organizes a club for that precinct. Above all, she emphasizes the importance of registration, frequently taking numbers of women to the Court House for that purpose, instead of waiting for the district registration.
>
> One committee woman helped to wash and dress the children and start them off to school, so that the busy mother might have time for the important duty of registering; another went into the kitchen and looked after the baking while the lady of the house attended to this formality.
>
> The Saturday and Monday before the election were busy days at the Women's Headquarters. . . . There were last orders to give, last assurances to be made doubly sure, last vacancies to fill where workers had dropped out. . . . On election day workers are always instructed to be at the polls at least fifteen minutes before they open. . . .

> The precinct committee women had . . . a "carriage list" . . . of the women voters . . . [and] . . . the hour at which they will be ready to go to the polls. . . . [W]hen it storms there are many who do not care to walk to the polling place.[9]

Women found the work of identifying and persuading voters to be agreeable, requiring both organizational and social skills. Men discovered that women excelled at crucial aspects of winning elections. Thus even in states where women could not vote, they were often preferred for the nuts and bolts of party work. A writer in the New York *Evening Post* said the campaign of 1900 was even more of a "petticoat campaign" than its predecessors.

> . . . to her is confided the difficult and delicate task of canvassing the slums and foreign quarters. It is conceded that the work is done far more tactfully and successfully than it was before her advent.
>
> Early in this campaign the State committee apportioned the lower part of the city among the members of the West End Women's Republican Club. . . . Their districts once assigned, with plenty of "literature" on hand, they pursue their own methods. . . .
> Visits are made to the Russian and Polish Jewish quarters, to Little Italy, Little Syria, and other foreign settlements. The number of men old enough to vote and the number of the unnaturalized are learned. The women of the Republican Club get this information from their foreign sisters rather than from the men themselves who are less approachable. But sometimes a wife does not know her husband's politics, and protests that he would beat her should she ask. The visitor inquires whether he would beat herself if she put the question, and usually receiving a negative answer, returns at meal-time. If she can gain his confidence, he will listen to her respectfully, and even seek enlightenment upon questions of the day, which it would lower his dignity in his own eyes to ask from another man. Literature is left, and knotty points explained in subsequent interviews. A daily report is sent to State headquarters, whence agents are dispatched to the addresses of unnaturalized men to urge them to take out their papers, and to facilitate the metamorphosis of the alien into the citizen by explaining the legal formalities that seem too formidable to the ignorant. His naturalization accomplished, it is easy enough to persuade the regenerated foreigner to register and vote—and "to vote right" from his sponsor's view point.
> Meanwhile the feminine campaigner is making herself agreeable to the woman of the tenement . . . [and] explains the doctrines of her party. Mrs. Cornelia S. Robinson, president of the West End Club, says that the women of the poorer classes are much quicker than the men to grasp the importance of the monetary question, accustomed as they are to handling all the money earned by the family. In the case of a sick baby a doctor may be sent, if the mother agrees, or at any rate an ordinary prescription is ordered from some neighboring pharmacy. If want is apparent, it is met with temporary

relief, and then called to the attention of the authorities. A women with half-a-dozen small children in need of food or clothing, will use all her influence for the first person who alleviates her sufferings, and can usually be counted upon to control her husband's vote.

. . . the three hundred members in the Women's Republican Club . . . [also] labor among clerks and factory hands of their own sex; handicapped, however by the attitude of employers, who fear that the girls might use their organization, even if ostensibly political, to make a united demand for better pay.

. . . In general, the women do all the tedious preliminary work in the wide area referred to, and the men follow up their efforts after the way has been opened.[10]

The 1900 Republican convention featured a record number of women, who had no official role. Besides the usual family members, there were "hundreds of women . . . who take an active interest in politics."[11] The campaign was a rematch between Bryan and McKinley, prompting a notable lack of interest by voters. Indeed, it often seemed that women were more interested in the campaign than men. Reported Carrie Chapman Catt:

Suffragists and anti-suffragists are alike donning McKinley and Bryan badges, and are joining McKinley and Bryan leagues. Last, but not least, the national committees are reported to be in a condition of despair, for, with all their effort and expense to place their respective arguments before the voters of the country, their speakers are frequently met by audiences a majority of whom are women.[12]

The McKinley campaign did not have a separate women's bureau as it had in 1896, but women worked locally. While J. Ellen Foster toured the Western states with Vice Presidential candidate Theodore Roosevelt, Helen V. Boswell organized women to canvass house-to-house throughout New York state. Even Mary Elizabeth Lease, who had seconded William Jennings Bryan's nomination at the 1896 Populist convention, campaigned for McKinley and the Republican Party, although Annie Diggs stayed faithful to the People's Party.[13] Lacking funds and organization, the Democrats used women orators extensively. The DNC hired two young women from Kentucky and Minnesota to travel around recruiting women. Helen Gougar completed her personal partisan realignment and campaigned for Democratic candidate Bryan because of his strong support for prohibition.[14]

Within the full suffrage states, party women concentrated their efforts on women voters. "Colorado women are actively interested in the present campaign, and are well organized. Women's Republican Clubs and Women's Bryan Clubs are keeping open headquarters, holding parlor meetings and mass meetings, distributing literature, and sending speakers to remote districts." Outside of these four states, women continued to try to influence men. In New York, the opening of Women's Republican Headquarters attracted numerous women and quite a few men. In Massachusetts, women organized to reelect the governor and to persuade towns to limit the sale of liquor. They held "rallies, arranged for effective speaking and music, distributed literature, invoked the aid of the ministers and churches, canvassed for votes, and supplemented the men with whom they worked in every way possible." In Minnesota a woman ran the Minnesota Republican State Central Committee during the 1900 campaign, commanding "over a hundred men and women." In California the Women's Republican State Central Committee was praised for its efforts on behalf of the party.[15]

Nor did party women rest after the 1900 election. The Women's Democratic Club of Chicago declared it would be permanent. Women's Roosevelt Clubs appeared soon after McKinley was assassinated in 1901.[16] In the 1901 New York City mayoral campaign, reformers and Republicans united to elect fusion candidate Seth Low. "Municipal League Working Hard to Secure Campaign Fund—Two Hundred Thousand Leaflets Distributed by Republican Women" wrote the *New York Tribune* in October. Women opened their headquarters in Democratic territory, determined to capture the foreign-born vote. Tammany bowed to the assault by promoting a Women's Democratic Club of the East Side, whose president was the wife of a Tammany assemblyman and mother of a Tammany alderman. However, there is no evidence that it did any actual campaign work. In 1903 the *New York Herald* devoted an entire page to "Women in the Political Campaign," commenting that "there are hundreds of these earnest feminine workers swarming all over the city like the traditional bee."[17]

As she had done previously, for the 1908 campaign Foster reconstituted the WNRA into the Committee on Women's Work of the Republican National Committee. Boswell was the organization secretary of both groups, though Foster employed Mary Garrett Hay to work in the New York headquarters as "Miss Boswell and myself are continually speaking." Hay, like Foster, had begun as a temperance worker and was a dedicated Republican. But most of her work was in suffrage; she was Carrie Chapman Catt's chief lieutenant and shared her home after Catt was widowed in 1905. Boswell organized noontime political meetings so the men could listen to women speakers after eating their lunch.[18]

After McKinley's reelection, party men settled into the pattern of asking women to help elect men but seldom rewarding them for their efforts. In 1900 there were eight women serving in the legislatures of Colorado, Idaho, and Utah; in 1905-8 there were none. Women's experience in politics was summed up by the New York *Sun* in 1900 when it reported that the Republican State Central Committee was finally giving the West End Republican women a "hall, and paying for the services of clerks. There is no quid pro quo about it, however, as there seems to be in things political where men are concerned. The women give their time, strength, and services voluntarily." Even in Colorado, where women could vote, Emily R. Meredith concluded in 1905 that "Men held all the offices previous to the enfranchisement of women, and they still hold them, as well as almost all the power that comes from official position. They controlled the party machinery, and still control it. . . ."[19] A few years later, another Denver woman confirmed that women "are more effective and efficient as workers in any department of political work than men, but women do the work and the men get the money and position nine times out of ten."[20]

THE ELECTION OF 1912

Women gradually increased their presence in party affairs during the first decade of the twentieth century, but for most, the campaign of 1912 was their political baptism. *Harper's Weekly* declared it "the first incursion of American womanhood into national politics." As had been true in the nineteenth century, reform was the main road to partisanship. Jane Addams wrote about those years that "social workers, with thousands of other persons throughout the nation, had increasingly felt the need for a new party which should . . . make social reform a political issue of national dimensions." In 1911, sensing the time was ripe to challenge the regular Republican leadership, Wisconsin Senator Robert LaFollette formed the National Progressive Republican League. His intention to challenge President Taft's renomination was upstaged by former President Theodore Roosevelt's decision to do it himself. Taft won the Republican Party nomination on the first ballot, 556 to 107, despite the fact that Roosevelt had won most of the 1912 primaries. The Progressives held their own convention and nominated Roosevelt and California Governor Hiram Johnson on the "Bull Moose" ticket. Progressive Party conventions were held in many states to nominate candidates for other offices. Women rallied to TR's candidacy; Woman's Roosevelt Leagues had formed many months before any party conventions.[21]

Women found a warmer welcome in the Progressive Party than they had ever had from the Democrats or Republicans. Theodore Roosevelt urged that women have a voice in party affairs even in states where they could not vote. Their presence in party bodies was a striking contrast to their rarity in the major parties. Between twelve and forty women were convention delegates, compared to two each at the Democratic and Republican conventions. Alice Carpenter sat on the Resolutions Committee; four other women served on the national Executive Committee, and quite a few were on state and local party committees. Several women were chosen as electors to vote for Roosevelt should he win that state's vote in the electoral college. Jane Addams seconded Roosevelt's nomination. The platform pledged the party "to the task of securing equal suffrage to men and women alike." It also supported "minimum wage standards for working women. . . . The general prohibition of night work for women and the establishment of an eight hour day for women and young persons." As usual, the Democratic platform had nothing on women. The Republican Party promised to "strive, not only in the nation but in the several states . . . to limit effectively the labor of women and children."[22]

The *New York Times* was quite taken by the "feminized campaign" of the Bull Moosers. Apparently oblivious to twenty years of party work by New York City women, it emphasized that Progressive Party women were working and making decisions, not just providing decoration and entertainment. "Women Rule Moose State Convention" headlined one story, noting that women were one-quarter of those attending the New York meeting. "Many Women in the Picture at the Roosevelt Convention" was the caption for a large photo of the national meeting held in Chicago on August 5–7. The first day's front page story ridiculed it as "a convention managed by women and has-beens. . . . About everybody here who wears trousers is an ex. There are ex-Senators, ex-Secretaries, and ex-Commissioners galore. Everybody who is not an ex is a woman." This theme continued throughout the fall. "Women and Girls, as Usual, Among Most Enthusiastic" said a story on Roosevelt's visit to Los Angeles in September.[23]

Spurred by the new interest by and about women, the Democrats and Republicans opened women's bureaus in their New York campaign headquarters in August, both to appeal to the 1.3 million women who could vote for President in six states and to recruit them as party workers. Florence Jaffrey Harriman, a New York socialite known to everyone as Daisy, organized and headed the Democratic women's bureau, called the Women's National Wilson and Marshall Association.[24] Harriman did not have a plan of action, declaring only that women "will have a large part to play in managing Governor Wilson's campaign in the [suffrage] states." She worked with the recently founded Women's National Democratic League (WNDL), whose members were mostly political wives. In August they brought a thousand women to Wilson's home in New Jersey for a little speech. In September, Harriman went to Illinois to organize more women for Wilson, but she didn't get to any of the states where women could vote for him.[25]

Republican women had the advantage of experience, having organized their own work in Presidential campaigns for two decades. After J. Ellen Foster died in 1910, her place as president of the WNRA was taken by Helen V. Boswell. She directed women's work for the Republican campaign. While Harriman was good at generating publicity, Boswell knew how to organize. Her plan was to organize women "in the counties of all the states where women have the ballot. These Committees will work in harmony with the respective County Chairmen and will devote their attention first to getting out the full registration. They will then show the women voters of the country why they must vote for President Taft in the interest of their homes, State and Union." Putting Mary Wood in charge of organization at the New York headquarters, Boswell spoke around the country. Before the end of the campaign "there was a strong organization of women in almost every state, seconding the efforts of the men," including an organization of African American women.[26]

Women organized everywhere. Jane Addams campaigned "from town to town in both Dakotas, in Iowa, Nebraska, Oklahoma, Colorado, Kansas and Missouri." She found that "many women are interested. . . . [T]here are active groups of women in politics everywhere—not only in Chicago or Boston but in the smaller places." While women had campaigned for men for decades, "It became the fashion at every big dinner or large gathering, to have women from the three parties present their reasons for loyalty to the party of their choice." Democratic and Republican women debated how the tariff—still the foremost issue of national politics—affected the family budget. Progressives appealed to women's concern for social justice. In states where women could not vote, they were asked to sway their men.[27]

Traditionally, New York City hosted the main campaign headquarters and Chicago a secondary one to ship materials and organize speaking tours to the western states. The Progressive Party's New York women's bureau was run by three women: two well-known reformers, Frances Kellor and Mary Dreier of Brooklyn, and Alice Carpenter, a "wealthy club worker" from Massachusetts. In Chicago, the party was influenced by Ruth Hanna McCormick, whose husband, Medill, managed the Chicago campaign office while also running for the Illinois legislature on the Progressive ticket. She, like Harriman and Boswell, was mostly a party woman. But unlike them she had lived in a settlement and observed first hand the working conditions of Chicago women. As a member of two important families, she knew everyone. Indeed, when Harriman got to Chicago, she asked McCormick "what Democratic women I ought to see."[28]

The women in these bureaus were almost heady with the idea that "the recognition of their ability to think and work along the same lines as men will do more to popularize the suffragist cause than anything that has happened in the history of the movement." However, the Presidential candidates preferred to avoid it. Roosevelt had declared for suffrage, but only "by states." Wilson's position was that he had no position. Taft was waiting for "the intelligent women" to demand suffrage, and even then was concerned with "the problem of entrusting such power to women."[29] Instead, women emphasized the "tariff issue as one of overshadowing importance to women voters" and each candidate's support for "laws to better the lot of women and children." Even the Bull Moose women did not base their appeal on suffrage but on social justice. Frances Kellor said, "One of the real accomplishments is the change of women's interest from the one interest, the vote, to the triple interest—the vote, the home, and women and children."[30]

While woman suffrage was still radical, whether women should be in politics was no longer. Women had argued for years that whatever affected the home concerned women, and what government did, or could do, affected the home. Progressive men, at least, now agreed. In one campaign speech, Roosevelt said women were welcome because "we intend from now on to make participation in 'politics' a method of applying ethics to our public life." Furthermore, "real issues affect women precisely as much as men. The women who bear children and attend to their own homes have precisely the same right to speak in politics that their husbands have." Even Woodrow Wilson, a progressive of a different stripe, was pushed to acceptance. He told the thousand women brought to his home in August by Harriman and the WNDL that he "rejoices" that "women come into politics." Since the Socialist Party and Prohibition Party had long supported women's involvement in politics, only President Taft was left with nothing to say.[31]

The gradual acceptance of women in politics seems due to three factors. One was experience. Reports from the full suffrage states generally confirmed that women's presence at the polls had a salutary effect, though there was an occasional article on female voter fraud.[32] In 1902, journalist Oswald Garrison Villard commented on the gradual acceptance of women's participation in politics even without the ballot.

> Twenty-five years ago such a thing as a woman's headquarters, distributing pamphlets, raising money, getting up meetings, supplying speakers, and furnishing one of the most effective arguments of the entire campaign, would have aroused a storm of indignation and scorn . . . ; and indeed in 1894 there were not a few protests. . . . In 1897 the women workers for the Citizens' Union were heartily welcomed . . . , but they were still regarded as curiosities. . . .
>
> In the campaign of 1901 public sentiment had been so far educated that [I] was unable to find a trace of a protest against women's taking part in the battle against Tammany.[33]

By 1912 most men outside the South had some exposure to politically active women. Reformers lobbied state legislatures; women campaigned to elect "good men"; suffragists appealed directly to voters in state referenda; women's groups were active in municipal reform movements; women had partial suffrage in over half the states and ran for school and municipal offices even where they couldn't vote. In New York City, where the major parties had their national headquarters, women had been working in campaigns for over twenty years. This city's major suffrage organizations, the Woman Suffrage Party and the Women's Political Union, were organized by political districts and by 1910 were targeting "antis" in the state legislature for removal campaigns.[34]

Equally important, the definition of "politics" was changing. During the nineteenth century, "politics" meant running for and serving in public office. However, as the state expanded its role in regulating public behavior and providing for the common good so did the definition of politics. By the twentieth century, "politics" encompassed civic improvement, an area that women claimed as their own under the rubric of "municipal housekeeping." It was accepted that those who educated the public on the desirability of certain public policies, and who pressured public officials to adopt them, were "in politics" as much as those who occupied public offices. In 1897, when suffrage was still limited, J. Ellen Foster informed the reading public that women were already in politics. In 1919 even anti- Alice Hay Wadsworth, President of NAOWS, admitted that she was "in politics."[35]

The third factor was diffusion from England. Cross ocean travel was common among elites; magazine and newspaper articles often commented that women were very influential in British politics, and were more advanced than American women in political organization. J. Ellen Foster acknowledged the influence of the Woman's Liberal Federation, which aided Gladstone on behalf of Irish home rule, in inspiring the formation of the WNRA. She may have also learned about "the recalcitrant voter being tracked to his lair by bands of enthusiastic and athletic Primrose Dames mounted on bicycles," when she visited England. Great Britain was a positive role model which many in the United States wanted to emulate and surpass. To elites at least, if women in politics was acceptable in England, it was acceptable in the United States.[36]

Suffrage, however, was another matter, even for English women. Politics was an elite activity, requiring no one's express permission, but voting was done by the masses, and required the sanction of state law. Corruption, the selling of votes for personal gain without regard to social impact, was a common complaint, as was the belief that "ignorant women" would only add to the existing problem. When suffragists argued that women would be no worse than men, the response was that women would double the costs of elections without affecting the outcomes.[37] Therefore suffragists argued that women voted "better" than men, though there was very little evidence to support this claim. Since Illinois had separate ballot boxes for men and women for seven years, its votes were scrutinized for signs. After Chicago elected a Republican machine candidate as mayor in 1915, Hull House resident Edith Abbott wrote that in the primary, 55 percent of the women compared to 44 percent of the men had voted for the progressive Republican, but he lost because twice as many men voted, leaving only a choice between two undesirable machine candidates in the general election. Observers agreed that the presence of women at the polls reduced rowdiness, parties paid more attention to personal character when picking candidates, and state legislatures put "women's issues" higher on their agenda. But, for the most part, "the ballot in the hands of woman has neither unsexed her nor regenerated the world."[38]

Whether woman suffrage made a difference was debated after the 1912 election. Wilson won with only 42 percent of the popular vote; Roosevelt came in second with 27 percent. Of the six woman suffrage states, TR won only in Washington and California where the Governor was his running mate—though some "pundits attributed [this] success to the work of newly enfranchised clubwomen," who had worked hard for the ticket. Despite the heated campaign, overall voter turnout continued its downward slide to less than 59 percent—the lowest since 1836. Why enfranchise women, when fewer and fewer men wanted to vote?[39]

Whatever it did for men, the election of 1912 was a boost for suffrage and a springboard for women's political activism. Roughly half of the 1.3 million women eligible to vote did so. That year, three more states enfranchised women and four elected women to their legislatures. In New York, the Progressives convinced both the Democratic and Republican parties to put in their state platforms a plank calling for a referendum on a state suffrage amendment. In Washington a woman ran for governor on the Socialist ticket. In Colorado— no stranger to women in politics—the *Denver Republican* reported that many women ran for city commissioners, aldermen, city clerks, and treasurers and only one was defeated. When Mrs. Gertrude Lee, vice-chairman of the Colorado Democratic state party, moved up in January of 1914 to become the first female state party chairman, it was reported by the *New York Times* as a major front page story.[40]

Quite a few California women ran for office, though not as successfully. Several filed for state Assembly in 1912, but since six were Socialists and one was a Democrat in an essentially Republican state, none won. In 1914, twenty women filed for state office though fourteen were on the Prohibition and Socialist tickets. Helen K. Williams excited many women when she sought the Republican Party nomination for lieutenant governor. Republican Women's Clubs rallied around her despite her history of supporting Democrats, until she was disqualified. Women did better in municipal races, which were nominally nonpartisan. Throughout the state, the vast network of women's clubs turned their attention to municipal affairs, providing an organizational base for many women to run for city council. Many won in small towns. In June of 1915, journalist Estelle Lawton Lindsey became the first woman elected to the L.A. city council. "Backed by socialists, the labor council, and women's clubs, Lindsey ran as a candidate dedicated to the empowerment and welfare of women, children, and the laboring classes."[41]

In Chicago, 78 percent of registered women voted in 1914, compared to 69 percent of registered men. Although none of the eight women who ran for alderman, mostly as Progressives, won, they were lauded for their spirited campaigning which decreased the vote for several machine hacks. Most women supported "good men" running against local party machines. The Municipal Voters' League credited them "with electing . . . seven of the better candidates." In the Seventh Ward, Republican women elected their candidate over the opposition of Republican bosses. In the Second Ward, the Alpha Suffrage Club ran an African American man as an independent and "came within 167 votes of beating the ward organization candidate." A year later the Republican organization bowed to popular demand and, with the help of the Alpha Suffrage Club, elected Oscar DePriest as the first black man on the Chicago City Council.[42]

THE ELECTION OF 1916

In 1916 Theodore Roosevelt led the Progressives back into the Republican Party, which nominated a nominal Progressive, Charles Evans Hughes, former governor of New York, in early June. Most of the prominent Progressive women who had supported TR, such as Margaret Dreier Robins, Alice Carpenter, Katherine Bement Davis, Maude Howe Elliott, and Cornelia Bryce Pinchot followed his lead, though not always with great enthusiasm. Katherine Philips Edson of California spoke for many when she wrote that it was "simply a choice with me between two rather undesirable candidates." The Progressive Party met separately, but, after Roosevelt declined its nomination, did not choose another candidate and essentially ceased to exist as a party.[43]

Reintegrating the Progressives into the Republican Party was not easy. Prodded by several women, Progressives formed the Hughes Alliance to work for his election but not that of other Republicans. The Women's Committee of the National Hughes Alliance, headed by Frances Kellor, opened its headquarters in July, a month before the parent organization was officially formed. After Hughes declared his support for a federal suffrage amendment on August 1, the Women's Roosevelt League, which Alice Carpenter had organized in May, became the New York City branch of Kellor's group.[44] The Hughes Alliance, "created for the purpose of attracting Progressive and other independent voters to the Hughes banner," was overshadowed by its female auxiliary in publicity and enthusiasm. Although the Women's Committee was supposed to "affiliate with the men's sections" to turn out the woman's vote in the suffrage states and work separately on "an educational campaign" in the rest, it ran its own operation with 191 branches and eleven field organizers, raised $132,000 from 1,100 contributors, held its own events, and published a weekly twelve-page magazine with campaign news and propaganda.[45]

On September 16 the Women's Committee announced that it would send a campaign train to a hundred cities in twenty-eight states, financed and managed solely by women. Having received the approval of the Republican National Committee for the trip, the women emphasized that they would only campaign for Hughes, not suffrage. However, all the women on it were suffragists. For the month after it left New York City on October 2, the women's train was greeted by large crowds and garnered daily publicity. The crowds were not always warm, and neither were the press reports. The consequent controversy led Kellor to publish two reports praising the work of the Women's Committee, one anonymously.[46]

Brass bands and breakfast for one thousand at the elegant Plaza hotel celebrated the train's departure from Grand Central Station with twenty-five female orators, including some of the better known Progressive women. Several major newspapers assigned reporters to ride the entire trip, and local press often rode along in each state, reporting on the women, their speeches, their reception, and of course, what they wore. The orators specialized in one of five campaign themes: nationalism, Americanism, industrial welfare of women and children, Wilson's Mexico policy, and "abolition of class legislation." At each of several stops made every day, the women were taken to street corners and meeting halls to speak. Sometimes there was a major meeting in the evening, often featuring prominent men campaigning for Hughes flanked on the stage by the train women. Several of the women addressed voters in ethnic neighborhoods in their own languages, especially Yiddish and Italian. Elizabeth Freeman specialized in "the colored vote." She spoke in black churches and neighborhoods, often departing from the five themes to denounce Wilson for failing to stop Southern lynching or costing black men their jobs in the federal civil service. The train returned to New York City thirty-three days later to a smaller welcoming party, and vociferous debate.[47]

Always well organized, Kellor had sent advance women to the cities designated as stops to arrange the meetings, rallies, and Republican reception committees. As she soon discovered, the Democrats also did some advance work. They sent telegrams to 7,000 local papers attacking the train, generating many stories and some paid adds. While Kellor boasted that the $48,000 to run the train came only from women, the attacks emphasized that "[t]he women who are financing the junket represent the largest fortunes in the country." Ridiculing the train as the "billionaire special," the Democrats identified the women sponsors by their rich male relations, even though the women riding the train were, with few exceptions, professional women who earned their own living. Wilson women often met the train and disrupted the Hughes women's meetings. The reception in labor towns was particularly hostile; several stops were canceled once this became clear. In the first Chicago stop women from the local Women's Trade Union League followed the motorcade with Wilson banners, even though one of the Hughes speakers was Margaret Dreier Robins, their national president. When the train returned to Chicago in November, the *Chicago Tribune* noted that "In all the seventy odd towns in which meetings have been held, the women have never been so rudely handled as they were in Chicago this morning." Press reports often highlighted train opponents, who heckled train speakers as the "women of Wall Street." The *New York Times* called the train the "sex solidarity special" of "petticoated politicians." While it did note that the Hughes women were "objects of a special animosity" not usually accorded to male campaigners, it seemed unaware that women heckling women was hardly an example of "sex solidarity."[48]

Evaluations varied widely of the first major campaign effort to be "organized, financed and managed by women." Kellor said "five hundred thousand people were reached directly" at the 328 meetings held "in factory, shop, railroad yard, school, or church." She appended seven pages of favorable comments from thirty-eight important people and thirty-five newspapers to her anonymous report. Suffrage writer Ida Husted Harper denounced the "Golden

Special" as costing Hughes "thousands of votes" by women. The *San Francisco Examiner* concluded that "Women Gain Friends in Great Campaign." The *New York Times* editorialized that "the interest they excited was not in what they said, but in the fact that they said anything. . . . [F]ew people, if any, paid real attention to what [the train orators] said. . . . [Though] the newspapers . . . gave them a good deal of space, no attempt was made anywhere to give even the substance of their speeches." Instead the coverage focused on the "discourtesies" and "mean little outrages." The *Times* editorial writer had not read the California press. If he had, he would have noted that the *San Francisco Chronicle* and the *Los Angeles Times* gave the women's train front page coverage that was substantive and positive when it visited these cities. The *Chronicle* headlined: "Fair Republican Spellbinders Take San Francisco by Storm," "Hughes Women Given Rousing Welcome by Cheering Thousands," "Riotous Greetings and Triumphant March Through Bay Cities Complete First Round of Greatest Political Campaign Ever Undertaken by Their Sex." The *Los Angeles Times* pronounced the "Nation's Brightest Women Plead the Cause of Hughes" and "In Brilliant Addresses Touching Every Phase of National and International Affairs Leaders of Their Sex Show Why Wilson Should be Defeated."[49]

Publicity about the "golden special" swamped the usual organizational work by Republican women, which was split between the Eastern and Western headquarters. Harriet Vittum directed work from Chicago while Boswell organized women in the East. Her National Women's Republican Association, which "controls all the Republican women's clubs and leagues in the U.S." announced in August that "suffragists and anti-suffragists [would] work together" for "Republicanism in the home, in the state, and in the nation." Although there was some competition between Boswell's and Kellor's groups—both organized campaign committees of business women in New York City—and Boswell did not think Kellor's was true-blue Republican, she allowed her name to be put on its stationery and cosponsored the women's campaign train, on which she rode part of the way.[50]

Democratic women also organized on several fronts. The WNDL announced the formation of Women's Wilson and Marshall Clubs. The Woodrow Wilson Independent League had a women's auxiliary. The Woman's Bureau in the New York Wilson headquarters wrote literature, but the task of winning votes for Wilson in the Western states was handled from the campaign's Chicago headquarters by Elizabeth Bass. Bass was a former president of the Chicago Women's Club and the General Federation of Women's Clubs who had worked for the 1913 Illinois suffrage law. She was appointed overall head of the campaign Woman's Bureau by her former school classmate, Senator Thomas Walsh of Montana, the man in charge of the Western campaign. With a budget of only $20,000 Bass looked to women's political clubs for help because there was "only sporadically and incidentally. . . any political organization of women." She asked Gertrude Barnum, daughter of a local judge, to organize women in industry, and later wrote that "[m]ore than anyone else, she spoiled the 'Hughes Special' because she made it ridiculous at almost its first stop, Chicago." The Democratic Woman's Bureau was derided by Kellor as "a model national feminine Tammany Hall." A few days before the election, Bass came to New York to debate Boswell at Carnegie Hall before an audience of women who could not vote.[51]

Now that four million women could vote for President in twelve states, able to choose ninety-one electors out of 531, the two major parties competed for women's votes. Large amounts of literature was written specifically for women. In 1912 the Democrats had touted Wilson's work in New Jersey for laws aimed at protecting women and children. Since laws like these could not be passed by Congress, in 1916 the literature emphasized how general federal laws passed during his administration had helped "First—The Children," "Second—The Women Earners," and "Third—The Home Women." The *Democratic Text Book* for 1916 devoted a page to suffrage, emphasizing that Wilson had voted for it in New Jersey's 1915 referendum, but Hughes had not voted at all in New York's. Republican literature had the same themes, particularly praising protective laws passed by Republican state legislatures. Women were mentioned for the first time in the 1916 *Campaign Text Book*, with two paragraphs on protection and one on suffrage.[52]

Women were also courted with symbolic support. Both parties seated more women at the conventions. The Democrats had eleven as delegates and another eleven as alternates, while the Republicans seated five and nine women respectively.[53] Both supported suffrage in their platforms for the first time, but neither supported a federal amendment. The Republicans "favor[ed] the extension of the suffrage to women but recognizes the right of each state to settle this question for itself." The Democratic plank, written by President Wilson to avoid stepping on states rights, said "We favor the extension of suffrage to women, state by state, on the same terms as men."[54]

The election was so close that the next day the *Los Angeles Times* declared "Victory for Hughes" and the *Chicago Daily News* proclaimed that "Nation Elects Hughes." It was three days before it was known that "peace and prosperity" had won it for Wilson by only twenty-three electoral college votes and 49 percent of the popular vote. Although overall voter turnout increased to 61.6 percent, a lot of voters in the Western states split their tickets. The *New York Times* headlined its post-election analysis: "Votes of Women and Bull Moose Elected Wilson." It claimed that the Progressives had returned to the Republican fold in the East, but not in the West. Wilson won California's thirteen electoral votes by only 3,200 votes, while Progressive Republican Hiram Johnson was elected to the Senate by over 300,000. The *Times* said "it is the opinion of expert calculators" that women even more than men had voted for Wilson; if they had voted like "their husbands," Hughes would have been elected President. It asserted that women reacted against the National Woman's Party, which "terrorized two conventions" with the club of "four million votes" and the "Golden

Special," which had provided ready fodder for the Democrats' propaganda machine. "The impression was created that the ladies of the stump speaking party were rich dilletants who had come to patronize the practical women of the West." The *San Francisco Chronicle* agreed that "Hughes Failed to Win Progressives" but only casually mentioned that "Labor and Pacifist Women Also Factor." The *Los Angeles Times* ignored the women's vote, saying only that "Johnson Machine is Blamed for Treachery." Subsequent analyses agreed that women's vote was crucial, but not as a reaction against the women who organized for Hughes. Raftery reported that "clubwomen had become so active in California's political life that many people held them responsible for the failure of the Republican Presidential candidate in 1916."[55]

For suffragists, the big news wasn't the possibility that women's votes may have re-elected the President. It was the election of Jeanette Rankin to Congress from Montana. Rankin was a Montana suffragist who won handily as a Republican in a state that voted for Wilson. Her victory thrilled suffragists, who thought the gates to political equality were finally opening. Montana had just granted full suffrage in 1914, though women had voted for school boards since 1889. Rankin spoke all over the state when campaigning for the referendum; when she ran for Congress the suffrage organization was still intact. She needed all of it, as well as the support of her large, politically inclined family, as both Montana Representatives ran statewide in a large, sparsely populated and mountainous state. She ran as a woman, promising "to work for a federal suffrage amendment, an eight-hour day for women, improved health care for mothers and infants, tax law reform, Prohibition, and a stronger national defense." A few days after she was sworn in, she was one of fifty Members of the House to vote "No" on the Declaration of War against Germany. As the only woman, she was singled out for opprobrium, and her vote against war was used against her when she unsuccessfully challenged Senator Walsh for his seat in 1918.[56]

Rankin's 1918 loss was disappointing, but only seemed a snag in women's steady march into the political house. New York women won full suffrage in a 1917 referendum—the first Eastern state to do so. Oklahoma, South Dakota, and Michigan women won full suffrage in 1918. North Dakota, and Nebraska granted Presidential suffrage in 1917, and Arkansas and Texas allowed women to vote in the primaries, the most important election in those one-party states, in 1917 and 1918 respectively. On January 5, 1917, President Wilson acknowledged women's growing importance by asking the Senate to confirm the appointment of Frances C. Axtell to the Employees Compensation Commission. Axtell, a Washington State legislator since 1912, had narrowly lost her own bid for Congress in 1916 by 3,000 votes when she ran as a Progressive and Democrat in a Republican district. So many California women ran for office in 1918 that some thought that the "merits of the individual and not the sex will be measured by the voter." A study released by the Leslie Bureau of Suffrage Education showed "record numbers" of women elected to county and

local offices in states where women could vote, and women in the state legislatures doubled their numbers from twelve to twenty-five.[57]

THE PARTIES RESPOND

Even as they resisted woman suffrage, the Democratic and Republican Parties
were preparing for it. Republican women met in New York City after the 1916
election to discuss a "proposed organization of women's work in the National
Republican Party." By "1918 brave efforts were made to get women into
[Democratic] party councils in all the states where they had even a partial vote."
They were pressed to do this not only by the party women in each state, but
by their National Committees. On February 26, 1919, the DNC passed a resolution recommending that the Democratic State Committees "take such practical action as will provide the women of their respective states with
representation, both as officers and as members thereof." On December 10,
1919, the RNC urged the state and county committees to select "one man and
one woman member" as the "principle of representation."[58] The National
Committees were already following their own advice.

After its December 1916 meeting the Democratic National Committee
announced that "Mrs. George Bass has just been selected chairman of a woman's
bureau of the Democratic National Committee. Mrs. Bass will organize and
superintend a campaign of education in the doctrines of the Democratic party,
in preparation for the Congressional elections in the suffrage States in 1918 and
for the presidential elections in 1920." Bass moved from Chicago to Washington
and hired a professional staff. As director of publicity she chose Ellis Meredith,
who had thirty years of experience as a suffrage leader, journalist, and party
activist in Colorado where she had successfully worked for equal representation of women on all party committees. Bass adopted this idea. In January of
1918 she proposed to the DNC Executive Committee that a non-voting
woman Associate Member be appointed from each state by that state's
Committeeman, in consultation with Mrs. Bass. On February 26, 1919, the
DNC agreed, effectively doubling its membership. Expansion moved slowly;
forty-two Associate National Committeewomen were chosen by September
1919, but only twenty-two came to the January 8, 1920, DNC meeting. On
September 27, 1919, the DNC Executive Committee voted to add seventeen
women to its ranks; DNC Chairman Cummings named eleven in February.
Twenty years later Eleanor Roosevelt picked this event to commemorate in an
annual celebration of Democratic Women's Day.[59]

Over three years Bass sent 12,000 letters to state, county, and precinct
chairmen looking for women willing and able to organize the woman voter on
behalf of the Democratic Party. To these women she sent over one million
copies of seventeen pamphlets on government and politics. At the February
1919 DNC meeting, she proposed a "Plan" for "General Political Organization

Among Women." Its essence was that a woman should be appointed in every state, "district, town, ward or precinct" by the relevant party committee or its chairman, "to be associated with the corresponding male official . . . and act under the general direction of the chairman." She also recommended the creation of Departments of Education on the national and state levels to develop "Women's Political Study Clubs." Each state should have a Women's State Executive Committee comprised "of the associate member of the National Committee, the State Vice-Chairman, and the Director of Education." Although the DNC formally adopted this plan, lack of money limited its execution. The DNC did create a Department of Education, and appointed Antoinette Funk, a Chicago lawyer and suffragist, as its director. She too wrote letters to women around the country. However, party men in the states were not very cooperative. In September of 1919 Bass reported that Democratic women were organized in only Colorado, Missouri, and New York, while in other states they were "repelled and discouraged by conditions in the regular organization." To party men she made "a very practical appeal to you again for your personal cooperation, which alone can breathe a spirit into this organization. Will you answer my letters, and will you comply with my requests for information and names, and will you realize that these requests are all to the definite end of binding fast to us the newly enfranchised women of the country?"[60]

The Republican National Committee was also concerned with "binding fast" the loyalty of women, but its organization was better financed, more thorough, and more effective. Soon after the national headquarters moved from New York City to Washington, D.C., in 1918, RNC chairman Will Hays asked Ruth Hanna McCormick to be chairman of the newly created Republican Woman's National Executive Committee (RWNEC). After helping to elect her Congressman husband as Senator from Illinois, McCormick wrote to "active worker[s] among women" all over the country asking them to join the Republican Party and to fill out questionnaires on their districts.[61]

On May 22 and 23, 1919, top Republican men and women met in Washington, D.C., to discuss how to bring about women's "full participation" in the Republican Party. The official policy was to have no separate women's organization, but pragmatism dictated at least a temporary one. The management of independent women's Republican clubs was left to the states. RWNEC recommended a tripartite organization of Republican women on the national level. In addition to itself, it asked the RNC to create a Woman's Division, to be chaired by Mrs. McCormick, "to carry on the work of organizing the women into the party's activities," and a "Republican Woman's National Council of one hundred" to "discuss the general policies of the party." Mary Garrett Hay, known as the "Big Boss" of the New York City suffrage organization, took over as head the RWNEC in June 1919. By the time the formal announcement was made on November 11, 1919, McCormick had resigned due to ill health. Mrs. John Glover (Christine Bradley) South, daughter of the first Republican Kentucky Governor, became the first chairman of the RNC Woman's Division.[62]

When the RNC met on December 10, it considered various proposals for female representation, and sent them to the Rules Committee. South and Hay wanted full and equal representation on the RNC from all states, and a fair share of delegates to the national convention. It would be four years before they got equal representation on the RNC, and it would never be fully achieved on all the state committees or at the national convention. Even though Republican women demanded, and Republican men often gave lip service to, the idea of equal representation, this was the one area in which women in the Republican Party lagged behind their Democratic sisters.[63]

By the time the Nineteenth Amendment was added to the U.S. Constitution, the political parties in many states had years of experience working with women and were ready to integrate them into the *formal* structures that ostensibly ran the parties. The national committees of both major parties were actively working to recruit and organize women. In their search for women leaders, reformers, suffragists, and party women were all asked to join and to bring other women with them. The party woman had emerged as a distinct type of political activist, and while she supported suffrage and might also support various reforms, her primary loyalty was to her party. However, party men did not always distinguish party women from others whose roots, and loyalty, were in the suffrage movement or various reform activities. Party men opened the door of the political house, and invited women into the foyer.

· *Five* ·

Making a Place:
The Women's Divisions

𝒯he strategy party women used to establish themselves in the political house was to stake out a territory as exclusively theirs. They argued that women brought to politics a unique perspective, that they were experts on issues that touched on children or the home, and that only women could organize the woman voter. It was a practical strategy because, as Emily Newell Blair explained, "men held the citadel, the only way women could get in was by making a place for women."[1] Specialized bureaus for groups of voters with common interests was a standard campaign practice, but the bureaus came and went with the campaigns. By 1920 the national committees wanted to form more stable organizations; a permanent place for party women was readily incorporated into their plans. They formed Women's Divisions to gain the loyalty and support of women voters and workers.

Experienced party women recognized that they could not just mobilize women during campaigns but had to provide ongoing programs to encourage women to stay active. They did this by organizing permanent women's political clubs with the same purpose women's clubs had had for thirty years: they were schools for women to educate themselves on issues and to learn practical skills. The Women's Divisions facilitated the clubs by sponsoring numerous conferences and writing many pamphlets on campaign techniques, organization, and how national issues affected everyday life. While their primary purpose was to utilize women for party work, the Women's Divisions also acted as advocates for women within their respective national parties. The more active division heads urged that more women be seated at the national and state conventions and in some cases pressured their presidents and governors to appoint more women. The Democrats and the Republicans followed roughly the same strategy, but not with the same emphasis. The Republicans stressed organizing women into clubs, and the Democrats stressed putting women onto existing party committees.

THE DEMOCRATS

After President Wilson won reelection in 1916 the Democrats asked Elizabeth Bass, who headed the campaign Woman's Bureau, to make it a permanent part of the DNC. "Permanent" was a relative term. Her work was suspended during the war and, after the Democrats suffered a resounding defeat in 1920, it was abandoned. Lack of funds left the DNC itself little more than a skeleton, but DNC Chairman Cordell Hull was determined to mobilize women for the Democratic party. In February of 1922 he asked Emily Newell Blair, the National Committeewoman from Missouri, to organize a new Women's Division. A writer by trade, Blair had worked in the Missouri suffrage movement since 1914 and moved into party politics only after 1920. Although she hailed from a Democratic family, she had been undecided as to her own party preference until 1919. She took over the difficult job of organizing Democratic women during a Republican decade when the DNC itself was barely able to survive. She started from scratch because "not so much as a scrap of paper remained from all of the splendid work of Mrs. Elizabeth Bass."[2]

Blair did find "many Democratic women's clubs left from the last campaign," and encouraged their growth by sending them material for monthly discussion meetings on such topics as the tariff, conservation, and the civil service merit system. In two years, she distributed 1,170,360 information pieces, including a twelve-page *Organization Primer* aimed at precinct workers. Mrs. Thornton (Laura) Brown was hired to organize more clubs. Blair thought the clubs could be "a proving ground for the development of woman leadership," but soon found that local party men, and some local party women, feared them as threats to their provincial power. Nonetheless, Missouri, Connecticut, Maine, and several other states started enough clubs to form state federations. Mrs. Halsey Wilson, well known as a superb orator, was hired to run Speakers Institutes around the country. These taught a large corps of Democratic women to talk up the virtues of Democratic candidates.[3] Democratic women also tried to educate Democratic men, though it's not at all clear how much the men listened. As the 1922 election loomed, a Tennessee organizer urged that

> The election officers must put women to work at every voting or registration place. This trains the woman precinct leader we need and makes it easier for the reluctant and timid women to attend the polls. You know how many women won't go to the polls because only men are there and tobacco smoke or worse (*sic*). Think how you'd feel if obliged to go into a women's pink tea parlor to vote and could only vote for women. . . . A woman candidate can bring out more women's votes than anything else, I have found out.[4]

The DNC gave Blair an assistant, Marion Glass Banister, sister of the Senator from Virginia. While Blair traveled the country making over two hundred speeches, Bannister wrote numerous pamphlets to persuade women to become Democrats and to explain national issues to local women voters. On July 8, 1922, they began publication of a mimeographed *Fortnightly Bulletin*. By the time No. 11 was issued on March 17, 1923, it had graduated to print and, by issue No. 32, its circulation was 19,500. It was a chatty newsletter, full of suggestions on how to organize, campaign tips, and club news. In 1923, the DNC acknowledged the importance of the Women's Division by making Blair a Vice Chairman. During 1923 and 1924 the WD held twenty-four conferences in seventeen states attended by several thousand party women. These "Schools of Democracy" instructed women in organization, public speaking, and Democratic policies. Nearly seven hundred women from twenty-eight states came to a National School of Democracy held in New York City from January 28 to February 3, 1923. At the DNC meeting on January 15, 1924, Blair reported that she had organized one thousand women's Democratic clubs. Blair trod a careful path between the Democratic women's clubs and the party committees, making it clear that "where women participated in the regular party organization, clubs . . . were volunteer auxiliaries." Don't "interfere in any way with the presence of women on the regular political committees!" she told club women. However, she thought the clubs did a better job of appealing to women not already committed to a political party "than party committees concerned primarily with party organization" because women were used to working through clubs.[5]

After the debacle of the 1924 election, the DNC suspended operations and Blair moved what remained of the DNC Women's Division to the Woman's National Democratic Club (WNDC), which she had asked Daisy Harriman to organize in 1922. Intended to provide "a Democratic oasis in a Republican desert," the WNDC quickly became "a national clearing house for women's party activities." In 1925 Blair returned to Missouri, using money from the DNC to hire Texas suffragist Minnie Fisher Cunningham as the WNDC's executive secretary. In 1926 the WNDC restarted the newsletter, renaming it *The Bulletin*. Copies were shipped to the women's division of each state party that had one so it could insert a sheet on local activities. Blair often wore two hats— she was secretary of the WNDC from 1923 to 1926 and president in 1928— but she had one goal, the education and organization of Democratic women.[6]

During the lean years of the mid-1920s the DNC was dependent on the volunteers at the WNDC for its own survival as well as that of the Women's Division. Harriman later recounted that "At the end of the Coolidge administration, about '26 or '27, the Democratic Party didn't have enough money to keep a headquarters. The Women's National Democratic Club had to take all the archives and put them in the attic of their club house. The Committee even kept their desks there, because they couldn't afford to have an office." Although Blair was not paid for her work, the DNC did provide some funds and also contributed to the mortgage on the large and elegant house the WNDC purchased in 1927 at 1526 New Hampshire Ave., NW, Washington, D.C. (which it has to this day). But most of her traveling expenses to make speeches, organize clubs, and supervise the Schools of Democracy came from herself and her husband; money for office expenses and salaries for part-time organizers was raised by her and other Democratic women.[7]

The WNDC was more active than the DNC. During the summers of 1926 and 1927 it ran a training school in political organization for women, with courses in campaign machinery, club and party organization, government activities, and public speaking. Over 55,000 copies of the monthly *Bulletin* were distributed. Primarily an outlet for Democratic Party propaganda, there were many articles denouncing the Republican Party, but few on "women's issues," including renewal of Sheppard-Towner and equalizing the nationality laws, which were major concerns to all women's organizations in the late 1920s. The WNDC's purpose was to help "keep the Democratic National organization alive and vital between campaigns" and *The Bulletin* was geared toward that goal, though it did report on women's activities in the party. Organizing Democratic women was like swimming upstream. Sue White recounted that "after the 1928 campaign there was little cohesion left among the rank and file of Democratic women," and in 1930 Harriman wrote "[t]hat there is much for us to do . . . is evidenced by the fact that in Minnesota there is one Democratic woman's organization and 1199 Republican."[8]

After Al Smith received the Democratic Party's nomination for President at the 1928 convention, he named John J. Raskob as the new chairman of the DNC. A rich businessman with no previous political experience, many thought he was a Republican. However, as chairman of the General Motors finance committee he could raise money and that was what the impoverished DNC needed most. Nellie Tayloe Ross became head of the Women's Division. Ross had become nationally prominent when she succeeded her deceased husband as Governor of Wyoming in 1924, but was defeated when she ran for reelection in 1926. Her skill was public speaking, not organizing. She was an effective campaigner for Smith, but the Women's Division remained unorganized until Sue White was hired as the Executive Director in 1930, a post she held until October 1933. After Raskob raised the $1,500,000 necessary to pay off the 1928 campaign debt he used his money and that of other rich men to create a permanent, professionally staffed, national organization. Some estimated that he personally contributed $15,000 to $30,000 a month to the DNC. Some of this was used to organize Democratic women.[9]

Ross continued Blair's policy of urging "women to seek representation in the regular organization of the party where control rested," but was less active in organizing clubs. She saw the purpose of the Women's Division "to introduce and make articulate the voice of Democratic Women throughout the entire range of party activities and to serve especially as a medium through which the party may be constantly making new contacts with the women of the electorate and representing the claims of the party to them." *The Bulletin* was renamed the *Democratic Bulletin*. While still officially published by the WNDC, it became a party organizational tool, running lists of discussion topics and references for club meetings, and recommendations for platform planks from Democratic notables and representatives of different organizations. By the June 1932 national convention, Democratic women had been contacted in 2,600 of 3,000 counties, including all the counties in twenty-two states.[10]

The election of 1932 convinced the Democrats of the value of permanent organization for women—which Republican women had been working on for years. After Roosevelt became President he made the DNC Women's Division a full-time department and, in October of 1933, put it into the hands of Molly Dewson, a dedicated supporter who had organized women for him in New York for the previous four years.[11] In the four years Dewson ran the division, she turned it from a struggling enterprise into a major institution. In 1942 the *Democratic Digest* wrote about her:

> To Democratic women everywhere Miss Dewson is "The General." In 1933, as Director of the Women's Division, she set both their pace and the course with her Reporter Plan, assisting them to understand and explain their policies. Changing conditions have ratified and expanded the original education plan, but basically it is still Miss Dewson's program. She retired in 1938.[12]

In many ways, Dewson was typical of the reform women that FDR brought into the government. Born in Massachusetts in 1874, her family was Republican but not politically active. After graduating from Wellesley in 1899, she became a social worker and an authority on minimum wage legislation for women. Many joked that her initials stood for "Minimum Wage" rather than Mary Williams Dewson. In 1913 she retired with her life-partner, Mary G. "Polly" Porter, whose independent income freed both from the need to work for money. She soon became a suffragist and a war worker. In the 1920s the Porter/Dewsons moved to New York City, where Dewson worked for Florence Kelley's National Consumers' League, quickly becoming lead lobbyist for the Women's Joint Legislative Conference, guiding its program for protective labor laws for women workers through the New York legislature. Eleanor Roosevelt recruited her for Al Smith's 1928 Presidential campaign and FDR's 1930 gubernatorial campaign. ER and Dewson became a political team.[13]

In the FDR administration, Dewson steadfastly pursued three goals: teaching women about the New Deal, political appointments for women whose political work deserved recognition (or their husbands, if they preferred), and "50–50," or equal representation of women on all party committees, national, state, and local. She was successful in all three areas, partially due to her own organizing abilities and partially due to the fact that she had the ear of the President and Eleanor Roosevelt.[14]

Dewson's first task after FDR's election was getting women into the government. As a result of her prodding the number of women receiving political appointments increased significantly. But by 1934 securing patronage for women was no longer a full-time job and Dewson turned to her real "obsession," educating women, and through them the rest of the country, about the programs of the New Deal. Believing that "elections are won between campaigns" she urged every county Democratic women's organization, particularly in small towns and rural areas, to appoint a local woman to be a "Reporter" on each of twenty-two New Deal agencies. These women had the responsibility of informing themselves about the work of "their" agency, and in turn speaking about it to local community groups. Reporters were to be "the mouth-to-mouth, house-to-house interpreters and apostles for the New Deal," Dewson argued. Begun only in February 1934, by September Dewson reported that 5,836 women representing forty-two states were Reporters and by late 1935, 15,000 women were active.[15]

> Molly Dewson herself went about the capital calling on the heads of agencies and establishing liaison for her women. She even sent [the reporters] sample letters showing how to ask for the information they wanted. . . . The result was that in every community where the Reporter Plan was in operation she had a group of women experts on the New Deal.[16]

The women were brought together in regional conferences to meet each other and hear prominent women from the New Deal agencies. The first was in Raleigh, North Carolina, on October 12, 1934, but the idea was so popular that dozens were held over the next few years. "[W]omen turned out in large numbers, even though they had to pay their own expenses. Presently the men leaders asked to be invited, too." They were also encouraged to subscribe to the WNDC's magazine, renamed the *Democratic Digest* in October of 1933. In March 1935 the Women's Division amicably took it over because Dewson wanted it as an organizing tool. Under her tutelage its circulation of 1,600 quickly increased to 13,000 in 1936 and 26,500 in 1938. Intended to complement the Reporter Plan, it featured articles on New Deal programs and New Deal women but had little about the activities of party women. There was a regular page about the WNDC.[17]

Dewson's achievements were not without resistance. She officially resigned as director in 1934 after DNC Chair Jim Farley refused to give the Women's Division the $50,000 she requested. President Roosevelt negotiated a compromise of $36,000 but Dewson insisted on resigning so that her salary of $7,500 would be free for other uses by the division. Carolyn Wolfe of Utah took over the title of director, but Dewson retained her actual power as chair and sole member of the newly created Advisory Committee to the Women's Division. President Roosevelt continued to support generous appropriations, and according to Secretary of Labor Frances Perkins, "backed the Division in everything it did."[18]

Although most Democratic party women united behind her leadership, Dewson faced some opposition from Emma Guffey Miller, the outspoken National Committeewoman from Pennsylvania. Miller, who dated her Democratic party activity from the election of 1880, when she was six, was organizing Democratic women when Dewson was still a Republican. As a delegate at the 1924 Democratic convention, Miller seconded the nomination of Al Smith for President, and herself received 1 1/2 votes. She seconded Smith again in 1928, and Roosevelt in 1932 and 1936. Moving to Washington in 1933, she first worked with and then challenged Molly Dewson for the unofficial leadership of Democratic women, arguing that the National Committeewomen should have been consulted before Wolfe was chosen to be director. Miller had some support among the National Committeewomen who felt that the (female) state vice chairmen threatened their position as top Democratic woman in their states. However, Eleanor Roosevelt's loyalty to Dewson did not waiver, making Miller little more than an irritant.[19]

The Reporter Plan was to prove women could be more than just "bands of party-rooters." It not only gave Democratic women an important role and generated publicity for the New Deal throughout the country, it trained them for the 1936 campaign. To raise money, the Women's Division produced Donkey Banks, which local activists could use to collect pennies for their local programs. The $60,000 women raised for the 1936 campaign bought their independence from party men. As a result of this focus on women, "By the time the 1936 campaign got underway it was becoming apparent even to the most purblind male leaders that Molly Dewson had a nationwide force of New Deal saleswomen. Respectfully they admitted her for the first time to policy conferences."[20]

Molly Dewson's strategy was to create her "salesforce" outside of the regular party. Blair was constantly hampered by local party organizations who wanted nothing that wasn't under their direct control. With the New Deal reporters, Dewson built a female army dedicated to FDR's reelection rather than local candidates. Her women answered to her, not to the local party leaders and they talked up FDR's policies, not the virtues of the Democratic Party and its local candidates. The message is clear in a pamphlet for "Democratic Victory" in 1936 that was "dedicated to Mrs. County Leader." In pictures and punchy word bites it told women how to organize other women in every precinct. It instructed her to find her own "live wire assistant[s]" if those "appointed by some man leader" didn't work out and to ignore "Mr. County Leader" if he "wants you to be a figurehead." After her precinct leaders were registered with the Women's Division in New York, they were sent packets of fliers to distribute without going through the state and local parties. Women were exhorted: "Don't Wait for permission from any high up chiefs to go out and WIN VOTES." The pamphlet told them to take responsibility for registering new voters, talk up the Roosevelt record, and educate women on the issues of the campaign.[21]

With the 1936 landslide, Dewson's army no longer needed its general. She was appointed to the Social Security Board in 1937 and retired in 1938. She was not replaced at the DNC with anyone of comparable stature, influence, or access. Instead the work of the division was carried on by her erstwhile assistant, Dorothy McAllister, a young mother of two children married to a Michigan Supreme Court judge. McAllister continued Dewson's programs, holding sixteen regional conferences and other events, all leading up to a three-day National Institute of Government in May of 1940. When over five thousand women defied all expectations and paid their own expenses to attend, it was national news. But this largest ever gathering of Democratic women preceded a decline rather than a breakthrough in their influence. "By the time the third term was really underway, . . . [t]he women's movement in the Democratic Party had . . . passed its peak."[22] The new chairman of the DNC, Edward Flynn, cooperated less with the Women's Division than Jim Farley had. FDR's successful election to a third term rendered women's role as political infantry unnecessary, and the gathering clouds of war shifted attention from domestic programs to foreign policy. After the 1940 campaign the Reporter Plan was dropped. Wartime travel restrictions made regional conferences impossible. Patriotism, not partisanship, was the message of the day.[23]

Gladys Tillett became head of the Women's Division in 1941. The daughter of a judge and the wife of a leading lawyer in Charlotte, North Carolina, Tillett had worked with the League of Women Voters (LWV) in the 1920s and 1930s to establish it as a presence in the state. However, women's influence stalled until 1945, when World War II ended and India Edwards took over the Women's Division. Edwards had been editor of the women's page of the *Chicago Tribune* prior to her third marriage in 1942. She moved with her husband to Washington, D.C., and began volunteering at the DNC in 1944 after being angered by a speech made by Congresswoman Clare Booth Luce (R. Conn.) at the Republican convention. By 1945 she was the executive secretary of the Women's Division and by 1948 its executive director. Edwards was there full-time, whereas Tillett lived in North Carolina. By the time she became top Democratic woman, Edwards had learned that "women were second class citizens in the opinion of the majority of male politicians." She believed "that helping to raise the status of women in our party was an important part of my duty." Edwards offered to resign when she found that she could do nothing without the approval of DNC Chairman Robert E. Hannegan, who was so unreachable that his secretary would not even grant requests for appointments with Tillett or other prominent women. This move impressed him sufficiently to give her room to develop a program. He left the DNC in 1947.[24]

In the next few years Edwards rebuilt the Women's Division "into an important organization; between campaigns it was virtually the national headquarters.

. . [doing] much of the work of the research and speakers' bureaus," in addition to publishing the *Democratic Digest*. She lobbied for appointments for deserving women and publicized women's work for the party. The invitation to a Women's Inaugural Meeting on January 21, 1948, to listen to President Truman and five prominent officials said: "Gentlemen admitted if accompanied by ladies." Afterwards she met with the state vice-chairmen and the national committee-women at the WNDC where they stressed the need of "women to achieve equal status with men in party matters."[25]

In 1950 Edwards replaced Tillett as vice chairman of the DNC, and kept the title until 1956. During her years at the DNC, she served under five chairmen, but turned down President Truman's offer to head the DNC herself. Edwards had become a close confidante of Truman after being one of the few politicians to "truly believe" he would be reelected in 1948, and as such was a logical choice to become DNC chair in 1951. She turned him down because "the men of our party are [not] ready to have a woman chairman. They would not work with her the way they would with a man." When he countered with the claim that "[t]hey would work with you that way after they discovered as I have, that you operate like a man," she closed the conversation by pointing out that the 1952 election was too close. "[Y]ou know I *would be so busy protecting my rear* I never could move forward."[26]

Had Edwards accepted the chair of the DNC she would have had little time to put her stamp on the party. Truman did not run for reelection in 1952, and the Democratic candidate that year, Adlai Stevenson, chose as the new DNC chair a colleague from his home state of Illinois, Stephen Mitchell, who proceeded to get rid of India Edwards. In January of 1953 Mitchell abolished the Women's Division, integrating its staff into the research, publicity, and organization departments. After many letters of protest, Mitchell created a small Office of Women's Activities (OWA) with little staff and no budget. A few months later he asked Katie Louchheim to run it, letting Edwards keep the title of vice chair.[27] Edwards's, final note to Louchheim in October lamented that "I'm not turning over to you a going concern, such as the W.D. used to be, only an office and a secretary and an assistant and several thousand names of women who are good Dems. And the goodwill which the W.D. has had for many years. . . ."[28]

Louchheim, like Edwards, got her start in party politics by volunteering at DNC headquarters. Unlike Edwards, she was a "professional volunteer" rather than a career woman. Her husband worked in Washington, and she helped in war relief, aided the LWV, and wrote a column for the American Federation of Labor's League for Political Education. A member of the 1952 Democratic Platform Committee, she developed a good working relationship with Stevenson, the party's titular head, but Stevenson was not President, so securing appointments for women was not an available activity. Since, as she later wrote, "[d]efending women, pressing their cause, is a role I never asked for or wanted" and the DNC was also deeply in debt, fundraising became her major focus.[29]

Mitchell was replaced two years later by Paul Butler, whose attitude towards women's activities was more generous. Until she got more money, Louchheim used her ingenuity to maintain a program, such as creating the Democratic Congressional Wives Forum for political wives to do what paid staff had done previously. She thought this group "really the best of my lot. They know politics, they don't have to be taken by the hand. They don't make extraordinary demands. They don't expect the impossible. . . . And they like what little I have tried to do for them." Eventually she restored the "Office of Women's Activities [to] an important unit in organizational matters, . . . serv[ing] the entire headquarters in the preparation of materials on campaign organization and techniques." It had five full-time paid staff during the 1954 campaign and eight during 1956.[30]

However, the *Democratic Digest* was a permanent casualty of "integration." Mitchell transferred it to a separate corporation where it was intended to be a self-supporting monthly edited by Clayton Fritchey, former DNC director of public relations. As Edwards predicted, *Democratic Digest* proved unable to be self-sustaining. It was reformatted and reduced after twenty-two months and died in 1961. Newsstands were reluctant to display it and a subscription quota for each state set up by the DNC was rarely met. The new magazine either ignored women or, as Edwards wrote Louchheim, mentioned them "in such a tone of ridicule and belittlement that I feel sure women are going to resent it."[31]

During Louchheim's first three years as director, the OWA raised about $100,000, which was split between the DNC and local Democratic parties. Democratic women stood on street corners urging passers-by to "Drop a Dollar in the Hat . . . Help Elect a Democrat." They also held "Teas for TV" and resurrected Democratic Woman's Day, a tradition begun by Eleanor Roosevelt in 1939 as "women's most important fundraising day of the year." In 1955 much effort went into several regional conferences to teach campaign techniques to Democratic women. These led to a national campaign conference in 1958 which was held biannually through 1966. Louchheim started a newsletter specifically *For and About Women.* While only four pages, it told its 25,000 readers what women were doing as candidates and elected officials, not just party boosters. Louchheim ran the programs for women at the 1956 and 1960 Democratic national conventions. At the DNC meeting held after the 1956 convention, Louchheim succeeded Edwards as the woman vice chairman of the DNC.[32]

Although Louchheim was careful not to publicly criticize the Democratic Party's treatment of women, she was quite aware of the ways in which women were ignored, condescended to, or put down, and sometimes let the press criticize the party for her. One of those times was the 1960 Democratic convention, where she was scheduled to speak about the work of Democratic women at the end of the opening ceremonies. As she began her speech the sound was turned off and the hall emptied. And she never forgot that at the dinner honoring DNC Chairman Paul Butler party men had not asked any party women to share the dais.[33]

Despite her original reservations about specializing in women, Louchheim was not happy to lose her job when the Kennedys took over at the end of the 1960 convention. Ten years later she wrote:

> The 1960 Democratic Convention in Los Angeles was all but over.... At precisely midnight the telephone in my office rang.... Bob Kennedy, in what could best be described as politely authoritarian tones, without any prefix or preamble, announced, "We're going to give your job to Margaret Price [then National Committeewoman from Michigan]...."
> ...That night on the telephone we talked tough.
> "You'll regret this," I said, feeling and sounding like a harridan. "I've got friends everywhere; I know the territory; I've got the workers with me, I've trained them. You're making a mistake."
> Bob growled back, "We don't like to be threatened.[34]

When he called her bluff Louchheim gave in. For the duration of the campaign she worked as Bobby Kennedy's assistant and afterwards was given an appointment doing public relations for the State Department.

Her successor, Margaret Price, kept the job of vice chairman in charge of women's activities under both Kennedy and Johnson in part because its importance had declined along with that of the DNC. Price continued the biannual Democratic women's campaign conferences and the celebration of Democratic Women's Day but added little new, even though she served in a Democratic administration. The Kennedy administration was not interested in women, and under Johnson the White House took over the key functions of publicity and patronage for women. Lady Bird ran luncheons for "women doers," and her friend and press secretary, Liz Carpenter, was put in charge of finding women for jobs. In 1968 Edwards filled in for Price, who was ill, and found "practically no staff and no material at the Committee in spite of there being many bodies floating around." In her book she wrote, somewhat sardonically, "the National Committee had fallen—or been pushed—into a state of desuetude. Only the Office of Women's Activities, ... functioned with any degree of efficiency." She measured the latter's influence by the fact that in Price's entire eight years as DNC vice chair and head of Democratic women she had never had a private interview with either Kennedy or Johnson.[35]

After a lengthy illness, Price died in 1968 and the Democrats lost the White House. Her successor, Geri Joseph of Minnesota, was appointed DNC vice chairman in charge of women's programs but by then there was little to supervise. Instead of programs for party women, she announced the formation of a committee to investigate why the number of women in elective office had declined and to encourage "greater numbers of qualified women" to run for office. She resigned in 1970 to help Hubert Humphrey make another run for the Presidency, and the new chairman of the DNC, Larry O'Brien, abolished the women's division once again.[36]

THE REPUBLICANS

In the campaign to recruit women into the parties, the Women's Division of the Republican National Committee had the advantage of a permanent National Committee headquarters, established in Washington, D.C., in 1918, ten years prior to that of the Democrats. Ruth Hanna McCormick organized Republican women while chairman of the Republican Women's National Executive Committee for half of 1919, and Mary Garrett Hay continued the work until the 1920 Republican convention when the RWNEC dissolved. The official head of the RNC Women's Division, Christine Bradley South, stayed in Kentucky. The two units were composed largely of the same people; indeed press reports described Hay as the leader of the G.O.P. women's division when she was forced out of the Republican Party for opposing the renomination of suffrage foe, New York Senator James W. Wadsworth Jr.

According to a *Report* distributed at the June 1920 Republican convention, RWNEC was very busy between its formation on September 3, 1918, and June 8, 1920. In January of 1920 it held three conferences in Chicago, Denver, and San Francisco for both men and women party leaders to discuss the degree of organization already achieved and the best way to bring more women into the Republican Party. By June, Republican women leaders had been found for over 30,000 precincts in 1,700 counties in thirty-eight states. Over half a dozen women were working as paid organizers in preparation for the 1920 campaign. One was responsible for the distribution of 3,700,000 copies of seven different leaflets. Two women wrote a semi-monthly *Republican National Bulletin,* and others traveled and wrote reports on state organization of women. RWNEC enlisted Republican women writers and, with the help of a press service, placed "something like one hundred articles" in magazines likely to be read by women. It also prepared a "weekly clip sheet . . . containing news of women's political activities" which was sent with the regular RNC press packet to over five thousand newspapers. RWNEC made a special effort to recruit "organized women" by attending national conferences of women's groups and asking likely prospects at these to join the Republican speakers bureau.[37] In addition

> A personal typewritten letter has been sent to all leading suffrage workers; to the ten thousand presidents of federated woman's clubs; to all women who served as county chairmen in the various State Councils of Defense; to members of the D.A.R., and on all other lists which were available, asking them to affiliate and help the Republican Party.[38]

After Hay was forced out, the RNC asked Harriet Taylor Upton to take over women's work for the 1920 campaign out of the Chicago headquarters.

Upton was a former treasurer of NAWSA and organizer of the Ohio suffrage campaign. Her father had been a Republican Congressman, but she didn't declare her party preference until early in 1920, when Ohio Republican leaders asked her to organize their women. Once he became the Republican nominee, Warren G. Harding suggested Upton for the national post. They both came from Marion, Ohio, and he thought she was "safe and sane." In 1921 Upton moved to Washington to supervise the work of organizing women into the Republican Party. She was appointed vice chairman of the RNC Executive Committee, a position she held without pay until June of 1924. To compensate her, President Harding agreed to appoint her husband to a position "worthy of his ability and education." However his efforts to do so were blocked by Ohio Senator Pomerene. The matter became moot when her husband died in April of 1923 and Harding died in August.[39]

The RNC Executive Committee was enlarged to nineteen members, adding eight more women, including Upton. They were: Mrs. Corrinne Roosevelt Robinson, New York; Mrs. Arthur L. (Henrietta) Livermore, New York; Mrs. Medill (Ruth Hanna) McCormick, Illinois: Mrs. Charles F. (Katherine Phillips) Edson, California; Mrs. Jeanette Hyde, Utah; Mrs. Manley L. (Carrie Secelia Jorgens) Fosseen, Minnesota; and Mrs. John Glover (Christine Bradley) South, Kentucky. These women divided the country into regions, with each taking responsibility for one. The Women's Division hired Betsey Edwards and Edna Annette Beveridge as organizers and for a year sent them to the states where the state party was weak or otherwise willing to accept them. Upton wrote long letters to the "Members of the Committee" describing their activities and how they were received by state party men.[40] Early in 1922 Upton summarized their experience: "The South, where we have little hope of accomplishing anything, is crying for our help and the doubtful northern states where the Republican Senator depends on the woman's vote, do not want us, or conditions are such we cannot go."[41]

In the middle of 1922, the organizers were let go and Upton's strategy shifted to organizing Republican women's clubs. Upton was frustrated because "almost all initiative is stifled" and she was "allowed to do . . . only . . . about one tenth of what I ought to do." Everywhere the men seemed afraid for the women to organize themselves. The women on the RNC Executive Committee planned to organize a national federation of women's clubs, but dropped the idea when informed that only the RNC had the power to make such a decision. By 1923 Upton had resigned herself to the fact that "each state is a law unto itself and the National work is general over-seeing and advising when asked."[42]

Upton and Blair often found themselves appearing jointly before women's groups, where they fell into a regular, somewhat humorous, routine while competing for women's support.[43] But unlike Blair, who concentrated on organizing women and writing propaganda, Upton found herself doing a little bit of everything. She tried to help along all Congressional action to which the Party was pledged, travelled [*sic*] and spoke for the Committee, tried to open new positions for women, tried to make men feel kinder to women, while my constant and particular job was seeing Republican women who came to Washington as visitors or those who needed political advice or wished political positions. Day after day my outer office was filled with people who awaited their turn. These visitors were not all women. Men who had tried everything, as a last resort appealed to me.[44]

At some point Upton began a bi-monthly newsletter on *What Republican Women are Doing*. She also arranged for a woman's page in *The National Republican* to reach a wider audience. Hays had moved the paper from Muncie, Indiana, to Washington in 1918 so that the RNC would have a dependable publicity outlet between campaigns. "Ties between the [paper] and the national committee were informal but close," its 200,000 subscribers often being the recipients of gift subscriptions from well-off Republicans. The weekly paper ran several series on women. Helen Varick Boswell contributed seventeen columns on "A Republican Woman in Politics" from November 1918 through April 1919. There was a series on Suffrage in 1920 and another on Women as Factors in American History in 1921. The Women's Division provided a weekly column on Activities of Organized Republican Women from February 1922 until it was expanded in August to a full page of news and commentary edited by Florence Riddick Boys, of the RNC publicity department. All this ended abruptly in December of 1924. After the campaign, the new RNC chairman "detached [the newspaper] from national committee operations." In March of 1925 it became an independent monthly magazine and women disappeared from its pages.[45]

Before the Republican convention of 1924 Upton announced that she would return to Ohio to run for Congress. Calvin Coolidge chose his old friend William M. Butler to run his campaign and to chair the RNC. Butler in turn picked three vice chairmen and reduced the Executive Committee to six. Mrs. Alvin T. (Sallie Aley) Hert of Kentucky, the one woman, was put in charge of the Women's Division—"Typically . . . without consulting the women members." Hert was a political widow; there is no record of any activity by her in reform, suffrage, or even the Republican party other than as a helpmate to her husband. He was a businessman who had run the Chicago headquarters of the 1916 Hughes campaign and served on the RNC Executive Committee until his death in 1921.[46]

Hert soon found that Republican women weren't very happy with their place in the party. In the May 1926 issue of the "Newsletter from the Women's Division, Republican National Committee" she wrote that "Many of the letters from the women have carried a discouraging note and even a tone of resentment because of the alleged lack of recognition or failure of their state organization to take them into full political fellowship." She told them to "Organize, work, build permanently, and don't complain to the men."[47]

Hert, like Upton, wanted women to form party clubs and the clubs to federate. She told the women that "Permanent local and state wide organization of both the men and the women of the Republican party is essential to party harmony, to party development, and to party success. . . ." She told the RNC that "year round organization" was necessary for women to have a "sustaining interest in our party" and to reduce "the great overhead and expense of constructing campaign machinery." But while the women formed clubs and some joined in state federations, the RNC did not authorize a national organization.[48]

The one exception was the National League of Republican Colored Women (NLRCW). In August of 1924, the two black women on the RNC, Mamie Williams of Georgia and Mary C. Booze of Mississippi, convened a meeting at the end of NACW's biennial convention to form the NLRCW. Its first president was Nannie Helen Burroughs, the founder and principal of the National Training School in Washington, D.C. Burroughs was not a party woman, having spent her life as an educator, social worker, and leader of the woman's missionary society of the Colored Baptist Convention; as a D.C. resident she could not even vote. The NLRCW only survived a few years. It remained separate from the Women's Republican National Political Study Club, founded by Jeanette Carter in 1923. She began *The Political Recorder* in 1925 and supplanted it with *The Women's Voice*, subtitled "A National Women's Magazine Published in the Interests of Republican Policies" in 1939. Like the NLRCW, it was an outlet for black Republican women. On March 26, 1939, Carter called a meeting in Washington, D.C., to form a national organization with Lethia C. Fleming of Ohio, who worked with her on the *Voice*, as chairman. In January of 1940 the *Voice* announced the National Association of Republican Women. However, neither the organization nor the magazine lasted past 1940.[49]

Burroughs was one of the national leaders who addressed the eighty-five women from thirty-two states attending the three-day conference Hert called for Republican women leaders in Washington in January of 1927. The women discussed the "problems of organizing women's Republican clubs, under the auspices of the Republican state committees, to function continuously, . . . questions of party loyalty, party integrity, the direct primary and representation of women in the party organization." This was followed by regional meetings as women organized the Mississippi Valley Republican Women's Conference, the New England Conference, and an Eastern States Republican Women's Conference. Some of these conferences became annual affairs.[50]

Republican women in most states did not need the help of the RNC Women's Division to organize themselves. Middle-class women had been organizing clubs for decades, and outside the South, the Republican Party was the party of the middle-class. It was easy for women with club experience to organize party clubs—indeed women in many states had been doing so for years. Nor did party women need to be persuaded about the value of political education. The Republican Party women who canvassed the tenements in the 1890s and early 1900s learned from experience that women needed "better and broader education along political lines" and that this required "campaigning all the year round."[51] Party women took on the task of educating women about politics. By helping other women become informed voters they eased their way into the Republican Party and created a niche for themselves.

One such group was the Women's National Republican Club (WNRC) formed by elite women in New York City after the 1920 Presidential campaign to provide a "permanent meeting place for women Republicans." Like the WNDC, it owns its clubhouse, currently at 3 W. 51st St. in New York City. In 1927 it started a monthly magazine, *The Guidon*, which it published through 1941. By 1928 it had three thousand members from forty-one states. Its founding mother was Mrs. Arthur L. (Henrietta Wells) Livermore. The daughter of a Massachusetts legislator, she graduated from Wellesley, married, and moved to New York City, where her interests moved from civic affairs, to suffrage, and then to the Republican Party. As the first president of the WNRC she made political education a priority, and subsequently became the director of the WNRC's School of Politics. For the next forty years thousands of women from New York and neighboring states took basic classes in American law and government and party organization and supplementary ones in public speaking. Special classes were held for women jurors, an evening school was opened for business and professional women, and a School of Political Science was started by its Young Women's Organization. Before major elections, women were trained in campaign methods and election law. By 1935, the WNRC was running schools in more than twenty states. They created a body of women trained in the political arts and eager to apply them for the Republican Party.[52]

Political education quickly became the primary activity of most Republican women's clubs, at least between campaigns. The Republican Women of Pennsylvania, also organized in 1920, had its own School of Politics, as well as "Political Breakfasts, Better Politics Week, Miniature National Conventions, [and] Legislative Conferences." The Minneapolis Republican Women's Club had "four major departments of study, including International, National, State and Municipal Affairs." In 1926, the Republican Woman's Federation of California (Southern Division) published a pamphlet on *Our Government: Ten Units of Study for Republican Study Clubs*. In 1931, Lenna Lowe Yost, the new director of the RNC Women's Division, wrote that "Every important Republican Women's Club of which we have knowledge is carrying some sort of an educational or legislative program. Several of the state publications print monthly programs of great value." She acknowledged that "Education-Organization, are the watchwords of the Women's Division of the Republican National Committee." In the 1960s Republican women were still running schools of politics to educate women in the arts of organization, persuasion and campaign techniques.[53]

Yost became the official director in August of 1930, when it became a salaried position with the RNC, although Hert retained overall direction of women's activities as vice chairman for another five years. Yost had been president of the Women's Christian Temperance Union in West Virginia and superintendent of the WCTU Legislative Department, making her the only woman with a background in reform to head the RNC Women's Division. Active in Republican Party politics for many years, she was the national committeewoman from West Virginia from 1924 to 1932 and had served on the state Board of Education. She replaced Louise Dodson, who had worked for the RNC after Upton brought her into the Women's Division. In 1935 Mrs. Robert Lincoln (Wilma D.) Hoyal, national committeewoman of Arizona, was appointed director of the Women's Division, but resigned early in 1937.[54]

Unlike Democratic women, whose clubs and organization disintegrated after losing the election of 1924, Republican women strengthened theirs even though Roosevelt's victories left the Republican Party in disarray. In 1934, Yost reported that there were "thirty-five State-wide clubs . . . thousands of local clubs, and the nearly fifty thousand women members of the regularly constituted Republican Party Committees. . . . Attendance records have been broken . . . two thousand at a banquet in Kansas. . . . A state rally in Columbus, Ohio brought over three thousand ardent Republicans. . . . Nearly a thousand at the annual luncheon meeting of the League of Republican Women in Washington. . . . More than a thousand Michigan women . . . at a great rally in Detroit." Women were clearly a force to be harnessed if the Republican Party was to make a comeback.[55]

After the 1936 Roosevelt landslide there were only eighty-nine Republicans in the House, sixteen in the Senate, and six Republican Governors. In only a few years the Party had gone from the majority party to one that could barely qualify as serious opposition. The new RNC chairman, John D. M. Hamilton, decided to rebuild it into the headquarters of a "loyal opposition," with regular funding, professional staff, and an ongoing program. As part of his plan he appointed Marion Martin as assistant to the chairman for Women's Activities in September of 1937. He told her to "devise a . . . method for the maximum utilization of the many Republican Women's Clubs." Martin, a national committeewoman from Maine, had spent the previous six years in both houses of the Maine state legislature. She found "that individual clubs were operating usually as single units without connecting ties to each other or to the party organization. As a consequence, some women's clubs were attempting to establish party policy; some were endorsing candidates in primaries; occasionally others were even working for favored Democratic candidates." In 1935, the RNC had established a Young Republican National Federation, whose elected chairman was director of the youth division at the RNC. This was both a precedent and a model.[56]

Martin called a meeting of the national committeewomen in Chicago on November 4, 1937, where, despite considerable opposition, she was "authorized to draw up a set of rules, governing the conditions under which a National Federation of Women's Republican Clubs (NFWRC) should operate." The rules she proposed a month later were clearly written to meet the political concerns of the RNC. The NFWRC "should be established for the express purpose of giving direction to the clubs, because under the set-up previous to that time there was no group that had any jurisdiction over them whatsoever, and therefore they could undertake anything they wished and sell it to the voters as Republican doctrine." The proposed federation would be an auxiliary of the RNC, all clubs applying for membership must have the approval of the national committeewoman and the state vice chairman, and must not have supported an opposition candidate within the previous two gubernatorial campaigns. The organization would be run by the assistant chairman in charge of Women's Activities (Martin's new title), assisted by an Advisory Committee of presidents of state-wide NFWRC organizations. Its purposes were:

- To foster and encourage loyalty to the Republican Party and the ideals for which it stands.
- To promote education along political lines.
- To encourage closer cooperation between independent groups and the regular party organization which are working for the same objective, namely, sound government. To promote an inter-change of ideas and experiences of the various clubs to the end that any policies which have proven particularly effective in one state may be adopted in another.
- To foster, in the broad sense, uniformity of purpose and ideals.
- To encourage a national attitude and national approach to the problems facing the Republican Party.[57]

After formal approval by the national committeewomen on January 1, 1938, Martin traveled the country speaking to Republican women. In a report to the RNC chairman subsequent to the first federation meeting in Chicago on September 23–24, 1938, she reported that "85 clubs representing approximately 95,000 members had affiliated, and delegates from 10 state-wide and 32 individual clubs were in attendance at the meeting." Martin's speech before that gathering made it clear that the federation should supplement and not usurp the work of the regular party organization. "The clubs should be a training ground . . . a rich source of help to the Regular Organization which, in a time of great activity, may turn to the clubs for additional volunteers to carry on their work." But they should maintain their separate identity so that they could make "a place within their ranks for every woman within their community" in order to "cement their loyalty." In an unintended swipe at "50–50" she pointed out that "making a place" was "impossible for the [Regular] Organization to do

because we can use just so many precinct committeewomen, so many city committeewomen, et cetera." She also attacked Dewson's National Reporter Plan
without mentioning it by name. "We have seen the country flooded with propaganda, designed to entrench the New Deal and all its fallacious doctrines, and
it is necessary for us to help combat its insidious effect." In her subsequent
report to the RNC chair she wrote that

> it is our objective . . . to give them the Republican viewpoint in order to
> help combat some of the New Deal propaganda. . . . With 100,000 club
> women informed as to Republican history and Republican accomplish-
> ments, we will at least have a nucleus of militant Republicans to carry the
> banner in an offensive campaign.[58]

Marion Martin wore two hats as head of the RNC Women's Division and
executive director of the NFRWC and she saw the two entities as playing different roles. The clubs were to be the point of entry for women to involve
themselves in the Republican Party; they would recruit and train women for
party work. But it was on the regular party committees that women would
exercise influence. These distinctions were spelled out in the *Handbook of
Organization* issued by the RNC in 1946. Chapter VI on "The Women's
Division" begins by stating that "Every Party Committee from precinct to state,
should have a woman's division, headed by the woman Vice Chairman" and
goes on to describe its duties. These were to fill all party offices "which should
be filled by a woman," support the chairman's "plan of organization," promote
"the interests of the women, seeing that they receive proper recognition for
their efforts" and promote "the advancement of qualified women in Party and
public office." At all times "the women's work supplements that of the men."
Four pages later it said the duty of "the women's Republican clubs is *political
education* for women." The clubs were to be "helpful to the Regular
Organization in campaign-time," by providing a "ready-made audience . . . and
a channel for taking the Republican story to the voters."

Although often referred to as auxiliaries, Republican's women's clubs had
their own program. Between campaigns the clubs often worked on issues, lobbying at state and national levels. In 1940, federation members urged "their representatives in Washington to hold free and open hearings and a full investigation
on the amendments to the Wagner Labor Relations Act, and to write their representatives during National Debt Week to impress them with the fact that constituents were concerned over the national debt." As long as they did not work
against an official party position, as expressed in the platform, the clubs were
free to choose their concerns. Several lobbied their legislatures on traditional
women's issues such as the provision of mother's pensions and jury service.
National officers often lobbied for the Equal Rights Amendment, which was
in the Republican Party Platform from 1940 to 1964 and endorsed by the
NFRW in 1956.[59]

For the next ten years Martin nursed the federation. By the 1946 Biennial Convention there were eighty individual clubs and twenty-seven state wide federations, representing a total of 400,000 Republican women in forty-one states. In November the Republican Party gained control of both houses of Congress for the first time since 1928, and after the December RNC meeting the new chairman, Carroll Reece, fired Marion Martin. According to one report he "walked into Miss Martin's office" and said: "You have enemies on the committee. I want harmony here; I will appreciate it if you would severe your connection with us as rapidly as possible." Her removal prompted a revolt by her creation. In 1948 the Advisory Board of the NFWRC changed the By-Laws so that it was no longer merely advisory to the executive director, and thus no longer under the direct control of the RNC chairman. Instead, "the Executive Director shall be the liaison between the Republican National Committee and the National Federation of Women's Republican Clubs; [and] shall carry out the policies of the Advisory Board and Executive Committee." This drastic shift of power was facilitated by the election of a new president at the convention the following day. As the wife of the Hawaiian delegate to Congress, Mrs. Joseph R. (Elizabeth) Farrington lived in Washington, D.C., most of the year and thus was able to take over direction of the federation.[60]

Although relations with the RNC appeared to be harmonious, in fact they were not. The assistant chair ceased to head the Women's Division in 1950, when Mrs. Gilford Mayes of Idaho took over the former position, and Bertha Adkins of Maryland became executive director of the latter. Both were national committeewomen from their respective states, though their predecessor, Mrs. Jane Hamilton Macauley of Iowa, was Martin's staff assistant when given her job. During her four years as president, Farrington expanded and strengthened the Republican women's organization. She started the eight-page *Washington Newsletter* which was distributed widely, and promoted numerous Schools of Politics to train more women for campaign work. At the July 1952 Biennial Convention, she led a move to make the federation autonomous and independent of the RNC. The office of executive director was dropped as was the Advisory Board. The renamed National Federation of Republican Women (NFRW) was governed by a Board of Directors with its president assuming the role of RNC liaison. The two women vice chairmen of the RNC were invited to attend meetings of the board, but only so long as the NFRW president retained ex officio membership on the Executive Committee of the RNC.[61]

In August of 1952 Ivy Baker Priest was appointed Women's Division director and assistant to the chair (another title change) of the RNC for the duration of the campaign. When Eisenhower appointed Priest to be Treasurer of the United States in January 1953, Bertha Adkins assumed her title and duties. Adkins came from a Republican family in Democratic Maryland. Her selection as national committeewoman by male party leaders in 1948 had incurred the ire of the Maryland Federation of Republican Women, who wanted the position to go to one of their own. However, two years of hard work by Adkins healed the breach and the Maryland federation supported her move onto the RNC staff and into the position of top woman at the RNC.[62] Noting the discomfiture of Democratic women at the recent abolition of the DNC Women's Division, Adkins promptly issued a statement that

> We do not go along with the theory that has been given out at Democratic national headquarters that by abolishing the Women's Division you are taking a step forward. We believe there is still need for a Women's Division, devoted to women's activities, to educate not only the women in politics, but the men as well. As I see it, a Women's Division not only is alert to the possibility of promoting well-qualified women in public service, but it also has the responsibility of giving the women information which they need to do their job better. And I think any honest person recognizes that women often approach problems with a different point of view than that of a man.[63]

In April, Adkins told the RNC that the "Women's Division is vigorous and healthy, in contrast to the deceased division of the opposition party." In May the new RNC chair, Len Hall, cut thirty-nine persons from the RNC staff and abolished most of the divisions, including the Women's Division. In their place he set up a "Special Activities Board" with the RNC executive director as its chair and Bertha Adkins as its vice chair. This board directed all activities aimed specifically at women, youth, minorities, farmers, labor, veterans, business and professional groups, and others. Hall claimed that this would give women a greater voice in RNC policy. Adkins did not let these changes interfere with her plans. She traveled widely, ran regional conferences on administration programs, party organization and campaign strategy, and produced pamphlets aimed at women. When Eisenhower presided at a series of stag dinners, Adkins leaked her displeasure to a friendly reporter, and then recommended that the President meet with important women so he could learn what they did. From these "doe breakfasts" came monthly and then weekly luncheons of the top women in the administration who wanted to talk to each other. Adkins organized a Republican Women's Conference in 1954 to provide organizational and campaign training that was so popular that the annual spring conference became a tradition. By 1956 there was once again a unit called the Women's Division, though it occupied women's place in the organization chart under the Special Activities Board; Adkins was director of special activities.[64]

The NFRW sat beside it as a separate unit, both on the chart and in the RNC's offices. Their relationship, at least in theory, was spelled out in the 1956 *Handbook for National Committeewomen and State Vice Chairmen*. Each State Committee was urged to have a Women's Division Committee, composed of the state vice chairman, the national committeewoman, the state federation president, and other women "appointed [who] represent ... every segment of voters in the State." The Women's Division was to work with women in the regular party organization while federation leaders were to work with the club women, who were to "serve as auxiliary workers in the regular precinct organization." All three heads were mandated to promote leadership among women, promote women for public office and convention delegate, and help with fundraising. Although efforts were made "to eliminate any residue of friction" between the clubs and the regular organization, since both were concerned with electing Republican candidates and turning out women voters, they remained "incongruously competitive."[65]

Although the RNC believed that the NFRW added to its strength, it acknowledged that there were problems. Clare B. Williams, who replaced Adkins in 1958, added a 1963 postscript to the official NFRW history identifying greater inclusion as a goal.

> There are some details of our inter-relationships as Republican women leaders, however, which need immediate and serious consideration for improvement. Across the country, included in the membership of the Executive Committees of the State Central Committees are only one-third of the State Federation Presidents, one-half of the National Committeewomen and even not all of the State Vice Chairmen.
>
> Included in the Executive Committees of the State Federations are less than half of the National Committeewomen and about two-fifths of the State Vice Chairmen.
>
> One hundred percent inclusion of all our women leaders in all these Executive Committees should be an immediate goal to further women's influence and effectiveness.[66]

The traditional problem for party women of who would select their leaders continued to haunt the NFRW in the 1960s, which depended on the RNC for "between two-thirds and three-fourths of the finances needed to operate" even though it had half a million members in four thousand clubs in fifty-one states.[67] This was brought to a head in 1967, when the heir-apparent was First Vice President Phyllis Schlafly, representing the conservative wing of the party which had brought it to ignominious defeat in 1964. Schlafly was a long-time Republican activist, having been a delegate to the 1956 and an alternate to the 1960 Republican Conventions, as well as president of the Illinois Federation of Republican Women. In 1964 she gained notoriety with the self-publication of a pro-Goldwater book, *A Choice Not an Echo*, that was widely read. In September of 1964, when the Goldwater forces were in control of the party, she was elected first vice president of the NFRW. This made her a logical candidate to be the organization's next president, but not the most desirable one from the perspective of the party leaders who had regained control of the national party machinery, though not the local NFRW clubs, after Goldwater's defeat. The men in the RNC prevailed on the NFRW nominating committee to pass over Schlafly in favor of Gladys O'Donnell, a conservative from California acceptable to them. Normally nomination was tantamount to election but Schlafly decided to contest the leadership's decision. Goldwater remained neutral; both women had supported his race for the Republican nomination. After a bitter campaign with numerous charges of procedural and voting irregularities Schlafly lost with 44 percent of the vote. Despite urging from many of her supporters that she form a rival organization, she dropped out of the NFRW (though not out of the Republican Party) and instead began publishing her monthly *Phyllis Schlafly Report* for the three thousand women who had supported her at the NFRW convention.[68]

The new NFRW president took office at a time that the new feminist movement was beginning to make headlines, and she quickly declared her support for many of its goals, especially passage of the ERA. In February of 1968, the NFRW replaced its four-page newsletter, *Republican Clubwoman,* with a larger, slicker magazine named *FOCUS.* It promoted both Republican women and the ERA. Its March 1969 cover declared that "Women" are "The Wave of the Future."

SUCCESS BUT NOT SURVIVAL

Writing in 1958, after both Women's Divisions had been officially abolished, political scientist Hugh Bone concluded that

> In any evaluation of the importance of the units in the national offices, the women's sections would rate very near the top. This is due to the great volume of publicity that they have been able to secure for their parties and to the help they render to women officeholders and national committeewomen. Their importance is also due to the catalytic and service functions that they perform in their relationships with state and local organizations.[69]

During the four decades after they were formed, the women's sections did much more than provide publicity and render service. To them fell the primary task of educating women to participate in electoral politics. To mobilize the woman voter they added several innovations to the repertoire of campaign tactics. One was the "political" party. Since women were used to entertaining guests at home, the women's divisions encouraged them to organize parties around political events. Radio parties to listen to candidates' speeches followed by issue discussions were started in the 1920s by Republican women and popularized in the 1930s by Democratic women. By the 1950s, coffee klatches had taken over, with candidates or their surrogates personally speaking with a group of neighbors in someone's home. Another contribution was the transformation of campaign literature from lengthy exegeses of political principles to short, cogent statements of facts. Democratic women introduced the Rainbow Fliers—one-page statements on specific issues printed on different colored paper—to FDR's 1932 campaign. The print equivalent of today's thirty-second sound bite, in

1936 these were 80 percent of the literature supplied by the DNC, and were picked up by the Republicans by 1940.[70]

In addition to mobilizing women voters, the Women's Divisions and their successors were the chief promoters of women within each party. Each used the achievements of the other to push their own party to pay more attention to women. One example of this is Louchheim's February 15, 1957, report on women's activities telling the DNC that the Republicans had "just issued a statement that they had a hundred more women in State Legislatures than we have." She urged the national committeemen and women attending "to increase the number of women office holders in the State Assemblies and to encourage them to run."[71]

The women's units of the National Committees survived many storms—changes in party chairs, budget cuts, electoral defeats, abolition, and being taken for granted. For over forty years they fought to make a place in the political parties for women and to train women to work in politics. They educated women about government and politics, provided a supportive environment for women to work for their party's success, advocated for women's greater inclusion on party bodies and in party affairs, urged that more women be selected to run for public office, and often acted as chief promoter for more appointments for women. Although they did not yet know it, the women's units would soon face still another challenge. A new feminist organization was founded in 1966, and one of the first things the National Organization for Women did was to recommend that the Women's Divisions be abolished.[72] The work of party women had made a place for women in the parties. And after years of struggle, new feminists were questioning whether that place had become a ghetto.

· Six ·

Party Organization:
The Evolution of Fifty-Fifty

𝒟uring the Populist and Progressive eras the political house was renovated. Plans were laid and new laws were passed that changed political parties from fundamentally private associations to quasi public ones. The state took over some party functions, and regulated others. In the nineteenth century conventions were the most common means of selecting party candidates, but these were often dominated by bosses who told their delegates how to vote. By 1914, seventeen states had a presidential preference primary, and others had direct primaries for at least some state and local elections. In the Western states, where Progressives were particularly strong, nonpartisan elections became the norm for municipalities. States also replaced long ballots with short ones, and party tickets with the Australian single ballot system. "Corrupt Practices" Acts forbade the selling of political favors or the purchasing of editorial endorsements, tried to limit the expenditure of money in campaigns, and provided some types of public financing. Voter registration laws were passed to eliminate "floaters" and "repeaters"—who voted at many polling places for a price. As "tickets" supplied by each party were replaced with a ballot printed by the state, more laws defined who could be on the ballot and how to get there. Other laws dictated party structure, including the number and type of party committees and officers.[1] The new laws did not eliminate corruption or party machines, though they did reduce their scope. Just as the South found ways to keep former slaves from voting despite the Fifteenth Amendment, the parties adapted to the new environment and learned to use the rules to their own advantage.

As women pushed open the door to the political house, they asked for and frequently received representation on party committees. Often this was specified in party rules, which might state that an equal number of men and women would represent a specific district, or that a committee would have a female vice chairman, or a vice chair of the opposite sex than the chairman. Initially party men appointed their female equivalents. Women chafed at not being allowed to select their own leaders, and as the states passed laws on party structure, demanded provisions not only specifying women's representation on different party committees but that these women would be elected, as were the men. Sometimes the laws on female representation codified existing practices or party rules, and sometimes they were passed to change the rules.

Exactly how many committees there were varied from state to state, but there was a common pattern. On paper, the structure of each party was hierarchical, with party committees having formal decision making power at every geographic level. In reality party organization is more accurately described as layered, with the connections between layers being somewhat tenuous. The primary party unit is the state party. Each party's state central committee is usually comprised of representatives from relevant units, which can be counties, assembly districts, or Congressional districts. At the bottom of the hierarchy, the basic unit is often the precinct or election district. The most important unit is usually the county committee, which is often but not always comprised of representatives from each precinct. Some county committees have so many members that they never meet, or meet only to rubberstamp decisions made by a ruling committee. The members of the national committee are chosen by the state party, though they are often officially elected by delegates to the quadrennial national nominating conventions. This convention is ostensibly the highest decision making body in each major party, with the national committee in charge between Presidential elections. Delegates to the national convention are chosen in accordance with rules written by each state party. [2]

Through the 1960s, state parties were autonomous, as were local units within the state. The locus of real power varied from state to state, but was only rarely in the formal governing bodies. Even more than in most organizations, power and influence traveled through informal networks and was a function of subjective feelings and personal relationships. These networks were male, and the attitudes of party men toward party women paralleled those of the rest of society. Indeed it was precisely because real influence arose from informal rather than formal relationships that women were so readily admitted onto the formal political committees. For many years, party men gave the women what they asked for: titles and positions. It would be several years before women realized that these brought little, if any, power to affect party decisions, and only the merest traces of that staple of party men, patronage. Some party women carved out a female sphere where they were able to exercise influence over other women, and a few became important figures in some campaigns. But party women remained in the political penumbra. They were inside the political house, but only as servants.

THE COLORADO PLAN

Colorado passed the first law requiring female representation on party committees in 1910, but its parties had been tinkering with representational schemes since women got full suffrage in 1893. According to Helen Sumner, "the

Populist Party organized its committees upon the basis of one man and one woman from each representative district, whether county or precinct, but in the other parties women have been obliged to bring pressure to bear to secure this dual system of representation." In preparation for the 1894 elections, the chairman of the Republican State Central Committee appointed women as vice chairmen of the state and county committees, with responsibility for organizing the new women voters into the Republican Party. The county committees were pressured to add at least one woman to each precinct committee, but not all did so. Ellis Meredith, a suffragist and Populist who became a Democrat when the two parties fused, wrote in 1895 that "In the People's party two women and three men form a precinct committee; the Democrats have a committee of three, one woman and two men, and the women have equal representation in the county and State Central committees." It was not until 1906 that the state conventions of both parties voted new rules requiring equal representation on the party committees, and these were not always followed. Nonetheless, women were well organized, having state leagues of both Republican and Democratic clubs with memberships in the thousands and clubs in the small towns as well as in Denver. In 1910 they took their demand to the legislature, which made equal representation on party committees part of the new primary law. [3]

Only a few state parties followed Colorado's lead before 1920. At the Idaho party conventions of 1898 the Democrats and the Silver Republicans, "the strongest two parties in the state numerically, selected their respective State Central Committees by placing upon them a man and a woman from each county, thus equally dividing the honors and responsibilities." There are no records of the early party rules, but between 1910 and 1920 two states passed laws requiring female representation on at least some party committees. Michigan, where women had full suffrage since 1918, required two men and one women on each Congressional party committee. Nebraska, which only gave women Presidential suffrage, specified that a man and a women must be elected from each district to the next higher one. [4]

By the time the National Committees were deciding how to admit women, "The Colorado Plan"—for every committeeman there would be a committeewoman—had become the model. It soon became known as "fifty-fifty," and for the next fifty years its attainment was high on the priority list of both Democratic and Republican women. [5]

THE NATIONAL COMMITTEES

At their 1920 convention, in anticipation of the ratification of the Nineteenth Amendment, the Democrats doubled the size of the National Committee by adding a woman from each state. They used this as part of their campaign for women's votes, but to no avail. [6] Convinced of victory, the Republican Party waited until 1924. Despite RNC Chairman Will H. Hays's statement that the rights of women in the Republican Party were equal to those of men, they were not even made associate members until 1923. After the 1924 convention adopted Rule XIV, authorizing each state to send one man and one woman to the National Committee, equal representation for men and women on the RNC remained the rule until 1952. [7]

Instead eight women were added to the RNC Executive Committee. They were not themselves members of the RNC (though some were later appointed as associate members). Nor did they officially reconstitute the defunct Republican Women's National Executive Committee, but they acted as though they were the committee in charge of Republican women, meeting separately from the men and making decisions about how to organize women. For its public face in the 1920 campaign, the Republican Party promoted these women as part of the "REAL COMMITTEE that does the work and controls the management" in contrast to the Democrats who put women equally on the DNC, "which meets only once in four years, and then only to fix the date and place of the next convention." [8] While Upton was still telling the public in 1923 that women "have as much influence and are as freely consulted as in the Democratic party," privately she wrote in 1922 that "Republicans will not get anywhere until women are on the National Committee. . . . The men on the Committee do not take us seriously and do not do for us or allow us to do for women of the Party what we ought to do. The Executive Committee is simply a servant of the National and as a rule it does not function between elections." She told RNC Chair John T. Adams that she had changed her mind about 50–50 and now thought it necessary "because in the states where the chairman had been strong enough to force an equal representation on the state committee, work had progressed and women were closely tied to Party machinery." [9] It would be several years before the women realized that the national committees themselves had no power. [10]

Upton may have been correct that women had as much influence in the Republican as in the Democratic Party despite their non-voting status on the RNC. As party historian Ralph Goldman pointed out, "the national committee tends to be more of a political environment than an operating agency." Usually, but not always, the chair is chosen by the party's most recent Presidential candidate and runs the National Committee through control of the staff and budget. If the party does not control the Presidency, the chair may be picked by its dominant faction and be someone who "is not necessarily in full accordance with the views of its titular leader." Florence J. Harriman became a Democratic national committeewoman in 1920; she was still there in 1950 when she described it as "rather a farce. . . . We're just figureheads. That's all. . . . The National Chairman and the Vice Chairman run it all." Perhaps because the National Committees are relatively powerless, with "little contact with the real world of issues and politics," women's first and easiest achievement was equal representation at the top. [11]

Despite the fact that being on the National Committee was not a source of much influence, women have been reluctant to see their participation diluted. In 1952 the Eisenhower forces persuaded the GOP to add to the National Committee those state party chairmen from all but solidly Democratic states. Although intended to lessen the weight of Southern committee members, women readily recognized that since the state chairs were male, it would lessen their influence as well. They protested strongly at the Republican convention that this proposal "creates inequality between men and women" and deprived women of equal rights and recognition. Nonetheless the voice vote in favor of the change was overwhelming. The *New York Times* reported that "[a]s a battle of the sexes it was rather one-sided. The women made the speeches and the men got the votes." In 1955, women on the RNC were "up in arms" that forty men had been added under the new rule, altering the "historic balance" between men and women. The South was also unhappy. In 1968, RNC membership was extended to all state party chairs, appeasing the South, but not the women. Women's demand that state vice chairmen (all women) also be added had been denied. [12]

THE COMMITTEE OFFICERS

Although the formal organization of the national committees has not remained constant, custom or rules of both parties since the early 1920s have required that at least one woman be a vice chair or assistant chair of each National Committee, usually with jurisdiction over party women. At the first meeting of the DNC after the 1920 convention, Charl O. Williams, national committeewoman from Tennessee, was elected vice chairman, the first woman so honored. She resigned in November 1922 to become the Washington field secretary for the National Education Association. [13] The following spring, DNC Chair Cordell Hull replaced her with the head of the woman's division, Emily Newell Blair. At that time the DNC had four vice chairmen. Since the party was encouraging the state and county committees to name women as vice chairmen with the responsibility of organizing party women, the 1924 national convention set an example by resolving that the *first* vice chair of the DNC should be a woman. [14] At the usual changing of the guard after the 1928 convention, the DNC added another woman vice chairman to the three men, and dropped the title "First." Blair was replaced with Nellie Tayloe Ross, formerly Governor of Wyoming, and Florence Farley, national committeewoman from Kansas. Belle Moskowitz became the only woman on the seven-person Executive Committee. [15]

Harriet Taylor Upton was both head of the Women's Division and vice chairman of the RNC Executive Committee between 1921 and 1924. But she wasn't a vice chairman of the RNC itself. Probably to maintain their public face as the party of women's rights, the RNC added a second vice chairman on June 8, 1921, specifying that the position be occupied by a woman. Upton

promptly nominated Mrs. Leonard Wood of New Hampshire, wife of a leading contender for the 1920 Republican Presidential nomination, adding that
she was recommended by the women on the RNC Executive Committee.
Wood was elected unanimously, but there is no record that she was more than
a name. Upton remained the woman in charge of Republican women until she
was replaced by Sallie Hert. When women became members of the National
Committee in 1924, Hert, the national committeewoman from Kentucky, was
elected a vice chairman of the RNC. [16]

National Committee titles do not tell much about real power or position.
Sometimes they are merely pats on the back, and sometimes they mean even
less. Frequently, half of the vice chairs have been women, though the
Republicans have been more faithful to this division than the Democrats. [17] Less
frequently women have held half the seats on the Executive Committee. At the
1936 convention the DNC expanded, temporarily, the number of vice chairs
to eighteen, eight of whom were women. This was a result of the friction
between Molly Dewson and Emma Guffey Miller over who should be the top
Democratic woman. DNC Chairman James Farley planned to appoint Dewson
to the one female slot in recognition of her *de facto* leadership, but Miller, and
her brother Senator Guffey, put on such a strenuous campaign for herself that
Dewson proposed the vast expansion so Miller could be elevated to "an empty
honor without responsibility or power." Farley then appointed a Democratic
National Campaign Committee, with himself as chairman, and Dewson as the
only vice chairman. By 1940, Dewson was the only women vice chairman of
the DNC. For the next two decades there was always one, but only one, woman
vice chairman of the DNC. [18] There has also only been one top Republican
woman at the RNC, but her title has varied. The 1936 Republican convention
began the tradition of having two of the four RNC vice chairmen be women,
neither of whom headed the Women's Division. After 1937 the woman in
charge of women on the RNC usually held the title of assistant to the chairman or assistant chairman and was paid for her services. In 1940 she became an
ex-officio member of the RNC Executive Committee. [19] In 1971 her title was
changed to co-chairman.

STATE AND LOCAL PARTY COMMITTEES

Both parties encouraged their state committees to follow their example. At
the 1920 Democratic convention DNC Chairman Homer S. Cummings
urged the delegates to "go home and adopt the fifty-fifty plan of organization, giving women equal representation with men in all party councils." [20]
But in 1922, when Emily Newell Blair asked the 3,000 Democratic county
chairman for the names of the women on their committees, only seven
replied, and one answered "None, thank God." To change this attitude, the
new DNC Chairman, Cordell Hull, wrote all of the state chairmen, urging

them to put women on their committees, even if that meant changing the state law. Only a few states passed statutes, but Blair reported early in 1924 that "in more than thirty States women have representation on state committees, and down through the county and ward to the precinct committees."[21] Republicans also approved of the plan. President Harding, who thought women should not organize politically outside of a political party, was enthusiastic about bringing women in. In 1923 Ohio State Senator Maude C. Waitt asked for his views on a 50–50 bill she had just introduced into the Ohio legislature. He gave his

> most cordial approval to a revision of our election laws which will make possible the representation of women from every district in the state central committee. This is an action we owe to the enfranchised women voters. It has been done in many states with an eminent degree of satisfaction. I should regret to see Ohio fall behind other states in granting full recognition to women in our party organization. [22]

The drive for 50–50 statutes in the 1920s was led by Republicans, in part because they controlled most of the state legislatures. Several states passed laws similar to Colorado's; some also required that the vice-chairmen of each committee be female, or of the opposite sex than the chairman, or that half the officers be female. Where 50–50 was not required by state law, it was often required by party rule. In 1927, the LWV found that "equal representation on the general party committees is now the prevailing though not universal practice, by party rule rather than by law." [23]

Women in states where the parties did not support equal representation on official party committees often organized separately. Indeed the RWNEC had proposed, and the RNC accepted, a plan recommending that "The Chairman and each State Central Committee shall appoint in consultation with the Woman's National Executive Committee, a State Executive committee of women numbering from five to fifteen members to act with the State Central Committee." By 1920, there were Republican Women's State Executive Committees in Arizona, Idaho, Illinois, Kentucky, Massachusetts, Montana, New York, Ohio, Tennessee, and Virginia. A report to the RWNEC described that of Illinois as "consisting of one woman from each congressional district the same as the men's state committee." The one in Idaho "holds its meetings and works entirely apart from the men's organization," while in Arizona "men and women working in perfect harmony," Indiana and Oregon women organized Advisory Committees, and Iowa and Maine created a Women's Division. A few states, such as Kansas, Missouri, and Wisconsin, couldn't be easily labeled, but Republican women were actively organizing in them. And in a few others, such as Minnesota and North Carolina, a woman leader was trying to organize from the top down, but slowly. New York abolished their Women's Executive

Committee in 1925 after a law was passed doubling the State Committee. Some state Democratic parties also created women's executive committees. [24]

In 1929 Blair assessed the effects of 50–50 as mixed. States that had not adopted 50–50 by law or rule showed no increase in the number of women on party committees; without a "special place" women did not get in at all. But entry did not mean women had influence or that they acted to represent women in the party or that they were rewarded proportionately for party service. In 1928 Eleanor Roosevelt had observed that "women who have gone into politics are refused serious consideration by the men leaders" and recommended that women organize women to back women political bosses. Blair concluded that showing such prowess only caused a backlash: "as soon as women used their knowledge to their own advantage against some men on the committees, they found themselves replaced by women who did not have such knowledge."[25]

Despite these less than glowing assessments, many party women in states that did not require 50–50 craved it. In Illinois, Republican women lobbied to add it to the state primary law, in part because they wanted to chose their own leaders rather than have them appointed by party men. They didn't get a law but they eventually persuaded both parties to require it by rule on some committees. In New York, Republican women said that "50–50 works." So dedicated were the New York parties to 50–50 that after the courts invalidated several laws permitting party rules to require it, they changed the constitution.[26]

When Molly Dewson took over the DNC Women's Division in 1933, she found Democratic women's "political participation was casual and spotty."

> Women political leaders at that period had little power. Outside of a few exceptions they were just figureheads, symbols acknowledging that women had the vote. They waited for the go-ahead signal from the man who was responsible for their appointment.[27]

Nonetheless, she instigated a major campaign to achieve 50–50 because she felt that it was the best means available for women to get responsibility in the party organizations. The Women's Division produced a study of state election laws and drew up model legislation which it urged Democratic women to have passed in their states. In August 1935 DNC Chairman Jim Farley sent a letter to all Democratic county chairmen giving his support for the plan, and asking theirs.[28] Each new victory was applauded in the Women's Division magazine, *Democratic Digest*.[29] In February 1937 it reported that "The fifty–fifty movement has gained considerable momentum during the last few years. . . . The prestige of fifty–fifty organization immeasurably increased because of its unbelievable efficiency during the last campaign."[30]

There was a significant increase in states with some form of 50–50 during Dewson's tenure, and little increase afterwards. In 1929 Blair reported that "in eighteen states there is some form of fifty-fifty organization in both major political parties."[31] In February 1939 the *Democratic Digest* reported that seventeen states had equal representation on all party committees, eleven by law and six by regulation, while twenty-two states had 50–50 on some committees, seven by law and fifteen by regulation. However, the *Democratic Digest* of March 1949 reported that there had been no further progress. A study done in 1947 found that the Republican Party provided for equal representation on all party committees only in the states where it was required by law, and on some party committees in another twenty-one states. "In only eight states—Arizona, Georgia, Maryland, Mississippi, Nevada, North Dakota, Virginia, and Wisconsin— has no systematic effort been made to secure equal representation in either party, either by statute or by party regulation."[32] More progress was reported in 1960 by a Democratic Party survey that showed 50–50 was required on all committees in twenty-one states, on some in nineteen and on none in ten.[33]

Dewson's success was due in part because she was realistic. Her concept of 50–50 acknowledged male predominance. A chart on how 50–50 should work was published in *Democratic Digest* in 1934 which showed parallel structures. Underneath the DNC were two separate hierarchies. In the male line were the chairmen of each geographic unit, ending with the "Men's Clubs." In the female line were the vice chairs, ending with the "Women's Clubs or study groups." The chart did not reflect actual party structure, but illustrated Dewson's understanding that making a place for women did not involve pushing out any men. She justified this special place by arguing that "Women have a different contribution.... The first duty of women is having her own home and keeping that home together; second we are interested in the training of the child, and the third big thing is peace.... If we work for these things we will get a position in politics."[34]

State party laws or rules often acknowledged that 50–50 was not equal representation. Some states defined the primary duties of the vice chair, or co-chair, as supervision of the party's women's clubs, and used the pronoun "she" to distinguish it from the supposedly generic "he." Others specifically made the female leader of a party unit subordinate to the male leader, even to the point of total exclusion from the ruling executive committee. When rules did require women on the executive committee, it was not in equal numbers with men. In the 1950s the RNC held an annual campaign school for its state chairmen; the women vice chairmen were not invited.[35] Nor was there any guarantee that positions provided for would be filled. After decades of lobbying, the constitution of the Maryland Republican Party was changed to require that each county have a woman vice chair. But a survey in June of 1967 disclosed that only ten counties plus Baltimore had women in this position.[36] But when there was no such requirement, there was often no one in charge of organizing women. In 1953 in the state of West Virginia, the Democratic vice chairman was a man, and there was one woman's Democratic club and no woman leader.[37]

With or without 50–50 requirements, women rarely replaced men. They could serve, but could not lead. One who tried was Iowan Minnette Doderer. Beginning as a Democratic precinct worker in 1952, she soon became county vice chairman. Noting that she was doing the work for which the four chairmen she served under got the credit, when the position next became vacant she decided it was her turn. Her closest friend told her she shouldn't run for the chairman because she was a woman, and organized their faction against her. She lost the party chairmanship, but won a seat in the Iowa state legislature in 1964.[38] The (male) respondents in a 1967 study of Colorado County Chairman agreed that "many times [women] actually do the work of the chairman with the title of vice chairmen," but few ever became county chairmen. Data on how many women chaired party committees in the roughly 3,000 counties were not collected and seldom reported. Throughout the 1940s and 1950s, the DNC usually said about one hundred county chairmen were women. In 1954, the Republicans claimed 300 were women. Neither party identified *which* counties were led by women. County chairman in an area dominated by the other party is a thankless job.[39] In 1951, a questionnaire answered by 423 Republican precinct committeemen out of over 1100 in King Co., Washington State showed that 42 percent were women, but only one of twelve district leaders was female. In 1926, a New York court invalidated a Republican Party rule that one of the two Assembly District leaders, who sat on the State Central Committee, must be female; a year later there were 141 women and 159 men.[40]

Women state vice chairmen could also do the work of chairmen, and sometimes served as temporary chairs, but it was rarely a stepping stone to the top job.[41] The first woman to be a state party chairman for a full term was Congresswoman Mary Norton (D. N.J.). She held the job twice, in 1932–35 and 1940–44, at the behest of her mentor, Jersey City boss Frank Hague. The second was Elizabeth Snyder, who headed the Democratic State Central Committee of California from 1954 to 1956. Unlike Norton, she was not put into office by a boss. Snyder, who had headed the Woman's Division, credits the "strong women" in the California party and India Edwards, then living in California, for pushing her to run. "We had an enormous group of solid, hard-working women that, believe me, were the guts of the Democratic party, too, when it came to the real hard work. They did fund-raising." The campaign was hard fought and nasty. During Snyder's two-year term, there was still a "Women's Vice Chairman," who was a woman. Only in the late 1960s did attitudes about woman's place melt enough for women to seriously aspire to be state party chairmen. Three Republican women chaired their state parties in 1966. Lorraine Orr of Nebraska was elected Republican chairman in 1967 and reelected in 1969, after serving as vice chairman for two terms.[42] In 1968 Koryne Horbal was elected chairman of the Minnesota Democratic Farmer/ Labor Party.

THE FUTILITY OF 50–50

Emily Newell Blair thought 50–50 would be "an opening wedge" to get women inside the political house until they became "powerful enough in politics to defeat men." Women soon discovered that the party committees did very little and that party men stacked the decks. In 1924 a member of the New Jersey Republican State Committee "found . . . that the Committee rarely met. When it did, a few resolutions of no importance were passed, and a motion made to adjourn. Then the men met privately and transacted the real business. The results were then handed to the whole Committee on a silver salver, as it were. We found that the members knew nothing of the finances of the Committee, and that apparently there were no printed rules." [44]

While the anecdotal evidence is spotty, it consistently discloses that regardless of the rules, major decisions were made by men. In 1928 it was major news that "7 G.O.P. Women Selected to Attend Conference on Picking Candidate," at the New York state convention because it was so common for everything to be "settled by groups of men leaders to whose conferences no women had been invited." In 1931, Sara Schuyler Butler, vice chairman of the New York State Republican Committee and daughter of the president of Columbia University, himself a power in the New York Republican Party, noted that a "forward step" was taken by state laws requiring that women be elected rather than appointed. "So long as they remained appointees they were not only under obligation to the man who named them but they had no constituency to which to appeal in case of necessity." But in 1933 New York's Republican state chairman selected Butler's replacement while slighting her candidate, who was supported by the prominent Republican women of the state. [45]

Women eventually learned that the committee chairman usually made all the decisions or they were made by the Executive Committee of the relevant party body, where 50–50 rules did not apply. Repeatedly women saw their recommendations ignored. As Democrat Louis Howe observed in 1935, "care is still taken that only such women as can be trusted to follow implicitly the orders of the local male boss are permitted to hold even these nominal positions of authority." Even the highest party women had little influence. In 1953 Jessica (Judy) Weis wrote the "Members of the Executive Committee" of the Monroe County Republican Committee to protest the fact that "45 MEN are meeting to-day to select the leader of the women of the County." Weis had been New York's national committeewoman for ten years and county vice chairman and head of the Women's Division for over fifteen years, but she did not sit on the County Executive Committee and was not allowed to participate in the meeting to select her successor. She was "deeply disturb[ed] . . . that women should have no part in choosing their own leader." [46]

While no one proposed that 50–50 be abolished, over time women became disenchanted with its actual results. In the early fifties Eleanor

Roosevelt, who supported the program, criticized it in terms very similar to Dewson's and Blair's years earlier.

> It looks better on paper than it has worked out in practice. Too often the vice chairmen and the committeewomen are selected by the men, who naturally pick women who will go along with them and not give them any trouble. . . . And a state vice chairman, even if she has ability and a mind of her own, finds herself frustrated by a kind of political protocol under which she is not permitted to choose the women with whom she is to work, but must accept those handed to her by the masculine-dominated county committee.[47]

The more experience women in both parties had with 50–50, the more they shared Roosevelt's dismay. In December 1929 Sophonisba Preston Breckinridge, former NAWSA vice president and founder of the School of Social Service Administration at the University of Chicago, was asked to prepare a factual study of the activities of women for President Hoover's Research Committee on Social Trends. As part of her research she sent questionnaires to the forty-eight women on each major party's national committee. Only twelve Republicans and eleven Democrats replied. Of these only one of the former and two of the latter were dissatisfied by the treatment of women by her party.[48]

But by the mid-1940s, when two political scientists repeated Breckinridge's survey, the national committeewomen in both parties were participating more and liking it less. Returns from eighteen of the forty-five Democratic women and twenty-three of the fifty-three Republicans surveyed showed that all but a few had worked their way up through other party offices both in the regular organization and in separate women's clubs, with an average of nineteen years in politics. Half had held public offices of some sort and all belonged to at least one women's organization, usually the General Federation of Women's Clubs. Their greater experience over those national committeewomen surveyed by Breckinridge had led to a greater cynicism. One third of the women of both parties "stated in rather strong terms that the influence of the women members was negligible." Some went so far as to say that women were "of less value today than 20 years ago." In 1933, when her research was published, Breckinridge's own assessment on the achievements of women in the parties was mixed. "The Committee woman is often the shadow of the Committee man; but she is a woman. The door has opened a little." The authors of the later study concluded that "the door has opened farther," but not much farther. [49]

National committeewomen have not been surveyed on their perceptions of their own power since 1944. But in 1963 data were compiled on all but four of the 686 people who had served on the national committees of the major parties between 1948 and 1963, including reports from "knowledgeable political observers and participants in the states." These informants were asked to rank the National Committee members on their importance in their own states. The authors concluded that

> By our ratings it turns out that national committee*men* are important figures in the state parties. Of the national committeemen for whom we have judgments, more than 90 percent in both parties are among the top twenty-five party leaders in the states; indeed, 42.1 percent of the Democrats and 35 percent of the Republicans are judged to be among the top half-dozen party leaders in their states.

> The national committee*woman*, however, enjoys very little power in her state party. Nearly one-third of the Republican women and nearly one-half of the Democratic are described by our informants as quite unimportant. . . . [It can be] inferred from the data, . . . that, if *these* women have little influence, then *no women have much influence in state political parties.* The national committeewomen are as important as any women in the parties, but of very little importance at all by comparison with the male party leaders. In most states, at most levels of party organization, women have *equal representation* with men; there is no evidence that they have ever had *equal influence.*[50]

This survey included evaluations of the state party chairmen—all men—who were found to be only slightly less important than the national committee*men*. In the only study done of county chairmen which included the vice chairmen, the latter were two thirds as likely to be actively involved in seeking candidates for public office, which is a primary job of a local party. Ironically, by the early 1960s when these studies were done, women were a majority of the staff in the many national and state party committee headquarters. Although female staff were paid for their work, as a group, women were still "making coffee but not policy." Elizabeth Gatov, California's Democratic national committeewoman from 1956 to 1965, commented that it was common to have male and female co-chairs for local committees: "the man for the name, and the woman for the work." More than forty years after party men opened the door of the political house, women could dust the furniture and wash the dishes, but could not sit in the rooms where the decisions were made.[51]

· Seven ·

Down Different Paths:
Women's Organizations and
Political Parties after 1920

After 1920 the braid that bound the Suffrage Movement together began to unravel as feminists, reformers, and party women went their separate ways. The rift between feminists and reformers quickly widened and deepened when the National Woman's Party introduced an Equal Rights Amendment into Congress. While both camps shared a desire to improve the status of women, they disagreed on the roles and nature of women and on how to achieve those goals they shared. Conflict over their different agendas polarized them into antagonistic camps for decades. They carried their debate over the right agenda for women into the parties, and to some degree polarized them. Although some prominent Democrats were feminists, by and large feminists had warmer relationships with the Republican Party, which they maintained through the 1960s. Reformers had been part of the Progressive wing of the Republican party, and while some retained their party loyalty, many did not. FDR's New Deal brought reformers, especially younger ones, into the federal government, and into the Democratic Party.

The major political parties first embraced then rejected former suffragists. They campaigned against a "woman's bloc," forcing political women to choose between their party and their sex. Those who became party women learned to confine their interests to winning elections and making a place for women within their parties. Nonetheless, some issues, particularly Prohibition and Repeal, sometimes realigned party women with their partisan adversaries. All three types of women were joiners, involving themselves in the many new women's organizations that flowered in the 1920s. They provided links between different groups of organized women, bringing their conflicts with them.

Over time, both feminists and reformers declined in numbers and strength, while party women increased in numbers if not in strength. During this period the Republican Party proved itself more hospitable to feminists, while the Democratic Party became home to most of the reformers.

123

THE LEAGUE OF WOMEN VOTERS

In March of 1919 Carrie Chapman Catt urged NAWSA to create an auxiliary organization in those states where women could vote. The new League of Women Voters (LWV) would maintain the momentum created by the fight for suffrage. A year later, before ratification was complete, NAWSA dissolved itself into the National League with a four member executive committee and a Washington office. The same convention voted to support protective labor legislation for women, social welfare bills, and removal of laws that discriminated against women. The new league also passed numerous resolutions on other issues, mostly reflecting the ideals of the Progressive Movement. Citizenship schools, to train women in their new responsibilities, were planned for the time between ratification and the 1920 elections.[1]

The major political parties reacted to the idea of a League of Women Voters with horror; they saw it as a competitor for women's loyalties. Party women took the lead in trying to prevent its formation. Even the party women on NAWSA's Executive Council—Republicans Mary Garrett Hay (N.Y.), Harriet Taylor Upton (Ohio), and Narcissa Cox Vanderlip (N.Y.) and Democrats Elizabeth Bass (Ill.) and Anna Pennybacker (Tex.)—argued against it. At the mere announcement that a such an organization was in formation, the Women's Republican Club of New York denounced it as a "nonpartisan party" that was a "menace to our national life and unAmerican in principle." The Democrats said it was "superfluous." Elizabeth Bass went further than mere argument; she joined with Ruth Hanna McCormick to try to block the formation of new state leagues.[2]

The League urged women to "Get into the Parties." *The Woman Citizen* ran a series of short essays on political parties, most on the theme of "Why I Joined My Party."[3] At NAWSA's Victory Convention, held in Chicago in February 1920, Carrie Chapman Catt sought to reassure the parties that the new league would not be a competitor by encouraging women to work within them. She said:

> opposition to the League of Women Voters . . . is . . . largely political. The people who are interested in enrolling large numbers [of women] in political parties . . . seem to think that it is going to keep women out of the political parties.
>
> It certainly was never any idea of the League of Women Voters that we voters should remain out of the parties and appeal to them for their help, for the things that we wanted to do. The only way to get things in this country is to get them on the inside of the political party. . . . [W]hen you enter the party . . . you will find yourself in a political penumbra where most of the men are. . . . [I]f you stay long enough . . . you will discover a little denser thing . . . the numbra of the . . . party, the people . . . planning the platform and picking out the candidates, doing the real work that you and the men sanction at the polls. You won't be so welcome, but there is the place to go.

If you stay there long enough and are active enough, you will see the real thing in the center, with the door locked tight, and you will have a hard, long fight before you get inside the real thing that moves the wheels of your party. . . . You must go into those parties.[4]

Some prominent women, such as Jane Addams, now a leader of the peace movement, warned that women's principles would be corrupted if they did not retain a separate identity. However, she did not advocate a separate women's party because she felt all political parties were essentially corrupt. The League's compromise was to urge its members to be active in the political party of their choice, while remaining "non-partisan and all partisan."[5]

Despite these overtures, the parties remained fearful. The president of the St. Louis, Missouri, LWV commented in 1920 that "Both major parties are a bit suspicious and very watchful lest the League of Women Voters should inter-fere in any plans they may have for organizing the women." When Emily Newell Blair was organizing women for the county conventions, party men told her she "could not be a Democrat and a worker for the League of Women Voters." At the 1920 Missouri State Democratic convention "the local politi-cians decided that it was a new women's party and proceeded to fight it and the women connected with it."[6]

Although both parties were cold to the League, the Republican Party was harsher. Ruth McCormick, the most prominent Republican woman of her day, led the attacks. In her history of the LWV Louise Young concluded that "[H]er antagonism was communicated . . . to the Republican leadership . . . [and] led to hostility that was not allayed for many years." The Republican Party may also have reacted to the NWP's targeting it in 1920 as the party "most guilty" for delay in ratification of the Suffrage Amendment. The NWP picketed the Republican convention in June and threatened to follow Harding on the cam-paign trail with pickets, hecklers, and embarrassing questions if he did not com-pel the Republican Governors of Connecticut or Vermont to make theirs the missing thirty-sixth state. When Harding declined, the NWP said it would cam-paign against all Republican candidates, as it had done against all Democrats in 1916. The NWP did not picket the Democratic convention, saying that Cox had a much better record on suffrage than Harding. While suffragists knew that the LWV was not the NWP, party women, and men, did not always distinguish between them. McCormick thought that even non-political women's groups like the GFWC undermined women's political influence.[7]

RNC Chairman Will Hays pursued "complete amalgamation" of women into the Republican Party "to check any tendency toward the formation of a separate women's party." Early in 1920 he told Republican women that "I would rather a woman join with our opponents than belong to no party." His successor, John T. Adams, told the WNRC in 1922 that "the best thing for a woman is to be a Republican partisan; the second best thing, a Democratic partisan; and about the poorest thing she can do, politically, is to be a non-partisan or a woman partisan."[8] During the 1920 campaign Warren G. Harding said: "Too much is heard of independence in politics." "[N]ew voters" should "join . . . some party and give . . . to the party of their choice their service, conscience, wisdom and loyalty." He lamented the possibility of a "selfish group allegiance. . . . It would be the supreme disappointment if the coming of women into our political life should mean the organization of any considerable part of them into a woman's party, built upon a spirit of demand."[9] Harding and other Republicans continued to harp on this theme even after the election. He had the same message for women whether he was speaking to women's Republican clubs or the LWV: join the political parties and avoid "sex organizations."[10]

Some State Republican leaders were quite hostile. The New York League—roughly two-thirds of whom were Republicans—invited the newly elected Republican Governor to address its convention in February of 1921. Ill and ordered by his doctor to rest, Governor Nathan L. Miller canceled all public appearances except this one. He rose before the assembled women and told them to disband. "Any organization which seeks to exert political power is a menace to our institutions unless it is organized as a political party," because it was not responsible to anyone. He further denounced the social welfare bills the league supported, in particular those that sought to limit women's night work and hours, as one group of women trying to make decisions for another.[11] The Republican members of the LWV replied with a letter that said their attempts to work within the parties had been "humiliating." "We are forbidden to exercise independence or judgment and are openly advised that there is no place in the party except for those who take orders." Republicans were not conciliatory. Even before Miller's speech, a convention of Republican women had passed a resolution stating that league members were not wanted in the Republican Party. One speaker at the New York Republican women's convention denounced the league as "the tail-end of the Socialist kite."[12]

The influential, pro-Republican Hartford *Courant* warned that women "are forming a new party—a woman's party."[13] The newspaper editorial voiced openly what Republican officials only hinted at in their steady denunciations of a separate women's political organization: that the LWV would follow the example set by the NWP in 1916 and campaign against the party in power and all of its candidates if that party did not support League positions. Now that the Republican Party dominated the federal government and women could vote in every state, it wanted to forestall any effort by organized women to influence elections. "Republican men," Harriet Taylor Upton reported in December 1921, "do not feel very kindly towards the League of Women Voters." They continued to warn women against the "error of 'non-partisan' organization."[14]

Their fears were not groundless. Some suffragists, such as the NWP's Anne Martin, wrote and spoke about the need for "sex solidarity" in politics. The

Pennsylvania LWV had declared that the parties were run by "selfish and powerful minorities."[15] Analyses of the 1915 Chicago elections, where men's and women's ballots were counted separately, showed that in primaries, where there was a real difference between candidates, and party was not a factor, women did not always vote like men.[16] Suffragists had shown they were willing and able to campaign vigorously against incumbents who opposed suffrage. In 1918, NAWSA targeted Senate opposition leaders Willard Saulsbury Jr. (D. Del.) and John W. Weeks (R. Mass.) for defeat. Weeks counted their activities as a major cause of his loss. New York women helped defeat four state legislators and Ohio women defeated the reelection of a three-term mayor.[17] In 1920, newly formed leagues worked against incumbents who had opposed suffrage and other LWV issues. Connecticut suffragists tried but failed to retire another anti- Senator. A 1922 newspaper article on how women helped overthrow machine politicians in the Pennsylvania and Indiana primaries was headlined "Women in Politics Bring Worry to Old Guard."[18]

Of all campaign efforts by women, that against Senator James W. Wadsworth, Jr. became a litmus test of party loyalty. Senator Wadsworth was from an old political family in upstate New York. He had led the opposition to the Nineteenth Amendment even after New York gave women suffrage in 1917 and the New York legislature asked him to vote for the federal amendment. The LWV marked him for defeat when he came up for reelection in 1920 even though the fate of the suffrage amendment was now out of his reach. That January the New York State LWV mailed a pamphlet on "The Case Against Senator Wadsworth" around the state. The National LWV offered its assistance at its February convention. In 1919, Mary Garrett Hay, head of the New York Suffrage party and a leader of Republican women, had stated that she would work against Wadsworth if he was the Republican candidate despite the fact that active opposition would endanger "her whole political career and reputation." Her actions did just that. Months before Wadsworth was reelected she was removed from all Republican Party positions, national, state, and local.[19]

Party women were not united in their objection to the league. Some saw it as a kindergarten for the real world of party politics. Katherine Edson wired the women on the RNC Executive Committee in 1921: "Please do not allow any attack by National Committee on National League of Women Voters. Such attack would alienate thousands of women all over the country from party." She later wrote Ruth McCormick that the LWV "will be the biggest feeder we can have for the Republican Party."[20] Democrat Daisy Harriman commented in 1923 that the League "has done a great work by giving women a preparatory school in which to learn a technique for making themselves felt when they do join the parties." Reflecting a still prevalent ambivalence, she quoted a New York Democratic woman as lamenting that "if party women would only realize it, the League is an immense help toward political education, a broad point of view, and fundamental preparation for our new duties."[21]

For several years the LWV's relationship to the parties remained problematic; it even delegated members to ask the parties why they were so hostile. In 1920 two members of the national board were on national party campaign committees and several state officers held party positions. While the League remained officially non-partisan, local leagues endorsed and openly worked for or against many candidates. The Ohio LWV helped elect Democrat Florence Allen to a judgeship in Ohio in 1922 and the Tennessee LWV worked to reelect Republican Harry Burns to the Tennessee legislature in 1920 (his last minute vote change made Tennessee the thirty-sixth state to ratify Suffrage). A few LWV officers ran for office themselves, with the help of local leagues. At the 1923 convention, "Marguerite Wells was appointed to chair a committee of three to identify ways of penetrating the parties." The National Board decided to let local leagues decide for themselves when officers could be active in parties, and when they had to resign if they wanted to be partisan.[22]

Many party women joined the LWV; in the 1928 party conventions, one eighth of the Republican women delegates and one sixth of the Democratic women were LWV members. But partisanship took its toll. The New York LWV was split when Hay opposed Wadsworth while most other prominent Republican women supported him. Other local LWVs had similar problems. National membership declined to 40,000 by the end of the decade. The national league commissioned a study in 1927 which revealed that quite a few local leagues were disrupted by partisan splits. It concluded that the LWV could best pursue politics by being nonpartisan.[23]

The League searched for a role in a hostile environment, eventually settling on political education and lobbying as the twin features of its program. After a vigorous Get Out the Vote campaign in 1924 which saw little change in women's turnout from 1920, new LWV President Belle Sherwin realized that women had to learn politics "from the alphabet upward" before they could be expected to fully perform their civic duties. It might be another generation before political equality would be a reality. In 1927 and 1928 the LWV broadcast weekly bipartisan speeches on national issues to seventeen million people listening to twenty-four radio stations. The president of NBC claimed this significantly increased the woman's vote in 1928. Success prompted the League to create a regular Voters Service project, which by 1930 "had organized nearly thirteen hundred institutes and schools on government and politics." It published annual reports on women in public office and encouraged women to run for office. It sent questionnaires to candidates to identify their opinions and proposals on issues relevant to the league's program. This method of gathering information—developed by suffragists during their state campaigns—became a model for other issue organizations for years to come. The LWV registered women to vote when the men ignored them and then invited all the candidates to speak to the new voters. In 1952 it expanded this strategy by inviting the Presidential candidates to participate in a "Citizen's View of '52" forum, for which it received national media coverage. This was a precursor for the tele-vised debates it sponsored eight years later. Over time the League expanded its reach, becoming best known for its careful, informed studies into important public issues. In 1946 it reorganized, and while it continued to promote "polit-ical responsibility through informed and active participation of citizens in gov-ernment," it dropped the emphasis on political education. By the 1950s the LWV had matured and institutionalized. Its membership ranged between 120,000 and 150,000 in roughly 1,200 local leagues, whose members debated issues endlessly before deciding whether to take a stand. While the LWV stayed out of the partisan cauldron in which it had been so badly burned in the 1920s, it did become what Harriman said it would be, a political "preparatory school" for women. Surveys of women holding public office repeatedly showed that work in the League was part of their training, and strengthened their motiva-tion for going more deeply into politics.[24]

THE NATIONAL WOMAN'S PARTY

Throughout 1920 the NWP leadership debated its future. At a three-day con-vention in February 1921 the NWP was refounded and rededicated to the prin-ciple of equality that had informed the spirit of the 1848 Seneca Falls conference. After deciding to remove women's legal disabilities, the NWP drafted model bills to eradicate sex specific laws which it sent to the state leg-islatures. The NWP soon decided that this strategy was too slow and uncertain. Alice Paul oversaw the preparation of another Constitutional amendment, which was announced at a major conference held in Seneca Falls on July 21, 1923. Later that fall the Equal Rights Amendment (ERA) was officially intro-duced into Congress by Rep. Daniel R. Anthony (R. Kans.), nephew of Susan B., and the Senate Republican Whip, Charles Curtis (R. Kans.), both of whom had been suffrage supporters. While the NWP did have other issues on its agenda—equalizing the nationality laws for married women, jury service, abo-lition of laws that penalized women's employment opportunities, adding "sex" to any law or program seeking equal rights for any other group—the ERA was always the priority; all other issues were "sideshows."[25]

Although it retained the name, the National Woman's *Party*, none of its refounders thought it should be a real political party, not even as much of one as the original NWP had been when it campaigned against all Democrats. The NWP disdained both Democrats and Republicans. Its president, Mrs. O.H.P. (Alva) Belmont, declared that "[w]e mean to free women from the indignity of hanging on to the old political parties." However, since its primary goal was another Constitutional amendment it could not avoid them. Every four years it sent delegations to each party's national nominating convention to lobby for a plank in support of the ERA. In states where there were local members it also lobbied the state parties to include it in their platforms, and in state legislatures it campaigned against all protective laws that applied only to women. It did not lobby for state ERAs. While the ERA dominated the NWP's agenda, it also formed some specialized groups. One of these was a Political Council to help women "force their way into the very heart of such old political parties as remain existent and such new ones as may arise." Its secretary was Sue Shelton White, and its focus was the election and appointment of women to any available governmental post.[26]

Like the LWV, the NWP made a brief foray into electoral politics during the 1920s. In 1924 Alice Paul urged the election of women who supported the ERA and a general feminist program in order to make women's vote count. The NWP sent leaders around the country to interview potential candidates, culminating in a major "Women for Congress" conference in upstate New York in July. Four parties had nominated ten women for Congress that year, all in districts completely dominated by another party. Convinced that the woman's vote would make a difference, the NWP decided to support all of them. It concentrated its efforts in Pennsylvania, where five women were running, sending Doris Stevens to Philadelphia to manage its campaign. The only woman who won was Mary T. Norton of New Jersey, the candidate of the boss of Jersey City. She held her seat for twenty-six years.[27] The NWP continued to support candidates for another ten years but with little noticeable success. Although it usually supported women who were also feminists, it opposed any candidate who was critical of the NWP, regardless of sex.

Party women and men disliked the NWP for the same reasons that they opposed the LWV, but they did not try to stop it because it was too small to be a threat. The NWP had garnered quite a bit of publicity during the final fight for suffrage, but the militant women who marched under its banner were a small percentage of the millions who supported NAWSA. Nonetheless, party women would have preferred that it cease to exist. Daisy Harriman reconciled herself to the LWV but not the NWP. In 1923 she wrote that

> I dislike very much the sex-conscious block that Alice Paul and her party
> have organized. I don't think they can ever be powerful enough on their
> own to accomplish anything, and I do think they stir up so much antago-
> nism in the men that it is very difficult for the rest of us to peacefully nego-
> tiate the things we want.[28]

Most NWP members were Republicans, though they were not active ones.[29] Quite a few hailed from Western states where the NWP had appealed to voting women before 1920, and which usually voted Republican. Many more came from Republican families. In general, campaigning against the Democratic Party had left a lingering dislike for and poor relationships with the party of the working man. During the 1920s the NWP could get an audience with the President or other high-ranking appointees through members with personal connections. Although none of these three Republican Presidents endorsed the ERA, none opposed it, and all expressed personal support when they received delegations from the NWP. President Roosevelt, on the other hand, never met with the NWP. He was described by an NWP publication as "a peninsula, almost completely surrounded by women who believe in protective labor legislation for women only." The distaste was mutual. Eleanor Roosevelt, FDR's liaison with women's groups, later characterized the NWP as "a perfectly useless organization."[30]

The Republican party led the Democrats in support for the ERA, the NWP's prime concern. The first major party candidate to endorse the ERA was Thomas Dewey in 1948. The first three Presidents to publicly support the ERA, while they were President, were Republicans: Eisenhower, Nixon, and Ford.[31] The Republican Party put the ERA into its national party platform in 1940, four years before the Democrats. Several Republican Congresswomen were NWP members, and until 1964 they were the chief sponsors of the ERA. When it was voted on in the Senate in 1946, 1950, and 1953, Republicans were much more likely than Democrats to vote in favor.[32] In part this was because the professional and business women who became the ERA's primary supporters after 1937 were more likely to be Republicans and were more successful with members of Congress from their own party. But conservative organizations like the National Association of Manufacturers, which opposed any law regulating industry, also supported the ERA. The NWP shared with the Republican Party a belief in legal equality and individual rights, and an opposition to government regulation, of which protective labor legislation was one form. After World War II, when the political atmosphere veered sharply right, the NWP went with it. In 1973 Alice Paul admitted that "almost all our members seemed to be of the conservative school."[33]

The NWP's only Presidential endorsement was in 1928 for the Republican Hoover-Curtis ticket. The primary reason for this move was opposition to the Democratic candidate—New York Governor Alfred Smith, a strong proponent of protective labor legislation. The NWP also wanted to support Hoover's runningmate, Charles Curtis, because of his steady support of suffrage and the ERA. Paul thought Hoover might be induced to publicly support the ERA because he had told an NWP delegation that "I agree with you in principle. . . . If I find this amendment is necessary to obtain equality of opportunity I will be with you." The endorsement backfired. Hoover won without any apparent need for the NWP's support, and never backed the ERA while in office. Twenty percent of the NWP Board had opposed the endorsement; some supported Smith and several resigned as a result, including committed Democrat Sue Shelton White. Hoover's failure to come out for the ERA, despite statements supporting "equality of opportunity for every boy and girl," discredited the action in the eyes of NWP members. The mistake was not repeated.[34]

This did not keep the NWP from relentless pursuit of endorsements for the ERA from the Presidential candidates, even ones it knew to be unsympathetic. Its effort to lobby Adlai Stevenson when he was the Democratic Party candidate in 1956 was described by Katie Louchheim, a member of his campaign entourage:

> Our great ordeal occurred five days before election; up till then the feminists promoting the Equal Rights Amendment had been put off. Every candidate for public office was and still is subject to their persistent lobbying. They had to be received. Eleven strong, they waited for Adlai in a Bellevue-Stratford parlor in Philadelphia; the hour was late, he had just delivered a major speech at the University of Pennsylvania at which student booing had again distracted the audience and disrupted the dearly bought TV time. Escorting him down the hall, I felt much like a jailor and said so. . . .
>
> My worst fears were soon realized. One persistent pleader sat not only beside him but practically upon him. Crossing her hands on her breast in martyr fashion, she bombarded him with long impassioned pleas and large pieces of paper with the signatures of prominent public figures. When Adlai finally broke in to relate his experiences as Governor, referring to the many organizations opposed to this legislation, Alice Paul, their statuesque spokesman, announced that the opposition had crumbled away. Opposition, apparently, these fourteen years later, is still crumbling. In the end it took a combined force of Mrs. Ives, Eugenie Anderson and TV newsman John Daly physically to pry the Governor loose.[35]

Although the NWP was heartened by Eisenhower's endorsement of "equality of rights for women" in the 1956 campaign, it came too late for the NWP to do much with it. The opportunity to make the ERA a campaign issue did not arise until 1968 when Eugene McCarthy (D. Minn.), then chief sponsor of the ERA in the Senate, ran for President. NWP members organized campaign committees for him during the primaries, distributed flyers, made phone calls, and paid for radio promotionals praising his support for the ERA. The *NWP Bulletin* claimed that the New Hampshire primary "marks the first time the issue of the Constitutional Rights of Women has ever been regarded as an issue of political significance in a Primary election" and cited McCarthy literature that listed his ERA sponsorship among his activities. In April, Emma Guffey Miller wrote him that several NWP members, "mostly Republicans," had traveled at their own expense to primary states to campaign for him.[36]

Despite the greater affinity of feminists for the Republican Party, two of the most partisan NWP members were Democrats: Sue Shelton White and Emma Guffey Miller. White inherited her party preference, being from Tennessee, where twelve years as a court reporter was "good training for a feminist." From more modest origins than the typical NWP activist, White chaired the state NWP in 1918, moved to Washington in 1919 to edit the NWP paper, the *Suffragist*, and was jailed for five days after burning a caricature of President Wilson. After attending Washington College of Law, she returned to Tennessee to practice law and became deeply involved in the Democratic Party. White left the NWP when it endorsed Herbert Hoover; she met Eleanor Roosevelt while working for Al Smith's 1928 campaign. Returning to Washington, she worked in the Women's Division of the DNC for three years, helping to organize Democratic women.[37]

Emma Guffey Miller was in her fifties when she moved to Washington, D.C., from her home in Pennsylvania. Born into a political family, she had long been an active Democrat, especially on behalf of her brother, Joseph Guffey, Pennsylvania Senator from 1935 to 1947. She maintained his home in D.C. and acted as his hostess. In 1932 she became the Democratic national committeewoman from Pennsylvania, a position she held at her death in 1970 at age ninety-three. By 1938 she had become an outspoken advocate of the ERA and joined the NWP. Although she chaired the NWP from 1960 to 1965, when she became life president, "she never sacrificed her partisan politics to her feminism."[38]

The NWP's best-known member was Perle Mesta, who inherited her husband's steel business before moving to Washington, where she made her reputation as "the hostess with the mostest." She joined the NWP in 1938, becoming a major contributor of both money and influence. In 1940 she was an active Republican, and lobbied the Resolutions Committee to include the ERA in the Republican platform. By 1944 she had switched to the Democratic Party. As a member of the convention Resolutions Committee that year, she pushed the Democrats to put the ERA in their party platform. After Harry Truman became President, he made her the Minister to Luxembourg, where she continued to speak out for women's rights.[39]

Despite the prominence of some of its members, by the 1950s the NWP had contracted to a small group in Washington, D.C., with a few more stalwarts around the country. Its journal, *Equal Rights*, ceased publication in 1954. The organization made little effort to recruit new members while its older ones were dying and retiring. It could get a Member of Congress to regularly introduce the ERA, and many more to sign on as sponsors, but could not get it out of committee. Instead it spent the limited time and energy of its few members on internal disputes and lawsuits. The NWP had never been much of a political force, but even as a carrier of feminist ideas, it no longer had much impact. It had a small revival in the 1960s when Emma Guffey Miller became president and Perle Mesta became vice president. At a dinner following its first convention in seven years, notables from the Democratic and Republican parties appeared or sent messages of support. Most were carefully worded to express support for women without mentioning the Equal Rights Amendment.[40]

THE WOMEN'S PROGRESSIVE NETWORK

The Suffrage Movement followed a different trajectory than the overall Progressive Movement of which it was a part. Progressivism probably peaked in 1912. By 1920 it was comatose. While it never died—its policy proposals became New Deal bills in the 1930s—it did decline. When Maud Wood Park, the new LWV president, led a delegation of prominent women to both parties' 1920 conventions she noted that "the League's moderately advanced social views found warm response in neither party. The change in public mood had been drastic; Progressive ideals now raised few echoes."[41] Suffrage activism crested in 1920 with the victory of the Nineteenth Amendment, but progressive women drew upon the energy it generated for a few more years. With the backlash against progressivism fed by the Great War, women's organizations were prominent targets. By mid-decade, women activists, worn out with years of sacrifice and assaulted from all sides, began to retreat into their own affairs, and by the Great Depression their concern for women's welfare was overshadowed by society's greater concern for men as family breadwinners.

Despite the backlash, the 1920s were a "seedtime of reform," as historian Clarke Chambers termed it. During the first half of this decade two of the most influential organizations acting on behalf of women were the National Consumers' League (NCL) and the National Women's Trade Union League (WTUL). Their chief activists had involved themselves in the suffrage struggle once that movement surged, but more than most suffragists they pursued the vote as a means to better achieve the goals for which their organizations were already working. Margaret Dreier Robins resigned from NAWSA's Committee on Women in Industry after it formed the LWV in 1920, "acknowledging that she had assumed the chair to make certain of the inclusion of the WTUL's own program in the League's agenda; she was too busy as WTUL president, she said, to give further time to the League."[42] Florence Kelley was a member of the NWP Executive Committee when it was debating what to do next. At the refounding convention she argued for support for protective labor legislation whether women "demanded it for themselves or not," and when the NWP did not comply she publicly denounced it for being unconcerned with the problems of working women.[43] When the new NWP adopted goals that conflicted with her lifelong pursuit of labor laws, she withdrew and became its foremost opponent. As leaders in the women's progressive network, the NCL and the WTUL had a great deal of influence on organized women outside of their own organizations.

In 1920 the LWV joined with the NCL, the WTUL, and other women's organizations to form the Women's Joint Congressional Committee (WJCC) to lobby Congress on public health and welfare bills. In its first five years the WJCC persuaded the Republican Congress to pass numerous social reform bills, including the Sheppard-Towner Maternity and Infancy Protection Act

(1921), the Cable Act to make married women's citizenship independent of that of their husband's (1922), and a Constitutional amendment to prohibit child labor (1924).[44] Similar coalitions of women's groups created Women's Legislative Councils (WLC) in several states, often at the instigation of the state LWV. In addition to the league, participants usually included the state federation of women's clubs, business women's clubs, the WCTU, the Mothers Congress (which became the National Congress of Parents and Teachers in 1924), and state chapters of the National Council of Jewish Women and the National Council of Catholic Women.

Organized lobbying by associations of women's groups had a lengthy tradition. According to Breckinridge, "as early as 1906 the reports of women's organizations contain references to Legislative Councils in which the constantly increasing number of women's organized groups united to advocate their common interests." The early WLCs evolved out of the legislative committees of the state federations of women's clubs in the 1900s. Historian Mary Ritter Beard, herself a Progressive and a feminist, concluded in 1914 that "not a single important [social legislation] statute has been enacted without the active support of women, organized and unorganized." However, most WLCs were formed in the early 1920s. Although composed of many women's organizations, it was LWV members who did the research, lobbying, and letter writing for the proposals a WLC supported, and monitored their progress through bulletins to WLC members. The state WLCs peaked in the 1920s but Breckinridge reported that in 1931 there were "at least eighteen states where women's organizations co-operated in support of desired legislation." They were part of the network that sustained the progressive impulse despite declining public support. This was the last comprehensive survey. The women's organizations that survived the 1930s seem to have diverted their energies into other areas than a woman's agenda.[45] Many, such as the Woman Citizens' Union of New Orleans that was founded in 1934, devoted their energies to promoting clean elections and creation of a state civil service.[46]

Though neither the largest nor the most prominent organization in the progressive network, the NCL played a key role largely due to the single-mindedness of Florence Kelley. At the end of the Great War, she rejoiced that the NCL "is still in existence and has 82 leagues in fifteen states and the District of Columbia." However, the NCL was soon pulled in too many directions for its resources. Its drive for more protective labor laws for women was slowed when the Supreme Court declared in 1923 that laws requiring minimum wages for women were unconstitutional and expressed a general hostility to state regulation of industry. The NWP's proposed Equal Rights Amendment undermined the NCL's claim that women were united on what legislation they wanted. While it scored some successes working with the WJCC, the effort to ratify the federal Child Labor Amendment exhausted the NCL's funds and literally wore Kelley out. Despite the organization's decline, many women who

had worked in local branches of the NCL went on to positions in state and federal agencies concerned with social welfare. Kelley's disciples carried her concern for protecting women into the government long after her death in 1932.[47]

Like that of the NCL, the influence of the WTUL was due to the drive
of its leaders. Herself a wealthy woman, Margaret Dreier Robins made a point
of bringing trade union women into the WTUL leadership. By the time she
became honorary president in 1922, most of the executive board members were
union women such as Rose Schneiderman. They reinforced the policy of the
WTUL to emphasize unionization of women workers. While legislation was
not its primary focus, the WTUL claimed to be the only organization representing women in industry when it testified before legislative bodies and thus
the authority on what wage earning women really wanted. As the voice of
working women it had a great deal of stature, but a weak foundation. Organized
labor treated it like a poor relation and the affluent women who had supported
it for two decades eventually lost interest in reform. In 1921 the WTUL canceled its biennial convention, and its monthly publication, *Life and Labor*, was
reduced to an occasional *Life and Labor Bulletin*. By 1926 it was active only in
New York, Chicago, and Washington. Margaret Dreier Robins was a committed Republican, staying loyal when the party turned conservative in the 1920s.
She campaigned for the Republican presidential ticket even in 1924 when
Progressive women such as Jane Addams were supporting Robert LaFollette, in
his quixotic campaign for President.[48]

The GWFC had been slow to board the Progressive train, but did become
a significant contributor. "Its enthusiasm for progressive reform hit a peak in
the period 1920–24" when it helped organize the WJCC and worked on several welfare and women's issues. It initially viewed the LWV as a competitor
but the two organizations quickly worked out an accommodation. By the end
of the 1920s they were going in different directions. The GFWC was one of
the first to withdraw from the WJCC. By 1930 it had given up reform and
returned to its original concerns with culture and the home.[49] This took it off
the hot-seat, but also drove away women who wanted to work on more serious issues. In the October 1929 issue of *Harper's*, journalist Anna Steese
Richardson asked, "Is the Woman's Club Dying?" She concluded that "Women
who participated in the 1928 presidential campaign found club activities rather
stupid in comparison. . . . [T]oday you find club leaders turning definitely to
city, county, state and national politics. The woman whose ambition it was to
be president of a district or state federation now wants to go to the state legislature or to Congress." She predicted that "the political party organization will
replace the cultural club." Indeed there is anecdotal evidence that politically
inclined women left GFWC clubs for party clubs during the 1920s, leaving in
the GFWC only those women primarily concerned with culture and the home.[50]

The National Association of Colored Women, with 50,000 members, first
expanded then contracted its program. It joined the WJCC in 1924 and with-

drew in 1927, when the GFWC and other large women's federations did so. In 1930 it reduced its extensive program to two departments: Mother, Home, and Child, and the Negro Woman in Industry; later adding one on Colored Girls. By 1939 the membership stabilized at 50,000 while geographic spread increased to forty-two state associations.[51] In 1924 the NACW became deeply involved in the Republican Presidential campaign when its outgoing president, Hallie Q. Brown, was appointed by the Republican National Committee as director of the Colored Women's Department of the Coolidge-Dawes campaign. Brown had been a teacher, lecturer, temperance worker, and organizer of women's clubs. She effectively diverted NACW's leaders, clubs, and magazine to aid the Republican Party. As a result, "during the Presidential race, the NACW's usual social service activities took a backseat to intense partisan politics" and its "nationally read magazine [became] a political organ for the Republican party."[52]

As in the LWV, partisanship by the NACW created internal conflict, and in 1928, now led by Mary McLeod Bethune, it stayed out of politics. Bethune, who founded and ran a school for African American girls in Florida which became Bethune-Cookman College, felt NACW had become both too political and too provincial. In 1935 she founded the National Council of Negro Women (NCNW) which she led until 1949. As NACW became less political and more conservative during the 1930s, the NCNW took its place in the progressive network. Bethune was a Republican in the 1920s and led a voter registration drive for black women in 1920, but was less partisan than the older generation of African American female leaders. She became friends with Eleanor Roosevelt in 1934, teaching her about the condition of blacks and learning from her to distrust the Equal Rights Amendment. Although she had supported Hoover in 1932, through ER she forged a link between the black community and the Democratic Party which no doubt contributed to black women voting Democratic in the election of 1936. During the New Deal the NCNW lobbied for the inclusion of African Americans on its many programs. When World War II began, it pressed for the inclusion of black women in the women's units of the armed forces. In 1957 Dorothy Height became the fourth president of the NCNW, having worked her way up through the ranks. For thirteen years she had been on the national staff of the YWCA, which paid her salary to organize for the NCNW. By the mid-1960s the organization had three million members through its affiliates in forty-seven states.[53]

The ranks of reform organizations were reinforced in 1920 by the creation of the Women's Bureau in the Department of Labor. Its mandate was to "investigate and improve the condition of working women" but its real purpose was to be an advocate for women in industry inside the government itself. Thus the Women's Bureau "developed warm, supportive work relationships with . . . advocates within social reform and women's organizations."[54] The WJCC lobbied hard to maintain the Women's Bureau budget. Mary Anderson was appointed by Wilson to be its first director in 1920, although she was herself a

Republican. She kept that position until 1944. As women's reform organizations declined, the Bureau assumed leadership of their mutual causes. Over time however, women's organizations were replaced by labor unions and mixed-sex liberal organizations as the signatories on anti-ERA efforts and other relevant items that came before Congress. Historian Cynthia Harrison called this the Women's Bureau coalition.[55]

As the aging activists of the progressive network retired and died, they were replaced by a new generation of women who had been foot soldiers in the suffrage movement. This new generation was smaller in numbers, and often found professional positions in the government agencies created by the pioneers. Newer reformers, like the older ones, were usually raised as Republicans. During the 1920s, as the Progressive tradition receded and became isolated within the Republican Party, they lost faith in the party of their birth. Many were excited by the nomination and election of Franklin Roosevelt to the Presidency in 1932. Quite a few accepted positions in FDR's administration, and, if they had not already done so, switched parties. As the New Deal promoted the programs they had advocated for so long, the progressive impulse shifted from the Republican to the Democratic Party.[56]

OTHER FEMINIST ORGANIZATIONS

The NWP was not the only feminist organization, though it was the only one to publicly embrace the feminist label. In the 1920s and 1930s, organizations of women in business and the professions were founded, grew, and worked for explicitly feminist goals, including removal of discriminatory laws and practices, jury service for women, the election and appointment of more women to public office, and eventually, the ERA. As the NWP shrank in size and focus to concentrate on Congressional passage of the ERA, these other organizations lobbied for changes in state laws more favorable to women as well as looked for opportunities to promote women on the national level and in the political parties.[57]

The largest and most active of these was the National Federation of Business and Professional Women (BPW). During the Great War the YWCA "believed that the war effort would be aided by mobilizing the special talents of the business and professional women." It called a national conference in May of 1918 and hired Lena Madeson Phillips to organize such women into their own association. At the June 1919 founding conference, Gail Laughlin, a lawyer and member of the National Woman's Party, became its first president. When the BPW joined the WJCC it remained neutral in the debate over protective labor legislation. Initially it was part of the progressive network, but, like the NWP, its members were more concerned with equality for women. Harriet Taylor Upton even thought BPW might "make us more trouble" than the LWV. The YWCA continued to focus on progressive reform issues but in 1937 the national BPW endorsed the ERA. Smaller groups, including service organizations such as the Soroptimists and Zonta, and occupational organizations of women lawyers, educators, dentists, osteopaths, real estate agents, accountants, and physicians, also endorsed the ERA. Many NWP activists were founders or members of these groups. In 1944, BPW decided to work for "the election and appointment of qualified women to local, state, national and international offices, boards and commissions." Two years later BPW added *endorsement* of specific women for specific offices, creating a Political Alertness project for this purpose. Its magazine, *Independent Woman*, extolled women's success in politics, and its chapters supported individual members' campaigns.[58]

PROHIBITION AND REPEAL

Prohibition and woman suffrage had been intertwined since the 1850s, even though proponents of both agreed that a discreet distance was necessary to achieve either. By the time Congress approved the Eighteenth Amendment in December of 1917, prohibition was no longer predominantly a woman's crusade. Support for prohibition was far more widespread than for woman suffrage, particularly among Southerners. Congressional opponents, in retreat from the claim that legal liquor would undermine the country's ability to fight the war, attached a clause requiring full ratification within seven years in hopes they could stall in the states. To their surprise, ratification was completed within thirteen months, most states voting on it after the war ended. By March of 1922, forty-five states had voted to add prohibition to the Constitution.[59]

Only as it was being ratified did opponents create an Association Against the Prohibition Amendment (AAPA), so confident had they been that it would never come to pass. It took many years of experience to convince most people that "the noble experiment" created more problems than it solved, including increased crime, government corruption, disrespect for law, infringement of civil liberties, and health problems from bad alcohol. The Republican Congress passed the Volstead Act in October of 1919, over Wilson's veto. By defining "intoxicating liquor" as any beverage with more than one half of one percent alcohol it covered beer and light wine, and was much more restrictive than many had expected. And more costly. By 1928, prohibition had cost almost a billion dollars in enforcement and lost revenues, and accounted for two-thirds of the criminal cases in the federal courts. The AAPA grew slowly, subject to the usual problems of single-issue organizations. In 1928 it was taken over by a small group of wealthy businessmen, who reorganized it to resemble a business enterprise and funded it accordingly. The AAPA began a massive propaganda campaign.[60]

The 1928 Presidential contest pitted wet Al Smith against dry Herbert Hoover, generating a furious public debate over prohibition. While Smith lost, the campaign revealed the growth of wet sentiment and persuaded the AAPA that repeal was realistic. The new chairman of the DNC, John J. Raskob, was a member of the AAPA and dedicated to repeal of prohibition. Backed by Al Smith, Raskob poured his considerable personal wealth into the DNC, while pressuring the Democratic Party to come out for repeal. The Eighteenth Amendment had passed Congress with strong bipartisan support, but after 1928 the major parties polarized. "While the Republicans enlarged their commitment to prohibition enforcement, the Democratic party shifted increasingly toward advocacy of repeal." At the 1932 Democratic convention, the applause was deafening when 80 percent of the delegates voted for an absolute repeal plank over a weaker one. This shift in opinion had many sources, but the Depression weighed especially heavily on the Democratic electorate. "The promise of re-employment and of the conversion of the profits of the bootleggers into taxes paid to the government was a matter of deep concern in those grey days to millions of voters." Repealing prohibition seemed like one path to economic recovery the Democrats could do something about. In 1932, "wets won by a considerable margin" the referenda on prohibition held in eleven states. Thus when the Democrats won the Presidency and almost two-thirds of both houses of Congress, many observers credited the party's support for repeal as a major reason. The lame duck Congress did not wait; in February of 1933 it sent the Twenty-First Amendment to the states, specifying that it be ratified by conventions called for that purpose and not by state legislatures. This was completed on December 5, 1933.[61]

Much of the speculation about women's votes derived from prohibition. A 1922 straw poll by the *Literary Digest* showed women somewhat dryer than men. In 1923 the *Christian Science Monitor* said women held the balance of power "primarily because of the wet and dry issue."[62] In 1928, speculation became reality. Prohibition brought women to the registration offices, to the polls, and in particular to Herbert Hoover. Several nonpartisan women's organizations formed to oppose Smith or support Hoover because of prohibition, but the best organized and the most active was the WCTU. The organization had grown steadily, reaching 600,000 members in 1930 by becoming even more "zealous in the field of moral reform." It "waged campaigns against patent medicines containing alcohol, against the sale of cigarettes, and in opposition to obscene literature." As it became apparent that prohibition would once again be on the policy agenda, the WCTU prepared for the 1928 elections by holding eleven regional meetings in January and February to stimulate women's interest. There, it introduced lists of acceptable and unacceptable candidates for each party. Herbert Hoover headed the first list; Al Smith headed the second. After the nominating conventions, the WCTU set up a presidential campaign committee for the first time in its fifty years. It collected money, printed literature, distributed two million window posters, held rallies, sent out speakers, ran training schools to teach women how to vote, and generated publicity around three themes: "Smith was wet, Hoover was dry, and

Tammany was evil." When the votes were counted, the WCTU was among those who claimed victory.[63]

The belief that "the Nineteenth Amendment protects the Eighteenth Amendment" was soon shattered. In April of 1929, Pauline Morton Sabin, affluent socialite and Republican national committeewomen from New York, "resigned her party office to organize a woman's protest against Prohibition." This dramatic move by someone known primarily for her party loyalty and Republican fundraising ability was made at a luncheon given in her honor by the Women's National Republican Club. As a result of the publicity, Sabin later said, "letters began pouring in from women all over the country saying that they also protested against Prohibition. . . . There was a large group ready to be organized, wanting to be organized. And the road before me was so plainly indicated I could not turn back from it." Raised in a Republican family—her grandfather had been Senator and Governor of Nebraska and her father Secretary of the Navy in 1904–5—Sabin had risen quickly in New York Republican circles even though her husband was a wealthy Democrat. She helped to found the WNRC and was its president and chief fundraiser from 1922 to 1926. As national committeewoman from New York, she co-chaired Senator Wadsworth's unsuccessful 1926 reelection campaign, and joined his criticisms of prohibition with her own. Her husband, Charles H. Sabin, had long been active in the AAPA and had recently joined its executive committee. Thus her departure from Republican orthodoxy did not entail a break from her immediate family and political associates. Indeed, she used them to recruit socially prominent, upper-class women, Democrats and Republicans, to her cause.[64]

On May 28, 1929, twenty-four such women met in Chicago to form the Women's Organization for National Prohibition Reform (WONPR). Repeal, like prohibition, made allies of natural enemies. The strongest supporters of the Eighteenth Amendment had been Progressive Republicans and Southern Democrats. The repeal effort combined conservative Republicans, especially business leaders and social elites, with liberal Democrats, particularly organized labor and urban ethnics. But, until WONPR was born, it was assumed by all that women, at least organized women, were solidly behind prohibition. When he learned the news, ex-Senator Wadsworth, who had fought the Eighteenth Amendment as he had the Nineteenth, exclaimed: "By heavens, there is a chance of getting repeal if the women are going to join with us!" Former New York Democratic Governor Al Smith later wrote that "When women entered the fight for Repeal, sanity began to return to the country."[65]

WONPR grew rapidly, reaching 100,000 members within a year, 300,000 within two years, 600,000 by its third birthday, and 1.5 million by the time it disbanded in December of 1933. Active state organizations increased steadily, though New York always had the most members and the South had the least. "While the national leadership included a large contingent of upper-class

Republican women, state leadership positions . . . were filled by roughly equal numbers of Democratic and Republican women and by women representing a variety of class backgrounds." Surveys showed that most members were house-wives, followed by teachers and others in female professions. Self-supporting women of lesser means were the least likely to join. Growth was aided by the policy of not charging dues; voluntary contributions financed WONPR's work. WONPR could dip into AAPA's deep pockets; it needed a large membership to legitimate its claims. WONPR's primary activity was to generate publicity on the "paralyzing and demoralizing effects" of prohibition in order to make repeal respectable, but it also engaged in direct political work. Borrowing strat-egy from the Suffrage Movement and the LWV, it demanded that incumbents and candidates declare their views and publicized the results. WONPR also worked to defeat drys and elect wets to office, claiming several victories in state and Congressional races. Prohibition was the most contentious issue at the June 1932 national party conventions where WONPR lobbied vigorously for repeal planks in the platforms. The Democrats welcomed the United Repeal Council (URC) and voted for repeal. The Republicans waffled on the welcome; their plank was described as "moist." On July 3, 1932, WONPR endorsed the Democratic nominee, Franklin Delano Roosevelt, for President. It was the only one of the five URC organizations to do so, though some endorsed wets run-ning for Congress. Two weeks later *Time* magazine put Pauline Sabin on its cover.[66]

In August of 1934, the key men of the AAPA and the women of WONPR reconstituted themselves as the American Liberty League (ALL). They hired Jouett Shouse, who had served as chairman of the DNC executive committee under Raskob, to be their president. ALL was ostensibly bipartisan, an image maintained by the active presence of Democrats Shouse, Raskob, and Al Smith, but in fact it was the voice of conservative businessmen, who viewed FDR as a class traitor and vehemently opposed the New Deal as a cancerous growth of federal power. One sign of partisan realignment as the Fourth Party System gave way to the Fifth was that many progressive Republicans joined FDR's admin-istration, and, outside the South, conservative Democrats began supporting Republicans. ALL functioned as a conservative think-tank, employing researchers and writers to prepare pamphlets and speeches attacking Roosevelt and the New Deal. By 1936, ALL was part of the Republican team in all but name: one-third of the members of the RNC finance committee were on the ALL exec-utive committee, and even Al Smith spoke out for Alf Landon.[67]

Although Pauline Sabin was on ALL's six-member Administrative Com-mittee and several women served on the larger Executive Committee, ALL was basically a male organization. But, as the AAPA had done, ALL encouraged satel-lite organizations. Sabin formed a Women's Division in 1934, but it was aban-doned after a year when "it was clear that the league's business-based philosophy had little appeal to large numbers of American women." In July of 1936 the Independent Coalition of American Women was formed in Toledo, Ohio.

Dubbed by Molly Dewson the "ladies' auxiliary of the Liberty League," its work to elect the Landon/Knox ticket brought it "the blessing of the Republican party," and funds from the same deep pockets that funded ALL and the AAPA. Before it dissolved a few months later, it had recruited women in twenty-five states, and sponsored Al Smith's speeches attacking Roosevelt.[68]

PEACE AND PATRIOTISM

The Great War and the Russian Revolution reshaped the political environment in which feminists, reformers, and party women operated. In 1930, Jane Addams wrote that

> Social progress during the decade from 1919 to 1929 was conditioned at every turn by the fact that we were living in the midst of post-war psychology.... Any proposed change was suspect, even those efforts that had been considered praiseworthy before the war. To advance new ideas was to be radical, or even a bolshevik.... Throughout the decade this fear of change, this tendency to play safe, was registered most conspicuously in the fields of politics, but it spread over into other fields as well.[69]

The progressive impulse had been under attack before the war, but, for women's organizations, it was peace versus patriotism that caused the greatest damage. On this issue the antis scored one of their few major victories, undermining the legitimacy of women's reform agenda and pushing the more cautious women's organizations out of the progressive network. Their assault was launched by the paranoia of the "red scare" in 1919 and 1920, in which labor unions, progressive organizations, and individuals were accused of aiding Bolshevism. Fear, fed by race riots and labor actions, resulted in thousands of arrests without evidence or concern for civil liberties. The replacement of Wilson by Harding provided only temporary respite. "Although the fever of the Red Scare subsided, the virus lived in the bloodstream of the nation." The brunt of these attacks shifted to progressive women, their organizations, and the reform agenda. In 1921, even women's colleges were denounced by Vice President Calvin Coolidge as hotbeds of radicalism.[70]

Not surprisingly, war and revolution fueled the antis. Under the leadership of Alice Hay Wadsworth, NAOWS departed from its conservative critique of suffrage to employ rhetoric filled with vitriol, innuendo, and character assassination. In April of 1918, *Woman's Protest* became the *Woman Patriot*, and proclaimed itself the "Home Defense against Woman Suffrage, Feminism and Socialism." NAOWS condemned all "three branches of the same tree of Social Revolution." Even when reformers and feminists split, the antis treated them as one, denouncing as subversive all who worked for peace, protection, the Child Labor Amendment, and the Equal Rights Amendment. Sheppard-Towner and the Child Labor Amendment were maligned as part of the government's attempt to take control of the family. In 1922 NAOWS became the Woman Patriot Corporation, with its paper edited by Alice Wadsworth and financed by Senator Wadsworth. Despite the antis' professed abhorrence of women in politics, "throughout the 1920s, the *Woman Patriot* encouraged political participation by patriotic women in order to counter radical women and their polluting influence in women's politics and organizations." Its final issue was published when FDR was elected.[71]

Peace and disarmament were on reform women's agenda before the war. In 1915 Carrie Chapman Catt and Jane Addams were among the founders of the Woman's Peace Party. But when the United States declared war, Catt supported the war effort, believing that to do otherwise would undermine the Suffrage Movement. Addams continued to work for peace, subjecting herself to vilification and costing her the elevated place in public esteem she had previously held. In 1919 the Woman's Peace Party became the American section of the Women's International League for Peace and Freedom (WILPF). It did not join the Women's Joint Congressional Committee (WJCC), but many of its members were involved with WJCC organizations; progressive women shared their concern for peace and welfare legislation, including cutting military appropriations.[72]

During the war, the Military Intelligence Division had collected material on "feminism" and had undercover agents among women war workers. In 1922 it turned its attention to women's political activities. President Harding and Secretary of War John W. Weeks, who blamed suffragists for the loss of his Senate seat in 1918, wanted continued conscription and increased appropriations, but Congress, tired of war and influenced by progressive and pacifist groups, cut the military budget instead. The role of the WILPF in this brought it into direct conflict with the War Department, and in 1922 Secretary Weeks and several generals began publicly denouncing pacifist groups and dismissing women opponents of military preparedness as hysterics. In addition to the WILPF, they also attacked the PTA, the YWCA, the WCTU, and the Girls' Friendly Society (an Episcopal Church group), all members of the WJCC.

In May of 1923, Lucia R. Maxwell, the librarian of the Chemical Warfare Service of the War Department, published a chart based on the department's files. In the center column was a list of the "Women's Joint Congressional Committee Participating and Cooperating Organizations in [the] National Council for Prevention of War." On the sides were listed prominent individuals along with summaries of their radical views and other organizational memberships. Lines linking these people and organizations gave it the name of the "Spider Web Chart." At the top, in big black letters, was a claim that "THE SOCIALIST-PACIFIST MOVEMENT IN AMERICA IS AN ABSOLUTELY FUNDAMENTAL AND INTEGRAL PART OF INTERNATIONAL SOCIALISM (Lusk Report p. 11)." At the bottom the librarian had written a poem.

Miss Bolsheviki has come to town,
With a Russian cap and a German gown,
In women's clubs she's sure to be found,
For she's come to disarm AMERICA.

She sits in judgment on Capitol Hill,
And watches the appropriation bill
And without her O.K., it passes—NIL
For she's there to disarm AMERICA.

She uses the movie and lyceum too,
And later text-books to suit her view,
She prates propaganda from pulpit and pew,
For she's bound to disarm AMERICA.

The male of the specie has a different plan,
He uses the bomb and the fire brand,
and incites class hatred wherever he can
While she's busy disarming AMERICA.

His special stunt is arousing the mob.
To expropriate and hate and kill and rob,
While she's working on her political job,
AWAKE! AROUSE!! AMERICA!!![73]

This chart was circulated widely and eventually printed in the March 1924 *Dearborn Independent* with an article entitled "Are Women's Clubs 'Used' by Bolshevists?" under the generalship of avowed socialist Florence Kelley. R.M. Whitney's book, *Reds in America*, which specifically attacked women's clubs and the organized remnants of progressivism, was also published in 1924. Joan Jensen argues that this timing was not a coincidence; the Republican Party was worried that a third party challenge from Senator Robert A. LaFollette in 1924 might have the same disastrous consequences that Roosevelt's did in 1912. Since Jane Addams and progressive women's organizations were among his supporters, attacking organized women in general and Addams in particular was an indirect way of undermining LaFollette. However, the WJCC ignored these political implications and a month later informed Secretary Weeks that the Chemical Warfare Service's attack was contemptible. It threatened reprisals from twelve million women. Weeks admitted the chart had errors, insisted the librarian had not published it in her official capacity, and ordered all copies destroyed. Despite this retreat, the chart found an eager audience and continued to be used by opponents of social reform legislation. Accompanied by charges of "bolshevism," "socialized medicine," and "nationalization of children," the Spider Web

Chart was read into the Congressional Record in 1926 in the effort to defeat renewal the Sheppard-Towner Act.[74]

The War Department soon realized that women's patriotic organizations were the best vehicles through which to oppose pacifist sentiments. Among the more vitriolic generals was Amos A. Fries, chief of the Chemical Warfare Service, which had "become a sort of collecting agency" of information on radicals. His wife was a member of the Daughters of the American Revolution (DAR) and in 1925 became its publicity chairman. Organized in 1890 as a protest against the exclusion of women from the Sons of the American Revolution, the DAR had gradually added social service activities and progressive goals to its patriotic and historic ones. Susan B. Anthony, Jane Addams, and Alice Paul were members. During the war it shifted emphasis to support of the military and after the war endorsed "preparedness." It didn't drop all of its progressive programs until 1923; in 1921 the DAR even supported Sheppard-Towner. Relationships between the DAR and patriotic groups strengthened during the early twenties. DAR members were encouraged to read the *Woman Patriot*, chapter programs featured professional patriots and red-baiters, and activities expanded to include blacklisting and loyalty oaths for public employees, especially teachers. By 1927, the DAR was leading the attacks on progressive women's organizations and the entire reform agenda.[75]

Charges of subversion that were ignored when they came from the *Woman Patriot* and appeared politically motivated when coming directly from the War Department were listened to when propounded by such respectable organizations as the DAR. But even its image was tarnished when Carrie Chapman Catt charged it with slander and witch-hunting while others labeled it "the blue menace." While the DAR dismissed the counter charges and purged dissenters, when the decade ended, red-baiting still remained rampant. WONPR's official history recounts the following:[76]

> Mrs. Langley, the first field organizer in New York State, began her work in Oswego County in August, 1930, and was promptly notified by the acting chief of police of Oneonta that she must get out of the county at once, as he had had word from the chief (then attending a police chief's conference in Rochester) that a Red organizer had been sent into the county and that he knew she was "it." An exchange of telegrams with the New York headquarters finally cleared the matter, and she was allowed to proceed with her canvass.[77]

These public fights took their toll on all women's organizations, prompting withdrawals from the WJCC, dissolution of WLCs, and retreats from legislative activities. State officers of the PTA wrote that they could no longer work "for things unAmerican." NAWSA's heir, the LWV, was often attacked—the State Regent of the North Carolina DAR publicly stated that it was a tool of the communists. A decade after universal suffrage, organized womanhood was retreating from political engagement. Women were still forming organizations and still going to meetings, but with a few exceptions, most of their energy focused on improving individual welfare and studying issues, not on making public policy, and definitely not on electing candidates for public office. Women's organizations were going down different paths. Most had heard the message of political leaders that women should not organize politically outside of a political party.[78]

· Eight ·

Building a Base:
Women in Local Party Politics

$\mathcal{A}$s suffrage became a reality, the ranks of party women mushroomed. Women rushed into the realm of practical politics with enthusiasm, eager to learn and do everything. A New Jersey Republican summed up their attitude when she wrote in 1924: "Women are the natural housecleaners. Get into your party and clean house. You cannot learn the real condition of affairs by standing on the outside and trying to look in through the windows. They are too dirty." Within a few years women learned that party men were willing to let them work, but not at cleaning the political house. As Eleanor Roosevelt explained in an April 1928 *Redbook* article, "Beneath the veneer of courtesy and outward show of consideration universally accorded women, there is a widespread male hostility—age-old perhaps—against sharing with them any actual control."[1] By 1930 women had been absorbed and co-opted; the parties digested women with only a few burps.

When women opened the door of the political house, the edifice they entered was not empty. It was a labyrinthine complex of many rooms, built largely by men for their comfort and convenience, full of the furniture brought there by past and present occupants, permeated by smoke, reeking with the fumes of alcohol, and rather messy. On every level, national, state, and local, women had to operate within existing political arrangements, most of which were unfamiliar to them, and had to deal with men far more knowledgeable of these arrangements than they were and with little inclination to share that knowledge. Women learned that despite their formal admission to the official party bodies, the actual decisions were made at times and places of which they were not even told, let alone invited to. The most important rooms of the political house were closed to them, often hidden from sight, and their ability to rearrange the furniture in the rooms they could occupy was not great. Party women set about educating themselves and other women in party and public affairs. They soon learned that they could make a place for themselves in the political house, but mostly as servants to party men. While they made the beds, tended the plants, and served the coffee, they also created their own spaces, infiltrated many interior rooms, and took over the basement.

Although the strength and organization of the major political parties varied from state to state, party leadership everywhere had the same attitude: They wanted women as voters and workers but not as leaders or decision makers. The few exceptions were women who demonstrated their loyalty to party men, usually to one man who acted as their sponsor and protector. Beyond this, few generalizations can be made because politics differed from state to state, and within each state. Some states and cities had strong party organizations, others relied on "friends and neighbors" politics, or were dominated by traditional elites whose economic interests were sustained through political control. Still others had a populist tradition, or had been suffused by progressive ideals that preferred weak parties. The limited evidence available does not show that women more quickly entered politics in visible positions in one type than in another. But it does indicate that where a party was strong, party leaders chose the women to organize and educate other women, and the women they chose were ones without competing claims on their loyalties. Where parties were weak, party men accepted help from their national committees, or asked suffragists and reformers to organize women for their party, or let women organize on their own. After these women succeeded enough to make demands, they were squeezed out of the party.[2]

BRINGING WOMEN INTO THE PARTIES

Party men in the states where women were not already organized invited well-known women with organizational experience to be their women leaders. Some Republican state leaders sought out prominent suffragists such as Harriet Taylor Upton of Ohio, Louise Dodson of Iowa, Lillian Feickert of New Jersey, and Nina Otero-Warren of New Mexico.[3] Quite a few Republican state party leaders drafted leaders of women's clubs. In Minnesota the "men's political organization" appointed Mrs. Manley L. Fosseen as "Chairman of the Women's Republican organization in Minnesota" in November of 1919. She had been president of the Dome Club of St. Paul, a club for the wives of state legislators.[4] In Connecticut, however, where the Republican Party had opposed suffrage, "the Republicans appointed former leaders of the anti-suffrage movement to the state central committee with the responsibility for overseeing its voter education program."[5]

Locales with strong parties were less concerned with organizational experience than with loyalty. Party bosses recruited women like themselves—ethnically and politically—to head their women's organizations. In 1920, Frank Hague, Democratic boss of Jersey City, appointed the wife of one of his staunch supporters, Mrs. James (Rose Anne) Billington, to be New Jersey's national committeewoman. She had been a suffragist. But as the leader of Democratic women, Hague chose Mary Norton, president of the Queens Daughters Day Nursery Association. Despite her lack of political experience, in 1921 he made Norton the vice chairman of the New Jersey State Democratic Committee. She served Hague and his Democratic machine loyally for decades and was appropriately rewarded. Four years later Hague had her elected to Congress where she served until 1951. He also arranged for Norton to become the first woman to chair a state Democratic Party for a full term, in 1932–35, and again in 1940–44.[6]

Where parties were weak, women often organized themselves. In Maryland, a Democratic state whose Governor had opposed suffrage, six suffragists decided to organize Republican women in November 1920 after several months of canvassing the state for Harding. Despite only token help from party men some of whom "were leery of women in 'a man's sphere' and others who looked with suspicion upon those women who were ardent members of the Women's Christian Temperance Union" they convened the first meeting of the Maryland Federation of Republican Women's Clubs in June of 1921.[7] In Missouri, Emily Newell Blair and her feminist friends traveled throughout the county looking for Democratic women and persuading them to go to the county convention to vote for their women candidates. They were so successful that the men withdrew the names of the wives and daughters they had thought to put into the new women's positions.[8]

In some states party strength varied by area, with the Democrats typically strong in large cities, and the Republicans strong elsewhere. In New York the Democratic party paid little attention to would-be party women until the 1917 referendum gave all women the vote; then it moved quickly. In December the Democratic State Executive Committee doubled its membership by authorizing the state chair to appoint women members. Over the next few months many County Committees followed suit, led by Tammany Hall and the regular Democratic Organizations in the other boroughs of New York City. Since all were boss controlled, the women had no power, but neither did most of the men.[9]

Democratic women in upstate New York were organized by reformers and suffragists, partly financed by party women in New York City. Harriet May Mills of Syracuse, former president of the New York Woman Suffrage Party, became chairman of the women's division of the New York Democratic State Committee. She enlisted Nancy Cook, a teacher, Mrs. Daniel (Caroline) O'Day, widow of a Standard Oil executive, and Eleanor Roosevelt, a prominent political wife who had been encouraged to "serve as [her husband's] proxy in politics" after he was stricken with polio.[10] Joined by Marian Dickerman, these women spent six summers in the 1920s traveling throughout upstate New York to organize women into the Democratic Party. They were not always welcomed by the local Democratic committees. By 1928 ER "had become well aware of an inherent masculine hostility toward women in politics, for they certainly did not roll out any red carpets for her and Mrs. O'Day." Nonetheless, the work of the women often galvanized the men. When her husband was elected Governor in 1928, James Farley credited ER for the "more efficient upstate organization work ... in rural Republican districts where the Democratic candidates had never before had help."[11]

New York Republican women organized quickly. Within days of the 1917 referendum giving New York women full suffrage, Republican Governor Charles Whitman asked the party's county chairmen to appoint women as associate chairmen and as co-leaders from each Assembly District in their counties. The women leaders then appointed captains for each election district to personally contact the new women voters. Women's many years of political experience made it easy to identify suitable chairmen, leaders, and captains. In April 1918, four months after Helen Varick Boswell became woman's chairman for New York County, she reported that 50 to 90 percent of her districts were organized. The Bronx leader asked Mrs. Cornelia S. Robinson to be the woman chairman. A former president of the WEA, which Boswell had founded, and founder of the Bronx County Woman's Republican Club, she was well situated to complete the organization of women in the Bronx.[12] Several county committees amended their rules to provide for one woman as well as one man from each election district, though the courts later invalidated this change, until sanctioned by legislation. The first such bill passed in 1922, sponsored by an Assemblyman Russell Livermore, son of Henrietta Wells Livermore, herself the chairman of the Republican Women's State Executive Committee.[13]

When women got the vote, Chicago was a city in transition. Until 1931, both major parties had strong organizations, but they were often torn by competing factions, as well as by competition between themselves. Progressives were also a factor for a few years. Thus the major parties were quick to organize women. In 1916 a student researching Chicago politics found that "in the Republican party we find the Illinois Republican League, representing only the women voters of that party in Cook county." Delegates were appointed by the ward committeeman and reflected their factional allegiances. The Democratic women's organizations were called "Ward Branches." While most were auxiliaries to the men's organizations, an Illinois Woman's Democratic League had its own monthly newspaper. These groups were decimated by the war, which turned women's attention from politics to patriotism. Afterwards Republican women reorganized, while Democratic women languished. All were gone within a few years. In 1927, the Democratic national committeewoman wrote that the "story of Democratic organization of women in Illinois is not a cheerful one." She lamented the lack of support by Democratic men in this "overwhelmingly Republican State."[14]

POLITICAL CLUBS

The woman's party club was modeled on the woman's club, not on men's party clubs. The latter generally started as social clubs in the nineteenth-century saloon. Indeed Tammany Hall, the first grand Democratic organization, was "practically conceived in a tavern; and ever since the eating-house and the saloon have been its chief supports." Writing in 1909, a foreign observer said that saloons were the only permanent party clubs, but he didn't have women in mind.[15] Women had organized campaign clubs since the 1840s and these flourished in the 1880s, but when J. Ellen Foster encouraged Republican women to form permanent organizations, she knew that alcohol would not be the glue that held them together. Women had already organized themselves into numerous clubs, largely for study and self improvement. The study of issues and the education of women about politics would be the task of women's Republican clubs between campaigns.

Although Foster began work for the RNC in 1888, it was on December 13, 1894, that the "first auxiliary of the Woman's Republican Association was organized . . . in the West Side Republican Club rooms," of New York City. Known as the West End Auxiliary (WEA), its purpose was "to unite the women of this community in educational and social influence for the maintenance of the principles of the Republican Party in the home, in the state and in the nation." Reflecting Foster's experience in the WCTU, Article VI of its Constitution declared: "Let it always be clearly understood that this organization is for the study of simple republicanism, that it is contrary to its design to attempt any diversion of the organization's work or influence to such reform movements as temperance, woman suffrage &c, with which many republican women are individually associated."[16] Within a year there were at least a dozen women's Republican clubs in New York City and seventeen clubs elsewhere in the state; Kate Bostwick described them, as well as the one she organized in Brooklyn, in her 1896 article on "Women's Political Clubs." By 1901 there were enough clubs for the Women's Republican Association of New York State to hold regular meetings.[17]

Foster was a traveling catalyst. She aided and encouraged the formation of Republican women's clubs, but it was local women who did the work. In 1894 she went to the National League of Republican Clubs (NLRC) meeting in Denver, and soon thereafter "Women's Republican Leagues were established in many towns throughout the state and in every district in Denver." As Colorado was a focal point of the 1896 realignment, women's Republican clubs were divided, and many dissolved. In Kansas, "women's Republican Leagues have been organized all over the State." In 1895 the NLRC met in Cleveland and Foster presided at the organizing meeting of the Ohio Woman's Republican Association. By 1900 there were ongoing Republican women's clubs in several states, including New York, Illinois, Colorado, Kansas, Utah, Wyoming, Idaho, Ohio, and California, mostly in cities and towns. Colorado formed a statewide Women's Republican League that year, and soon had "the only permanent headquarters maintained by a political party." As Republican women organized, they debated whether to be independent or auxiliaries to men's clubs. Foster suggested that women should form separate clubs to study politics, but cooperate with men in campaigns; by and large that is what they did. Nonetheless the conflict between independence vs. cooperation (or subservience) would continue for many decades, with local politics and individual personalities usually being the determining factor.[18]

Lacking support from their National Committee, and seldom favored by their state committees, Democratic women took longer to form ongoing organizations. Since the social base of the Democratic Party outside the South was urban, ethnic, and working class, the saloon played a much greater role in party organization than in that of the Republican Party. Outside the four full suffrage states, there appear to be few Democratic women's clubs, other than temporary campaign clubs, prior to 1912. There were at least one, maybe two, Democratic women's clubs in New York City and a couple in Illinois that continued to work between campaigns, but most Democratic women did other things.

In the suffrage states it was largely on the coattails of Populism that women gained a voice in the Democratic Party. Democratic women were strongest in Colorado, founding the Colorado Women's Democratic Club on May 24, 1894. Although it was the first woman's club to be duly enrolled in the National Association of Democratic Clubs, it disintegrated in 1895 after a factional dispute. Populist women had organized clubs even before getting the ballot and achieved some representation on party committees. The 1896 fusion brought many into the Democratic Party. After the 1896 election, many clubs fell apart as the parties realigned, but by 1900 they were on the rise again. Helen Sumner reported that "the most important of the Democratic women's organizations in 1906 was the Jane Jefferson Club, which was founded about 1898. The Democratic women, apparently, do not pay as much attention to local precinct organizations as do the Republican, but concentrate all their efforts upon the one large club."[19] The Woman's Democratic Club of Utah was organized in 1895, the year before Utah became a state, as an auxiliary to the County Committee. It declared its independence in 1899 after proving its mettle during the 1896 campaign for Bryan and "Free Silver." Despite some lean years, in the mid-1960s it was thriving.[20]

While campaign clubs of women flourished at every election, ongoing clubs and statewide federations were harder to sustain in the states where women did not have full suffrage. In Cincinnati, Ohio, Republican women thought they "established the city's first official women's political organization" in 1920. And in 1927, when four hundred women formed the Ohio Council of Republican Women they thought they were the first state organization of

Republican women.[21] Similarly, it appears that the California women's Republican Clubs faded after 1900, then reappeared in 1914, when Democratic women organized numerous clubs and Republican women formed two competing state organizations. These did not last, and party women reformed their organizations again after 1920.[22] Only in the 1920s, when the RNC, the DNC, NAWSA, and its successor the LWV all encouraged women to join political parties, did club organization increase exponentially. Encouraged by the national parties, and sometimes by the state parties, women in many states turned their 1920 campaign organizations into permanent ones.

Not all clubs were begun by the regular party organizations; indeed competing clubs were sometimes created by local factions, or even by women who wished to remain independent of partisan in-fighting. In Chicago multiple factions were the norm. In 1916, Yount found that "both parties and every faction maintain women's clubs in every ward where they have men's organizations." Since the Democrats were better organized, that meant there was "a woman's club in practically every ward of the city," but only one of the three main Republican factions had the strength to cover every ward. In 1921, women who had once worked for the Progressive Party founded the Woman's Roosevelt Republican Club in Chicago so they could have a club "controlled and conducted by themselves and independent of the regular party organization." This club made a point of endorsing candidates in the Republican primary, and once, when there were none to its liking, endorsed the Democratic candidate for Illinois governor. Ruth Hanna McCormick was one of its founders, though this was only one of the clubs she organized in her state. She was a loyal Republican, but was at odds with all of the Chicago factions of her party and didn't trust any of them to support her husband when he ran for reelection to the Senate in 1924.[23]

This kind of independence was exactly what party men feared the most. They wanted women to work loyally for party nominees in the general election, but not to take sides in primaries. An April 1924 article on "Women's Party Clubs" in the *National Republican* said there was "great variety" in their organization, describing some of the patterns. Clubs were more common in cities, "while rural districts keep to the regular party organizations." And "in some states there is rivalry between what is called the women's division and the women's clubs." In some states, the state committee divided the territory up among the women vice chairmen; in others they sent out their own organizers. Independence from the state party was discouraged as leading to disharmony. Indeed clubs which "try to . . . map out a program of their own . . . may be a menace. It has happened, in some cases, that women have organized so effectively that they became a great power, . . . demanding this and that regardless of party decisions. . . . Some . . . have operated as a belligerent anti-man league, a female bloc, whose chief function was to grasp for the sex offices and power in the party and in the government." Women's clubs were urged to be "helpful" to the party; they were not to be a "machine."[24]

When Marion Martin surveyed the Republican woman's clubs in 1937 she found two types: "(1) those that had been established as auxiliary units to the local or state organizations and which were working in close harmony with the same, such as the Pennsylvania Council of Republican Women; and (2) those that had been established as a protest to the manner in which the Republican Party functioned in their state." The latter in particular were a problem. Forming the NFRW was a way to harness them all for the good of the Republican Party.

There were a couple of attempts to form a national organization of Democratic women, but none were successful. In 1912 the Women's National Democratic League (WNDL) organized in Washington, D.C., and incorporated in New York. Its officers and directors were almost all wives of Members of Congress; there is no record of its existence after 1918.[25] Early in 1920, several New York City women obtained a charter for Women Democrats of America, which they expected to become a national organization. Mrs. Bass, then speaking for the Women's Division of the DNC, objected, and it did not survive. Subsequently some states formed federations of Democratic women's clubs, or Democratic federations including women's clubs, but there was no systematic effort by the national party to organize Democratic women into clubs as there was for Republicans.[26]

Early in 1922, the Republican Woman's Club of St. Louis began publishing a magazine entitled *The Elephant*. Soon there was a *California Elephant*, a *Massachusetts Elephant*, and a *Pennsylvania Elephant*. Republican women in several other states began their own magazines; Pennsylvania and Illinois both called theirs *The Republican Woman* while New York's was *The Woman Republican*. By 1926, the RNC Women's Division identified eleven "official publications now being published by Republican women in the various states" and printed "news items" from active women in twenty-four states. In 1927 there were fifteen state and local publications, including ones in Illinois, New York, Kansas, New Jersey, Rhode Island, Maryland, and Ohio. While there was no truly national magazine, the WNRC's *Guidon* carried regular reports from the state vice chairmen on what Republican women were doing in their states.[27] These publications were not mere mimeographed newsletters, but slick magazines, supported by ads from Republican candidates and elected officials. They were full of articles about what state agencies did, statements by and about men and women candidates, exhortatory pieces to women to become more involved, and information on party activities and on legislation of interest to women. The latter included bills affecting women directly, such as 50–50, jury service, and protective labor laws, and bills affecting traditional "women's interests" such as schools, charities, and welfare. Most of these magazines survived only a few years; the last three ceased publication in 1941.

Democratic women relied on the national magazine published by the DNC Women's Division and the WNDC, into which they often put state inserts, but they had fewer state publications than did Republican women. In

1916 the Illinois Woman's Democratic League published a monthly *Woman's Democratic Press*. Between 1925 and 1935 the Women's Division of the New York State Democratic Party put out the *Women's Democratic News*; the United Democratic Women's Clubs of Maryland began *The Maryland Democrat* in 1925; and in the 1930s, the Democratic Woman's Club of Kentucky published *The Democratic Woman's Journal* four times a year.[28]

The number of women's political clubs rose and fell, often so rapidly that the Women's Divisions could not keep track of how many there were. A lot depended on the political environment, both nationally and locally. But for a given time and place, Republican women were much more likely to form political clubs than Democratic women and their clubs had a greater geographic spread. The New Jersey Women's Republican Clubs (NJWRC) claimed sixty thousand members in 1922. The New Jersey state Democratic Party had no equivalent organization, and indeed made little effort to recruit women at all, merely advising them to join the regular Democratic organization. In Maryland women of both parties quickly organized clubs, but Democratic women only did so in Baltimore.[29]

The different patterns are partially a reflection of the different social base of each party. Club women were mostly middle-class women, and the Republican party was the party of the middle class. While there were middle-class women in the Democratic Party, and wealthy women as well, they weren't as numerous and were more likely to be found in cities, especially Democratic cities with strong party organizations that disfavored women they could not control. As Republican women repeatedly pointed out, it was "not possible for all women of fine executive ability . . . to find an outlet for their energies through the official Party organization." Perhaps the party committees provided enough places for Democratic women, but Republican women wanted more opportunities for "Party service."[30]

However, the attitude of the national parties also played a role. Blair's reports and those in the DNC and WNDC publications demonstrate that the number of Democratic women's clubs ranged between 1,000 and 2,500 in the early 1920s, but declined after 1924. In 1930, Daisy Harriman could find only three hundred clubs.[31] The formation of women's party clubs continued to be important to Republican women, but after Blair left the DNC, Democrats didn't even count them, let alone encourage them. The *Democratic Digest* is full of stories on women's entrance onto party committees, women's work as reporters, and their participation in conferences, but clubs are barely mentioned, and then only as affiliates of the WNDC.[32]

In contrast, Republican women regularly reported, indeed bragged, about how many clubs they had. Upton wrote in 1924 that New Jersey had 100,000 Republican women in 308 "active local units," Illinois had 24,000 in 82 "chapters," the Pennsylvania Council of Republican women claimed "105 branches in 43 of 67 counties," Utah had 78 clubs with 2,000 members, Connecticut had

75 clubs with 14,000 members, Rhode Island "has 3,500 Republican club women," West Virginia had organized 15 clubs, Indiana had 50 clubs and Washington had 34 with 2,000 members. In addition there were uncounted Republican women's clubs in Alabama, Texas, California, Kansas, Arkansas, Mississippi, and New York.[33] The WNRC reported in 1927 that "There are Republican women's clubs in 18 states, and federations in three, [with] approximate membership of 150,000 women." Two years later Sallie Hert wrote that "our organized effort has [resulted in] clubs in twenty-eight states. . . . I am taking up with our chairman the club idea in a stronger way and he is heartily in accord with it." And in 1933 Mrs. Yost reported to the WNRC that there were "thirty state organizations of Republican women."[34]

The Democrats left club organization up to the women in each state. In 1955, the DNC's Katie Louchheim told *The Evening Star* that there were "several hundred, maybe thousands" of Democratic women's clubs, but she really didn't know. The last published report comparing the clubs of both parties was a 1958 article in *Good Housekeeping*. It said that NFRW "has about 4,000 clubs and about half a million members," while the Democratic Office of Women's Activities reports that "about 2,500 to 3,000 clubs have a total of 100,000 members, but explains that thousands of Democratic women are active in regular party groups not limited to women."[35]

Although women's political clubs flourished in the 1920s and 1930s, they were never systematically studied. When Roy Peel, a professor of political science at New York University, researched *The Political Clubs of New York City* between 1927 and 1932, he saw women's clubs only as auxiliaries to the 1,200 regular male clubs.

> Nearly every club has such an auxiliary, and nearly every male leader whom the writer has interviewed has expressed his wholesome disrespect for them. Publicly, male politicians are reconciled to woman suffrage. Privately, they consider all women politicians as unmitigated nuisances and all women voters as utterly unreasonable and stupid additions to the electorate.[36]

If Peel shared this attitude, perhaps that explains why he was completely oblivious to the existence of separate women's political clubs even though New York City newspapers frequently reported their meetings and work well into the 1940s, and the three magazines published by New York party women had regular reports on club activities. During these years the WNRC and several woman's Republican clubs in New York counted their members in the thousands, and certainly did not think they were auxiliary to the men. The Woman's Republican Club Mrs. Wentz founded in 1900 survived until 1941. The Republican Business Women's Club, founded in 1926, was soon copied throughout the state.[37]

Nor did Democratic women view themselves as mere subsidiaries, even though they were more likely to be in auxiliary clubs *as well as* completely independent women's clubs. The largest was the Woman's Democratic Club with a membership of over two thousand in 1928, whose activities and conflicts were regularly reported in the press. It was founded in 1905 by Mrs. John Sherwin (Nellie Fasset) Crosby, who observed the activity of Republican women but found no women working for the Democratic Party. The founding members were not associated with Tammany Hall, but after women got suffrage in 1917, Tammany women took it over, electing as its president the sister of a Tammany boss. In 1931 three Tammany women fought for the club presidency. In 1935 the club claimed 1,600 members, and officers from all five boroughs.[38]

This was not the only large club of Democratic women. The Democratic Union of Women of New York was founded in 1922 by women supporters of Al Smith, including future Labor Secretary Frances Perkins. Its president was the vice-chairman of the Tammany Executive Committee, and it thrived while Smith was Governor. In 1925 the Women's Democratic League of Kings County, Inc. formed to resist the invasion of Tammany clubs.[39]

Although New York Democratic women, like those in Colorado, tended to prefer a few big clubs to many little ones, there were quite a few neighborhood Democratic women's clubs that held regular functions. These clubs were more common in Brooklyn and Queens than in Manhattan, but they were not just auxiliaries to the men's clubs; they often organized independently and resisted subordination. In 1928 the Jackson Heights (Queens) Democratic Club split over this issue. "'The men in the old Democratic Club are a little old-fashioned,' Mrs. Williams said. . . . 'They wanted us to form an auxiliary but we didn't want to be subject to the men's organization. We have a strong separate vote and we need a strong separate organization.'" After the men's club denied the new Women's Democratic Club of Jackson Heights the use of its clubrooms they rented space for their meetings.[40]

While it is not clear how many of the New York City women's political clubs were independent and how many were auxiliaries to men's clubs, there does not appear to have been any movement for integration. Some clubs had men's divisions and women's divisions, which met on separate nights, sharing occasional social activities and campaign duties. Most clubs were strictly single sex. Since admission to regular clubs required sponsorship and approval from the district leader, there wasn't much chance that a member of one sex would stray into a club run by the other. Party men and party women lived in different worlds. In the male world, politics, liquor, and occasional "anti-social" activities were linked a way that was alien to the female world. The link was reinforced by prohibition, which "drove the saloons out of business and threw their habitues into the clubs. Scores of new clubs were established." Some had bars in their headquarters, or readily accessible through a door to the adjacent building.[41] Peel asked

> Why do men forgather in the club rooms of the party and jealously guard
> these quarters against the intrusion of females? Only on certain evenings,

sometimes only in certain rooms especially reserved for them, are women tolerated in about half of the political clubs of New York. They are admitted during the afternoons and evenings when programs are being rendered, or campaigns are in progress, but always under certain restrictions. The sociologist, Moskowski, was of the opinion that in primitive society the male club house originated "in certain strivings of the men to emancipate themselves from the tyranny of women." Apartment life in the city probably occasions the same sort of domestic tensions as were observed in primitive society, and on this assumption one might conclude that the male clubs are today havens for oppressed heads of families.[42]

Nor were the women anxious to join the men. In 1930 the Republican Business Women, Inc. of New York City surveyed its six hundred members "comprising lawyers, secretaries, nurses, teachers, saleswomen," etc. on the limited interest of women in politics. Half of those who replied went to political meetings, one quarter belonged to their local party organization, and 20 percent "rendered service."

> The replies are overwhelming testimony to the fact that women are conscientious about voting, but are far from satisfied with present political organizations. . . . [One woman said] "It still remains a club for men. Since I do not spit or play poker, there is little to interest."[43]

Despite prohibition, it would take many years to separate politics from male social rituals, in particular that of alcohol consumption. In the 1940s Katherine St. George was told she could not become chairman of the Orange County (N.Y.) Republican Party because she "won't be able to go into the saloons with the boys." As late as 1970 a Chicago alderman told two female political scientists that women were handicapped as members of the City Council because so much of its business was discussed in bars, often at night. In his mind politics and the saloon were both part of the male domain.[44]

Outside of Manhattan it was more common for party clubs to have both men and women members, but the women were still expected to serve and obey the men. When Shirley Chisholm joined the Seventeenth Assembly District Democratic Club in Brooklyn in the 1940s, she observed that the club was "exploiting the women," who were mostly "the wives of officeholders or other party faithful." Women ran the annual party and raffle which provided the club's funds that the men spent, but the men wouldn't even give them a budget to run it with.[45]

In 1972 Adler and Blank repeated Peel's study. Much had changed. By then there were only three hundred party clubs in New York City, affiliated with three parties. The Italians had replaced the Irish as the dominant ethnic group, and the Democrats were divided into "regular" and "reform" factions. The great women's clubs, which had thrived during the years Peel was doing his research, were gone, as were most of the men's. Only eight of 254 clubs which provided membership information were limited to men; seven were Democratic clubs and one was Conservative. Six clubs claimed female membership between 80 and 100 percent—five Republican and one Democratic—but only the Women's Republican Club of Staten Island kept "women" in its name. Among the rest, women averaged half the membership of Republican clubs but only a third of the Democrats. In the forty years since Peel surveyed the political landscape, women had changed the shape of both major parties, but the Republicans still had more women.[46]

Until the 1960s single-sex clubs were still common, especially in urban areas. Initially women's clubs met in the afternoon and men's clubs in the evening. But separation continued even when it was not dictated by different life styles. A 1958 report on the East Brunswick (New Jersey) Democratic Women's Club of one hundred members, said that "the township's Democratic men's club meets upstairs at the same time the women meet downstairs." Separate might not mean equal, but only in separate organizations, or units, could women hold leadership positions and not just be servants.[47]

Clubs were often ethnically homogenous as well as sex specific. Nationality and racial groups of women met separately as did those of men. Sumner wrote in 1909:

> In the fall of 1906 there was a Woman's Republican Club of Colorado and women's Republican clubs in every ward in Denver, as well as in many of the smaller towns. A Colored Woman's Republican Club ... gave occasional rallies, with both white and colored speakers of both sexes. There was also an Italian Women's Republican Club with about forty members, a Swedish-American club with about sixty members, and a German club.[48]

Indeed, the first Republican women's club in New York was the Colored Women's Republican Association, started in 1892 by Mary L. Hall. Hall had served for sixteen years as an assistant to the African American male leader in her district, but had a falling out with him. Encouraged by J. Ellen Foster, she set up her own organization of women and, with financial help from Republican women, became "a power" in her district. In an 1895 parade her voters club carried a banner reading "As she wishes, So we vote."[49] Statewide organization lagged until July of 1938 when Jane Todd, who had recently become vice chairman of the Republican State Committee and head of its Women's Division, set up a Colored Women's Division, led by Maria C. Lawton of Brooklyn. During the fall campaign, each borough in New York City had its own vice chairman. Afterwards the CWD worked to recapture the loyalty of black women for the Republican Party by fostering clubs and activities, holding its first State Conference of Republican Colored Women in Westchester County on October 18, 1939.[50]

In Denver, Elizabeth Ensley and Ida DePriest founded the Colored Women's Republican Club in 1894. In Chicago, black women started several political organizations after getting partial suffrage, including the Colored Women's Party of Cook County. The Alpha Suffrage Club became a major power in the Republican Party of the Second Ward by 1915, though it appears to have subsequently vanished.[51] By 1920 there were Colored (or Negro) Women's Republican Clubs in Texas, Rhode Island, California, Ohio, and Maryland.[52] Soon there were more. Suffragist Florence Randolph, president of the New Jersey Federation of Colored Women's Clubs, began to organize Republican women's clubs in 1920. In 1922, Laura Thomas held the first meeting of the Central Republican Women's Club No. 1 of East St. Louis, Illinois, in a storefront. Daisy Lampkin chaired a women's Republican club in Pittsburgh before becoming vice chairman of the Colored Voter's Division of the 1928 Presidential campaign.[53] In 1939 there were at least seventy-one clubs of black Republican women throughout the country.[54]

After the National League of Republican Colored Women was founded in 1924, many state leagues formed. Among the most active was that of Illinois, which already had many local clubs when Irene Goins brought them together into the Colored Women's Republican Clubs of Illinois. After Goins's death in 1929, Irene McCoy Gaines, a social worker and wife of a state legislator, became president. She soon became a well-known Chicago politician in her own right. Most league clubs were affiliated with their local Republican organizations and reflected the factions of their districts; at least one was independent. The league was powerful enough to regularly elect a woman to the Republican State Central Committee from the heavily black south side of Chicago. Gaines held that position in 1928 and Cornelia J. Pickett was elected in 1939.[55]

Although ethnically distinct organizations were normal in the Democratic Party, it was rare for this to be proclaimed in their names. Party clubs did not need to publicize their ethnicity; it was simply common knowledge which were Italian, Jewish, or Irish. Insofar as women's clubs were auxiliaries to men's, they would be attached to those of the same ethnicity rather than designated an "Irish women's club." One exception was black women, for which there was limited Democratic interest until FDR became President. A Colored Democratic Woman's Club was organized in Denver in 1902, but such clubs were rare until the 1930s, when women such as Crystal Bird Fauset organized the Philadelphia Democratic Women's League.[56] Unlike Republican women, black female Democrats did not create their own national organization. There were some state groups, such as the Ohio State Council of Negro Democratic Women, "sparked by Jean Capers, member of the Cleveland City Council" in 1948.[57] There may have been many black women's Democratic clubs, but they were not disclosed by descriptions such as that for the State Federation of Democratic Clubs of Delaware, which said in 1954 that it "will include all Democratic clubs in Delaware—women's clubs, men's clubs, clubs with men and women, Young Democratic clubs, and negro clubs."[58]

KEEPING WOMEN IN THEIR PLACE

After a few years the party men who had appointed suffragists to be their woman leaders realized that they had made a mistake. The best party women were not those who had learned their craft in service to a great cause, whether suffrage or reform. Such women were just not party loyalists. Party men replaced them with their own women, frequently wives of party men or major contributors, whom they could control. The Republican Party of New Jersey concluded that Lillian Feickert was too independent because she demanded that the party support certain legislation, insisted on planks in the party platform, and refused to submit to party discipline. In 1924 she and other suffragists were targeted for removal from the party state committee. Despite her defeat, she continued as president of the NJWRC. However her successor as vice chairman of the state committee organized women into "official" Republican women's clubs. By 1925 women's planks had disappeared from the state party platform. The last suffragist was removed from the state committee in 1928. And in 1929, the official Women's State Republican Club of New Jersey was created; the NJWRC disbanded in 1930. Loyal party women had eclipsed suffragists in the New Jersey Republican Party.[59]

Republican women in New York had a similar experience. Party men had been quite horrified by suffragists when Mary Garrett Hay spoke against the reelection of Senator Wadsworth in 1920. They much preferred party women like Helen Varick Boswell and Sarah Schuyler Butler who never questioned the qualifications of *any* Republican. Being a suffragist practically become a disqualification for high party office, even after years of party work. On September 6, 1929, the Republican State Committee met to pick a successor to Pauline Sabin who had resigned as national committeewoman to organize WONPR. Henrietta Wells Livermore, founder of the WNRC, had "strong backing among the women."[60] But newly elected Congresswoman Ruth B. Pratt was chosen, even though she had not sought the office. She had worked in the trenches of the Republican Party for ten years, without a background in suffrage or reform. Livermore's friends later wrote:

> Mrs. Livermore was one of the foremost leaders of the woman suffrage movement in New York. After the suffrage amendment was passed she sacrificed herself to organize women within her party, rather than to take leadership in the League of Women Voters, which did nothing to strengthen the party. We can guess why she came to loggerheads with the gentleman in her own county, petty self-interest and factional bickering are not in Mrs. Livermore's box of tricks, she is deeply patriotic and considers her country's interests of paramount importance.[61]

Even grassroots clubs were dependent on the approval of party men for success and survival. The few histories of women's clubs within the parties are replete with stories of how they were decimated when the state chairman appointed a woman to organize party women after a dispute with the existing women leaders. For example:

> The Woman's Republican League of Colorado, perhaps the largest and most powerful political organization of women that has ever existed in the state, was formed in 1900. . . . [I]n one week it announced nine different meetings to be held under its auspices. This organization held its power until the fall of 1902, when it went to pieces as the result of trouble with the new state chairman, who superseded the president of the league by appointing a woman vice-chairman of the State Central Committee, to whom he gave charge of the work among women.[62]

In Maryland, of which Upton had written, "There is no use in our trying to deceive ourselves—men in the machine in the state do not want women butting in,"[63] the Maryland Federation of Republican Women's Clubs was told by male party leaders "that we could come to (their) meetings if we did not make a debatable motion." The women were determined not to be an auxiliary existing merely to help the men, "A carpet for the men to walk on." But when several women leaders ran for the Maryland House of Delegates in 1921, the men ignored them and all the Republican women lost. They also lost their first party battle in 1923. While the women debated who among them should become the woman associate member of the National Committee, the men selected the wife of a rich and influential Republican Party man. Generally the early organizers of the Maryland Republican Women's Clubs felt the men did not consult them and "did not want them."[64]

Congresswoman Mary Norton of New Jersey was the kind of woman that party men wanted. She believed that women should gain

> their political education through involvement in the day-to-day political work, however menial. This work was to be done in existing political clubs or in women's auxiliaries closely allied with the regular party organization. Women were Democrats first, Democratic women second. Initially, men were to be the teachers, women the pupils. Women need not initiate legislation. Party programs and politics were to be accepted. Norton was confident that, as women's political experience grew, the party leadership would give them increased responsibilities—political jobs and political office.[65]

POLITICAL MACHINES

During the first half of the twentieth century there were at least a dozen states with party organizations strong enough to be called machines by political analysts.[66] Although political parties were hierarchically organized, with the State Central Committee being the highest official body, machines were generally organized at the county level and the party county leader was the machine boss.

Sometimes there would be bosses at other levels, such as the Assembly District, or Ward, even the city, but it was usually as head of a county committee that a boss ruled. The oldest and most famous machine, Tammany Hall, dominated only the Democrats in New York County, one of five boroughs that made up Greater New York City after consolidation in 1898. Even Chicago's boss ran the party as chairman of the Cook County Democratic Committee. There were some state party bosses in the nineteenth century, such as Hanna of Ohio and Platt of New York. But only a few state machines survived well into the twentieth century.

At the bottom of the hierarchy were the precinct captains or sometimes the captain's assistants. Precincts—called Divisions in Philadelphia and Election Districts in New York—are voting districts of several hundred voters. Precinct captains generally resided in their voting districts, were of the same ethnicity as their voters but a slightly higher economic status. They helped them with their problems with government and their personal needs. On election day they brought their voters to the polls.[67] A typical precinct captain viewed his job as helping the people of his district 364 days of the year; on one day they helped him. A machine politician was a professional politician. Machines could only flourish where there was enough patronage to compensate the captains, largely with low-level government jobs that left them with plenty of time to serve their districts. Some captains worked for the love of politics or the sense of power it gave them to rub elbows with public and party officials, but most expected some reward—jobs, clients or contracts.

In some of these machines individual women made their mark. Many worked with their husbands, to whom the material reward usually went. In none were women as a group recognized as a political force. Few studies of party machines have even mentioned women, let alone described their experiences. The one exception is Sonya Forthal's monograph on Chicago in 1927. In addition, Gosnell's book on Chicago described the activities of one woman in the Democratic Party machine and Salter's book on Philadelphia profiled a Republican woman. Machines were commonly grounded in immigrant, working-class populations, which tended to vote Democratic, but some were Republican. Chicago did not become a Democratic city until the election of Anton J. Cermak as mayor in 1931. Philadelphia was solidly Republican from the Civil War through the 1940s.

Sometime between 1928 and 1936 Gosnell interviewed one very successful woman precinct captain whom he called, "Mrs. Smith, an official co-captain of a precinct in the Fifteenth Ward and a veteran of many political battles."[68]

> This neat, elderly, garrulous woman was responsible for the women's votes only, and left the rest of the work to the male captain. For many years she had been an active feminist. In fact, she took part in the agitation for woman suffrage in Illinois before 1913. When partial suffrage was granted after that

date, she helped to organize the women and get them out to vote. In those early days, when a woman pleaded she could not vote because she was washing or had to look after the baby, Mrs. Smith would help finish the washing or mind the baby. In that way the women became accustomed to vote, and now they do it as a matter of course.

A separate women's organization was set up because Mrs. Smith found that a woman could do a lot more to get other women to vote than a man could. Some men even did not like to have the male precinct captain talking to their wives. The women organized card parties and dances. One dance was held at a downtown hotel at which the attendance reached seven hundred. The men always contributed to the expenses of such functions. Mrs. Smith was soon interested in political work for its own sake. She enjoyed getting out and talking to people and thought that many more women would like it if only they once tried it. Women were somewhat limited in what they know about such things because they spent so much time at home and heard of developments only through their men folks. At the card parties the women started to gossip about politics among themselves and thus acquired a desire to have something to say about how things are run. Once women got used to taking an active part, there was no difficulty whatsoever in keeping them interested in seeking ways to be of service.[69]

Mrs. Smith was older and more experienced than the typical women Forthal interviewed. The latter were found in middle-class and poor areas, not the richer ones, but otherwise "showed no significant differences in characteristics and activities from the men." Half were between forty and fifty in age, and the rest were younger. One third were housewives, one third clerical workers, one fifth held government jobs, and "the remainder held miscellaneous jobs. Their motive was generally economic; in only two instances were the women imbued with idealistic motives."[70]

During the 1930s the Democratic machine banished the Republicans from any hope of ever gaining political office in Chicago. Based on a coalition of ethnic voting blocs, it was run by the Irish who shared major offices with Poles and Jews and minor ones with African Americans and Italians. The last of the big bosses was Richard J. Daley, mayor from 1955 until his death in 1976. Even though women did not constitute a political bloc, a few were always slated for public office. Porter and Matasar described the typical "Daley woman" as unquestionably loyal, ethnic, from a long-trusted political family or a reliable political sponsor, and preferably able to finance her own campaign. Such women need not rise through the political ranks, since they might have office but would never have influence. Instead there was a "woman's route" through involvement in church and community affairs in order to demonstrate a concern for people. Good women in the Daley organization were servants of the people, not power brokers, and were expected to specialize on issues suitable to women. However, the organization did welcome women as precinct workers; by 1970 some 3,500 were organized into the Cook County Democratic Women's Club. Placed at their head was the one woman ever to become a ward committeeman.[71]

In Salter's 1932 study of Philadelphia he identified seven women among the 2566 Republican division leaders and profiled one of them, Rosie Popovits:

> Several months later I asked Rosie if she, as a ward politician, were confronted with any special disadvantages because of her sex. She said that there were certain difficulties on this score. Three lesser and rival politicians in the division tried to start a whispering campaign against her. The nub of the argument was "I am a married woman, having two children, and my place was at home, and not at the polls."
>
> John Tollagrata, the leader of a small anti-Vare faction in the division, sent word to Mr. Griffiths that, if the ward leader would replace Rosie with a man, then Tollagrata would return to the fold and bring his friends along. The leader told Mr. Tollagrata to go to hell and he told Rosie that so long as she kept up the good work he was 100 percent behind her. She added with a smile, "You see, that this so-called 'feminine charm' does not mean a thing in politics, and jealousy is the chief obstacle in a woman's path to success."[72]

Even the Old Regular (Democratic) Machine of New Orleans found a place for a few loyal women. The Pilsbury sisters were prominent among them. Mary Ellen Pilsbury served as its "lady leader" for almost forty years. She began in 1922 when she substituted for her husband as a poll commissioner, and was eventually promoted to president of the Third Ward Women's Regular Democratic Organization. She was employed in patronage jobs controlled by the city machine. Her sister Edna was more active in women's clubs than in local politics but did sit on the Democratic State Committee. In 1930 they helped the machine control dissident women by taking over the New Orleans chapter of the League of Women Voters, using the usual tactic of packing the membership right before elections were held. Their success drove out the better educated, affluent women commonly found in LWV chapters, and left it tainted even after the national withdrew recognition in 1936. Both sisters were president of the city Federation of Women's Clubs.[73]

Unlike Chicago or Philadelphia, New York City was dominated by Democratic Party machines throughout all five party systems, though it was greatly weakened in 1933 when Republican Congressman Fiorello LaGuardia was elected as a fusion mayor. None of the books on machine politics in New York City said much about women despite numerous press reports on their activities. Peel merely commented that "for every assembly district leader and election district captain there is a woman lieutenant" and women were "also given some representation on committees and at conventions" but he neither counted nor interviewed any of these women.[74] News stories on the Woman's Democratic Club after 1920 usually identified the club president as a Tammany woman, with a job in city government or married to a judge or other elected official. The Women's Democratic Union was created to mobilize female support for Al Smith during the 1920s. Women were active in the New York City Democratic machines, and to judge by the press reports, got a share of the low level patronage jobs in city government and the courts.

The press did a better job than Peel of finding women. In 1919, the *New York Times* wrote an article on the "Women Sachems in Tammany's Wigwam," and in 1924 it interviewed "The Three Women of Tammany" who sat on the Committee of Seven District Leaders which advised Tammany boss Charles Murphy. Miss Elizabeth M. Barry was asked by Murphy himself to organize women in her district and given a patronage job in the courts when she proved adept at her political duties. Mrs. Ernestine Stewart was asked by her district leader to be a co-leader after she proved herself as a captain.

> She commands a small army of forty-six election captains, who know every inch of the ground in her territory. "My women can enter apartment buildings to interview voters where a man could not get by the elevator boys and the superintendents."

The third, Barbara Porges, was born into politics and known as the "boss" of her district by the early 1900s. Believing that "women make better politicians than men," she made her husband an alderman and continued dispensing favors and collecting votes until she died in 1936. She never asked anything for herself, nor did she attempt to specially organize women. When suffrage was on the ballot in 1915, she urged men to vote against it because the women "in our district aren't ready for the vote."[75]

The top Tammany woman was Elisabeth Marbury. The daughter of a Tammany chieftain, she was already well known in New York City as a play-broker and author's representative when she became the first national committeewoman from New York, a post she held until her death in 1933. Marbury had not taken a position on suffrage and had no interest in feminism or reform. Although herself unmarried, she thought a woman's highest calling was to be a wife and mother. Her first political venture was in Al Smith's 1918 gubernatorial race. While she faulted women for their lack of political impact, she observed that "the majority of men consider our entrance into politics as either a nuisance or a joke." Marbury could be counted on to support Tammany's every decision and to entertain district leaders or visiting dignitaries on request. She was accorded the minor honors that normally came with such loyalty.[76]

Women like these were exceptions. Most precinct captains, leaders, and bosses were men. Gosnell estimated that women were 5.1 percent of the Chicago precinct captains in 1928 and 11 percent in 1936, though they were as much as 25 percent in the "colored wards." He did not count those women who ran a precinct with their husbands, or in their husbands' name.[77] No one

else counted the women, individually or in clubs, so there is no way of knowing if women did better in one area, or party, or machine, than in another. Blair
felt that "generally speaking, the boss-controlled machines have been more hospitable to women than those led by more idealistic politicians." But Boswell
observed that male captains were still given twice the money to get out their
vote that women got.[78] Beyond this there is little evidence that strong party
machines had different attitudes toward women than weak party organizations.
Some women were chosen for positions by bosses, some achieved recognition
through their work, a few were elected to office, and many more got patronage jobs. More important to the male bosses than sex was loyalty. If women had
to be given a place, then so be it, as long as they were loyal women.

Although women did work in and for political machines, they also organized against machines. This was particularly true of elite women, for whom
machines represented everything that was bad about politics. The municipal
reform movements of the 1890s and early 1900s saw the formation of separate
women's organizations through which women worked to elect candidates as
good-government reformers alongside of the men's organizations. The Women's
Municipal League of New York, founded in 1894 by Josephine Shaw Lowell,
was one of these. So was the Women's Campaign Committee founded in 1908
in San Francisco. Sometimes party women organized against the machines in
their states. When progressive Gifford Pinchot ran in the Republican primary
for governor of Pennsylvania in 1922, the vice chairman of the Republican
State Committee "led the vice chairmen of most of the county committees,
who are women, against the machine candidate." This was rare. More commonly, nonpartisan political clubs, such as the Women's Citizens Committee
formed in 1949 in Gary, Indiana, provided a way for women to be involved in
politics who did not want to be party women, or who lived in times and locales
where parties did not offer suitable opportunities for female participation.[79]

In the 1930s, 1940s, and 1950s, elite women in New Orleans worked
through a succession of organizations to defeat politicians they thought were
corrupt. The political machine created by Huey Long, elected governor of
Louisiana in 1928, and his successors, effectively bifurcated state politics into
Longs and anti-Longs for several decades. In 1933 Hilda Phelps Hammond
formed the Women's Committee for Louisiana to protest the election of a Long
machine Senator with stuffed ballot boxes. Active until Long was assassinated
in 1935, the committee provided a basic education in practical politics for New
Orleans women "of brains and standing." One of these was Martha Robinson,
who turned the Women's Division of the Honest Election League into the
independent Woman Citizens' Union (WCU) in June of 1934. As women, the
WCU lobbied for clean election laws, registered voters, removed false names
from the registration lists, and monitored the polls on election day. Because the
WCU did not support candidates, the Independent Women's Organization
(IWO) was formed in 1939 to endorse an anti-Long for governor. He won the

primary held early in 1940 and the IWO became a major player in state politics. It could field a corps of campaign workers valuable to any candidate committed to good government and, as a result, was listened to on both policy and appointments. In 1946 it helped elect a reformer as mayor of New Orleans. While it could elect and influence good men, when the IWO ran Martha Robinson for City Council in 1954, it foundered. The reform mayor saw a strong independent woman on the Council as a threat to his power, and the voters saw her as a threat to traditional ideas about women. In the 1960s, the IWO declined in effectiveness. Women going into the labor force deprived it of volunteer workers, and conflicts over race eclipsed good government issues. As the Fifth Party System slipped into the Sixth, many of the oldest and most active IWO members joined the Republican Party.[80]

SEX SOLIDARITY AND SEX PREJUDICE

During the 1920s whether or not women would vote as a bloc was argued as ideology more than as fact. By 1920 sufficient women had voted long enough for political analysts to know that they voted pretty much like everyone else in their immediate communities; region, race, and religion shaped women's political opinions just as they did men's. Although most women did share some life experiences, eventually becoming wives and mothers, this had limited effect on their candidate preferences, despite a persistent belief that there were "women's issues" that would bring them to the polls. Other issues, partisanship, and factionalism also took their toll. Wrote the *National Republican* in 1924:

> Already we have forgotten "women's rights;" even passed beyond the thought of the "privilege" it is; and are now at the stage of reminding ourselves that it is a responsibility. . . .
>   There is no such thing today as "woman solidarity" in the United States. Having attained the right to vote, we have left that behind. Women of one section, class or group want the same things as the men of their section, class or group, rather than clinging with their sex on a feminine program. Some of the leading questions affecting only women have brought out wide differences of opinion among the women themselves, as the question of a blanket amendment wiping out all the special legislation regarding women.[81]

Despite the ambiguity of the evidence and the lack of polls, many women candidates believed that women were crucial to their election, as workers if not as voters. In 1918 Mary M. Lilly was chosen by Tammany Hall to run for the State Assembly in one of the few Republican districts in New York City. She thanked women for her 174 vote plurality.[82] Judge Florence Allen credited her election to the Ohio Supreme Court in 1922 and 1928 in a nonpartisan race to the work by committees of women she had organized while working for suffrage. However, she lost the 1926 primary election for the Democratic Senatorial nomination because of opposition by the party organization.[83] When Representative Margaret Chase Smith (R. Maine) ran for the Senate in 1948 she faced primary opposition from three Republican candidates and the GOP establishment. She was elected in a Democratic year. "Women came out to vote in unprecedented numbers. The city clerk of Portland reported that more women had voted than ever before in the city's history."[84] Ivy Baker Priest reported that she was asked to run for Congress in 1950 by prominent Republican men because the female incumbent, Reva Beck Bosone, had "mobilized the women to win the election by an overwhelming majority, and during two years in Congress, had kept them pretty well behind her."[85] Clare Boothe Luce's biographer wrote that when she ran for Congress from Connecticut in 1942, "there was a stalwart core of Republicans who were appalled at the idea of a woman candidate." However,

> Clare's own reason of why she won the campaign is the women. "It is simply not true," she says, "that women prefer to vote for a man. Women will vote for a woman rather than a man provided they are convinced that she is competent. I went out to organize women—working women. For instance, I gave a big dinner for working girls in Bridgeport, told them my qualifications, and asked them to vote for me. In the end I cut down the big Democratic lead there by exactly the number of women I had thought could be changed."[86]

In spite of scattered signs of sex solidarity, division among women was more common than unity. Even for feminists, some female candidates presented problems. Texas women were particularly challenged by the candidacy of Miriam "Ma" Ferguson for Governor in 1924. Not only was she a stand-in for her husband, who had been impeached for corruption, but both had ardently fought woman suffrage; Jim had led the opposition to it at the 1916 Democratic convention. However, her opponent in the runoff for the Democratic nomination (which would determine the winner in this one-party state) was the candidate of the Ku Klux Klan. Faced with such a choice, women's organizations and leaders splintered.[87]

In 1928, three "Ruths" were elected to Congress: Ruth Hanna McCormick, (R. Ill.), Ruth Bryan Owen (D. Fla.), and Ruth Baker Pratt (R. N.Y.). All were opposed by at least one organized women's group, in this or subsequent years. In 1928 the NWP opposed McCormick in her race for Congressman-at-Large and in 1930 it even endorsed two men—Socialist journalist Heywood Broun, husband of NWP activist Ruth Hale, and Democrat Louis Brodsky—running against incumbent Pratt. Both women had openly criticized the NWP. Both won without concern for the NWP's opposition.[88]

Of these three, McCormick was the only one who had actively organized women into politics. As chairman of RWNEC in 1918, regional director of the

RNC Women's Division from 1920 to 1924, and Republican national committeewoman from Illinois from 1924 to 1928, she had created a network of Republican women's clubs, especially in rural Illinois. This gave her something of a female political machine, albeit one without patronage. In her victory speech she said, "There is no doubt that it was the women who gave me my chance in the primary." But factional loyalties trumped sex. In 1930 she ran for the U.S. Senate, defeating Senator Charles S. Deneen in the primary. He was a regular Republican leader who had defeated her husband for that same office in 1924. When McCormick brought Mary Church Terrell to Illinois to campaign for her among African Americans, she was attacked by Ida B. Wells-Barnett for importing an outsider. Not mentioned in these attacks was the fact that Wells-Barnett was part of the Deneen faction. Both she and her husband had once obtained jobs from Senator Deneen—she as a parole officer and he as an assistant states attorney. Wells-Barnett's loyalty was not reciprocated; she ran for the state senate that year but Deneen supported a black man. As Republican women soon discovered, factional loyalties also trumped party. After defeat in the primary, the Deneen Republicans did not practice the party loyalty they had long preached to the women. They attacked Ruth McCormick, whose supporters condemned "the selfishness and lack of loyalty of the men."[89]

McCormick was also opposed by WONPR, even though she and its founder, New Yorker Pauline Sabin, had served together as members of the Republican National Committee. After McCormick won the Republican primary, WONPR, according to its official history,

> launched a campaign to induce the [Illinois] Republicans to adopt a wet plank in their platform, which had always been dry . . . [but] the Republican leaders [were] unconvinced.
> . . . the WONPR decided to throw all its influence in favor of the Democratic candidate. It was the first case in which the WONPR, though composed of both Republicans and Democrats, gave its endorsement to the candidate of one of the parties because of his stand for Repeal. Moreover, ironically enough, it committed a woman's organization to an active battle against a woman candidate—a stand which cost her the support even of many of her personal friends.[90]

When McCormick lost the Senate race, WONPR claimed credit, though more should be given to the Depression; 1930 was not a Republican year. The Democrats reclaimed the House (though not the Senate) for the first time in twelve years. However, unlike the NWP, WONPR's political work had more than rhetoric at its disposal. As *Time* magazine pointed out, "the group is happily supplied with rich husbands." In 1932 it helped defeat two Democratic women and elect former Senator James W. Wadsworth, Jr. to the House from upstate New York, even though it was a Democratic year. As the daughter of William Jennings Bryan, Representative Ruth Bryan Owen was a determined dry. She was also very popular among her constituents and in 1930 was reelected without opposition. In 1932, WONPR persuaded a wet man to oppose her in the Democratic primary. With repeal as the main issue, Owen lost by two-to-one. In Ohio, WONPR campaigned against Judge Florence Allen, a dry Democratic nominee for Congress, who was opposed by a wet Republican.[91]

The limited evidence shows a vast gulf in sex solidarity between women campaign workers and women voters. The kind of people, particularly women, who campaigned for candidates were usually more educated, economically better off, and more attuned to issues than the typical voter. Particularly in the 1920s, there was a large cadre of women who had been trained in political work by the Suffrage Movement, who could readily transfer their loyalties and skills to women candidates. But the mass of women voters had the same attitudes as the mass of men voters. In the political world, as in the rest of society, there were men's jobs and women's jobs. Executive positions and seats in the upper house belonged to men. Ruth McCormick hit this barrier when she ran for the Senate, plus the problems of prohibition, Depression, and fickle factionalists. In the 1920s, even such progressives as Senator Hiram Johnson (R. Calif.) didn't think women should be Senators. As for the Illinois voters, Ruth's supporters believed "that many women in the last election did not vote for Mrs. McCormick just because she was a woman."[92]

McCormick was not the only woman who ran for the Senate in the 1920s, but she was probably better prepared than any other to overcome these prejudices. As the daughter of Senator Mark Hanna and the wife of Senator Medill McCormick, she had spent her life in politics. She was a well-known fixture in Illinois, had organized women throughout the 1920s, and had her own money to spend (for which she was investigated by the Senate Campaign Fund Investigating Committee) and family in important places. But she couldn't break through the social barriers about what was the right job for a woman. After World War II some prejudices about what women could do began to decline. In 1948, when Representative Margaret Chase Smith of Maine ran for the Senate, her opponents declared that the Senate was no place for a woman. But "the women of Maine got mad" and elevated her.[93] Nonetheless, not until the 1980s could a woman run for the Senate without her sex being raised as an objection.

In the forty years after suffrage, the sex solidarity that had been built by women's clubs for the previous thirty years and saw its greatest achievement in the final drive for the Nineteenth Amendment, slowly degenerated. It didn't disappear. Individuals and some organized women, particularly the Women's Divisions, the NWP, and the BPW, continued to urge women to run for office, lobbied for more appointments for women, and helped in campaigns. Women in some states worked together to interest women in politics. But "political sisterhood" did attenuate and was dishonored while sex prejudice remained strong and sex barriers moved only a little. Journalists, authors, and politicians readily admitted that politics was "really a man's world." The only question debated was whether women could become "a real political force" or whether they even wanted to.[94]

ILLUSION AND DISILLUSION

By the end of the 1920s many women were disillusioned with the major political parties. While some were disappointed that they got work but no "plums," the most unhappy were those who had cut their political teeth in reform or suffrage movements but heeded the call to join a political party rather than remain nonpartisan or work through women's organizations. They had believed that women could make a difference, and mostly found that they were used. Winifred Starr Dobyns, a progressive Chicago Republican, resigned after several years as the woman state vice chairman, quoting the famous limerick about "The Lady and the Tiger." In a January 1927 article with that title, she explained that she now knew that "the aim of the political organizations is not good government, patriotic service, [or] public welfare. . . . [M]achines are . . . highly efficient business organizations" operating in the self interest of their leaders. Women were welcomed because "once in the organization, we could be controlled. Our nuisance value was gone." She concluded that "the political machine is the greatest menace to democracy that exists today," and that it could not be reformed from within.[95]

She was answered a few months later by Emily Newell Blair, who was still the vice chairman of the DNC. She wrote that women needed to fight longer and harder, or not fight at all. Power could only be won through fear. If women wanted recognition, they must organize a following, and try, try again. In December of 1927 New York Republican leader Henrietta Wells Livermore told Republican women: *Don't Resign—Fight!* "Until politicians treat women fairly and do not discriminate against them because they are women, women must go into politics with the backing of women. . . . [They] . . . must learn solidarity in order to overcome these special temporary handicaps." In April of 1928, Eleanor Roosevelt, experienced party woman and prominent political wife, combined cynicism and hope. Summarizing the complaints of women from both parties who worked hard but were ignored when important decisions were made, she confirmed that "Politically, as a sex, women are generally 'frozen out' from any intrinsic share of influence in their parties." She acknowledged that an occasional woman was elected to public office, but for the most part, party men were recognized and taken care of, while women "are generally expected to find in their labor its own reward." Her solution was for women to organize as women, select competent women as "bosses," and follow their lead as they bargained and dickered in "the hard game of politics with men." But, she cautioned, women should do this within the parties and should not organize a "Woman's Party."[96]

Women expressed their dissatisfaction more explicitly in private. In January of 1931, prominent Republican women from twelve Eastern and Midwestern states gathered in New York for the first meeting of the National Council of the Women's National Republican Club. Virtually all complained of being ignored and unappreciated by party men. But they didn't know what to do. Mrs. Parker of New Hampshire asked "if we could force ourselves into the confidence of the men," or should wait "until they finally do recognize [our] contribution." Mrs. Frank Kellogg of Minnesota said they should ask the men to cooperate more. Henrietta Wells Livermore replied that "That was the attitude we took ten years ago," but it didn't work. "[M]any men acquire reputation and power by exercising their nuisance value. That is distasteful to women." The representatives from three states—Pennsylvania, Ohio, and New Jersey—were more optimistic, largely because of thorough organization and a sympathetic state chairman.[97]

By 1931 the director of the DNC Women's Division, Nellie Tayloe Ross, publicly admitted that men only regarded women as political auxiliaries. Even Blair was "Discouraged About Women in Politics." Politics was still a "male monopoly." Indeed women's participation had declined since 1920. In particular, the "higher type" of woman who worked for other women had been replaced by the women "who do what they are told . . . to do, and who are without achievement or previous leadership of women." The women who succeeded in politics were those who ignored other women and depended on men for their advancement. Such women "have no use for feminism . . . women's measures or movements." Blair called for "women candidates who will campaign frankly on the issue of women's right to participate equally with men in politics." Her call came too late. The women's movement had long since peaked, feminism was under assault from all sides, and female consciousness was disappearing.[98]

For the next three decades party women, and some party men, chided the parties for their failure to recognize women's work and to provide opportunities for office and advancement. In 1937, Dewson admitted that "women [still] do not have a fair share of the patronage . . . a fair chance to run for congress . . . nor for the state legislature." In a 1939 speech Monroe (N.Y.) County Republican Vice Chairman Judy Weis told her organization that "men seem to have a deep seated distrust of us in politics. They hate to see their cozy club invaded." In 1945 the president of the NFWRC told the RNC that Republican women "have had too little opportunity to prove their worth," and Marion Martin emphasized that "there are in many instances at the present time a seething and a boiling on the part of the women because they feel they have been given the doorbell ringing jobs to do, but are never given a voice." India Edwards later observed that the professional world acknowledged women more than the political world. "The kind of treatment I and the other women received at the *Trib* did not prepare me for the way in which women were discriminated against in politics."[99]

Their pleas must have fallen on deaf ears. "Within the orbit of the political party," Lou Harris wrote in 1954, "women were still definitely second-class citizens." Perhaps those who seethed dropped out, while those who stayed were those who found party work to be its own reward. Barbara Kerr observed in 1956 that "Politicians will cheerfully continue to exploit women's genius for dreary detail. Over 8,000,000 dedicated ladies will toil in this year's campaigns for long hours, no wages and no visible rewards. But let a woman talk strategy or policy, issues, patronage or money, and men's faces freeze; they are repelled by any such presumption of political equality." Studies of state and local party officials repeatedly showed that women worked harder and longer than equivalent men, even though they had lower offices, lesser influence, and fewer opportunities to advance. Cotter and Hennessy found in 1963 that within state parties, only .7 percent of Democratic national committeewomen were ranked among the top six party leaders of their state, 7.5 percent among the top twelve, and 21.8 percent among the top twenty-five. Republican women comprised 8.1 percent, 18.2 percent, and 24.2 percent of these categories. And many women who held party office still shared the experience of Jane Richardson, member of a Maryland Republican County Committee in the 1950s "who soon found that she was not always notified of its meetings, and when she did attend, she was 'a voice without a vote.'"[100]

FEMALE INFILTRATION

During World War II "much of the hard, gruelling work of Party organization fell upon women." After the war, women kept their stake in the "bottom rung of the political ladder" as election clerks and inspectors, poll watchers, and vote pullers. By the 1950s women had taken over most of the grunt work of canvassing, telephoning, and mailing. One reason for this was that they were good at it. Party leaders constantly commented on women's superior "people" skills. Another was that they were cheap. As Jim Farley found in the 1930s, women worked for "the cause" more than for jobs. By the postwar period the continual assault on patronage and party prerogatives begun by Progressives had significantly reduced the available jobs for party service and consequently the number of available men. Postwar prosperity made it easy for men to get jobs without party help. Women, on the other hand, were told to go home and give up their paid jobs to men. For ten to twenty years, until women regained their place in the labor force, many more women than men were available for volunteer work of all types.[101]

Among younger women, decades of exhortation to participate in the political process saw fruit; as party work lost its image as a male domain, it became less of a male domain. Women in the 1950s, like the educated, middle-class woman of the 1890s, found party work to be a pleasant way to spend their discretionary time. It was mildly challenging, provided social contact, and since it was unpaid with flexible hours, did not conflict with family obligations or incur the social disapproval that came with paid employment. Housewives flowed into the vacuum created by the departure of men. By the 1950s they were doing most of the campaign work and were often the only workers sustaining the parties between campaigns. This was just as true of black women as of white, even though the former were more likely to be in the paid labor force. Clare Williams said three million Republican women were active in the 1958 campaign. Six million women volunteers was the estimate for the 1960 Presidential campaign. By 1962 even Attorney General Robert Kennedy, who admitted he had no great love for women, agreed "that men do ninety percent of the talking in the campaign and women do ninety percent of the work." In 1971, RNC Chairman Robert Dole told the RNC that "women do 90 percent of the work, they should get 50 percent of the delegates."[102]

Unlike earlier decades, the new party women were just as likely to be Democrats as Republicans. After losing the Presidency in 1952, a reform movement swept the Democratic Party. Adlai Stevenson's wry humor, elegant speeches, and image of intelligence and integrity reinvigorated the Democratic Party. During his campaign thousands of political clubs were founded throughout the country. The Stevenson campaign and the subsequent reform movement brought into Democratic Party politics a new breed, the amateur Democrat, who was educated, middle-class, professionally employed (and/or married to a professional), and motivated by ideals more than patronage. These "ardent amateurs" set up their own organizations to combat the regulars for control of the Democratic Party. In New York City, reform clubs admitted both men and women members, but elsewhere separate clubs were often founded. Elizabeth Snyder, southern chairman of the California Democratic Women's Division from 1952 to 1954, said in 1977 that the Stevenson campaign was "when we formed many of the women's clubs that are still in existence today."[103]

Not all reformers were young amateurs. In Texas, redoubtable Minnie Fisher Cunningham organized the Texas Democratic Women's State Committee in the 1950s and helped found the liberal "Democrats for Texas."[104] Eleanor Roosevelt encouraged the New York City Democratic reform movement and personally campaigned to defeat the New York County Democratic boss, Carmine DeSapio, in 1961.[105]

In New York City women flocked to join reform clubs. Wilson observed in his 1960 study that "Women play an active and vocal role (at least three club presidents are young ladies)." By 1972, women were 45 percent of Democratic reform club members. The kind of women who became reform Democrats in the 1950s were like those who had worked for municipal reform and for the Populist Party in the 1890s and became progressive Republicans in the 1910s— educated, articulate, and idealistic. They worked with men, but did not always follow them. Wilson noted that: "on several occasions, the male and female leaders from reform clubs have taken conflicting positions . . . in meetings of the county executive committee." This was unheard of in the regular Democratic organization where the woman co-leader was often chosen by and always subordinate to the male district leader. For some women, the reform clubs were launching pads for political careers. Carol Greitzer and Shirley Chisholm were among those who joined or switched to reform clubs; the former was elected to the NYC City Council in 1969, and the latter to the New York State Assembly in 1964 and to Congress in 1968.[106]

In California, the reform movement helped women recapture the political toehold they had lost in the 1930s and 1940s. By 1950 the Democratic Party was in a state of disarray; Republicans held most offices even though 60 percent of the voters registered Democratic. In order to make pre-primary endorsements of generally liberal candidates, the clubs that had formed to elect Stevenson in 1952 joined into the California Democratic Council (CDC) in 1953. Aided by National Committeewoman Clara Shirpser's efforts to organize women's clubs, CDC brought many women into local politics who then moved into key positions in local campaigns, or ran for office themselves. In 1951, the state BPW Federation decided to promote one BPW woman in each party for election to the California Assembly from newly reapportioned districts. By concentrating their efforts, raising money, and flooding the districts with members to ring doorbells, BPW elected Democrat Dorothy M. Donohoe the following year, bringing to three the number of women in the eighty-member assembly. In 1953 Rosalind Wyman became the second woman elected to the Los Angeles City Council at the tender age of twenty-two, and kept her post until 1965. By 1961, Elizabeth Rudel Smith, recently appointed Treasurer of the United States, said of her home state, "I can recall only one headquarters in northern California in the last campaign which was NOT directed by a woman."[107]

Throughout the 1960s the lower ranks of the Democratic Party expanded with women and men who were inspired by the social movements of that era, particularly civil rights and anti-war. There were still plenty of traditional party women who put electoral success above all else, but they were facing competition from a new strand of reformers who brought concern with issues over candidates into their party activities. This new generation aggressively pushed into the middle ranks of party activists—becoming delegates to conventions and serving on State Committees. In the 1970s these "amateurs" would reform the Democratic Party. The Republican Party was not consumed by a reform movement that decade, but it did attract young idealists, many of whom joined the NFRW. They weren't part of the Sixties social movements; often they opposed them. But among the Republican idealists were many who were sympathetic to feminist causes, even though the very term "feminist" was then in disrepute. Some of the most outspoken supporters of the ERA and the legalization of abortion in the 1970s and 1980s began their political careers as "Goldwater Girls."[108]

· Nine ·

Doing Their Bit:
Women in National Party Politics

$\mathcal{W}$omen's expectations were high when they went to the 1920 national nominating conventions. They felt the parties had thrown open the doors to the political house even though the Nineteenth Amendment had not yet been ratified and there was a distinct possibility that the thirty-sixth state would not be found in time for the 1920 elections. They soon learned that the door was only open a little. For the next five decades women struggled to find a place for themselves in national politics as well as in the local parties, even though opportunities to do so presented themselves only every four years. Women were usually more visible at the national conventions than in the Presidential campaigns because the Women's Divisions continually lobbied their respective national committees to put more women on the program. The states selected the delegates, but the national party allocated space and time for activities. In general, delegate selection followed the same pattern as suffrage: the Western states included more women, and the Southern states had fewer.

Women's role in the campaigns was idiosyncratic. Through the 1950s most campaigns had one woman in charge of organizing women, but the influence of that woman, or the presence of others, varied considerably. Presidential campaigns, even as they became large and quasi-bureaucratic, reflected the personal relationships and proclivities of the men on the ticket, and those candidates who had women in their entourage or had learned to appreciate their value locally, gave them important roles in their campaigns above and beyond organizing women voters. Women's opportunities were somewhat affected by the social mores of the times but it was individual attitudes that mattered most. These attitudes changed with time and circumstances. World War II syphoned off men, leaving women to fill the vacuum for volunteers. Once accepted, women stayed, taking over the bulk of grassroots campaign work for Presidential campaigns as well as local campaigns. As the Fifth Party System shifted into the Sixth, the nature of Presidential campaigns also underwent transformation. Professionals took over more and more tasks, replacing volunteer time with services bought by money raised by other professionals.

THE NATIONAL CONVENTIONS

The number of women delegates and alternates jumped dramatically in 1920 and again in 1924. It dropped in 1928, just as women were beginning to feel accepted "more as a matter of course than they were at the first." While women were still noticeable at both conventions, a new consensus was solidifying on their place in the political house: women would get a share of the available positions, but nowhere near 50–50. From 1932 to 1960 women were roughly 12 percent of Democratic delegates, except in 1936 when Molly Dewson's personal efforts brought them to 15 percent. They increased to 14 percent in 1964 and declined to 13 percent in 1968. The Republican pattern was a gradual but erratic increase from 6 percent of the delegates in 1928 to 11 percent in 1952; it fluctuated between 15 and 18 percent from 1956 through 1968. Democratic conventions had more delegates than the Republicans, so even when their percentages were lower, the Democrats could claim to have more women. Both parties lumped delegates and alternates together when issuing press releases, conveniently ignoring the fact that the latter couldn't vote. Since women have constituted between 20 and 29 percent of the alternates, this contributed to political puffery. The Democrats have also blown up their numbers by the use of divided votes, without mentioning that women were more likely to share a vote than were men. The Republicans did not divide votes, so women's totals were a better reflection of their actual voting strength.[1]

Equal representation at the conventions has been a constant goal of party women. At its January 15, 1924, meeting Blair persuaded the DNC to ask each state to send eight rather than four delegates-at-large to the national convention, each with a half vote, and that four of these be women. As a result, the number of women delegates more than doubled even though some states did not send four women. This was repeated in 1928 and 1932 with varied results. On January 9, 1932, the DNC once again resolved "to give adequate representation to women without disturbing prevailing party custom" at the urging of the national committeewomen, who had met the day before. The RNC enlarged the total number of delegates to the 1924 convention to create places for women, but in 1928 men retook these seats and reduced the number of women. Although Republican women urged that state delegations have equal numbers of men and women they didn't do so as publicly as Democratic women. Some states tried harder than others. Both Florida parties had equal division. Montana, Minnesota, Michigan, California, Texas, and the Canal Zone often sent a well above average proportion of women to the conventions as delegates.[2]

At most conventions the women's division organized a special program for women, depending on the funds and available space. If there was competition for the nomination or other controversial issues, publicity for and about women was buried. Given that it's hard to judge programs that aren't publicized, the high point for Democratic women was probably in 1936 and for Republican women in 1956—the years FDR and Ike were renominated. Dewson used the 1936 convention to organize women and to publicize their achievements. All four days of convention week began with a breakfast rally for women from a different region featuring a speaker on a New Deal program and Dewson on the upcoming campaign. The Reporter Plan had focused women's attention on issues, so their convention activity centered on getting into the platform planks of special interest to women written by a Women's Advisory Committee that was appointed by Dewson. Women's participation on convention committees also peaked that year, until 50–50 brought their numbers closer to men's. Of over fifty seconding speeches for FDR, eight were by women.[3]

The 1936 Republican convention did not have a woman's program. Instead, WD director Mrs. Hoyal told the press that women should participate as delegates rather than as women. Several prominent Republican women lobbied for positions on convention committees and a few for platform planks, but other than that, "concerted feminine activity during the day was conspicuous by its absence."[4]

For the 1956 conventions, the women's divisions of both parties dueled with "Ladies' Days," but the Republicans trumped the Democrats in the battle for favorable publicity. Being in power enabled the GOP to vaunt the women in the Eisenhower administration, fifteen of whom spoke to the convention. Several gave a "briefing brunch" for six hundred Republican women attending the convention. The RNC also touted the top convention jobs held by women for the first time. By 1956, both conventions commonly scheduled a string of female speakers, vying for number and prominence. However, with few exceptions the women appeared at afternoon sessions when the audience was thin. That year the Democrats put seven Congresswomen on stage, introduced by Katie Louchheim. Eleanor Roosevelt, a sure-fire favorite, spoke at another hour. When Louchheim went to the podium, reporters turned to interview the few delegates in the hall, while others read and chatted among themselves; no one paid attention to the women speakers. "Din But No Crowd Greet the Ladies," wrote the *New York Times* the next day, while the *Herald Tribune* observed "Women Have Day, Only 10% of Delegates Show Up, and They Talk or Read Papers."[5]

In 1960, Washington reporter Isabelle Shelton, who covered women in politics, wrote that

> both parties are firmly eschewing the long lackluster parade of women speakers which in the past has constituted their chief bow to the gentler sex. The ladies have not been at their best in these clusters, to put it mildly. Television ratings showed this to be the low point of viewing.[6]

Instead of decorating the main event, programs for women became sideshows. At the 1960, 1964, and 1968 conventions, the women's divisions sponsored press conferences, receptions, delegate lounges, and even some light entertainment. In 1960, the Republicans publicized the large number of important jobs women would hold at their convention, but the program for women was a fashion show in which political wives paraded in gowns modeled after those of Republican First Ladies. More and more women came to the conventions as delegates, party officials, and even office holders, but as a group women faded into the background.[7]

Although each party's Presidential candidate generally picks his running mate, in the Democratic Party at least, token nominations for Vice President are often made by states who wish their favorite sons to be recognized at the conventions. It was also used to honor favorite daughters. Mrs. Leroy Springs (S.C.) received thirty-eight votes at the 1924 Democratic Convention and Nellie Tayloe Ross (Wyo.) got thirty-one votes for Vice President in 1928.[8]

Occasionally organized interests used this to honor one of their own. The first effort to honor specific women in this way was instigated by BPW in 1952. Begun by the New York Executive Committee largely as a means of honoring BPW's outgoing national president, Judge Sarah Hughes, the campaign quickly broadened to include token nominations of women at both party conventions. Senator Margaret Chase Smith (R. Maine) was the obvious choice for the Republican Party, and former Congresswoman Clare Booth Luce (R. Conn.) agreed to make the nomination. Word of this reached Democratic Party activists long before BPW's formal endorsement at its July 1952 convention, and they were not thrilled that such an honor should go to someone who was not a party activist. Julia Crews of New York began her own campaign to secure the nomination of DNC Women's Division head India Edwards. "We had nothing against Sarah Hughes," she explained later, "except that she was not well enough known among our women leaders in the party."[9]

The idea received little support until Crews persuaded Congresswoman Mary Norton (D. N.J.) that the time had come to nominate a woman. A joint letter was sent to all the national committeewomen. Once they realized that BPW had its own campaign and its own candidate for Vice President they united behind one of their own. However, Edwards did not want any conflict over what was an honorary gesture, so both women were nominated at the Democratic convention, with short speeches and great acclaim. The campaign for Senator Smith was buried by the Republican fight between supporters of Robert Taft and Dwight D. Eisenhower. In the Republican Party token nominations are often imbued with a political significance that they don't have in the Democratic Party. After rumors floated on what *were* the women doing, Smith asked that her name be withdrawn and Luce made a speech from the convention floor that the women had abandoned the nomination in the interest of party harmony.[10]

Smith's turn came in 1964, only five years after Jim Farley declared that "We'll Never Have A Woman President." On January 27, 1964, she stood before the Women's National Press Club and announced that she was running for the top job. Of the five reasons she gave for her decision, number two was "to break the barrier against women being seriously considered for the presidency of the United States." When Margaret Chase Smith became the first woman to seriously campaign for a major party nomination she had already broken several barriers. Although she followed her husband into the House of Representative after his death in 1940, she was elected to the Senate on her own in 1948 and reelected three times, making her the first woman to be elected to the Senate for a seat not created by the death of her husband. While building a respectable record in the House, she achieved national prominence on June 1, 1950, when she issued her Declaration of Conscience against Senator Joe McCarthy (R. Wis.) and the witchhunt he was leading under the guise of anti-Communism. By 1964, her credentials for the Republican Party nomination were as good as those of any male politician. Although Senator Barry Goldwater (R. Ariz.) sewed up the nomination early, Smith received twenty-seven delegate votes at the Republican Convention.[11]

THE CONVENTION COMMITTEES

There are four convention committees: Credentials, Platform (or Resolutions), Rules, and Permanent Organization. How important a committee is varies with the politics of each convention. With a few exceptions, at least one woman was on each committee at each party convention from 1924 on. The committee that regularly had the fewest was Resolutions, and that was the one women wanted most. Shortly after the 1924 Democratic convention, where women felt cut out of the platform-writing process, the DNC voted that at the next convention there should be a man and a woman from each state on the Resolutions Committee. However, nothing happened in 1928, and only one woman was on the 1932 Platform Committee. In 1936 Molly Dewson had women named as alternates to the Platform Committee so they could vote when their male delegate was not present. Finally, the 1940 convention endorsed a unanimous DNC recommendation made the previous February to double the size of the Platform Committee by adding a woman from each state, and in 1944 there were forty-two women on the Democratic Platform Committee. This did not mean that women's influence was equal to men's. The platform, usually proposed by the candidate-to-be, first went through the ministrations of a much smaller drafting committee, which never had as many women as men.[12]

In the Republican Party, Maine National Committeewoman Marion Martin led a similar movement. At her urging, the RNC adopted a resolution in December 1936 favoring equal representation on committees, but it was not enforced in 1940. A resolution recommending that the Resolutions Committee have a male and female delegate from each state was passed by the RNC on June 21, 1944, and confirmed at subsequent conventions. Most states named a woman to the committee, though several couldn't comply because they had no women in their delegations; only thirty women served on the Resolutions Committee in 1944. The composition of the convention committees was not in the permanent rules; each convention passed a new resolution, though a perfunctory one. Beginning in 1944 Republican Conventions voted that each state could place one man and one woman on the Resolutions Committee. In 1959 the DNC voted for equal representation on all committees at the 1960 convention, and the Republican Convention that year adopted Rule 14(a) to mandate equal representation beginning in 1964.[13]

Equal representation did not actually mean that women would be half of the voting delegates on the committees; it meant that each state had the right to send one female and one male delegate to each committee. States that had no women delegates, or did not appoint one, simply lost a vote, and there were several states in every convention that chose that option. For some conventions the Democratic rules allowed delegations to select two members of the same sex for each committee "for which one of each sex was not available." As late as the 1968 convention, twenty-two Republican and thirteen Democratic delegations did not have the four women necessary for full representation on the four convention committees.[14]

WOMEN'S WORK IN PRESIDENTIAL CAMPAIGNS

As states ratified the Nineteenth Amendment, excitement built among party women for the 1920 elections. In January, Elizabeth Bass announced the formation of an executive committee to organize Democratic women. In May, Mabel Gilmore Reinecke, executive secretary of the Republican Women's National Executive Committee, claimed that "the Republicans will have 50,000 women speakers in the field this year." However, when Harriet Taylor Upton took over organizing women for Harding after the June Republican convention, she found that "few states had women's political organizations of any great strength."[15] This time Bass ran her campaign from New York, and Upton from Chicago.

The Harding campaign appointed Mary Church Terrell as director of Work among Colored Women in the East. One of the most prominent women of her day, Terrell was president of the Women's Republican League of Washington when she was called to the campaign headquarters in New York. The black vote was small but growing. During the war, close to 450,000 African Americans had migrated north to fill jobs opened up by the draft. Still less than 3 percent of the population in Chicago and New York, they remained faithful to the "party of Lincoln." In some places, black women registered at higher rates than white women.[16] Terrell worked in the Colored Division, writing letters and making speeches; race trumped sex in the Republican Party's division of labor. This was not a problem in the Democratic Party because both voters and staff were virtually all white.

Both parties urged the states to ratify the Suffrage Amendment, and both competed for women's votes. Even if the amendment had not been ratified in time, women could vote for President in twenty-nine states with 306 electoral votes. The Republicans bragged that when the Democrats controlled Congress, the Suffrage Amendment failed to get the necessary two-thirds vote, but when the Republican Party regained control its very first act was passage of the Nineteenth Amendment. It proudly declared that twenty-nine of the first thirty-six states to ratify it had Republican legislatures.[17] The *Democratic Text Book* mentioned suffrage three times and gloated over the greater number of women at their convention and their addition to the DNC as full members. It claimed that the Democratic Platform supported all but one of the proposals in the "Woman's Platform," while the Republican Platform only endorsed half.[18] Harding's managers had decided on a "front porch" campaign; he would stay home and give speeches to select delegations of visitors. Upton insisted on one day for women. Eventually called "Social Justice Day," delegations of women came on October 1 to hear Harding give lukewarm support for a variety of welfare measures. The Republican Party issued pamphlets on "The Woman, the Child and the Republican Party."[19]

Despite Upton's late start, the Republican Party devoted more campaign resources to women. Bass later wrote about the Democrats:

> [I]t was a rather sad campaign. . . . our coffers were empty and little money in sight. The Woman's Bureau organization, however, did a good piece of work and had many speakers in the field. We started the campaign in New York in July and collected most of our own campaign fund. . . . Then we gave all the money we had left, some eight or ten thousand dollars, to the head-quarters as a gift. Election night came . . . and the Woman's Bureau turned its face to the wall and died.[20]

Harding and Coolidge trounced Cox and Roosevelt, getting 60 percent of the vote compared to their 34 percent, but the election was a great disappointment to everyone else. Despite the excitement over suffrage, women did not flock to the polls and men didn't either. Less than half of those eligible to vote did so; roughly one third were women. Women had been voting for many years in the Western states and two or three years in several other Northern states, yet the combined turnout rate in these was no higher than in Northern states where women voted for the first time.[21] There was much debate as to *how* women voted. In a pre-election poll, Ohio women favored Harding two to one, which was viewed as stronger Republican sentiment than that of men. But only Illinois separated men's and women's ballots. In every county but two, 3 percent more Illinois women than men voted for Harding.[22] A statewide election in Maine in September prompted many to observe that women had overwhelmingly voted Republican because the Democratic vote remained the same as in previous years while the Republican vote soared. However, a new law required city voters, mostly Democrats, to register, but not rural voters, mostly Republicans. And the Democrats had done little to organize women.[23] As Southern whites had predicted, black women tried to vote throughout the South. As black leaders had predicted, Southern whites stopped them. Southern white women did what their men had long predicted and mostly stayed home.[24]

Many men also stayed home on election day. The drop in voting stimulated a vigorous debate about who didn't vote and why. The RNC commissioned a study by Washington lawyer Simon Michelet on the "stay-at-home" voter. The Republicans expected a third party challenge in 1924 which would "make heavy inroads into normal Republican states of the Northwest and industrial centers of the East." The RNC wanted to compensate by bringing to the polls Republicans who did not normally vote, such as women.[25] In 1923, University of Chicago political scientists Charles Merriam and Harold Gosnell asked 5,310 Chicago citizens why they did not vote in the mayoralty election of April 3, 1923. Of the 1.4 million people who could have voted in that election, only 900,000 had registered and 723,000 went to the polls. Three-fourths of the unregistered adults and two-thirds of the nonvoters were women.[26]

Women gave different reasons from men, but "newness" was not their primary reason for not voting. Instead, 11.4 percent of the women did not believe women should vote—politics was men's business—and another 1.5 percent didn't vote because their husbands objected. Twice as many women as men gave general indifference (30.4 and 14.6 percent), ignorance or timidity (8.3 and 4.6 percent), or illness (13.8 and 8.6 percent) as their explanation. Among women, the younger generation was more likely to vote; the opposite was true for men. Ethnicity also mattered. "In both the presidential and the mayoralty elections, the adult female citizens of German, Polish, Scandinavian, Russian and Italian stock showed less interest in voting than did the women of native-white or Irish stock. Indeed, the one-third of nonvoting women who gave "indifference as a reason for not voting were white women of foreign parentage, not registered, having little voting experience, living in the poorer sections of the city, and having no occupation but housework." On the other hand, "Colored women from the South shared with their men folks an intense interest in politics." The ballot box was a symbol of emancipation because they were denied it in the South.[27] Registration laws were also blamed for reducing the electorate and in particular for discouraging women voters. Simon Michelet wrote that "marriage, child-birth and domestic duties make it more difficult for women to comply with the restrictive provisions of the registration laws. Those states that have property-owning and tax-paying requirements as a basis for registration make it difficult for women to qualify."[28]

The 1924 Presidential campaign was rather lackluster. The Democrats, decimated by their fractious convention, nominated a candidate more conservative than Coolidge. The Republicans, confident of victory, were more interested in saving money than in maximizing their vote.[29] Coolidge stayed in the White House, making a few speeches over the new device called the radio, while his campaign was run from Chicago. Different party resources dictated different strategies for organizing women. Sallie Hert of Kentucky replaced Harriet Upton as the "Vice Chairman in Charge of Women's Work" for the Republicans. Under her direction, women RNC members headed different geographical divisions, with separate divisions for farm and business women. Over five hundred women enrolled as campaign speakers. The Democrats did not have a separate women's division, putting a man at the head of each department—e.g., organization, publicity, speakers, education—with a woman vice chairman. The Progressive Party, reincarnated to run Wisconsin Senator Robert LaFollette for President, mirrored the Republicans, with a separate organization of women under the general direction of Mable Costigan. It did have one woman, Frances Axtell of Washington State, at the head of a state organization, running the men as well as the women.[30]

The biggest change from 1920 was the increased participation of black women under the leadership of Hallie Q. Brown. African Americans had continued their trek to the North, recruited by manufacturers when new laws closed down foreign immigration. There they could register and vote, and were becoming an important voting bloc in some cities. According to historian Evelyn Higgenbotham:

Black women's Republican clubs sprang up everywhere—led by clubwomen already in the vanguard of the civic and political affairs of their communities. The overall operation included precinct captains; ward chairmen; city, county, and district chairmen; together with state chairmen and national organizers and speakers. Each state chairman developed circulars and bulletins for her own territory and sent reports to the black press "with accurate and encouraging accounts of women's campaign activities."[31]

Both parties made a special appeal to women, as reflected in their campaign text books, but the Democrats went one step further. Marion Glass Banister wrote a 142-page *Democratic Women's Campaign Manual*. This was the last time the Democratic Party devoted special pages of its campaign text book to women. "Women" is not even in the index of subsequent volumes.

In the 1924 general election, voter turnout dropped again, to 48.9 percent overall. In the Southern states turnout was in the low teens; in South Carolina it was 6.4 percent. Several small studies tried to ascertain who did and did not vote. After the 1924 election Arneson interviewed 4,390 residents of Delaware, Ohio, home of Ohio Wesleyan University, and reported that 57.1 percent of women and 72.9 percent of men had voted. The turnout for the entire state of Ohio had been 57.8 percent. He didn't separate men's reasons from women's, but did observe that the poor and uneducated were less likely to vote than others.[32]

The apathy that reigned in the 1924 campaign receded in 1928 when 56.9 percent of the voting age population went to the polls. The increase was mostly women. "From all parts of the country county clerks reported the greatest women's registration in history." Two weeks before the balloting, the *New York Times* predicted "This Year's Woman Vote to Set a High Record."[33] The race to the registrar wasn't strictly spontaneous. Herbert Hoover had been "building his own organization of women in California as an asset for a future Presidential nomination campaign as early as 1924. . . . In early 1928, Hoover-for-President Committees of women were organized throughout the states." After the convention, Hoover insisted that organizing women be a campaign priority, and put former suffragist Louise Dodson of Iowa in charge. Many women had been favorably impressed with Hoover when he was food administrator during the Great War. But more were spurred to action by the unique nature of the 1928 contest. A wet Catholic pitted against a dry Quaker made liquor and religion—more commonly found in local politics than national—dominant campaign issues, despite disavowals by both candidates that they were important.[34]

The Republican Women's Division was "besieged by unprecedented numbers of women who wanted to participate in the campaign." Although the National Woman's Party was the only women's organization to officially endorse Hoover, so many other organization women supported him that he was often referred to as "the woman's candidate." Officers of the DAR, the PTA, the GFWC, and the BPW signed ads endorsing Hoover. Carrie Chapman Catt and the LWV's first president, Maud Wood Park, were on his official Advisory Committee. Many well-known women, such as Jane Addams and M. Carey Thomas, publicly gave him their approval. Even Mrs. Samuel Gompers, widow of the president of the American Federation of Labor, endorsed him. Of course the WCTU actively campaigned for Hoover; several state conventions officially endorsed him and President Ella Boole urged women to vote for him, even though the national body did not discuss it. Other women's organizations that supported prohibition acted similarly.[35]

As in previous campaigns, the RNC Women's Division was in charge of appealing to women voters. Sallie Hert announced that Republican women would work with men on a "50–50" basis. Women were divided into interest groups—homemakers, professional, rural, industrial—each with its own nationally renowned chairman. Margaret Dreier Robins headed the department of industrial women, and the former president of the GFWC, Mrs. Thomas G. (Alice Ames) Winter, directed homemakers. Republican stalwart Helen Varick Boswell ran the women's speaker's bureau for the eastern states.[36] Daisy Lampkin of Pennsylvania, chairman of the NLRCW's executive committee, was appointed to organize black women voters in the East, and Letitia Fleming in the West (out of the Chicago office) though both worked in the Colored Division, not the Women's Division. Hallie Q. Brown became vice chairman of the Speakers Bureau in that division. Other prominent black women, such as Terrell, Bethune, and Burroughs, actively campaigned for Hoover, concerned that "Smith in the White House means the South in the saddle."[37]

In the Democratic Party, New York Governor Al Smith was the candidate of the urban "wets," who had spent the last four years slowly taking over the northern branch of the party. This prompted the wife of DNC chairman Clement Shaver to co-found the National Woman's Democratic Law Enforcement League (NWDLEL) in May of 1927, with the avowed purpose of nominating a "dry" at the Democratic Convention. The virulent attacks by this group on Smith made the WCTU, who sent a few women to "protest, pray and influence" the Democrats to stay dry, appear moderate and balanced by comparison. Despite numerous charges that he was a "machine" candidate, Smith easily captured the nomination at the June convention in Houston. He conceded to the "drys" a promise in the platform to make "an honest effort to enforce the Eighteenth Amendment," and chose a dry Protestant from Arkansas as his running mate. But Smith picked John J. Raskob, a committed wet and wealthy Catholic, as the new DNC chairman.[38]

"Although it seemed hopeless to expect any general feminine support for the Democratic candidate," a few women did make "powerful pleas." Two days after her appointment as head of the DNC Women's Division, Ross announced that "no separate campaign will be conducted among women. . . . [A]ctivities designed to influence feminine voters will be co-ordinated with the general plan of the DNC." Instead, Raskob and Ross appointed a Women's Advisory Committee, with Eleanor Roosevelt as chairman. ER "appointed a woman to cooperate with the men in organizing the women in [several] fields. These women were designated as vice-chairmen to work with the men chairmen." The divisions were: Independent Smith-for-President Clubs, Business and Professional Women's Leagues, College Women's Leagues, Women in Industry Clubs, Social Workers, Doctors, New Voters League, Women's Speakers Bureau, and Women's Publicity. Even Representative Mary T. Norton was only vice chairman of the Women's Speakers Bureau, and that for Doctors had no woman at all.[39]

ER's most valuable recruit was a retired social worker, Molly Dewson, whom she sent to St. Louis to run the Southern campaign because the women there would not work together. Dewson sent the feuding women on speaking tours and took over the task of organizing. The Democrats did little to mobilize women beyond making speeches. Ross spent her time on the speaker circuit and ER had campaign duties as the wife of the Democratic candidate for New York Governor. The *Chicago Tribune* accused that city's Democrats of neglecting to register women because of "a fear that some of these Democratic women would vote against Smith." Press releases to the contrary, the Democrats appear to have conceded the woman's vote to Herbert Hoover.[40]

One of the most powerful persons in either campaign was Belle Moskowitz, who had been a close personal advisor to Al Smith since she helped him win women's votes when he first ran for Governor in 1918. Her background was in social reform. She had worked for TR's Progressive Party, and husband Henry had run for Congress in New York City on the Progressive Party line. In 1916 she was a member of the Women's Committee of the Hughes Alliance. Officially in charge of publicity, she was "generally conceded to be Governor Smith's No. 1 advisor on politics as well as social legislation. She ran national Democratic headquarters in his campaign for President in 1928, the only woman ever to attain a position of such authority."[41]

The Socialist Party, which had backed LaFollette in 1924, ran Norman Thomas on their own ticket in 1928. But unlike LaFollette's campaign, the SP had no separate women's division, believing that men and women should be in the same organization and listen to the same pleas.[42]

Considerable publicity was directed at women. NBC gave the LWV weekly radio time to educate listeners on politics. Radio speeches and dramatizations of the candidates became the rage; women were urged to invite their friends and neighbors over for radio parties to listen to these programs. The *Woman's Journal* published monthly articles by party women on why women should vote for their candidate. The Republicans printed reams of material directed at women with special pamphlets on separate issues and planted articles in women's and other popular magazines. The GOP ran a "kitchen" campaign, pitching their message to women as homemakers and reminding them that it was by following Hoover's instructions that housewives had helped win the Great War. The Democrats printed only a few pamphlets. The 1928 *Republican Campaign Text Book* devoted 25 of 425 pages specifically to women and what the Republicans thought were issues of particular concern to women. The 1928 *Democratic Text Book* had nothing.[43]

Whatever else was said by or about either candidate, it was prohibition that evoked the most emotion. Principle trumped party loyalty as dry Democrats and wet Republicans had to explain themselves. Quite a few party women "trampl[ed] across party lines into the enemy camp." Mrs. Clem Shaver, still the wife of the now former chairman of the DNC, attacked Smith as though she were Carrie Nation axing a saloon. Even the more moderate speeches made headlines. It was both legal and expected that Presidential appointees would campaign for their party, and one of the most prominent was Assistant Attorney General Mabel Walker Willebrandt. Her spirited speeches urging vigorous law enforcement and condemning the laxity of New York with its Tammany Governor Al Smith raised such a ruckus that she was called "the most notorious woman in America."[44] Outside the South, prohibition drove a wedge into black loyalty to the Republican Party. Ida B. Wells-Barnett, appointed by the Hoover campaign as Organizer of Negro Women for Illinois, reported that "there are thousands of Negroes from the Atlantic to the Pacific who are going to vote the Democratic ticket . . . [due to] belief that . . . Al Smith will modify or repeal the Volstead law." Despite this discouragement, she wrote a pamphlet on "Why I am for Hoover" and paid from her own pocket to print 3,000 copies.[45]

Whether one counted speakers, organizers, workers, or merely showing up, women blossomed in the 1928 campaign. Emily Newell Blair claimed "there were as many women as men active as organizers and as speakers." One reporter for the *New York Times* noted that "if anything, women outnumber men at political meetings, and women speakers are becoming as numerous as men" and another that there was a 20 percent increase in demand for women speakers over 1924. A retrospective reviewer wrote that "in the state and local organizations . . . women workers assumed a far more prominent share than . . . ever . . . before."[46] Barnard heralded the campaign as women's political arrival:

> Over night the psychology of the situation was reversed. Woman, who for eight years had done little more than wash the political dishes, now suddenly was set on a cushion and fed upon strawberries, sugar and cream. Down at Republican National Headquarters in Washington, sixteen of the thirty-two rooms were given over to the women's activities. . . . Newspapers bristled daily with headlines of the women's drives. Into the movies and the rotogravure sections moved the pictures of the women party leaders. For the first time they were of major importance, because for the first time they had a constituency.[47]

All this attention to women paid off. Almost seven million more people voted for President than had done so in 1924, and ten million more than in 1920. Most of the newly mobilized voters were women. "Virtually every Republican respondent agreed that women experienced a remarkable political renaissance in 1928, voting in unprecedented numbers."[48] Michelet estimated that "women cast 45 percent of the total vote in 1928, as compared with 35 percent in 1924" and 30 percent in 1920, though it varied enormously in different areas. He agreed that organization as well as issues brought women to the polls. Every "city, county, town or hamlet [had] . . . active women campaign organizations, while in larger cities a central women's organization might have local branches in every ward and precinct."[49]

Lacking scientific polls or separate ballot boxes, *how* women voted was harder to estimate. By 1928 newspapers and magazines were conducting large pre-election straw polls with increasing sophistication, and reporting the results as they came in. The *Chicago Tribune* reported on October 24 that "Women Favor Hoover 3–2, in Chicago poll."[50] Sampling was not yet a science, but a straw poll of forty-six states conducted by the Hearst newspapers was the most accurate of the many done that year. It predicted that 60 percent of women and 56 percent of men would vote for Hoover.[51] After the election both press and party leaders were impressed with women's contribution to Hoover's victory, though he won among men as well. Party leaders collected the best judgments of experienced local party workers. Some estimated that as many as 65 percent of women voted for Hoover, including many otherwise Democratic voters. The research director of the RNC concluded that

> Most conspicuous and important was the support given President-elect Hoover by the women. . . . [T]he militant support of Mr. Hoover by America's womanhood was constant in every state. Indifference or aversion to political activity . . . was overcome, and hundreds of thousands of women who had never participated in politics and never voted were brought into the campaign as zealous workers in behalf of Mr. Hoover. . . . The enthusiasm of women for him cut across party lines, broke down sectional barriers and prejudices of 50 years duration and survived the blight of religious intolerance. Hoover's support by women was the one constant, dominating factor in every state making a report—in many states women offsetting all losses of normal Republican votes due to variously assigned causes.[52]

Democrats bemoaned the fact that normally Democratic wives did not vote like their husbands. They blamed it on prohibition, religion, and Smith's personal style. Some recognized the importance of organization. They "complained that the opposition could turn out the women's vote more effectively than could the Democrats. Upper-class, Republican women . . . controlled most women's organizations in the United States and used their positions to promote the Republican Cause." An Indiana woman wrote:

> Do you know that the greater part of Federation of Clubs, League of Women Voters, the D.A.R.'s, the Council of Jewish Women, the Business and Professional Women, W.C.T.U., are composed mostly of Republican women throughout the United States? . . . There is not the slightest doubt that the Republican Party distributes much political propaganda thru all local women's clubs.[53]

Daisy Harriman asked the Democratic national committeewomen "in the ten states which unexpectedly went Republican" why Smith lost. Only Tennessee's answered; she blamed the party's failure to organize and inform women. A few months later the WNDC wrote to "leading women Democrats in all 48 states." "Hundreds" of responses pointed the arrow at "lack of organization."[54] Southern women were not the only traditional Democrats suspected of desertion. "Party lines were ruthlessly cut adrift by voters of both sexes; but even to a larger degree in the case of women than of men." Catholic women were a large group of first-time voters; many of their votes went to Hoover.[55]

Hoover clobbered Smith, getting 58 percent of the total vote to Smith's 41 percent. Prosperity and prohibition kept the Republicans in power. The solid South cracked; Smith got a majority in only five Southern and one border state, for which the Republicans thanked women. Smith even lost New York, where Democrat Franklin Delano Roosevelt won the governorship. But beneath this facade was another story. Smith won in areas with a heavy immigrant population: Rhode Island, Massachusetts, and the twelve largest cities. Except in 1912, the Republicans hadn't lost these two states since the party was founded. While "old" voters went to the polls in larger numbers than in 1924, an even larger number of "new" voters, mostly immigrants and the children of immigrants, shifted the balance of power. In 1930, after the stock market crashed and the economy began a downward slide, even more of these new voters gave the House of Representatives back to the Democrats. And in 1932, the Fifth Party System poked its head above the surface of the Republican ocean.[56]

It was not until the 1932 Presidential campaign that the Democrats seriously tried to mobilize Democratic women. Jim Farley, Roosevelt's campaign manager, had found the work of women in the gubernatorial races of 1928 and 1930 "quite amazing." When compared with past elections, "the total party vote picked up anywhere from 10 to 20 percent, after a women's organization had been established." FDR's overwhelming reelection in 1930 made him the leading contender for the Democratic Presidential nomination because political observers were impressed with his "feat in carrying the Republican up-state territories." Few besides Farley acknowledged how much this was due to the years of work by ER and Democratic women. Farley "also learned that the feminine workers . . . were apt to be more faithful than the men in distributing literature and doing the other little irksome tasks that are so necessary for victory." Molly Dewson was put in charge of the Women's Division for the 1932 and 1936 Roosevelt campaigns.[57]

Dewson believed that women should be treated like other voters. She discouraged FDR and other Democratic speakers from speaking about "women's issues" or specifically to women as Hoover did. FDR concurred that women were as concerned with cheaper water and power, farm relief, and economic recovery as men were. As in 1928, there were no pages in the 1932 *Democratic Text Book* aimed at women. Nellie Tayloe Ross, still head of the DNC Women's Division, put out a pamphlet on "Pertinent Facts for Practical Women" arguing that the Democratic Party had recognized women more than the Republicans. But the primary literature prepared by the Women's Division of the campaign were the Rainbow Fliers. First used in FDR's 1930 race, they showed how abstract policies impacted on people's everyday lives. Packets were sent to women county and precinct leaders wherever they could be found, along with a personal letter from Dewson asking women to call on their neighbors and talk about Roosevelt's plans. Six million fliers were distributed in 1932, but they did not identify the Women's Division as the source. "Because we feared some men might be prejudiced by material put out over the Women's Division name they carried the label of the Democratic National Campaign Committee only."[58]

Dewson decided that the path of least resistance was "to make the men find working with women easy, pleasant and profitable." She told Farley that "nothing we did would bother the machines." This meant that the Women's Division stayed out of the cities and concentrated on rural areas and small towns in the North. This was Republican territory, the same Republican territory that ER and New York women had organized for FDR in 1928 and 1930. It was a formidable task, because, except for a few states like New York, Democratic women were largely unorganized. There were some Democratic women's clubs, and some women trained in politics from Blair's efforts in the 1920s, but "Practically, [the Democratic women's clubs] had advanced little beyond the social stage, for, being separate from the regular party organization, they could have little political power or influence." As an example, she later wrote, "In 1932 I was delighted to receive a complete roster of county vice-chairmen from the Michigan Democratic State Committee, but when I wrote these women about plans, I found one had died, some had moved, others were sick and hardly a single one considered her county vice-chairmanship was more than a recognition of herself or her husband, involving little if any responsibility." With little money and only a few reliable women, Dewson put together a women's campaign organization, woman by woman and county by county. She insisted on direct contact with Democratic women rather than going through the state and county chairmen. Although her strategy wouldn't be fully realized for another four years, Louis Howe concluded that he "would rather have a half dozen women field workers than a hundred men any day."[59]

The RNC Women's Division was not starting from scratch, having a wide network of Republican women's clubs and well-trained party workers. Even before the campaign started, Republican women were "holding meetings, sometimes attended by as many as 5,000 women." For the 1932 campaign it repeated many of the things it had done in 1928. The Chicago headquarters named women leaders to head different sections, including the past president of BPW and a farm woman who had become a radio personality. As before, the endorsement of "nationally known women" was sought, but this time they were appointed to an RNC approved Board of Counselors. No distinction was made between those who had married important men (former first ladies, Mrs. Thomas A. Edison, Mrs. Henry Ford) and those who had achieved in their own right. Among the latter were suffrage leader Carrie Chapman Catt and LWV President Maud Wood Park, WTUL founder Margaret Dreier Robins, several past presidents of the DAR, the GFWC, writers, and college presidents. Other women headed divisions elsewhere. Mary Church Terrell became "director of work among colored women of the East," working out of the New York office. Dr. Lillian Gilbreth was president of the Women's Division of the Engineers' National Committee for Hoover.[60]

When the votes were counted, observers recognized that the political terrain had shifted. Overall turnout remained the same as in 1928, but the

Democrats took 57 percent of the almost forty million votes cast for President while Hoover got less than 40 percent. The Republicans won in only six states—five small northeastern states plus Pennsylvania. The Democrats captured both Houses of Congress, by three to one in the House and two to one in the Senate. There was one Congressional district, in Connecticut, where an incumbent Democrat was replaced by a Republican; the Fairfield County Republican Women's Association took the credit.[61]

How and how many women voted was no longer news and little space was spent in speculation. General consensus held that women had cast only 40 percent of the total vote. There was still a gender gap, but it wasn't known how much of one for some time. Random sample polling did not become an election staple until 1936, when voters were asked how they voted in 1932. Of those who said they had voted, 63 percent of the men were for FDR, but only 57.5 percent of the women. Only 35 percent of the men said they voted for Hoover, compared to 41 percent of the women. The six percent difference between male and female voters is corroborated by local studies. Gosnell's analysis of numerous variables that correlated with the FDR Chicago vote in 1932 showed that in areas where women were a higher percentage of the total registered voters, the vote for FDR went down.[62]

For the next four years Molly Dewson dedicated herself to turning women on to the New Deal and turning them out for FDR. By 1936 she had identified "sixty thousand party representatives" to woman her campaign. At the 1936 convention the Women's Division put a packet of Rainbow Fliers on every delegate's seat, and acknowledged its authorship. Over 83 million of these were eventually distributed around the country. They were so successful and so cost efficient that the DNC continued the practice for many years to come. In 1940, a corps of women volunteers researched and wrote separate Rainbow Fliers for virtually every *county* on local New Deal achievements.[63]

The 1936 campaign saw more attention to women than any time since 1928, but this time it was the Democrats who led the way. Dewson turned her reporters into precinct workers, telling them to personally visit every prospect in their districts, organize radio parties, and distribute Rainbow Fliers. The WD prepared speakers' kits and publicity ideas, sending "Grass Trampers" to neighborhood meetings and "Visitors" to the homes of those who didn't go to meetings. Once again, Dewson later wrote, "we campaigned hardest where our popularity was weakest. . . . Practically none of our material was sent into the overwhelmingly Democratic States." This time the WD also created committees with prominent women at their head. Many well-known women, especially social workers, who had supported Hoover in 1932 went over to Roosevelt in 1936, generating much publicity.[64]

In 1936 the Democratic campaign made its first serious appeal to African American voters, who were already voicing their approval of FDR's New Deal. Democratic activist Crystal Bird Fauset of Philadelphia became the first Director of Colored Women's Activities. The Republican Party sought to lure Southerners from their traditional Democratic loyalties, sitting lily-white delegations from the South at its national convention and otherwise downplaying black participation. Mary Church Terrell's offer to the RNC to organize women as she had in past campaigns was ignored; the head of the campaign's Colored Division chose one of his own. Black women responded to this shift in party appeals by voting Democratic. Subsequent Republican campaigns continued to have special units for African Americans, but their role and influence in the party declined. By 1948, there was no longer a director in charge of organization of black women; instead several black assistants worked for the Women's Division.[65]

Despite occasional predictions of a Landon victory, the election of 1936 was a landslide for Roosevelt. Overall turnout increased to 61 percent, with 60 percent of all votes going to FDR. Only in Maine and Vermont did a majority vote for the Republican ticket. The Gallup Poll showed no difference in the Presidential preferences of men and women. Gosnell's study of Chicago showed the same positive relationship between districts with high female registration and Republican votes. Republican women might still have an edge in turnout, but there was no longer a preference effect.[66]

The Presidential campaign of 1936 was the last one in which much ado was made about women. The campaigns continued to have special units of women, but they focused less on the woman voter. More and more women took over the nuts and bolts throughout the campaign organization while men retained control of decisions. In 1940, the Democratic Women's Division once again prepared most of the campaign literature, issuing fifty million Rainbow Fliers. It also organized campaign schools for precinct workers in 112 crucial Congressional districts in fifteen states. In the Republican Party, the NFWRC became the major provider of women campaign workers, often taking on tasks, such as massive telephone polls, otherwise beyond the reach of campaigns. But the NFWRC stayed in the background, never getting the kind of publicity or post-election acknowledgement given to Republican women in 1928 or Democratic women in 1936. It also became less common for the top party woman to head the campaign women's division, that task going to someone appointed just for the campaign.[67]

Despite decreasing publicity, what there was indicated that women were increasing their participation in political campaigns. Shortly after the 1940 election, Edward J. Flynn, the new chairman of the DNC, told a conference of Democratic women that women were better organized than the men and asked them to do more.[68] In an October 30, 1944, story, the *New York Times* reported that "More Women Than Ever are Campaigning in Partisan or Independent Groups This Year." After surveying party and nonpartisan groups, the reporter wrote that

All agreed that women's divisions of national committees, special women's groups and individual women workers were to a great extent responsible for the large registration figures. All credited women with excellent work in helping to get absentee ballots to servicemen, conducting polls, canvassing, speech-making and arranging political meetings. The most important job of all—to see that every registered voter gets to the polls on Nov. 7—will be to a large degree undertaken by women.

Marian Martin said five million women were working for the Republican Party. The Democrats did not give out numbers, but said there were more women than ever before. In New York City, the American Labor Party claimed four to five thousand women were campaigning for its candidates. Even the Congress of Industrial Organizations had a women's division to mobilize the 25,000 local women leaders on its mailing list.[69]

In the 1950s, Republican women out organized Democratic women nationally as well as locally, relying on the many Republican women's clubs for personnel. While Democratic "women's activities were 'well integrated' with those of the party as a whole," the Republican Party still bid for the woman's vote. In preparation for the 1956 campaign the RNC set up a special unit exclusively of women to do grassroots fundraising for TV time. The year before, its women's division had conducted a poll, using 15,000 Republican women to interview 250,000 voters in forty-seven states on how they felt about the Eisenhower administration. While this many interviews may not have provided a more accurate reading than a much smaller standard sample, it did bring more voters into contact with Republican women. In the capital, the D.C. League of Republican Women volunteered to do the secretarial work of the Republican Members of Congress who were up for reelection. This meant that more constituents had more letters answered and received more Congressional mail than normal in the crucial months prior to the election. A few days before the election, the Eisenhower campaign bought thirty minutes of afternoon TV time, when housewives were watching, to broadcast a panel discussion with seven women.[70] During the 1960s the role of women in the Presidential campaigns moved from mobilizing the woman's vote to providing support services for the overall campaign. Women took over grassroots contact and grassroots fundraising. When Pat Hitt organized Women for Nixon-Agnew in 1968, its primary purpose was to raise money. She later claimed that it "was the only campaign support organization that more than paid its own way."[71]

While women's numbers in Presidential campaigns increased, the way in which campaigns portrayed women and their political roles narrowed. Political women were displaced by political wives, and the concerns of working women were displaced by the concerns of housewives. This shift could be seen both in the women's programs at the conventions and in the women who were publicized by the campaigns. Programs for women delegates in the 1920s and 1930s emphasized issues. While these included traditional female areas such as children and welfare, the message was that women could be effective actors in changing laws and educating voters. By 1960, convention programs highlighted women's role as helpmates to their husbands, who were the candidates and officials. In the 1920s and 1930s women public officials campaigned for their party's ticket; in the 1950s and 1960s the most prominent women campaigners were candidates' wives. Their job was to tell the voter that their husbands were good family men.[72]

The change was gradual. In 1946 the DNC Women's Division ran a speaker's school "to help women help their husbands . . . in the 1946 congressional elections." The 1948 campaign asked "Housewives for Truman" to blame the Republican Congress for the high cost of living. In 1956 four car caravans toured several states with carloads of Congressional wives bringing publicity to Democratic candidates. This was repeated in 1964 with cabinet wives added to the mix. Half of the 1960 convention program for Democratic women was for political wives. In 1960 the Nixon campaign introduced a separate "Pat for First Lady" campaign "to help channel the enthusiasm of women." According to Women's Division director Clare Williams "we are giving women a chance to have fun while doing . . . the grubby work of doorbell ringing and canvassing." It also sent out a "flying squadron of influential women"—all political wives and widows—to be the featured guests at political events.[73]

This shift in image did not represent women's numbers or roles in politics, which were expanding and diversifying. It did reflect the post–World War II view that woman's place was (only) in the home; the good woman was devoted to her family, not to issues; she promoted her husband, not herself. The rising prominence of political wives also came from their increasing importance to the success of their husbands' campaigns. For this, Eleanor Roosevelt set the precedent for the political "team."[74] Previously, wives were not expected to campaign publicly. Some stumped, but most stayed out of sight, or appeared demurely at their husband's side at receptions. ER's courting of public opinion for her causes and her husband was initially scandalous, but after FDR's death she became an icon and her public activity *the* model for political wives. More and more, political wives took to the campaign trail, first with their husbands and then independently. After Louchheim organized the Democratic Congressional Wives Forum, political wives campaigned for other women's husbands as well as their own.

In the 1956 campaign Pat Nixon and Mamie Eisenhower toured with their husbands; Stevenson's sister (he was divorced) campaigned both with him and independently, while Nancy Kefauver stayed home. In 1960, a pregnant Jackie Kennedy stayed home while Pat Nixon became a frequent flyer. In the 1964 campaign, the wives took off on their own. Lady Bird Johnson toured the South by train for a month before the election, preceded by an advance team that organized women's campaign groups at every stop. The other three wives also traveled on their own, as well as with their husbands. To some extent wives specialized in appeals to women, freeing their husbands for other tasks.[75]

The result of these changes was to create two classes of party women: the workers and the wives. Most of the work done during elections, and between them, was done by women, especially ordinary housewives, but the most influential women and the most celebrated were the wives of candidates, elected officials, and other important men. Workers shifted to the background of campaigns while wives were glamorized. Given the paucity of women in policy and decision making posts, the message that was conveyed to party women was that who you married was more important than what you did. Instead of the "voice" in party councils that Marion Martin had asked for in 1945, the doorbell ringers were given the chance to admire the wives of important political men. As women took over work in the basement of national as well as local campaigns, their routes to the top were reduced.

THE WOMAN'S VOTE?

From 1936 onward voters were asked repeatedly before each Presidential election if they were going to vote and how. In-depth research analyzing how different groups voted began in 1940. Accurate estimates of voter turnout were available for 1948. Even when "party managers . . . [made] special appeals to the feminine vote," these surveys showed no significant differences in how men and women voted. They did show that 3 to 13 percent fewer eligible women voted than men. Quite a few women still believed that "voting is for the men." More important, women's turnout varied significantly by age, education, and economic status. Younger women voted at higher rates than older women; those with more income and education voted more than those with less. This pattern favored the Republican Party. It wasn't that more women were voting Republican (though sometimes they did) but that more Republican women were voting.[76]

In 1952 a new gender gap appeared—the first serious sex difference in votes for President since Herbert Hoover. Polls of voters done before and after the November election found women were 5 percent more likely to vote for Eisenhower than were men, though both gave him a majority. Like Hoover, Eisenhower particularly attracted new women voters from traditional Democratic constituencies such as the South and labor union families. Interest in the woman voter increased, as pollsters, politicians, and pundits speculated on why women liked Ike. Republican women gleefully claimed "The Ladies Elected Ike," and this belief soon became "firmly enshrined among American political lore." Lou Harris's analysis of the Roper/NBC polls found a difference in male and female votes of 9 percent for those with high incomes, 6 percent for those with middle incomes, and 3 percent for those with low incomes, with women in all three groups more likely to vote for Ike. Harris attributed this to more women than men blaming the Democratic party for the Korean War, inflation, and corruption in Washington. Others argued that more women than men liked family men and father figures. But journalist Marion K. Sanders credited the "well trained Republican women. . . . The telephone . . . was used on a scale never before attempted. California . . . was blanketed by a telephone chain organized by three hundred Republican Women's Clubs." Even top Democratic woman Katie Louchheim acknowledged "that the fervor and enthusiasm with which women worked for Eisenhower last time was a factor in his victory." While the polls indicated there was a preference effect, these comments imply a turnout effect as well—a likely result from the intensified work of the NFRW in the previous few years. In the 1930s and 1940s the DNC Women's Division had worked hard to organize women and mobilize the Democratic woman voter. This was not done in the 1950s, when Republican women's clubs were flexing their muscles. Overall turnout went from 53 percent in 1948 to 63 percent in 1952.[77]

In the 1956 election both parties paid more attention to women. Despite efforts by some Democratic groups, especially labor unions, to recapture its portion of the female vote, the gender gap increased to 6 percent, though more men as well as women voted for Eisenhower than in 1952. Overall turnout dropped to 60 percent.[78]

Although some were still asking "Will Women Decide the Election?" in 1960, the gender gap dropped to between 2 and 3 percent—too small to be statistically significant but implying that women still voted more frequently for the Republican candidate. Democratic women dismissed the very idea of a woman's vote. Republican women flouted it. The GOP women's division proudly declared that in these three Presidential elections a majority of women voted for the Republican Party and a majority of Republican votes came from women. Nonetheless, its 1962 pamphlet on *Win With Womanpower* was directed only at male candidates for public office. "Who is the most important woman on your campaign team?" it asked. "Your wife, of course."[79]

In 1964 as in 1960 the gender gap of 2 to 3 percent was too small to be significant, but it was notable because, for the first time, women were more likely than men to vote for the Democratic Presidential candidate. In 1968 43 percent of both men and women said they voted for Nixon. But men were 4 percent more likely to vote for George Wallace (16 percent to 12 percent) while women were more likely to vote for Humphrey (45 percent to 41 percent). In the same polls, the traditional relationship between SES and party preference disappeared. High SES women were 3 percent more likely to vote Democratic than low SES women. Something was happening to the woman voter, but it was not clear just what.[80]

Throughout the 1950s and into the 1960s there were rumblings of discontent among party women. Not that party women had ever been complacent. But for decades they had heard men say that they would get more recognition if they only worked harder, built up more experience, were more loyal, and in general acted more like party men—without losing their femininity or ceasing to be ladies. By the 1950s, party women no longer believed these old bromides. They knew they worked harder and deserved more; they just didn't know how to get it. Most did not admit their discontent publicly because they did not want to give ammunition to the opposition. But it seeped out. At a 1952 women's leadership conference held at Bethune College, India Edwards told the crowd, "The men don't want women messing around in politics," while Bertha Adkins informed them that "there's still that feeling that women haven't quite the ability that men have."[81]

In December of 1958 *U.S. News and World Report* put those leaders' successors as top party women, Clare Williams and Katie Louchheim, on its cover to highlight lengthy interviews on "What Women Do in Politics." Williams emphasized that "Women are now a greater voting force than men." Since women had more time than men to go to meetings and study issues, Williams said, husbands were more likely to ask wives how to vote than the other way around. She believed that even though "there are still shortsighted men," the parties took women more seriously than ever before. But what did women do? The workers at "the lowest level" were "almost entirely women," she said. "The farther up the political ladder you go, whether it is a party office or whether it is an elected office, the fewer women become." And, she added, "it is wrong." Williams walked a fine line in her efforts to get party men to reward party women without ruffling any feathers, telling the RNC in 1959 that "It's a man's world, and we, as women are very glad of it; but … in 1952 and 1956 the women of America deserve a lion's share of the credit for those Republican victories." Yet in 1960 she and the RNC chairman lamented the fact that fewer women had been selected as delegates to that year's nominating convention.[82]

Louchheim was a bit more circumspect. Democratic women were 75 to 80 percent of "active campaign workers" and their tasks included providing "political know-how" and campaign management, she said. Throughout her tenure in the DNC Woman's Division she had argued that there was no woman's vote or women's issues. "Brains has no sex" was her constant refrain, along with "women are people." She viewed it as a "handicap" for women to be "lumped" together into a "reserved section" for women. To Louchheim, the "place" for women that her predecessors had built had become a jail. She thought the typical male politician was condescending, viewing all women as either "feminists" or "featherbrains," "fluttery females" or "bespectacled battleaxes." When invited to introduce several men to a Democratic women's meeting in 1960, she informed them that they could not "talk about (a) motherhood, (b) how pretty we all are, (c) the Red, White and Blue, (d) what lovely hats we are wearing or (e) how nice your chairman is." In order to undermine the male stereotype about party women, she used her "party office to destroy this illusion of a women's voting bloc."[83]

Despite their dismay at condescension, stereotyping, and exclusion, party women probably received more recognition on the national level in the 1950s than in the 1960s, when newspapers wrote that "Fewer Women Try for Congress," and journalists observed that women "seem to be less effective, politically," than ever before.[84] The men who ran for President, or ran their campaigns, and the men who ran the national committees did not go out of their way to appeal to women. They did recruit woman as volunteers to staff headquarters, raise money, and ring doorbells, but as the idea of the "woman's vote" faded, professional pollsters convinced political managers that there were no approaches or issues that made a difference. On the local level women were running campaigns and running for office, but on the national level they were being replaced by media buys. TV seemed a more cost-effective way than the precinct worker to reach the most voters in national and statewide campaigns, and the professionals who made and bought the spots were men. As the Fifth Party System disintegrated, women's small but hard fought place in the national parties deteriorated with it. Women took over the basement of Presidential campaigns, and then the basement shrank.

· Ten ·

Having a Say:
Women's Issues in the Party Platforms

$\mathscr{P}$arty platforms are rarely taken seriously by anyone except those who write them but at every party's quadrennial convention everyone wants a say. Women were no exception when they could not vote, and they continued to pursue their issues long afterwards. Writing the quadrennial platform was one more battleground for the ongoing fight between feminists and reformers. While party women often agreed on traditional women's issues, the ERA frequently forced them to chose sides.

LWV Chairman Maud Wood Park brought "the first Woman's Platform" to the 1920 party conventions. Its six planks on Child Welfare, Education, The Home and High Prices, Women in Gainful Occupations, Public Health and Morals, and Independent Citizenship for Married Women reflected the concerns of Progressive women reformers.[1] This platform was presented to the Republican Resolutions Committee by prominent Republican women and to the Democratic Platform Committee by Democratic party women. Several of the proposals found their way into the final platform of each party, but not because of the eloquence of their presenters. Harriet Taylor Upton, who made the presentation to the Republican Resolutions committee, wrote that only diligent detective work disclosed when and where it was to meet. When she was finally allowed to appear before the committee she found that "the resolutions had been drafted and decided upon previous to the convention. In fact, they were printed and lying on the table before us."[2] While neither party put women's issues high on their agenda, neither did they give women's proposals the cold shoulder of which NAWSA had long complained. Both platforms had several paragraphs on women in industry, citizenship for married women, and child labor. This was the last time women's organizations agreed on what they wanted.

By 1924 feminists and reformers had distinct and competing agendas. NWP members appeared in force at the conventions. They testified before all the 1924 platform committees, interviewed delegates, and draped the hotel lobbies with their banners. Despite this strong presence the NWP was successful in getting support for the ERA only from the national Farmer/Labor Party. Several state delegations to the Democratic and Republican national conventions gave it their backing, but the national party platforms only welcomed "the women of the nation to their rightful place by the side of men" (Democrats) and congratulated them on attaining "full equality" (Republicans).[3]

Reform women's organizations fared no better despite seemingly greater access. The LWV prepared four proposals and asked Vice President Julia Lathrop, former director of the Children's Bureau, to present them to both conventions. However, both parties insisted on the women's planks being screened by a committee of party women. The chairman of the DNC appointed Eleanor Roosevelt to head a Woman's Advisory Committee, which held hearings on planks of interest to women. Numerous women's organizations and Democratic clubs testified, and those proposals that had the most support were published, along with a list other planks (e.g., the ERA) proposed by other groups. This list reflected the pantheon of reform causes, including entry to the League of Nations, reduction of the tariff, better treatment for Indians, elimination of exemptions to the civil service, prison reform, and child welfare. Also included were removal of women's legal disabilities except for special treatment in the realm of labor, social welfare, and family law. Despite all this work and publicity, ER was not allowed to present her committee's recommendations to the all-male Resolutions Committee. After waiting outside the door of the hearing room for many hours she handed them to a man from New York as he entered the closed hearing room but never found out if they were even discussed. Torn apart by debate over the League of Nations and a proposal to condemn the Ku Klux Klan, the 1924 Democratic convention paid no attention to the women's proposals. Reform organizations made similar demands on the Republican Party, but Republican women concentrated their efforts on gaining equal representation on the National Committee. On issues of "special interest to women" there was no real difference between the parties.[4]

The 1928 platforms were equally undistinguished. No state delegations pledged support for the ERA; nor did the national party platforms. The Democrats came out for "equality of men and women in all political and governmental matters" in a section on Women and Children, and the Republican party proclaimed that it "accepts wholeheartedly equality on the part of women." Although lauding mention of the word "equality" by both parties as a step in the right direction, the NWP was particularly incensed at the Democrats for putting women in the same section as children.[5]

In 1932 four state delegations endorsed the ERA, but neither of the major national parties, despite the fact that each party's platform committee had a woman member for the first time and that woman was a supporter of equal rights. The NWP placed its table at a conspicuous spot at each convention's headquarters hotel and lobbied delegates vigorously both for the ERA and for elimination of the final discrepancies in the citizenship rights of men and women. By then, one NWP member sat on the Democratic National Committee and two others on the Republican National Committee. Six NWP members were delegates to the 1932 Republican Convention, and three speakers presented the NWP's case at each party's platform hearings. Their efforts were to no avail. Women, let alone the ERA, were not so much as mentioned in either party's platform in 1932.[6]

In 1936 the NWP, the LWV, and BPW went to the conventions with different agendas and came away with different achievements. The LWV had shifted its focus from women's issues to good government concerns; its priority was endorsement of the merit system in the civil service. BPW demanded repeal of Section 213 of the National Economy Act, which prohibited husbands and wives from both working in the federal civil service. Although neutral in language, it was used to fire married women from their jobs. The Republicans rejected the ERA on grounds it would lead to a proliferation of other constitutional amendments. Instead, its platform favored protectionism. While the LWV was gratified that Alfred Landon, the Republican candidate, publicly supported the merit system, they thought the platform "lacked force and specific recommendations." New York Assemblywoman Jane Todd was the prime mover for BPW. Unsuccessful in persuading the Platform Committee to oppose discrimination, she appealed to Mrs. Eugene (Agnes) Meyer, wife of the owner of the *Washington Post*, who made a personal call to Landon. He in turn told the committee chairman to put in a supportive plank. Opposition to "legislation which discriminates against women in Federal and State employment" was put into the Republican platform.[7]

Women's proposals to the Democratic Party Platform Committee were screened by Molly Dewson, who formed a Committee to Suggest Platform Planks of prominent Democratic women. Although she solicited widely for proposals, all recommendations had her approval, and the only one aimed at women's problems rather than women's "special interests" was the one to repeal Section 213. Mindful of what had happened in 1924, Dewson persuaded the DNC to designate a women alternate from every state to the Platform Committee. Since there were no controversial issues at this convention, men often missed the Platform Committee meetings so several women were able to offer and vote on Dewson's recommendations. Nonetheless, neither repeal of 213 nor support for the Child Labor Amendment made it into the platform, though the former had the support of all women's organizations and the latter was the single most popular issue of all those women whose views were sought. Dewson put a positive front on these rejections, writing later that her Women's Committee was "delighted because the platform did not mention woman even once. We are now persons." In fact, women weren't "persons" in the platform but only worker's wives.[8]

Four years later a breakthrough for the ERA came at the 1940 Republican convention even though there were no women on the Republican Platform Committee that year. For the first time the platform of a major political party explicitly stated that "[w]e favor submission by Congress to the States of an amendment to the Constitution providing for equal rights for men and women." This news made the front page of the *New York Times*. In the preceding four years interest in the ERA had grown. The BPW endorsed it in 1937 and the Senate Judiciary Committee considered it. The Republican Party was looking for a way to challenge Roosevelt's campaign for an unprecedented third term, and appealing to women through support of the ERA was one more way to do it. At the usual hearing, none of the women's organizations opposed to the ERA were present to speak against it. The NWP gave credit to two prominent Republicans, Alf Landon of Kansas and Senator Wharton Pepper of Pennsylvania, though it certainly didn't hurt for the chair of the Resolutions Committee, Herbert Hyde of Oklahoma, to speak in its favor. The following day the *New York Times* reported the opposition to the ERA by the NCL and the WTUL in a story on candidate's wives.[9]

The Democrats didn't follow suit, despite intensive lobbying by Emma Guffey Miller, national committeewoman from Pennsylvania, whom Frances Perkins called "a great power in the Democratic Party." Dorothy McAllister, director of the DNC Women's Division, appointed a Democratic Women's Advisory Platform Committee composed of Congresswomen and representatives of the national women's organizations opposed to the ERA. It recommended an alternative plank which committed the party to "equality of opportunity for men and women without impairing the social legislation which promotes true equality by safeguarding the health, safety and economic welfare of women workers." A statement by Eleanor Roosevelt that the ERA would be "a grave mistake" was read to the platform committee. She said that "until women are unionized to a far greater extent than they are at present an equal rights amendment will work great hardship on the industrial group, which after all is the largest group of wage-earning women." The platform committee accepted the Democratic women's proposal.[10]

Feminists were more successful in persuading the Democrats to finally oppose employment discrimination. BPW proposed that "the right to work for compensation should not be denied or abridged by reason of race, religion, sex, economic or marital status." Section 213 had been repealed in 1937, but twenty-four state legislatures were still debating bills denying married women the right to work. McAllister found that phraseology alarming and circulated it to ERA opponents for commentary. She eventually obtained an opinion from Dean Acheson, an attorney who argued cases for the NCL, that such a proposal might lead to moves for a constitutional amendment, and any amendment prohibiting denial of the right to work for compensation might endanger protective labor legislation for women. McAllister recommended to Congresswoman

Mary Norton that the Women's Advisory Platform Committee she chaired pre-empt this possibility by proposing alternative language. The Democratic platform for 1940 stated that the "right to work for compensation in both public and private employment is an inalienable privilege of women as well as men, without distinction as to marital status." BPW not only accepted this alternative, but took credit for it.[11]

By 1944, the NWP was involved in a major campaign to get the ERA passed by Congress. Obtaining endorsements from both parties in their platforms was considered a crucial step, particularly since each state could now appoint a woman and a man to the platform committees. Local NWP members lobbied state delegations for both parties, and Alice Paul personally interviewed the members of both resolutions committees. The Republican victory was overwhelming, with all the women members voting in favor of the ERA and only three men opposed. Former President Herbert Hoover "went out of his way to support us," Paul said. Once again it was reported by the *New York Times* but this time it was on the engagement page.[12]

The Democratic convention reflected the changing temper of the times. Although Secretary of Labor Frances Perkins and Mary Anderson, recently retired as director of the Women's Bureau, actively opposed the ERA, many other opposition leaders had left the field. Protective labor laws had been waived in the interest of wartime production so their retention was no longer a viable objection. Endorsements of the ERA by women's organizations had increased, though only the GFWC actually switched sides. The opposition was still led by Dorothy McAllister, but she was no longer director of the DNC Women's Division. Its director, Gladys Tillet, kept out of the fight. Instead, two NWP Council members, Emma Guffey Miller and Perle Mesta, sat on the Platform Committee. Eleanor Roosevelt anticipated that the ERA would not be adopted but left her position unclear. McAllister read a letter reaffirming her 1940 statement, while Miller read one specifying that Roosevelt was making "no statement on the Equal Rights Amendment since I cannot decide what I think in peace time, and in war time all restrictions seem to be off." Many notables, including Senator Harry Truman (D. Mo.), who was on the Resolutions Committee, expressed support. Frances Perkins later wrote that "the women of the Democratic Party were very much divided . . . [but] I couldn't keep it out . . . because Emma Guffey Miller . . . was . . . a powerful force in Democratic politics." When the Republican Party once again endorsed the ERA, Democratic Party leaders worried that it would attract women's votes. The final plank adopted by a two-thirds vote of the committee read "[w]e recommend to Congress the submission of a Constitutional Amendment on equal rights for women."[13]

The NWP used endorsement by both party platforms to persuade the Senate to vote on the ERA in 1946. Democratic opponents argued that the 1944 platform only supported "*a* constitutional amendment on equal rights," not *the* ERA. While the ERA did not pass, citation of the platforms prompted ERA opponents to redouble their efforts to remove endorsement in 1948. The National Committee on the Status of Women recommended to both parties that they drop the ERA in favor of a plank for "sound and effective legislation to remove discriminations against women." But its chair, Mary Anderson, no longer had the official position, or the connections, she had during the Roosevelt administration, and the director of the DNC Women's Division, India Edwards, was pro ERA. This time inertia favored the NWP. The Platform Committee of the Republican Party re-adopted the ERA plank unanimously, candidate Thomas E. Dewey endorsed the ERA shortly thereafter, and the fact that their convention preceded the Democrats' that year kept the ERA in the Democratic platform over some opposition. As before, Emma Guffey Miller and Perle Mesta worked on the Democrats, and Mesta also contacted her personal friends on the Republican Platform Committee. At the Republican convention the NWP campaign was run from the hotel room of Pearl Sayre, an NWP Council member who was also a Republican national committeewoman from Oklahoma and an RNC vice chairman. Phone calls to delegates were made in her name. The NWP was well aware of the importance of these people. Anita Politzer wrote Mildred Palmer that the successes of 1944 and 1948 would not have occurred without insider support. She gave particular credit to Perle Mesta, who had friends in both parties.[14]

The 1952 and 1956 platform hearings saw little open opposition. Emma Guffey Miller sat on the Democratic Platform Committee in 1952, and Jane Todd, a New York assemblywoman and staunch ERA supporter, chaired the relevant Republican subcommittee. Since Eleanor Roosevelt had withdrawn her opposition to the ERA in 1951, and India Edwards still headed the DNC Women's Division in 1952, Miller was even able to strengthen the Democratic plank by adding the word "endorse" to recommend, though the Platform Committee did refuse to add "unqualified" in front of "equal rights." The Republican plank was not changed, and there "wasn't the first concern" about its inclusion among platform committee members, in part due to the solid support of such insiders as Katharine St. George (R. N.Y.), Sayre, and Todd.[15]

Nonetheless, the NWP did not rest easy, and in 1956 once again solicited its members to write to their state's Platform Committee members. Alice Paul claimed that there was a move by the Women's Bureau to substitute an equal pay plank for the ERA, even though the Bureau's director, Alice Leopold, was an ERA supporter, and both planks had been in both parties' platforms since 1944. Katie Louchheim, the Director of the Office of Women's Activities of the DNC, was an ERA opponent, but she ignored the Democratic platform. The hearings were short and perfunctory, with no one speaking in opposition, though Walter Reuther of the United Auto Workers sent written testimony to both parties which included opposition to the ERA. BPW President Hazel Palmer testified favorably at both conventions. The president of the National

Federation of Republican Women testified in favor of the ERA, and her organization endorsed it the following month. Miller chaired the Democratic hearing as a member of the Platform Committee, which she orchestrated as an ERA rally. Resistance was expected on the drafting committee as it contained among its members arch ERA foes Congressman Emmanual Celler (D. N.Y.) and Mildred Jeffrey of the United Auto Workers, whom Alice Paul described as a "violent opponent" of the ERA. But the vote was unanimous and nothing changed. Both major parties endorsed the ERA *and* equal pay.[16]

In 1960 support for the ERA began to erode as opponents renewed their active opposition. The Republican Party platform contained the usual endorsement plank, but only after the Resolutions Committee, at the urging of former BPW President and Platform Committee member Hazel Palmer, removed an amendment added by a subcommittee to the effect that any constitutional amendment should not affect "present health and safety laws." The Democratic platform contained a compromise that removed explicit reference to a constitutional amendment while retaining support for "legislation which will guarantee to women equality of rights under law, including equal pay for equal work." Esther Peterson, representing the Industrial Union Department of the AFL-CIO had proposed the opponents' standard plank from the 1940 Democratic platform with an additional sentence on equal pay. This was accompanied by a statement to the Platform Committee signed by the officers of twenty-four organizations urging that the ERA plank be dropped. In addition to the AFL-CIO and several unions, the opponents included the American Civil Liberties Union, the liberal Americans for Democratic Action, American Federation of Teachers, American Nurses Association, the Women's Division of the Methodist Church, and the National Councils of Jewish, Catholic, and Negro Women. Privately, the NWP stalwarts were "shocked" by the "lack of mention of women and their place in the scheme of things" but publicly they put on a positive face by declaring that the language included the possibility of a constitutional amendment to bring about equality under law. They did not comment on the irony of the platform's title: "The Rights of Man." To compensate, Emma Guffey Miller altered a letter from candidate Kennedy to make it appear as if he had endorsed the ERA and had it typed at the DNC on campaign stationery. The campaign chose to ignore the forgery, but it and more traditional ERA opponents were unhappy with both the platform and the NWP. Esther Peterson later said the platform was an "embarrassment" to President Kennedy.[17]

This embarrassment was removed in 1964, even though Kennedy was no longer President and President Johnson had been a sponsor of the ERA. The Democratic platform that year merely advocated "ending discrimination" and affirmed support of "legislation to carry forward the progress already made toward full equality of opportunity for women as well as men." Johnson didn't want any debate over or changes in *his* platform so the draft that was, as usual, prepared beforehand was pushed through a convention he controlled. The sections on women were written under the supervision of Secretary of Labor Willard Wirtz, who shared Peterson's antipathy toward the ERA. Nonetheless there were hearings to build a record, at which Peterson cited the opposition of the President's Commission on the Status of Women to an amendment as the means to obtain legal equality. Emma Guffey Miller submitted testimony from twenty people in favor of the ERA even though Johnson had told her privately in June that the plan was to "tie our plank in with the whole Civil Rights issue." The NWP blamed Peterson and complained that the platform committee was stacked against any plank endorsing the ERA.[18]

The ERA was not actually dropped from the Republican platform, but it did disappear, even though *all* of the candidates for the Republican nomination in 1964 (Goldwater, Rockefeller, Scranton, Smith) and all of the women on the Platform Committee supported it. The committee voted its approval of the 1960 plank, but "in the interest of brevity," the 1964 platform did not "repeat the commitments of . . . 1960." Instead it incorporated "into this Platform as pledges renewed those commitments which are relevant to the problems of 1964." In place of explicit support for the ERA, the 1964 Republican platform pledged "continued opposition to discrimination based on race, creed, national origin or sex." Although the NWP considered this a victory, it was a frustrating one. It tried to have "our 1960 Plank printed as a footnote, or in an appendix to the 1964 Platform" without success. Republican officials said they would try to help, but RNC staff insisted that would be amending the platform, which could not be done. The following year, when the NWP sent out its standard ERA pledge cards to be signed by supportive Members of Congress, they no longer contained excerpts from the party platforms endorsing the ERA.[19]

After the 1968 conventions, even the NWP had to publicly admit that the ERA had been dropped by both parties, despite its support by all but one of the major candidates for President that year, and in spite of testimony from Betty Friedan, president of the new National Organization for Women. An ERA plank was submitted to the Republican Platform Committee by NWP Vice Chair Louise Gore, who was also a State Senator from Maryland and head of the women's division of the Nixon campaign, but it was passed over in favor of an expression of "concern for the unique problems of citizens long disadvantaged in our total society by race, color, national origin, creed or sex." The Democratic Platform didn't go that far. Although NWP members were on the Platform Committee, and claimed their presentation was well received, the only concession was the insertion of the words "and other" in the pledge "to wipe out once and for all the stain of racial and other discriminations." For the first time since 1936 any mention of women was completely omitted from the Democratic platform. The NWP found this "incomprehensible."[20]

It's more comprehensible if one looks at the pattern of appearances and disappearances of the ERA and other references to women over the entire

period since 1920. By and large the issues and the language in the party platforms reflect the prevailing opinions of the time. Occasionally one party is pre-
scient enough to take a position on an issue whose time has not yet come. More
often issues remain in the platform after their time has passed. Both of these
happen when there is key insider support and no real opposition. Party platforms usually show a "cyclical movement" in which one party leads on an issue,
and the other follows within an election or two. Occasionally a party plank will
break from past pronouncements and those of the other party, usually when
new interest groups or coalitions gain sufficient power at the quadrennial conventions to make their appearance felt. But most changes are gradual, reflecting the essential stability of the important groups within each party.[21]

The references to women in the platforms of the twenties and thirties
reflect the prevailing concern with protecting women in industry, and a distaste
for the fact that women must work at all. This key goal of the Progressive
Movement outlasted Progressivism. Planks on equal citizenship rights for resident American women married to aliens (Dem. and Rep. 1920) and the Child
Labor Amendment (Dem. and Rep. 1924) were 1920s issues. It is in citizenship
rights that the idea of equality first slips in, though it is also given an honorable
mention in the rhetoric, not the programs, of both parties in 1928. By and large,
the Republican Party was the leader on issues involving equality. "Equal pay for
equal service" first appears in the Republican platform of 1920, though it was
limited to the federal government. The Democrats finally followed in 1928,
without the limitation. After that, equal pay disappears from the platforms of
both parties until 1944 (it was a war issue) when it became a permanent fixture through 1960 (the Equal Pay Act was passed in 1963). The right of married women to keep their jobs first appears in the Republican platform of 1936
(though it's expressed as a general opposition to legislated employment discrimination), followed by a more specific reference in the Democratic platform
of 1940 (after the federal discriminatory provision had been removed in 1937).[22]

The 1940s, dominated as they were by the war, showed a clear shift away
from protecting women and in favor of equal opportunity. Once again the
Republicans led the way, with the 1940 Republican platform reflecting the
future and the 1940 Democratic platform the past. The opposition to the inclusion of the ERA in the 1940 GOP and 1944 Democratic platforms was
defeated by the major public campaign for the ERA that the NWP orchestrated, with endorsements by major newspapers and public figures. The coalition of anti- organizations, mostly reform women's groups and the Women's
Bureau, had not been influential in the Republican Party for many years and
was by now politically weak. In contrast, several NWP members were active in
both parties and had established personal relationships with key members which
they used to gain votes. By the 1960s it was the NWP that was weak, while
labor's traditional opposition to the ERA had been trained on the platforms by
Esther Peterson after she became a CIO lobbyist in 1957. Consequently, the

ERA was finessed out of the platform of the Democratic Party, and faded out of the Republican's. In 1964 the Republican Party followed the Democratic lead not by removing the ERA, but by not printing it. Since it is not influenced by organized labor as are the Democrats, had there been much of a public outcry, this omission would probably not have stood the test of time. But the NWP was isolated, the older generation of Republican supporters was gone—even Representative Katherine St. George (R. N.Y.) had lost her seat in 1964—and the new generation did not see the ERA as relevant. In 1968 the plank that had come in as front page news went out without even a notice.

Replacing the ERA was the inclusion of "sex" in the litany of prohibited discriminations. Again the Republican Party was first when its 1956 platform vowed to continue the "fight for the elimination of discrimination in employment because of race, creed, color, national origin or sex," and the Democrats followed with similar sentiments in 1960. Both repeated this pledge in 1964, but in 1968 the Democrats dropped specific mention of sex discrimination, even though new troops were carrying the feminist banner at the hearings. Perhaps the GOP would have followed the Democrats' lead and dropped this issue in 1972 as it had on the ERA, had public consciousness of sex discrimination remained at the same low level. But the rise of a new movement for women's liberation ensured that this did not happen.[23]

· Eleven ·

Claiming a Share:
Presidential Appointments of Women

Political women have shared with political men the belief that appointments to government office matter. Although party women have had much more influence on which women get what than women without party service, that has not deterred other women from trying to influence the appointments process. Despite public statements that merit is all that matters, most Presidents have listened and responded to outside pressure. Many have told their personnel staffs to be "representative," though what that means varies with each administration.

Appointments matter for several reasons. Although the spoils system was undermined by the advent of civil service, participants in the political system still regard patronage as part of the process. Not only is it good politics to reward supporters, but it's good administration to put into key positions people who are sympathetic to the President's philosophy and subject to his (or her) control. Appointments also have symbolic value. They signal to members of a particular group, at least those who consciously identify with that group, that the President considers them important. And they signal to group leaders, when consulted on the appointment, that their opinion is important. But group demands for appointments, whether by party or interest group organizations, are rarely made for purely symbolic reasons. Those who do not claim a share strictly as a reward for their contribution to victory demand it in order to affect public policy. There has been a pervasive assumption, rarely tested by serious analysis, that in order to have a voice in government, one must also have a presence.[1]

Women have been no exception. One of the arguments for giving women the vote was that their participation would lead to more honest administrations. But even anti-suffragists thought women had a place in public affairs and should be appointed to positions where they could influence issues within their sphere. Breckinridge identified three other reasons frequently advanced for putting women into public office: 1) Women's domestic experience particularly suited them for positions involving care of or decisions over other women, children, the aged and infirm. 2) Women should have a role in legislation because it often affected families, their sphere in the world. 3) Holding office would "widen women's general opportunity for employment."[2]

EXPANDING WOMEN'S SPHERE

Education was the first field in which women moved into public office. Since the proper raising of the child was acknowledged as within woman's sphere, supervision of the schools was a natural expansion of her role after primary education became a public responsibility. Many states let women vote on school matters long before they could vote on anything else. Even when they could not vote, women were elected or appointed as school administrators. Estelle Reel, elected Wyoming's superintendent of public instruction in 1894, was appointed by President McKinley to be superintendent of Indian schools in 1898. By 1896 there were enough women in high public service positions for a survey of "The New Woman in Office," though it included elected women.[3]

Some women received appointments from state governors in the nineteenth century, especially for unpaid positions. Commissioners of charity or supervisors of schools were considered proper places for women's influence. Josephine Shaw Lowell was appointed to the New York State Board of Charities by Governor Tilden in 1876 and served until 1899. Mary Elizabeth Lease was appointed to the Kansas Board of Charities in 1893, but only lasted one year. In 1893, as the Depression deepened, "the Governor of Illinois appointed [Julia Lathrop] to the Illinois Board of Charities, a commission charged with oversight of the county institutions that Lathrop already abhorred." He also appointed Florence Kelley as a factory inspector.[4] This pattern continued in the twentieth century, with some expansion to positions overseeing women's prisons and public welfare.

Robyn Muncy has described how women built a "female dominion" as the policy experts on women and children. Women's clubs moved from investigating the problems of women and children to lobbying for new laws to improve schools, food, sanitation, the lot of women in industry, etc. At the same time, educated women created new professions for themselves that required "new areas of expertise in which they did not compete with men for jobs or training." When state governments created commissions and investigating agencies within these areas, women's clubs lobbied for the appointment of women experts. For some time, the calls of "patronage" and "expertise" competed for priority in state appointments. The next governor of Illinois gave Kelley's and Lathrop's jobs to party men as patronage appointments.[5] As the Progressive Movement compelled governments to make merit the main criterion, women moved into professional positions in government. Indeed they were so successful that by the late 1920s male professionals decided to retake the territory.

PRESIDENTIAL APPOINTMENTS

When the Children's Bureau was created in 1912, President Taft selected Julia C. Lathrop of Illinois to be its director. She was reappointed by President Wilson and served until 1921. Wilson appointed nine more women beginning in 1917, when demands for suffrage were escalating. The most prominent of these was Annette Adams who became U.S. attorney for the Northern District of California and was promoted to assistant attorney general in 1920. Elizabeth Bass, the director of the DNC Woman's Bureau, frequently wrote Wilson urging him to appoint, or not appoint, various women. She opposed the choice of Mary Anderson to head the Bureau of Women in Industry (later the Women's Bureau of the Department of Labor) and supported other women for various commissions than the ones that Wilson picked. In addition to the expected appointments of women to the Women's Bureau and the D.C. Juvenile Court, Wilson began the tradition of appointing women to the Civil Service Commission and the U.S. Employees' Compensation Commission. Between 1917 and 1953 there was always one woman on the latter commission—usually as chairman. The Civil Service Commission had five women between 1920 and 1961. Helen Gardener, a NAWSA vice president, was appointed by Wilson specifically "to secure in that body the woman's point of view."[6]

After Gardener's death in 1925, President Coolidge promised to nominate a woman to replace her. He was petitioned by both the LWV and the NWP to pick one of their own. His choice was Jessie Dell, chair of the NWP's Government Worker's Council, who had served in the War Department for twenty-five years. Her confirmation by the Senate was nearly thwarted by the Woman Patriot Publishing Company, whose letterhead proclaimed it was "Opposed to Feminism and Communism." It persuaded the Senate to reopen its confirmation with a petition claiming Dell was planted by the NWP, a socialistic organization. Until then, the NWP had not been tarnished by the Red Scare as had the organizations in the WJCC. Now it found itself accused of using "sinister pressure" on the Senate as part of its "concealed design to establish a tyranny of women in the guise of equality." Although Dell was confirmed and the NWP continued to press for appointments for its members, it did so quietly to avoid more such publicity. It did obtain some minor positions and appointments to international conferences, but it wasn't until the Truman administration that the NWP again secured a major one.[7]

Government jobs were one more arena in which feminists and reformers battled. When Harding indicated that he would appoint another woman to replace Adams as assistant attorney general, the NWP promoted Gail Laughlin, then an attorney in California and president of the new National Federation of Business and Professional Women. Katherine Edson, one of California's most respected progressives, wrote in opposition, calling her an "extreme feminist" and a troublemaker. Mabel Walker Willebrandt, who had made her reputation as a public defender with special responsibility for cases involving women, got the appointment. She was not affiliated with either side of the feminist/reformer rift, though she had lobbied the state legislature for a married woman's property bill.[8]

Harriet Taylor Upton felt Harding was quite sympathetic to her pleas to appoint more women and would have appointed even more had he lived longer. Sometimes she spoke to him about jobs for specific women, such as postmistresses, but usually when she "talked with the President about a woman . . . I did not discuss with him at all who the person should be provided he appointed a woman."[9] Under the Coolidge administration there was no one who thought getting more appointments for women was part of her job. His only major appointment was Genevieve Cline, who became the first woman on the federal bench when she joined the U.S. Customs Court in 1928. However the number of women in lower level positions, such as collector of customs and recorder of land grants, slowly rose during these Republican administrations. Women postmistresses, a common patronage job, "increased from little more than one-tenth in 1920 to nearly a fifth in 1930" though women were concentrated in the smaller towns.[10]

The possibility of a woman in the Cabinet was frequently speculated about during the 1920s. Harding said he would appoint a woman to head a Department of Education or Social Service, if either was created. Expectations were high that President Hoover would claim "first" honors since so many women had worked for his election. Assistant Attorney General Mabel Walker Willebrandt was widely promoted, especially by drys. Social reformers campaigned for Grace Abbott, graduate of Hull House and chief of the Children's Bureau, to be his Secretary of Labor. Republican women speculated that he would appoint RNC vice chair Sallie Hert as secretary of the interior, or Margaret Dreier Robins as Secretary of Labor. Although he was deluged with letters and petitions, Hoover chose no woman. Willebrandt was not even discouraged from resigning her old job, though Abbott was retained in hers.[11]

When Roosevelt became President he placed patronage for women in the hands of Molly Dewson, head of the DNC Women's Division. This began a tradition that lasted almost thirty years of the top party woman in the country being designated the "gatekeeper" for Presidential appointments of women. Upton had been influential while head of the RNC's Women's Division, "constantly trying to see what the party could do for women which would be helpful and creditable to the party," but she didn't have the veto power over major appointments of women that Roosevelt ceded to Dewson. Dewson had her own ideas about who was suitable for what. Her nod did not merely go to those who had supported Roosevelt, though they weren't ignored, but to those who would support the social reform programs to which she had devoted her life. Her goals were to "demonstrate the value of women's contributions to the public sphere" and "to build up the women's side of the Democratic party." Her first and highest achievement was the appointment of Frances Perkins as Secretary of Labor. Indeed, Dewson "practically made a career out of promoting Frances Perkins," pressing Roosevelt to appoint her as state industrial commissioner while governor of New York, and organizing a national lobbying campaign on her behalf even before Roosevelt was nominated for President.[12]

In the two years she devoted to placing women in federal positions, their numbers leaped. Dewson began with a list of sixty-five "key women" whose political work deserved recognition and went on from there. The "firsts" for which she was responsible in addition to Secretary Perkins, were U.S. Circuit Court of Appeals (Sixth Circuit) Judge Florence Allen in 1934; Ruth Bryan Owen, appointed minister to Denmark in 1933 after being defeated for reelection to Congress; Director of the Mint Nellie Tayloe Ross; and Assistant Treasurer Marion Glass Banister. She also pushed women into positions of responsibility in the new independent agencies set up to administer the New Deal, and found jobs for hundreds of politically active women as postmistresses and collectors of customs in the states. In her autobiography she listed over one hundred women whose jobs she was responsible for. Many of Dewson's protégées in turn recruited other women. The highest concentration of women employees in the New Deal was in the Departments of Labor, State, and Treasury and in the independent agencies. Unfortunately, the latter were also the first to be cut back when Congress sought to curb the New Deal. The more stable agencies saw very little turnover, and when Dewson left the DNC in 1937, women lost their advocate. The only major Presidential appointments after her departure were Daisy Harriman as minister to Norway (1939) and Marion J. Harron as judge of the U.S. Tax Court (1942). Several attempts to promote women already in government service failed, including a small boomlet to appoint Judge Allen to the Supreme Court when two vacancies appeared in 1939.[13]

Dewson's technique was to identify deserving women and the jobs for which they would be best suited. In this endeavor she relied on advice from Nellie Tayloe Ross, Eleanor Roosevelt, and Sue Shelton White. Although these women had been party activists, other party women, such as Emily Newell Blair, complained that women who had worked hard in the campaign were getting less attention than they deserved. Once Dewson found a "match" she used her knowledge of decision making points in the Roosevelt administration to know whom to persuade and whom to pressure. When necessary she generated letter writing campaigns from women in her social reform and political networks throughout the country and planted newspaper stories. And she relied heavily on Eleanor Roosevelt, whose intervention was often crucial. Once *her* women were taken care of, Dewson had no objection to the "girlfriends" of the boys receiving a few crumbs, but used her okay as leverage for other concessions. "I would also be opposed to Mrs. O'Conner's being given a job," she wrote Eleanor Roosevelt on April 27, 1933, "until the Kentucky men promise to give 50–50 representation in the Party to the women and to allow the women to choose their own state vice chairwoman."[14]

Although Republican women obviously did not benefit from federal appointments in a Democratic administration, that did not stop them from making their claims on Republican governors. At the RNC meeting of November 29, 1938, Marion Martin told the national committee members:

> What we need from you is this: We have elected a good many Republican Governors. We are proud of it. We think the women had quite a bit to do in the matter of their election. We feel we are not asking too much if we ask you to consider giving some jobs to women.[15]

When Truman took over in 1945, several prominent Democratic women importuned him to give jobs to women. Eleanor Roosevelt wrote letters and the chair of the DNC Women's Division, Gladys Tillet, made suggestions. Nothing worked until India Edwards assumed the job of top Democratic woman and gatekeeper. She had supported Truman since 1944 and he listened to her. One of the first things she did was to *prevent* Marion Martin, recently ousted from the RNC, from being appointed to the Federal Communications Commission because she didn't think Truman's first major female appointee should be a Republican. The first woman on that commission, Frieda Barkin Hennock, was finally appointed by Truman in 1948. Edwards was more successful than Tillet in placing women in part because of her relationship with Truman, and in part because she used the same techniques that Dewson had used. Tillet had prepared lists of qualified women for the President's perusal.[16] Edwards looked for a qualified woman for every position that opened up and organized a campaign to clear her candidates with those whose political approval was required and to sell them to the President. She summed up the process and her tactics:

> Getting anyone appointed to high office is such a complicated and difficult procedure that few persons understand it. When a woman is involved, the appointment is even more complicated and difficult. For every post there are many names presented by state political leaders, Congressmen and interested organizations. The Cabinet member, who will make the recommendation to the President, the White House staff personnel and the chairman and vice chairman of the National Committee must make every effort to see that anyone accepted by the President as a nominee is able to convince the Senate committee empowered to turn down the nominee or present his or her name to the full Senate for confirmation, that he or she is well qualified for the post and politically acceptable to the political leaders of his or her state. Anyone who has not been concerned with this kind of patronage work finds it hard to understand why it is so hard for a woman to be named to a high-ranking post. Someone interested in her appointment has to work day and night, sometimes subtly and tactfully, sometimes in an aggressive way, and

always with patience. This effort must be backed up by the knowledge that until the appointment has been confirmed by the Senate it may not materialize no matter how certain it seems along the way.[17]

The importance of political support is illustrated by an appointment that never happened. Mabel Walker Willebrandt achieved a major reputation as a litigator in her seven years as assistant attorney general in charge of prohibition cases. It was enhanced during her subsequent thirty years of private practice. She was active in Republican Party politics during her entire career, initially as a public campaigner for Republican Presidential candidates in the twenties. Her aspiration to be a federal judge was never achieved, despite her acclaim while a federal prosecutor and her record in arguing over forty cases before the Supreme Court. Harriet Taylor Upton urged Harding to appoint her in 1923 when women were still viewed as a political force, and believed he would have made the appointment had he not died in August. A possible appointment by Coolidge was stymied by the opposition of one of her home state's (California) Senators. He didn't want any federal appointments to go to the other Senator's protégés. Both Willebrandt and Florence Allen were mentioned by the *Christian Science Monitor* for a vacancy on the Supreme Court in 1930, but Hoover considered neither. Nor did he accede to Willebrandt's request that he recommend her for a judgeship to President Truman in 1948. By the time Eisenhower was elected, Willebrandt had soured on her original progressive Republicanism and supported his rival, Taft, for the nomination. After Harding died she never again had the insider support and absence of political enemies necessary to get a high federal office.[18]

Even with insider support, women faced barriers unknown to men, including the fact that they were women. In the 1940 Presidential campaign Wendell Willkie promised to put a man rather than a woman at the head of the Department of Labor. He thought this would aide his candidacy. Edwards' memoirs contain numerous descriptions of her campaigns to get appointments for women. Some of the problems particular to women she described included an unwillingness of men (particularly judges) to have a female colleague, allegations of lesbianism, opposition of the national committeewoman of the candidate's state on the grounds that she had not worked long and hard enough in the party, and expectations of qualifications and a virtuous lifestyle higher than those for a man. Her campaign to have Judge Allen appointed to the Supreme Court was vetoed by Chief Justice Fred Vinson because a woman in their midst "would make it difficult for them to meet informally with robes, and perhaps shoes, off, shirt collars unbuttoned, and discuss their problems and come to decisions." She finally persuaded Truman to appoint Mrs. Eugenie Anderson as ambassador to Denmark despite the fact that her husband was alive and well; protocol had no place for the *husband* of an ambassador.[19] She also had her own standards, which were described by a columnist and reprinted in her memoirs:

India has only three "musts" for her protégés. First they must be capable. . . . Second, they must be presentable. Mrs. Edwards is not interested in the Phi Beta Kappa or a diamond-in-the-rough type. She also bars those who rely on willowy hips and sidelong glances to win friends and influence people. . . . Third, the candidate must be acceptable to their Senators.[20]

Edwards was the first Women's Division head to favor the ERA, and as a result she got on much better with Emma Guffey Miller than had her predecessors. Miller was always pushing NWP activists for positions in the government and Edwards helped her with two of them in 1949. One was easy, as Perle Mesta was a friend and fundraiser for Truman and he wished to reward her. The only problem was thinking up a suitable position for someone who had never held a paying job and whose reputation was based on being "the hostess with the mostest." Edwards persuaded Mesta and Truman that she should be the minister to Luxembourg. There was some opposition in the Senate, but she was confirmed and was warmly received.[21]

The appointment of Burnita Shelton Matthews to be the first woman federal District judge (one level lower than the Circuit Court judgeship which Florence Allen held) was hampered by the fact that she was a Republican. As general counsel to the NWP during the twenties she had not been a major Republican activist, but she had authored such pamphlets as "What the Republican Party Has Done for Women." Initially Edwards told the NWP that such a major appointment of a Republican was impossible, but relented when Miller persuaded her that the DNC was supportive. Since Matthews had lived and practiced law in the District of Columbia for decades, she was proposed for a position in the D.C. judicial district. With no elected officials, there was one less barrier to surmount. Support was obtained from her "home-state" Senators from Mississippi, who were Democrats. After a six month campaign, in which Matthews employed an assistant to line up endorsements, her name was included among four women Edwards recommended to Truman at a time that he was to name twenty-seven new judges, though she only expected one of the women to be appointed. The day before the final list was to go to the Senate, Edwards found out that no women were on it. She decided to go to bat for Matthews alone and wrote letters to the DNC chair and to Truman pleading for the appointment because "there will be unfavorable reactions if not one woman is among the twenty-seven new judges nominated." When the list was released the following day, Matthews was on it.[22]

Matthews's appointment removed her from active work for women, though she did hire a series of women law clerks, but Mesta's did not. In her autobiography she wrote that while minister to Luxembourg she was frequently asked to speak in Western European countries and liked to talk about women's rights.

I was asked to give a speech of this sort in Switzerland, but the sponsors, who had seen newspaper accounts of my previous talks, told me I must not mention women's rights. Women did not even have the vote in their country, they said, and there was no use in reminding them of the fact. I replied that if I could not speak about women and women's rights, I wouldn't speak at all. And I didn't.[23]

Mesta's feminism did not hamper her diplomatic career, but her party affiliation did. Although she had once been a Republican and still had many friends in the Republican Party, including newly elected President Eisenhower, when the Democrats lost power, so did she. Two months after his inauguration

> I received a perfunctory cable from John Foster Dulles saying that my resignation had been accepted, effective April 13. I had been fired with the minimum two weeks' notice—although Luxembourg was not sent another minister for eight months. Later I found out that President Eisenhower had been under heavy pressure from the women's division of the Republican National Committee to get rid of me. . . . The reason for this, I determined later, was that the Republican women's organization didn't want a Democratic appointee to be representing the U.S. Government at the coronation in England the first week in May.[24]

As had Truman, Eisenhower vested control of women's appointments in the head of Republican women at the RNC. Like India Edwards, Bertha Adkins had no illusions about the difficulties that faced her. Although she didn't have the trust and confidence of Eisenhower that Edwards had from Truman, in some ways her task was easier, as Eisenhower let the RNC clear patronage appointments. Although Adkins was not responsible for his most prominent selections, such as Oveta Culp Hobby to be secretary of health, education and welfare, Ivy Baker Priest to be treasurer, and Clare Booth Luce to be ambassador to Italy, she was behind the women appointed to many lesser positions.[25]

Adkins's techniques were similar to Edwards's, though from her own description she was not as aggressive in "matching" and "selling." She solicited recommendations of qualified women from state political leaders, nonpartisan women's organizations and her own network, engaged in preliminary screening to make sure they were suitable and available, then made them known to White House staff, cabinet officers and others whose endorsements were needed. Although not as "pushy" as Edwards, Adkins was numerically more successful; indeed her ultimate achievement was her appointment as undersecretary of H.E.W.[26] According to historian Cynthia Harrison

> the General's appointments of women exceeded Truman's in most instances. In roughly the same amount of time, Eisenhower named twenty-eight women to Senate confirmed posts, compared to twenty for Truman. . . . Eisenhower also edged Truman out slightly in terms of "first" appointments—ten for the General and nine for Truman. . . . The Republican bested Truman's annual average of Senate-confirmed appointments by .5—2.75 up

from 2.25. The percentage of women serving in both Senate-confirmed and
other appointments equaled Truman's 2.4 (84 out of 3491 total positions).[27]

Adkins could achieve more with less effort than Edwards because she was
working with a more receptive audience and the pool of potential applicants
was larger. Well-educated, professionally employed women with careers were
more likely to be Republicans than Democrats. After the 1952 election
Republican women argued that Ike owed his election to women. Republican
women had lobbied for decades for more appointments, using the argument
that giving important appointments to women would win the support of
women voters and grassroots party workers. Since this could never be proved,
the only measures of success were the voiced opinions of party women and
publicity. Eisenhower's appointments achieved both. Indeed they were so highly
publicized that the DNC was worried about their effect.[28]

President Kennedy did not alleviate this worry, but neither was he concerned about the DNC. Margaret Price, DNC vice chairman in charge of
women, had no influence, nor did she use the effective tactics of her predecessors. Instead she prepared a list of jobs in which she thought women could serve
and attached to it the resumes of about two dozen women. She did form "sort
of a search committee" from those women Kennedy did appoint by asking them
to look for others, but they "had a difficult time finding people that he could
consider appointing." Kennedy's initial appointments were so few that journalists rebuked him, and Democratic women such as Eleanor Roosevelt and Emma
Guffey Miller wrote protest letters and sent him names of women he should
appoint to something. Kennedy's only notable appointments were Esther
Peterson as assistant secretary of labor, Eugenie Anderson to be minister to
Bulgaria, and Sarah Hughes to be a federal district judge in Texas. Anderson had
already been an ambassador under Truman, and Hughes, a state judge, was
appointed at the behest of Vice President Johnson. In July 1963 an aide, Clayton
Fritchey, suggested that a few notable appointments would generate good publicity, but Kennedy ignored this. Harrison has calculated that while his Senate-
confirmed appointments were only two-thirds those of his predecessors, women
still held the same 2.4 percent of all appointed positions. Although Kennedy's
failure to place women has often been explained as due to his personal attitude,
Harrison argues that it was primarily a function of his personnel selection system. In his drive to hire "the best and the brightest" he looked for relatively
young achievers in places women were unlikely to be found—elite universities, major corporations, and top law firms. This process created a form of institutional discrimination that even Esther Peterson, who also tried to place some
women, could not overcome.[29]

This quickly changed after Johnson was sworn in as President by Judge
Sarah Hughes on November 22, 1963. Although a party man himself, he did
not look to the decimated DNC for advice. Instead he relied on that of an old

family friend, Liz Carpenter, who was already in the White House as Lady Bird's press secretary. In her memoirs she describes how she was recruited to find more women in January of 1964.

> On one memorable day, President Johnson decided that women were being discriminated against in getting high level government jobs. . . . I was waiting at the elevator . . . when the doors opened. He stepped out, and I found myself propelled along by his Long Arm toward his office. . . . He was talking as fast as he was walking.
>
> "Anna Rosenberg Hoffman tells me that we need more women in government," he said, accepting it as a fact, and embracing it as his cause, because of his great respect for this long time friend and top management expert. "Call Esther Peterson and both of you be at the Cabinet meeting at ten o'clock in the morning, and we'll do something about it."
>
> We were there. We had worked all night on our presentation. And we assured the Cabinet that all brains didn't come in male packages.
>
> Then Johnson took over. "I'm sure there are plenty of high level positions available for qualified women in your departments. And I am sure there are many women already on your payrolls who have been waiting for promotions for a long time. So, go back to your departments and see what you can do. Then, report back to me next Friday how many you have placed."
>
> Those were the magic words—"report back to me." The program began to move. All over the government, personnel officers who had been ignoring their women employees for years suddenly had a wolflike gleam in their eyes. The hunt was on.[30]

After the Cabinet meeting Johnson told the directors of twenty independent agencies to hire more women and told the press he intended to appoint fifty women to policy-making posts. Although most stories on women rarely got past the women's pages, this one made it to the front page—at least in Washington.[31]

> By April 1965 a good many appointees, all female, were sworn in by a woman, Judge Burnita Matthews. The President in his informal remarks, expressed the hope that all the husbands in the room would find it in their heart to forgive him by next November.[32]

Johnson kept up his campaign to end "stag government" for almost another year, then his attention turned elsewhere. According to Zelman, this interest was stimulated in part by his personal experiences with "women doers" and his belief that they should play a greater role in the government. But it was also prompted by his need to create favorable publicity and loyal supporters in an administration that was not yet his.[33] Therefore, he did not stop with an announcement. According to Carpenter

> The President joined the talent search for women. . . . He was determined to get more women in government. Every time there was a vacancy, I was

asked to supply some women's names. The problem about luring women into government is that though people talk a lot about it, there are few women who can put aside family obligations, or leave a more lucrative business position. But I didn't want to pour cold water on the President's enthusiasm. We searched, and we found, quite a few—more than 150 new appointees and eight hundred promotions within a few months. We followed every lead, no matter how fruitless.[34]

Not all of these appointees were to the significant policy making posts Johnson had targeted; in fact the statistics were blown up for publicity purposes. Despite this tactic, and the fact that Johnson didn't have the clean slate of a newly elected President, there was sharp improvement in the numbers of women serving, and, more important, in the attitude towards women's claims for inclusion. Esther Peterson, whose own agenda for women did not give any priority to appointments, felt Johnson's campaign was an affirmation of the work of the President's Commission on the Status of Women. Women's organizations were enthusiastic. The personal attention of the President gave women's employment issues a status never before seen.[35]

After Nixon was elected President, Elly Peterson, former chairman of the Republican Party in Michigan, became assistant chairman at the RNC. As the top Republican woman, she said more jobs for women would be her priority. Although she had ridiculed Johnson's program as "very definitely a political gimmick," she was quick to propose her own. Her plan was to "go after a specific job, finding the right woman" for that job—the same strategy her most successful predecessors had used. In 1970, with most top jobs filled, she lamented her lack of success.[36] However, the task of recruiting women for the Nixon administration had been given to Pat Hitt, a Californian who had organized Women for Nixon-Agnew. A few weeks after the election she gave the White House a list of 250 women "eminently qualified for some position." She later said:

> But the unfortunate part of it was: in all honesty, neither Bob Haldeman nor John Ehrlichman were very sympathetic toward women. What they did they did because of my needling or something like that. But they really weren't gung ho. I think Nixon was more than they, but was too busy to do much, and not really all out. Pat [Nixon] had been a housewife. His whole experience had been mostly with housewives. That's what he really thought of women, mostly, as.
>
> I'd have to say I really didn't have the greatest cooperation in the world, though [Richardson] and Finch were both strong for women. They both helped.[37]

Hitt was successful with some appointments, including one for herself as assistant secretary at the Department of Health, Education and Welfare. But she was not the only one pushing for appointments for women. Indeed it seemed that organized women everywhere were pressuring the Nixon administration to appoint more women.[38]

Presidential appointments of women was the one area in which there was steady progress from Taft's appointment of Lathrop in 1912. The only decline was under President Kennedy. Women also increased in the civil service and Congressional office staff. Over the years women slowly filtered into the government, in part because the civil service relied on objective tests and quantifying qualifications, and in part because the lower pay made the jobs less attractive to men, and the regular hours made them more attractive to women. Few of these women knew the long history of women's struggle, and only some were conscious of how much discrimination there was. But when the women's liberation movement emerged in the late 1960s, they were well positioned to push for its goals. Once the rights of women became a public issue, for the second time in the twentieth century, government feminists came out of the woodwork and acted as social change agents from the inside. They made it possible for the new feminist movement to bring about a small revolution in public policy on women in only a few years.[39]

· Twelve ·

Conclusion

If one could plot women's entry into politics on a graph, one would see long periods of slow but steady increase, punctuated by a sharp rise for a few years, followed by a bit of a decline and another slow, steady increase. Some women were actively campaigning in the 1840s and 1850s, but it was in the 1880s that women's work in the political parties flowered, and even then it was more in the minor than the major parties. This crested in 1900, as the Populist Movement ended and the Fourth Party System settled into place. For the next twelve years, women moved more slowly into party work in those locales where they could move at all. They were particularly active in the full suffrage states and in major urban areas. The party woman, as a distinct type from the feminist and the reformer, took her place on stage, but not equally in every place. In some areas, such as Colorado and New York City, party women became conspicuous in the 1890s and were quite ordinary by 1900. In others, especially the South, they would be barely noticeable until well after suffrage. In 1912, the Progressive Movement brought women into all the parties in numbers too big to ignore. Full suffrage for women moved from the back burner onto the national agenda. The Suffrage Movement maintained its momentum even after the Progressive Movement dwindled. But by 1920, when equal suffrage was achieved, Progressivism was in steep decline and a backlash was growing. The new woman voter entered the electorate in an era that discouraged any political activity outside of narrow, conventional channels.

Different groups of political women had different trajectories. For reformers, 1924 was probably their peak, as measured by legislative successes, nationally and in the states. Afterwards the backlash wore down their optimism, their drive, and their success rate. The star of Republican women rose until the election of 1928, the "year of the woman voter," when large numbers of women who had not previously voted supported Hoover and Prohibition (or opposed Smith and Tammany). Democratic electoral successes in the 1930s dampened their opportunities, though their level of activity flattened more than declined. For Democratic women, 1936 was their best year. Their curve was flatter, with success measured by the fact that more Democratic women attended their party's national convention and voted than had in the past. During and after World War II the participation of women rose in both parties, but not recognition of their work. As for feminists, their electoral and legislative success was small in the period under study, but their success in raising the consciousness of parties and politicians probably peaked in the mid-1940s when the ERA was put in the platforms of both major parties and the Senate cast its first vote on the proposed Equal Rights Amendment. Their trajectory was long and low, with barely a peak at all. The feminist hour would not come until the 1970s, with a new social movement cluster, a new party system, and new feminists.

When women joined the electorate, the parties actively recruited women while simultaneously discouraging any participation in non-party organizations with a woman's agenda. Women were wooed with specialized bureaus aimed at mobilizing and educating the woman voter to support each party's candidates and a message aimed at what each thought were women's special interests. The Republicans were particularly vigorous in this pursuit, and were also blessed with greater financial and organizational resources than the Democrats. The "golden era" for party women was in the 1920s; while feminists and reformers were attacked, they were courted. Later, party men began to be more selective even of loyal party women, preferring the pure party woman to those who had other agendas, and the woman who followed more than the woman who led.

During the 1930s, 1940s, and 1950s, party women used two means to slowly but steadily organize women: putting them on the party committees and creating separate political clubs for women. The first gave select women official titles and responsibilities, and the second provided a place for any woman willing to work. A key difference between the official committees and the clubs was that the clubs elected their own leaders, while committeewomen were generally chosen by men. Although both parties used both strategies, the Democrats emphasized the former and the Republicans the latter. From the perspective of the mid-1960s, neither strategy was particularly successful in giving women influence or recognition, though one could argue that both were quite successful for the parties since women did lots of work for few rewards. Nonetheless, for party women, the Republican strategy was a bit more successful. Women had a little more say in the Republican Party than among the Democrats.

Party women were usually careful not to alienate men. Women who would not cooperate, or complained too much, were simply removed and replaced with more compliant women. The successful party woman emphasized that women were to serve the party, not themselves or any special interest. Consequently their public image was one of worker bees, who gratefully made coffee but not policy. However, this is not the whole story. Party women also fought big battles and little ones to establish their own place in the parties and prepared many women to play a larger role should opportunity present itself. Party women educated women for politics, legitimated their presence in political work, undermined the assumption that politics was a male preserve, and infiltrated the political organizations. By the 1960s, women were the workhorses of the major political parties. While most still served party men and male candidates, party women had left the foyer, permeated other rooms in the political house and taken over the basement. They made a place for themselves, and made themselves indispensable.

Democratic and Republican party women competed with each other and used their competition as leverage within their respective parties. While both specialized in the organization of women, Republicans displayed more gender consciousness and sex solidarity than did Democrats. Their magazines, their campaign literature, and their general admonitions were more likely to treat women as a group, with specific interests or a special viewpoint, deserving of special representation, than those of the Democrats. Although women of both parties were constantly told to put party loyalty above all else, to serve the party faithfully and ask nothing for themselves, they in fact did make demands, and usually backed them up not by threats to sit on their hands, but by allusions to a mythical woman voter who would support the party that elevated the women within it. Because more women voted Republican, the banner of the "woman voter" was more likely to be waived by Republican party women. Democratic women more often claimed her to be a myth, alleging no difference between the sexes in party loyalty. In both major parties, slowly, over time, women's numbers among workers and their appointments in governments controlled by their party increased. Their rewards were never equal to the work party women did—men always got the lion's share—but they did increase. Insofar as data are available, Republican women got a little more than did Democratic women. They got more recognition, more jobs, received more appointments, elected more officials (especially state legislators), and had a few more votes at party conventions.

OPPORTUNITIES AND CONSTRAINTS

When women entered the political house they initially thought they would be accepted as full and equal partners by party men. As in a marriage, their duties and roles would be different, but their contribution would be important enough for the men to solicit their advice and pay attention to their concerns. It took several years for party women to realize that they were naïve. The experience of women in the parties, as in marriages, varied considerably; a lot depended on the proclivities of individual party men. Working in the parties was like a traditional marriage and, for most women, not a very good one. Men were still head of the household and made all the important decisions, but, as in a bad marriage, women did not run the home; they were largely servants.

Women initially thought that just as the vote made them full citizens, allowing them to elect their government along with men, obtaining positions on the official party committees would make them colleagues, selecting candidates and exercising leadership along with men. It took some time for women to learn that party committees were not where the real decisions were made. Political parties, more than most other entities, rely on informal networks rather than formal institutions to educate acolytes, spread information, and reach decisions. These networks were male. There was no formal route for entry. As in a sorority, fraternity, or private club, those on the inside opened the doors to those whom they chose, or those whom they felt necessary to choose. Only occasionally were these doors opened to women. Women, often chosen by men, might sit on party committees or head women's divisions, but with occasional exceptions, their advice was not solicited or paid much heed.

Of course, party men welcomed women as workers. They assigned them the more difficult tasks that men did not want and denied them the rewards that party men took for granted. When Republican women enlisted in New York City campaigns in the 1890s, the men sent them to canvass the most intransigent Democratic districts that were loyal to Tammany Hall. When New York Democratic women began to organize on their own in the mid-1920s, they skirted the big city machines for traveling throughout rural New York looking for Democratic women in Republican territory. When Harriet Taylor Upton hired women to recruit and organize Republican women in the early 1920s, Republican men wanted them only to work in the South and other areas where Republicans were hard to find. Molly Dewson's strategy for the Presidential campaigns of 1932 and 1936 was to mobilize Democratic women in the Northern rural areas that were traditionally Republican. Despite these difficulties, party women accepted the challenges thrown to them and often excelled.

For a few years after women gained full suffrage in each state, some local parties sought out some women to run for some offices. When they learned that voters were not eager to see women expand on their traditional role by reaching for offices held by men, the parties lost interest. There was no electoral advantage in challenging prejudices. At the same time, by attacking "sex solidarity" as unpatriotic, the parties contributed to the demise of female consciousness necessary to chip away at those prejudices.

The male response to party women was pretty much the same as their response to women's invasion of other male domains: a few women were rewarded as individuals, but the doors of opportunity were closed to women as a group. They were invisible, except when wanted for work. After the thrill had worn off, women met the same fate in the parties as they had in male-dominated occupations, or the paid labor force in general: overt resistance was replaced by accommodation, stratification, a decline in status, and lower compensation. "Politics," Emily Newell Blair wrote in 1937, "is a man's game. A woman on her own had as much chance in them as a Dupont to sit in President Roosevelt's cabinet."[1] The main difference between the political world and the business world was in the rhetoric. Since our democratic values praise participation and glorify representation, male resistance was thickly wrapped in words of flattery and approbation. Party men did not publicize their distaste for women as leaders and office holders, though they conceded it in private. Instead they praised women while ignoring and isolating them in the lower ranks and female ghettos.

There are two routes to influence in electoral and party politics: the individual and the organized bloc route. The individual route requires sponsorship. This is particularly important for outsiders who are not members of the dominant group. Someone on the inside has to anoint the aspiring politician as desirable to open any doors. Sponsors often educate their protégés into the real world of politics as well. The stronger the sponsorship, the more ready the acceptance, and the easier the access. The alternative route is to organize a bloc of people with a valuable resource—votes, time for party work, money—who are willing to act together. This has been the classic route to ethnic success in politics. But empowerment requires group solidarity and resources. Both of these routes were fraught with problems for women and neither was readily available.

Sponsors were hard to find. By and large men would not sponsor women; even when the men were willing, sexual mores made such relationships suspect. Thus the women with the best chance for sponsorship were family members of politicians. Even when their husbands or fathers did not sponsor them directly, the associations built up over the years and the family name served to legitimate them to the male politicians as well as to voters. Above all else parties want to win elections, and politicians know that voters favor familiar names. Of the first fourteen women elected to Congress (between 1917 and 1932) six were widows of incumbents.[2] The rest included: one who succeeded her father,[3] the daughter of a Congressman who replaced her husband after his conviction for violating Prohibition,[4] Ruth Bryan Owen, the daughter of a three-time Democratic candidate for President,[5] and Ruth Hanna McCormick, the daughter of one Senator and the widow of another.[6] The only real success among the remaining four was Mary Norton, whose sponsor was Boss Hague. The others were short-term Members of Congress; one served only one term and two served two terms.[7] Only three of these first fourteen women served long enough to have political careers and gain enough seniority to have any political influence.[8]

The two women elected governor in the 1920s, and the third elected in 1966, replaced their husbands: one had been impeached; one died while running for reelection; and one could not succeed himself but in fact ran the state.[9] Of the first ten women to serve as U.S. Senators, five were appointed to fill vacancies and seven served less than a year. While not all seven were widows, all were elected or appointed solely to hold the seat open for the men who were expected to run for it. All three who served a full term succeeded their husbands. Hattie Caraway (D. Ark.) initially filled her dead husband's term but was reelected after Senator Huey Long (D. La.) became her sponsor and campaigned vigorously for her. Margaret Chase Smith (R. Maine) succeeded her husband in the House, then ran for the Senate on her own. Maurine Neuberger (D. Ore.) replaced her incumbent husband when he died two days before the deadline to file for reelection.[10]

Men did not sponsor just any woman. They sponsored women who were loyal and accommodating. While party men might tell women that to get ahead they had to act like men, by and large male politicians did not feel comfortable with women who acted as they did; they preferred women who brought traditional feminine qualities to the political sphere. Thus, with rare exceptions, the women tapped to run for electoral office or who otherwise acquired political influence were not women who were aggressive, personally ambitious, or who had competing loyalties. Belle Moskowitz was typical of the few women with real influence in the post-suffrage era. Her biographer (and granddaughter) described her approach to advising Governor Al Smith as that of a

> sister, mother, wife; controlling her environment through subtle manipulation; loyal and selfless, or at least to all appearances not self-interested—by following the models women had traditionally observed in the private sphere of the family Belle Moskowitz remained in safe territory. Although her sphere was now public, she conformed to roles that made herself and Smith feel comfortable.[11]

Elected women recognized the necessity of being what men wanted them to be. In a 1939 speech on women in politics, Judy Weis, who would later serve two terms in Congress (R. N.Y.), simultaneously lamented women's lack of progress and recommended "a little bit of feminine helplessness applied at the right moment" over "strong arm methods" for women to achieve proper recognition. Maurine Neuberger commented in 1951 when a member of the Oregon state legislature: "in politics . . . the woman intruder is most effective when she is seen but rarely heard, . . . [w]ithout sacrificing any of the qualities which make women attractive in men's eyes."[12] These women were not exceptions; successful female politicians saw conforming to men's expectations as the way to get ahead in a man's world.

While sponsorship may work for those individual women who can inherit, marry, or otherwise find sponsors, it creates a classic free rider problem. A free rider is someone who benefits from the collective goods gained by the efforts of others. Often the free rider doesn't even realize that the work of others made the collective good possible and thus feels neither responsibility nor gratitude to the group, let alone the active individuals, which made her success possible.[13] Thus women who attained political influence through male sponsors were more likely to be accountable to their sponsors, or the party organizations through which they worked, rather than to women as an abstract group or the women's movement. For a group to hold members accountable to it for their actions is a long-standing problem faced by all identifiable groups, but it has been a particularly difficult one for women. Thus sponsorship by an insider in politics may be an individual route to influence, but it does not lead to group influence. In order to attain group influence, there must be an organized group supported by group consciousness.

Politicians expressed fear that women would organize independently of the parties. They campaigned hard against the formation of the LWV and charged the NWP with fostering "sex antagonism." Since women had been voting for many years in many states prior to 1920, party men knew that women did not vote as a bloc. But party men and women wanted to be the sole organizers of women voters and workers because that was the way to control them. The same people who spoke against the LWV and the NWP were eager to organize separate women's bureaus, departments, etc. as long as they were *within* the parties. They lectured women constantly about the importance of party loyalty.[14]

Separate institutions in the parties did provide women with a place of their own. Some women were able to use them as a base from which to launch political careers. Caroline O'Day (D. N.Y.) and Helen Gahagan Douglas (D. Calif.) headed the women's divisions of their state parties; Judy Weis (R. N.Y.) ran that of her county; and Ruth Baker Pratt (R. N.Y.) was a co-leader of her district. Katherine St. George (R. N.Y.) was a rare female county chairman. All these women were elected to Congress. Nina Otero-Warren was head of the New Mexico Republican Party women's division when she ran for Congress, and lost, in 1922.[15] But separate institutions brought burdens as well as benefits. On the one hand they provided opportunities for women to learn organizational skills, practice leadership, and develop group cohesion. But while they could run their own organizations, they could never exercise leadership over men, who ran the parties. Separate bureaus and clubs could be a political base, but they could also be a ghetto.

The structure of our electoral system created more barriers to group mobilization. Our legislative bodies are based on representation by geographic district, not identity, interests, or ideology. The single member district favors candidates who represent a majority, not a minority, of voters in a district, or at least a majority of the voters in the dominant party's primary. Ethnic groups could organize and elect one of their own when they were geographically concentrated—and even then each new group took decades to crack the barriers of existing party leadership. Women are geographically dispersed, making it hard to mobilize the majority necessary to be elected. Women are more likely to win elections in multi-member districts, but these have not been common.[16]

This structural problem was compounded by the lack of party competition in most places in the Fourth and Fifth Party Systems. When local parties put together slates of candidates, they include representatives from identifiable groups to appeal to their voters. But only if they face real competition from another party do they seek out new voters; otherwise they slate candidates representing vested interests and turn out the votes they know they can rely on. Women's claim for representation was undermined by the fact that they were the last group to be enfranchised; by the time they could vote, extensive areas of one party dominance made women's votes unnecessary to win local elections.[17]

Added to structural factors were social and economic ones: voters thought men better suited to hold office, women's competency was constantly undervalued, their resources were limited and "sex solidarity" repeatedly attacked. The fact that most women live with men and share common interests worked against the group consciousness necessary for group mobilization. While women, at least middle-class women, often had more time than men, they had considerably less disposable income in a system where it was accepted that "money was the mother's milk of politics." All these factors made the organized bloc route to political power rarely more than wishful thinking.

WHAT WOMEN ACCOMPLISHED

If becoming an organized force in politics was not possible for women between 1920 and 1970, what then did political women do?

First of all the presence of women helped civilize politics, as it was intended to do. During the nineteenth century, campaigns were a form of ritualized combat between competing organizations. The outcome was determined not by persuading voters to support a party's candidates, but by persuading partisans to come to the polls and opponents to stay away. Party conventions were marked by spitting, smoking, drinking, and fighting. Elections were all-day festivals rife with liquor and rowdiness. "Key men" took "floaters" to vote early and often. Votes could be purchased or otherwise controlled. Opposition voters could be discouraged through threats and intimidation. Since each party supplied its own ballot with only its own candidates on it, party men generally knew how many were actually cast, and by whom.

When women began to vote, change began to happen. Smoking and spitting were banned from party meetings. Polling places were moved from the saloon, barber shop, and livery stable into churches and schools.[18] This was accelerated when women also became election judges and poll watchers. Tyler's description of how change happened in New Orleans applies to other places at other times:

> These incidents illustrate the threatening and decidedly masculine atmosphere still prevalent at the polls in the 1940s. In places where swaggering policemen boldly flaunted their allegiance to one faction, where mayhem was not uncommon, where the simple act of placing a paper ballot into a wooden box could be accompanied by taunts, leers, threats, or even fisticuffs, numbers of women certainly hesitated to cast votes. Having other women

physically present at the polls served to allay hesitations and fears in many women voters. For this reason, the women activists of New Orleans deserve credit for changing with their very presence the threatening atmosphere at the polls and making it possible for all women to vote with greater peace of mind.[19]

And, Tyler might have added, women made it easier for men as well.

What happened in the polling places also happened in other rooms of the political house, but more slowly. The addition of women was part of a vast change in political culture that took place gradually over several decades. The "domestication" of politics that Baker describes taking place in the nineteenth century didn't stop in 1920.[20]

Second, party women accelerated the shift in campaign techniques from emotional appeals to an emphasis on facts. Women initially campaigned through parlor meetings, with women speakers and question periods. Soon candidates came, pursuing the woman's vote by subjecting themselves to her scrutiny. According to Louis Howe, FDR's chief political advisor, women "revolutionized the character of our campaign literature." He observed that "the average man . . . is willing to accept his leader's statements without further inquiry," but "if you are going to gain a woman's vote, . . . you must have some real arguments." He credited the DNC women's division for the Rainbow Fliers and the LWV for promoting candidate debates. Louchheim noted in 1958 that women "popularized the candidate questionnaire, the coffee hour, the political panel discussion, and they demanded the audience question period."[21] Women insisted that candidates offer the voters more than patronage and pablum, and sometimes they did.

Finally, the women who went into the parties did in the twentieth century what organized women—especially the WCTU and the women's clubs— did in the nineteenth century: they laid the foundation. They prepared women for political work and enlarged their sphere of activity. They did this through education, legitimation, and infiltration. When the political opportunity structure opened up, women in both parties were ready to take advantage of it. Just as suffrage moved rapidly after 1910, when it could ride the coattails of the Progressive Movement, women's entry into politics moved rapidly after 1970, as it rode the wave of the Sixties movements, and especially the Women's Liberation Movement. If the foundation had not been laid in the preceding decades, none of these movements would have facilitated women's entry into the political house. But if these movements hadn't come along, women would still be waiting for the woman's hour that never came. Party women did what was possible to do in the conservative period between social movement clusters. And by doing what was possible, women went into politics the same way they got suffrage: slowly and persistently, with great effort, against much resistance, a room at a time.

Sources, Citations, and Abbreviations

The full citations for most of the sources used are in the References. Sources fully cited in the notes are not separately listed in the References. These include manuscript collections and short published items cited only once, such as newspaper stories and brief periodical references, particularly ones that have no specific author. The References contain a few publications not specifically cited in the notes that provide valuable background or overviews. They are not cited in the notes because they cover areas for which I did my own research in original materials. Few party women left personal papers, but in the nineteenth and early twentieth centuries party activities were heavily covered by newspapers, which often had partisan leanings. Wherever possible, newspaper citations include section number (if there is one), page, and the column in which a story or quote appears in this form: V:3:2. Some newspapers use letters instead of section numbers. If there is no section, only arabic numerals are used. Many newspaper clippings were found in archives and in morgues. These rarely had section or page numbers, and more rarely column numbers. I cited all information available to me. The newspaper morgues I mined are described below.

When citing manuscript collections where I looked at the original documents I also cite the library in which they are held. When citing those on microfilm, I do not cite the library in which I saw them, because they are available elsewhere. The Library of Congress has both the originals and a microfilm copy of the early Presidential papers and does not allow researchers to look at the actual papers. For those, I cited the Reel number rather than the Box number, but indicate that they are held in the Library of Congress.

All election data not otherwise cited are from the *Historical Statistics of the United States: Colonial Times to 1970*, from the section on Elections and Politics, Series Y 1-271, pp. 1067-85. Turnout computations are based on the voting age population for a given year and state. Restrictions due to age, citizenship, and sex were factored into the calculations. Indirect ones, such as registration requirements and poll taxes, which often curtailed voting by specific racial or ethnic groups, were not.

National Party Conventions is the source of all uncited information on the conventions, candidates, and delegate votes. This book is updated every four years by Congressional Quarterly, Washington, D.C. Page numbers do not remain the same, so none are cited. Information not repeated in each edition is cited to a specific year and page.

National Party Platforms, compiled quadrennially by Donald Bruce Johnson and Kirk H. Porter, was the source for most of the information in these documents. The page numbers remain the same in each edition, so I did not include a year of publication in the citation. I did discover a few omissions so other sources are occasionally cited.

Some other reference books were particularly useful for background information. Deserving of special mention are *Political Parties & Elections in the United States: An Encyclopedia*, ed. by L. Sandy Maisel and Charles Bassett (New York: Garland 1991); *The National Party Chairmen and Committees: Factionalism at the Top*, Ralph M. Goldman (Armonk, N.Y.: Sharpe, 1990); *History of American Presidential Elections 1789–1968*, Arthur M. Schlesinger Jr., general editor (New York: Chelsea House, 1971, 4 vols.); *History of U.S. Political Parties*, Arthur M. Schlesinger Jr., general editor (New York: Chelsea House, 1973, 4 vols.).

The following abbreviations are for sources or organizations used more than once.

AIPO—American Institute of Public Opinion, otherwise known as the Gallup Poll.

Bancroft—The Bancroft Library at the University of California at Berkeley. The Regional Oral History Office sponsored two series of interviews relevant to this book, one of Suffragists and one of California Women Political Leaders. I read most of them, but not in Bancroft, as copies are available in other libraries.

BDE—Brooklyn Daily Eagle, the largest circulation newspaper in Brooklyn, N.Y., is indexed from 1891 to 1902. Its morgue in the Brooklyn Public Library covers roughly from 1904 until it died in 1955. It was an independent Democratic paper.

BWA—Black Women in America: An Historical Encyclopedia, ed. Darlene Clark Hine, (Brooklyn, N.Y.: Carlson, 1993).

ChiTrib—The *Chicago Daily Tribune* began publication on June 10, 1847. Always a Republican paper, it shifted from radical Republican during the Civil War, to progressive through WWI, to arch conservative during the New Deal. It supported woman suffrage.

CHS—Chicago Historical Society.

CSM—Christian Science Monitor, founded in 1908 by Mary Baker Eddy, founder of the Church of Christ, Scientist. Never partisan, it featured articles of general public interest for an international audience. Its index begins in 1960.

DCPL—Public Library of the District of Columbia, Washingtonia Collection.

DCWF—Democratic Congressional Wives Forum, formed by Katie Louchheim in 1953. See References for full cite.

DB—The *Democratic Bulletin* was published by the WNDC from February 1926 through September 1933. It was called *The Bulletin* through August of 1929.

DD—Democratic Digest, official publication of the Women's Division of the Democratic National Committee from March 1935 to February 1953. From October of 1933 through February 1935 it was published by the WNDC.

DNC—Democratic National Committee.

ER—Equal Rights—The official newsletter of the National Woman's Party; began publication on February 17, 1923, and ceased in 1954. Initially it was a weekly, but in the 1930s cut back to semi-monthly and then monthly. It was succeeded by an occasional *NWP Bulletin*. Both are in the NWP Papers on microfilm.

ER and ER papers—Eleanor Roosevelt (1884–1963); a collection of her papers is on microfilm.

FB—The *Fortnightly Bulletin* was published by the Women's Division of the DNC from July 8, 1922, through November 4, 1924. An incomplete set is in the WNDC archives.

FDRL—Presidential library of Franklin Delano Roosevelt in Hyde Park, N.Y.

HSTL—Presidential library of Harry S Truman in Independence, Mo.

HWS—History of Woman Suffrage. See References for full citations of all six volumes. In the notes, the volume number precedes and the page number follows the source.

LAT—The *Los Angeles Times* began publication on December 4, 1881. It is a Republican paper.

LD—*Literary Digest*—a weekly compendium of ideas and information from other periodicals published from March 1, 1890, to February 19, 1938.

LoC—Library of Congress. Microfilmed papers cite the Reel number and original papers cite the Box number for the collections used.

LWV papers—Papers of the League of Women Voters. The originals are in the LoC. Microfilm is widely available.

MSRC—Moorland-Springarn Research Center, Howard University, Washington, D.C.

NAW—*Notable American Women.* There are four volumes; the volume number precedes and the page number follows the source. Although the authors signed each biography, none are listed in the References. The first three volumes include women who died before 1950. The fourth volume adds women who died before 1975.

NPC—*National Party Conventions*, published quadrennially by Congressional Quarterly.

NR—*The National Republican*, a national weekly review of American history, public policy, and public affairs; was an informal organ of the RNC from 1918 through 1924. An incomplete set is on microfilm.

NWP papers—Papers of the National Woman's Party. Originals are in the LoC; microfilm available elsewhere.

NYH—The *New York Herald*, which published from May 6, 1835, until it merged with the *Tribune* on March 19, 1924. NYPL has a handwritten index covering from 1835 to 1917 and partly to 1918. It was a Republican paper.

NYHT—The *New York Herald-Tribune*, published from March 19, 1924, until April 24, 1966. It continued as a Republican paper.

NYPL—The Research Library of New York Public Library at Fifth Avenue and 42nd St. in New York City.

NYSun—The morgue of *The* (New York) *Sun* in NYPL covers from roughly WWI until it merged into the *New York World Telegram* in 1950, through there are a few items from earlier years. *The Sun* was an independent newspaper with Republican leanings.

NYT—The *New York Times* is indexed from September 18, 1851, until the present and is widely available on microfilm. It was a conservative Democratic paper but independent of the New York City Democratic machines. It opposed woman suffrage even after New York enfranchised women in 1917.

NYTrib—The *New York Tribune* published from May 10, 1841, until it merged with the *Herald* on March 19, 1924. An index from 1875 to 1906 is on microfilm. It was a Republican paper and opposed woman suffrage.

PP—*National Party Platforms*, compiled quadrennially by Donald Bruce Johnson and Kirk H. Porter; Urbana: University of Illinois Press. The latest platforms are added to each edition, but the page numbers remain the same.

RMN—*Rocky Mountain News* began publishing in Denver, Colorado on April 23, 1859. It was a Democratic paper, pro woman suffrage, and quite sympathetic to Populism.

RNC—Republican National Committee.

RP papers—Papers of the Republican Party, Part I: Meetings of the Republican National Committee, 1911–1980, Series A, 1911–1960.

RWI—*The Republican Woman*, published monthly by the Illinois Republican Women's Clubs from 1922 to 1931. Its name officially changed to *The Republican Woman of Illinois* in May of 1930.

RWP—*The Republican Woman*, published monthly by Republican Women of Pennsylvania, Inc. from 1923 to 1941.

SFC—The *San Francisco Chronicle* began publication on January 16, 1865. It was a Republican paper with a progressive orientation.

SFCall—The *San Francisco Call* published from December 1, 1856, until it became the *San Francisco Call and Post* on December 9, 1913. It was an independent newspaper with Republican leanings.

SFEx—The *San Francisco Examiner* began publication in January 16, 1865. It was an independent newspaper, but its owner, William Randolph Hearst, was a Democrat.

SI—Division of Social History, Political Collection, Smithsonian Institution, Washington, D.C.

UCLA—Papers found in the Special Collections of the research library of the University of California at Los Angeles.

WDN—*Women's Democratic News* was published monthly by the Women's Division of the New York State Democratic Party from 1925 through 1935.

WJ—*The Woman's Journal* was started by Lucy Stone and Henry Blackwell in 1870 and published weekly. They also founded the American Woman's Suffrage Association. In 1910 it became the official publication of NAWSA, which did not subsidize it as regularly as promised. In 1917 it was purchased by the Leslie Woman Suffrage Commission, established by a bequest from Mrs. Frank Leslie, and merged with two other suffrage publications.

WC—*The Woman Citizen*, subtitled "A Weekly Chronicle of Progress," took over from *WJ* on June 2, 1917. After ratification it became a monthly magazine. In 1928 it resumed the title of *Woman's Journal* and kept it until folding in mid-1931. During the last ten years of its life the League of Women Voters subsidized the magazine in exchange for two pages of news, but this was discontinued in 1930 when the LWV decided to put out its own publication.

WES—Washington, D.C. *Evening Star* or *Sunday Star*, a daily newspaper that published from December 16, 1852, through August 7, 1981. Its morgue in DCPL covers roughly from the 1930s through 1972. Non-partisan in origin, it became very conservative by the twentieth century.

WP—The *Washington Post* of Washington, D.C., started on December 6, 1877, as a Democratic daily. It was purchased at a bankruptcy sale in 1933 by a rich Republican and is run by his descendants.

WNDC—Women's National Democratic Club, maintains archives in their clubhouse at 1526 New Hampshire Ave., NW, Washington, D.C. 20036.

WNRC—Women's National Republican Club, located at 3 W. 51st St., New York, NY, 10019, does not have an organized archive. The papers and scrapbooks in its file cabinets and closets are not publicly available although I was permitted to read them.

WRNY—*The Woman Republican* published its first issue on January 13, 1923, and its last in December of 1941. Originally a biweekly sponsored by the New York Republican Women's State Executive Committee, it became a monthly put out by the state Women's Division in 1926 when its first publisher terminated. In 1933 the New York Republican State Central Committee withdrew financing, but the magazine continued for another eight years, supported by the personal resources of its editors.

WTUL-MDR papers—Papers of the Women's Trade Union League and its Principle Leaders, for Margaret Dreier Robins, are on microfilm. The original Robins papers are at the University of Florida.

Notes

NOTES FOR THE INTRODUCTION (PAGES 1 TO 7)

1. Harriman 1923, 351.

2. O'Neill is the chief exponent of "the failure of feminism" school, 1969, viii. See also Lichtman 1979, 238: "If rank and file women did not simply vote the preferences of their fathers, husbands, and brothers, neither did they become the infantry of a renewed campaign for progressive reform." Terborg-Penn 1978, 237: "Despite the rhetoric of woman suffrage as an instrument of reform, political observers now know that suffragists failed to organize an effective mechanism for mobilizing women's voting strength to solve society's problems, for the female vote had very little effect on the politics of the nation."

3. Wheeler 1995, 253.

4. Both Frank Kent, an experienced political journalist, and Louis Howe, FDR's top political advisor, wrote that politicians assumed that women would vote like their fathers or husbands; Kent 1923, Chapters 26–27; Howe, 1935. Indeed one of the main arguments against woman suffrage was that allowing women to vote would double the cost of an election without affecting the outcome.

5. Wilson 1921. Drexel 1923. "Woman Suffrage Declared a Failure," 1924. Russell 1924. Tarbell 1924. Selden's 1924 *Ladies Home Journal* article gave a balanced view.

6. See statements in *WC*, Sept. 8, 1923, 7–11, 23; Nov. 3, 1923, 14–15; March 22, 1924, 7–9, 29; April 5, 1924, 8–10, 30; April 19, 1924, 14–16; May 17, 1924, 24; May 31, 1924, 19, 33; June 14, 1924, 16. Longer treatments in Breckinridge 1933, 1972; League of Women Voters 1927; Smith 1929. See also Cox 1997, 100–102 for a list of forty "Assessments After National Suffrage." Catt 1925, pointed out that most of these negative judgements came from people and publications that had opposed woman suffrage.

7. *BDE*: "Divorce Women and Politics Is Advice of Sage of N.Y.U.," May 24, 1931, 13:4; "Moley Calls Women Failure in Politics," June 4, 1931, 28:6. Lippmann 1928. Quote in Ross 1936, 215. But see the anniversary editorial in *Ladies' Home Journal*, August 1930, 22, a suffrage opponent whose current editor observed that suffrage's "great leaders did not make the rosiest promises" and were "wise" not to do so.

8. For discussions of these trends see Baker 1984; Lebsock 1990; Skocpol 1992; Sklar 1993; Andersen 1996.

9. This is a generic statement; if one looks at distinct groups of women in different states, the timing is different. Religion, region, race, and class affected when, where, and what women engaged in politics. The term "feminist" did not become common until 1910; Cott 1987. I am using it somewhat anachronistically to refer to those women for whom women's

rights were paramount to other concerns, and who worked for women's independence, autonomy, and equality. Stanton and Anthony were most certainly feminists, even though they did not adopt the label.

10. First quote from address by Emily Dean to the third annual convention of Illinois Republican Women's Clubs, Nov. 30, 1925; Folder 8, Emily Dean Papers, CHS. She was president of the Illinois Republican Women's Clubs, 1924–38. Second quote from Pratt 1928, describing her experiences as New York City's first woman alderman. Her article is one of many that urged women to act as individuals even though they were treated as females.

11. *Notable American Women* only includes women who died before 1975, so a couple more may be added to future volumes. Classification of the women who died before 1950 is in Vol. III, 723, 272, and of the rest is in Vol. IV, 764, 765, 771–72. The suffragists who were also party workers were: Clara Shortridge Foltz (R. Calif.), Mary Garrett Hay (R. N.Y.), Harriet Taylor Upton (R. Ohio), Sue Shelton White (D. Tenn.), Emily Newell Blair (D. Mo.), Minnie Fisher Cunningham (D. Tex.), Molly Dewson (D. Mass.), Emma Guffey Miller (D. Pa.), Cornelia Bryce Pinchot (R. Pa.). Jeannette Rankin (R. Mont.) was the only suffragist elected to Congress, serving two separate terms. Nellie Nugent Somerville (D) served four years in the Mississippi state legislature and Gail Laughlin (R) twelve years in Maine's. The editors of *NAW* did not list as suffragists some politically active women for whom suffrage was only a small part of their life work, such as Ruth Hanna McCormick (R. Ill.) and Katherine Philips Edson (R. Calif.). There were many suffragists active in their own states who weren't prominent enough to make it into *NAW*. Identification of these and analysis of their subsequent political activity requires more research.

12. Because *NAW* lists different types of reformers, it's harder to assess the potential universe. One hundred women are listed as social and civic reformers, forty worked in temperance, prohibition, and repeal, forty-three in labor and labor reform. Some women are in more than one category, and several women worked in other types of reform work. Civic and social reformers who were party workers are: Katherine Philips Edson (R. Calif.), Annie LaPorte Diggs (P. Kans.), Belle Moskowitz (D. N.Y.). Caroline O'Day was elected to Congress (D. N.Y.). Party women involved in alcohol reform were: J. Ellen Foster (R. Iowa), Mary Garrett Hay (R. N.Y.), Helen Gougar (various parties, Ind.), and State Senator Belle Kearney (D. Miss.). The advocates of Prohibition Repeal, Pauline Sabin (R. N.Y.) and Emma Guffey Miller (D. Pa.), were party women first. Other reformers in *NAW* who were active in the parties and/or elected to public office include: Ida B. Wells-Barnett (R. Ill.), Louise DeKoven Bowen (R. Ill.), St. Leg. Anne Wilmarth Thompson Ickes (R. Ill.), Eleanor Roosevelt (D. N.Y.), Mary Church Terrell (R. D.C.), St. Leg. Crystal Bird Fauset (D. Pa.), Irene McCoy Gaines (R. Ill.), Daisy Lampkin (R. Pa.), Mary Elizabeth Lease (P. Kans.), Alice Dunbar Nelson (R. Del.).

13. Baer 1993.

NOTES FOR CHAPTER ONE (PAGES 9 TO 25)

1. Reichley 1992, quotes on 4, 5. Reichley also calls these the republican and liberal traditions, terms I avoid because they are loaded with other meanings. He argues that "the most important institutional reason for the continued dominance of the two-party system in the United States is the electoral college," 1992, 33.

2. Freeman 1986, quote on 329.

3. The party systems are described by Chambers and Burnham 1967. Critical elections were first defined by Key 1955, 3–4, as "a sharp alteration of the pre-existing cleavage within the electorate ... [that] seems to persist for several succeeding elections." Kleppner 1987, 18, defines it as "a macrolevel phenomenon involving an abrupt and durable change in the partisan balance at the electoral level." Burnham 1970, devotes his first ten pages "Toward a Definition of Critical Realignment." See Sundquist 1983, Chapters 1–3, for a detailed explanation of all of these concepts. Political scientists rediscovered realignment in the 1950s by analyzing voting statistics. Contemporary observers knew that something unusual was happening, and even used the term "realignment." They seem less aware than scholars that rapid realignment was usually the result of long term changes; Key 1959; Gamm 1989, 3–4. Carmines and Stimson, 1989, have called such gradual change "issue evolution."

4. Sisson 1974, 11, attributes the term to Jefferson.

5. Formisano 1981.

6. Formisano 1981, 67. The Anti-Masonic Party held the first national political convention. A few months later the National Republican Party held the second. The Democratic Party elected the first national chairman and committee.

7. Ireland's potato famine drove over a million Irish immigrants to the U.S. after 1847, expanding the electorate and prompting strong anti-Irish attitudes. Henretta 1987, 426.

8. Reichley 1992, 121.

9. Kleppner 1981, 124. The seven Republican states were Minnesota, Iowa, Nebraska, Kansas, Vermont, Rhode Island, and Maine; Kleppner 1979, 38.

10. Kleppner, who has devoted his professional life to exploring the historical relationship between religion and party, distinguishes between pietists and ritualists to explain why some Protestant denominations voted Democratic along with the Catholics; 1979, 180–97. For my purposes simple distinctions are sufficient. On Jews see Fuchs 1956, 32.

11. Kleppner 1987, Chapter 4. The 1892 Populist Presidential candidate won in Kansas, Colorado, Nevada, and Idaho. In 1894, as the Depression deepened, the Populist vote increased by 40 percent, sending six Senators and seven Representatives to Congress. Although the populists nominated Bryan for President in 1896 to avoid splitting the "free silver" vote, they ran a separate candidate for Vice President—Southerner Thomas E. Watson. The People's Party ran presidential tickets for the next three elections, but never received more than 0.8 percent of the popular vote. "Populist Party" in Maisel 1991, 849–51. The Eastern Democrats were "goldbugs" and could not remain in a party favoring silver. On New York City, see Goldschmidt 1972, 520–32.

12. Burnham 1981, quote on 164. Sundquist 1983, 161. Burnham 1970. Cotter 1991, 1048. There was great variation by state, with turnout in Southern states sometimes only in the single digits. Reynolds 1988, demonstrates how New Jersey Democrats clung to power by emphasizing local concerns and distancing themselves from the national party.

13. Lubell 1956, 31–42. Andersen 1979. Henretta 1987, 726–29. Some have argued that newly mobilizing ethnic women contributed more than men to the New Deal realignment; Lubell 1956, 42. This is disputed by Gamm 1989, 162–66, who microanalyzed ethnic voters in Boston and concluded that ethnic men mobilized for 1928, while ethnic women waited until 1932 and 1936. No one has examined the Western states to see who were the newly mobilized voters, but Gosnell 1937, 1, pointed out that after 1929, "voters in the New England states and the rural sections of the northeast ... changed their political attitudes least." Between 1928 and 1936 "Maine shows a shift of only 10 percent away from the Republican party" while California shifted 34 percent.

14. Lubell 1956, 49. Lubell identified 1935 as the year in which class consciousness drowned out religious, racial, and cultural cleavages among the working class. Gamm 1989, 55, noted that Jews were an exception. In the 1920s class divided Jewish votes; after 1936 virtually all Jews voted Democratic.

15. "States' Rights Party" in Maisel 1991, 1074–75.

16. Carmines and Stimson 1989, describe the change in Congressional voting patterns as "issue evolution." My interpretation is elaborated more thoroughly in Freeman 1995, 1999.

17. Freeman 1998.

18. Suffrage referenda in McDonagh and Price 1985. Religion of temperance and suffrage leaders in Giele 1995, 85, 132; that of anti-suffragists in Jablonsky 1994, 53–57.

19. Robb 1942, 131, gives a similar explanation for why nineteenth century English women were more active in the Conservative Party than the Liberal Party, and least seen (or least written about) in labor organizations.

20. Cooper 1892, 139, quote on 140. Hall quote in "Two Women in Politics," *NYH*, Nov. 3, 1895,VI:9:5. Gamm 1989, 100–101.

21. Generalizations about voting patterns are based on more extensive analyses by Abbott 1915; Eckhert 1916;Toombs 1920; Lape 1922; Merriam and Gosnell 1924; Gosnell 1927; Berelson and Lazarsfeld 1945; Gosnell 1948; Harris 1954; Lynn 1979; Lichtman 1979; Andersen 1979; Baxter and Lansing 1983; Goldstein 1984; Gamm 1989;Andersen, 1996.

NOTES FOR CHAPTER TWO (PAGES 27 TO 45)

1. Gertzog 1990.According to an 1858 paper, women, including "women of color," first voted in 1797; I *HWS* 1881, 447–50. Some women could also vote in colonial Massachusetts, when few men could do so; I *HWS* 1881, 208.

2. List of partial suffrage states with dates in NAWSA 1940,Appendix 5.

3. Quote in IV *HWS* 1902, 1042. Matthews 1992, 116.

4. Lerner 1979, xxix, 114. Ginzberg 1990, second quote 71, first and third quotes from Grimké to Beecher, 84. In 1837 Catherine Beecher and Angelina Grimké exchanged letters over the propriety of petitioning by women. Beecher maintained that petitioning was "entirely without the sphere of female duty," though she herself had done it; Ginzberg, 67. The abolitionists sent millions of signatures to Congress in the late 1830s and 1840s. Gerda Lerner estimated that 70 percent of those signing the 1838 petitions were women; 1979, 126.

5. Lerner 1979, 126. Ginzberg 1990, 99–100. Liquor could still be imported or made for private consumption.

6. First quote from Earhart 1944, 138. Massey 1966, Chapter 8. Second quote from II *HWS* 1882, iii.

7. Quotes from Bordin 1981, 156, xviii. Flexner 1959, 1968, 182. Lebsock 1990, 38.The crusade began in the small towns of Ohio and spread east for about six months, as bands of women marched on saloons, knelt to pray that they close, and sometimes invaded so that they did so; Bryce called it the Women's Whisky War, 1886, II:292, 586. Earhart 1944, 139–43; Bordin 1981, 15–33; Blocker 1985; Garner 1997–98.The WCTU was founded in Cleveland, Ohio, in November 1874, but soon moved its headquarters to Chicago.

8. Rose 1996, 12. Earhart 1944, 184–91. Quote in Bryce 1888, II:586.WCTU Pledge in IV *HWS* 1902, 1046.

9. IV *HWS* 1902, 1046.

10. Lee 1980. Bordin 1981. Giele 1961, 1995. Willard's endorsement of suffrage caused conservative members to withdraw; Bordin 1981, 119. The Georgia WCTU was decimated when excluded from Methodist churches because of a disagreement over woman suffrage; Rose 1996, 159n59.

11. IV *HWS* 1902, 1043. This volume has a thirty-page listing and description of "National Organizations of Women" at the beginning of the new century. See also Chapter 13 in Flexner 1959, 1968, and Breckinridge, 1933, 1972, passim.

12. Quote from Terrell's autobiography, 1940, 148. See also Breckinridge 1933, 1972, 24–25, 77–78; Evans 1989, 152; O'Neill 1969, 87–88; White 1993. Membership figures from IV *HWS* 1902, 1051. Terrell bio in IV *NAW* 1980, 678–80; *BWA* 1993, 1157–59; obit in *NYT*, July 29, 1954, 23:4. Terborg-Penn 1998, 88, says NACW had a Suffrage Department "from the onset." However, it is not mentioned in the summary of NACW's work in IV *HWS* 1902, 1051, written by NACW's vice president and editor of its official organ.

13. Harper 1898, I:185–86.

14. Kraditor 1965, 145–52, 221–22. The founding of the AERA is described in II *HWS* 1882, Chapter 18; the founding of the AWSA in Chapter 26. Although the editors/authors of *HWS* were the founders of the NWSA, this is described only on 400.

15. The Wyoming territorial legislature adopted woman suffrage on Dec. 10, 1869 and a convention put it in the constitution with which it became a state in 1890. The Territory of Utah enacted a similar statute in 1870, but in 1887 Congress abolished woman suffrage as part of its effort to eradicate polygamy and punish those who practiced it; Edmunds-Tucker Act, 24 *Stat.* 635. Woman suffrage was assumed to increase the voting strength of Mormon husbands. It was restored by the Utah constitutional convention of 1895 and Utah entered the union in 1896 as the third full suffrage state; White 1974, 344–69. See III *HWS* 1886, 725–31 for Wyoming and IV *HWS* 1902, 936–56 for Utah; Bryce 1888, 427–28; Beeton 1986, Chapters 1 through 5; Grimes 1967, Chapters 2 and 3; Catt 1940, Chapter V; Catt and Shuler 1923, 1926, 74–85, 127–29.

16. IV *HWS* 1902, 967–69, 1096–98. Suffrage was granted on Nov. 23, 1883. Challenged by saloon owners, the state supreme court initially voided the Suffrage Act as procedurally defective in 1887. The legislature passed it again, but in early 1888 the court ruled that the Congressional Act that created the Territory of Washington only gave its legislature the authority to enfranchise male citizens.

17. Quote from Beard and Beard 1930, II:563. Catt and Shuler 1923, 1926, 117–19, 122; Beeton 1986, Chapters 6 and 7. Colorado and Idaho were the first states to enfranchise women by popular vote. Idaho had considered enfranchising women in 1889 when it drew up a constitution to apply for statehood, but instead limited the franchise to non-Mormon men. By 1896 Mormon men could vote in Idaho and were a major contributor to the favorable referendum outcome; Beeton 1986, 124, 132. In Colorado, Populism was the crucial factor. The Governor of Colorado wrote in 1894 that "The Populists in the General Assembly nearly all supported the [suffrage] bill, but a majority of the members of both the old parties voted in opposition. The law was recommended by a Populist governor, the bill was introduced by a Populist Representative, at the general election the Populist part in the State supported the measure; but nearly all the Republican counties and all the Democratic counties voted largely against it"; reprinted in 272 *North American Review Heritage*, Sept. 1987, 48. For an insider's view of Colorado suffrage, see Reynolds 1909. For the relationship between Suffrage and Populism see Edwards 1997, Chapter 5.

18. IV *HWS* 1902, xxi lists the following: Kansas, 1867/94; Michigan, 1874; Colorado, 1877/93; Nebraska, 1882; Oregon, 1884/1900; Rhode Island, 1886; Washington, 1889/98; South Dakota, 1890/98; California, 1896; Idaho, 1896. These are described in *HWS* and by Catt and Shuler in Chapter IX of their book; 1923, 1926. See also Beeton 1986.

19. On the "doldrums" see Anthony 1954, 415.

20. The leading role of the WCTU is evident in the description of activities in each state in IV *HWS* 1902. The authors/editors, who were suffrage's chief agitators, give the WCTU major credit for many state campaigns. In 1881 the National Brewers' Congress came out against woman suffrage; Brown 1916. Marilley 1986, identified WCTU support as crucial to Colorado's granting of suffrage in 1893. Gullett describes how temperance agitation in California led women to demand suffrage as early as the 1870s; 1983, 31. By the 1896 California referendum WCTU support was such a liability that Anthony asked Willard to move the WCTU national convention to another state even though the California suffrage leaders were all WCTU officers; R. Davis 1967, 95. As Earhart pointed out, the WCTU was often active in a state long before any suffrage association, Chapter 12. It was not uncommon for the head of the WCTU suffrage department in each state to found and often head the equal suffrage association in that state. Dr. Anna Howard Shaw headed the national WCTU's suffrage department from 1888 to 1892. Between 1904 and 1915 she headed NAWSA. Quote on Gougar in Kriebel 1985, 139. According to Bordin, citing Giele 1961, 83, NAWSA had only 13,000 paid members in 1895. The Senate floor discussion and vote on a suffrage amendment held on Jan. 25, 1887 is described in IV *HWS* 1902, 110–11. Flexner 1959, 1968, 173–75.

21. First quote from Zagarri 1999, 124. Last quote from Gertzog 1990, 55.

22. First and third quotes from Dinkin 1995, 31, 33, 41–43. Second quote from Gunderson 1957, 136. See also Matthews 1992, 98; Lerner 1979, 125; Edwards 1997, 17, 25. Ryan 1990, 136, says the Democrats "were only slightly tardy in adding feminine political symbolism to their campaign," giving an 1840 visit by Andrew Jackson to New Orleans as an example. Dinkin 1995, and Edwards 1995, found little evidence of involvement by Democratic women until after the war, and always less than by Republican women. DeFiore 1992, says that in Tennessee the Whigs initiated female involvement in 1840, the Democrats followed in 1844, but by 1848 Southern women withdrew largely because the Seneca Falls conference in July identified female activity with abolitionism. Varon's research on antebellum Virginia concurs that the Whigs initiated women's welcome into partisan activities. "The Democrats seem to have finally come around by the campaigns of 1848, 1852, and 1856"; 1995, 516. Kenney wrote pamphlets for the Democrats in the 1830s, but switched after the Whigs offered her $1,000 for her services; Varon, 497. For an explanation of Whig leadership on women, see Varon 1998, 82; Basch 1993; Kincheloe 1981.

23. "Female Politicians" 1852, 356. "Tippecanoe" was the nickname for William Henry Harrison, successful Whig candidate for President in 1840. Hale 1852, 293.

24. Dinkin 1995, 44–49. Carroll's life is documented by Coryell 1990. Both Carroll and Fillmore had been Whigs. Fillmore succeed to the Presidency in 1850 after the death of Zachary Taylor, but the party declined to nominate him in 1852. The Know-Nothings were one response to increased Irish immigration in the 1830s and 1840s. Virulently anti-Catholic, the party elected candidates in five states in 1854, and was absorbed into the Republican Party after 1856.

25. Coryell 1990, Chapter 4. II *HWS* 1882, 40–50 describes some of Dickenson's exploits and has a copy of her invitation to address Congress. Bio in I *NAW* 1971, 475–76. Chester

1951, is her only book-length biography. Chapters 3, 8, and 13 describe her campaign speeches. She campaigned for Democrat and Liberal Republican Presidential candidate Horace Greeley in 1872, otherwise for Republicans. She was a paid speaker, though occasionally she donated her services.

26. First quote in anonymous article on "Women in Politics" in New York published in *The Daily Picayune* of New Orleans, Nov. 2, 1880, 6. Gougar quote from her column on "Women in the Campaign," *Our Herald*, Nov. 25, 1882, cited in Kriebel 1985, 84; her switch from Republican to Prohibition Party is recounted in Chapter 13. Gougar bios in Willard and Livermore 1897, 327–28; II *NAW* 1971, 69–71. Third quote in Edwards 1997, 43. On Willard see Willard 1889, 377, quote on 407. She lost power when she tried and failed to merge the Prohibition Party with the Populists in 1892; Earhart 1944, 211–12, Chapter 14. IV *HWS* 1902, 438. "Prohibition Party" in section on Party Profiles; *NPC* 1997, 273. "Election of 1884," "Prohibition Party," and "Woman's Christian Temperance Union" in Maisel 1991, 296–98, 891, 1230. See Gullett 1983, Chapter 1, for details on how WCTU activity by California women led them into politics. Last quote in "Women in Politics," *WJ*, Aug. 6, 1888, 318.

27. Prohibition voters were largely Republicans; Edwards 1997, 41. Democrat Grover Cleveland won New York by 1,147 votes, giving him all of its 36 votes in the electoral college, where he won the Presidency by only 37 votes. The Prohibition Party candidate got 24,999 votes in New York; *Congressional Quarterly Guide to U.S. Elections* 1985, 341.

28. On Republican clubs generally see Ryan 1888; McGerr 1986, 80. After announcing the formation of the NLRC in its Feb. 1888 issue, the *North American Review* published a series of letters in March commenting on whether such clubs were desirable or were a threat to regular party organization. Edwards has found Republican women's campaign clubs mentioned in local newspapers in the 1880s and 1890s in New York, Massachusetts (down to the ward level in Boston), Ohio, Iowa, Illinois, Indiana, Michigan, Wisconsin, Kansas, Nebraska, Wyoming, Colorado, California, Utah, Idaho, Washington, Oregon, Kentucky (in at least one district), and possibly others (Rhode Island, Maine); personal communication, Oct. 17, 1997. Reynolds, who admits New Jersey was "a laggard in political innovations," says "a few Republican clubs included a women's auxiliary"; 1988, 12, 29. His cites to 1880 and 1884 newspapers imply these were campaign clubs. Quote from *NYTrib*, July 12, 1888, 2:6, which says there were already a few Republican women's clubs in Iowa. On July 19, 1888, Foster wrote a long letter to Republican Party candidate Benjamin Harrison analyzing the Prohibition vote. In a P.S. she reported that "I am now busily engaged in making plans for the organization of women's republican clubs. ... I have the kind approval and co-operation of the National Committee"; Reel 10, Harrison Papers, LoC. *NYTrib*, Aug. 18, 1888, 2:1 reprints WNRA circular to appeal to women. *WJ*, Sept. 1, 1888, 276, announced "Women's National Republican League" as outcome of Foster's observations in England. WNRA discussed in Edwards 1997, 75, 83–87. Adams and Foster's nephew wrote a short biography of Foster which identifies Clarkson as her friend, but does not clarify who initiated the idea for women's Republican clubs; 1913, 265. As RNC chairman from July 1891 to May 1893, Clarkson could support Foster's work. While Foster was an important Republican, some scholars have overestimated her work, stating that she was the initiator of one thousand local women's Republican clubs; I *NAW* 1971, 651–52; Dinkin 1995, 94. Even counting temporary campaign clubs, I've found no credible evidence of this many clubs.

29. Foster quote in Harper 1898, 785. On Gougar see Kriebel 1985, 116. On the Nonpartisan WCTU see Rose 1996, 24–25. Foster's friendship and then rivalry with Willard

is discussed in Earhart 1944, 217–18, 222–24; and Bordin 1981, 125–29. An Oct. 26, 1886, leaflet protesting the WCTU's affiliation with the Prohibition Party written by Foster is on Reel 10 of the Benjamin Harrison Papers, LoC. *NYT,* March 8, 1891, 3:3, reviews criticism of her, noting that "In 1881 she was a partisan Prohibitionist." Several close associates as well as her husband held different federal patronage appointments during Republican administrations. The Benjamin Harrison Papers reveal a successful demand for a job for him soon after Harrison's election; Foster letter of Jan. 1, 1889, to BH, Reel 14 and undated 1889 letter to E. W. Halford, Reel 24. Undated 1889 news clipping says: "Husband of J. Ellen Foster, Mr. E. Foster, has been appointed Register of the Treasury. The salary is $4,000 a year."; Reel 20, Harrison Papers, LoC. Her Iowa background is reviewed in Mott 1933 and career and ideas are discussed in Edwards 1997, 49–50; Gustafson 1999. See also Willard and Livermore 1897, 296–97; I *NAW* 1971, 651–52.

30. Hanley 1941, 23, 30.

31. *NYH* wrote several stories on Ormsby and her group. The last one was in March of 1893, even though the fight appeared to be just heating up; 1892: June 30, 3:5; July 3, 5:6; Aug. 22, 9:2 (Cleveland letter); Sept. 28, 5:5; Oct. 2, 15:5; 1893: Feb. 15, 10:6, Feb. 18, 7:6; March 14, 5:2; March 19, 19:6; March 20, 10:4; March 25, 10:1. *BDE* wrote one describing the circulars she was mailing; Oct. 25, 1892, 4:3. See also the *NYTrib,* 1892: July 1, 6:4; July 10, 8:2 (Cleveland letter). Hoey claimed Dickinson gave Ormsby $1,000 but that she didn't use most of it for the campaign. Ormsby admitted receiving money, but not how much, and said it went to pay Hoey.

32. Edwards 1997, Chapter 5. Frances Willard was a vice president of the founding convention that met in St. Louis in February 1892 and authored a minority report from the Resolutions Committee that endorsed woman suffrage. Her effort to put woman suffrage and prohibition planks into the Populist platform failed because the Prohibitionists refused to participate in the convention on the grounds that these planks were not strong enough, and without the Prohibition votes Southern opposition could not be overcome; Earhart 1944, Chapter 14. Quotes from IV *HWS* 1902, 438. Bryan 1896, 288–90, lists the members of the People's Party National Committee, including two women out of dozens. Lease is remembered for the admonition that "farmers should raise more hell and less corn," but Edwards found no evidence that she ever uttered those words; personal communication, July 21, 1997.

33. Dinkin 1995, 97. Woman suffrage was not the topic of Bryan's speech to fifteen thousand people at Monmouth, in Warren Co., Ill., even though women sponsored the meeting and paid all the expenses; Bryan 1896, 572–73; Hanley 1941, 30. Kriebel, 1985, 162. First quote from Bostwick 1896, 304–5; second in *NYTrib,* Aug. 22, 1896, 2:2. NYC canvassing reported in *NYTrib,* Aug. 29, 1896, 4:5; Syracuse work on Sept. 19, 1896, 3:2; Boswell, *NR,* Dec. 7, 1918, 8. See also *WJ,* 1896: Oct. 10, 321; Oct. 17, 333. On Foster's campaigning see *WJ,* Oct. 24, 1896, 340, excerpting from *The Kansas City Journal. NYT,* Oct. 23, 1897, 2:5, reported that the president of the Women's Health Protective Association told three thousand assembled women that "We women who are working without a vote can multiply it about twenty times." Seth Low, reform candidate for mayor, then observed: "From looking at this audience, each of you represents forty votes at least."

34. Foster 1892, 251. *WJ,* Nov. 10, 1894, 353–54, lists the known women candidates for office. See also Lockwood 1893.

35. Reynolds 1909, 351. IV *HWS* 1902, has a report on each state as of 1901. Cox 1996, lists the women legislators in each state. *SFEx,* Nov. 4, 1894, 17, describes "Colorado's Queer

Campaign Where the Polls Are Open to Both Sexes, How the State Has Been Stumped and Stirred Up by the Petticoated Politicians." *NYTrib*, Nov. 20, 1898, II:7:1, profiled the woman elected Colorado superintendent of public instruction, called "the little Professor," and her staff. *WJ*, Jan. 5, 1899, 96, reprinted an article from the *SFCall* on the new Idaho superintendent.

36. IV *HWS* 1902, 478, 486, second quote on 488. R. Davis 1967, 66, lists twelve women who ran for office in San Francisco in the 1890s on third party tickets. Gullett found that women's political efforts originated with nonpartisan organizations of women, who then sometimes obtained party endorsement for their candidates; 1983, 278–81. She observed that the "Los Angeles political system was more responsive to . . . organized women than was the San Francisco political establishment in the last two decades of the nineteenth century" because it was more homogeneous, Protestant and Republican, 1983, Chapters II and III, 144. This is consistent with other analyses, both contemporary and current. Even in the highly partisan Third Party System, California political culture was relatively nonpartisan. The only reference I've found to the Women's Republican State Central Committee of California is in the *NYTrib*, July 28, 1900, first quote on 7:2. Clara Shortridge Foltz campaigned for the Republican Party in the 1880s; I *NAW* 1971, 641–43.

37. The 1894 Kansas campaign, including office holders, is described in IV *HWS* 1902, 638–64, and Goldberg 1994. Woman suffrage "was endorsed in the platforms of the People's and Prohibition parties, ignored in the Republican and opposed in the Democratic"; *WJ*, Nov. 10, 1894, 354. Diggs bio in Willard and Livermore 1897, 247; I *NAW* 1971, 481–82; obit in *NYT* Sept. 9, 1916, 11:4. Johns bio in Willard and Livermore 1897, 420. Emery bio in I *NAW* 1971, 582–83. Lease bio in II *NAW* 1971, 380–82. Wells bio in III *NAW* 1971, 565–67; *BWA* 1993, 1242–46. On women running small towns, see W. Smith 1984; Gehring 1986; Moss 1987; *NYTrib* editorial, "Women in Western Towns," May 20, 1896, 6:4, which commented on how common it had become. Four "Women in Politics" were profiled in the *NYTrib*, Sept. 13, 1896, 3:7. Eisenhuth in IV *HWS* 1902, 551.

38. The Prohibition, Republican, and Democratic parties nominated women for trustee, while the Populist Party nominated a woman for state superintendent of instruction. Republican Lucy Flower won. Democrat Dr. Julia Holmes Smith was appointed trustee by the Governor to fill a vacancy and served for a while, but lost at the polls; *WJ*, Oct. 13, 1894, 322; IV *HWS* 1902, 604–6. *WJ*, Nov. 10, 1894, 354, describes suffrage and other political activities in several states, including Illinois. See also "Women at the Polls," *ChiTrib*, Nov. 7, 1894, 11:4. On Wells-Barnett's experiences, see her autobiography, ed. by Duster 1970, 243–44. The Republican women who sponsored Wells' campaign tour were white.

39. Edwards 1997, 134–35; IV *HWS* 1902, 463, 506, 551, 561, 636, 657, 675, 779, 890, 979.

40. Brown 1994. Edwards 1997, 35–38.

41. "Women in Politics," dated New York, Oct. 27, 1880, in *The Daily Picayune* of New Orleans, Nov. 2, 1880, 6. On Southern Populism see Shaw 1984, 176–78. On women, "white and colored," in the Tennessee prohibition referendum, see Isaac 1965, 52–60, quote on 58. The argument that women didn't belong in politics was still being made in 1903 and 1908, thus implying that women were still there; Issac, 1965, 153–54, 164. On New Orleans, see IV *HWS* 1902, 679–83. *WJ*, reported on Sept. 14, 1912, 292, that "The New Orleans women got the special tax voted, but they could not vote for the men who were to spend the money . . . . [and] the promised improvement has never been completed." On Felton, see Willard and Livermore 1897, 286–87; Talmadge 1960; Chamberlin 1973, Chapter 2; Whites 1993; I *NAW* 1971, 606–7; obit in *NYT*, Jan. 25, 1930, 15:3. Dinkin 1995, 98, says Southern women were publicly supporting candidates by the 1890s.

42. First quote called an "old saying" when used by speaker in anti-Tammany rally held by the Women's Municipal League; "Women Pursuing the Tiger," *NYTrib*, Oct. 31, 1894, 7:1; "Women Against Misrule," *NYT*, Oct. 31, 1894, 5:1. Second quote in "Woman Suffrage in Colorado," 57 *The Outlook*, June 12, 1897, 406. On Jane Addams in Chicago see A. Davis 1967, Chapter 8. "Ladies' Committee" covered in *NYT*, Oct. 1890: 22, 5:2, 27, 4:2; *NYH*, Oct. 27, 1890, 3:4. BWHPA activity reported in *NYT*, Oct. 1893: 7, 8:3; 20, 9:3. Schieren acknowledged women's assistance in a letter to Rev. Charles H. Parkhurst, published in the *NYT*, Sept. 26, 1894, 2:7. Brooklyn became one of five New York City boroughs in 1898. In Sept. 1898, 2:3 *Municipal Affairs* published a special issue on "Women's Work on City Problems," with articles from New York, Philadelphia, Boston, Chicago, New Orleans, Washington, Denver, and Indianapolis.

43. On the WML see Monoson 1990; Edwards 1997, 118–19; Dinkin 1995, 113–16. WML sponsored meetings in *NYT*, Oct. 1894: 13, 9:4; 20, 9:5; 26, 9:5; 27, 5:3; 31, 5:1; and Nov. 1, 5:2. Evaluation of "Women's Work in Politics," *NYT*, Nov. 4, 1894, 18:1. WNRA sponsored meetings in *NYT*: Oct. 1894: 25, 9:3; 27, 5:3. One meeting for "colored women" sponsored by the Johanna Women's Anti-Tammany League is in *NYT*, Nov. 1, 1894, 5:2. Parkhurst motivation in *NYT*, 1894: Sept. 26, 2:7; quote in Oct. 5, 8:1. Parkhurst anti-suffragist articles and pamphlets are listed in Marshall's bibliography, 1997, 322–23. Second quote in Bostwick 1896, 306, who called herself a "rabid Republican" in 1899; *NYTrib*, June 21, 1899, 7:3.

44. Boswell interview in *NYH*, May 28, 1895, 5:6; bio in *Brooklyn Eagle Magazine,* Sept. 19, 1926, 11; obit in *NYT,* Jan. 6, 1942, 23:3; family background in Boswell, NR, Nov. 23, 1918, 8. Quote in *NYH*, Oct. 11, 1894, 12:2. See also the series of "Political Episodes" written by Boswell for the 1935 issues of *WRNY*.

45. Women's Republican club meetings described in: *NYT*, May 23, 1895, 8:3; Oct. 5, 1895, 2:7; July 12, 1896, 8:1; Aug. 22, 1896, 2:3; *NYTrib*, Dec. 14, 1894, 5:5; Sept. 18, 1896, 3:2; Nov. 17, 1896, 5:6; June 19, 1897, 5:1; Sept. 11, 1897, 5:1; Oct. 30, 1897, 5:1. "Colored Women Aroused, Too," *NYTrib*, Oct. 31, 1894, 7:1. Boswell's activities described in *NR*, Dec. 21, 1918, 7; *NYH*, 1895: Feb. 26, 10:1; May 28, 11:1; June 15, 7:1; July 2, 7:2; Sept. 11, 11:1; Oct. 18, 3:1; Nov. 6, 5:6; June 27, 1896, 10:1: *NYTrib*, June 15, 7:4, 1895; Nov. 3, 1895, 10:1; Aug. 22, 1896, 2:2; Oct. 24, 1896, 5:1; Nov. 17, 1896, 5:6; May 19, 1897, 5:6; Oct. 5, 1898, 5:1; March 7, 1899, 5:2; Sept. 17, 1899, III:5:5; *NYT*: May 28, 1895, 9:4; Oct. 18, 1895, 6:2. Boswell, *NR*, Dec. 21, 1918, 7, recounts her selection as a delegate to the NLRC convention. Despite much publicity at her presence, she only went once. At least five states sent women as delegates to this convention: New York, Illinois, Ohio, Colorado, and Wyoming; *Cleveland Plain Dealer,* June 19, 1895, 3:5.

46. Low women's meeting in *NYT*, Oct. 23, 1897, 2:5. *NYTrib* 1897: "They Fight Over Low," Oct. 2, 5:5; "Trouble in the West End," Oct. 16, 5:1; "Ellen Foster Talks," Oct. 30, 5:1; middle quotes in "Women's Part in Politics," Nov. 15, 1897, 5:5. The Republican Union League Club of Brooklyn's court fight was over who would get the silver coffee urn; *NYTrib*, Sept. 28, 1898, 5:3; June 21, 1899, 7:3; May 4, 1901, 5:1; Dec. 6, 1901, 14:1; *NYT*, June 21, 1899, 3:6. First and last quotes in *NYH*, Sept. 19, 1897, V:12, which devoted a full page to "Leaders of the Women in Politics." Low was an independent Republican. He came in second in a field of four; the regular Republican was third; the Tammany candidate won.

47. *NYT*, Oct. 28, 1897, 2:2. IV *HWS* 1902, 872, mentions the Democratic club without context or comment. I have been unable to find reports of its activities in NYC newspapers, which don't report a permanent women's Democratic club until 1905–6.

48. "The Woman and the Vote," *SFEx*, Nov. 4, 1894, 17.

49. On the Whigs, see Varon 1995, 489. On the Republican Party, see Dinkin 1995, 44–45. 1868 Democratic Convention in II *HWS* 1882, 343. *NYTrib*, "Women in Politics," Sept. 8, 1900, 7:1.

50. Mary Marjorie Stanton, "The Woman Suffrage Movement in Ohio Prior to 1910," M.A. Thesis, Ohio State University, 1947, 39–40, cited in Blocker 1985, 220. First quote in *WJ*, Nov. 10, 1894, 354. Second quote in 44:2285 *Harper's Weekly*, Oct. 6, 1900, 950. *NYH*, Oct. 7, 1900, V:3:1, also credited the Populists, but said the Republicans were divided and the Democrats opposed to woman suffrage. IV *HWS* 1902, 518, credits only the Populists. On Illinois voting women see *ChiTrib*, Oct. 17, 1894, 1:3, but see "Democratic Women not Idle" which lists six locations where the "Democratic Woman's Campaign committee announces the following meetings," 2:4; Nov. 7, 1894, quote on 11:4. On California see IV *HWS* 1902, 486–88.

51. On the Seneca Falls signatories, see Paulson 1973, 36. Post-Civil War attitudes in Edwards 1997, Chapter 2; quoted in 1995, Chapter 2. However, in 1884 five members of the Woman Suffrage Party of New York issued a broadside with nine "reasons why New York suffragists should prefer" Democratic candidate Grover Cleveland, even though the WSP convention had decided to remain uncommitted. No. 1 was that "He is Governor of our State"; Oct. 13, 1884, Reel 2, Cleveland Papers, LoC.

52. Harper 1898, 723–74.

53. The full 1872 "call" is in II *HWS* 1882, 517–20. A more detailed description of Anthony's efforts is in Harper 1898, 416–23. The "splinter" in the 1872 Republican Party Platform says: "The Republican Party is mindful of its obligations to the loyal women of America for their noble devotion to the cause of freedom; their admission to wider fields of usefulness is received with satisfaction; and the honest demands of any class of citizens for equal rights should be treated with respectful consideration." Meetings in New York, Massachusetts, Pennsylvania, Illinois, Michigan, Connecticut, Maine, Rhode Island, and California are reported in *WJ*, Oct. 5, 1872, 317; Oct. 12, 1872, 324; Nov. 2, 1872, 349. Dinkin 1995, 68, describes Anthony's 1872 campaigning. For 1876 see Harper 1898, 476; and III *HWS* 1886, 22–27. Quotes and other information from "Suffrage Work in Conventions" which is Chapter 23 of IV *HWS* 1902, 434–49. See also *WJ*, June 30, 1900, 204.

54. Letter to Henry Blackwell in Harper 1898, 420. Anthony wrote similarly to Stone in August 1878, 499. Quote from letter to Stanton in Barry, 1988, 249; original in Huntington Library, San Marino, Calif.

55. Harper 1898, 594. The manifesto was printed in numerous Republican papers; see *NYTrib*, Aug. 1, 1884, 2. Blackwell letter of Aug. 26, 1889, in Earhart 1944, 225–26. Lucy Stone expressed similar sentiments in a letter written to Willard on Sept. 2, 1889.

56. IV *HWS* 1902, xviii.

57. IV *HWS* 1902, 150.

58. IV *HWS* 1902, 173–74.

59. Harper 1898, 785, 793–94, 928.

60. Anthony, "Political Women," *The Daily Times*, September 11, 1900, reprinted in Harper 1898, III:1214–15. This diatribe reflects Anthony's opinion more than the actual facts. V *HWS* 1922, 702, reports that the Prohibition Party "always advocated woman suffrage in its national platform except in 1896, when it had only a single plank, but this was supplemented by resolutions favoring equal suffrage." This volume does not mention the People's Party, which ran Presidential candidates through 1908. The lack of an official Women's Bureau in the 1900 McKinley campaign did not keep J. Ellen Foster and Republican women from actively cam-

paigning; *NYTrib*, Sept. 8, 1900, 7:1. Stanton letter to Lowell reprinted in *NYT*, Oct. 11, 1894, 9:7; quote in *NYH*, Oct. 7, 1900,V:7:2, as part of a full-page story on "The Woman in Politics."
    61. Sent to the *Denver News*, reprinted in *WJ*, Nov. 10, 1894, 356.

NOTES FOR CHAPTER THREE (PAGES 47 TO 61)

    1. The best explanation of Progressive men's interest is in Duncan-Clark's 1913 book, which devoted one chapter to "Women and the Progressive Movement." "The welcome to women . . . was due to their sudden sense of need for woman's political comradeship." He believed that "Woman's happiest and most useful sphere is the home," from which "it is impossible to divorce politics." Therefore, "The votes of women will hasten [the] end . . . [of] political indifference to the home." Theodore Roosevelt wrote the Introduction to this book, indicating its views were common to Progressives; 1913, 99, 103–7.
    2. Beard and Beard 1930, II:539. See also Reichley 1992, 183.
    3. DeWitt 1915, Chapters 8, 10, and 11 discuss the movement's political reform measures. Quote from Reynolds 1988, 137, who argues that the transformation of voting had to occur before woman suffrage became acceptable, at least in New Jersey.
    4. Quote in DeWitt 1915, 196. The Populists began the process of redefining the electorate to include women in the 1890s, but Progressives completed it. Historians of Progressivism acknowledge woman suffrage as one of "the democratic innovations" of the Progressive era though they don't always credit its populist roots; Faulkner 1931, 85; Hofstadter 1955, 265; Morgan 1972, 72–73; Grimes 1967, 100–101; Sundquist 1983, 177.
    5. Quote in Dorr 1924, 219. The Woman Suffrage Party held its organizing convention the same week in the same place as Mrs. Pankhurst's first New York speech. Similar organizations were soon formed in San Francisco, Baltimore, Philadelphia, Boston, and Chicago and the states of New York, Massachusetts, and Illinois; Peck 1944, 168–73. VI *HWS* 1922, 445, 460. Flexner 1959, 1968, 254. Graham 1997, 55–60. In New York, Assembly Districts are the primary unit of political organization, selecting the district leaders who sit on the State Central Committee. Each is composed of numerous election districts.
    6. Wiebe 1967, 208. Key 1964, 615. Reichley 1992, 197. The Alaska territorial legislature gave women full suffrage in 1913. The connection in California was particularly close, largely because all these measures were part of a packet of reforms promoted by progressive Republican Governor Hiram Johnson. See Key and Crouch 1939. In Idaho and Colorado women voters were credited for bringing the initiative, referendum, and recall in 1910 and 1912. A 1912 suffrage campaign in Michigan, which had the initiative and referendum, narrowly failed. New Mexico was the only Western state never to grant women suffrage. Jensen attributes this to the fact that the 1910 constitutional convention created a state constitution that was almost impossible to amend but she doesn't explain how the initiative and referendum were added in 1911; Jensen 1986, 305. Faulkner lists several other states with these measures that did not give women suffrage: Maine (1908), Missouri (1908), Arkansas (1910), Nebraska (1912), Ohio (1912), North Dakota (1914), Maryland and Massachusetts (1918). In addition, Louisiana and North Dakota permitted the recall.
    7. The Seventeenth Amendment for direct election of U.S. Senators was sent to the states by Congress on May 13, 1912, and ratified by May 31, 1913. On March 19, 1914, woman suffrage passed the Senate by 35 to 34—short of the two-thirds necessary—51:V *Congressional Record*, 5108, and on Jan. 12, 1915, was defeated in the House by 174 to 204, 52:II

Congressional Record, 1483–84. This was the first Congressional vote since 1887. The aye votes were mostly from the twenty-one Western states; women had full suffrage in eleven of these. It is likely that passage of a federal suffrage amendment required a critical mass of U.S. Senators needing women's votes to be elected.

8. Flexner 1959, 1968, 261. Buechler 1986, 178. Trout 1920. In fact the Illinois law granted suffrage for all offices and purposes (e.g., referenda, municipal suffrage) not identified in the state constitution. The Illinois Supreme Court upheld this law in 1913, ruling that the state constitution granting suffrage to men over age twenty-one only applied to elections mentioned in that document. A similar law passed by the Indiana legislature in 1917 was rejected by that state's highest court; Cushman 1917, 633–34. "Piecemeal enfranchisement" continued even as momentum for a federal amendment increased. Twelve more states granted Presidential suffrage between 1917 and 1920; NAWSA 1940, 162–64. Peck credits the victory in New York to the city's Woman Suffrage Party, whose thorough organization persuaded the political machines to stay out of the 1917 referendum after defeating it in 1915; 1944, 278.

9. First quote in Scott 1970, 170. Second quote from a leaflet on "Some Facts About Suffrage Leaders" signed by J.B. Evans; SI, n.d. but after 1916. The quote specifically refers to Anthony and Dr. Anna Howard Shaw. The leaflet also denounces Elizabeth Cady Stanton for being anti-Christian, Vira Boorman Whitehouse and Alice Carpenter for being socialists, and Mrs. O.H.P. Belmont, "the woman of divorce fame." Stanton died in 1902 and Anthony in 1906; the others were still active suffragists. This leaflet was written to object to a suffrage meeting being held at a high school auditorium in Selma, Alabama.

10. Georgia Senator Joseph E. Brown read an 1884 report signed by himself and Senator Francis M. Cockrell (D. Mo.). It is reproduced in IV *HWS* 1902, 94–100; quote on 97–98. In 1912 Louisiana suffragist Kate Gordon "had grown so tired of hearing from the opponents of woman suffrage that their objection rested solely upon the fact that negro women would be enfranchised, that . . . she offered as a substitute for the full suffrage bill one limiting it to the white primary elections. This novel offer was received with great applause by the assembled members of the two [Louisiana] Houses, but was not accepted; VI *HWS* 1922, 222.

11. Studies of Southern state suffrage movements make it clear that the "specter of black voters was raised again and again"; Roydhouse on North Carolina, 1980, 134; Morgan 1972, 108–9. However, some Southern Congressmen did vote for the Suffrage Amendment in 1919; V *HWS* 1922, xxii, 647. On use of racial arguments by suffrage opponents: Camhi 1994, 130–2, 138–41; Marshall 1997, 211–15; Jablonsky 1994, 45–47; Lebsock 1993, 70–75.

12. Kentucky suffrage quote in IV *HWS* 1902, xxvii, 674. Fear of Negro voting was a prominent argument in the ratification debates by Southern states. Catt and Shuler 1923, 1926, 476, quote a Georgia Senator: "The sole intent of this voting privilege is to equalize white women with Negro women." Louisiana Ex-Governor Pleasant said: "Ratification of the Nineteenth Amendment not only would give suffrage to the white women but to the Negro women of the State. If we ratify the Nineteenth Amendment we ratify the Fifteenth and give suffrage to the Negro man"; 483. Allen 1958, 83–99. Borah quote in V *HWS* 1922, 413. As a young lawyer Borah had worked for state suffrage in 1896; Beeton 1986, 130. Despite his otherwise Progressive mantle, and the fact that women voted in Idaho, he voted against the Suffrage Amendment repeatedly. Map of ratification states in VI *HWS* 1922, 628. The Southern suffrage movement, like the South, was Negrophobic; the Northern movement was not. After 1903, in order to encourage suffrage clubs to form in the Southern states, NAWSA took the position that admission of colored women's clubs was up to each state

suffrage association;V *HWS* 1922, 83. Impact of Southern racial phobia on NAWSA strategy is in Morgan 1972, 88–97, 106–7, 112–13, 122–23. Women in these five border states already had partial suffrage. Virginia was the first Southern state to ratify, in 1952, and Mississippi was the last, in 1984.

13. Terborg-Penn 1983, 256; citing 19 *The Crisis*, November 1920, 23–25 and *The Negro Year Book, 1921*, 40.

14. Walsh recounts the "close affinity between suffragettes and temperance advocates in Indiana since the 1850s"; 1987, 171. Tyer 1916, credits Idaho's early grant of woman suffrage to a belief that women would vote in prohibition. Later studies of referenda in states with woman suffrage substantiated women's greater support for prohibition. Ogburn and Gotra 1919, 413, 433. Gardner 1920, 26. Goldstein 1984, 168–75. The difference was particularly clear in Illinois because women's votes were counted separately from men's through 1920. After getting partial suffrage in 1913, women were credited with voting sixteen more counties "dry" in 1914; *NYT*, April 9, 1914, 2:3. See also the *NYT* article on the spread of prohibition, April 19, 1914, VI:10:1. In an April 1, 1919, referendum on the issue "Shall Chicago Become Anti-Saloon Territory?" 79.8 percent of the men but only 62.7 percent of the women said no; Gosnell 1937, 145.

15. Catt and Shuler 1923, 1926, give great credit to the "liquor interests" for defeating woman suffrage in numerous state campaigns and describe how both suffrage and temperance leaders tried to avoid public association of the two issues. Wesser 1986, 199, confirms the success of this strategy in New York, viewing the two issues as "distinct" which "took different paths."

16. McDonagh and Price 1985, 415–35. Marshall 1997, 160–62, 180–81.

17. Park 1960, 177, said of that stalwart foe from Massachusetts: "Senator John W. Weeks, for example, admitted in a frank moment that he would favor woman suffrage if it could be limited to taxpaying women or to those with a high educational qualification." Ida Husted Harper wrote of the suffrage opposition: "Its leaders were for the most part connected with corporate interests and did not believe in universal suffrage for men"; "Introduction" to V *HWS* 1922, xix.

18. Flexner 1959, 1968, 296. Marshall 1997, Chapter IV, analyzes who made which arguments against suffrage.

19. Cleveland, May 1905, 3. Apparently his views had changed. In 1884 five members of the New York Woman Suffrage Party urged suffragists to support his election as President, claiming that "last winter . . . he voluntarily and publicly promised to sign any woman suffrage measure we could get the Legislature to pass"; Printed letter addressed to "Good Friend," Oct. 13, 1884, Cleveland Papers, LoC, Reel 2.

20. "'Votes for Women'—As Seen by Edward W. Bok," *NYT*, April 18, 1909, V:3:1,3. Bok was a dedicated anti-suffragist who wrote many anti-articles in *LHJ*, some of which were reprinted by anti-suffrage organizations. See Marshall's bibliography for a list, 1997, 303.

21. McDonough and Price 1985. Grimes 1967. This is also consistent with Giele's analysis of suffrage leaders; 1995, 85, 132–33. See also *ChiTrib,* Oct. 17, 1894, which reported that efforts to register women to vote (for university trustee) were slow in the German wards. "There was a feeling that they would be held back by their husbands, and this seems to have been largely the case." German Catholics usually voted Democratic.

22. Flexner 1959, 1968, 299. Marshall, who argued that ethno/religious effects on suffrage referenda varied with time and place, still found that areas with more Catholics recorded higher opposition to suffrage; 1997, 156–58, 162. Kenneally summarized the Catholic posi-

tion by paraphrasing the Archbishop of Boston's comment in 1885: "The Church does not involve itself in political questions; therefore it 'leaves alone' the issue of woman suffrage; on the other hand, the archbishop cautioned, women should not take part in politics," 1967, 43. In the 1896 California referenda, woman suffrage lost in the counties of San Francisco, Oakland, and Alameda, which had a high concentration of working class Catholics, and won in Los Angeles County, which was more heavily Protestant; IV *HWS* 1902, 493, 500. This pattern repeated itself in the successful referenda of 1911, but by then the Southern California population had grown sufficiently to give suffrage a margin of victory of 3,587; R. Davis 1967, 134. Camhi 1994, 111–15, links the Church's position to birth control advocates' endorsement of woman suffrage. Jablonsky 1994, 67–69, links it to traditional views of the family and woman's place.

23. McDonagh and Price 1985, 431. But they "report with surprise our finding that the Progressive vote in 1912 (for Theodore Roosevelt) was not significant as an intervening variable influencing suffrage support." However, the rural California counties that voted for suffrage in 1911 also voted for Roosevelt in 1912; Reichley 1992, 228; Flexner 1959, 1968, 257.

24. Camhi 1994, quote at 2, 88, 240. Jablonsky 1994, second quote at 19, 20, 75–77, 84, 105. He points out that while anti- leaders, like the suffragists, were old-stock Anglo-Saxon, they were from more conservative denominations (Presbyterian and Episcopalian), and were less likely to have college educations and jobs; 53–57. Marshall 1997, has a very perceptive analysis of the relationship between class, gender, and suffrage. See also Vose 1972, 48–53; Flexner 1959, 1968, Chapter 22. The eight founding states were Massachusetts, New York, Pennsylvania, Maryland, Rhode Island, Illinois, Oregon, and California. Dodge bio in I *NAW* 1971, 492–93. Alice Hay Wadsworth bio in Cameron and Lee 1924, 32. Her father, John Hay (1838–1905), served under McKinley and Roosevelt. Her husband was from a distinguished old-money family in upper New York State. Kilbreth obit in *NYT*, June 28, 1957, 23:5.

25. The House vote on May 21, 1919, was 304 to 89. The Senate vote on June 4, 1919, was 56 to 25 before pairing, and 66 to 30 afterwards. Before the new Congress took its seats in March 1919, the old, Democratically controlled Congress voted on the amendment one last time. On Jan. 10, 1918, the House voted 274 to 136, more than two-thirds. On Feb. 10, the Senate defeated it by 55 to 29, or 63 to 33 after pairing. V *HWS* 1922, 636, 642, 644, 646.

26. NAWSA 1940, 53.

27. Calculated by Ford 1991, 3, from Stevens, 1920.

28. Evans 1989, 148–51. A. Davis 1967, Chapter 8.

29. On Kelley and protective labor laws see Baker 1925; Nathan 1926; Goldmark 1953; Sklar 1995; O'Neill 1969, 96–98; Muncy 1991, 26–46; Lehrer 1987; and Vose's chapter on the minimum wage, 1972. Dorr 1910, Chapter V, describes the first Consumers' League that formed in New York City in 1890. Kelley liked to be called *Mrs.* Kelley although that was her mother's name. Her former husband's name was Wischnewetzky. Her father William was known as "Pig Iron" Kelley (R. Pa.). Bio in II *NAW* 1971, 316–19; obit in *NYT*, Feb. 18, 1932, 19:2; editorial on Feb. 29, 1932, 18:3.

30. First quote in O'Neill 1969, 98. Last quote in Lebsock 1990, 52. The WTUL's early history is described by Wertheimer 1977, Chapter 15, and its later history by Foner 1980, Chapter 6 and passim. In time the reformers came to dominate, and changed its focus from organizing women into trade unions to investigation and education. For short histories of

the WTUL see O'Neill 1969, 98–102, 114–17, 153–60, 220–21, 240–49; Chafe 1972, 69–79. For longer histories see Dye 1980 and Lehrer 1987. The official name of the WTUL was the National Women's Trade Union League, and it is often indexed under "N" rather than "W." Margaret Dreier Robins was married to Raymond Robins, one of the more important Progressive reformers, and lived with him in Chicago settlements. Her bio was written by her sister, Dreier 1950; also in III *NAW* 1971, 179–81; obit in *NYT*, Feb. 22, 1945, 22:1. Dreier bio in IV *NAW* 1980, 402–6; obit in *NYT,* Aug. 17, 1963, 19:1.

31. Flanagan 1990, describes the Chicago City Club, and Perry 1990, that of New York. Quote from Perry 1984, 28.

32. First quote from the Proceedings of the 1904 Biennial, cited in Breckinridge 1933, 1972, 258. Information on woman's clubs and GFWC in Dorr 1910, Chapter II, "From Culture Clubs to Social Service"; Wells 1953, 200–2, 206–6; O'Neill 1969, 84–90; Blair 1980, 97; Evans 1989, 150; Scott 1991; Skocpol 1995, Part III; Daggett 1913, 155. Roydhouse recounts how the North Carolina Federation of Women's Clubs involved women in lobbying in the 1910s, and their "experience soon convinced women [that] without the vote they could only rely upon the good will of the male legislators," 1980, 125. Cleveland quotes in Cleveland, May and Oct. 1905. Last quote from Beard in Lane 1977, 93.

33. Wells 1953, 205. Blair 1980, 5, 96–97, 113. O'Neill 1969, 259. Rejection of the suffrage resolution at the 1912 Biennial in Edson 1912.

34. Wells 1953, 204. O'Neill 1969, 87. Blair 1980, 109. Scott 1991, 127, reports that a compromise offer was made to seat the organizer of the black women's club as a representative of the Massachusetts State Federation, but she refused. "A Protest Against Color Line," *WJ*, June 16, 1900, 189. Jane Addams and Florence Kelley tried to block the GFWC's racial exclusion strategy, but only shifted it to an informal practice rather than a formal policy.

35. GFWC membership from Breckinridge 1933, 1972, 30. First quote in Raftery 1994, 144. Second in Braitman 1986, 84, quoting the *Pacific Empire Express Reporter* 1913, 8. Third in Jensen and Lothrop 1987, 64. Gibson was appointed to the Immigration and Housing Commission in 1913, and Edson to the Bureau of Labor Statistics and then to the Industrial Welfare Commission where she served from 1914 to 1931; Raftery 1994. Colorado quote in Dorr 1911, 432. Edson bio in I *NAW* 1971, 562–64; Braitman 1988.

36. On NACW, see Scott 1991, 146–49, 180. Terborg-Penn 1978, 1983, 1995, 1998 describes black women's suffrage activities. California suffragists paid Naomi Anderson to solicit black men's votes during the 1896 California referenda; IV *HWS* 1902, 480; Guellet 1983, 306. Some spoke out for woman suffrage during Reconstruction, and a few afterwards, but a major appeal to black (male) voters didn't appear until the 1910s. See Logan 1905, 1912. In 1915, W.E.B. DuBois published a symposium on "Votes for Women" in his magazine *The Crisis*. Camhi 1994, 236–37, describes the Back Bay Pilgrims as a black women's anti- organization which first appeared at a Massachusetts legislative hearing in 1913, and expanded statewide. Black newspapers analyzed by Beatty 1978. New Jersey referendum analysis by Reynolds 1988, 162. Terborg-Penn lists several states with black woman suffrage clubs, mostly in woman suffrage states. Like the Alpha Suffrage Club, their purpose was to encourage black women to use the vote already obtained. Most of the others in her list are Republican clubs or general women's clubs that had suffrage sections; 1978, 131, 179. When she organized the Alpha Club, Wells-Barnett had been a member of the Illinois Equal Suffrage Association for twenty years and it became a constituent club. Squires was a white friend of Wells. First quotes in Williams 1916, 12; second in Duster 1970, 345–46. Prior to World War I the northern black population was small. In the Southern states, suffrage agitation by

women was discouraged and by blacks was punished. In the northern states, black women interested in suffrage could join a state Equal Suffrage Association, as Wells-Barnett did or participate in the Suffrage Department of NACW.

37. Quote in Bordin 1981, xvii. V *HWS* 1922, 215, 247, reports "greetings" from the WCTU to the NAWSA conventions of 1908 and 1909, but none afterwards. The Anti-Saloon League was founded in Ohio in 1892 to pressure legislatures to enact prohibition and local option laws.

38. Buenker 1971; 1973, 156–62. Addams 1910. Perry 1987, explains how reformer Belle Moskowitz influenced Al Smith. In 1917, New York voted for full suffrage after rejecting it in 1915. Flexner 1959, 1968, 290, credits Tammany Hall's withdrawal of active opposition for the 100,000 vote margin for suffrage in New York City. In NAWSA's official history on the New York referendum, credit is given to the mutual influence of "working girls" on "women of means" working for suffrage and vice versa; 1940, 112.

39. Cott 1987, 24–28. Flexner 1959, 1968, 25, 250–52. Quote from Blatch and Lutz 1940, 92.

40. Flexner 1959, 1968, 252–54. Ford 1991, 33. DuBois 1991, 169. Nichols 1983, 13–14. The Pankhursts, in turn, were inspired by Susan B. Anthony when she visited London in 1899 and 1904; Ford 1991, 24, 36. Thus female militancy wasn't purely a British import; it just skipped a generation in the United States.

41. First quote from Ford 1991, 27. Second from Dorr 1924, 158. Chapter 9 of Dorr's autobiography describes of the effect on her of hearing the Pankhursts speak in London in 1906. Dorr later became the first editor of the Congressional Union's newsletter, *The Suffragist*.

42. More accurately, this is the percent of women who completed four years of college, whether or not they graduated. Feminism also appealed to educated men. In 1910, 3.4 percent of men over age 25 had completed four years of college; in 1920, 3.9 percent had done so. Younger people were more likely to have gone to college than older ones. Women with four years or more were 2.6 percent of the 25–29 age group in 1910 and 3.4 percent in 1920. Men were 4.1 percent and 4.9 percent respectively. Educational attainment was not asked by the U.S. Bureau of the Census until 1940; these figures are estimates based on later censuses by John K. Folger and Charles B. Nam, U.S. Bureau of the Census, *Education of the American Population,* 1967.

43. Quote in Cott 1987, 40–41. Evans 1989, 167–68. Cooley 1913, 8.

44. Ford 1991, 18–30 describes their experiences and how these radicalized them. Alice Paul was the daughter of a Quaker banker, who grew up in New Jersey and went to study at the London School of Economics after obtaining her B.A. from Swarthmore in 1905. In 1912 she received her Ph.D. in Political Science from the University of Pennsylvania after writing a dissertation on *The Legal Position of Women in Pennsylvania.* Lucy Burns was the daughter of a Catholic bank president in Brooklyn, N.Y., who received her B.A. from Vassar in 1902. Martin's father was also a banker. She was raised in Nevada and obtained both a B.A and an M.A. from Stanford University in 1896 and 1897.

45. Kraditor 1959, 1969, 262–67. Ford 1991, 46–59. Miller 1992, 83–92. Ruth's father was Marcus Hanna, Senator from Ohio, 1897–1904 and Chairman of the Republican National Committee 1896–1904. He is credited with electing William McKinley as President, and with putting the national Republican Party on a sound financial basis by requiring corporations to donate a percentage of their earnings to the party coffers. In both *WJ* 1900, 337, and in *Collier's Weekly* 1900, 18, Catt described him as having a "well-known antipathy to the woman in politics." The eldest son of the *Tribune*'s owners, Medill McCormick went into politics over his family's objection. He and Ruth were active in the Illinois Progressive

Movement and the Progressive Party. He was elected to the Illinois House in 1912, the House of Representatives in 1916, and the U.S. Senate in 1918. Ruth's granddaughter, Kristie Miller, published her biography in 1992.

46. Irwin 1921, 1964, 152–66. Ford 1991, 59–64. On the 1914 Arizona campaign see Snapp 1975. The CU's victory claims were hollow; its impact on the elections was minimal.

47. First quote from speech of April 8, 1916, by Alice Paul, reproduced in Irwin 1921, 1964, 154. On 1916 and 1918 campaigns, see Irwin 1921, 1964, 152–62, 175–83, 390–92. On Wilson leagues, see Snapp 1975, 136, for Arizona, and *SFEx*, Sept. 6, 1916, 6:1, Sept. 28, 1916, 4:1, for California.

48. *NYT Magazine*, Sept. 1, 1912, V:9.

49. V *HWS* 1922, xxi, 324, 342 (first two quotes, third quote in note), 412, 424, 426, 434, 461, 464, 471, 490, 574 (fourth quote). *WJ*, Feb. 28, 1914, 65, reported that "Many suffrage leaders, including Mrs. Grace Wilbur Trout, president of the Illinois Equal Suffrage Association, . . . urged the women to refrain from voting at the primaries." Addams's partisanship prompted many stories and comments in *WJ* throughout 1912. Wilson administration warning in *NYT*, Aug. 17, 1916, 7:3. See also the *NYT* editorial, "Party Politics and the Women" which lauded defeat of the NAWSA resolution restricting officers; Nov. 27, 1912, 12:2.

50. V *HWS* 1922, 702, 707.

51. Platform fights in Peck 1944, 244–53; V *HWS* 1922, 711–13; Dreier 1950, 129. Democratic Southerners continued to oppose woman suffrage because it would mean Negro suffrage. Senator John Sharp Williams of Mississippi proposed a plank that read "The right of no white person to vote shall be denied or abridged on account of sex," because, he said, "the same means that have been resorted to cut down the vote of the Negro men would not be applicable for Negro women"; Morgan 1972, 108–9. Hughes quotes on why he supported the federal amendment in RNC 1916, 17. See also the report of his speech to Republican women announcing his conversion in the *NYT*, Aug. 2, 1916, 1:2. "Press Full of Comment on Hughes' Declaration," *WJ*, Aug. 12, 1916, 258, reviewed the responses. *NYT*, June 9, 1916, 3:1, story on the Republican platform wrangle reported the vote as 26–21; this was only the initial vote, the final one was 35 to 11. Lovell 1980, 72–76, describes suffragists' efforts to obtain support from the candidates. For an analysis of Wilson and suffrage see Lunardini and Knock 1980–81.

52. Catt and Shuler 1923, 1926, 107.

NOTES FOR CHAPTER FOUR (PAGES 63 TO 83)

1. First quote Foster, 1892. Second quote in *RMN*, Nov. 4, 1894, 1:2. Reports on Woman's Democratic Club, "Captured the Club," and "Enthusiastic Supporters of the Tax-payers' Ticket," *RMN*, Oct. 25, 1895, McCormick quote in Miller 1992, 120.

2. McGerr 1986, 206.

3. Rose 1996, 17, summarizes the rise and decline of saloons and drinking. Roosevelt 1886, 79, discusses their role in sustaining political machines. Edwards 1999, describes the "transformation of electoral campaigns" by the urban middle class; quote on 21.

4. VandeCreek 1999.

5. *WJ*, June 23, 1900, 196, 199, "Two Utah Women in Politics." IV *HWS* 1902, 439. Breckinridge 1933, 1972, 276–77. In an interview with *WJ*, Jones said her husband had no interest in politics, except to vote, and she had no interest until Utah gave suffrage to women, when she "became fascinated with the work"; June 30, 1900, 201. "New Woman at Kansas

City," *NYTrib*, July 7, 1900, 7:3 describes Cohen as she demonstrated for Bryan. Quote from Catt 1900, 337.

6. *WJ*, July 9, 1904, 224, "Women in National Republican Convention," describes the Colorado women. *WJ*, June 25, 1904, 204, "An Idaho Delegate," describes West, as "a forceful factor in securing suffrage for the women of Idaho" and "the first woman to receive her credentials as a delegate to a National Convention" in 1900. *NYT*, June 21, 1904, 1:6, describes her as the one woman delegate, but other records indicate she was an alternate.

7. *The Denver Times*, Jan. 20, 1902. Beswick held the office of "County Investigator," though this article does not describe her duties.

8. First quotes in Runyon 1908. Last quote in Sumner 1909, 64. Like other workers, women canvassers were paid less than men.

9. *WJ*, April 14, 1900, 111–12.

10. *The Evening Post* (New York), Oct. 18, 1900, 8:1, devoted its regular column on "Women and Their Work" to campaign activities. It was reprinted in *WJ*, Nov. 3, 1900, 348, under the heading "New York Women in Politics."

11. "Women at the Convention," *NYTrib*, June 21, 1900, 9.

12. Catt wrote these words for *Collier's Weekly*, 18, and *WJ*, 337.

13. On Lease, see Blumberg 1978, 12, 14. She campaigned for Teddy Roosevelt when he ran as a Republican in 1904, and as a Progressive in 1912. In between she spoke for the Socialist Party. On women's work in the 1900 campaign, see *NYTrib*, Sept. 8, 7:1; Oct. 13, 7:1; Oct. 21, 1900, II:6:2; *BDE*, Sept. 8, 5:4; Oct. 26, 18:3–6; Boswell, *NR*, Feb. 22, 1919, 7:6.

14. Kriebel 1985, 189–90. "Women in Politics," *NYTrib*, Sept. 8, 1900, 7:1 (last paragraph). "Women Orators of the Three Leading Parties," *BDE*, Oct. 26, 1900, 19:3–6. Catt 1900.

15. *WJ*, Nov. 3, 1900, 345; Sept. 15, 1900, 292; quote from Mary A. Livermore, Sept. 22, 1900, 300; Sept. 10, 1904, 292. "Campaign Headquarters," *NYTrib*, Oct. 13, 1900, 7:1. Article from *The Minneapolis Journal*, as reprinted in *WJ*, Nov. 10, 1900, 352. "California Women in Politics," *NYTrib*, July 28, 1900, 7:2. "Women in Politics," *NYTrib*, Sept. 9, 1900, 7:1.

16. IV *HWS* 1902, 612. Chicago had a Woman's Roosevelt Club in 1902; Folder 11, Emily Dean Papers, CHS. Dean was the President of the Illinois Republican Women's Clubs from 1924 to 1938.

17. "To Work for Low," *NYTrib*, Oct. 9, 1901, 7:2; "Municipal League. . ." *NYTrib*, Oct. 25, 1901, 7:1. "Women in the Political Campaign," *NYH Magazine*, Oct. 26, 1903, 8. When interviewed by the *Herald* about the Tammany women's club, Mrs. Julius Harburger mistakenly claimed that it was a "first" for women in the history of the Democratic Party. The Tammany club was probably more show than substance. Its only other mention in the newspapers was a 1904 interview with "Women Helping in the Campaign," *NY World*, Aug. 28, 1904, 7:1. Villard, a reform, pro-suffrage journalist said that "no body of women worthy of notice has yet been got together to campaign for Tammany Hall"; 1902, 78.

18. Compare the names on the letterhead stationary in Reels 86 and 96 of the Taft papers, LoC. Quote from Foster letter of Oct. 5, 1908 to Taft, Reel 96, Taft Papers, LoC. Taft's reply is on Reel 477. Hay bio in II *NAW* 1971, 163–65; obit in *NYT*, Aug. 21, 1928, 19:3. Boswell remembered the 1908 campaign in *NY Sun*, Oct. 10, 1921.

19. Cox 1996, 327. *NYSun* quote reported in *WJ*, Nov. 10, 1900, 357. Second quote by Meredith, *WJ*, Oct. 2, 1905, 72.

20. Quoted in Sumner, 1909, 62, from a survey she did on the consequences of suffrage in Colorado. A Denver Politician 1909, 70, also noted that "the women who do the real political work prior to and on election day more often than not are forgotten when it comes to allotting the political positions."

21. "Women in Politics in the Presidential Campaign," 56 *Harper's Weekly*, Nov. 9, 1912, 12. Addams 1930, 23. Reichley 1992, 198–200. Burckel 1991, 695–96. Women's Roosevelt Leagues reported in the *SFCall* 1912: March 17, 43:1; March 26, 2:6; March 29, 7:3; Sept. 28, 11:3; Nov. 2, 11:1, and in 12:16 *California Outlook*, April 13, 1912, 16.

22. TR letters on women mentioned in *ChiTrib*, Sept. 3, 1912, 5:5. *NYT* 1912: editorial, "Women as Party Workers," Aug. 12, 8:3; Sept. 1, 5:9:3; Oct. 7, 9:3. Daggett 1913, 151, wrote that there were twenty women delegates, "coming even from states that have not yet admitted women to citizenship." Breckinridge 1933, 1972, 278–79 claimed twelve. Carpenter was from Massachusetts. The four women on the Executive Committee were Jane Addams of Chicago, Frances Kellor of New York, Isabella Blaney of California, and June Gordon of New Orleans (who soon resigned); Daggett 1913, 153. From various sources, Gustafson estimated that there were from sixteen to forty women delegates and five to twenty women alternates; 1993, 199, 226–29. Gable is "certain" there were at least fifteen; 1978, 267n, see also 40, 58, 76, 107. Gustafson identified women on the state committees of California, New York, Connecticut, Maryland, New Hampshire and Rhode Island, and "other states;" 1993, 265–66. The press claimed Addams was the first woman to second a nomination, ignoring Elizabeth Cohen's brief remarks for Bryan at the Democratic convention in 1900, though some pointed out that Mary Lease had seconded James Weaver's nomination at the 1892 Populist convention, and Bryan's in 1896. No one remembered that Frances Willard had seconded the nominations of the Prohibition Party's candidates in 1884 and 1888; Bordin 1986, 130–35. Note that "equal suffrage" does not mean support for a federal amendment; V *HWS* 1922, 705–7. Duncan-Clark named only Addams and Kellor in his chapter on "Women and the Progressive Movement"; 1913, 106–7.

23. *NYT* 1912: Aug. 1, 3:3; Aug. 4, 4:1; Aug. 5, 1:1; Aug. 7, 2:2–7; Sept. 1, V:9:1; Sept. 4. 11:1; Sept. 5, 3:5; Sept. 17, 3:2. See also, Miller 1992, 48–57. Elinor Carpenter's appointment to the New York State Executive Committee was described as "The feminization of the Bull Moose Party"; Aug. 12, 6:3; "feminized" and "feminization" appear repeatedly in *NYT* coverage.

24. Harriman was an early Wilson supporter; *BDE*, Nov. 9, 1924. She wrote Chairman W.F. McCombs for his endorsement of her plan, which she received on Aug. 5, 1912; *NYT*, Aug. 7, 1912, 4:3. It was common to name campaign organizations for the candidates. California women worked under the auspices of the Woman's Woodrow Wilson League; *SFCall*, July 9, 1912, 5:3. See also Harriman 1923; bio in IV *NAW* 1980, 314–15; *NYT* obit, Sept. 1, 1967, 28:6.

25. The *NYT* described it as "the most ambitious bureau of them all . . . for the wives of many of the Democratic National Committeemen have allied themselves with the bureau and are working hard"; Sept. 1, 1912, 5:9:1. *NYT* 1912: Aug. 18, 4:3; Sept. 17, 3:5. See also Miller 1999.

26. *NYT*, first quote in Aug. 20, 1912, 18:2; Sept. 15, 1912, 2:9 includes reports from Washington and California where women would vote in their first Presidential election. "Women Politicians Open Headquarters," *BDE*, Aug. 10, 1912, 14:6. Second quote from Boswell, *NR*, March 1, 1919, 7. California Women's Taft Club activities in *SFCall* 1912: March 5, 1:4; May 1, 5:1,2; May 2, 16:2,3; May 5, 40:2; May 12, 18:2. Boswell describes the Republican women's campaign in *NR*, March 8, 1919, 8; "Political Episodes XII," 13:5 *WRNY*, May 1936, 9.

27. First Addams quote in Addams 1930, 38. Second in *NYT*, Sept. 26, 1912, 5:2. Third quote is Boswell's; *NR*, March 1, 1919, 7. Daggett 1913, 153–54, described women's campaign propaganda. See also *NYT*, Sept. 1, 1912, V:9:1.

28. See Ray 1924, 169, on campaign customs and party organization. On McCormick see Miller 1992, 37–38, 48, 54–57; III *NAW* 1971, 293–95; *NYT* obit, Jan. 1, 1945, 21:3. Harriman quote in Harriman 1923, 112.

29. First quote from *NYT*, Sept. 1, 1912,V:9:1. Roosevelt wrote to his state and county chairmen on July 20, 1912: "Gentlemen: I favor woman suffrage by states"; *NYT*, Aug. 6, 1912, 2:2. He was not new to this issue. When he was Governor of New York, Roosevelt had urged gradual extension of the suffrage to women; *NYT*, Jan. 6, 1899, 5:2. Taft quotes from his speech to NAWSA's 1910 convention; in 1912 he said he was still waiting; V *HWS* 1922, 270–71, 708. Wilson, *ibid.* and *NYT*, Aug. 18, 1912, 4:3.

30. *NYT* 1912: Aug. 12, 3:2; Kellor quote, Sept. 1,V:9:1; Oct. 11, 1:2. See also editorial on "The Wilson Women," *NYT*, Sept. 5, 1912, 8:2.

31. Quotes from a Roosevelt speech made in Vermont and reported in the *NYT* of Aug. 31, 1912, 2:4. Wilson quote *NYT*, Aug. 18, 1912, 4:3. See *NYT* editorial "Women as Party Workers," Aug. 12, 1912, 8:3. Taft didn't support woman suffrage until Congress sent it to the states in 1919; Catt and Shuler 1923, 1926, 238.

32. Favorable reports include Borah (1910) and Tyer (1916) on Idaho; Slocum (1903), Creel and Lindsey (1911), Dorr (1911), and Taylor (1912) on Colorado; and Edson (Oct. 1912) on California. In 1915 the California legislature praised the workings of woman suffrage; resolution reprinted in Coolidge 1916. The *NYT* published a lengthy report on women "floaters" and other frauds in Colorado, Feb. 21, 1904, 3:1:4, "When Lovely Woman Stoops to Politics"—"Her Methods Are So Up-to-date that the Male Graduate of the 'Practical' School Can Learn From Her." *Outlook*, which, like the *NYT*, opposed suffrage, emphasized suffrage's failings, arguing that respectable women did not vote, or voted like their husbands, and "vicious women" followed a boss; Lewis 1906.

33. Villard 1902, 79.

34. Flexner 1959, 1968, 256. Women's Political Union; n.d. (1912); SI. In 1910, the Supreme Court of Nebraska held that women could be elected to offices for which they could not vote; *Jordan v. Quible*, 86 Neb. 417 (1910). Jordan was elected county treasurer after serving for seven years as deputy, but the outgoing treasurer refused to turn over the records or money until the court ruled her election valid. Other states had long elected women to school boards and as state superintendents of public instruction even when they could not vote for those offices.

35. Foster 1897. Alice Hay Wadsworth letter of Sept. 4, 1919, to Ruth Hanna McCormick, asking her to oppose Ann Martin, who was running for the Senate in Nevada; Box 13, Hanna-McCormick Papers, LoC. Wadsworth's name appears on a members' list of the 1916 Women's Committee of the Hughes Alliance, though there is no evidence that she did anything in this campaign.

36. Bryce commented in 1888 that American women's participation in politics had not yet caught up with that of English women; II: 172, 586. When Story 1903, compared British and American women in politics, he noted, as Bryce had, that the former were ahead of the latter and both were far ahead of their European counterparts. He identifies 1881 as the year "that women became an active feature in British politics," 259, but appears unaware of how involved American women were in electoral and party politics by 1903. Miller 1896, was more aware that American women weren't too far behind English women. On Foster and the WLF, see *Chicago Inter-Ocean*, Sept. 29, 1888, 12. Edwards 1997, 83, believes that the Republican Party arranged for her to travel to England, but credits the Conservative Party's Primrose League rather than the Liberals for her inspiration. Quote from a speech given in

1898 in Robb 1942, 121. The *NYTrib* regularly wrote about British women's political work, noting that men thought them much better at house-to-house canvassing, Aug. 25, 1895, 6:5; "Titled English Women Who Have Been Taking an Active Part in the Recent Elections," Oct. 21, 1900, II:6:3. Its story on J. Ellen Foster's proposal to organize Republican women said the new clubs would "do work similar to that carried on by the English women"; July 12, 1888, 2:6. See also: *NYT*, July 22, 1903, 2:2; April 24, 1907, 4:1; *NYH*, Oct. 20, 1895, VI:9;1.

37. The *NYT* repeatedly editorialized that women should only be allowed to vote if they could prove they would vote better than men but ignored any evidence that they might do so. Compare the editorial of Feb. 14, 1900, 6:2 with letters from Wyoming officials on Feb. 23, 1900, 6:5, attesting to the beneficial effects of woman suffrage. After the 1916 election the *NYT* complained that in Illinois women voted exactly like men; Nov. 8, 1916, 12:1. The paper's election analysis four days later credited women voters for Wilson's victory in California, and hence the election, because they didn't vote just like men; Nov. 12, 1916, 1:1. *ChiTrib*'s Oct. 17, 1894 front page story on the registration of women to vote on "educational affairs" said they were "Treated as Queens," and included "the most cultured and thoughtful women" rather than the "disreputable" whom, it was feared, might "overcome the votes of the members of good society." As a woman suffrage supporter, its coverage was quite different than that of the *NYT*.

38. Abbott 1915. Coolidge 1916, argued that California women used the vote to educate themselves and improve municipal government. Quote from William Macleod Raine, in the (Utah) *Deseret News*, Feb. 13, 1902, cited in Beeton 1986, 136, who reviewed the studies and commentaries on the impact of woman suffrage in the four early suffrage states. *NYTrib* and *NYH* generally reported during the 1890s and 1910s that women's presence brought order to the polls, as did Whelpley 1900.

39. "What the Election Did for the Cause of Suffrage," *NYT Magazine*, Nov. 10, 1912, V:1. Quote from Raftery 1994, 154.

40. Daggett 1913, 151. The Census Bureau estimated that 1,346,925 women were eligible and at least 680,000 voted; *NYT*, Nov. 9, 1912, 10:6. Women were elected to their state legislatures in Colorado, Utah, Washington, and Wyoming; Cox 1996. On New York, see Wesser 1986, 200. Colorado election results as reported in *WJ*, April 12, 1913, 120. "Colorado Elects Woman Chairman," *NYT*, Jan. 16, 1914, 1:5. Three months later another front page story was headlined "To Depose Woman Leader," but it was small and below the fold. It said: "Because the rules of the Democratic Party will not allow a woman to manage a campaign, Mrs. Gertrude Lee, it is said, will be deposed as Chairman of the State Democratic Committee. Organized Democrats are preparing to attend a meeting of the State Committee next month, to name Mrs. Lee's successor in ample time to arrange for the fall campaign;" *NYT*, March 12, 1914, 1:4. However, stories in *RMN* indicate she held onto the chairmanship longer; "Mrs. Lee Defies Men to Oust Her," April 1, 1914, 1.

41. California 1912 Assembly races reported in column by Florence Collins Porter, in 13:6 *California Outlook*, Dec. 3, 1912, 10. Municipal elections reported in *WJ*, Dec. 13, 1913, 400. The 1914 candidates listed are in Coolidge 1916, 5. Williams candidacy reported in *SFEx* 1914: May 12, 5:1; June 19, 6:1; June 20, 10:6; July 9, 5:3; July 24, 20:1; Aug. 25, 7:7; Sept. 16, 9:6. Lindsey win is in *NYT*, June 3, 1915, 20:2. Quote from Katz 1996, 1999, 23. See also Gustafson 1997.

42. Twice as many men registered as women; final returns reported by Chicago Election Board in *Survey*, July 25, 1914, 442; early reports in "50,000 Women in Chicago Primary,"

45:9 *WJ*, Feb. 28, 1914, 1. Quote in Taylor 1914, 70. Wendt and Kogan 1943, 1971, 305. The Seventh Ward was in a fine residential district just south of the University of Chicago. Its leader was the wife of U.C. professor J. Paul Goode, Republican Party Alderman Charles E. Merriam was an advisor and its members were "ministers' wives, presidents of social clubs, civic club presidents, heads of card clubs, etc"; Ray 1924, 185–86, citing Yount 1916, 54–56. The Second Ward was also on the south side of Chicago, but further north in what was becoming a black ghetto; Goldstein, 1984, 236. Duster 1970, 346. Hendricks 1990, 168–69, 180–89 says that three black men ran in the Republican primary for the Second Ward in 1915, dividing the efforts of women, but that the Alpha Suffrage Club still supported DePriest. He did not run for reelection in 1917, after much bad publicity from a trial for gambling, bribery, and other offenses; Hendricks 1990, 206.

43. Nominations in *NYT*, June 11, 1916, 1:8. List of Progressive women who worked for Hughes in Gustafson 1993, 352. Edson to Harriet Vittum, Sept. 6, 1916, Box 1, Folder 4, Edson Papers, UCLA. Jane Addams supported Wilson's reelection, but didn't campaign for him as she had for TR.

44. On the Women's Roosevelt League, see the *NYT*, 1916: May 24, 6:5; June 1, 5:2; June 28, 8:5; July 13, 2:5; July 14, 20:5; Aug. 4, 5:6. Formation of the Women's Committee of the Hughes Alliance covered by *NYT*, July 1916: 2, 9:1; 3, 5:3; 8, 5:4. Alice Carpenter was also a member of Alice Paul's Congressional Union. Hughes was prodded by TR to endorse woman suffrage; Gustafson 1993, 353. On April 28, 1916, TR told a delegation from the CU that he supported a federal amendment; *NYT*, April 29, 1916, 18:3.

45. Quotes from the *NYT*, July 8, 1916, 5:4,5. Other reports on July 10, 7:1; July 25, 9:4; July 28, 9:7; Aug. 5, 4:4; Aug. 6, 5:2. *NYH* July 1916: 4, 6:1; 8, 6:2; 13, 6:1. See Women's Committee 1916 and Kellor 1917 for a detailed description of its activities. The former says thirteen issues of the magazine were each sent to between 25,000 and 50,000 persons. I haven't found any copies.

46. "G.O.P. Women's Special," press release signed by Frances A. Kellor, n.d. "for release anytime after Sept. 16"; SI. *NYT*, Sept. 17, 1916, 12:2; *NYH*, Sept. 21, 1916, 2:7. Letters to the editor identified all the members of the Train Committee as suffragists, but the stationary of the Women's Committee lists antis among its members; *NYT*, Sept. 24, 1916, 7:3; *NYH*, Sept. 24, 1916, 3:2; O'Shaughnessey Papers, Box 5, NYPL. The anonymous report was a 38-page pamphlet, *Women in National Politics*, published by the Women's Committee, National Hughes Alliance. Kellor's 1917 article was later reprinted as a pamphlet.

47. Both the *NYT* and the *NYH* published stories virtually every day of the month-long trip. Too many to list here, they are cataloged separately under "Hughes Alliance" in the 1916 *NYT Index*, and integrated under "Hughes, Charles E.", in the 1916 *NYH Index*. Half of the Women's Committee pamphlet is about the train; its appendix includes five pages of editorial comments from local papers. Journalist Rheta Childe Dorr rode the train as an official speaker for Hughes *and* as a newspaper correspondent reporting on the trip. Her autobiography summarizes her experiences, 1924, 315–18. Other descriptions of the campaign train are in Braitman (on California) 1986, 92–93; Bates (Montana) 1987. The first three of the five campaign themes reflect Kellor's priorities, though no doubt the RNC sanctioned them. Kellor bio in Fitzpatrick 1990; obit in *NYT*, Jan. 5, 1952, 11:2.

48. The *NYT*, which supported Wilson, was quite hostile to the women's train, much more so than local papers. See particularly *NYT*, Oct. 1916: 5, 3:3; 6, 4:2; 8, 4:2; 10, 11:3; 12, 24:2; 15, 6:3; 18, 4:4; Nov. 20, 8:1 and the editorials of Oct. 4, 10:4,5; Oct. 5, 10:4, and Nov. 6, 10:4. *SFEx*, in contrast, wrote that "Women Stir Ohio Crowds for Hughes," Oct. 4, 1916,

4:1. *ChiTrib*, which declared "Hughes Women Found Chicago Battle Ground," Nov. 2, 1916, 3:4, nonetheless concluded that "Illinois Women Turn to Hughes," Nov. 3, 1916, 5:1. Robins' biography describes her wonderful reception and ignores the heckling; Dreier 1950, 129–30. Roosevelt told a crowd at Denver on Oct. 24 that he knew "that every woman on the train is a wage earner, except two that are married"; Women's Committee 1916, 31.

49. Kellor quotes and other comments are in Women's Committee 1916, 19. Husted quote in letter to *NYT*, Nov. 16, 1916, 10:7. *SFEx*, Nov. 8, 1916, 5:5. The *NYT* editorial, Nov. 6, 1916, 10:4. Train coverage in the *SFC*, Oct. 18, 1916, 1:1 and the *LAT*, Oct. 19, 1916, 1:1. *LAT* also reported that the women "captivated Pasadena": "They came, they saw, they conquered"; Oct. 20, 1916, 6:1; "Women Hoodlums Fail to Mar Great Ovation," Oct. 19, 1916, 6:4, and "Women's Day in Politics;" Oct. 19, 1916, 7:1. Both California papers supported Hughes and had opposed woman suffrage prior to its victory in 1911. See also Wood 1999.

50. *NYT* 1916: Aug. 5, 4:4; Aug. 17, 7:5; Oct. 10, 10:6. Press release of Sept. 16, 1916, announced the train sponsors as "The Republican Women's Campaign Committee and the Women's Committee of the Hughes Alliance." Kellor's post-election diatribe accused the Republican Party of putting the Chicago HQ "in charge of . . . a man who had long been an anti-suffragist in his own State"; 1917, 234. *NYT*, Aug. 17, 1916, 7:3, identified him as Alvin T. Hert of Kentucky. His widow would later head the RNC Women's Division. Kellor did not mention Vittum. Boswell only expressed her disapproval of Kellor, the Woman's Committee, and the train, which she left after four days, twenty years later; "Political Episodes XIII," 13:6 *WRNY*, June 1936, 6.

51. Breckinridge 1933, 1972, 281. On the Democratic Woman's Bureau, see "Major Parties Appeal To Women As Never Before," *WJ*, Aug. 12, 1916, p. 262; Bass 1940, 17, 39, quote from Bass "Report," 1919, Financial Report. On Bass see DCWF 1960, 31; NWPC–Dem 1980, 4; V *HWS* 1922, 464, 567; VI *HWS* 1922, 155; obit in *NYT*, Aug. 26, 1950, 13:5. On the WNDL, see the *NYT*, Aug. 4, 1916, 5:6. Independent League in the *NYT*, Aug. 24, 1916, 5:4. Bass letter of June 15, 1918, to "Mr. President," Wilson Papers, Reel 377. Kellor quote in Kellor 1917, 237. Carnegie Hall debate reported in *NYT*, Nov. 5, 1916, 4:1, which failed to note the futility of women debating before an audience of women in New York City where they could not vote, rather than in Chicago, where they could.

52. "Wilson or Hughes? The Difference it Makes to The Women," three-page pamphlet, 1916, SI. The four million woman voters was calculated from the 1910 census showing 3,665,445 women over twenty-one in these twelve states; *ChiTrib*, Nov. 5, 1916, 3. The *Times* calculated that between 1.5 and 2 million women might vote; *NYT*, Oct. 29, 1916, 14:1. DNC 1916. RNC 1916, 16, 17, 260, 363.

53. Breckinridge 1933 and 1972, 275–77. The *NYT*, June 8, 1916, 5:5, reported that the Democrats had fourteen women delegates and nine women alternates from eight states.

54. V *HWS* 1922, 711, 714.

55. *LAT*, Nov. 8, 1918, 1; Nov. 10, 1916, 1:3. The *Chicago Daily News* headline was actually printed on election day, as it was an evening newspaper. Its headline on Nov. 8 said "Hughes Leads; West to Decide," and "Women Vote Like Men." *SFC* opined "Hughes Probably Elected—California Apparently is Safely Republican," Nov. 8, 1916, 1:1; Nov. 11, 1916, 3:1. Of these papers, only *NYT* had extensive election analysis, even of California; *NYT*, Nov. 1916: 12, 1:1. 20, 8:1. Last quote Raftery 1994, 146.

56. Chamberlin 1973, 3–17, quote on 6. The *NYT* reported her negative vote on the war resolution on the front page, April 6, 1917, 1:8, and later used that as one more reason why the federal suffrage amendment should not be passed; editorial of Nov. 3, 1917, 14:2.

57. On Axtell see "Two Women for Congress," *WP*, Nov. 10, 1916, 2. "Woman is Given High Office," *WJ*, May 19, 1917, 115; *WC*, April 10, 1920, 1106. Quote from "Many Women Candidates for Election," *SFEx*, July 28, 1918, 8:1. Leslie study reported in *WC*, Dec. 28, 1918, 636. On women state legislators, Cox 1996, 327. Full suffrage required a state's male voters to pass a referendum. Partial suffrage only required legislative action.

58. First quote from an untitled, undated "call" for a meeting on Nov. 23rd, in the Edson Papers, UCLA. It contains an "outline of the proposed organization" and states that "every effort should be made to make Miss Rankin's work in Congress effective," implying a 1916 date. Second quote from Meredith July 1933, 7. Democratic resolution reprinted in Blair 1929, 218; Republican resolution in Good 1963, 11.

59. Quote in "Mrs. George Bass Heads Bureau to Teach Women Beliefs of Democratic Party"; *WJ*, March 10, 1917, 57. Bass explained her move as a pre-emptive strike, prompted by Theodore Roosevelt's suggestion to the RNC Chairman that women be added to the RNC; letter of Jan. 21, 1918 to "Mr. President," Wilson Papers, Reel 94. Clement 1936, 28. DNC 1945, 4. Bass 1919; 1940, 39. DCWF 1960, 31. Feb. 26, 1919, resolution in Breckinridge 1933, 1972, 281; DNC 1919; *NYT*, Feb. 27, 1919, 8:1. *WES*, Sept. 28, 1919, 1:5,6; *WP*, Sept. 28, 1919, 2:6. *NYT*, Feb. 16, 1920, 15:4 lists the eleven women added to the DNC Executive Committee and 65 *LD*, May 29, 1920, 69–70, profiles them. Four of these are mentioned in *HWS* indicating some suffrage activity. Democratic Women's Day was celebrated with fundraising events; *For and About Women*, Sept. 1956, 2; Box 17, Louchheim papers, LoC. Edwards 1977, 101.

60. Middle quote in one of two Bass "Reports," 1919, 7, describing her work and assessment of state activity, in the Josephus Daniels papers, Box 705, LoC. Other quotes from DNC "Plan," 1919, 6; reported in *NYT*, Feb. 27, 1919, 8:1. Antoinette Funk's letter of Aug. 29, 1919, to Mrs. W.E. Brown reads like a form letter and was probably sent to thousands of women. Mrs. Brown sent it to Ruth McCormick, then in charge of organizing Republican women; Box 13, Hanna-McCormick Papers, LoC. Funk's letterhead stationary identifies her as "Director of Education" but does not indicate that she was in the Women's Bureau, as the "Plan" had proposed. The DNC papers from this period have been lost, so information on what happened when is sketchy.

61. "Democratic and Republican Women Working for Suffrage Amendment," *WC*, Jan. 5, 1918, 108–9 identifies Boswell as heading the GOP Women's Division but she is not mentioned in Good's semi-official *History*, which only names McCormick; 1963, 9–10. There were no copies of McCormick's form letter and questionnaire in her papers, but I found one of each, dated March 11, 1919, addressed to "My dear Miss French," plus several replies, in Box 5 of the Edson Papers, UCLA. The committee members listed on RWNEC's letterhead stationery in March of 1919 were Mrs. Medill McCormick, Chairman, Mrs. Florence Collins Porter, California, Miss Mary Garrett Hay, New York, Mrs. Margaret Hill McCarter, Kansas, Mrs. Josephine Corliss Preston, Washington, and Mrs. Raymond Robins, Illinois. Later stationary added the names of Mrs. John Glover South, Kentucky, Mrs. Thomas H. Carter, Montana, and Miss Maude Wetmore, Rhode Island. McCormick wrote Alice Hay Wadsworth in Sept. 1919 that "WE HAVE THREE anti suffragists on the committee and the members have been selected by the men in the Rep. organization and endorsed by the Natl. Committeeman and State Chair men from their respective states" (sic). These are in Box 13, Hanna-McCormick Papers, LoC.

62. Women came from every state except Mississippi and Texas. Coverage of the conference is in *NR*, May 31, 1919, 1, 8. First quote from Chairman Will Hays on "Woman's Place

in the Republican Party," *Ibid.*, 8; Hays 1955, 258. "Report" and "Recommendations" of the RWNEC, n.d. but probably May 1919, Reel 15:620, WTUL-MDR papers. Letter of Sept. 5, 1919 from Will H. Hays to McCormick and Hay; Box 13, Hanna-McCormick Papers, LoC. RWNEC "Report" of June 8, 1920, 4; Reel 15: 609–14, WTUL-MDR papers and Hay scrapbook, NYPL. The official reason for McCormick's resignation was illness, but her biographer says "Ruth was not happy with this new arrangement;" Miller 1992, 120–21. Hay and South appointments in *NYT*, Nov. 11, 1919, 4:2, Jan. 6, 1920, 1:2. The members of the RWNEC after Hay became chairman were: Mrs. John G. South, Kentucky; Mrs. Thomas Carter, Montana; Mrs. Margaret Hill McCarter, Kansas; Mrs. Florence Collins Porter, California; Mrs. Josephine Corliss Preston, Washington; Mrs. Raymond Robins, Illinois; Mrs. C.A. Severance, Minnesota; Miss Bina West, Michigan; Miss Maude Wetmore, Rhode Island; and Mrs. Geo. Reinecke, Executive Secretary. In Republican literature South is always listed as Mrs. John, but when she contributed a short statement to *WC* on "Why I Joined My Party" she signed it with her own name; Feb. 21, 1920, 894. Background on South in *NR*, Aug. 27, 1921, 8:4.

63. Women's demands reported at a conference for Midwestern women held in Chicago on Jan. 5, 1920; *NYT*, Jan. 6, 1920, 1:2; *WC*, Jan. 17, 1920, 722, 727. Hay demands: *NYT*, June 2, 1920, 3:1. Minutes of the Dec. 10, 1919, RNC meeting are in the RP Papers, Reel 1:325; see also Good 1963, 11; Livermore 1925; *NYT*, Dec. 11, 1919, 1:4.

NOTES FOR CHAPTER FIVE (PAGES 85 TO 108)

1. Blair 1929, 219.

2. Bass 1940, 17, 39. Quote from Blair 1940, 15. Gruberg 1968, 54. Information on Blair is in her unpublished autobiography, 1937, and IV *NAW* 1980, 82–83; obit in *NYT*, Aug. 4, 1951, 15:3. I read the former at the WNDC. Blair describes her indecision about party preference at 133–34, and her selection by Hull because "of all the women mentioned, most people wanted you," at 150. Both her parents and her husband were Democrats. Andersen 1999.

3. Blair 1940, first quote on 15; 1937, second quote on 152, 173. *FB*, July 8, 1922, 2. Blair's *Organization Primer* in WNDC archives.

4. *FB*, Oct. 7, 1922, 6; WNDC archives.

5. Blair later said there were 2,500 Democratic Women's Clubs by the end of 1924, but I've used the number as of January in DNC, "Blair Report" 1924, which she also reported in *NYT*, March 16, 1924, IX:18:1. The additional 1,500 clubs were most likely temporary campaign clubs rather than permanent ones. "Democracy Schools" described in Blair 1937, 173, which says they were modeled on the LWV citizenship schools. NYC "School" in *NYT* 1923: Jan. 22, 14:7; Feb. 4, 7:1; *FB*, No. 11, March 17, 1923, 1;, WNDC archives. Local clubs also ran their own "Schools"; *BDE*, Sept. 1, 1923, 24:7; *NYWorld*, Oct. 11, 1925. First and third quotes in Blair 1940, 15. Second quote from *FB*, Oct. 7, 1922, 6. Information on Bannister is in her papers in the LoC and in Ware 1981, 144.

6. First quote in Blair, "Looking Forward," *DB*, June 1928, 8. Second in Blair 1940, 38. "The Story of the Woman's National Democratic Club," *DD*, April 1935, 19–20. DCWF 1960, 39. Cunningham bio in I *NAW* 1971, 176–77; *NYT* obit., Dec. 12, 1964, 31:5. WNDC origins in Blair 1937, 167–68; as confirmed by Harriman in Frances Lide, "Honored Guest at Club Tea," *WES*, Sept. 23, 1954. On state inserts see Wolfe 1978, 94. State libraries that have copies of *The Bulletin* and the *Democratic Bulletin* generally have the inserts for their state.

7. Quote in Harriman oral history 1950, 35. "An Appreciation," *The Bulletin,* June 1928, 9. "Annual Report," *The Bulletin,* February 1929, 26. According to Mrs. Charles S. Hamlin, the house was bought in May 1927 with a $13,000 gift from the DNC and a $20,000 private loan; "Women's National Democratic Club," *DB,* March 1933, 14. Blair says the DNC contribution was only $5,000; 1940, 38. Fenzi 1997, 5–6. Blair's 1924 report to the DNC says she raised $27,755, other Democratic women contributed $7,215 and the DNC provided $25,108; 1924, 1098–99. In 1937, 153, she wrote that she raised $80,000. Blair made some money of her own from writing about women and politics during these years and traveled on a railroad pass available through her husband, who was a railroad lawyer.

8. Cunningham 1926. "Annual Report for 1926–27," *The Bulletin,* February 1927, 5; July 1927, 3. First and third quotes in Florence J. Harriman, "Extracts from the Report of the Board of Governors," *The Bulletin,* March 1930, 29–33. Second quote in White 1932, 37.

9. *The Bulletin,* August 1928, 4–5. DCWF 1960, 39. *NYT,* July 14, 1928, 4:3. Dewson 1949, I:123. On Raskob see Goldman 1990, 323–24; Kyvig 1979, 101, 144; McManus 1931. Raskob had voted for Coolidge in 1924 and Wilson in 1916. He said he had no fixed party identification, but *Who's Who* said he was a Republican. He supported FDR in 1932, but Landon in 1936. On Ross, see Scharff; obit in *NYT,* Dec. 21, 1977, B:11:4–5. Recruited by Smith advisor Belle Moskowitz, Ross announced her support of Smith in February 1928; *NYHT,* July 29, 1928. That the DNC finally realized the necessity of organizing women is seen in "The Democratic Women Must Organize," by Jouett Shouse, who was hired by Raskob to be Chairman of the DNC Executive Committee in charge of day-to-day operation; 5:3 *WDN,* July 1929, 1.

10. First quote in Ross, *DD,* May 1940, 13. *DD,* March 1931, 10. Second quote in *DD,* June 1932, 12–13. "Program for Democratic Clubs," *DB,* January 1931, 21–23. White 1932.

11. Dewson 1949, I:123.

12. *DD,* Jan. 1942, 7.

13. Dewson bios in Ware 1987; IV *NAW* 1980, 188–91; obit in *NYT,* Oct. 25, 1962, 39:1.

14. Roosevelt and Hickok 1954, 15. Schlesinger, Jr. 1960, 439–40. Even though the DNC was in Washington, Dewson kept her main office in New York City, where she lived with Polly Porter. When in Washington, she stayed at the White House. Dewson 1949, I:123.

15. *DD:* "The Reporter Plan," Sept. 1934, 14; "Army of Women Work Under Reporter Plan," Jan. 1935, 10; "What the Women Could and Should Do for the Democratic Party," March 1935, 17. Ware 1981, 68–73. Dewson's view reflected FDR's. After losing the 1920 election, he wrote that "our weakness in the past has been due largely to the fact that we have conducted our campaigns in most places only during the two or three months before election," FDR to John P. Hume, Nov. 8, 1920, Box 16, FDR papers, FDRL.

16. Roosevelt and Hickok 1954, 17–18.

17. Quote in Roosevelt and Hickok 1954, 20. Ware 1981, 73–74. *DD:* May Thompson Evans, "Institute for Democratic Women Launches Reporter Plan in North Carolina," Dec. 1934; "A New Deal for the *Democratic Digest,*" March 1935, 3; "The Richmond Regional Conference Opens First Institute of Government March 7–8," March 1935, 12–13; "Second Regional Conference in Detroit," April 1935, 7; "The First Regional Conference—A Milestone in Women's Evolution," April 1935, 12–13; "State Meetings Draw Enthusiastic Crowds," May 1935, 7; "Enthusiasm of Regional Conferences Spreads from Coast to Coast," June 1935, 16–17, lists eighteen regional and district conferences between April 22 and May 24, 1935. The magazine "costs the National Committee $2.00 for each annual subscription and the subscription price is only $1.00"; Dewson 1940, 90.

18. Ware 1981, 72. Roosevelt and Hickok 1954, 20. Quote in Perkins 1946, 121. Dewson 1949, II:37. Although Wolfe was the official head of the Women's Division from 1934 to 1936, when she met Jim Farley at an official dinner shortly after her appointment, he didn't know who she was; Wolfe oral history 1978, 86. Pamphlets from the Woman's Division had both her name and Dewson's on them.

19. Molly Dewson to Eleanor Roosevelt, April 17, 1937, and June 22, 1937; Molly Dewson to Jim Farley, Sept. 22, 1937; Reel 7, ER papers. Miller bios in IV *NAW* 1980, 476–78; *WES*, April 2, 1964.

20. Quote in Roosevelt and Hickok 1954, 18. Wolfe describes the Donkey Bank campaigns; 1978, 121–24. Fundraising figure from Dewson 1936, 5.

21. "Democratic Victory," sixteen-page pamphlet; 1936, SI. This pamphlet also describes the Donkey Banks and the Rainbow Fliers. A quarter million were printed. Dewson had little to say about Democratic women's clubs, but she wrote that in the 1936 campaign they were "outdated" and just "confused the party organization"; 1936, 5.

22. *DD* reported on the institute in its June/July 1940 issue, 62–67. See also *NYT*, May 1940: 2, 25:8; 3, 5:1, 12:3; 4, 7:1; 5, 47:7. Column by Jay Franklin chides DNC chairman for his absence: "Farley Misses Trick by Failure to Explore Rising Trend of Women's Political Activity," *WES*, May 9, 1940. Quote from Furman 1949, 284. Information on McAllister in Blair 1937, 150; Ware 1981, 148.

23. Ware 1981, 3, 126. Roosevelt and Hickok 1954, 21–22.

24. On Tillett, see Roydhouse 1980, 257–59, who interviewed her on July 25, 1975; bio in *DD*, Jan. 1941, 4; obit in *NYT*, Oct. 3, 1984, IV:27:6. Roosevelt and Hickok 1954, 26–27. Edwards 1977, 9, 91, 94–95. Edwards died at age 94; obits in *WP*, Jan. 16, 1990, B:5; *NYT*, Jan. 17, 1990, B:10:1; *LAT*, Jan. 18, 1990, A:26:1. Luce's speech criticized FDR for bringing the U.S. into WWII after promising not to do so in the 1940 campaign; Edwards' son was killed in battle in 1943; *NYT*, June 28, 1944, 15:1,2.

25. First quote in Bone 1958, 108. Former Congresswoman Chase Going Woodhouse (Conn.) was the official Director of the Women's Division in 1947–48, but Edwards ran it. Woodhouse "hated" the position, feeling that "Patronage was the whole business. Nobody was interested in issues." Woodhouse oral history, 1977–79, 261–62. Edwards' view is summarized in Morgan 1984, 298. "To the Ladies—and By and For Them," *DD*, Feb./March 1949, second quote on 18, third quote on 19. Edwards 1977, 125–26.

26. Edwards 1977, 7, quotes on 141–42, emphasis in original. Edwards later confessed that "not accepting his offer was one of the great mistakes of my life, but I did what I thought at the time was the best for the Democratic Party." Goldman 1990, 433–44, said Edwards was Truman's second choice for DNC chair; his first choice also turned him down.

27. Edwards wrote that Mitchell thought she wanted his job and had too much support on the National Committee; 1977, 202–3, 258. Copies of the protest letters, Edwards' resignation, and the DNC press releases of Jan. 26 and Oct. 7, 1953, announcing the changes are in the Edwards papers, HSTL. Edwards wrote an article for *DD*, April 1953, 18, putting a positive face on "integration." According to *Newsweek*, May 9, 1955, 31, Louchheim served without pay, though Edwards had received $14,500 annually. According to Louchheim the OWA did not have a separate budget and funds raised were turned over to the DNC; letter of Sept. 5, 1956, to Senator Albert Gore; Box 18, Louchheim Papers, LoC.

28. Letter is in the India Edwards file, Box 3, Louchheim Papers, LoC, undated but clearly written in October 1953. On Nov. 2, 1953, Edwards wrote Louchheim, "The more I think of how little I had to turn over to you, the more I realize how completely the Women's

Division had been integrated, or disintegrated. I am shocked at myself for allowing such a thing to happen for we really had a going concern until Steve decided to do away with it. . . . I look back with shame and horror at the last year but the years before were challenging and worthwhile and I loved every moment of them in spite of the hard work and the frustrations which were bound to occur." This file has many letters between the two women, implying a more cordial relationship than that hinted at in their books. However, Louchheim's journal makes it clear that she did not care for Edwards and thought she was interfering; Louchheim Papers, Box 122, 21.

29. Biographical Note on Register of Louchheim Papers, LoC. Quote in Louchheim 1977, 31–33, 235. She added that "Somehow it [pressing women's cause] has pursued me." Louchheim oral history for HSTL 1972, 53; Box 95, Louchheim Papers, LoC. Louchheim, who lived to age eighty-seven, was forever identified with this cause; obits in *NYT*, Feb. 12, 1991, D:20:1; *WP*, Feb. 12, 1991, B:6.

30. Mitchell ruffled a lot of feathers, but the drive to oust him was led by California National Committeewoman Clara Shirpser after he publicly repudiated two Democratic Congressional candidates, including one incumbent, and treated her like a nonentity; Sanders 1956, 23. Well covered in the press, Shirpser's version is in her oral history 1975, 302–21. Louchheim quote from her journal, Jan. 29, 1956, 20; Louchheim Papers, Box 122, LoC. Last quote from Bone 1958, 108–9.

31. Roosevelt and Hickok 1954, 29–31. Edwards 1977, 203–4. Bone 1958, 76–77, 109. *CQ Weekly Report*, Aug. 21, 1953, 1104. Quote from Edwards letter of Feb. 10, 1954, to Louchheim, Louchheim Papers, Edwards File, Box 3, LoC.

32. In 1956, $100,000 would buy an hour of network TV time. The following are all in the Louchheim Papers, LoC: A file containing *For and About Women* from its beginning in February 1955 through November/December 1958 is in Box 17. Box 16 has clippings on the 1958 Campaign Conference for Democratic Women Leaders, as well as the annual Democratic Women's Days. Numerous reports on the activities of the OWA are in Box 18, and scrapbooks on each regional conference are in Boxes 69–76. "Democratic Women Plan Conferences," *WES*, March 20, 1955. National conferences in *WES*, April 20, 1958; May 3, 1960. When the first Democratic Women's Day was announced, it was not clear if the funds raised were for the WD or the DNC; "Radio Party Series to Aid Democrats," *WES*, Sept. 10, 1939; *NYT*, Sept. 1939: 1, 38:3; 10, 1:4; 16, 8:6. "Fund-Raising Day Set by Democrats," *WES*, Sept. 9, 1956.

33. Louchheim oral history for Kennedy library, 1968, 35–36; Box 57, Louchheim Papers, LoC. Inez Robb, "Women Workers Expendable," *Louisville Times*, July 4, 1960; Box 81, Louchheim Papers, LoC. The only woman sitting with the top Democratic party men was the girlfriend of comedian Mort Sahl. Of course, as the top Democratic woman, Louchheim should have been there. Shirpser said this was a common experience in the 1950s because party men hogged the seats at the head table no matter how much work women did to put on an event; oral history 1975, 650–51.

34. Louchheim 1970, 245–45. At JFK's request the DNC officially elected Price as the vice chair in charge of women's activities on July 16, 1960. She was a friend of Michigan Governor G. Mennen Williams and on the national board of the YWCA. *CQ Weekly Report*, July 22, 1960, 1306.

35. First quote from Edwards letter to Margaret Kuh, Sept. 30, 1975; Edwards file, WNDC archives. Second quote in Edwards 1977, 104, 252. Price bio in Shalett 1960, and Price file, *WES* morgue, DCPL. Her husband was an executive with Mercedes Benz Corp. in Brazil.

Reports on her Democratic women's campaign conferences in WES: May 21 and 22, 1962; April 14, 1964; April 11, 1966; April 18, 1966; April 20, 1966. Price issued a newsletter called Capital Capsule. Lady Bird's luncheons mentioned in NYT 1964: Jan. 17, 22:4; Feb. 20, 15:7; July 30, 25:2; Aug. 17, 11:2.

36. Price obit in NYT, July 24, 1968, 41:3; WES, July 23, 1968. "Geri Joseph Gets Key Job," WES, Aug. 31, 1968. Quote in "Women-in-Office Drive Slated," WES, April 24, 1969, C:4:3. Joseph was a close personal friend and political supporter of the Humphreys. "Giant Jump for Women," WES, July 21, 1970. NYT, July 21, 1970, 49:1, announced that Mary Lou Burg of Wisconsin had been named DNC vice chairman to replace Joseph. Harriet Cipriani ran women's activities for the DNC under both Joseph and Burg. O'Brien reorganized and consolidated DNC units to save money to pay off the ten million dollar debt; NYT, May 17, 1970, 43:3. India Edwards took over Price's job at the DNC in May and organized women's activities at the 1968 convention; "India Edwards Will Return for Party Convention Role," WES, May 28, 1968.

37. RWNEC Report, 1920, 1:7. RNB, May 15, 1920, Reel 15:630–33; and "Confidential Report. Status Organization on Republican Women by States. for Members Republican Women's National Executive Committee," n.d. (1920), Reel 15:634–40, WTUL-MDR Papers.

38. RWNEC Report, 1920, 9.

39. Upton reports that TR's sister, Corrinne Roosevelt Robinson, was the RNC's first choice, but she declined. First quote in Upton 1926, XXV:6, 8. Upton was not a party woman: "My work for the Republican Party prior to the national convention of 1920 amounted to nothing;" Upton 1926, XXV:1. Second quote in Upton to Harding, March 29, 1922, Reel 300, Harding Papers, LoC. There is a lot of correspondence between Upton and Harding, his secretary George Christian, and Postmaster General Will Hays concerning her husband's promised appointment in the file titled "Republican National Committee." Senator Pomerene (D. Ohio) opposed suffrage and the women's agenda, so was certainly no friend of Upton's; Lemons 1973, 105. Upton bio in III NAW 1971, 501–2; obit in NYT, Nov. 4, 1945, 44:1.

40. The women members of the RNC Executive Committee are listed in Good 1963, 14, 52, and on the committee's letterhead stationary; Hanna-McCormick Papers, Box 13, LoC. There were only six regions; Corrinne Roosevelt Robinson was exempted from organizing responsibility. The lists of states in each region are attached to various Upton letters and are in the Minutes of the Meeting of March 4, 1921. These and one map in Box 13 indicate that the regions were fluid and states shifted on request. While Upton's letters are addressed to Members of the Committee, their content implies that they were sent only to the women members. I found these letters in the Hanna-McCormick Papers but not in the Edson Papers, UCLA, even though both women were "Members of the Committee." Harvey 1995, 159–68, has a more extensive description of early efforts to organize Republican women, relying on Upton's letters in the Harding Papers and stories in the NYT. RNC Executive Session of March 3, 1921 created a permanent Women's Division with space and staff; RP papers, Reel 1:370–6.

41. Upton letter of Feb. 1, 1922, to Members; Box 13, Hanna-McCormick Papers, LoC.

42. The two organizers were fired partially because state Republican leaders objected to national interference, and partially to save the $12,000 per year Upton estimated they cost in salary and traveling expenses. First quotes in Upton letter of June 20, 1922, to Members of the Committee; Upton letter of June 16, 1922, to Mrs. McCormick; last quote in Upton letter of June 17, 1923, to Mrs. McCormick; Box 13, Hanna-McCormick Papers, LoC. Prior

correspondence contains numerous references to a proposed national federation of Republican women, and on Aug. 27, 1921, *NR*, 8, published an article announcing the National Republican Federation, "an organization of all Republican women for political education." That was the last public reference.

43. Blair 1937, 153–54.

44. Upton 1926, XXVII:11.

45. I've seen only one copy of Upton's newsletter, from the Lola Pearson Papers, Western History Collection, University of Oklahoma, Box 44, Folder 3. Dated Feb. 15, 1924, it does not have an issue or volume number. Upton letters to "Members of the Committee," Feb. 1, 1922, March 2, 1922, on the *NR* column; Box 13, Hanna-McCormick Papers, LoC. Quotes from Goldman 1990, 294, 369. Hays was originally from Indiana, and no doubt had some connection with the owners of what was then called the *Indiana Journal*. When it became an independent monthly magazine, its name changed again to *The National Republic*.

46. *WC*, June 14, 1924, 22. Upton lost the Republican primary; *NYT,* 1924: June 6, 3:2; Aug. 13, 1:2. Quote in Goldman 1990, 369. Hert bio in *NR*, June 28, 1924, 17; *NYT* obit, June 9, 1948, 29:1.

47. First quote in "Newsletter," Vol. II, No. 2, May 1926, 1. Second quote in "Summarized Report of the Conference of Republican National Committeewomen, State Vice chairmen and State Club Presidents, January 12, 13, 14, 1927—Carlton Hotel, Washington, D.C.," 3. Both in Box 324, Burroughs Papers, LoC.

48. First quote in "Summarized Report." 1927, 2. Second quote from Hert speech at RNC meeting of Dec. 16, 1931, reporter's minutes, 105–6, National Archives.

49. Minutes of formation of the NLRCW are in Box 309 of the Nannie Helen Burroughs Papers, LoC. Higginbotham 1990, 208–12. Burroughs bio in Clarke 1924, 239; *BWA* 1993, 201–5; *NYT* obit, May 22, 1961, 31:5. Information on the Study Clubs and copies of the two magazines are at MSRC. Organizing meeting in 1:1 *The Women's Voice*, May 1939, 18; announcement in 1:9, *ibid.*, Jan. 1940, 12–13. The June 1940 issue reports that "Republican Women's Club of the District of Columbia Joins National Federation of Republican Women's Clubs," implying that the NARW folded. *Ibid.*, 9.

50. "Women Leaders Meet," *The Guidon*, Feb. 1927, 1. "Coolidge Praises Women in Politics," *NYT,* Jan. 13, 1927, 3:6. Quote from "Summarized Report." 1. Invitations were extended to the state vice chairs, the national committeewomen, and state club presidents, but the women who came did not all hold these titles. Massachusetts, New York, Maryland, and North Carolina were particularly oversubscribed. The first Eastern States Conference is described in 5:4 *RWP*, June 1927, 1–5, and the second "Interstate Conference of Republican Women" in 6:4 *RWP*, June 1928, 4–8. Three regional conferences mentioned in McCormick, July 1928, 7.

51. Quotes from interview with Mrs. Cornelia Robinson, of the West End Women's Republican Association, based on her "ten years of active experience in political work by women"; *NYH Magazine*, Oct. 25, 1903, 8:4,5.

52. WNRC origins in Whitney 1928, quote on 1; Chittenden 1927; Miller 1921, who said it was intended to duplicate for women "the famous National Republican Club, which Republican men long ago established." Henrietta Livermore rarely used her own name, preferring "Mrs. Arthur L. Livermore." Her bio is in Cameron and Lee, 1924, 305–6; obits in *NYT*, Oct. 16, 1933, 17:4; *NYHT*, Oct. 15, 1933. Contemporary writers often confuse her with Mary Livermore, suffragist of Massachusetts, who died in 1905. Livermore was succeeded at the WNRC by Alice Hill Chittenden (1926–28), who had gained renown as an

avid and active anti-suffragist; interview in *NYT Magazine,* June 17, 1917, 7; obit in *NYT,* Oct. 3, 1945, 19:1. On the Schools of Politics see *Guidon,* Jan. 1927, 4; Oct. 27, 4; April 1928, 7; *NYHT,* Aug. 21, 1924; Sept. 9, 1928; *NYSun,* April 2, 1934; May 3, 1935; Sept. 14, 1937; Nov. 7, 1935; July 25, 1938. *RWI* occasionally mentions a Woman's National Republican Club of Chicago, but does not say if it was related to the one in New York or merely used a similar name.

53. "The Republican Women of Pennsylvania Enters on Its Tenth Year," 7:4 *RWP,* Oct. 1929, 1–4. Remington 1920, 22. Yost quote in Yost 1931, 5. Hosmer oral history 1983, 87–89, describes the "traveling schools of politics" she organized in San Mateo County (CA) in the 1950s. The WNRC continued its school through the 1960s and the *Republican Clubwoman* listed schools of politics in several states in its 1960s calendars.

54. Good 1963, 20–22. Gruberg 1968, 55–56. Between 1928 and 1930 the work of the Women's Division was done by Louise M. Dodson, who had been an Associate Member of the National Committee from Iowa before women became full members in 1924. She only held the official position briefly in 1930 after Hert resigned and before Yost was appointed; *NYT:* Jan. 19, 1930, 24:2; Aug. 14, 1930, 2:2; Aug. 21, 1930, 5:6; Dec. 17, 1934, 17:6; Dec. 22, 1934, 7:5. *NYSun:* Jan. 23, 1930, 10:1; Aug. 6, 1930; Aug. 15, 1930; June 14, 1932; Aug. 26, 1932. *CSM,* Aug. 22, 1932. Yost bios in *WES,* Aug. 17, 1930, July 22, 1932; resignation in *NYT,* Dec. 1934, 17, 17:6; 22, 7:5; obit in *NYT,* March 8, 1972, 40:4.

55. Yost 1934, 4.

56. Good 1963, 22. Quotes from Williams 1962, 7. Martin bio in Marston 1952. On Hamilton, see Goldberg 1990, 397–402; "Urges Salaries for Politicians," "Hamilton Speaks at School for Republican Women"; *NYSun,* May 1, 1939.

57. Williams 1962, 7–12; first quote and NFWRC purposes on 11. Second quote from "Report of the Assistant Chairman in charge of Women's Activities" (Marion Martin) to the RNC, Nov. 29, 1938, RP papers, Reel 5:943. Some of this opposition may have come from the fact that the national committeewomen had already made organization plans with the RNC chairman the previous August, which were probably preempted by Martin's; 12:1 *The Guidon,* Oct. 1937, 34.

58. Williams 1962, quotes on 15, 17, 18.

59. Quote from a three-page undated leaflet on "The National Federation of Republican Women: Background on the NFRW" which I picked up at the 1980 Republican National Convention. Information on work for "women's bills" is reported in the various state Republican women's magazines and on the ERA in the NWP Papers.

60. Membership given by NFRW President Marie Suthers to RNC Executive Session, Dec. 8, 1945, RP papers, Reel 7:842–55. First quote in Doris Fleeson, "Clash Within Party— Question of G.O.P. Policy Is Raised as Miss Martin Is Fired by Reece"; *WES,* Dec. 17, 1946, A:11. Reece's "words" were probably leaked by Martin. Edwards later wrote that Martin lost her job because "Senator Robert Taft did not appear to like her brand of politics," even though she pointedly did not favor any candidate for the Republican nomination, 1977, 97–98. Other stories identified her enemies on the RNC (the main one was Ohio National Committeewoman Katherine Kennedy Brown): *WES,* "Firing of G.O.P. Women's Head Laid to Feud," Dec. 12, 1946. Williams 1962, 29, second quote on 30. Martin returned to Maine where she became Commissioner of Labor; Marston 1952. Her position in the national party was not restored by the defeat of the Taft faction of the Republican Party at the 1952 convention. She died at age eighty-six; obit in *NYT,* Jan. 11, 1987, 22:6.

61. "G.O.P. Picks Mrs. Gilford Mayes to Head Women's Activities," *WES*, Jan. 22, 1950; Doris Fleeson, "G.O.P. Women Angry," *WES*, Jan. 23, 1950. Brandon 1950. Williams 1962, 30–32. Macauley was the cousin of John Hamilton, and got her first job at the RNC when he was RNC Chairman, 1936–1940; *NYT*, Jan. 31, 1947, 27:4. "Mrs. Macauley Named As Taft Denies Part in Ousting Miss Martin," *WES*, Dec. 19, 1946. Farrington and Mayes reported on the schools and the effective work they were doing at a variety of RNC meetings and conferences, from which they appear to be joint projects; RP papers, Reel 10:209, 218–21, 339–42.

62. *NYT*, Aug. 16, 1952, 12:6. Helmes 1983, 10–17. *CQ Weekly Report*, Jan. 23, 1953, 124. Priest bio in IV *NAW* 1980, 562–63; *NYT* obit, June 25, 1975, 46:1. Adkins obit in *NYT*, Jan. 15, 1983, 11:1.

63. Quoted in Roosevelt and Hickok 1954, 32.

64. Adkins oral history 1968, 46, 53, 55. Adkins quote from Report to the RNC, April 10, 1953, RP papers, Reel 14:19–23. *CQ Weekly Report*, May 1, 1953, 588; May 8, 1953, 600. Adkins kept her salary of $12,000 a year; *Newsweek*, May 9, 1955, 31. RNC press releases and news articles said she was in charge of the Women's Division; Adkins file, *WES* morgue, DCPL. Changes to the RNC Rules in 1956 restored the title of Assistant Chairman; Good 1963, 37. Bone 1958, 43, 61, has organization charts. Roosevelt and Hickok 1954, 33–35. Sanders 1956, 114–15; Shelton, "'Breakfast With Ike'—Here's What It's Like," *WES*, May 29, 1955. Spring conferences and campaign schools reported in *WES*, April 4, 1954, Feb. 12, 1956, March 5, 1956, B:5, April 12, 1959, March 27, 1960, April 3, 1960, March 5, 1961, April 18, 1962, April 5, 1964, April 23, 1968, April 18, 1969.

65. First and second quotes in *Work and Win: A Handbook for National Committeewomen and State Vice-Chairmen of the Republican Party*, 1956, Weis Papers, Reel 4:395–400. See also *"Work and Win" An Organization Manual for Women*, 1956, Weis Papers, Reel 4:403–409. Williams 1962, third quote on 33, 36. Last quote in Cotter and Hennessy 1964, 152. Bone 1958, 53.

66. Williams 1962, 37. Williams remarried and retired from politics in 1963; obit in *St. Petersburg Times*, Feb. 20, 1996, 7.

67. Membership from President Dorothy A. Elston, in Williams 1962, 34; quote from Williams' 1963 postscript, 37. The District of Columbia counts as a state. Baer 1991, reports that "in 1977 the NFRW became completely self-sustaining financially" even though it had considerably fewer members.

68. Felsenthal 1981, 165–67. Schlafly's version is in "The Purge," Chapter XII of her self-published book, *Safe—Not Sorry*, Alton, Ill.: Pere Marquette Press, 1967, 146–70. Schlafly claimed that the first vice president traditionally succeeded to the presidency, but in fact only two had done so. Hitt, a key organizer of O'Donnell's campaign, recounts a different version in her oral history, 1977, 41–51.

69. Bone 1958, 111.

70. Rainbow Fliers were first used by the Suffrage Movement to defeat Sen. John W. Weeks (R. Mass.) in 1918; Ware 1981, 85; 1987, 160, 170. Their introduction into the 1932 campaign is described by Howe 1935, 10. The WNRC has a collection of Republican rainbow fliers produced by them for the 1940 campaign.

71. Quote from Louchheim report in DNC 1960, 1964, 413. See also the RNC press releases for 1962 on the "record number of GOP women candidates" for various offices; Box 59, Louchheim Papers, LoC.

72. NOW press release of Nov. 20, 1968, 1.

NOTES FOR CHAPTER SIX (PAGES 109 TO 121)

1. DeWitt 1915, 151, lists California, Illinois, Iowa, Maryland, Massachusetts, Michigan, Minnesota, Montana, Nebraska, New Hampshire, New Jersey, North Dakota, Ohio, Oregon, Pennsylvania, South Dakota, and Wisconsin, as having presidential preference primaries. See Chapter Ten for his discussion of "Measures of Control Over the Nomination and Election of Officials." The populists had advocated many of these reforms but in the 1890s they were seen as too radical; Goldman 1952, 1956, 60. There is no comprehensive overview of these legal changes, but they are discussed by Ranney 1975, 18, 80–81; and Merriam 1908, 9–62.

2. Key, Jr. 1964, Chapter 12.

3. *NYT*, Nov. 25, 1894, 18:5. *SFEx*, Nov. 5, 1894, 17. Irving Howbert was the Republican state chairman. Sumner quote, 1909, 58. Meredith quote, 1895, 706. See also: Wixson 1902, 414; Vaile and Meredith 1927; Meredith 1934, 10–11. *DD*, Jan. 1939, 14. *RMN* 1894: Aug 24; Aug. 29; Aug. 30; Aug. 31; Sept. 2; Sept. 4, 2; Sept. 6, 1,8; 1906: Sept. 13, 1:4,5; Sept. 15, 7:3; Sept. 23, 1:2; Sept. 24, 3:1,2. *Denver Republican*, Nov. 14, 1894, 2; Sept. 15, 1906, 5:5, 12:1,2; Sept. 16, 1906, 5:4,5. Meredith was a leader in the Colorado suffrage movement and served on the Democratic Party State Central Committee between 1904 and 1908.

4. Quote on Idaho in letter to *WJ*, Oct. 8, 1898, and to *NYTrib*, Oct. 22, 1898, 5:3. "Confidential Report. Status. Organization on Republican Women by States. For Members Republican Women's National Executive Committee." n.d. but clearly Spring 1920, Reel 15:634–40 WTUL-MDR Papers.

5. Vaile and Meredith 1927, 1134. Meredith June 1933, 19.

6. *NYT*, June 26, 1920, 2:6. DCWF 1960, 27.

7. Hays statement in *NYT*, Jan. 6, 1920, 1:2. Republican women's expectations described in *WC*: Jan. 17, 1920, 722; Jan. 24, 1920, 752. "Women to help run the G.O.P." reported that women would be appointed as advisory members of the RNC; 78:1 *LD*, July 14, 1923, 15. Good 1963, says there is no record of an RNC meeting creating the associate members, but the first appointments were in July 1923. She lists them on p. 46, followed by a list of all the national committeewomen who served between 1924 and 1964. On Dec. 12, 1923, the RNC recommended that the 1924 Republican convention adopt equal division; RNC Minutes for Dec. 12, 1923, 132–33, RP papers, Reel 1:621–22. The 1924 *Proceedings* includes the announcement that the Rules Committee "has given to the ladies equal representation on the RNC" and a copy of Rule XIV; RNC, *Proceedings*, 1924, 90, 93. The equal representation rule changed numbers in subsequent conventions, eventually ending up as Rule 23, which was modified by a new Rule 22 in 1952 and returned to Rule 14 in 1960. The struggle for equal representation on the RNC is summarized in Andersen 1996, 81–84, and Harvey 1995, 299–305.

8. *NYT*, June 1920: 9, 2:3; 10, 3:3. "Women Members of Republican National Executive Committee," ad signed by Harriet Taylor Upton in *WC*, Oct. 9, 1920; and leaflet in Box 5, Edson Papers, UCLA.

9. First Upton quote in 78:1 *LD*, July 14, 1923, 23. Second in Upton letter of June 20, 1922, to Members of the Committee, Box 13, Hanna-McCormick Papers, LoC.

10. Cotter and Hennessy's 1964 book on the national committees is aptly titled *Politics Without Power*.

11. First quote in Goldman 1990, xiv. Second quote in Bone 1958, 7. Third quote in Harriman oral history 1950, 29. A prominent Democratic woman during the Wilson admin-

istration, Harriman became an alternate member of the DNC from the District of Columbia in 1920 and a full member in 1924; 13. Fourth quote in Saloma and Sontag 1973, 92.

12. RNC, *Proceedings* 1952, 278–98, Rules 22 and 23. Cotter and Hennessy 1964, 21. First quote, *NYT*, July 11, 1952, 1:4. Other quotes in Isabelle Shelton, "G.O.P. Women Now 'Boiling' Over '52 Committee 'Padding,'" Feb. 17, 1955, *WES*. See also: Ruth Dean, "Women's Influence Fight Is On in G.O.P. Committee Circles," *WES*, Jan. 10, 1964. On 1968 change, Saloma and Sontag 1973, 95.

13. Williams 1940, 38.

14. Blair 1940, 38.

15. *DB*, August, 1928, 4–5.

16. Minutes of the RNC meeting of June 8, 1921, RP Papers, Reel 1:465–66. RNC Executive Committee members did not have to be RNC members. Good's semi-official history fails to make this distinction, sometimes listing both Upton and Woods (incorrect spelling) as vice chairmen; 1963, 13, 14, 52. Gruberg 1968, 55 accurately distinguishes their positions, relying on Upton 1926, XXVII:9. Upton's letterhead stationary identifies her as vice chairman of the RNC Executive Committee, as does Goldman 1990, 300. The RNC letterhead for that period lists no vice chairman under Will Hays, and only Ralph Williams as vice chairman under John T. Adams. I didn't see Wood's name on any stationery.

17. Cotter and Hennessy 1964, 20, 34. See also Breckinridge 1933 and 1972, 279–83.

18. Dewson 1949, II:151–52. "Equal Number of Men and Women Appointed National Vice Chairmen," *DD*, August 1936, 8–9. Furman 1949, 242–44. The women are named in DCWF 1960, 40. There were supposed to be eight men and eight women in 1936, but Farley added a couple of extra men at the last minute.

19. *NYT*, June 1936: 10, 1:4; 13, 10:5. Good 1963, 52–54 lists those who served until 1963.

20. Quote in DNC, *Democratic Women March On* 1945, 5.

21. First quote Blair 1940, 15. However, Blair 1937, 152, says eleven answered her letter. See also Blair, June 9, 1923, 1. Second quote in *NYT*, March 16, 1924, IX:18:2.

22. March 5, 1923, telegram from Ohio State Senator Maude C. Waitt to Warren G. Harding, and night letter reply; Reel 231:0391–2, Harding Papers.

23. LWV 1927, 4. Livermore 1925. Whitney 1927.

24. "Plan of Organization as Adopted by the Republican National Committee, January 10, 1919" on back of leaflet headed "Republican Women's National Executive Committee" in Box 111, Hanna-McCormick Papers, LoC, and also in RWNEC Report of 1920, 3–4. "Confidential Report" to RWNEC, 1920; WTUL-MDR Papers, Reel 15:634–40. There were no reports from some states where there were established organizations of Republican women (e.g., California and Pennsylvania). Democratic women mentioned in Williams 1977, 51.

25. Roosevelt 1928, quote on 78. Blair 1929, quotes on 220, 224, 227. Both ER's and Blair's analyses of women's failure to achieve any real power in the parties are blunt and perceptive, but their recommendations are rather naïve. Catt, who did not join a party, was more realistic in her analysis; 1925.

26. "What Do We Mean When We Say 50–50?," *RWI*, Feb. 1931, 4. "50–50 Works in New York," *RWI*, April 1931, 7. See Fisher 1947, 89–90, for chart of 50–50 states. The New York legislature passed several laws permitting party rules to require 50–50, but the actual rules were found by various state courts to be in violation of other state laws. New York Constitution, Article XIII, § 1 was added at the 1938 Constitutional convention, and later approved by the voters.

27. Dewson 1949, first quote I:54, second quote, I:21.

28. *DD,* "Chairman Farley Asks Fifty-Fifty," Aug. 1935, 31.

29. *DD,* "44 and 50–50," Feb. 1935, 8; "Mrs. Johnesse gets 50–50 Representation: She's A Pioneer—Generally," June 1935, 21; "Women Must Be Given Equal Representation With Men on All Party Committees," Feb. 1937, 8; "South Dakota and Oregon Pass Bill for 50–50 Representation of Women and Men on Party Committees," March 1937, 9; "Democratic Women's Days Shine On in Texas While The State Passes the 50–50 Bill," June 1937, 8; "50–50 for California: The Fight That Won the Victory," July 1937, 28; "Now It's 50–50 in Alabama," March 1938, 36; "50–50 for Minnesota Women," August 1938, 27; "50–50—The First Step for '40," Feb. 1939, 22; "50–50 Progress," April 1939, 23.

30. *DD,* "Women Must Be Given Equal Representation With Men on All Party Committees," Feb. 1937, 8.

31. Blair 1929, 223.

32. Dorothy S. McAllister, "50–50—The First Step for 40," *DD,* Feb. 1939, 22. Fisher 1947, 89–90. DD, February-March 1949, back cover.

33. DCWF 1960, 42. *For and About Women* reported in June/July 1958 that the Vermont Democratic State Committee had just voted in full 50–50 and that Arizona passed a law requiring women county vice chairmen. This resulted in twenty full 50–50 states, eighteen partials, and ten with no such requirement. "None" increased because Alaska and Hawaii became states in the 1950s and had no rule on equal representation for the Democratic Party.

34. Chart in *DD,* Aug. 1934, 11. Dewson lecture at the Women's National Democratic Club, quoted by Ellis Meredith in "What Can One Woman Do?" *DB,* May 1933, 18.

35. Segal 1971, 9896–97. Eileen Summers, "Women Long Way From Top," *Washington Post,* August 1954; clipping in Box 58, Louchheim Papers, LoC.

36. Helmes 1983, 30, who added that an appeal by the president of the Maryland Federation of Republican Women's clubs resulted in more women being made county vice chairmen. She doesn't say what year the Republican constitution was changed.

37. DNC Inter-Office memorandum to Hy Raskin from Katie Louchheim, Nov. 4, 1953; Box 40, Louchheim Papers, LoC.

38. Doderer 1992, does not give the year she ran for county chairman, but told me May 6, 1999, that she thinks it was 1962.

39. Eileen Summers, "Women Long Way from Top," *Washington Post,* August 1954, reports 300 Republicans and "a fair number" of Democrats. Shaffer 1956, 125, says "[h]ardly more than 100 women occupy county chairmanships in the country's 3,072 counties," but doesn't say in which party. Democrat Katie Louchheim claimed "we have 91 women county chairman in 36 states" in "What Women Do in Politics," 1958, 79. Carter 1971, quote on 19. He reports that the 1967 list of chairmen in the 63 Colorado counties had three women Democrats and one Republican; 20n13. More interesting are the reasons the 100 chairmen and ex-chairmen he interviewed gave for lack of women: 40 said tradition or habit and 25 didn't know. Only eight said men are the political leaders and two that women will not follow women; 106, Table III-5. Braitman 1999, 179, reports that in 1954 both parties had three women as California county chairs, and in 1962 the Democrats had six and the Republicans eight.

40. Bone 1952, 10, says equal division was not the rule at this time. He does not identify the legislative district used as the organizational unit. King Co. includes Seattle. *Burton v. Schmidt,* 128 Misc. 270, 218 N.Y.S. 416 (1926). Whitney 1927.

41. A telegram in 3:2 *DB,* Feb. 28, 1928, 5, said two women had been temporary chairs in New York and Texas, overlooking Gertrude Lee's lengthy service in Colorado. Gruberg 1968, 66–67, identifies women in Iowa (1928), Kansas (1930), Idaho (1934), and Oregon (1937)

who served as temporary Democratic state chairs, but doesn't give a source. *DD*, June, 1946, 13, reports "Mrs. Mary Johnesse was elected Chairman of the State Committee in Idaho in 1934, having filled out the term of the Chairman beginning in 1932. Several women have been promoted to the position ... when a vacancy was created in that office." In New York, Sarah Schuyler Butler was titular head of the Republican State Committee for ten days after the chairman died while Caroline O'Day was already acting chairman of the Democratic State Committee, due to the resignation of the male chair. Both were active and prominent party women; neither was even considered for permanent chairman; *NYT*, Aug. 16, 1928, 1:6; *BDE*, Aug. 16, 1928, 2:6; *NYHT*, August 19, 1928; Barnard Sept. 1928, and Feb. 1931; *WJ*, Sept. 1928, 32.

42. On Norton, see Chamberlin 1973, 53–59. On Snyder, see Snyder 1977, quote on 103; Braitman 1993; letters about her campaign and California politics by India Edwards, in Edwards file, Box 3, Louchheim Papers, LoC. On July 7, 1954, Edwards wrote, "I am convinced [opposition to Liz Snyder] is mainly because she is a woman although no one out here agrees with me."

43. Wiggins and Turk 1970; Huckshorn 1976, 25–26. One was Elly Peterson of Michigan, who had been the assistant chairman to the RNC and Director of the Women's Division for six months in 1964, and would hold that position again from 1969 to 1971. Gov. George Romney made her state chairman after she ran a futile race against incumbent Democratic Senator Philip Hart to aid his gubernatorial campaign; "Elly Peterson Breaks New Ground," *WES*, Feb. 14, 1965.

44. First quotes from Blair 1929, 218–19, 223. Second quote from Lippincott 1924, 6.

45. Headline and first quote in *BDE*, Sept. 1928, 2:6. Butler quote in Butler 1931, 14, 39. "Macy Selects Lillian Garing—Queens Woman Gets Post on State Committee—Miss Butler Is Disappointed—Vice-Chairman Had Demanded Mrs. Whitney Be Named," *NYSun*, Feb. 3, 1933; *NYT* 1933: Feb. 3, 19:3; Feb. 4, 5:1; March 12, 27:4. Butler resigned after ten years to marry and move to England. Her father was Nicholas Murray Butler, who replaced Seth Low when he resigned to run for mayor of New York City, and was himself a candidate for the 1920 Republican Presidential nomination. Garing bio in 9:10 *WRNY*, March 4, 1933, 12. She was succeeded a year later by Virginia M. Bacon, wife of an M.C. A month later Macy ceased sponsorship of *WRNY*, which Whitney had been publishing, and dropped from the state party payroll the three women editing it. Rosalie Low Whitney continued publishing it under the aegis of the Republican Women's Educational League; *NYT*, March 11, 1933, 15:2.

46. Howe quote in Howe 1935. First Weis quote from letter of May 18, 1953; Weis Papers, Reel 1:714–15. Second quote in letter of April 2, 1953 to "Fred," the County Chairman; Reel 1:707–8. Weis urged the selection of Helen Power as her successor, claiming she had the backing of a majority of organization women. Her papers do not explain why Weis was resigning, or who was selected in her place.

47. Roosevelt and Hickok 1954, 16, 38.

48. Breckinridge 1933 and 1972, 293.

49. Breckinridge quote 1933 and 1972, 288. Other quotes from Fisher and Whitehead 1944, 900–3.

50. Cotter and Hennessy 1964, 44, 57, 58–59. Emphasis in original.

51. This 1961 questionnaire study was only of party leaders in Oklahoma, but listed responses separately by party and office; Patterson 1963. A review of then existing studies of women as local party leaders was made by Conway 1979. Bone 1958, 107. Quote from Gatov oral history, 1978, 211.

NOTES FOR CHAPTER SEVEN (PAGES 123 TO 147)

1. Young 1989, 33–38.

2. Lemons 1973, 52–53. Young 1989, 34–36. Republican quote in *NYT*, April 2, 1919, 1:2. Democratic quote in *NYT*, Feb. 13, 1920, 1:4.

3. *WC* 1920: Feb. 14, 841, 869; Feb. 21, 894–95; "Getting into the Parties," May 29, 1319.

4. Catt 1920, 946. Reprinted in Peck 1944, 325; Ware 1989, 165–66.

5. Chafe 1972, 34–35. Quote is from Catt's 1920 speech. Catt herself never joined a political party, preferring to work in the peace movement, but she did lend her name in support of Presidential candidates, including Cox in 1920 and Hoover in 1928 and 1932; Peck 1944, 325. Young 1950, 180; 1989, 36.

6. First quote Gellhorn 1920, 356–57. Blair 1937, 143, 138.

7. Quote in Young 1989, 34. McCormick's attitude in Miller 1992, 121, 130, 137. Personal feelings toward the LWV should not be ruled out; McCormick had chaired NAWSA's Congressional Committee and left under less than pleasant circumstances. NWP attacks in *NYT* 1920: May 31, 3:1; July 11, 14:1; July 23, 2:6; June: 2, 3:1: 3, 1:2; 5, 2:4; 6, 5:1; 9, 3:6; 12, 3:3; 13, 3:1; 19, 2:8; 23, 3:1. Hays 1955, 260.

8. First Hays quote 1955, 258; second in *WC*, Jan. 17, 1920, 722. Adams quote in *NR*, Jan. 21, 1922; "The outstanding feature of the luncheon was the series of criticisms . . . against the League of Women Voters." See also *NYT*, Jan. 15, 1922, II:2:2.

9. First quote, *NYT*, Sept. 16, 1920, 3:1. Second quote, *NYT*, Oct. 19, 1920, 2:2.

10. In November of 1921 the Governor of Iowa read a speech by President Harding to a regional meeting of the LWV in which he said: "I hope the thoughtful womanhood of your region will play its full part in developing the conscience and in making the politics of our political parties. Nothing could be more unfortunate than to give our limited assent to the proposal of organizing our citizenship into groups according to sex." *NYT*, Nov. 23, 1921, 19:2. In May of 1922 Harding told the women Republican clubs of New Jersey: "women can play their part fully and best only when they play it in connection with recognized political organizations"; "New Voters Told to Avoid Blocks and Sex Organizations," *NYH*, May 13, 1922.

11. Membership estimate in *BDE*, Feb. 4, 1921, 6:3. Miller speech in *NYT*, Jan. 28, 1921, 1:6. Miller defeated incumbent Governor Al Smith on Harding's coattails, but lost to him in 1922. Both had opposed woman suffrage at one time, but Smith supported protective labor laws.

12. *NYT*, Jan. 1921: first quote 29, 1:1; second quote 21, 5:2.

13. Quoted and cited by Nichols 1983, 44, who does not give the date; probably in 1921.

14. First quote in Upton letter to Members of the Committee, Dec. 14, 1921; Box 13, Hanna-McCormick Papers, LoC. Second quote in "Women Urged to Stand for Party Loyalty," *NR*, Jan. 21, 1922. There are fewer public anti-LWV statements by Democrats.

15. Martin 1925; quote in Anderson 1988, 31; bios in Howard 1985; II *NAW* 1971, 459–62. LWV quote in Young 1989, 87n13.

16. Abbott, 1915, 437–38. Eckert, 1916, 109. Actually, Democratic women voted like Democratic men; Republican women favored the more progressive candidate. In these years progressivism was still alive, if not well, especially in Chicago.

17. Lemons 1973, 93–96. Flexner 1959, 1968, 310–11. Morgan, 1972 133. Kenneally 1967, 55, citing personal communication from his son, Sinclair Weeks, on the effectiveness of women's opposition. The Democratic winner in Massachusetts, former Governor David I. Walsh, was a devout Catholic who, despite opposition from many in the Church hierarchy,

supported woman suffrage in the 1915 Massachusetts referendum. John W. Weeks generally opposed Progressive measures and suffrage was not the only reason for his defeat. President Harding appointed him as Secretary of War in 1921. On Ohio see Toombs, 1920.

18. On LWV work in campaigns see Young 1989, 47; Lemons 1973, 96–97. "Women in Politics Bring Worry to Old Guard," *BDE,* June 2, 1922, C:5:1–7. See also Lape 1922; Pinchot 1922.

19. On Wadsworth see Flexner 1959, 1968, 302; Kyvig 1979, 75–78; and his oral history 1952, which does not mention his anti-suffrage activities. On Hay and Wadsworth, see Lemons 1973; 93–96; Young 1989, 47; Perry 1999. *WC* 1920: "The Case Against Senator Wadsworth," Jan. 17, 727; "A Non-Partisan Pledge," Feb. 21, 895. *NYT,* "Women Urge Defeat of Wadsworth Here," Feb. 17, 1920, 17:4. Quote in "Suffragists First," *WC,* Dec. 13, 1919, 557. WCTU President and Brooklyn resident Ella Boole lost to Wadsworth in the 1920 Republican primary, and again in November as the Prohibition Party candidate, running on the slogan "Send a Mother to the Senate." However, he was finally defeated in 1926 when the Prohibition Party took enough Republican votes away to elect the Democrat, Robert Wagner; Lemons 1973, 96; Kyvig 1979, 77; Rose 1996, 76. Boole bio in IV *NAW* 1980, 91–92. In 1932, Wadsworth was elected to the House from upstate New York and served nine terms.

20. Edson telegram reported in the Minutes of the meeting of March 4, 1921, Women Members of the Republican Executive Committee, and letter of June 8, 1921 to Ruth McCormick; Box 13, Hanna-McCormick Papers, LoC.

21. Harriman 1923, 354.

22. Young 1989, 46, 48, quote on 73. Lemons 1973, 91–100. Harvey 1995, 193–96. October 1923 Board resolution in LWV pages in *WJ,* Nov. 1928, 28. LWV officers who ran include Wisconsin LWV President Jessie Jack Hooper who ran for the Senate against incumbent Robert LaFollette in 1922; Gruberg 1968, 123. One LWV officer, Mabeth Paige, was elected to the Minnesota legislature in 1922 and served until 1944; Young 1989, 73. Several Alabama LWV members ran for office and one was elected to the state legislature in 1922 and served for two terms; Thomas 1992, 212. Cox 1996, 47, 165. In the early 1920s, the Maryland LWV gave lunches for all women candidates, Republican and Democratic; Helmes 1983, 4–5. The Hay scrapbook, NYPL, contains an NYC-LWV press release of Sept. 21, 1921 endorsing three men running for New York City offices, and a clipping from the *NYTrib,* Sept. 23, 1921, reporting this action.

23. Delegate numbers in *WJ,* Nov. 1928, 28. Lemons 1973, 94. Young 1989, 94–95.

24. Young 1989, 74, first quote on 81, 85, 89, 91, 94, second quote on 99n3, third on 146, 153, 170. LWV GOTV campaign in Frazer 1924. LWV work for the 1928 election in Barnard Nov. 1928, 554; Morrison 1978, 177–216. LWV work in North Carolina is in Roydhouse 1980, 257–59. On LWV work as the precursor for women going into politics, see Lamson 1968; Kirkpatrick 1974; Diamond, 1977; Mandel 1981; and sources cited in Gruberg 1968, 87–94.

25. Lunardini, 1986, 153–56, 162. *ER,* July 28, 1923, 189. Becker, 1981, 19. Alice Paul oral history, 1972–73, 17–73, 615, 622, 624.

26. *ER,* March 3, 1923, 22. Ford 1991, 229. Belmont 1922.

27. *ER,* July 9, 1924, 179; July 26, 1924, 187; Aug. 9, 1924, 205; Aug. 30, 1924, 229; Sept. 6, 1924, 237; Sept. 13, 1924, 243; Sept. 27, 1924, 260; Oct. 11, 1924, 275; Nov. 8, 1924, 309. Becker, 1981, 99–100.

28. Harriman 1923, 354.

29. Letters of Alice Paul to various Republican elected officials in 1969 state that she is a lifelong Republican and a member of the National Federation of Republican Women; Reel 111, NWP papers. Other women were similarly identified.

30. First quote in Becker 1981, 202. Paul oral history 1972–73, 488. Eleanor Roosevelt quote in her letter of March 12, 1952, to Gertrude W. Fairbanks, Katherine St. George papers, Manuscript Department, Cornell University Library.

31. Pardo 1972, 151. Both Hoover and Truman endorsed the ERA in 1944, when neither was President or a candidate for President. Truman did not repeat his 1944 endorsement in 1948.

32. Republican MCs who were NWP members include Winifred Mason Huck (Ill. 1923), Clare Booth Luce (Conn. 1943–47), Katherine St. George (NY, 1947–65), Catherine May (Wash. 1959–71). ERA votes in II:3 *Congressional Quarterly*, July–Sept. 1946, 568; 6 *CQ Almanac*, 1950, 420, 539; 9 *CQ Almanac*, 1953, 386.

33. Quote in Paul oral history 1972–73, 436. On the NWP after WWII see Rupp and Taylor 1987, 136–44.

34. *NYT* Sept. 1928: 15, 4:4; 28, 7:1, Cott 1987, 62–64. Becker 1981, 93–96. *ER*, Sept. 22, 1928, 258–61; Sept. 29, 1928, 269; Oct. 13, 1928, 285. Pardo 1979, 56. *The Nation*, Oct. 1928, 312, has an unsympathetic report of the Hoover endorsement. Pardo reports that NWP officials met with Hoover several times seeking endorsement of the ERA. While he continued to voice a commitment to equal opportunity, he stated that there was insufficient national support and the Democratic Congress wouldn't accede to Republican leadership on the issue; 49. During the first two years of Hoover's administration the Republicans controlled both Houses. Nonetheless, Alice Paul continued to think very highly of Hoover; *ER*, May/August 1948, 29.

35. Louchheim 1970, 80.

36. Eisenhower's statement in "Memorandum concerning the Two Major Political Parties and the Equal Rights Amendment," Nov. 3, 1956, 2; Reel 103. 3:1 *The NWP Bulletin*, Winter 1968, 9; Reel 158. Ruth Gage Colby to Edith, April 1, 1968, on primary activities; Emma Guffey Miller to Eugene McCarthy, April 15, 1968; report by Margery Leonard, Chairman of Women's Committee for McCarthy; Reel 111. All in NWP papers. The ERA was *not* an issue in the 1968 campaign. Robert Kennedy was the only declared major party candidate who did not express some support. Supporters included Ronald Reagan, George Wallace, Richard Nixon, Lyndon B. Johnson, and Hubert Humphrey.

37. White's autobiography is in Showalter 1978, 45–52; bio in III *NAW* 1971, 590–92; *NYT* obit, May 8, 1943, 13:3.

38. Quote in Rupp and Taylor 1987, 124–25. Miller bio in IV *NAW* 1980, 476–78; *NYT* obit, Feb. 25, 1970, 51:2.

39. Mesta 1960, 79, 98, 130–34. The RNC Women's Division "Organization News," Sept. 24, 1932, 1, mentions her "fine work in the Oklahoma headquarters in 1928." Bio in IV *NAW* 1980, 470–71; obits: *NYT*, March 17, 1975, 1:5; *WP*, March 18, 1975, C:6:1.

40. Rupp and Taylor 1987. The NWP's 1960 convention was well reported. Isabelle Shelton, "Too Many Cliches About Women Seen," *WES*, Jan. 6, 1960, C:4. Marie Smith, "Equal Rights Victory Seen in New Session," *WP*, Jan. 6, 1960, B:4.

41. Quote in Young 1989, 46.

42. Chambers 1963. Quote in Young 1989, 39.

43. Lunardini 1986, 153, 160, 161; Kelley 1921; Kirchwey 1921.

44. The WJCC and its members are discussed by Breckinridge 1933, 1972, Chapter XIV; Johnson 1972; Selden 1922. Social welfare bills in Johnson 1972, 51–53; Lemons 1973, 56–57; Breckinridge 1933, 1972, 261–62.

45. The Women's Legislative Councils have received limited attention from historians. Two journalists credit the GFWC for early legislative activity; Dorr 1910; Richardson 1929. Young 1989, does not mention them as an LWV activity even though it was usually the most important member. On early Colorado see Dorr 1911, 432–33, who does not give dates of origin, and 1905 interview with Mary C.C. Bradford who describes Federation meetings with legislators; *NYH*, July 30, 1905, 6:1. Scott 1970, 187–88, describes the activities of several Southern WLCs. Sims 1997, 48, 51, and Roydhouse 1980, 141–43, 227–78, examine North Carolina's, active from 1921 to 1931. Thomas 1992, 211–12, devotes two paragraphs to Alabama's; founded in 1921, it declined after the LWV left in 1927. Carver 1979, 944, wrote that Florida's was "set up in 1921 under the auspices of the League of Women Voters and the Florida Federation of Women's Clubs" and "was active only in the 1920s and early '30s." In 1918, the Women's Joint Legislative Conference (WJLC) was formed in New York "at the request of the State Federation of Labor, to formulate and push a program of women's labor bills"; Baker 1925, 171–72. Quite a bit was written about the California WLC in local newspapers between 1915 and 1922. A file on the "Business Women's Legislative Council of California," beginning in 1927, is in the Huntington Library in San Marino, CA. Skocpol 1992, 453, 462, mentions the earlier California State Legislative Council of Women, a coalition of fifty-three women's organizations. See Gordon 1986, on New Jersey, and Nichols 1983, on Connecticut. The WLCs also served as an entry into the political arena. Ivy Baker Priest, Treasurer of the United States under Eisenhower, started her political career on the Utah WLC while a housewife in the 1930s; Priest 1958, 94. Eleanor Roosevelt analyzed proposals before the New York State Legislature for the New York LWV and the WJLC; Young 1989, 51. Breckinridge quotes, 1933, 1972, 258, 270. Beard 1914 quote in Lane 1977, 93. A study done of league members in 1956 found that only 4 percent saw legislation as its primary purpose; Ware 1990, 6, citing *Report I*, "The League Member Talks About the League," Oct. 1956, 57; LWV Papers, LoC.

46. Tyler 1996, 87–96.

47. O'Neill 1969, 232–36. Lemons 1973, 122. In *Adkins v. Children's Hospital*, 261 U.S. 525 (1923) the Supreme Court declared the D.C. minimum wage law "simply and exclusively a price-fixing law, confined to adult women . . . , who are legally as capable of contracting for themselves as men."

48. O'Neill 1969, 114–17, 240–49. Lemons 1973, 122–23. Her sister says she spent more time working for the Child Labor Amendment than for Coolidge; Dreier 1950, 198.

49. Lemons 1973, 54–55, 123. O'Neill 1969, 259–61. Breckinridge 1933, 1972, 260.

50. Richardson 1929, 607. My impression from reading many short descriptions of party women in their publications is that most had a background in the GFWC rather than in suffrage or reform. Remington, 57, made a similar observation in 1920.

51. Breckinridge 1933, 1972, 77–78. Stewart 1939, 3. While part of the WJCC, the NACW had sided with the NWP on the ERA. Its founder, Mary Church Terrell, had picketed the White House with Alice Paul, for which she was honored by the NWP in 1921; Terrell 1940, 316–17.

52. Quotes from Higginbotham 1992, 206. A 1939 report by Mary C. Booze, Republican national committeewoman from Mississippi, said that members of NACW "are predominantly Republican"; "Tour Completed: Colored National Committeewoman Reports to

Chairman Hamilton, Summer Activities," 1:6 *The Women's Voice*, Oct. 1939, 8, MSRC. Brown bio in I *NAW* 1971, 253–54; *BWA* 1993, 176–78.

53. Bethune bio in I *NAW* 1971, 76–80. She is listed among those on the Board of Counselors of the RNC Women's Division in 1932; *Organization News*, Oct. 22, 1932, 2, Burroughs Papers, LoC.

54. The Women's Bureau was created by 41 *Stat.* 987, approved on June 5, 1920. Its formation is described in Sealander 1983, Chapter 2; quotes are on 3, 28. A more personal view is given by its first director, Mary Anderson, in her 1951 autobiography. Breckinridge 1933, 1972, 265.

55. Anderson 1951. This change can be seen by looking at the organizations in the National Committee to Defeat the Un-Equal Rights Amendment (NCDURA) which formed late in 1944. Only a few of them were in the WJCC. Harrison 1988, 20; 1982, 71–72.

56. Perkins was raised a Republican, as was Dewson. After FDR was nominated, Edith Abbott wrote Mollie Dewson that she was a "life-long Republican by heritage, education, and years of allegiance," but saw hope for the social welfare measures she advocated only with FDR's election; letter of July 5, 1932, Costin 1983, 212. Older reformers such as Margaret Dreier Robins and Maud Nathan continued to support Republican candidates until they died; they never supported FDR.

57. Lemons 1973, 42–43; list of women's professional associations at 58n8. Breckinridge 1933, 1972, chapter 12. Rupp 1982, 49, argues that by the 1950s "feminism" had become so stigmatized that even the NWP only used it internally.

58. Paul oral history 1972–73, 440–42. Becker 1981, 197–99, 226–27. Lemons 1973, 43–46, 203–4. Rawalt 1983, 52. Breckinridge 1933, 1972, 63–64. Upton quote in letter of Dec. 14, 1921 to Members of the Committee"; Box 13, Hanna-McCormick Papers, LoC. BPW resolution in Fahy 1956, 8, and Rawalt 1969, 11–12.

59. The House passed the resolution on Dec. 17 by 282 to 128 and the Senate on Dec. 18 by 48 to 8; *Congressional Record*, 65th Cong. 1st Sess, 5648–66. The three holdouts were Illinois, Indiana, and Rhode Island. Only Rhode Island rejected the Eighteenth Amendment. Eight Southern and border states voted to reject the Nineteenth Amendment.

60. Kyvig 1979, 69, 72, 91–95, 106–8. Wolfskill says the takeover occurred in 1926, and was only formalized in 1928; 1962, 39.

61. Kyvig 1979, first quote, 143; third quote, 168. Chapter 8 covers the rapid partisan polarization between 1928 and 1932, and chapter 9 the actions by Congress and the states. Second quote in Root 1934, 105. The Twenty-First Amendment was ratified by thirty-eight states; only South Carolina officially rejected it.

62. *LD*, Sept. 9, 1922, 11–13. *CSM* quoted in 78:1 *LD*, July 14, 1923, 15.

63. First quote and figures in Breckinridge 1933, 1972, 58. Second quote and WCTU campaign work in Morrison 1978, 59–62, 155–64.

64. First quote from Munro 1928, 261. Second quote from *RWI*, Oct. 1929, 8. Third quote in Root 1934, 4. On Sabin see IV *NAW* 1980, 617–18; *Time*, July 18, 1932, 8–9; Kyvig 1976; Whitney 1928; *NYT* obit., Dec. 29, 1951, 23:1. On AAPA see Kyvig 1979.

65. Kyvig 1979, 126, identifies the quote as Wadsworth's, but his 1952 oral history, 359, attributes it to "a lot of men." Smith quote in Smith 1933, 10. Rose 1996, 2, credits WONPR as being the "decisive" factor in prohibition repeal. Organizations pro and con the Eighteenth Amendment are in Root 1934, 105; Rose 1996, 52–62. What Progressive Republicans and Southern Democrats who supported prohibition shared was evangelical Protestantism. The Methodist Church was the strongest and most consistent supporter of prohibition. Other

denominations with a missionary, moralistic impulse, such as the Baptists, also supplied many troops. There were a few women's organizations organized for repeal prior to WONPR, but Kyvig says they were small, "meagerly financed," and had no "noticeable impact;" 1979, 48; Rose 1996, 66–69, 72–78. Many prominent businessmen and their wives changed their minds on prohibition after a few years of seeing it in practice; Sabin 1928; Root 1934, 85. So did organized labor, which split over the Eighteenth Amendment, but united behind the Twenty-First; Rose 1996, 57–59. Quite a few WONPR leaders were related to men in the AAPA. Root, who wrote the official history, was the daughter-in-law of Elihu Root, who represented the brewers before the Supreme Court in their efforts to block the Eighteenth Amendment; *National Prohibition Cases*, 253 U.S. 350 (1920), *U.S. v. Sprague*, 282 U.S. 716 (1931). He and Senator Wadsworth had been outspoken anti-suffragists.

66. First quote from Rose 1996, 79–80. Important Democratic women included Emma Guffey Miller (Pa.), Belle Moskowitz (N.Y.), and Cong. Mary Norton (N.J.). Root 1934, membership on xii–xiv, 11, 18, 56, 86, 103, 132; publicity work on 27–35, 57–59; second quote on 29; political work on 36–45, 59–64; demands for legislators' views and responses on 48–55; the 1932 platform planks are on 81–84; endorsement and response on 90–104, the endorsement resolution led to "150 resignations and . . . 137,000 new members"; 103, pp. 332, 348. Resignations reported in *NYHT*, July 13, 1932, *pp.* 332, 338. AAPA support of WONPR "with material and document" in Wadsworth oral history 1952, 358. WONPR queried candidates' views not on liquor vs. prohibition, but on whether or not the issue should be voted on by the people, via a repeal amendment that had to be ratified by state conventions, not legislatures. By doing this it was pushing them to agree that the people should decide on prohibition regardless of the legislator's personal persuasion. The convention method of ratification provided by Article V of the Constitution had never been used before and has not been used since. At that time states were not required to reapportion after each decennial census, and legislators often represented "acreage over people." Rural voters, and the state legislators they elected, were more favorable to prohibition than the under-represented urban voters. The URC consisted of four repeal organizations, the AAPA, WONPR, Voluntary Committee of Lawyers, and the Crusaders, plus the American Hotel Association. A group formed by the AFL, Labor's National Committee for Modification of the Volstead Act, declined to join. Rose 1996, 7; Kyvig 1979, 153; *Time*, July 18, 1932.

67. Kyvig 1979, 191–95. Wolfskill 1962, 40, 55, 63, 207–9. Quite a few wealthy men financed the AAPA and the ALL, but the deepest pockets belonged to the DuPont family, with whom Raskob had long been associated, first as an employee and then as a business partner.

68. Wolfskill 1962, 60, 195–96, 208. In addition to Sabin, Rose identified two WONPR officers on the initial seventeen-member ALL executive committee, though others may have been added later; Rose, 1996, 133–34, first quote on 140. Dewson quote *NYT*, Oct. 2, 1936, 5:6. Independent Coalition of American Women in *NYT* 1936: July 1, 19:2, July 2, 6:6; July 14, 9:3; July 29, 6:2; Aug. 23, 34:4; Sept. 20, 1:6; Sept. 22, 6:4; Sept. 24, 6:2; Oct. 1, 15:4; Oct. 2, 1:8; Oct. 2, 5:6; Oct. 3, 2:4; Oct. 20, 4:7; Oct. 24, 9:5; Oct. 31, 1:5; Nov. 1, 1:4; Nov. 4, 18:3.

69. Addams 1930, 153–55.

70. Nielsen 1996, 87, 93, 105–6. Lemons 1973, 207, quote on 210. Lash 1971, 263–64. Gibbs 1969, 105. Calvin Coolidge, "Enemies of the Republic: Are the 'Reds' Stalking Our College Women?" 98 *The Delineator*, June 1921, 4–5, 66–67, was the first of a three-part series.

71. On the shift in leadership and tone, see Jablonsky 1994, Chapter 7. First quote in 11 *Woman's Protest*, Feb. 1918, 7, cited in Lemons 1973, 10. O'Neill 1969, 228. This was the last

issue under that name. Harriet Taylor Upton wrote to Mrs. Medill McCormick that anti-suffragists were outspoken opponents to the Sheppard-Towner Act in Congressional hearings; Upton letter of May 24, 1921, Box 13, Hanna-McCormick Papers, LoC. Nielsen 1996, 79, second quote on 81, 209–10. The antis challenged the constitutionality of the "Federal Baby Act"; Marshall 1997, 219.

72. Addams 1930, 122–52. When the United States entered the war, Addams worked with the Department of Food Administration, headed by Herbert Hoover, which probably explains why she endorsed him when he ran for President in 1928.

73. I found the version described here in the Swarthmore College Peace Collection; it's reproduced in Cott 1987, 242. There are other versions.

74. Lemons 1973, Chapter 8; Jensen 1983, 213; Johnson 1972, 47–48; Anderson 1951, 188–92; Addams 1930, 180–81; O'Neill 1969, 229n2. Several progressive women formed a Woman's Committee for Political Action in 1919, which aided the formation of the Conference for Progressive Political Action that sponsored the Progressive Party that nominated LaFollette. Whitney 1924, describes the CPPA as having "frankly communistic connections and with a program which parallels in many respects that of the Communist Party;" 48. Infiltration of women's clubs, particularly the WTUL, is on 177–83.

75. In 1912, at the peak of Progressivism, the DAR opposed child labor and unfair labor standards, and supported peace and protective labor legislation; Gibbs 1969, 78–84, 108–17. Breckinridge 1933, 1972, 23, 45–48. Addams 1930, 181. Lemons 1973, 123–24, 223–24. Quote in Jensen 1983, 211. Nielsen 1996, 159, 168. Paul oral history 1972–73, 436. Becker 1981, 4–5.

76. Carrie Chapman Catt's rejoinder was published in WC: "Lies At Large," June 1927, 10–11 and "An Open Letter to the D.A.R.," July 1927, 10–12; discussed in Peck 1944, 426–28, and Lemons 1973, 223–24. Gibbs 1969, 118–34. Villard 1928, wrote about the "Blue Menace."

77. Root 1934, 25.

78. On the PTA, see Lemons, 1973, 215. On North Carolina see Roydhouse, 1980, 302, citing Mary O. Cowper to Gladys Harrison, Feb. 13, 1927, Box 123 Series II (1926–28), LWV papers.

NOTES FOR CHAPTER EIGHT (PAGES 149 TO 178)

1. New Jersey quote, Lippincott 1924, 6. Roosevelt 1928, 79.

2. Mayhew 1986, reviews party organization in the fifty states as of the late 1960s, supplemented by historical material. Based on his estimates, roughly two-fifths of the American population lived in states with strong parties in the 1920s, with a small but steady decline thereafter.

3. Upton 1926, XXV:1. On New Jersey, see Gordon 1986, 78–79. On Dodson, "To Direct Women's Campaigning," NY Sun, Jan. 23, 1930, 10:1. Upton and Dodson soon left their states to work for the RNC, though Dodson returned. On Otero-Warren, see Salas 1999, 165.

4. Quotes in Remington 1920, 50, who observed "that a large number of women who have led in political organizations received their first public training in the Federated Women's Clubs"; 57.

5. Nichols 1983, 40.

6. Gordon 1986, 81, 89, 97; Gruberg 1968, 153; Chamberlin 1973, 54–55. Billington was active in the NWP, but still kept her place on the DNC until 1942. Norton was a party

woman who had never been involved with reform or suffrage. Hague was mayor of Jersey City, but dominated the state Democratic Party. With only a sixth grade education, he was known as a "Dictator—American Style." He freely admitted that Norton gave "respectability to his machine politics," but he was one of the rare bosses who rewarded his women as he did his men. Both were Irish Catholic. Chafe 1972, 38, quotes Molly Dewson saying that "Mayor Hague did not want any rival in his field and felt safer with the Congressman from Jersey City a woman." Despite this inauspicious background, Norton was a strong supporter of New Deal legislation. As Chair of the House Labor Committee, she shepherded the Fair Labor Standards Act through Congress in 1938; Ware 1982, 105.

7. Helmes 1983, 1–2.

8. Blair 1937, 13.

9. *NYT*, Dec. 12, 1917, 10:1; 1918: Jan. 28, 14:6; Feb. 22, 1:4; March 1, 20:4; March 13, 7:7; April 8, 8:5. *WC*, Jan. 4, 1919, 656, announced equal representation for women in Queens County.

10. "Financial Aid," 1:2 *WDN*, June 1925, 9. Davis 1974, 7, 12–13, 25–26. O'Day superseded Mills as state women's chairman; bios in Chamberlin 1973, 112–18; II *NAW* 1971, 648–50. ER's personal account is given in 1937, 341–42, as well as in a short biography by her friend Lorena Hickok in Roosevelt and Hickok 1954, 259–62. Quote in Lash 1971, 264, 277–78, 288.

11. First quote in Roosevelt and Hickok 1954, 261; second in Farley 1938, 54–55. Blair 1937, 181–82. Farley, FDR's campaign manager, specifically credits "Mrs. Roosevelt and the other women at headquarters who helped organize the feminine vote" but seems unaware that she had been doing this for six years. The spade work of New York Democratic women can be seen in the county reports of *WDN*. FDR won New York State by 25,564 votes while Al Smith lost it by over 100,000. "Upstate" refers to all of New York State outside New York City, including Long Island.

12. *NYT* 1917: Nov. 15, 6:4; Dec. 21, 11:3; 1918: Jan. 18, 10:6; March 13, 8:2; March 22, 24:1; March 24, 24:1; April 18, 12:8; June 21, 8:1. Boswell defined complete organization as a woman district leader and a woman captain in every election district. On Robinson, see 6:12 *WRNY*, Dec. 1928, 2.

13. *BDE*, Jan. 25, 1922, 4:3; 1:12 *WRNY*, July 7, 1923, 1; Livermore 1925. *In re Slawson*, 111 Misc. 271, 181 N.Y.S. 81 (1920), invalidated the initial party rules. The Livermore bill was passed as Election Law of 1922, chapter 588.

14. Yount was a graduate student at Northwestern University when he did research for his master's thesis under the supervision of Professor P. Orman Ray; 1916, 42–44, 52–57. Quote from Mrs. Kellogg Fairbanks, "The Work of Democratic Women of Illinois," 3:6 *WDN*, Oct. 1927, 10. See Bass's 1919 Report on Illinois, which was her home state.

15. History of political clubs in Peel 1935, Chapter III; quote on 33. Ostrogorski 1910, 168.

16. First quote in *NYTrib*, Dec. 14, 1894, 5:5,6. Second from *Constitution and Bylaws of the West End Auxiliary, Woman's Republican Association of the United States*, Organized 1894; NYPL. Helen V. Boswell started this club; *NYT*, Jan. 6, 1942, 23:3. Mrs. Clarence Burns, a well-known charity worker, was its first president.

17. *NYT*, May 28, 1895, 9:4. *NYH*: May 28, 1895, 11:1; Sept. 19, 1897, V:12:1,2. The same by-law was adopted by Syracuse women when they organized their club in 1896; *NYTrib*, Sept. 19, 1896, 3:2. Bostwick, 1896. "New York Republican Women Form A State Society for Political Work," *NYTrib*, April 24, 1901, 5:1.

18. *NYTrib*, July 28, 1900, 7:2, "California Women in Politics" reported that "the Women's Republican State Central Committee of California, which was organized six years ago in San Francisco." On Wyoming, see *ChiTrib*, July 10, 1892, 10. On Kansas, see state report in *WJ*, Nov. 10, 1894, second quote 354. On Ohio see *WJ*, June 29, 1895, 201, "Republican Women Organizing." On Illinois see *WJ*, Nov. 10, 1894, 358, "Republican Women at Work." On Colorado see Sumner 1909, first quote 67, 69. "Leaders in Colorado's Republican Woman's Club," *Denver Times*, Oct. 7, 1900. Third quote and photos of clubhouse in Wixon 1902, 414. IV *HWS* 1902, 520, 522, credits Mrs. Frank Hall, vice chairman of the Republican State Committee, for organizing women in Colorado, and the silver issue for recombining women's party clubs in ways too complex to go into. Yost wrote in 1931 that Utah, "organized in 1899 and incorporated in 1901," had the oldest Republican Club still in existence.

19. Sumner 1909, 1972, 66, 70. Edwards 1997, 105–6, 198n46. *WJ*, Nov. 10, 1894, 353. The first president of the Colorado club was Mary V. Macon. Its founder and most prominent member was Mary C.C. Bradford. Both resigned. For reports on initial activities see: *RMN* for 1894: May 25, Sept. 2, Sept. 4; Oct. 5, 5:1,2; Oct. 25, 1895. *Denver Post* for 1894: Oct. 13, 3:1; Oct. 20, 4:3; Nov. 23, 2:2; Dec. 1, 2:1. IV *HWS* 1902, 521 summarizes the political forces rupturing the women's Democratic clubs.

20. *Woman's Democratic Club, Year Book, 1913–1914*, seventeen-page booklet with history, officers, and constitution. *Women's Democratic Club, Sixty-Seventh Year, 1965–1966*, Salt Lake City, Utah, thirty-one-page booklet. Both in Women Democratic Clubs, Utah Historical Society, Salt Lake City. The history of the club in the latter is slightly different than in the former, and appears less accurate.

21. Quote in Williams 1977, 52. LeVan 1928, 4. LeVan was the Republican national committeewoman for Ohio, 1926–28. See also *The Republican Woman* (of Ohio), Founder's Issue, November 1927.

22. This is derived from somewhat inconsistent news stories in *SFEx* about the California Women's Republican Club, the Women's State Republican League, and the Women's State Democratic Club: June 27, 1914, 6:2; June 28, 1914, 57:2; July 2, 1914, 1:8; July 9, 1914, 5:2; July 16, 1914, 6:1; July 22, 1914, 7:8; July 30, 1914, 6:5; Sept. 9, 1914, 6:5. Apparently all of these dissolved. The end of the Women's Democratic Club is reported on May 28, 1922, 12:1, and the founding of the Women's Democratic Council on April 4, 1924, 6:2. There are no news stories on the Republican groups after 1916. A "History of California Federation of Republican Women" prepared by Jean Miles in 1974–75 says the first club was founded in Los Angeles in 1920 by Florence Collins Porter as a study club; reprinted in Hosmer oral history, 1983, 168.

23. First two quotes from Yount 1916, 52. Third quote in McCormick May, 1928, 2. The election in which the Republican club supported the Democratic candidate is not identified.

24. "Women's Party Clubs," *NR*, April 12, 1924, 17–18.

25. The Women's National Democratic League organized in May of 1912 and incorporated in the state of New York on June 27, 1912. Mrs. Crosby, who had initially used the same name for her NYC club, was one of the first officers, the rest were almost all wives of Members of Congress; *NYT* 1912: June 1, 4:2; June 28, 7:12; Aug. 4, 5:3; Sept. 21, 11:5; Oct. 10, 6:3; Jan. 10, 1913, 3:2; Jan. 8, 1914, 10:7; Aug. 4, 1916; 5:6; *SFCall*, June 28, 1912, 6:2. Rep. Stephen B. Ayres of New York, husband of the corresponding secretary (identified only as Mrs. Ayres), put the Constitution and Bylaws of the WNDL into the *Congressional Record Appendix* for

1912, 62nd Congress, 2nd Session,Vol. XLVIII, Pt. 12, 509–11.A year later, Mrs.Ayres defeated Mrs. Crosby for WNDL President—the only contested office.The latest mention I've found is in *WC*, Dec. 28, 1918, 628, on its forthcoming convention in Washington, D.C.

26.WDA in *BDE* 1920: Jan. 27, 6:6; Feb. 5, 20:5; Feb. 10, 20:6; *NYT* Feb. 1920: 5, 8:8; 6, 3:2; 7, 6:5. I've seen references to state federations in the archives I've searched but never a list. Even the Louchheim papers in the LoC have no such list, though her speaking schedules include appearances before state federations as well as individual clubs.

27. "Newsletter from The Women's Division, Republican National Committee, Washington, D.C.,"Vol. II, No. 2, May 1926, 18, 22–27. "Summarized Report of the Conference of Republican National Committeewomen, StateVice Chairmen and State Club Presidents, January 12, 13, and 14, 1927—Carlton Hotel, Washington, D.C.," 9. Both in Burroughs Papers, Box 324, LoC.Ten publications are listed in *RWP*, Feb. 1927, 10; I've found others.

28.The Illinois publication is identified and cited byYount 1916, 44, and the Maryland magazine by Weaver 1992, 214, but I haven't seen copies. *WDN* is in NYPL. I foundVol. 9, No. 1 for January 1939 of the Kentucky *Journal* in the WNDC archives. I have not found a list of Democratic women's publications.

29. On New Jersey see Gordon 1986, 79–80. On Maryland, see Weaver 1992, 216.

30. Quotes inYost October 1931, 14.

31. Florence J. Harriman, "Extracts from the Report of the Board of Governors," *DB*, March 1930, 29–33.These clubs were encouraged to affiliate with the WNDC for an annual fee of $12.00, but only twenty-six did so.

32. Neither Dewson nor Edwards wrote about Democratic women's clubs, though there is a mildly disparaging statement in Dewson's *DD* article on the 1936 campaign. Reports in the WNDC archives list affiliated clubs in twenty-nine states between 1935 and 1937, but these are only a small fraction of clubs known from other sources.

33. Untitled Upton article in *NYT*, March 16, 1924, IX:18:4–6. She and Blair published joint articles with much the same information in several newspapers in the spring of 1924. The headline varies.That in the *Kansas City Star*, May 3, 1924, 8:2, says "WomenVoters Line Up." *NR*, Nov. 8, 1924, 14:3, reports: "Connecticut has an enrollment of 30,000 women; Rhode Island has 36 clubs;Virginia, 29; Louisiana, 13; Oklahoma, 22; New Mexico, 23; Oregon, 23;Washington, 16 and some states several hundred."

34. *The Guidon*, Feb. 1927, 1. Letter from Mrs.AlvinT. Hert, vice chairman of RNC to *RWI*, Jan. 1929, 6.Yost statement in Minutes of the National Council of the Women's National Republican Club, Inc., October 16, 1933;WNRC, 34. Since she said there were thirty-five state federations in 1931, this indicates a decline after FDR's 1932 victory;Yost 1931.

35. Shelton 1955, D:1. "A Political Club forWomen Only," 1958.

36. Peel 1935, 248.This was all Peel had to say about women's political clubs. He explained that "this book does not treat of women's auxiliaries, since the subject of women in politics would require a volume." It is unfortunate that women's clubs weren't on his research agenda because the volume he thought necessary was never written, perhaps due to the absence of women from political science faculties. Peel did include chapters on "Nationality Clubs" and "Minor Party Clubs," which presumably did not require an entire volume.

37. Peel identified 2,819 political clubs in five parties in NewYork and New Jersey for the years 1930–32.While he counted clubs by party and whether or not they had their own

clubhouse, he didn't distinguish among the 1,200 auxiliaries so one cannot tell how many were women's, youth, etc. See Table XII—Number of Clubs in New York City and Its Environs (as of 1930–2); 1935, 34–5. The New York women's party magazines were *WDN*, *WRNY,* and *Guidon*. The *NY Telegraph* for May 1, 1927, identified all the women's Republican clubs organized by Mrs. Wentz alone. On the Republican Business Women, see 6:12 *WRNY*, Dec. 1928, 2; *NYT* 1926: July 21, 3:3; July 29, 15:1; July 31, 12:3; Oct. 30, 2:8.

38. Originally called the Women's National Democratic League, its name soon changed; *NYTrib* 1905: Aug. 15, 5:1; Sept. 15, 5:1; Oct. 7, 5:4. There are regular press reports of its meetings before and after it incorporated in 1912 as the Woman's Democratic Club of New York City; *NYT*, Feb. 9, 1912, 6:4. Mrs. Crosby was president until defeated in 1918 by Mrs. G.H. Childs, sister of Tammany leader John Curry (who was boss in 1929–34); *NYT*, April 13, 1918, 22:1. She was expelled in 1920 for supporting the Republican ticket; *NYH*, Oct. 22, 1920, 1. When she died, Crosby was eulogized as "the mother of New York Democrats"; *NYT*, Jan. 31, 1924, 15:6. Membership reports in "Largest Women's Political Club in America All for Governor Smith," *NYSun*, Oct. 11, 1928; and "Women's Democratic Club Takes Up Cause of Unattached Woman," *NYSun*, May 21, 1935. Presidency fight in *NYSun*, May 8, 1931; *BDE*, May 9, 1931, 24:3. See also: *NYT*, April 3, 1906, 6:3; June 1, 1912, 4:2; Jan. 10, 1913, 3:2; Nov. 1, 1913, 3:1; July 11, 1914, 5:4; Dec. 11, 1915, 7:6; April 18, 1920, 1:6; March 9, 1926, 23:2; May 15, 1927, 1:4; June 11, 1927, 21:2; Feb. 25, 1928, 2:7. *BDE*: Dec. 15, 1912, II: 8:3; April 18, 1920, 6:3:1; Oct. 22, 1922, 10:4:1; April 8, 1923, 5:7:1; Sept. 23, 1923, 8:4:1. "Women Democrats Cheer Tammany," Oct. 21, 1923, 22:5a; March 22, 1925, 7:1:a; June 17, 1924, 3:2; June 12, 1927, 8:2:1; Oct. 28, 1928, 18:1:1. The last press report of a meeting that I found was in 1946. The New York State Dept. of State reports that this club was incorporated on Feb. 8, 1912, and dissolved on Oct. 15, 1952.

39. *NYH*, June 28, 1922. *BDE*, Dec. 11, 1925.

40. "Women Win Right to Meet as Real Political Unit"—"Ousted by Jackson Heights Democratic Men, Secure New Quarters," *BDE*, April 18, 1928, LI:1:6. Peel mentions this club on 76 but was unaware that it was not an auxiliary.

41. Peel 1935, 38, 39, quote on 42, 130–1, 233. Chapter 8 describes the clubhouses; Chapter 12 the general activities; Chapters 15 and 16 the social activities; and Chapter 21 the "Anti-social Activities."

42. Peel 1935, 127–28.

43. "Political Clubs Are All for Men, Women Protest," *NYHT*, Sept. 15, 1930; *NY Sun*, Sept. 13, 1930.

44. Quote from Grafton 1962, 158, who doesn't specify the year; St. George did become county chairman. Porter and Matasar 1974, 97.

45. Chisholm 1970, 45. Wakefield 1959, 310. The Brooklyn organization was separate from Tammany Hall.

46. Adler and Blank 1975, 67–68, 165. Peel included clubs organized for the Socialist, Communist, and Socialist Labor Parties; Adler and Blank found that the Conservative Party was the only minor party with clubs. They said that in the 1930s and 1940s, as the machines slowly collapsed, political clubs came under the influence of organized crime, which would be one more reason for women to stay out; 22.

47. "A Political Club . . ." 1958, quote on 131.

48. Sumner 1909, 70. Edwards reports that ethnic women's Republican Clubs existed in the 1890s, 1995, chapter 5.

49. "Club of Colored Women," *NYH*, Sept. 27, 1892, 6:5. Boswell, *NR*, March 8, 1919, 8:6.

Interviews with Hall in *NYT*, Oct. 18, 1895, 8:1; *NYH*, Nov. 3, 1895,VI:9:5. Banner in *NYH*, Nov. 5, 1895, 5:5. See also *NYH* 1895, Oct. 12, 4:3; Oct. 18, 4:3; Nov. 3,VI:9:5; and Sept. 19, 1897,V:12:7. The voters club obviously had to be a men's club, and thus separate from the CWRA.

50. Lawton wrote four short pieces on the CWD in 1938 and 1939; 15:10 *WRNY*, Oct. 1938, 15–16; 16:5 *WRNY*, May 1939, 20; 1:2; *The Women's Voice*, June 1939, 11, 21; 16:12 *WRNY*, Dec. 1939, 23. Lack of further mention probably means the CWD didn't survive very long.

51. Thompson 1990, 129. Hendricks 1990, 167–75; 1999, 57. Ensley bio in *Colorado Suffrage Centennial* 1993, 17.

52. Terborg-Penn 1978, 178–79, 256; 1998, 103, 105.

53. On Randolph, see Gordon 1986, 78. Club No. 1 "Celebrates 18th Anniversary," *The Women's Voice*, June 1940, 5, MSRC. On Lampkin see IV *NAW* 1980, 406–8; *BWA* 1993, 690–93.

54. Rymph 1998, 139, citing a NFWRC survey of clubs affiliated with state federations; there probably were additional, unaffiliated, clubs.

55. On the Colored Women's Republican Clubs of Illinois, see Gaines 1929, 5. On Gaines, see IV *NAW* 1980, 258–59; *BWA* 1993, 476; her papers are at CHS. Picket mentioned in "Illinois Woman On Republican State Committee," 1:1 *The Women's Voice*, May 1939, 5, 24, MSRC.

56. "Colored Democratic Women Organize," *RMN*, Sept. 4, 1902, 6. On Fauset and her club see IV *NAW* 1980, 224.

57. Quote in DNC Inter Office Memorandum from Katie Louchheim to The Chairman, Oct. 29, 1953; Box 40, Louchheim Papers, LoC.

58. "Notes on Delaware Situation" by Ethel V. Weiss, two-page memo of April 14, 1954, in Box 18, Louchheim Papers, LoC.

59. Gordon 1986, 90–1, 93, 96. *NYT*: July 3, 1925, 5:1; April 15, 1928, X:6:1; Nov. 9, 1929, 9:6; Feb. 15, 1930,9:8; obit, Jan. 22, 1945, 17:5. *NYHT*, July 13, 1929, July 21, 1929.

60. *BDE*, July 9, 1929, 7:3; Aug. 19, 1929, 3:1.

61. "Can Men Pick Leaders for Women?" 7:1 *RWI*, Oct. 1929, 8. Mrs. Livermore was vice chairman of the Republican Westchester County Committee.

62. Sumner 1909, 1972, 70.

63. Upton Letter of Nov. 26, 1921; Box 13, Hanna-McCormick Papers, LoC.

64. Helmes 1983, 2–4.

65. Gordon 1986, 89, citing *Jersey Journal*, April 7, 1926.

66. Mayhew's extensive review of the structure of state and local parties as of the mid-sixties restricts the term "machine" to "a party organization that exercised overall control over government at a city or county level," 1986, 21. The popular view used the term much more liberally, probably including all of those organizations which he labeled strong "traditional party organizations." He summed up his assessment in 1991, 762, "thirteen states supported arrays of strong 'traditional party organizations' as late as the 1960s; Rhode Island and Connecticut in southern New England; New York, New Jersey, Pennsylvania, Maryland and Delaware (for which the evidence is notably scanty) in the Middle Atlantic area; Ohio, Indiana, and Illinois in the southern Midwest; and the noncoastal border States of West Virginia, Kentucky, and Missouri. The pattern is substantially specific to each state." While he didn't describe the pre-1960s pattern, Mayhew also said "a geographic pattern of party organization had coalesced by 1900, one that resembled the later 'traditional party organiza-

tion' map of the 1960s"; 766. A few states had strong party organizations in at least part of the state for some of the decades between 1900 and 1960. These include Tennessee, Louisiana, New Mexico and to a lesser extent, Arkansas, Texas, Virginia, and Georgia.

67. Gosnell 1937, Chapters 3 and 4, describes the character and activities of Chicago precinct captains, as does Forthal 1946. Salter 1935, Part II, provides "sketches" of nine Philadelphia division leaders. For a more personal description see Riordon (Plunkett) on New York City 1963; Wendt and Kogan on Chicago 1943, 1967.

68. Gosnell 1937, quote on 62. Gosnell interviewed Chicago precinct captains in both 1928 and 1936. It's not clear when this one was done; she may have been interviewed both times. In Chicago the main political unit was the ward, the equivalent of a city council district. Ward leaders were the primary party leaders, the permanent foundation of the party machine. They recruited precinct captains for each of the many precincts in their wards; after women could vote, they sought women co-captains to organize women. Even under Mayhew's restricted definition, Chicago and Philadelphia had party machines.

69. Gosnell 1937, 62–63.

70. Forthal 1946, 44.

71. Porter and Matasar 1974. Their interviews of living office holders were done in 1972. For information on others they relied on obituaries. Ward committeemen are the key party officials. The one woman, Lillian Piotrowski, refused to be interviewed.

72. Salter 1935, 203. The Vare brothers ran the Philadelphia machine when Salter did his research. Anti-Vares toppled it in 1933; Maisel 1991, 1171.

73. Tyler 1996, 79–80, 87–88. Both sisters were named Culligan before they married; although not mentioned in their obituaries, they most likely married brothers. *New Orleans Times-Picayune*, Nov. 7, 1930, 34:2 describes the LWV takeover with voters whose dues were not paid until the day of the election; March 15, 1952, I:3:3 has obit of Edna Pilsbury, 61; Feb. 22, 1963, I:18:1 has obit of Mary Pilsbury, 74.

74. Peel 1935, 62. LaGuardia's election cost Democrats the patronage of city jobs. Of the five borough bosses only Ed Flynn of the Bronx had supported FDR in 1932, so all federal patronage went through him; he followed Farley as DNC chairman in 1940. The other regular Democratic organizations "starved" in the 1930s; Adler and Blank 1975, Chapter 2.

75. "Women Sachems in Tammany's Wigwam," *New York Times Magazine*, June 8, 1919, VII:9:1–4. "The Three Women of Tammany," *NYT*, June 1, 1924, VIII:9:3. First Porges quote in *NYWorld*, Aug. 28, 1904, 7:1; second in *NYSun*, Oct. 21, 1931. Murphy died in 1924.

76. Dubuc 1920, 1. Byrnes 1924, 2. *Daily News*, April 29, 1931; *NYT*, May 3, 1931, 21:5. Quote from column she wrote for 7:2 *WDN*, June 1931, 10, 23, on "The Old Order." Marbury's entry in II *NAW* 1971, 493–95 has little on her political work; *NYT* obit, Jan. 23, 1933, 1:4.

77. Gosnell 1937, 61–62. Although Forthal 1946, also found only 5 percent of the precinct captains were women in 1927, her inclusion of the work of wives makes it clear that more women were active party workers than those who were official captains.

78. Blair 1937, 182. Boswell's observation was made at a meeting of the National Council of the Women's National Republican Club, Jan. 10, 1931; reporter's minutes, 7, WNRC. It's unclear whether she is referring to Tammany or Republican politicians, or both.

79. Monoson 1990. *SFCall* 1908: March 21, 8:2; March 29, 27:1; April 12, 30:3; Oct. 17, 7:2. Pinchot wrote about "The Influence of Women in Politics" as a result of his victory, 1922, quote on 12. "What Women Did in Gary," 68 *Ladies Home Journal*, October 1951, 51.

80. Tyler 1996, passim. The quote is from the title of Chapter 3. *New Orleans Times Picayune*: "Women Prove Factors in Primary," Feb. 4, 1940, II:2:1,5:1. "Fair Sex Lend Aid in Election," Jan. 20, 1946, III:1:1. Monroe 1946, describes how women elected Mayor Morrison.

81. "Four Years of Suffrage for American Women: Some Anniversary Thoughts," *NR*, Aug. 16, 1924, 17:2.

82. "'Women Elected Me' Mrs. Lilly Declares," *BDE*, Nov. 7, 1918, 8:1. She lost her seat the following year.

83. Allen 1965, 63–71, 76–77. Dickinson 1926.

84. Graham Jr. 1964, 57.

85. Priest 1958, 134. Priest lost in 1950, but Bosone was defeated by a man in 1952 when many Republicans rode into office on Eisenhower's coattails.

86. Hatch 1955, first quote 149, second quote 151.

87. Young 1999.

88. *ER*, Feb. 27, 1928, 21; Nov. 8, 1930, 318. Becker 1981, 103–4.

89. McCormick quote in *Chi Trib*, Nov. 8, 1928, 3:4. Medill McCormick committed suicide after losing to Deneen in 1924; Miller 1992, 151. Ruth had concentrated her organizing efforts on Illinois in the expectation that women would help reelect her husband, a Progressive and staunch supporter of woman suffrage. After the 1930 primary she was attacked for "excessive spending" and even investigated by the Senate; Miller 1992, Chapter 8 on "The Senate Campaign." On Deneen and the Barnetts; Gosnell 1935, 204, 206; Thompson 1979, 109, 119, 125. On Wells-Barnett and McCormick, see newspaper clippings in Irene McCoy Gaines papers, CHS, with resolution from six Colored Women's Republican Clubs that "we resent this put upon the Negro women of Illinois, whose vote she solicits, by the employment of an outsider to influence that vote." Wells-Barnett was one of the signatories. McCormick bowed to the attacks and replaced Terrell with Gaines. Note that Wells-Barnett had unsuccessfully run against Terrell for president of the NACW. Quote from "Have Women Political Power?," *RWI*, Jan. 1931, 5.

90. Root 1934, 39–40.

91. Chamberlin credits the Depression as well as McCormick's support for prohibition for her loss, but only prohibition for Owen's. Deneen supported prohibition so it was not an issue in the Illinois Republican primary. Ironically, the winning Democrat, James Hamilton Lewis, had been defeated by Medill McCormick for the same seat in 1918, which was a Republican year. Florida was a Democratic state, so the rejection of Republican rule prompted by the Depression was not a factor. *Time*, July 18, 1932, 9. Root 1934, 39–40, 63, 106. Pratt was also defeated in 1932, not a good year for a Republican to run in New York City. The three Congresswomen are profiled in Chamberlin 1973. Owen bio (under Rohde) in IV *NAW* 1980, 591–3. Allen bio in IV *NAW* 1980, 11–13.

92. Last quote in "Have Women Political Power?" *RWI*, Jan. 1931, 5. Johnson letter of April 9, 1930, quoted in Miller 1992, 223. *FB*, July 22, 1922, 4, said that Ruth's own husband objected to women serving in the Senate, and her brother-in-law's newspaper, *The Chicago Daily Tribune*, was "rather restrained" in its endorsement; Gosnell 1937, 164–65.

93. Smith 1952, quote on 50.

94. "It's a Man's Game, But Woman Is Learning," Dougherty 1946. "Really a Man's World—Politics," Samuels 1950. "Key Political Force—the Ladies," French 1956. These authors were journalists, but they quote politicians to make their point. Politician Farley 1959, maintained "this is still a man's world." Hitt emphasized how masculine the political

world had been in her oral history; 1977, 30–31. Polls in races with women candidates some-times asked voters about attitudes toward women.The only published comparison I've found was in 1964 when Democrat Genevieve Blatt challenged Republican Senator Hugh Scott. Of those polled, 10 percent were "pro-woman" and 17 percent were "anti-woman" (no other information provided); Falco 1980, 114. However, the Louchheim Papers, Box 59, LoC, con-tain a memo of a telephone conversation between Louchheim and Cong. Edith Green about a poll taken for her 1954 Congressional race which showed that 8 percent favored her because she was a woman, and 8 percent opposed her for the same reason. Non-party women's groups included Michigan's Women's Advisory Council, active in the 1950s and 1960s; "New G.O.P. Aide Wants More Women in Politics," *WES*, Dec. 4, 1963.

95. Egan 1920, 185. Dobyns 1927. The poem goes: "There once was a lady from Niger, who smiled as she rode on a tiger. They came back from the ride, with the lady inside, and the smile on the face of the tiger."

96. Livermore 1927, 4. Blair 1927. Roosevelt 1928. There were attempts to organize women outside the parties for electoral work, but none lasted. See "Women, Go Into Politics!," about the "Multi-Party Committee of Women, a non-partisan organization formed to encourage the participation of women in politics." Its founder, Edesse Dahlgren, explained that "it is not a feminist organization" but wanted to see that "women candidates get the recognition and support they deserve"; *NYSun*, Feb. 5, 1947.

97. Minutes, National Council, Jan. 10, 1931, quotes on 4–5; WNRC. Included in this meeting were five national committeewomen, two state vice chairmen, and four presidents of state club federations.

98. Ross statement in speech to United Women's Democratic Clubs of Maryland; *NYT*, May 22, 1931, 13:3. Blair 1931. See "Women Must Drop Feminism in Politics, Says Miss Butler," *BDE*, Dec. 28, 1926, 4:5. She repeated this in a reply to Blair in *RWI*, April 1931, 7.

99. Dewson quote from speech at the Northeast regional conference, reported in the Norwich Connecticut *Bulletin*, June 16, 1937; Reel 7, ER papers. Weis quote in Weis Papers, Reel 1:368; she compared lack of progress in politics with women's "tremendous strides in other fields of endeavor." NFWRC quote from Marie Suthers to the RNC Executive Session, Dec. 8, 1945; RP Papers, Reel 7:842–55. Martin quote from her report to the RNC, Dec. 7, 1945; RP papers, Reel 7:788–97. Good 1963, 31, quotes RNC Chairmen Hugh Scott, August 4, 1949, and Guy Gabrielson, Jan. 26, 1951, on the need for greater recogni-tion for women, but does not include the Suthers and Martin statements in her history. Edwards 1977, 68.

100. Harris 1954, 106. Kerr 1956, 4, was the Public Affairs editor for *Woman's Home Companion*. Costantini and Craik 1972, studied California party activists in the 1960s. Jennings and Thomas 1968, examined 1964 Michigan convention delegates. They also found a party difference with Republican women engaged "in proportionately more party service activity than Democratic women, but at the same time Republican men are more dominant than Democratic men," 484. However they appear to have measured number and type of positions rather than years of service or hours of work. Clarke and Kornberg 1979, interviewed several hundred party officials in Seattle, Minneapolis, Vancouver, and Winnipeg. Cotter and Hennessy 1964, 58. Maryland quote in Helmes 1983, 19. Although Sanders 1955, 21, confirms Blair's assessment of compliant party women, she also reports on a Midwestern woman who "enforced a women's boycott of state headquarters when she found that all the hot questions of strategy, candidates and patronage were being set-

tled at stag sessions."

101. First quote, *DD*, "Fifty-Fifty," June, 1946, 12. Second quote in Fisher 1947, 87. Farley 1938, 55. Young 1950, 81. Dougherty 1946, 17. Salisbury 1965–66. Ducas 1936, describes the experiences and motivations of three types of party women as they took over the work of party drones. Early in 1941, DNC Chairman Edward J. "Flynn Advises Women to Assume Heavier Role in Party Work" in a talk before the WNDC; *WES*, Jan. 19, 1941. Baker 1999 makes similar observations on the change in the party work force.

102. Those who commented on women's takeover of campaign and party work include: Dougherty 1946, 17; Sanders 1956, 31; Grafton 1962, 156, 120; Gruberg 1968, 52–53; Smith 1992, 148. Bone found in 1951 that "both Republican and Democratic headquarters during elections appear to be staffed, in the main, by middle-aged and elderly women, and women play a most active part in the organization." Eighty percent of these were housewives; 1952, 10–11, 18. Louchheim said that women campaign workers "outnumber the men by two or three to one," in Shelton, "Women, Once Ignored, Play Vital Role in Politics Today," *WES*, Oct. 3, 1954. On black women see, Clayton 1964, Chapter 7, especially quote from Cong. William Dawson (D. Ill.), 122: "the Negro woman has been the salvation of Negroes politically." 1958 estimate in "What Women Do in Politics," Dec. 1958. 1960 estimate in Sanders 1963, who divided the volunteers into three types: "Issues Girls, Club Ladies, [and] Camp Followers." Kennedy quote from "Comments . . . Before the CONFERENCE ON EMPLOYMENT OPPORTUNITIES FOR WOMEN," Sept. 24, 1962; Box 58, Louchheim Papers, LoC. Jackie Kennedy repeatedly told women's groups that President Kennedy thought "One woman is worth ten men in a campaign"; *WES*, Nov. 30, 1960, C:4:1. Dole quote in *WES*, "More Women, Dole Says," Dec. 10, 1971, and "'Distinction' for Women," Feb. 3, 1972.

103. The term is in Sanders 1955, 29–32. Quote in Snyder, who gives a first-person account of Stevenson's magnetism, 1977, 80. Snyder thought women did more campaign work in 1952 than in 1977; 83.

104. On Cunningham see IV *NAW* 1980, 176–77. She ran for office several times without success, then switched to writing a newspaper column.

105. Lash 1972, 271–72.

106. On amateur Democrats, see Wilson 1962, 1966; quotes on 132, 235. Wilson studied reform Democrats in New York, Chicago, and California, but mentions women only in New York City. Wakefield 1959, 310, found attitudes toward the role of women in politics to be part of the cultural conflict between reformers and regulars. Wilson 1962, 235n, reported that when DeSapio's coleader was asked if she ever voted contrary to his wishes, she replied "God forbid!" Comparison of the sex composition of reform and regular clubs is in Adler and Blank 1975, 191–92. Carol Greitzer told me (phone interview, June 25, 1998) that reform clubs automatically included both men and women, it was never questioned; indeed the presence of members of the opposite sex was one reason for joining.

107. Shirpser oral history 1975, 237, 240. Governor Hiram Johnson instituted cross-filing so he could run for the Senate in 1916 as both a Progressive and a Republican. Subsequent candidates could run in both the Democratic and Republican primaries and the better financed Republicans often won both nominations. Crawford 1953, describes BPW's California campaign. Republican Evelyn E. Whitlow lost narrowly to an incumbent; Donohoe served four terms. Wyman oral history 1977–78. Smith quote in Isabelle Shelton, "The Sky's the Limit for Political Women," *WES*, Feb. 7, 1961. California's first assemblywoman was elected in 1918; the first female State Senator was elected in 1979; Cox 1996,

63–66.

108. Among these was Hillary Rodham Clinton. An important Goldwater woman was Mary Dent Crisp, who was cochairman of the RNC from 1977 to 1980. She, like Goldwater, was pro-choice and pro ERA. Feminists were still active in the Republican Party in the 1970s, but were squeezed out in the 1980s.

NOTES FOR CHAPTER NINE (PAGES 179 TO 202)

1. Quote from Blair 1929, 220. The number of Democratic delegates was only slightly more than the Republicans until 1964 when it almost doubled; *NPC* 1997, 9. Statistics on women delegates from several sources, including DCWF 1960; Breckinridge 1933, 1972, 289; David, Goldman, and Bain 1960, 328; Fisher 1944, 896; Lynn 1979, 404.

2. Blair 1924, 21; 1940, 15, 38. Quote in *ER*, "Women in the National Conventions," Feb. 20, 1932, 20–21. Blair 1937, 188–89, describes how the resolution was passed despite opposition. Various papers (e.g., Louchheim's) contain lists of state delegations and the number of women in each one. Convention proceedings and some news stores gave women by state; *NYT*, Aug. 19, 1956, 66:8. David, Goldman, and Bain 1960, 515–16, lists the 1952 state delegations; Segal 1971, lists the 1968 state delegations; *Republican Clubwoman* for Oct. 1967 has a table of delegates and alternates to GOP conventions for 1956, 1960, and 1964. Georgianna Miles, president of the Women's State Republican Clubs, unsuccessfully demanded equal representation on the New Jersey delegation to the 1932 Republican convention; Gordon, 1986, 164.

3. Ware 1981, 80–82. Roosevelt and Hickok 1954, 16. Dewson 1940. Schlesinger, Jr. 1960, 597–98. Furman 1949, 241–43. *DD*: "Program for Democratic Convention Week," July 1936, 8; "Women Have Pride in Platform Contribution," August 1936, 6–7. "Table of Women on Major National Convention Committees," DCWF 1960, 30.

4. *NYT* June 1936: 7, 33:1; 9, 17:5; 10, 1:4; 11, quote on 16:1; 12, 17:5. *The Woman Republican* also wrote about personalities but not program; "Women in the Spotlight at the National Convention," 13:7 *WRNY* July 1936, 9.

5. "2 G.O.P. Women Get Top Convention Roles," *WES*, June 23, 1956. *NYT*, June 23, 1956, 9:3. They were Gladys Knowles, convention secretary, and Rep. Katharine St. George (R. N.Y.), parliamentarian. Items on the 1956 convention in Boxes 16 and 76, Louchheim Papers, LoC. See also: "Women Rallying for Convention—Showcase Prepared," *NYT*, Aug. 1, 12:1; "Ladies Are Greeted by Noise But No Crowds," *NYT*, Aug. 15, 1:8, 14:2–5; *NYHT*, Aug. 15, 1956. Compare with "Ladies Day at G.O.P. Convention," *NYT*, Aug. 22, 14:8; "G.O.P. Women Cautioned on Complacency," *NYT*, Aug. 22, 18:3–6; "15 Women Leaders Speak on Administration's Record," *NYHT*, Aug. 22, 1956. 1956 was not unusual: "Lateness of Women's Talks At Democratic Convention Hit," *WES*, July 24, 1948.

6. Isabelle Shelton, "A Long, Hard Row to Hoe, Women's Political Progress Is Slow," *WES*, July 10, 1960.

7. "Women Hold Key Jobs at G.O.P. Convention," *WES*, June 24, 1960. "'Great Ladies' to Parade," *WES*, July 24, 1960.

8. DCWF 1960, 27–8. Three women also received votes for the presidential nomination at the 1924 Democratic convention, including Emma Guffey Miller (Pa.); David, Goldman, and Bain 1960, 329.

9. Rawalt 1969, II:129. "Their hats were in the ring," *Independent Woman*, Aug. 1952, 226.

Dorothy Titchener, "Our woman-for-vice-president campaign," *Independent Woman*, Sept. 1952, 260. Quote in Roosevelt and Hickok 1954, 67, which contains a lengthy description of Crews life and Democratic Party activities.

10. Roosevelt and Hickok 1954, 66–68, 236. Good 1963, 33–34. Graham, Jr. 1964, 90–91. Luce's speech in *NYT*, July 1, 1952, 15:2.

11. *NYT*, Jan. 28, 1964, 1:2, speech excerpts 17:4. The 1959 Farley article quotes Eleanor Roosevelt, President Eisenhower, *and* Senator Smith on why women can't be President. "Question of Merit, says Senator Margaret Chase Smith of Maine. 'Let's not vote for a woman,' she says, 'just because she is a woman, when we have an able man filling the job.'" Nomination in *NYT*, July 16, 1964, 16:2. Smith was defeated for reelection in 1972 but lived until age ninety-seven; bios and career in Graham 1964; Lamson 1968, 3–29; Chamberlin 1973, 143–55; Sherman 1993; obit in *NYT* May 31, 1995; B:6:1.

12. 1924 DNC resolution in Blair 1940, 38. "Fifty-Fifty Representation at National Convention," *DD*, March 1936, 24. DNC meeting of Feb. 5, 1940, in DNC 1940, 49–50. DCWF 1960, 29–30. *NYT* July 1940: 17, 1:6; 18, 5:1.

13. Good 1963, 25–26, 41–42. The table in DCWF 1960, 30, gives somewhat different numbers for women on Republican committees than appear in Good, though the latter are not in tabular form nor complete for each year. See also RNC *Proceedings*, 1944, 32, 36–37 for resolution creating the Resolutions Committee and a list of the members for that year; subsequent *Proceedings* have similar ones. *CQ Weekly Report*, Sept. 25, 1959, 1307.

14. Segal 1971, 9896. Quote from Clarence Cannon, "Democratic Manual for the Democratic National Convention, 1960," 25. The 1948 convention only required those states having women delegates to choose a woman for the Platform Committee; DNC 1948, 59–60. At the 1996 Republican convention, West Virginia asked the Republican Party Rules Committee to amend Rule 17 requiring equal division on the four convention committees because it did not have four women in its delegation to fill all the slots. This motion was defeated without discussion in a voice vote by roughly two to one; personal observation.

15. *WC*: Jan. 17, 1920, 722; May 29, 1920, 1319, identified Reinecke as a "member of the State Board of the Illinois Equal Suffrage Association, who is executive secretary of the National Republican Women's Committee"; Mrs. Geo. Reinecke is also listed on the RWNEC stationary. Upton quote 1926, XXV:8–9.

16. Terrell 1940, 1986, 308–14. Henretta 1987, 692. The black population was higher in Washington, D.C., where no one could vote, black or white, male or female. The Cincinnati *Commercial Tribune*, Oct. 1, 1920, commented on higher registration by black women in Ohio, cited in Williams 1977, 60.

17. See the table in "Which Party Did It?," *WC*, Sept. 18, 1920, 422–27. However, note that in the Fourth Party System the Republicans dominated most state legislatures outside the South, which was anti-suffrage. In earlier Congressional votes on the Suffrage Amendment there was a partisan division in the Eastern states, with proportionately more Republicans in favor than Democrats. By the final vote, Southern Democrats were the last solid block of opponents; remove them from the Congressional and state voting columns and the pattern is not partisan.

18. DNC 1920, 67, 117, 365, 436–50.

19. Republican Party pamphlets are in the Harding Papers, Reel 195:0034–0063. Harding speech in *NYT*, Oct. 2, 1920, 2:2.

20. Bass 1940, 39.

21. One-third is the popular estimate of women's vote in 1920; it appears in numerous journalistic references, but without a source. In 1924 Michelet calculated that women were 37 percent of "1920 Total Vote Cast" in forty-two non-Southern states, 7. He estimated that 43 percent of the female voting age population (in forty-two states) went to the polls. His base was "native and naturalized white women only, 21 years of age and over, according to Census of 1920." State calculations ranged from 29 percent to 45 percent. Rice 1928, 245–47 calculated that in the Northern and Western states women cast between 34.7 and 46.5 percent of the 1920 vote. Overall voter turn out was 49.2 percent, the lowest since 1824 for a Presidential election. Several political scientists have challenged the idea that non-voting women significantly lowered overall turnout rates because the men's rate had been falling for two decades; Burnham 1974, Kleppner 1982. Andersen 1996, 52, 74, reviews these and other studies. Some women were still ineligible to vote. Georgia and Mississippi required voters to register several months in advance and women could not do this prior to the August 26 certification of the Nineteenth Amendment; Catt and Shuler 1923, 1926, 172. Women married to aliens were deemed disqualified, even when born and residing in the United States, because Congress had passed a law in 1907 requiring married women to take the citizenship of their husbands—though the Massachusetts ballot law commission ruled that an otherwise eligible woman who had married an alien prior to 1907 could still vote; "Legal Decisions for Women Voters," *WC*, Oct. 31, 1920, 607.

22. Ohio poll taken by the Cincinnati *Enquirer*, Nov. 2, 1920, and reported in Williams 1977, 63. Illinois vote in Rice and Willey 1924; Rice 1928, 1969, 176–79. Statewide, 74.6 percent of women and 71.4 percent of men voted for Harding over Cox. This gender gap was consistent for 100 of 102 counties, including Cook County (Chicago). Elizabeth Bass, director of the Democratic Women's Bureau for the 1920 campaign, wrote Wilson that he had lost the vote of Irish and German women due to the League of Nations; letter of Nov. 30, 1920, Wilson papers, Reel 374.

23. "Woman's Hand in Maine," 66 *LD*, Sept. 25, 1920, 13–14, summarizing reports from several newspapers.

24. Pickens 1920, 372–73. *NYT*, Nov. 3, 1920, 18:3. Sims 1997, 186. Michelet found that the 1920 vote increased very little over former elections by men only in Arkansas, Louisiana, Texas, Mississippi, Georgia, and South Carolina; 1924, 7.

25. Quote in *NYT*, "Plan to Bring Out Stay-At-Home Vote," May 11, 1924, I-2:5:1. Two years later the "Republicans Seek Stay-at-Home Vote" because of worry they might lose control of the Senate in the off-year election; *NYT*, April 26, 1926, 5:1.

26. Merriam and Gosnell 1924, 250–51.

27. Merriam and Gosnell 1924, 30, 37, 164, 230. Last quote in Gosnell 1935, 19.

28. Michelet 1928, 2, commenting on the elections of 1920 and 1924.

29. *LD*, July 21, 1928, 9, reported calculations by the *Boston Globe* that in 1924 the Coolidge campaign spent $3,663,952 and Davis spent $903,908, less than either party spent in 1920 or 1916, and for the Democrats, less than in 1912 (the only year it outspent the Republican Party).

30. *WC*, Nov. 1, 1924, 22. *NR*, Sept. 20, 1924, 14. Letter of Sept. 8, 1924 from Mrs. Hert to Mrs. McCormick; Box 13, Hanna-McCormick Papers, LoC. The 1924 Progressive Party drew more supporters from the Democrats than had its 1912 predecessor, and heavily from the Socialists, Farmer-Labor, and Non-Partisan League, but its voters were mostly disenchanted progressive Republicans.

31. Higginbotham 1992, 206–7; same quote in 1997, 141–42.

32. Arneson 1925, 819.

33. Barnard, Nov. 1928, 553. The *NYT* claim was based on a review of the voter registration figures where they were kept separately by sex; *NYT*, Oct. 21, 1928, X:8:1. This was one of many news stories predicting women's surge to the polls.

34. California women for Hoover mentioned in Hosmer oral history, 1983, 168. Quote in Harvey 1995, 204, who said that Hoover "personally directed the organization of 'club' women for the campaign"; 210. However, she underestimates the importance of prohibition; 221–23. Peel and Donnelly 1931, 52, 71, identified eight campaign issues, but concluded that "the only real issues were prosperity, prohibition and religion." Morrison wrote that among women, prohibition, and Smith's relation to Tammany Hall were the most frequent reasons given for opposing him; 178, 151. Lichtman also argues that "the issues of religion and prohibition seem to have been most important in drawing out the woman voter"; 1979, 238. Most contemporary commentators wrote that prohibition, religion, and Tammany Hall were the key issues for all voters, or at least the issues that evoked the strongest responses.

35. First quote in Morrison 1978, 84. *NYT* 1928: Oct. 18, 4:5; Oct. 26, 2:4; Nov. 1, 7:1. Phrase used by Anne McCormick 1928, 22, and Ethel Smith 1929, 126; Barnard, Nov. 1928, 555, says "it was women themselves, and not men press agents in their behalf, who first created the slogan." Hert wrote in *WJ* for August 1928, 6, that Hoover's nomination "was in no small measure due to the support given his candidacy by women." Her November article on "Women's Work for Herbert Hoover" gave five reasons on why she thought women were particularly impressed with Hoover. See also *NYT* editorial on "Women Voters in Ohio," Feb. 25, 1928, 16:3. Compare the ad: "Thirty-seven Leading Women tell why they will vote for Herbert Hoover" in *WJ*, Sept. 1928, 51, with the one on "Why Women Should Vote for Alfred E. Smith" which has no signatories; *WJ*, Oct. 1928, 51. "WCTU Plea for Hoover," *NYT*, July 8, 1928, 2:4. Extent of WCTU activity in Morrison 1978, 155–64; Boole bio in IV *NAW*, 1980, 91; *NYT* obit, March 14, 1952, 23:1.

36. Morrison 1978, 80, 86. *NYT* 1928: July 8, 2:4, Aug. 15, 2:4, Aug. 17, 2:2, Oct. 21, 26:4. *WJ*, Sept. 1928, 32. Robins was very active in the Hoover campaign; written remnants of her work, including a pamphlet on "Why the Industrial Women of the Country are for Herbert Hoover," are in the WTUL-MDR papers, Reel 15:716–94. Dreier summarizes her sister's 1928 activities, 1950, 209.

37. Higginbotham 1990, 211. Morrison 1978, 91–98, describes the extensive work black women did for Hoover, based on files on the 1928 election in the Claude Barnett Papers, CHS. Slogan comes from Nannie Helen Burroughs, "Summary of Report" of her 1928 speaking tour for Hoover-Curtis, Box 309, Burroughs Papers, LoC. She described the audiences for her speeches as "large and biracial" but didn't mention their sex composition.

38. Morrison 1978, 52–62. The cofounder of the NWDLEL was Mrs. Jesse W. Nicholson of Baltimore. Peel and Donnelly 1931, 34, 39. Goldman 1990, 321–25. Raskob was high in the councils of the AAPA, which Smith joined after his defeat.

39. First quote from Peel and Donnelly 1931, 83–84. Third quote from ER's official report on her activities; 3:10 *DB*, Dec. 1928, 19. Ross quote, *NYT*, July 14, 1928, 4:3. ER announcement, *NYT*, July 19, 1928, 3:5.

40. Ware 1981, 39–40. Harvey also found the Democratic women's campaign to be little more than speakers; 1995, 235, 237–39. Morrison says the "two most popular speakers were Ross and Emma Guffey Miller"; 1978, 119. Smith's campaign relied heavily on party women; the Hoover women came from everywhere. Ida Tarbell, a muckraking journalist who had opposed suffrage, was an exception; see "A Woman Looks at Smith," reprinted by the DNC

from *Collier's*, May 19, 1928, as a fourteen-page pamphlet, SI. When much-loved social worker Lillian Wald sent letters throughout the country in support of Smith, she was inundated with critical responses; Daniels 1989, 58. *ChiTrib*, Oct. 24, 1928, 1:7,10. New York State was especially active; "What the Woman's Speakers Bureau Did," 4:7 *WDN*, Nov. 1928, 20.

41. Roosevelt and Hickok 1954, quote on 205. Barnard, Dec. 1928, 44, says she sat with five men on "the innermost policy-making body." The 1928 *Campaign Book* lists her as one of seven on the Democratic Party Executive Committee. Bio in II *NAW* 1971, 589–91. Her granddaughter's biography makes it clear that she had no aspirations for political influence, but saw herself solely as a servant to Smith and to the social reform causes that had brought her to him; Perry 1987. After losing the Presidential race, Smith tried to "plant" her as Roosevelt's secretary while Governor of New York. FDR saw through this and declined the recommendation despite Moskowitz' well-known expertise. She had no further impact on politics. Her obituary on the front page of the *NYT*, Jan. 3, 1933, described her as the most powerful woman in American politics.

42. *WJ*, Nov. 1928, 30.

43. Morrison 1978, 102, 141, 143, 179–207. Harvey 1995, 216, 221. On radio parties see *WJ*, Nov. 1928, 30. The *WJ* candidate series ran April through November in 1928. Sally Hert wrote all those for the Republican position. Democratic authors included Emily Newell Blair, Marion Bannister, Daisy Harriman, Nellie Tayloe Ross, Eleanor Roosevelt, and Elinor Morganthau. The *Democratic Text Book* did include the Democratic Party platform, which had a few paragraphs on "Women and Children."

44. First quote in editorial on "Beliefs First, Party Second," *WJ*, Oct. 1928, 26, which also lists some women party shifters. NWDLEL attacks are in *NYT* July 7, 1928, 14:3. Ross 1928, explained how a dry could support Smith. Willebrandt's campaign speeches and the reaction to them are described in Chapter Six of her biography; Brown, 1984. Second quote by syndicated columnist Frank Kent originally appeared in the *Baltimore Sun*, cited in Brown, 173, and also used in *NYT* editorial, "The Problem of Mabel," Dec. 31, 1928, 14:6. See also Morrison 1978, 165–74.

45. Letter of Oct. 19, 1928, from Ida Wells-Barnett to Mr. (Claude) Barnett; Barnett Papers, CHS. In 1928 black elites were disgruntled with the Republican Party because it was pursuing a "Southern strategy."

46. Blair quote in Blair 1929, 224. See also Breckinridge 1933 and 1972, 286. *NYT* quote by A. McCormick 1928, 3. "Women Speakers Enroll in Campaign," *NYT*, Sept. 23, 1928, II:1:5. Some of the GOP speakers were paid; all the Democrats were volunteers. Third quote in Munro 1928, 253.

47. Barnard, Nov. 1928, 554.

48. Henretta 1987, 734. Quote in Lichtman 1979, 162. H. Smith 1929.

49. Michelet 1929, 13, did not explain why his 30 percent estimate was less than his previous 37 percent for the 1920 female vote but adding in the excluded six Southern states would bring it down. Morrison reports that women cast 42 percent of the vote in San Francisco and Cleveland and 41 percent in Chicago; 1978, 248.

50. *ChiTrib*, Oct. 24, 1928, 1:7, also said that "the comments of the women indicate that the wetness of Al Smith is largely responsible for the lead accorded to Hoover." Women were 43.21 percent of Chicago's registered voters. *ChiTrib* reported its final "straws" on Saturday before the election, but not by sex; nor did it break out the Chicago vote by sex, which Smith narrowly won.

51. Robinson 1932, 92, compared the many polls and concluded that the Hearst poll was the most reliable. It was conducted by sending out postcard ballots for informants to return, supplemented by personal inquiries. The 1928 predictions were based on roughly 1.2 million responses. Arkansas and Louisiana were the two missing states. *LD* had the best known poll, but Robinson found it less accurate when compared with the actual results, and it didn't separate responses by sex.

52. Harvey 1995, 253, citing J. Bennett Gordon to Lawrence Richey, Jan. 3, 1929, Campaign and Transition Papers, Box 157; and Lichtman 1979, 163, citing Republican National Committee, "Summary Report on the 1928 Campaign," Pre-Presidential, Box 89. Whatever the box, both agree this report is in the Hoover Papers, Hoover Presidential Library. Harvey reviewed responses to the RNC's information request in her 1995 dissertation, 247–55. The RNC said that reports were to be private, "as we desire to avoid publicity." Lichtman has excerpts from the Republican survey in his appendix, 291–3. Earle Kinsley, an aide to the RNC chairman, said that "In the South, as throughout the country, the women were to a large extent responsible for the results," *NYT*, Nov. 8, 1928, 9:2–3.

53. Morrison 1978, 263, and Lichtman 1979, quote on 163, cite reports in the FDRL. That club women were mostly Republicans was not a revelation. The Republican Party estimated that 80 percent "of the leaders among the club women are Republican" and this was probably true of members, at least outside the South, as well; *NR*, Nov. 15, 1924, 14.

54. Letter from Ethel Bailey Childress, National Committeewoman for Tennessee, Dec. 23, 1928, published in *DB*, Jan. 1929, 24–25. Some of the other letters were reprinted in *DB*, July 1929, 14, 28. The respondents to FDR's letters also complained about a general lack of organization.

55. Quote from Munro 1928, 253. The evidence on Catholic women is inferential, but both anecdotal and statistical. For the former see Walter Davenport, "Down the Home Stretch," 82 *Collier's*, Nov. 3, 1928, 8–9. Lichtman 1979, 160–61, used regression analysis to conclude "that women were more likely to vote for Republican candidate Herbert Hoover than were their male counterparts." Gamm, however, argues that in Boston, Irish women were already voting and Italian women abstained until the 1930s; 1989, 148, 163–64.

56. Smith won in Arkansas (home state of his running mate), Alabama, Georgia, Louisiana, Mississippi, South Carolina, plus Massachusetts and Rhode Island. As Lubell pointed out "Before the Roosevelt Revolution there was the Al Smith Revolution"; 1951, 34–35. Andersen 1979, discusses the importance of the immigrant vote.

57. First and third quotes from Farley 1938, 160. Gubernatorial terms were only two years until 1938. FDR's 1930 victory margin of 725,001 attracted nationwide attention; 61. Farley credits ER's organizational work for turning New York into a Democratic state; 353. He doesn't mention WONPR, but he acknowledges that repeal and economic recovery were the key issues in 1932; 112. Second quote from Peel and Donnelly 1935, 31, who intensively studied the Presidential campaigns of 1928 and 1932, but barely mention women's work in either one.

58. Dewson 1940. Dewson 1949, I:59–60, quote on 63. Howe 1935.

59. Quotes in Dewson 1949, I:44, 46, 55. Dewson 1940. Ware 1987, 158–72. Howe 1935, quote on 10.

60. First quote by Yost, in "Femininity of Woman Leader Hides Executive Ability," *WES*, July 22, 1932. Second from report by Yost to the RNC Executive Committee on Aug. 11, 1932; reporters' minutes, 3–4, National Archives. Good 1963, 21. Names from RNC Women's Division "Organization News," Sept. 24, 1932, 2–3; Oct. 22, 1932, 1–4, found in Box 324,

Burroughs Papers, LoC. Terrell quote 1940, 1986, 412. Yost headed the campaign women's division. Boswell was once again head of the Speakers' Bureau of the Eastern Division. She told the National Council of the Women's National Republican Club that the campaign would not pay the women to make speeches, but did pay some of the men; minutes of meeting of Jan. 21, 1933, 31, WNRC.

61. Minutes of the meeting of the WNRC National Council for Jan. 21, 1933, report of Mrs. Theodore L. Pomery of Connecticut, describes the "Factors Contributing to the Successful Campaign of the Republican Women's Association of Fairfield County, Connecticut," 19–25, WNRC. These can be summed up as thoroughness of organization.

62. The 40 percent comes from Robinson, 1933, 92, who attributes it to professional politicians. AIPO (Gallup) Poll #53 in 1936 queried voters on their 1932 votes. The lack of consistency between this poll and the actual vote is accounted for by time, failing memory, and the tendency of respondents to remember voting for the winner. Gosnell 1937, 1968, 109.

63. Ware 1981, 85–86. Roosevelt and Hickok 1954, 18–19. Dewson 1940. Schlesinger, Jr. 1960, 597. Furman 1949, 282–83. The Rainbow Fliers were written by Mary Chamberlain, who had worked as circulation manager for two magazines; *DD*, Dec. 1936, 7–8; Dewson 1940, 61; Wolfe 1978, 117.

64. "Women—It's Up To You," *DD*, Aug. 1936, 20. "Democratic Victory," sixteen-page pamphlet, 1936, SI. *DD*, Sept. 1936, has several articles on the campaign including: "Women You Hear About in The 1936 Campaign," profiles of Mrs. Charles W. Tillett, Jr., "chairman of the important Speakers' Bureau," Mrs. Henry W. Morgenthau, Jr., "Chairman of the Radio Program Committee;" novelist and playwright Alice Duer Miller, "heads the Author's Committee," and Grace Abbott "will be Chairman of a National Committee of Welfare Workers," 7; "The 'Grass Trampers' Are On the March," 8; "Mightier Than An Army Is An Idea Whose Time Has Come," on Reporters and Rainbow Fliers, 24; "Democratic Clubs and the Campaign," 25. Dewson quotes in "Our Part in the Campaign of 1936," *DD*, Dec. 1936, 5–6. The South did not get Rainbow Fliers though it "did join in the radio parties." "Votes by Wireless," 6; "Diary of a Speakers' Bureau," 8; "Publicity That Won," 9.

65. On Democratic efforts to appeal to blacks, see Schlesinger, Jr. 1960, 598–600. Fauset bio in IV *NAW* 1980, 224–25; *BWA* 1993, 410–11; *NYT* obit in March 30, 1965, 47:4. In 1938 Fauset became the first black woman to be elected to a state legislature. She won with the backing of the local Democratic Party in a district that was two-thirds white. She resigned in 1939 to work for the WPA. Gamm 1989, 101, argues that in Boston, black men gradually increased their support for the Democrats throughout the 1920s, but that "black women were permanently mobilized with a rush . . . in 1936." The *NYT* of Aug. 10, 1936, 10:2, reports "Frances E. Rivers, director of the Colored Eastern Division, announced the selection of Mrs. Maude B. Coleman of Harrisburg Pa. as women's director." Memo of Oct. 5, 1948 from Mrs. Robert W. Macauley, and Mrs. Charles W. Weis, Jr. to Mr. Herbert Brownell, Jr., identifies the four "negro women as 'Assistants in the Women's Division' to work more or less on a regional basis"; Weis Papers, Reel 2:678.

66. AIPO Poll #60, December 1936. Gosnell 1937, 109.

67. This assessment is based on newspaper coverage. The *NYT index* has two pages of entries on women in the 1936 presidential campaign but nothing comparable for the subsequent campaigns. The items in the *NYSun*, *BDE*, and *WES* morgues also imply less coverage, though computations are impossible. I examined the Guide to Thomas E. Dewey's papers at the University of Rochester and was impressed by the paucity of entries on women. Nor was there much on the 1948 campaign in Judy Weis' papers, and she was associate cam-

paign manager and head of the women's division in the 1948 Dewey campaign. I don't believe women's participation went down—if anything it increased—but their work was less publicized. *DD* continued to highlight the work of Democratic women until removed from control of the DNC Women's Division; see the many stories in the Jan. 1941 issue. The fewer stories in Dec. 1944, 14–17, and Dec./Jan 1949, 18–22, indicate smaller women's divisions and less effort focused on the woman voter.

68. "Flynn Advises Women To Assume Heavier Role in Party Work," *WES*, Jan. 19, 1941.

69. *NYT*, Oct. 30, 1944, 12:6. DNC Vice Chairman and Women's Division head Gladys Tillett had already claimed "a great increase in the number of women serving as precinct and county leaders and running for office on the party's local and state tickets"; *NYT*, Aug. 30, 1944, 32:6.

70. First quote from Louchheim, *NYT*, Sept. 14, 1956, 10:2. "Thank You, Mr. President from the Women of America, . . . The Republican Women's Fund Raising for the 1956 Campaign," Weis Papers, Reel 4:447–9; Isabelle Shelton, "A New Political Job Found for Women," *WES*, Nov. 27, 1955, D:4:1. Poll reported in *WES*, Nov. 2, 1955, and Weis Papers, Reel 4:446, 4:690. Results not given by sex. D.C. League work in *WES*, May 26, 1956. Paid TV ad in *NYT*, Oct. 25, 1956, 1:2, 22:1.

71. Hitt oral history 1977, 120.

72. Wives were not the only women speakers, but apart from ER, they got the most publicity; "Women Near End of Busy Campaign," *NYT*, Nov. 4, 1956, 69:8.

73. "Democratic Woman Speakers Get Campaign Tips at School," *WES*, May 20, 1946. WD director Tillett claimed this school was "the first of its kind arranged by a national party organization." "Housewives" in Edwards 1977, 118–19; DNC 1948, 48–54; *DD* 1948: Aug., 2, Sept./Oct., 3, Nov., 14–15, 23. "Crossroads Tour Aimed At the Women's Vote," *WES*, Oct. 15, 1956. The wives were from the DCWF. See also *NYT*, Oct. 1956: 15, 12:4,5; 18, 27:5. "Women to Carry Message," *WES*, Oct. 7, 1964, D:4:1. OWA-DNC "summary report . . . for the 1956 campaign" lists even more activities in which political wives predominated; Box 18, Louchheim Papers, LoC. Williams quote from her press conference describing a one a.m. phone call with Richard Nixon, in Isabelle Shelton, "Women Will Decide Election, Vice President Convinced," *WES*, Sept. 13, 1960. "'Flying Squadron' Takes Off," *WES*, Sept. 25, 1968. Daily meetings for women at the 1960 Democratic convention were: "Women on the Convention Scene" featuring women officials and wives; "How to Get into Politics," "My Husband Is 'a man who . . . ',""I'm Running for Office," and "I Married a Politician." News release on the 1960 convention program from Publicity Division, July 6, 1960; Box 17, Louchheim Papers, LoC.

74. Craig 1940, 143, credits ER with starting "team" politics.

75. Other women in JFK's large family campaigned for him, and Jackie did some TV appearances. "Lady Bird Special Building Up Steam," *WES*, Oct. 6, 1964. "The Campaign Trail, Distaff Side—Four Wives, Thousands of Miles," *WES*, Oct. 4, 1964.

76. First quote in Fisher and Whitehead 1944, 895. Data on turnout rates by sex and other categories from surveys conducted by the Center for Political Studies, Inter-University Consortium, University of Michigan are in Lynn 1979, 406–7, and Lansing 1974, 8. Harris 1954, 108, contains turnout data for 1940, 1948, and 1952 from Roper/NBC polls which show both men and women voting at considerably lower rates than the Michigan surveys. Earlier reports estimated turnout from voter registration totals where they were available by sex. From 1964 onward, the Bureau of the Census asked about voting in its post-election Current Population Survey and reported the results in *Population Characteristics*, Series P-20,

various numbers.Women's turnout rate equaled men's in 1980, and surpassed it thereafter. Preference data is in AIPO polls: 150, 183, 248, 263, 283, 290, 337, 339, 340, 341, 433, 436, 509, 510, 511, 512, 513, 574, 578, 579, 580, 638, 640, 641, 642, 645, 701, 702, 705, 771, 774, 775, 776, 780. Second quote from Berelson and Lazarsfeld, 1945, which reports a fall 1944 study of 2,000 women in four major cities.The major difference between these and the 1923 Merriam and Gosnell study is that ethnicity is not a factor (or it wasn't studied) and non-voting rates among young women more closely resemble those of young men, creating a curvilinear rather than unilinear relationship.

77. Priest, 1953, who headed the women's division of the 1952 campaign, agreed with Harris on why women preferred Ike. First and last quotes from Shelton 1955, D:1. Gallup 1956, 4, said that in 1948 46 percent of women and 44 percent of men voted for Dewey but this difference is too small to be statistically significant. Gallup Opinion Index, December, 1972, Report No. 90 says that in 1952, 53 percent of men voted for Eisenhower and 47 percent for Stevenson, compared to 58 percent and 42 percent of women; "The Vote by Sex in Presidential Elections, 1952–72" in Lynn 1979, 409.The Roper-NBC polls showed a similar response; Harris 1954, 112–13, 116, 222. Sanders 1955, quote on 118. Lynn found that 10 percent fewer women than men voted in 1948, 1952 and 1956, implying no turnout effect; Lynn 1979, 406.

78. For the 1956 campaign, reporters interviewed voters to find out why more women supported Eisenhower than men: NYT, Oct. 1956: 9, 22:3; 14, 49:2; 22, 1:3, 20:3; 23, 1:3; 26, 16:1. Brown 1956 and French 1956, interviewed politicians and pollsters.

79. "Will Women Decide the Election?" U.S. News and World Report, Oct. 3, 1960, 61–65. In almost every interview Louchheim said there was no woman's vote; see also DCWF 1960, 38. Despite the better organization of GOP women,Assistant RNC Chairman Elly Peterson admonished them to organize better in 1964 because their failure to bring more women to the polls cost the GOP the 1960 election; "GOP Women Held Responsible for 1960 Defeat," Hartford Times, Jan. 7, 1964.

80. In a 1960 article in the NYT Magazine, Philip C. Hastings, identified as the director of the Roper Public Opinion Research Center, wrote that "5 percent more women than men voted the Republican ticket in the 1954 Congressional election, [and] . . . surveys show about 4 percent more females than males preferring the Republican party." Presidential votes from the Gallup Polls, reported in Lynn 1979, 409 and Lansing 1974, 15.White women's votes by SES reported in Ladd and Hadley 1978, 240. Since black women voted heavily Democratic in 1968 and were more likely than white women to be low SES, their inclusion would obscure the change.Votes for Congress in 1968 showed the usual pattern, but it was less pronounced than previously; ibid., 243.

81. NYT,April 6, 1952, 36:1. Party women's discontent was usually transmitted through friendly reporters who could print anecdotes and complaints without tying them to one person. Columnists Isabelle Shelton and Doris Fleeson frequently acted as their mouthpiece. See also Kerr 1956; Shalett 1960; and the statements of Mrs. Mayes, head of the Women's Division, to the RNC meeting of Jan. 18, 1952, RP Papers, Reel 11:718–23; and of Mrs. Charles R. Weis, speaking for the national committeewomen, to the RNC Executive Committee asking for more inclusion and consultation, Jan. 17, 1953; RP papers, Reel 13:843–47.

82. "What Women Do in Politics," 1958, quotes on 72, 73, 76. Quote from RNC meeting of Jan. 23, 1959; RP papers, Reel 16:241–71. Committee on Arrangements; June 9, 1960; Reel 18:731–32.

83. Louchheim quotes throughout "What Women Do in Politics," 1958, 77–79; and in Shalett 1960. See also her article for the 1960 *Convention Book*, "DNC 1960," Box 17, and an unpublished speech of 1963/64, Box 63, both in Louchheim Papers, LoC. Louchheim's journal for February 1957 describes the grumbling at one meeting of what was most likely Democratic committeewomen; Box 123, LoC. Louchheim was not anti-feminist, but anti-stereotype. When feminism became a major force at the 1972 Democratic convention she wrote laudatory articles for *CSM*.

84. Frances Lewine, "Fewer Women Try for Congress," *WES*, Oct. 31, 1964. Second quote by Leighton 1968, 4.

NOTES FOR CHAPTER TEN (PAGES 203 TO 212)

1. "The First Woman's Platform," *WC*, May 15, 1920, 1254. Dreier 1950, 149.

2. Blair 1920, 27b–c. Quote in Upton, 1926, XXV:3.

3. Pardo 1979, 19. *ER*: "Republicans Refuse Equal Rights Plank," June 21, 1924, 147–49; "Farmer-Labor Party Endorses Equal Rights," June 28, 1924, 157–58; "Before the Democratic Platform Committee," July 5, 1924, 163. *PP*, Dem. quote, 248. The GOP plank is strangely omitted from *PP* but is in Breckinridge 1933 and 1972, 282 and referred to in the 1928 GOP platform.

4. Young 1989, 84. Ware 1981, 39. Roosevelt and Hickok 1954, 266. Dewson 1949, II:128. *NYT* June 1924: 1, VIII:4:6; 8, II:1:2; 10, 3:5; 18, 21:7; 25, 4:2. The 1924 Democratic convention lasted seventeen days and 103 ballots, making it the longest and one of the most divisive ever held.

5. Pardo 1979, 36. *ER*: "Our Speakers at the Republican Convention," "Equal Rights and the Republican Convention," June 23, 1928, 155–57; "The Woman's Party at the Democratic Convention," July 7, 1928, 171; Sue S. White, "Observations of a Democrat," *ER*, July 14, 1928, 181. *PP*, 276, 290.

6. Pardo 1979, 55. Breckinridge 1933 and 1972, 290. Becker 1981, 128. *ER*: "The Woman's Party at the Chicago Conventions," June 11, 1932, 147; June 25, 1932: "The Republican Hearing on the Equal Rights Plank," 163–64, "Sidelights on the Republican National Convention," 164–65, "GOP Platform Disappoints Feminists," 165; July 2, 1932: "The Democratic Hearing on the Equal Rights Plank," 171–72, "Garfield Opposed to Equal Rights Plank," 174, "Sidelights on Democratic National Convention," 175; July 9, 1932, "How They Held the Fort in Chicago," 179. The women members of the platform committees were Dr. Martha Robert de Romeau for the Republicans, and Jean Whittemore for the Democrats. Both were national committeewomen from Puerto Rico.

7. Pardo 1979, 80. *PP*, 367, 370. *NYT* 1936: May 31, III:7:8; June 9, 17:2; June 10, 1:4; June 12, 17:5; June 13, 10:5. *WES*, June 14, 1936, B:1:2. On Section 213 see Scharf 1980, 46–47.

8. Ware 1981, 80–82. *PP*, 361, demands "an end to the sweated labor of his [i.e., the worker's] wife and children." Suggestions and final recommendations of the Women's Committee are in Box 6, DNC Women's Division papers, FDRL. More suggestions and Dewson's letter to Charl Williams of July 10, 1936, are in Box 277. Caroline O'Day, "Women have Pride in Platform Contribution," *DD*, Aug. 1936, 6. *NYT*, June 1936: 21, 25:2; 22, 4:2; 23, 14:1; 24, 15:2, 18:2; 25, 1:6, 15:2; 26, 14:4; 27, 9:3. *WES*, June 1936: 22, A:5; 23, A:8; 24, A:6; 25, A:7; 26, A:8.

9. Pardo 1979, 101–2. *PP*, 393. Alice Paul gives Perle Mesta primary credit for getting the ERA in the 1940 GOP platform by persuading Hyde, an old friend from her home state, to replace vaguer language with explicit support. Paul was in Europe at this time and had no first-hand knowledge; Paul oral history 1972, 513–14. Mesta, best known as a Washington hostess, was a major contributor to and dedicated member of the NWP, but in her own book is quite modest about her role, 1960, 79. *NYT*, June 1940: 27, 1:6; 28, 5:1.

10. Pardo 1979, 101–2. Harrison 1982, 32–33. Perkins oral history 1955, 444. *PP*, 384. *NYT*, July 16, 1940, 5:1. "The Report of the Democratic Women's Advisory Platform Committee," July 13, 1940, Box 278, DNC Women's Division Papers, FDRL. See also McAllister's letter of Aug. 3, 1940, to Molly Dewson, Box 292, in which she crows that "you will be struck by the number of phrases, sentences and whole paragraphs taken from our platform suggestions."

11. *PP*, 384. Dorothy D. Crook, Director of Legislation and Public Affairs, BPW, to Mrs. McAllister, Feb. 23, 1940; Dean Acheson to Mary N. Winslow, Legislative Chairman of WTUL, April 16, 1940, Box 278; Mrs. McAllister to Cong. Mary Norton, June 19, 1940, enclosing Acheson letter, Box 281; DNC Women's Division papers, FDRL. *NYT*, July 15, 1940, 5:1.

12. Pardo 1979, 122–23. *ER*, Aug.–Sept. 1944, 56–58. *NYT*, June 27, 1944, 15:1. Paul oral history 1972, 490. *PP*, 412.

13. Pardo 1979, 122–23. *NYT* July 1944: 18, 9:3; 21, 12:6. Perkins quote in Martin 1976, 457–59. Anderson 1951, 259. Mesta 1960, 98, had switched parties since 1940. GFWC endorsement in *ER* Aug.–Sept. 1944, 58–60; *NYT*, April 27, 1944, 20:1. *Congressional Digest*, December 1946, 299, 301. *PP*, 403. Eleanor Roosevelt to Molly Dewson, July 3, 1944; Reel 7, ER papers. Eleanor Roosevelt to Emma Guffey Miller, Jan. 29, 1944; Reel 13, ER papers. Paul oral history 1972, 268. Perkins oral history 1955, 532, 534.

14. Mrs. Thomas F. McAllister to DNC Chair Robert E. Hannagan, June 15, 1946, emphasis in original; Box 72, Perkins Papers, Columbia University Library. Harrison 1982, 94–97. Pardo 1979, 151, 154. *PP*, 435, 453. Paul oral history 1972, 385. Anita Politzer to Mildred Palmer, June 6, 1952; Reel 98, NWP papers.

15. Harrison 1982, 114–15. *PP*, 486, 504. "Our planks in the party platforms," *Independent Woman*, Sept. 1952, 260. Unsigned letter to Ethel Ernest Murrell, June 6, 1952, regarding a meeting with India Edwards on the Democratic Platform; Mildred Palmer to Alice Paul, July 11, 1952; Ethel Ernest Murrell to Mrs. William Kent, July 15, 1952; Reel 99, NWP papers.

16. Harrison 1982, 139–40. *PP*, 532, 537, 549, 554. Congressional Chairman (Alice Paul) to Marjorie Longwell, Aug. 3, 12, 1956; same to Ernestine Bellamy, Aug. 16, 1956; sections 11 and 12 of NWP's "Memorandum concerning the Two Major Political Parties and the Equal Rights Amendment," Nov. 3, 1956; Reuther testimony; Reel 103, NWP papers. Palmer testimony reported in "Legislative Victory at both Political Conventions," 35 *Independent Woman*, Oct. 1956, 7, 28.

17. 3:3 *NWP Bulletin*, Fall 1968, 2; Reel 158, NWP papers. Rawalt 1969, II:192. Jane Grant to Emma, July 1960; testimony of Esther Peterson before hearings of the Democratic Resolutions Committee on July 7, 1960; Reel 106, NWP papers. Opponents listed at 106 *Cong. Rec.*, July 2, 1960, 15682. Peterson interview with Patricia Zelman on January 7, 1978, cited in Zelman 1980, 24. Harrison 1982, 368–74, 1988, 118, unearthed the altered document which made it clear that Kennedy's endorsement was not genuine. 1960 *CQ Almanac*, 772, said the platform represented a "victory for Northern Democrats" and gave credit for it to Resolutions Committee chair Chester Bowles "who drew heavily on subpanels of the

Democratic Advisory Council." Although Bowles had been an ERA sponsor in Congress, Northern Democrats by and large opposed the ERA and followed the wishes of the AFL-CIO. Mary Keyserling was one of the opponents on the Platform Committee this year; Keyserling oral history 1982, 178. *PP*, 589, 614.

18. *PP*, 645. Zelman 1980, 89–90. Letters of Aug. 29, 1964, from Emma Guffey Miller, and of Sept. 1 and 4 from Ruth Gage Colby, Mary Kennedy and others, to President Johnson; Miller described the Johnson conversation in a letter to Judge Sarah Hughes on Dec. 4, 1964; transcripts and testimony also on Reel 109, NWP papers.

19. *PP*, 682–83. Memo from Alice Paul of August 9, 1964, and other untitled documents on Reel 109, NWP papers. In the spring of 1984 I interviewed the chair and staff director of the 1964 Platform Committee, Melvin Laird and William Prendergast. Neither had any recollection of the fate of the ERA in 1964. Marjorie Longwell, in charge of the NWP's 1964 GOP effort, complained to Alice Paul that Republican women were apathetic; letters of June 25 and July 22, 1964, Reel 109, NWP papers.

20. 3:3 *NWP Bulletin*, Fall 1968, 2–3; and Spring/Summer 1968, 2–3; Reel 158, NWP papers. *PP*, 734, 749. The major Presidential candidates in 1968 were Richard Nixon, Nelson Rockefeller, George Romney, Ronald Reagan, George Wallace, Lyndon Johnson, Eugene McCarthy, George McGovern, Hubert H. Humphrey, and Robert F. Kennedy. All but Kennedy had expressed support for the ERA, and McCarthy was its chief Senate sponsor. Friedan's testimony included support for the eight items in NOW's Bill of Rights, but by far the bulk of her statement was devoted to the ERA; the EEOC ran a distant second. Nonetheless, Emma Guffey Miller reprimanded Betty Friedan "for supporting both the ERA and abortion and thus linking the amendment to an even more unpopular issue," even though abortion was barely mentioned at the end of her testimony; Rupp and Taylor, 1987 127. Ernestine Powell wrote Alice Paul on Nov. 20, 1968, that Friedan had sabotaged the ERA; Reel 111, NWP papers. Friedan's testimony to the Democratic Platform Committee, "A Bill of Rights for Women in 1968," Aug. 22, 1968; she found the Republican response more favorable than the Democrats', minutes of NOW Board meeting, Sept. 14–5, 1968; author's files.

21. Polsby and Wildavsky 1984, 240, 258–59. Pomper 1971, Chapters 7 and 8.

22. *PP*, 219, 236, 238, 248, 252, 262, 276, 290, 361, 367, 370, 384, 403, 410, 433, 453, 481, 504, 532, 549, 589, 610.

23. *PP*, 549, 583, 645, 683, 749.

NOTES FOR CHAPTER ELEVEN (PAGES 213 TO 225)

1. Mackenzie 1981, xix–xxi.

2. Breckinridge 1933 and 1972, 295. *WJ*, Feb. 13, 1909, 26, quotes a letter from the New York State Association Opposed to Woman Suffrage (NYSAOWS) to Gov. Charles Evans Hughes: "Earnestly believing that the serious purpose, ability and experience to be found among women in many walks of life, should be used for the benefit of the community . . . we hope you will make such appointments of women as are possible under the laws of the State of New York."

3. On Reel see *NYH*, Oct. 7, 1900, V:7:6; IV *HWS* 1902, 1010. The 1896 survey was by Miller.

4. On Lowell see Monoson 1990, 103–4, and Lowell bio in II *NAW* 1971, 437–39. On

Lease see Blumberg 1978; II *NAW* 1971, 380–82. Quote in Muncy 1991, 32. Lathrop bio in II *NAW* 1971, 370–72; *NYT* obit in April 16, 1932, 18:1.

5. Muncy 1991, 20, 30–33.

6. It is always difficult to ascertain what appointments should be counted as significant, since Presidents make many minor ones. I am relying on a list compiled by Karen Keesling and Suzanne Cavanagh of the Congressional Research Service of the Library of Congress, *Women Presidential Appointees Serving or Having Served in Full-Time Positions Requiring Senate Confirmation 1912–1977*, March 23, 1978. They relied on Breckinridge 1933 and 1972, 305–10 for pre-New Deal appointments, and both miss some women mentioned by Becker 1981, 103, as appointments promoted by the NWP. Several Bass letters are in the Wilson papers, on various reels. Lemons 1973, 73, Gardener quote at 75. Born a Republican in Virginia, the first Democrat that Gardener supported was Bryan, in 1900; *NYH*, Oct. 7, 1900, V:7:5. She was a personal friend of Wilson's. Gardner bio in II *NAW* 1971, 11–13. Adams bio in I *NAW* 1971, 3–5.

7. Becker 1981, 102–3. *ER*: Feb. 14, 1925, 3; Sept. 26, 1926, 259; Sue White, "A Victory for Women," Oct. 17, 1925, 283; Jan. 16, 1926, 389. The petition is reprinted in *ER*: March 6, 1926, 30–31; March 13, 1926, 38–39.

8. On Laughlin see II *NAW* 1971, 410–11; *NYT* obit, March 14, 1952, 23:4. Laughlin moved around quite a bit, practicing law in four states and eventually serving in the Maine legislature. Edson telegram to U.S. Attorney General Harry M. Daugherty of Aug. 11, 1921 and letter of Aug. 29, 1921, in Edson Papers, UCLA. Willebrandt bio in IV *NAW* 1980, 734–37.

9. Upton 1926, XXVII:15. Upton wrote in a letter dated Aug. 30, 1921: "When I began work here I saw that my time could not be given to helping people to get positions ... [but] when I was asked for my opinion as to the capabilities of two or three candidates for an office I have given it." In her unpublished autobiography she said her primary role was getting appointments for women. Upton quote from letter of Aug. 12, 1921, to "Members of the Committee"; all letters in Box 13, Hanna-McCormick Papers, LoC.

10. Breckinridge 1933, 1972, 311. Cline bio in IV *NAW* 1980, 153–54. She had also been a Harding appointee, as appraiser of imported merchandise in Cleveland, after years of work in women's clubs and for the Republican party.

11. Lemons 1973, 110. Chambers 1963, 246–47. Ware 1981, 46. Brown 1984, 175. "Women Leaders at Odds on Question of Place for One of Sex in Cabinet," *NYSun*, Jan. 22, 1929. Upton had also been "prominently mentioned" as the most likely woman for Harding to appoint to his Cabinet; *NYT*, Nov. 29, 1920, 21:4. *RWI*, Jan. 1929, 6. It would be forty-five years before another woman was appointed assistant attorney general.

12. Quote in Upton 1926, XXVII:4. Ware 1981, 45–47, 56. Last quote from Roosevelt and Hickok 1954, 187. Martin 1976, 235–41.

13. Dewson 1949, I:124. Roosevelt and Hickok 1954, 15. Ware 1981, 53, 55, 61–65, 119–20. Allen 1965, 110. Allen bio in IV *NAW* 1980, 11–13. "Marion Harron Appointed to Board of Tax Appeals," *DD*, Sept. 1936, 14. Dewson was herself appointed to the Social Security Board in 1937.

14. Ware 1981, Chapter 3, describes Dewson's patronage activities. Dewson frequently wrote Eleanor Roosevelt about her desires; see Reels 6 and 7, ER papers. Perkins oral history 1955, 4: 239–41, 256–57, 268, describes Dewson's claims on Labor Department jobs. Occasionally she kept Perkins from abolishing superfluous positions Dewson needed to reward her workers.

15. Good 1963, 24. RP Papers, Reel 5:944.

16. Harrison 1982, 206–9; 1988, 54–56. Edwards 1977, 97–98.

17. Edwards 1977, 186–87. Edwards diplomatically downplayed her role when talking to the press. In an interview with Dorothy Brandon she gave credit to party leaders for recommending women; "How Women Get Important Government Jobs," *NYHT*, Nov. 20. 1949.

18. Brown 1984, 109–16, 151, 173, 216–18, 249–50. "A Woman on the Supreme Bench," *CSM*, March 12, 1930.

19. Willkie promise mentioned in the New York *Daily News*, Nov. 5, 1940, 8:2. Edwards 1977, 171–72, 183, 187–91. To appoint Anderson, State Department rules had to be changed; Poling, 1952, 36. Her predecessor as Ambassador to Denmark, Ruth Bryan Owen, had resigned on marrying Capt. Rohde.

20. Tristram Coffin in *Coronet*, date unknown, reprinted in Edwards 1977, 144.

21. Mesta wrote that the idea was India's daughter's; 1960, 128, 130–34. Edwards 1977, 172–73.

22. Paul oral history 1972, 643–47. Edwards 1977, 184–86. A brief description of the campaign can be found in Mabel Vernon's letter of Feb. 10, 1950, to Anne Martin, Box 76/178, Mable Vernon Oral History 1972–73. Matthews oral history 1973, 41, credits Edwards, but appears unaware of the major campaign she instigated. Edwards told the press that Matthews' nomination came from the District of Columbia Bar Association; Poling, 1952, 15. Bio, Pollitzer, 1951; obit in *NYT*, April 28, 1988, IV:27:1.

23. Mesta 1960, 174.

24. Mesta 1960, 182.

25. *CQ Weekly Report*, July 20, 1956, 858. Mackenzie 1981, 18. Harrison 1982, 230–33; 1988, 60–62. In fact, Ivy Baker Priest had run the women's division during the Presidential campaign and drew up the initial "list of Federal positions that could be filled by capable Republican women" as well as obtaining one for herself; Priest 1958, 186.

26. Adkins oral history 1968, 48, 50–51. Appointment announced: *NYT* 1958: July 22, 29:7; Aug. 14, 31:5; Aug. 15, 1:4, bio at 12:2. Adkins said her primary function at H.E.W. was public relations, not policy. She initiated monthly luncheons of Eisenhower's women appointees, which were so popular they were increased to weekly affairs; 53, 58.

27. Harrison 1982, 238–39.

28. *CQ Weekly Report*, July 20, 1956, 857. Adkins oral history 1968, 42. Harrison 1982, 231–34, 237. The Aug. 15, 1958 *NYT* story on Adkins' own appointment was headed "Tactful and Tenacious." Privately, Republican women were concerned that their work would not be adequately rewarded with jobs; see Jessica Weis' letter of Jan. 11, 1953, to Edward Willis at Eisenhower campaign headquarters on the great "unease building up in women" followed by recommendations of women to be appointed; Weis Papers, Reel 1:676.

29. Quotes from Gatov oral history, 1978, 398. She was U.S. Treasurer under her prior name of Smith but resigned when she found it was a ceremonial "turkey"; 305. Harrison 1982, 262–79, 311–12; 1988, 75–81. Zelman 1980, 25–26, 37–38. Lash 1972, 312. Mackenzie 1981, 21–31. Some stories on women's demand for jobs from the Kennedy administration: "Where Are Jobs for the Women?" *WES*, March 5, 1961; "Press Secretary Defends Record," *WES*, March 20, 1961; "John Bailey Queried on Job Record," *WES*, April 11, 1961. Emma Guffey Miller wrote Louchheim that "all Margaret Price knows [about women's appointments] is what she sees in the newspapers"; letter of Jan. 26, 1962, Box 23, Louchheim Papers, LoC.

30. Carpenter 1970, 35–36.

31. Zelman 1980, 45. *WP*, Jan. 18, 1964, 1. *WES*, Jan. 29, 1964, 1.

32. Louchheim 1970, 184.

33. "LBJ Search Still On For Women for Jobs," *WES*, Feb. 13, 1965. Zelman 1980, 37–44.

34. Carpenter 1970, 36–37. Gatov, Democratic National Committeewoman 1956–1965, and U.S. Treasurer in 1961–2 (under the name of Smith), also commented on the problem of finding women who were not just qualified, but available to drop everything and move to Washington; oral history 1978, 307.

35. Harrison 1982, 504–6; 1988, 174–75. Zelman 1980, 40, 51–53. Rawalt oral history 1980, 633. Rawalt, then assistant head of the civil division at the Internal Revenue Service, lobbied for an appointment to the Foreign Claims Settlement Commission. She did not receive it despite her personal access to her fellow Texan in the White House, and never really knew why; Paterson 1986, 123.

36. First quote in "Federal Appointments Criticized," *WES*, March 17, 1964. Second in "She'll Push Jobs for Women," *WES*, April 12, 1969. See also: *WES*, March 30, 1969, E:16; Sept. 15, 1969; March 18, 1970.

37. Hitt oral history 1977, 181. She echoed Carpenter's complaint that most of the qualified women were not available to pull up roots and move to Washington on request; "Patt Hitt Defends Nixon," *WES*, Feb. 13, 1969, explaining the small numbers of women appointed to high positions.

38. Freeman 1975, 205–7. Rawalt oral history 1980, 695. May 1969.

39. Freeman 1975, Chapters 6 and 7.

NOTES FOR CHAPTER TWELVE (PAGES 227 TO 235)

1. Baker 1999, also argues that campaign work changed with the entry of women in ways similar to male jobs such as clerks and telephone workers, becoming a stool rather than a ladder. Quote in Blair 1937, 139.

2. Mae Ella Nolan (R. Calif.) 1/23/23–3/4/25, Florence Prag Kahn (R. Calif.) 2/17/25–1/3/37, Edith Nourse Rogers (R. Mass.) 6/23/25–9/10/60, Pearl P. Oldfield (D. Ark.) 1/9/29–3/4/31, Willa B. Eslick (D. Tenn.) 8/4/32–3/2/33, Effegene Wingo (D. Ark.) 11/4/30–3/4/33. Chamberlin 1973, 46–53, 59–63, 68, 85–89; Gruberg 1968, 152–56.

3. Winifred Sprague Mason Huck (R. Ill.), served 11/7/22 to 3/4/23, and failed to secure reelection. Chamberlin 1973, 44–46; Gruberg 1968, 152.

4. Katherine Langley (R. Ky.) 12/5/26–3/4/31, ran as her husband's surrogate, and lost to a Democrat when he tried to take the seat back from her after finishing his sentence. Chamberlin 1973, 65–67; Gruberg 1968, 154.

5. Ruth Bryan Owen, (D. Fla.) 3/4/29–3/4/33, daughter of William Jennings Bryan. Her daughter, Rudd Brown, ran for Congress in California in 1960, and lost. Chamberlin 1973, 75–81; Gruberg 1968, 155.

6. Ruth Hanna McCormick (R. Ill.) 3/4/29–3/4/31, daughter of Mark Hanna of Ohio and wife of Medill McCormick of Illinois. Chamberlin 1973, 69–74; Gruberg 1968, 154; Miller 1992.

7. Jeannette Rankin (R. Mont.) 3/4/17–3/4/19 and 1/3/41 to 1/3/43, organized the Montana branch of NAWSA. Alice M. Robertson (R. Okla.) 3/4/21–3/4/23, was the only anti-suffragist elected. Ruth Baker Pratt (R. N.Y.) 3/4/29–3/4/33, was a New York City alderman when she ran for Congress. Chamberlin 1973, 3–17, 38–44, 81–85; Gruberg 1968, 151–56.

8. Florence Prag Kahn (R. Calif.), twelve years; Edith Nourse Rogers (R. Mass.), thirty-five years; Mary Norton, (D. N.J.), twenty-six years. Kahn was the first Jewish Congresswoman; Matthews 1999.

9. After her husband was impeached, Miriam A. "Ma" Ferguson of Texas was elected in 1924 on the slogan of "two governors for the price of one." She served from 1924 to 1926, was defeated but then reelected in 1932, and served until 1936; Young 1999. Nellie Tayloe Ross was elected Governor of Wyoming in 1924 after the death of her husband and served one two-year term; Scharff, 1995. "Being in mourning, Mrs. Ross did no active campaigning. Her campaign manager was Joseph O'Mahoney, who later became a U.S. senator. She had had no previous political experience." After Governor George Wallace of Alabama couldn't get the state constitution changed to permit him to serve more than one consecutive term, he ran his wife. "Lurleen Wallace, a former dime store clerk whose only political experience had been visiting the 67 counties of the state in her husband's 1962 campaign, admitted that she would only serve as caretaker, a vote for her would be a vote for him. Their slogan was 'Let George do it.'" Gruberg 1968, 189–90.

10. Gruberg 1968, 132–128; Chamberlin, 1973, Appendix. Caraway was actually *elected* rather than appointed to serve out her husband's term of one year, after nomination by the Democratic State Committee. She surprised everyone when she decided to run for a full term.

11. Perry 1987, 155. See also Young 1999, and Salas 1999, for descriptions of how female candidates projected a traditional image of womanliness as their campaign strategy. Women did this more often than they relied on images of competency and experience typical of male candidates.

12. Wise quote in Weis Papers, Reel 1:367–68. Weis served from 1959 to 1963. Neuberger quote in Neuberger 1951, 18. Between 1950 and 1954 Richard and Maurine Neuberger both served in the Oregon legislature, he as a State Senator and she as a Representative.

13. The classic description of the free-rider problem was given by Mancur Olsen in 1969.

14. "There has been more talk about party loyalty since 1920 than in the fifty preceding years"; Catt 1923, 14. Le Van 1928, 10. Young 1989, 73.

15. There are probably many more women like these, but short biographies rarely mention party service and book-length ones are rare. On Douglas, see Scobie 1992. On Otero-Warren, see Whaley 1995.

16. Rule 1994.

17. See VandeCreek 1999, for a comparison of how women candidates were treated by the Colorado parties in 1912 and 1916, which illustrates this point.

18. Upton 1924, 19. "The Woman in Politics," *RMN*, Oct. 1, 1895, 1:2.

19. Tyler 1996, 132.

20. Baker 1984. Edwards 1999, analyzes the changes that took place in the 1890s as an attack on male privilege and the prerogatives of working class men. Tyler 1996, describes New Orleans women's efforts to clean up the election process in the 1930s and 1940s.

21. A Denver Politician, 1909, 22. Howe 1935. "How Far to Equality," 1958 speech, Box 67, Louchheim Papers, LoC.

References

A Colorado Woman, "Women's Political Work in Colorado," *The Woman's Journal*, April 14, 1900, 111–12.

A Denver Politician, "Votes for Women: What They Look Like from the Inside," *Woman's Home Companion*, November 1909, 22, 70–71.

"A Political Club for Women Only," 146 *Good Housekeeping*, Feb. 1958, 131–32.

Abbott, Edith, "Are Women a Force for Good Government? An Analysis of the Returns in the Recent Municipal Elections in Chicago," *National Municipal Review*, 1915, 437–48.

Adams, Elmer C., and Warren Dunham Foster, *Heroines of Modern Progress*, New York: Sturgis & Walton, 1913.

Addams, Jane, "Why Women Should Vote," 27 *Ladies Home Journal*, January 1910, 21–22. Reprinted with commentary by Victoria Bissell Brown in Wheeler, 1995, 179–202.

———, *The Second Twenty Years at Hull-House: September 1909 to September 1929*, New York: Macmillan, 1930.

Adkins, Bertha, *The Reminiscences of Bertha Adkins*, oral history interview by John T. Mason, Jr., on December 18, 1967; Oral History Research Office, Columbia University, New York, 1968.

Adler, Norman M., and Blanche Davis Blank, *Political Clubs in New York*, New York: Praeger, 1975.

Allen, Florence E., *To Do Justly*, Cleveland: Western Reserve University, 1965.

Allen, Lee Norcross, "The Woman Suffrage Movement in Alabama," 11 *Alabama Review*, April 1958, 83–99.

Andersen, Kristi. *The Creation of A Democratic Majority: 1928–1936*, Chicago: University of Chicago Press, 1979.

———, *After Suffrage: Women in Partisan and Electoral Politics Before the New Deal*, Chicago: University of Chicago Press, 1996.

Anderson, Kathryn, "Anne Martin and the Dream of Political Equality for Women," 27:2 *Journal of the West*, 1988, 28–34.

———, "Evolution of a Partisan: Emily Newell Blair and the Democratic Party, 1920–1932," in Gustafson, Miller and Perry, 1999, 109–20.

Anderson, Mary, *Woman at Work*, Minneapolis: University of Minnesota Press, 1951.

Anthony, Katharine, *Susan B. Anthony: Her Personal History and Her Era,* New York: Russell and Russell, 1954.

Anthony, Susan B. Collection, microfilm, Manuscript Division, Library of Congress, Washington, D.C.

Arneson, Ben A., "Non-Voting in a Typical Ohio Community," 19 *American Political Science Review*, Nov. 1925, 816–25.

Baer, Denise, "National Federation of Republican Women," in Maisel, 1991, 683.

———, "Political Parties: The Missing Variable in Women and Politics Research," *Political Research Quarterly*, Sept. 1993, 547–76.

Baker, Elizabeth, *Protective Labor Legislation*, New York: Columbia University Press, 1925.

Baker, Paula, "The Domestication of Politics: Women and American Political Society, 1780–1920," 89 *American Historical Review*, June 1984, 620–47.

———, *The Moral Frameworks of Public Life: Gender, Politics and the State in Rural New York, 1870–1930*, New York: Oxford University Press, 1991.

———, "She Is the Best Man on the Ward Committee": Women in Grassroots Party Organizations, 1930s–1950s," in Gustafson, Miller, and Perry, 1999, 151–60.

Barnard, Eunice Fuller, "Women Who Wield Political Power," *The New York Times Magazine*, September 2, 1928, 6–7, 23.

———, "Madame Arrives in Politics," 226 *North American Review*, November 1928, 551–56.

———, "Women in the Campaign," *The Woman's Journal*, December 1928, 7–9, 44–45.

———, "Miss Butler Blazes A Political Trail," *New York Times Magazine*, February 8, 1931, 11, 19.

Barry, Kathleen, *Susan B. Anthony: A Biography of a Singular Feminist*, New York: Ballantine, 1988.

Basch, Norma, "Marriage, Morals, and Politics in the Election of 1828," 80 *The Journal of American History*, December 1993, 890–918.

Bass, Elizabeth, "Advance of Democratic Women," 17:2 *Democratic Digest*, February 1940, 17, 39.

Bass, Mrs. George, "Report of Mrs. George Bass, Chairman Woman's Bureau of the Democratic National Committee," Atlantic City, N.J., September 26, 1919.

———, "Report of the Woman's Bureau of the Democratic National Committee covering Period from December 1916 to September 26, 1919"; 17 pages on organization in the states.

Bates, J. Leonard, and Vanette M. Schwartz, "Golden Special Campaign Train: Republican Women Campaign for Charles Evans Hughes for President in 1916," 37 *Montana, the Magazine of Western History*, Summer 1987, 26–35.

Baxter, Sandra and Marjorie Lansing, *Women and Politics: The Visible Majority*, rev. ed., Ann Arbor: University of Michigan Press, 1983.

Beard, Charles A., and Mary R. Beard, *The Rise of American Civilization*, New York: Macmillan, 1930, two volumes.

Beard, Mary, "The Legislative Influence of Unenfranchised Women," 56 *The Annals of the American Academy of Political and Social Science*, November 1914, 54–61.

Beatty, Bess, "Perspective on American Women: The View from Black Newspapers, 1865–1900," 9:2 *The Maryland Historian*, Fall 1978, 39–50.

Becker, Susan D., *The Origins of the Equal Rights Amendment: American Feminism Between the Wars*, Westport, Conn.: Greenwood Press, 1981.

Beeton, Beverly, *Women Vote in the West: The Woman Suffrage Movement, 1869–1896*, New York: Garland, 1986.

Belmont, Mrs. O.H.P., President of the Woman's Party, "Women as Dictators," *The Ladies' Home Journal*, September 1922, 7, 43.

Berelson, Bernard, and Paul F. Lazarsfeld, "Women: A Major Problem for the PAC," 9 *Public Opinion Quarterly*, Spring 1945, 79–82.

Blair, Emily Newell, "Women at the Conventions," 13 *The New York Times Current History*, October 1920, 26–28.

———, "How the Democratic Party Has Organized Women," *The Fortnightly Bulletin*, No. 17, June 9, 1923, 1.

———, *Organization Primer*, Washington, D.C.: Democratic National Committee, n.d., probably 1923; 12-page pamphlet.

———, "On to the Conventions," *The Woman Citizen*, April 19, 1924, 20–21.

———, "Boring From Within," *The Woman Citizen*, July 1927, 49–50.

———, "Women in the Political Parties," *Annals of the American Academy of Political and Social Science*, May 1929, 217–29.

———, "Why I am Discouraged about Women in Politics," 16 *The Woman's Journal*, January, 1931, 20–22, 44–45.

———, *Gamma's Story*, unpublished autobiography, Books I and II, Schlesinger Library, Cambridge, MA, and Case Western Reserve Library, Cleveland, OH, 1937.

———, "Advance of Democratic Women" 17:4 *Democratic Digest*, April 1940, 15, 38.

Blair, Karen, *The Clubwoman as Feminist: True Womanhood Redefined, 1868–1914*, New York: Holmes and Meier, 1980.

Blatch, Harriot Stanton, and Alma Lutz, *Challenging Years: The Memoirs of Harriot Stanton Blatch*, New York: Putnam's, 1940.

Blocker, Jack S., *"Give to the Winds Thy Fears": The Women's Temperance Crusade, 1873–1974*, Westport, Conn.: Greenwood Press, 1985.

Blumberg, Dorothy Rose, "Mary Elizabeth Lease, Populist Orator: A Profile," 1:1 *Kansas History*, 1978, 1–15.

Boal, Sam, "India Edwards: Distaff Democrat," *New York Times Magazine*, February 3, 1952, 45.

Bone Hugh A., *Grass Roots Party Leadership (A Case Study of King County, Washington)*, Seattle: University of Washington Bureau of Governmental Research and Services, October 1952 40-page pamphlet.

———, *Party Committees and National Politics*, Seattle, Wash.: University of Washington Press, 1958.

Bordin, Ruth, *Woman and Temperance: The Quest for Power and Liberty, 1973–1900*, Philadelphia: Temple University Press, 1981.

Borah, William E., "Why I am for Suffrage for Women: The Views of a Man Who Lives Where Women Have It," 76:2 *The Delineator*, August 1910, 85, 142.

Bostwick, Kate M., "Women's Political Clubs," 13:5 *Monthly Illustrator*, December 1896.

Boswell, Helen V., "A Republican Woman in Politics," a series of 17 short articles in *The National Republican* from November 28, 1918, through April 5, 1919.

———, "Political Episodes," *Woman Republican*, March 1935 through September 1936.

Braitman, Jacqueline R., "A California Stateswoman: The Public Career of Katherine Philips Edson," *California History*, May 1986, 92–95, 151.

———, *Katherine Philips Edson: A Progressive-Feminist in California's Era of Reform*, Ph.D. Dissertation, History, UCLA, 1988.

———, "Elizabeth Snyder and the Role of Women in the Postwar Resurgence of California's Democratic Party," *Pacific Historical Review*, November 1993, 197–220.

———, "Legislated Parity: Mandating Interation of Women into California Political Parties, 1930s–1950s," in Gustafson, Miller, and Perry, 1999, 175–86.

Brandon, Dorothy, "The Amazing Mrs. Mayes," *Herald Tribune Magazine*, May 11, 1952, 16, 32.

Breckinridge, Sophonisba Preston, *Madeline McDowell Breckinridge: A Leader in the New South*, Chicago: University of Chicago Press, 1921.

Breckinridge, Sophonisba Preston, *Women in the Twentieth Century: A Study of Their Political, Social and Economic Activities*, New York: McGraw-Hill, 1933; reprinted by Arno Press, New York, 1972.

Brown, Dorothy M., *Mabel Walker Willebrandt: A Study of Power, Loyalty and Law*, Knoxville: University of Tennessee Press, 1984.

————, *Setting a Course: American Women in the 1920s*, Boston: Twayne, 1986.

Brown, Elsa Barkely, "Negotiating and Transforming the Public Sphere: African American Political Life in the Transition from Slavery to Freedom," 7 *Public Culture*, 1994, 107–46.

Brown, L. Ames, "Suffrage and Prohibition," 204 *North American Review*, December 1916, 93–100.

Brown, Nona B., "Women's Vote: The Bigger Half?" *New York Times Magazine*, October 21, 1956, VI:28, 63–67.

Bryan, William J., *The First Battle: A Story of the Campaign of 1896*, Chicago: W.B. Conkey Company, 1896.

Bryce, Lord James, *The American Commonwealth*, 2 vols., London and New York: Macmillan, 1888.

Buechler, Steven M. *The Transformation of the Woman Suffrage Movement: The Case of Illinois 1850–1920*, New Brunswick, N.J.: Rutgers University Press, 1986.

Buenker, John D., "The Urban Political Machine and Woman Suffrage: A Study in Political Adaptability," 33 *The Historian*, February, 1971, 264–79.

————, *Urban Liberalism and Progressive Reform*, New York: Charles Scribner's Sons, 1973.

Buhle, Mari Jo, *Women and American Socialism, 1870–1920*, Urbana: University of Illinois Press, 1983.

Burckel, Nicholas, "National Progressive Republican League," in Maisel, 1991, 695–96.

Burnham, Walter Dean, "The Changing Shape of the American Political Universe," 59 *American Political Science Review*, March 1965, 7–28.

————, *Critical Elections and the Mainsprings of American Politics*, New York: Norton, 1970.

————, "Theory and Voting Research: Some Reflections on Converse's 'Change in the American Electorate,'" 68 *American Political Science Review*, 1974, 1002–23.

————, "The System of 1896: An Analysis," in Kleppner et al., 1981, 147–202.

Byrnes, Marion T., "Elisabeth Marbury on the Non-Voting Women," *Sunday Eagle Magazine*, June 15, 1924, 2.

Butler, Sarah Schuyler, "I Am Not Disappointed in Women in Politics," *The Woman's Journal*, April 1931, pp. 14, 39.

Cameron, Mabel Ward, and Erma Conkling Lee, eds., *The Biographical Cyclopaedia of American Women*, 2 vols. New York: The Halvord Publishing Co., 1924; reprint, Detroit: Gale Research Co., 1974.

Camhi, Jane Jerome, *Women Against Women: American Anti-suffragism, 1880–1920*, Ph.D. Dissertation, Tufts University, 1973; Brooklyn, N.Y.: Carlson, 1994.

Carmines, Edward G., and James A. Stimson, *Issue Evolution: Race and the Transformation of American Politics*, Princeton, N.J.: Princeton University Press, 1989.

Carpenter, Liz, *Ruffles and Flourishes*, Garden City, N.Y.: Doubleday, 1970.

Carter, Carrol Joseph, *The Colonels of Politics: The Local Political Leadership of Colorado County Chairmen*, Ph.D. Dissertation, University of Colorado, 1969. Reprinted by the Bureau of Governmental Research and Service, University of Colorado, Boulder, 1971.

Carver, Joan S. "Women in Florida," 41 *Journal of Politics*, August 1979, 941–55.

Catt, Carrie Chapman, "Women in Politics," *The Woman's Journal*, October 27, 1900, 337–38.

———, "Woman's Place in Politics," 26:3 *Collier's Weekly*, October 20, 1900, 18–19.

———, "On the Inside," Speech Delivered Before the League of Women Voters, Feb. 14, 1920, in *The Woman Citizen*, March 6, 1920, 947.

———, "Are Women Disappointed in Politics?" *The Woman Citizen*, November 3, 1923, 14–15.

———, "What Women Have Done with the Vote," 115 *Independent*, October 17, 1925, 447–48, 456.

———, "Wyoming, The First Surrender," in NAWSA, 1940, 59–68.

Catt, Carrie Chapman, and Nettie Rogers Shuler, *Woman Suffrage and Politics: The Inner Story of the Suffrage Movement*, New York: Charles Scribner's Sons, 1923, 1926.

Chafe, William, *The American Woman: Her Changing Social, Economic and Political Roles, 1920–1970*, New York: Oxford University Press, 1972.

Chamberlin, Hope, *A Minority of Members: Women in the U.S. Congress*, New York: Praeger, 1973.

Chambers, Clarke A., *Seedtime of Reform: American Social Service and Social Action, 1918–1933*, Minneapolis: University Minnesota Press, 1963.

Chambers, William N., and Walter Dean Burnham, eds., *The American Party System: Stages of Political Development*, New York: Oxford University Press, 1967.

Chester, Giraud, *Embattled Maiden: The Life of Anna Dickinson*, New York: G.P. Putnam's Sons, 1951.

Chisholm, Shirley, *Unbought and Unbossed*, New York: Houghton Mifflin, 1970.

Chittenden, Alice Hill, "A National Club for Republican Women," 5:5 *The Republican Woman* (of Pennsylvania), October 1927, 1–2.

Clarke, Harold G., and Allan Kornberg, "Moving Up the Political Escalator: Women Party Officials in the United States and Canada," 41 *Journal of Politics*, May 1979, 442–77.

Clarke, Ida Clyde, ed., *Women of 1924: International*, New York: Women's News Service, Inc., 1924.

Clayton, Edward T., "The Woman in Politics," in *The Negro Politician: His Success and Failure*, Chicago: Johnson Publishing Company, 1964, 122–48.

Clement, E(llis) M(eredith), "Women at Past National Conventions," *Democratic Digest*, July 1936, 28–29.

Cleveland, Grover, "Woman's Mission and Woman's Clubs," 22:6 *Ladies' Home Journal*, May 1905, 3–4.

———, "Would Woman Suffrage be Unwise?" 22 *Ladies' Home Journal*, October 1905, 7–8.

Colorado Suffrage Centennial, 1893–1993, Denver: Colorado Committee for Women's History, 1993; 22-page pamphlet.

Conway, M. Margaret, "Women as Voluntary Political Activists: A Review of Recent Empirical Research," in Bernice Cummings and Victoria Schuck, eds., *Women Organizing: An Anthology*, Metuchen, N.J.: Scarecrow Press, 1979, 298–303.

Cook, Blanche Wiesen, *Eleanor Roosevelt, 1884–1933*, Volume 1, New York: Viking, 1992.

Cooley, Winifred H., "The Younger Suffragists," *Harper's Weekly*, Sept. 27, 1913, 7–8.

Coolidge, Mary Roberts, *What the Women of California Have Done With the Ballot*, San Francisco: California Civic League, 1916; 8-page pamphlet.

Cooper, Anna Julia, *A Voice from the South by a Black Woman of the South*, Xenia, Ohio: The Aldine Printing House, 1892.

Coryell, Janet L. *Neither Heroine nor Fool: Anna Ella Carroll of Maryland*, Kent, Ohio: Kent State University Press. 1990.

Costantini, Edmond, and Kenneth H. Craik, "Women as Politicians: The Social Background, Personality, and Political Careers of Female Party Leaders," 28:2 *Journal of Social Issues*, 1972, 217–36; reprinted in Githens and Prestage, eds., 1977, 221–40.

Costin, Lela B., *Two Sisters for Social Justice: A Biography of Grace and Edith Abbott*, Urbana: University of Illinois Press, 1983.

Cott, Nancy F., *The Grounding of Modern Feminism*, New Haven, Conn.: Yale University Press, 1987.

———, "Across the Great Divide: Women in Politics Before and After 1920," in Tilly and Gurin, 1990, 153–76. Reprinted in Wheeler, 1995, 353–73.

Cotter, Cornelius P., and Bernard C. Hennessy, *Politics Without Power: The National Party Committees*, New York: Atherton Press, 1964.

Cotter, Cornelius P., "State Party Committees," in Maisel, 1991, 1047–58.

Cox, Elizabeth M. "The Three Who Came First," 20:11 *State Legislatures*, November 1994, 12–19.

———, *Women State and Territorial Legislators, 1895–1995*, North Carolina: McFarland and Co., 1996.

———, *Women in Modern American Politics: A Bibliography, 1900–1995*, Washington, D.C.: Congressional Quarterly Press, 1997.

Craig, Elisabeth May, "Politics Bloom in the Spring—!" *Independent Woman*, May 1940, 143, 152.

Crawford, Marie Adams, "Political pioneering in California," *Independent Woman*, February 1955, 44–46, 54.

Creel, George, and Judge Ben B. Lindsey, "Measuring Up Equal Suffrage," 77 *Delineator*, February 1911, 85–86, 151–52.

Cunningham, Minnie Fisher, "A Democratic School of Politics at Washington, D.C.," 2:4 *Women's Democratic News*, August 1926, 11.

Cushman, Robert E., "Woman Suffrage on the Installment Plan," 105 *The Nation*, December 6, 1917, 633–64.

Daggett, Mabel Potter, "The New Chapter in Woman's Progress," 56 *Good Housekeeping*, February 1913, 148–55.

Daniels, Doris Groshen, *Always a Sister: The Feminism of Lillian D. Wald*, New York: The Feminist Press, 1989.

David, Paul T., Ralph M. Goldman, and Richard C. Bain, *The Politics of National Nominating Conventions*, Washington, D.C.: Brookings, 1960.

Davis, Adalyn, *The Woman's National Democratic Club: The Place Where Democrats Meet*, Washington, D.C.: Woman's National Democratic Club, 1992; 56-page pamphlet.

Davis, Allen F., *Spearheads for Reform*, New York: Oxford University Press, 1967.

Davis, Kenneth S., *Invincible Summer: An Intimate Portrait of the Roosevelts, based on the Recollections of Marion Dickerman*, New York: Atheneum, 1974.

Davis, Reda, *California Women: A Guide to Their Politics, 1885–1911*, San Francisco: California Scene, 1967.

Democratic Congressional Wives Forum (DCWF), *History of Democratic Women*, 43-page pamphlet prepared under the auspices of the Democratic National Committee, 1960.

Democratic National Committee, *Women's Political Organization*, Plan Recommended to the States by the Democratic National Committee, February 26, 1919; 12-page pamphlet. Copies in the Schlesinger Library, Cambridge, MA, and on Reel 936, #7997, *History of Women*, New Haven, Conn.: Research Publications, 1977.

Democratic National Committee and Democratic Congressional Committee, *The Democratic Text Book, 1916*, Washington, D.C., 1916.

——, "Democratic Party Real Friend of Woman's Cause," *The Democratic Text Book, 1920*, Washington, D.C., 1920, 436–50.

——, "How the Democratic Party has Organized Women," by Emily Newell Blair, *Democratic Campaign Book, 1922*, 89–91.

——, "Women in the Democratic Party," *Democratic Campaign Book—1924*, Washington, D.C., 273–80.

——, *Women's Democratic Campaign Manual*, 1924; 142-page booklet.

——, "Report of Mrs. Emily Newell Blair, Vice-Chairman, Democratic National Committee," *Official Report of the Proceedings of the Democratic National Convention, June 24 . . . July 9, 1924*, Indianapolis: Bookwalter, Ball, Greathouse Printing Co., 1924, 1093–99.

——, *The Campaign Book of the Democratic Party, Candidates and Issues in 1928*, Washington, D.C., 1928.

——, *Official Report of the Proceedings of the Democratic National Convention*, Washington, D.C., 1940.

——, Women's Division, *Democratic Women March On*, 1945; 20-page booklet.

——, *Democracy at Work, Being the Official Report of the Democratic National Convention, Philadelphia, Pennsylvania, July 12 to July 14, inclusive, 1948*, Philadelphia, Pa.: Local Democratic Political Committee of Pennsylvania, 1948.

——, *Official Report of the Proceedings of the 1960 Democratic National Convention and Committee*, Washington, D.C.: National Document Publishers, 1964.

DeWitt, Benjamin Parke, *The Progressive Movement*, New York: Macmillan, 1915; reprinted by the University of Washington Press, Seattle, 1968.

Dewson, Mary W., "Our Part In the Campaign of 1936," *Democratic Digest*, December 1936, 5.

——, "Advance of Democratic Women," 17:6 *Democratic Digest*, April 1940, 61, 90–91.

——, *An Aid to the End*, unpublished autobiography in two volumes, 1949. Copies are in FDRL and the Schlesinger Library, Cambridge, Mass.

Diamond, Irene, *Sex Roles in the State House*, New Haven: Yale University Press, 1977.

Dickinson, Agnes Bryant, "Judge Allen's Glorious Defeat," *The Woman Citizen*, October 1926, 10–11, 39ff.

DeFiore, Jayne Crumpler, "COME, and Bring the Ladies: Tennessee Women and the Politics of Opportunity during the Presidential Campaigns of 1840 and 1844," 51 *Tennessee Historical Quarterly*, Winter 1992, 197–212.

Dinkin, Robert J., *Before Equal Suffrage: Women in Partisan Politics from Colonial Times to 1920*, Westport, Conn.: Greenwood Press, 1995.

Dobyns, Winifred Starr, "The Lady and the Tiger, Or, the Woman Voter and the Political Machine," *The Woman Citizen*, January 1927, 20–21, 44–45.

Doderer, Minnette, interview with Louise R. Noun, in *MORE Strong-Minded WOMEN: Iowa Feminists Tell Their Stories*, Ames: Iowa University Press, 1992, 158–74.

Dorr, Rheta Childe, *What Eight Million Women Want*, Boston: Small, Maynard and Co., 1910.

———, "'The Women Did it' in Colorado," 26:4 *Hampton's Magazine*, April 1911, 426–38.

———, *A Woman of Fifty*, New York: Funk & Wagnalls Co., 1924.

Dougherty, Page H., "It's a Man's Game, But Woman Is Learning," *New York Times Magazine*, Nov. 3, 1946, VI:17, 54, 56.

Dreier, Mary E., *Margaret Dreier Robins, Her Life, Letters and Work*, New York: Island Press Cooperative, 1950.

Drexel, Constance, "Have Women Failed As Citizens?" 71 *Collier's*, May 13, 1923.

DuBois, Ellen Carol, *Feminism and Suffrage: Emergence of an Independent Women's Movement in America, 1848–1869*, Ithaca: Cornell University Press, 1978.

———, ed. with commentary, *Elizabeth Cady Stanton, Susan B. Anthony, Correspondence, Writings, Speeches*, New York: Schocken Books, 1981.

———, "Harriot Stanton Blatch and the Transformation of Class Relations Among Woman Suffragists," in Dye and Frankel, 1991, 162–80.

Dubuc, Frances Fisher, "New York's 'Big Three' Women," *The Evening Post Magazine*, March 5, 1920, 1, 7.

Ducas, Dorothy, "All for the Party," 129 *Delineator*, Oct. 1936, 10–11, 50.

Duncan-Clark, S. J., *The Progressive Movement: Its Principles and Its Programs*, Boston: Small, Maynard and Co., 1913.

Duster, Alfreda, ed., *Crusade for Justice: The Autobiography of Ida B. Wells*, Chicago, 1970.

Dye, Nancy Schrom, *As Equals and As Sisters: Feminism, the Labor Movement, and the Women's Trade Union League of New York*, Columbia: University of Missouri Press, 1980.

Dye, Nancy S., and Noralee Frankel, eds., *Gender, Class, Race and Reform in the Progressive Era*, Louisville: University Press of Kentucky, 1991.

Earhart, Mary, *Frances Willard: From Prayers to Politics*, Chicago: University of Chicago Press, 1944.

Eckert, Fred W. "The Effect of Woman Suffrage on the Political Situation in the City of Chicago," 31 *Political Science Quarterly*, March 1916, 105–21.

Edson, Mrs. Charles Farwell (Katherine Philips), "Woman Suffrage at the Biennial," 13:3 *California Outlook*, July 23, 1912, 10.

———, "Actual Operation of Woman's Suffrage in Pacific Coast Cities," 1 *National Municipal Review*, October 1912, 620.

Edwards, India, *Pulling No Punches: Memoirs of a Woman in Politics*, New York: G. P. Putnam's Sons, 1977.

Edwards, Rebecca R., *Gender in American Politics: 1880–1900*, Ph.D. Dissertation, Dept. of History, University of Virginia, 1995.

———, *Angels in the Machinery: Gender in American Party Politics from the Civil War to the Progressive Era*, New York: Oxford University Press, 1997.

———, "Gender, Class, and the Transformation of Electoral Campaigns in the Gilded Age," in Gustafson, Miller, and Perry, 1999, 13–22.

Egan, Eleanor Franklin, "Women in Politics to the Aid of Their Party," 192 *Saturday Evening Post*, May 22, 1920, 12–13, 185–86, 189–90.

Evans, Sara, *Born for Liberty: A History of Women in America*, New York: Free Press, 1989.

Fahy, Evangeline H., "A Political Challenge In a Presidential Campaign Year," 35:5 *Independent Woman*, August 1956, 8–9, 29.

Falco, Maria J., *Bigotry!: Ethnic, Machine, and Sexual Politics in a Senatorial Election*, Westport, Conn.: Greenwood Press, 1980.

Farley, James A., *Behind the Ballots: The Personal History of a Politician*, New York: Harcourt, Brace and Co., 1938.

———, "Why We'll Never Have A Woman President," *This Week Magazine*, January 18, 1959, 8–9, 36.

Faulkner, Harold V., *The Quest for Social Justice, 1898–1914*, New York: Macmillan, 1931.

Fay, James S., "The Legal Regulation of Political Parties," 9 *Journal of Legislation*, 1982, 263–81.

Felsenthal, Carol, *The Sweetheart of the Silent Majority: The Biography of Phyllis Schlafly*, Garden City, N.Y.: Doubleday, 1981.

"Female Politicians," 30 *Democratic Review*, April 1852, 355–59.

Fenzi, Jewell, "WNDC Founders Emily Newell Blair and Daisy Harriman: A Study in Contrasts," paper given at the Oral History Association, New Orleans, LA, Sept. 25, 1997.

"50–50 Takes On New Importance Now," *Democratic Digest*, March 1941, 25.

"Fifty–Fifty," *Democratic Digest*, June 1946, 12–13.

Fisher, Marguerite J., and Betty Whitehead, "Women and National Party Organization," 38 *American Political Science Review*, October, 1944, 895–903.

Fisher, Marguerite J., "Women in the Political Parties," 251 *Annals of the American Academy of Political And Social Science*, May 1947, 87–93.

Fitzpatrick, Ellen, *Endless Crusade: Women Social Scientists and Progressive Reform*, New York: Oxford University Press, 1990.

Flanagan, Maureen A., "Gender and Urban Political Reform: The City Club and the Woman's City Club of Chicago in the Progressive Era," 95:4 *American Historical Review*, October 1990, 1032–50.

———, "Anna Wilmarth Ickes: A Staunch Woman Republican," in Gustafson, Miller, and Perry, 1999, 141–50.

Flexner, Eleanor, *Century of Struggle: The Woman's Rights Movement in the United States*, Cambridge, Mass.: Belknap Press, 1959; New York: Atheneum, 1968.

Flower, Lucy, "Women in Public Life," 57 *The Outlook,* June 12, 1897, 400–4.

Foner, Philip S., *Women and the American Labor Movement: From World War I to the Present*, New York: Free Press, 1980.

Ford, Linda G., *Iron Jawed Angels: The Suffrage Militancy of the National Woman's Party, 1912–1920*, Lanham, Md.: University Press of America, 1991.

Formisano, Ronald P., "Federalists and Republicans: Parties, Yes—System, No," in Kleppner et al., 1981, 33–76.

Forthal, Sonya, *Cogwheels of Democracy: A Study of the Precinct Captain*, New York: William-Frederick Press, 1946.

Foster, J. Ellen, "Work of Republican Women," address before the 1892 Republican National Convention," June 6, 1892, in Francis Curtis, *The Republican Party: A History of its Fifty Years Experience and a Record of its Measures and Leaders, 1854–1904*, 2 vols. New York: G. P. Putnam's Sons, 1904, 251–53.

———, "Woman's Political Evolution," 165 *North American Review*, November 1897, 600–9.

Frazer, Elizabeth, "The Rising Tide of Voters," 41 *Ladies Home Journal*, August 1924, 21, 132–34.

Freedman, Estelle, "Separatism as Strategy: Female Institution Building and American Feminism, 1870–1930," 5 *Feminist Studies*, 1979, 512–52.

Freeman, Jo, *The Politics of Women's Liberation: A Case Study of an Emerging Social Movement and Its Relation to the Policy Process*, New York: Longman, 1975.

320   *References*

———, "The Political Culture of the Democratic and Republican Parties," 101:3 *Political Science Quarterly,* Fall 1986, 327–56.

———, " 'One Man, One Vote, One Woman, One Throat': Women in New York City Politics, 1890–1910," 1:3 *American Nineteenth Century History,* Autumn 2001, 101–23.

———, "Sex, Race, Religion and Partisan Realignment," paper given at the New York State Political Science Association, April 1995, New York. Abridged version in *We Get What We Vote For . . . Or Do We? The Impact of Elections on Governing,* ed. Paul Scheele, Westport, Conn.: Greenwood, 1999, 167–90.

French, Eleanor Clark, "Key Political Force—The Ladies," *New York Times Magazine,* March 11, 1956, VI:14, 32, 34.

Fuchs, Lawrence H., *The Political Behavior of American Jews,* New York: Free Press, 1956.

Furman, Bess, *Washington By-Line: The Personal History of a Newspaperwoman,* New York: Knopf, 1949.

Gable, John, *The Bull Moose Years: Theodore Roosevelt and the Progressive Party,* Port Washington, N.Y.: Kennikat Press, 1978.

Gaines, Irene M., "Colored Women's Republican Clubs," 7:1 *The Republican Woman of Illinois,* October 1929, 5.

Gallup, George W., "An Appraisal—1920 to 1956," in *Women in Politics: Their Achievements and Their Opportunities,* The Eighth Annual Barnard Forum, 1956, 3–8.

Gamm, Gerald H., *The Making of the New Deal Democrats: Voting Behavior and Realignment in Boston, 1920–1940,* Chicago: University of Chicago Press, 1989.

Gardner, C. O. *The Referendum in Chicago,* Philadelphia: University of Pennsylvania Press, 1920.

Garner, Nancy G., "The Significance of Gender in the Kansas Woman's Crusade of 1874," 20:4 *Kansas History,* Winter 1997–1998, 214–29.

Gatov, Elizabeth Rudel, *Grassroots Party Organizer to Treasurer of the United States,* oral history interview by Malca Chall in 1975–76 for the Regional Oral History Office, the Bancroft Library, University of Berkeley, California, 1978.

Gehring, Lorraine A., "Women Officeholders in Kansas, 1872–1912," 9 *Kansas Historical Quarterly,* Summer 1986, 48–57.

Gellhorn, Edna Fischel, "Ratification, Schools, and the League of Women Voters," in Mary Semple, ed., 1920, 349–61.

Gertzog, Irwin N., "Female Suffrage in New Jersey, 1790–1807," 10:2 *Women and Politics,* 1990, 47–58.

Gibbs, Margaret, *The DAR,* New York: Holt, Rinehart and Winston, 1969.

Giele, Janet Zollinger, *Social Change in the Feminine Role: A Comparison of Woman's Suffrage and Woman's Temperance 1870–1920,* Ph.D. Dissertation, Radcliffe College, 1961.

———, *Two Paths to Women's Equality: Temperance, Suffrage, and the Origins of Modern Feminism,* New York: Twayne, 1995.

Gill, Gerald R., "From Progressive Republican to Independent Progressive: The Political Career of Charlotta A. Bass," in Gordon, 1997, 157–71.

Ginzberg, Lori D., *Women and the Work of Benevolence: Morality, Politics, and Class in the 19th-Century United States,* New Haven: Yale University Press, 1990.

Githens, Marianne, and Jewell Prestage, eds., *A Portrait of Marginality: The Political Behavior of American Women,* New York: McKay, 1977.

Goldberg, Michael L., "Non-Partisan and All-Partisan: Rethinking Woman Suffrage and Party Politics in Gilded Age Kansas," 25 *Western Historical Quarterly,* Spring 1994, 21–44.

————, *An Army of Women: Gender and Politics in Gilded Age Kansas*, Baltimore and London: The Johns Hopkins University Press, 1997.

Goldman, Eric, *Rendezvous with Destiny: A History of Modern American Reform*, New York: Vintage, 1952, 1956.

Goldman, Ralph M., *The National Party Chairman and Committees: Factionalism at the Top*, Armonk, N.Y.: M.E. Sharp, Inc., 1990.

Goldschmidt, Eli, "Labor and Populism: New York City, 1891–1897," 8 *Labor History*, 1972, 520–32.

Goldstein, Joel H., *The Effects of the Adoption of Woman Suffrage: Sex Differences in Voting Behavior—Illinois, 1914–21*, New York: Praeger, 1984.

Goldmark, Josephine, *Fatigue and Efficiency*, New York: Charities Publications Industries, 1912.

————, *Impatient Crusader: Florence Kelley's Life Story*, Urbana: University of Illinois Press, 1953.

Good, Josephine L., *The History of Women in Republican National Conventions and Women in the Republican National Committee*, Washington, D.C.: Republican National Committee, April 1963; 54-page pamphlet.

Gordon, Ann D., ed., with Bettye Collier-Thomas, John H. Bracey, Arlene Voski Avakian, and Joyce Avrech Berkman, *African American Women and the Vote, 1837–1965*, Amherst: University of Massachusetts Press, 1997.

Gordon, Felice D., *After Winning: The Legacy of the New Jersey Suffragists, 1920–1947*, New Brunswick, N.J.: Rutgers University Press, 1986.

Gosnell, Harold F., *Getting Out the Vote*, Chicago: University of Chicago Press, 1927.

————, *Negro Politicians: The Rise of Negro Politics in Chicago*, Chicago: University of Chicago Press, 1935.

————, *Machine Politics: Chicago Model*, Chicago: University of Chicago Press, 1937, 1968.

————, *Democracy: The Threshold of Freedom*, New York: Ronald Press, 1948. Chapter 4 on "Women Go to the Polls," and Appendix A, Tables I and II.

Grafton, Samuel, "Women in Politics: The Coming Breakthrough," 89 *McCalls*, September 1962, 102–3, 156, 158, 160.

Graham, Jr., Frank, *Margaret Chase Smith: Woman of Courage*, New York: John Day, Co. 1964.

Graham, Sara Hunter, *Woman Suffrage and the New Democracy*, New Haven: Yale University Press, 1997.

Grimes, Alan P., *The Puritan Ethic and Woman Suffrage*, New York: Oxford University Press, 1967.

Gruberg, Martin, *Women in American Politics: An Assessment and Sourcebook*, Oshkosh, Wisc.: Academia Press, 1968.

Gullett, Gayle Ann, *Feminism, Politics, and Voluntary Groups: Organized Womanhood in California, 1886–1896*, Ph.D. Dissertation, University of California at Riverside, 1983.

Gunderson, Robert Gray, *The Log-Cabin Campaign*, Lexington: University of Kentucky Press, 1957.

Gustafson, Melanie Susan, *Partisan Women: Gender, Politics and the Progressive Party of 1912*, Ph.D. Dissertation, History, New York University, 1993.

————, "Florence Collins Porter and the Concept of the Principled Partisan Woman," 18: 1 *Frontiers*, Summer 1997, 62–79.

————, "Partisan and Nonpartisan: The Political Career of Judith Ellen Foster, 1881–1910," in Gustafson, Miller, and Perry, 1999, 1–12.

————, Kristie Miller, and Elisabeth I. Perry, eds., *We Have Come to Stay: American Women and Political Parties, 1880–1960,* Albuquerque: University of New Mexico Press, 1999.

Hale, Sarah, "How American Women Should Vote," 44 *Godey's Lady's Book,* April 1852.

Hanley, Sarah Bond, "Political Pioneering in '88," *Democratic Digest,* February 1941, 23, 30.

Harper, Ida Husted, *Life and Work of Susan B. Anthony,* 3 vols., Indianapolis: Hollenbeck Press, 1898. Reprinted by Salem: Ayer Company, 1983.

———, "What the Election Did for the Cause of Suffrage," *New York Times,* November 10, 1912, Magazine Section, V:1.

Harriman, Florence (Daisy), *From Pinafores to Politics,* New York: Henry Holt, 1923.

———, *The Reminiscences of Florence Jaffray Harriman,* oral history interviews by Allan Neving, Dean Albertson, and John D. Kennedy in April 1950; Oral History Research Office, Columbia University, New York, 1950.

Harris, Louis, "Women: A New Dimension in Politics," Chapter VII in *Is There a Republican Majority? Political Trends, 1952–1956,* New York: Harper & Brothers, 1954, 104–17.

Harrison, Cynthia, "A New Frontier for Women: The Public Policy of the Kennedy Administration," 67 *The Journal of American History,* December 1980.

———, *Prelude to Feminism: Women's Organizations, the Federal Government, and the Rise of the Women's Movement, 1942–1968,* Ph.D. Dissertation, History, Columbia University, 1982.

———, *On Account of Sex: The Politics of Women's Issues, 1945–1968,* Berkeley: University of California Press, 1988.

Hartmann, Susan M., *The Home Front and Beyond: American Women in the 1940s,* Boston: Twayne, 1982.

Harvey, Anna L., *The Legacy of Disfranchisement: Women in Electoral Politics, 1920–1932,* Ph.D. Dissertation, Dept. of Politics, Princeton University, 1995.

———, "Culture or Strategy? Women in New York State Parties, 1917–1930," in Gustafson, Miller, and Perry, 1999, 87–96.

Hastings, Philip K., "Hows and Howevers of the Woman Voter," *New York Times Magazine,* June 12, 1960, VI:14, 80–81.

Hatch, Alden, *Ambassador Extraordinary: Clare Boothe Luce,* New York: Henry Holt, 1955.

Hays, Will H., *The Memoirs of Will H. Hays,* Garden City, N.Y.: Doubleday, 1955.

Helmes, Winifred G., *Republican Women of Maryland, 1920–1980;* 39-page pamphlet, no publisher, 1983.

Hendricks, Wanda Ann, *The Politics of Race: Black Women in Illinois, 1890–1920,* Ph.D. Dissertation, Purdue University, 1990.

———, "African American Women as Political Constituents in Chicago, 1913–1915," in Gustafson, Miller, and Perry, 1999, 55–64.

Henretta, James A., W. Elliot Brownlee, David Brody, Susan Ware, *America's History,* Chicago: The Dorsey Press, 1987.

Herberg, Will, *Protestant, Catholic, Jew,* Garden City, N.Y.: Anchor, 1955.

Hert, Sally, "Women's Work for Herbert Hoover," 13 *The Woman's Journal,* November 1928, 21.

Hewitt, Nancy A., and Suzanne Lebsock, eds., *Visible Women: New Essays on American Activism,* Urbana: University of Illinois Press, 1993.

Higginbotham, Evelyn Brooks, "In Politics to Stay: Black Women Leaders and Party Politics in the 1920s," in Tilly and Gurin, 1990, 199–220.

———, "Clubwomen and Electoral Politics in the 1920s," in Gordon, 1997, 143–55.

Hine, Darlene Clark, ed., *Black Women in the United States,* 16 vols., Brooklyn, N.Y.: Carlson, 1990.

———, ed., *Black Women in America: An Historical Encyclopedia,* Brooklyn, N.Y.: Carlson, 1990.

History of Woman Suffrage, 6 vols. Unabridged republication of the original editions, 1970, New York: Source Book Press. Vol. I, 1848–1861, ed. by Elizabeth Cady Stantion, Susan B. Anthony, and Matilda Joslyn Gage, New York: Fowler & Wells, 1881, 878 pp.; Vol. II, 1861–1876, ed. by Elizabeth Cady Stanton, Susan B. Anthony, and Matilda Joslyn Gage, New York: Fowler & Wells, 1882, 952 pp.; Vol. III, 1876–1885 ed. by Elizabeth Cady Stanton, Susan B. Anthony, and Matilda Joslyn Gage, Rochester, N.Y.: Susan B. Anthony, 1886, 1013 pp.; Vol. IV, 1883–1900, ed. by Susan B. Anthony and Ida Husted Harper, Indianapolis: Hollenbeck Press, 1902, 1144 pp.; Vol. V, 1900–1920, ed. by Ida Husted Harper, NAWSA, 1922, 817 pp.; Vol. VI, 1900–1920 (Woman Suffrage in the States), ed. by Ida Husted Harper, NAWSA, 1922, 899 pp.

Hitt, Patricia, *From Precinct Worker to Assistant Secretary of the Department of Health, Education, and Welfare*, oral history interview by Miriam Stein for the Regional Oral History Office, the Bancroft Library, University of Berkeley, California, 1977.

Hoff-Wilson, Joan, ed. *Without Precedent: The Life and Career of Eleanor Roosevelt*, Bloomington: Indiana University Press, 1984.

Hofstadter, Richard, *The Age of Reform*, New York: Vintage, 1955.

Hosmer, Lucile, *A Conservative Republican in the Mainstream of Party Politics*, oral history interview by Malca Chall in 1975–76 for the Regional Oral History Office, the Bancroft Library, University of California at Berkeley, 1983.

Howard, Anne B., *The Long Campaign: A Biography of Anne Martin*, Reno: University of Nevada Press, 1985.

Howe, Louis McHenry, "Women's Ways in Politics," 62:6 *Women's Home Companion*, June 1935, 9–10.

Huckshorn, Robert J., *Party Leadership in the States*, Amherst: University of Massachusetts Press, 1976.

Irwin, Inez Haynes, *The Story of the Woman's Party*, Penobscot, Maine: Traversity, 1921, 1964.

Isaac, Paul E., *Prohibition and Politics: Turbulent Decades in Tennessee, 1885–1920*, Knoxville: University of Tennessee Press, 1965.

Jablonsky, Thomas J., *Duty, Nature and Stability: the Female Anti-Suffragists in the United States, 1894–1920*, Ph.D. Dissertation, University of California at Los Angeles, 1978; published as *The Home, Heaven, and Mother Party: Female Anti-Suffragists in the United States, 1868–1920*, Brooklyn, N.Y.: Carlson Publishing Inc., 1994.

Jaquette, Jane S., ed., *Women in Politics*, New York: Wiley, 1974.

Jennings, M. Kent, and Norman Thomas, "Men and Women in Party Elites: Social Roles and Political Resources," 12 *Midwest Journal of Political Science*, November 1968, 469–92.

Jensen, Joan M., "All Pink Sisters: The War Department and the Feminist Movement in the 1920s," in Scharf and Jensen, eds., 1983, 199–221.

———, "Disenfranchisement is a Disgrace: Women and Politics in New Mexico, 1900–1940," in Joan M. Jensen and Darlis A. Miller, *New Mexico Women: Intercultural Perspective*, Albuquerque: University of New Mexico Press, 1986.

Jensen, Joan M., and Gloria R. Lothrop, *California Women: A History*, San Francisco: Boyd & Fraser, 1987.

Johnson, Donald Bruce, and Kirk H. Porter, compilers, *National Party Platforms*, Urbana: University of Illinois Press, multiple dates.

Johnson, Dorothy, "Organized Women as Lobbyists in the 1920's," 1:1 *Capitol Studies*, 1972.

Katz, Sherry, "Socialist Women and Progressive Reform," in William Deverell and Tom Sitton, eds., *California Progressivism Revisited*, Berkeley: University of California Press, 1994, 117–43.

————, "Redefining the Political: Socialist Women, Party Politics, and Social Reform in Progressive-era California," paper given at the 1996 meeting of the American Historical Association; revised as "Redefining 'The Political': Socialist Women and Party Politics in California, 1900–1920," in Gustafson, Miller, and Perry, 1999, 23–32.

Kelley, Florence, "The New Woman's Party," 65 *Survey*, March 5, 1921, 827–28.

Kellor, Frances A., "Women in the Campaign," 6 *Yale Review*, January 1917, 233–43.

Kenneally, James J., "Catholics and Woman Suffrage in Massachusetts," 53 *Catholic Historical Review*, April 1967, 43–57.

Kent, Frank, "How the Machine Handles the Woman Vote" and "Effect of Women on Machine Strength," Chapters 26 and 27 in *The Great Game of Politics*, New York: Doubleday, 1923.

Kerr, Barbara Wendell, "Don't Kid the Women," *Woman's Home Companion*, October 1956, 4, 6.

Key, Jr., V. O., and Winston W. Crouch, *The Initiative and Referendum in California*, Berkeley: University of California Press, 1939.

Key, Jr., V.O., "A Theory of Critical Elections," 17:1 *Journal of Politics*, February 1955, 3–18.

————, "Secular Realignment and the Party System," 21:2 *Journal of Politics*, May 1959, 198–210.

————, *Politics, Parties and Pressure Groups*, New York: Crowell, 5th ed., 1964.

Keyserling, Mary, oral history interview for Women in Federal Government Project, Schlesinger Library, Cambridge, Mass., February 1–4, 1982.

Kincheloe, Joe L., Jr., "Transcending Role Restrictions: Women at Camp Meetings and Political Rallies," 40 *Tennessee Historical Quarterly*, Summer 1981.

Kirchwey, Freda, "Alice Paul Pulls the Strings," 112 *Nation*, March 2, 1921, 332–33.

Kirkpatrick, Jeane J., *Political Woman*, New York: Basic Books, 1974.

Kleppner, Paul, *The Third Electoral System, 1853–1892*, Chapel Hill: University of North Carolina Press, 1979.

————, "Partisanship and Ethnoreligious Conflict: The Third Electoral System, 1853–1892," in Kleppner et al., 1981, 113–46.

————, "Were Women to Blame? Female Suffrage and Voter Turnout," 12 *Journal of Interdisciplinary History*, Spring 1982, 621–43.

————, *Continuity and Change in Electoral Politics, 1893–1928*, New York: Greenwood, 1987.

Kleppner, Paul et al., *The Evolution of American Electoral Systems*, Westport, Conn.: Greenwood Press, 1981.

Knoles, George Harmon, *The Presidential Campaign and Election of 1892*, Stanford: Stanford University Press, 1942.

Koven, Seth, and Sonya Michel, eds., *Mothers of a New World: Maternalist Politics and the Origins of Welfare States*, New York: Routledge, 1993.

Kraditor, Aileen S., *The Ideas of the Woman Suffrage Movement, 1890–1920*, New York: Columbia University Press, 1965.

Kriebel, Robert C., *Where the Saints Have Trod: The Life of Helen Gougar*, West Lafayette, Ind.: Purdue University Press, 1985.

Kyvig, David, E., "Women Against Prohibition," 28 *American Quarterly*, Fall 1976, 465–82.

————, *Repealing National Prohibition*, Chicago: University of Chicago Press, 1979.

"Ladies at Roslyn," *Time*, July 18, 1932, 8–9.

Ladd, Everett Carll, and Charles D. Hadley, *Transformations of the American Party System*, 2nd ed., New York: Norton, 1978.

Lamson, Peggy, *Few Are Chosen: American Women in Political Life Today*, Boston: Houghton Mifflin, 1968.

Lane, Ann J., *Mary Ritter Beard: A Sourcebook*, New York: Schocken Books, 1977.

Lansing, Marjorie, "The American Woman: Voter and Activist" in Jaquette, 1974, 5–24.

Lape, Esther Everett, "Women's Vote Revolt—How They Turned the Tide against Machine in Pennsylvania and Brought Victory to Pinchot," *New York Times*, May 28, 1922, VII:2:6.

Lash, Joseph P., *Eleanor and Franklin: The Story of Their Relationship Based on Eleanor Roosevelt's Private Papers*, New York: W.W. Norton, 1971.

——, *Eleanor: The Years Alone*, New York: W.W. Norton, 1972.

League of Women Voters, Committee on the Legal Status of Women, "The Legal and Political Status of Women in the United States: A Summary of the Outstanding Facts in the Present Situation," Washington, D.C.: LWV, 1927; 15-page pamphlet.

League of Women Voters papers, 1918–1974, microfilm, University Publications of America.

Lebsock, Suzanne, "Women and American Politics, 1880–1920," in Tilly and Gurin, eds., 1990, 35–62.

——, "Woman Suffrage and White Supremacy: A Virginia Case Study," in Hewitt and Lebsock, 1993, 62–100.

Lee, Susan Earls Dye, *Evangelical Domesticity: The Origins of the Woman's National Christian Temperance Union Under Frances E. Willard*, Ph.D. Dissertation, Northwestern University, 1980.

"Legislative Victory at Both Political Conventions," 35 *Independent Woman*, October 1956, 7, 28.

Lehrer, Susan, *Origins of Protective Labor Legislation for Women: 1905–1925*, Albany: SUNY Press, 1987.

Leighton, Frances Spatz, "Women could get anywhere in politics—if they had more guts," *THIS WEEK Magazine*, December 1, 1968, 4–5.

Lemons, J. Stanley, *The Woman Citizen: Social Feminism in the 1920s*, Urbana: University of Illinois Press, 1973.

Lerner, Gerda, "The Political Activities of Antislavery Women," in *The Majority Finds Its Past: Placing Women in History*, New York: Oxford University Press, 1979.

Lewis, Lawrence, "How Woman Suffrage Works in Colorado," 82:4 *Outlook,* January 1906, 167–78.

LeVan, Wilma Sinclair, "Republican Women of Ohio Organize," 5:7 *The Republican Woman* (of Pennsylvania), January 1928, 4, 10.

Lichtman, Allan J., *Prejudice and the Old Politics: The Presidential Election of 1928*, Chapel Hill: University of North Carolina Press, 1979.

Lippincott, Mrs. A. Haines, "Independence Within the Party," 2:1 *The Republican Woman* (of Pennsylvania), March 1924, 6.

Lippman, Walter, "Lady Politicians: How the Old-Fashioned Illusion That Women Would Redeem Politics Has Been Destroyed," 29 *Vanity Fair*, January 1928, 43, 104.

Livermore, Henrietta W., "The Election of Women on State Committees," 3:2 *The Woman Republican*, February 7, 1925, 2.

——, "Women's Place in Political Parties," 5:5 *Republican Woman* (of Illinois), December 1927, 4–5.

——, "New York State Republican Women 1919–1929: Ten Years of Education in Citizenship," 7:11 *The Woman Republican*, December 1929, 3, 9.

Lockwood, Belva A., "Women in Politics," 2 *American Journal of Politics*, April 1893, 385–87.

Logan, Adella Hunt, "Woman Suffrage," 9 *Colored American Magazine*, September 9, 1905, 487–89.

———, "Colored Women as Voters," 4 *The Crisis*, September 1912, 242–43.

Louchheim, Katie, *By the Political Sea*, Garden City, N.Y.: Doubleday, 1970.

Lovell, S.D., *The Presidential Election of 1916*, Carbondale, Ill.: Southern Illinois University Press, 1980.

Lubell, Samuel, *The Future of American Politics*, Garden City, N.Y.: Doubleday Anchor, 1951, 1952, 1956.

Lunardini, Christine A., and T.J. Knock, "Woodrow Wilson and Woman Suffrage: A New Look," 95 *Political Science Quarterly*, 1980–81.

Lunardini, Christine A., *From Equal Suffrage to Equal Rights: Alice Paul and the National Woman's Party, 1910–1928*, New York: New York University Press, 1986.

Lynn, Naomi, "American Women and the Political Process," in *Women: A Feminist Perspective*, ed. by Jo Freeman, Palo Alto, Calif: Mayfield Publishing Co., 2nd ed. 1979, 404–29.

MacAdam, George, "Getting Behind Hoover in the Kitchen: Women Should Manage Servants Rather than Go "Milling About" to Get Men's Places, Says Miss Chittenden," *New York Times Magazine*, June 17, 1917, 7.

Mackenzie, G. Calvin, *The Politics of Presidential Appointments*, New York: Free Press, 1981.

Maisel, L. Sandy, general editor, *Political Parties and Elections in the United States: An Encyclopedia*, 2 vols., New York: Garland Publishing, 1991.

Mandel, Ruth, *In The Running: The New Women Candidates*, New Haven: Ticknor and Fields, 1981.

Marilley, Suzanne M., "The Role of Temperance and Organizational Resources in the Colorado Woman Suffrage Victory of 1893." Paper given at the 1986 meeting of the American Political Science Association.

Marshall, Susan E., *Splintered Sisterhood: Gender and Class in the Campaign Against Woman Suffrage*, Madison: Wisconsin, 1997.

Marston, Doris Ricker, "Maine's Commissioner of Labor," *Independent Woman*, January 1952, 5–6.

Martin, Anne, "Feminists and Future Political Action," *The Nation*, February 18, 1925, 185–86.

Martin, George, *Madam Secretary: Frances Perkins,* Boston: Houghton Mifflin, 1976.

Massey, Mary Elizabeth, *Bonnet Brigades*, New York: 1966.

Matthews, Burnita Shelton, *Pathfinder in the Legal Aspects of Women*, oral history interview by Amelia Fry, Suffragists Oral History Project, Regional Oral History Office, the Bancroft Library, University of California at Berkeley, April 29, 1973.

Matthews, Glenna, *The Rise of Public Woman: Woman's Power and Woman's Place in the United States, 1630–1970*, New York: Oxford University Press, 1992.

———, "'There is No Sex in Citizenship': The Career of Congresswoman Florence Prag Kahn," in Gustafson, Miller and Perry, 1999, 131–40.

May, Catherine, "The Outlook for Advancement of Women," 50 *National Business Woman*, October 1969, 11–13.

Mayhew, David R., *Placing Parties in American Politics*, Princeton: Princeton University Press, 1986.

———, "Party Organization in Historical Perspective," in Maisel, 1991, 761–69.

McBride, Genevieve G., *On Wisconsin Women: Working for Their Rights from Settlement to Suffrage*, Madison: University of Wisconsin Press, 1993.

McCormick, Anne O'Hare, "Enter Women, the New Boss of Politics," *The New York Times Magazine*, October 21, 1928, 3, 23.

McCormick, Mrs. Medill (Ruth Hanna), "The Reason for Women's Republican Clubs," 1:11 *The Republican Woman* (of Pennsylvania), January 1924, 3.

———, "The Women's Roosevelt Republican Club," 6:2 *The Republican Woman* (of Pennsylvania), May 1928, 2, 10.

———, "United Effort Will Bring Recognition," 6:11 *The Republican Woman* (of Illinois), July 1928, 7.

McDonagh, Eileen L., and H. Douglass Price, "Woman Suffrage in the Progressive Era: Patterns of Opposition and Support in Referenda Voting, 1910–1918," 79:2 *American Political Science Review*, June 1985, 415–35.

McGerr, Michael *The Decline of Popular Politics: The American North, 1865–1928*, New York: Oxford University Press, 1986.

McManus, Robert Cruise, "Raskob," 231 *North American Review*, January 1931, 10–15.

Meredith, Ellis, "Equal Suffrage in Colorado," 8:10 *The New Cycle*, April 1895, 705–9.

———, "The Party Organization and the Club," *The Democratic Bulletin,* June 1933, 19, 30.

———, "Still Harping on Organization," *Democratic Digest*, July 1933, 7.

———, "Again—and Yet Again—Organize," *Democratic Digest*, May 1934, 10–11.

Meredith, Emily R., "Women in Colorado Politics," 36 *The Woman's Journal*, October 1905, 72.

Merriam, Charles E., and Harold F. Gosnell, *Non-Voting: Causes and Methods of Control*, Chicago: University of Chicago Press, 1924.

Merriam, Charles E., *Primary Elections*, Chicago: University of Chicago Press, 1908.

Mesta, Perle, with Robert Cahn, *Perle: My Story,* New York: McGraw Hill, 1960.

Michelet, Simon, *American Women at the Ballot,* Washington, D.C.: National Get-Out-The-Vote Club, 1924; 8-page pamphlet.

———, "Women at the Ballot," 4:5 *The Republican Woman*, Feb. 1927, 7, 12.

———, *Women Delegates at National Conventions,* Washington, D.C.: National Get-Out-The-Vote Club, 1928; 7-page pamphlet.

———, *Election of 1928,* Washington, D.C.: National Get-Out-The-Vote Club, 1929; 20-page pamphlet.

———, "Minnesota Women Voters in 1928," *The Minnesota Election: 1928,* Washington, D.C.: National Get-Out-The-Vote Club, 1929, 7–8.

Miller, Amanda M., "The Women's National Republican Club," 7:51 *The National Republican*, March 26, 1921, 5.

Miller, Joseph Dana, "The New Woman in Office," 132:787 *Godey's Magazine,* January 1896, 59–67.

Miller, Kristie, *Ruth Hanna McCormick: A Life in Politics, 1880–1944,* Albuquerque: University of New Mexico Press, 1992.

———, "Eager and Anxious to Work: Daisy Harriman and the Presidential Election of 1912," in Gustafson, Miller, and Perry, 1999, 65–76.

Monoson, S. Sara, "The Lady and the Tiger: Women's Electoral Activism in New York City Before Suffrage," 2:2 *Journal of Women's History*, Fall 1990, 100–35.

Monroe, Jr., William B., "Women with a Broom," *Ladies' Home Journal*, May 1946, 34, 208–10, 212.

Morgan, David, *Suffragists and Democrats: The Politics of Woman Suffrage in America*, East Lansing: Michigan State University Press, 1972.

Morgan, Georgia Cook, "India Edwards: Distaff Politician of the Truman Era," 78 *Missouri Historical Review*, April 1984, 293–310.

Morrison, Glenda E., *Women's Participation in the 1928 Presidential Campaign*, Ph.D. Dissertation, History, University of Kansas, 1978.

Moss, Rosalind U., "The 'Girls' from Syracuse: Sex Role Negotiations of Kansas Women in Politics, 1887–1890," in Susan Armitage and Elizabeth Jameson, eds., *The Women's West*, Norman: University of Oklahoma Press, 1987, 253–64.

Mott, David C., "Judith Ellen Foster," 19:2 *Annals of Iowa: A Historical Quarterly*, October 1933, 126–38.

Muncy, Robyn, *Creating a Female Dominion in American Reform, 1890–1935*, New York: Oxford University Press, 1991.

———, "Women Demand Recognition: Women Candidates in Colorado's Election of 1912," in Gustafson, Miller, and Perry, 1999, 45–54.

Munro, William B., "The Campaign in Retrospect," 18 *Yale Review*, December 1928, 246–61.

Nathan, Maud, *The Story of an Epoch-Making Movement*, New York: Doubleday, Page & Co., 1926.

National Anti-Suffrage Association, *The Case Against Woman Suffrage*, Boston: National Anti-Suffrage Association, n.d. but about 1915; 32-page pamphlet in the Political Collection, Division of Social History, Smithsonian Institution.

National Party Conventions: 1831–1996, Washington, D.C.: Congressional Quarterly, 1997.

National Party Platforms, compiled by Donald Bruce Johnson and Kirk H. Porter, Urbana: University of Illinois Press, updated every four years.

National Woman's Party Papers, 1913–1974, microfilm, University Publications of America.

National Women's Political Caucus, *Democratic Women Are Wonderful: A History of Women at Democratic National Conventions*; 36-page pamphlet prepared by Lee Novick for the NWPC, Washington, D.C.: NWPC, 1980.

National Women's Political Caucus, *Republican Women Are Wonderful: A History of Women at Republican National Conventions*, unpaginated pamphlet prepared by Rebecca K. Leet for the NWPC, Washington, D.C.: NWPC, 1980.

NAWSA (National American Woman Suffrage Association), *Victory: How Women Won It*, New York: H.W. Wilson, 1940.

Neuberger, Maurine, "Footnotes on Politics By a Lady Legislator," *New York Times Magazine*, May 27, 1951, VIII:18.

Notable American Women, 1607–1950: A Biographical Dictionary, Cambridge: Belknap Press of Harvard University Press, Vols. 1–3, 1971. *The Modern Period*, Vol IV, 1980.

Nichols, Carole, *Votes and More for Women: Suffrage and After in Connecticut*, New York: Haworth Press, 1983.

Nielsen, Kim, *The Security of the Nation: Anti-Radicalism and Gender in the Red Scare of 1918–1928*, Ph.D. Dissertation, University of Iowa, 1996.

Ogburn, W.F., and I. Gotra, "How Women Vote: A Study of an Election in Portland Oregon," 34 *Political Science Quarterly*, September 1919.

Olsen, Mancur, *The Logic of Collective Action*, Cambridge: Harvard University Press, 1969.

O'Neill, William L., "Feminism as a Radical Ideology," in *Dissent: Explorations in the History of American Radicalism*, ed. Alfred F. Young, DeKalb: Northern Illinois University Press, 1968.

O'Neill, William L., *Everyone was Brave: The Rise and Fall of Feminism in America*, Chicago: Quadrangle Books, 1969.

Ostrogorski, Moisei I., *Democracy and the Party System in the United States*, New York:

Macmillan, 1910; reprinted by New York: Arno Press, 1974.

Pardo, Thomas C., *The National Woman's Party Papers 1913–1974: A Guide to the Microfilm Edition*, Sanford: Microfilm Corporation of America, 1979.

Park, Maud Wood, *Front Door Lobby*, Boston: Beacon Press, 1960.

Paterson, Judith, *Be Somebody: A Biography of Marguerite Rawalt*, Austin, Tex.: Eakin Press, 1986.

Patterson, Samuel C., "Characteristics of Party Leaders," 16:2 *Western Political Quarterly*, June 1963, 332–52.

Paul, Alice, *The Legal Position of Women in Pennsylvania*, Ph.D. Dissertation, University of Pennsylvania, 1912.

———, *Towards Equality: A Study of the Legal Position of Women in the United States*, D.C.L. Dissertation, American University School of Law, 1928.

———, *Conversations with Alice Paul: Woman Suffrage and the ERA*, oral history interview by Amelia Fry, Suffragists Oral History Project, Regional Oral History Office, the Bancroft Library, University of California at Berkeley, November 1972, May 1973.

Paulson, Ross Evans, *Women's Suffrage and Prohibition: A Comparative Study of Equality and Social Control*, Glenview, Ill.: Scott, Foresman and Co., 1973.

Peck, Mary Gray, *Carrie Chapman Catt: A Biography*, New York: H. W. Wilson Co., 1944.

Peel, Roy V., and Thomas C. Donnelly, *The 1928 Campaign: An Analysis*, New York: Richard R. Smith, 1931.

———, *The 1932 Campaign: An Analysis*, New York: Farrar & Rinehart, 1935.

Peel, Roy V., *The Political Clubs of New York City*, New York: Putnam's Sons, 1935.

Perkins, Frances, *The Roosevelt I Knew*, New York: Viking Press, 1946.

———, *The Reminiscences of Frances Perkins*, interviews by Dean Albertson, between 1951 and 1953; Oral History Research Office, Columbia University, New York, 1955.

"Permanent Republican Clubs," 146 *North American Review*, March 1888, 241–65, is a series of letters from Republicans in different states.

Perry, Elisabeth Israels, "Training for Public Life: ER and Women's Political Networks in the 1920s," in Hoff-Wilson, 1984, 28–45.

———, *Belle Moskowitz: Feminine Politics and the Exercise of Power in the Age of Alfred E. Smith*, New York: Oxford University Press, 1987.

———, "Women's Political Choices After Suffrage: The Women's City Club of New York, 1915–1990," 62:4 *New York History*, October 1990, 417–34.

———, "Defying the Party Whip: Mary Garrett Hay and the Republican Party, 1917–1920" in Gustafson, Miller, and Perry, 1999, 97–108.

Pickens, William, "The Woman Voter Hits the Color Line," 3 *Nation*, October 6, 1920, 372–73.

Pinchot, Gifford, "The Influence of Women in Politics," *Ladies Home Journal*, September 1922, 12, 116.

Poling, James, "Washington's 'Queen-Maker,'" *Herald-Tribune Magazine*, April 27, 1952, 15, 36.

"Politics and the Woman," *The Woman Citizen*, December 28, 1918, 628.

Pollitzer, Anita, "Her Honor—The Judge," 30:1 *Independent Woman*, January 1951, 11–12, 31.

Polsby, Nelson W., and Aaron Wildavsky, *Presidential Elections*, New York: Scribner's Sons, 6th ed. 1984.

Pomper, Gerald M., *Elections in America: Control and Influence in Democratic Politics*, New York: Dodd, Mead, 1971.

Poole, Keith T., and L. Harmon Ziegler, *Women, Public Opinion and Politics: The Changing*

Political Attitudes of American Women, New York: Longman, 1985.

Porter, Mary Cornelia, and Ann B. Matasar, "The Role and Status of Women in the Daley Organization," in Jaquette 1974, 85–108.

Pratt, Ruth, "The Lady or the Tiger," 45 *Ladies' Home Journal*, May 1928, 8, 119.

Priest, Ivy Baker, "The Ladies Elected Ike," 76:350 *American Mercury*, February 1953, 23–28.

———, *Green Grows Ivy*, New York: McGraw-Hill, 1958.

Ranney, Austin, *Curing the Mischiefs of Faction: Party Reform in America*, Berkeley: University of California Press, 1975.

Raftery, Judith, "Los Angeles Clubwomen and Progressive Reform," in William Deverell and Tom Sitton, eds., *California Progressivism Revisited*, Berkeley: University of California Press, 1994, 144–74.

Rawalt, Marguerite, compiler, *A History of the National Federation of Business and Professional Women's Clubs, Inc.*, Vol. II, 1944–1960, Washington, D.C.: NFBPW, 1969.

Rawalt, Marguerite, *The Reminiscences of Marguerite Rawalt*, oral history interview by Harry Secord between 1978 and 1980; Oral History Research Office, Columbia University, New York, 1980.

———, "The Equal Rights Amendment," in Irene Tinker, ed., *Women in Washington*, Beverly Hills: Sage, 1983, 49–78.

Ray, P. Orman, *An Introduction to Political Parties and Practical Politics*, New York: Scribner's Sons, 1913, 1917, 1924.

Reichley, A. James, *Religion in American Public Life*, Washington, D.C.: Brookings Institution, 1985.

———, *The Life of the Parties: A History of American Political Parties*, New York: Free Press, 1992.

Remington, Pauline E., *Politics and Tea: Being a Brief History of the Activities of the Minneapolis Republican Women's Club since its Organization in May, 1920*, Minneapolis: Colwell Press, 1920.

Report of the Republican Women's National Executive Committee Acting with the Republican National Committee, from September 3, 1918 to June 8, 1920; 11-page pamphlet; copies are in the Hay scrapbook, NYPL; Reel 54:978–83, Harding Papers; and Reel 15:609–14, WTUL-MDR Papers.

Republican National Committee, *Campaign Text Book—1916*, Washington, D.C.: Republican National Committee, 1916.

———, "Women and the Republican Party," Chapter XIX of the *Republican Campaign Text-Book, 1924*, Washington, D.C.: Republican National Committee, 1924, 295–97.

———, *Official Report of the Proceedings of the 18th Republican National Convention held in Cleveland, Ohio, June 10, 11, & 12, 1924*, New York: Tenny Press, 1924.

———, "The American Home: Record of the Republican Party in Behalf of Childhood, Womanhood and the Home," Chapter XV of the *Republican Campaign Text-Book, 1928*, Washington, D.C.: Republican National Committee, 1928.

———, *Official Report of the Proceedings of the 23th Republican National Convention held in Chicago, Illinois, June 26, 27, & 28, 1944*, Washington, D.C.: Judd & Detweiler, 1944.

———, *Official Report of the Proceedings of the 25th Republican National Convention held in Chicago, Illinois, July 7, 8, 9, 10, & 11, 1952*, Washington, D.C.: Judd & Detweiler, 1952.

———, Women's Division, *Women in Public Service*, Washington, D.C., various dates.

Republican Party Papers, Part I: Meetings of the Republican National Committee, 1911–1980, Series A, 1911–1960, University Publications of America.

Republican Woman's Federation of California, Southern Division, *Our Government: Ten Units of Study for Republican Study Clubs*, Los Angeles, Calif.: Gem Publishing Co., 1926; 31-page pamphlet.

Reynolds, John F., *Testing Democracy: Electoral Behavior and Progressive Reform in New Jersey, 1880–1920*, Chapel Hill: University of North Carolina Press, 1988.

Reynolds, Minnie J., "The Recollections of a Woman Campaigner," 74 *Delineator*, October 1909, 250–51, 299.

Rice, Stuart D., and Malcolm M. Willey, "A Sex Cleavage in the Presidential Election of 1920," 19:148 *Journal of the American Statistical Association*, December 1924, 519–20.

Rice, Stuart D., *Quantitative Methods in Politics*, New York: Russell & Russell, 1928, 1969.

Richardson, Anna Steese, "Women At Two Conventions," *New York Times*, July 11, 1920, VII:2:6.

———, "Is the Woman's Club Dying?" 159 *Harper's Magazine*, October, 1929, 605–12.

Riordan, William L., *Plunkitt of Tammany Hall: A Series of Very Plain Talks on Very Practical Politics*, New York: Dutton, 1963.

Robb, Janet Henderson, "The Primrose Dame," in *The Primrose League 1883–1906*, New York: Columbia University Press, 1942, 106–37.

Robinson, Claude E., *Straw Votes: A Study of Political Prediction*, New York: Columbia University Press, 1932.

Robinson, Edward S., "Trends of the Voter's Mind," 4 *Journal of Social Psychology*, August 1933, 265–84.

Roosevelt, Eleanor, "Women Must Learn to Play the Game as Men Do," *Redbook*, April 1928, 78–79, 141–42.

———, *It's Up to the Women*, New York: Frederick A. Stokes, 1933.

———, *This Is My Story*, New York: Harper & Bros., 1937.

Roosevelt, Eleanor, and Lorena A. Hickok, *Ladies of Courage*, New York: G.P. Putnam's Sons, 1954.

Roosevelt, Eleanor, papers, 1933–1945, microfilm, University Publications of America.

Roosevelt, Theodore, "Machine Politics in New York City," 33 *The Century Magazine*, November 1886, 74–82.

———, "Women and the New York Constitutional Convention," 107:14 *Outlook*, August 1, 1914, 796–98.

Root, Grace, *Women and Repeal: The Story of the Women's Organization for National Prohibition Reform*, Authorized by Mrs. Charles H. Sabin, New York: Harper and Brothers, 1934.

Rose, Kenneth D., *American Women and the Repeal of Prohibition*, New York: New York University Press, 1996.

Ross, John Gordon, "Ladies in Politics: The Gentle Experiment," 96 *The Forum*, November 1936, 209–15.

Ross, Nellie Tayloe, "Why a Woman 'Dry' Supports Governor Smith," 13 *The Woman's Journal*, September 1928, 18.

———, "Women and the Democratic National Convention," *Democratic Bulletin*, July 1932, 18–19, 48–49.

———, "Woman Power of the Democratic Party," *Democratic Bulletin*, March 1931, 10.

———, "Democratic Women's Work Valuable," *Democratic Bulletin*, June 1932, 12–13.

———, "Advance of Democratic Women," 17:5 *Democratic Digest*, May 1940, 13, 37.

Roydhouse, Marion W., *The "Universal Sisterhood of Women": Women and Labor Reform in North Carolina, 1900–1932*, Ph.D. Dissertation, History, Duke University, 1980.

Rule, Wilma, "Women's Underrepresentation and Electoral Systems," 27:4 *P.S.: Political Science and Politics*, December 1994, 689–92.

Runyon, Alfred Damon, "The Woman Boss of Denver," 52:2 *Harper's Weekly*, December 26, 1908, 8–9, 28.

Russell, Charles Edward, "Is Woman-Suffrage a Failure?," 107 *Century*, March 1924, 724–30.

Rupp, Leila, "The Survival of American Feminism: The Women's Movement in the Post War Period," in *Reshaping America: Society and Institutions, 1945–1960*, in Robert H. Bremner and Gary W. Reichard, Columbus: Ohio State University Press, 1982, 33–65.

Rupp, Leila, and Verta Taylor, *Survival in the Doldrums: The American Women's Rights Movement, 1945 to the 1960s*, New York: Oxford University Press, 1987.

Ryan, Daniel J., "Clubs in Politics," 146 *North American Review*, February 1888, 172–77.

Ryan, Mary P., *Women in Public: Between Banners and Ballots, 1825–1880*, Baltimore: Johns Hopkins University Press, 1990.

Rymph, Catherine Elaine, *Forward and Right: The Shaping of Republican Women's Activism, 1920–1967*, Ph.D. Dissertation, History, University of Iowa, 1998.

Sabin, Pauline Morton, "I Change My Mind on Prohibition," 149:7 *The Outlook*, June 13, 1928, 254, 272.

Salas, Elizabeth, "Soledad Chavez Chacon, Adelina Otero-Warren, and Concha Ortiz Y Pino: Three Hispana Politicans in New Mexico Politics, 1920–1940," in Gustafson, Miller, and Perry, 1999, 151–60.

Salisbury, Robert H., "The Urban Party Organization Member," 29 *Public Opinion Quarterly*, Winter 1965–66, 550–64.

Saloma III, John S., and Frederick H. Sontag, *Parties: The Real Opportunity for Effective Citizen Politics*, New York: Vintage Books, 1972, 1973.

Salter, J. T., *Boss Rule: Portraits in City Politics*, New York: Whittlesey House, 1935.

Samuels, Gertrude, "Really a Man's World—Politics," *New York Times Magazine*, October 15, 1950, VI:17, 51–53.

Sanbonmatsu, Kira Leigh, *The Politics of Women's Place: Gender Roles, Public Opinion, and the American Party System*, Ph.D. Dissertation, Political Science, Harvard University, 1998.

Sanders, Marion K., *The Lady and the Vote*, Cambridge: Houghton Mifflin, 1956.

———, "Issues Girls, Club Ladies, Camp Followers," *New York Times Magazine*, December 1, 1963, 38, 63, 65–66.

Savage, Sean J., *Roosevelt: The Party Leader, 1932–1945*, Lexington: University Press of Kentucky, 1991.

Scharf, Lois, *To Work and To Wed: Female Employment, Feminism and the Great Depression*, Westport, Conn.: Greenwood, 1980.

Scharf, Lois, and Joan M. Jensen, eds., *Decades of Discontent: The Women's Movement, 1920–1940*, Westport, Conn.: Greenwood Press, 1983.

Scharff, Virginia, "Feminism, Femininity, and Power: Nellie Tayloe Ross and the Woman Politician's Dilemma," 15:3 *Frontiers*, 1995, 87–106.

Schlesinger, Jr., Arthur M., *The Politics of Upheaval*, Volume III of *The Age of Roosevelt*, Boston: Houghton Mifflin, 1960.

———, general editor, *History of American Presidential Elections 1789–1968*, New York: Chelsea House, 1971, four vols.

———, general editor, *History of U.S. Political Parties*, New York: Chelsea House, 1973, four vols.

Schuler, Loring A., editorial on "Ten Years of Suffrage," *Ladies' Home Journal*, August 1930, 22.

Scobie, Ingrid Winther, *Center Stage: the Life of Helen Gahagan Douglas*, New York: Oxford University Press, 1992.

Scott, Anne Firor, *The Southern Lady: From Pedestal to Politics 1830–1930*, Chicago: University of Chicago Press, 1970.

———, *Natural Allies: Women's Associations in American History*, Chicago: University of Illinois Press, 1991.

Scott, Mary Semple, ed., "History of Woman Suffrage in Missouri," 14 *Missouri Historical Review*, 1920, 281–384.

Sealander, Judith, *As Minority Becomes Majority: Federal Reaction to the Phenomenon of Women in the Work Force, 1920–1963*, Westport, Conn.: Greenwood Press, 1983.

Segal, Phyllis N., "Women and Political Parties: The Legal Dimension of Discrimination," unpublished paper inserted into 117 *Congressional Record*, April 6, 1971, 9896–7, by Rep. Martha Griffiths (D. Mich.).

Selden, Charles A., "The Most Powerful Lobby in Washington," 39 *Ladies Home Journal*, April 1922, 5, 93, 95–96.

———, "Four Years of the Nineteenth Amendment," 41 *Ladies Home Journal*, June 1924, 27, 138, 140.

Shaffer, Helen B., "Women in Politics," 1:7 *Editorial Research Reports*, Washington, D.C.: CQ Press, February 20, 1956, 119–36.

Shalett, Sidney, "Is There a 'Women's Vote'?" 233 *Saturday Evening Post*, Sept. 17, 1960, 31, 78–80.

Shaw, Barton, *The Wool-Hat Boys: Georgia's Populist Party*, Baton Rouge: Louisiana State University Press, 1984.

Shelton, Isabelle, "Spotlight Pinpoints the Woman Voter, Though '56 Campaign Is Still Off Stage," Women's World column, *The Sunday Star*, May 15, 1955, D-1.

Sherman, Janann M., *Margaret Chase Smith: The Making of a Senator*, Ph.D. Dissertation, History, Rutgers—The State University, 1993.

Shirpser, Clara, *One Woman's Role in Democratic Party Politics: National, State, and Local, 1950–1973*, oral history interviews by Malca Chall for the Regional Oral History Office between May 11, 1972, and July 31, 1973, the Bancroft Library, University of California at Berkeley, 2 vols., 1975.

Showalter, Elaine, ed., *These Modern Women: Autobiographical Essays from the Twenties*, New York: The Feminist Press, 1978.

Sims, Anastatia, *The Power of Femininity in the New South: Women's Organizations and Politics in North Carolina, 1880–1930*, Columbia: University of South Carolina Press, 1997.

Sisson, Daniel, *The American Revolution of 1800*, New York: Knopf, 1974.

Sklar, Kathryn Kish, "Historical Foundations of Women's Power in the Creation of the American Welfare State, 1830–1930," in Koven and Michel, 1993.

———, *Florence Kelley and the Nation's Work: The Rise of Women's Political Culture, 1830–1900*, New Haven: Yale University Press, 1995.

Skocpol, Theda, *Protecting Soldiers and Mothers: The Political Origins of Social Policy in the United States*, Cambridge: Harvard University Press, 1992.

Slocum, Mary G., "Women in Colorado Under the Suffrage: Another Point of View," *Outlook*, Dec. 26, 1903, 997–1000.

Smith, Alfred E., "On the Way to Repeal," *New Outlook*, August 1933, 10–11.

Smith, Ethel M., *Toward Equal Rights for Men and Women*, Washington, D.C.: Committee on the Legal Status of Women, National League of Women Voters, May 1929.

Smith, Helena Huntington, "Weighing the Women's Vote," 151 *Outlook and Independent*, January 23, 1929, 126–28.

Smith, Margaret Chase, "No Place for a Woman?," 68 *Ladies Home Journal*, February 1952, 50, 83.

Smith, Mary Louise, interview with Louise R. Noun, in *MORE Strong-Minded WOMEN: Iowa Feminists Tell Their Stories*, Ames: Iowa University Press, 1992, 146–57.

Smith, Wallace, "The Birth of Petticoat Government," 10 *American History Illustrated*, May 1984, 50–55.

Snapp, Meredith A., "DEFEAT THE DEMOCRATS: The Congressional Union for Woman Suffrage in Arizona, 1914 and 1916," 14 *Journal of the West*, October 4, 1975, 131–39.

Snyder, Elizabeth, *California's First Woman State Party Chairman*, oral history interview by Malca Chall for the Regional Oral History Office, the Bancroft Library, University of California at Berkeley, 1977.

Stanton, Elizabeth Cady, and Susan B. Anthony, *Correspondence, Writings, Speeches*, edited by Ellen Carol DuBois, New York: Schocken, 1981.

St. George, Katherine, oral history interview by Fern S. Ingersoll, May 10, 1979, Library of Congress, Washington, D.C.

Stevens, Doris, *Jailed for Freedom*, New York: Schocken Books, 1920; reprinted 1976.

Stewart, Sallie W., "Growth Among Negro Women: Eliminating Departments Permits Club Women to Grow in Value and Power," 1:2 *The Women's Voice*, June 1939, 2–3, 20–21.

Story, Douglas, "The Woman in Politics," 29:2 *The Mumsey*, May 1903, 256–63.

Sumner, Helen L., *Equal Suffrage: The Results of an Investigation in Colorado Made for the Collegiate Equal Suffrage League of New York State*, New York: Harper and Brothers, 1909. Reprinted New York: Arno Press, 1972.

Sundquist, James, *Dynamics of the Party System: Alignment and Realignment of Political Parties in the United States*, Washington, D.C.: Brookings, 1983.

Talmadge, John E., *Rebecca Latimer Felton: Nine Stormy Decades*, Athens: University of Georgia Press, 1960.

Tarbell, Ida M. "Is Woman's Suffrage a Failure?" 79 *Good Housekeeping*, October 1924, 18–19, 237–39.

Taylor, Edward, "Speech in the House of Representatives," *Congressional Record Appendix*, April 24, 1912, 62nd Congress, 2nd Session, Vol. XLVIII, Pt. 12, 509–11.

Taylor, Graham, "Women's Voting Significantly Tested in Illinois," 32 *Survey*, April 18, 1914, 69–70.

Terborg-Penn, Rosalyn Marian, *Afro-Americans in the Struggle for Woman Suffrage*, Ph.D. Dissertation, Howard University, 1978.

———, "Discontented Black Feminists: Prelude and Postscript to the Passage of the Nineteenth Amendment," in Scharf and Jensen, 1983, 261–78.

———, "African American Women and the Woman Suffrage Movement," in Wheeler, 1995, 135–55.

———, *African American Women in the Struggle for the Vote, 1850–1920*, Bloomington: Indiana University Press, 1998.

Terrell, Mary Church, *A Colored Woman in a White World*, Washington, D.C.: Ransdell, 1940. Reprint: Salem, N.H.: Ayer Co., 1986.

Thomas, Mary Martha, *The New Woman in Alabama: Social Reforms and Suffrage, 1890–1920*, Tuscaloosa: University of Alabama Press, 1992.

Thompson, Mildred I. *Ida B. Wells-Barnett: An Exploratory Study of An American Black Woman,*

1893–1930, Ph.D. Dissertation, George Washington University, 1979. Reprinted in Vol. 15 of *Black Women in U.S. History*, Brooklyn, N.Y., Carlson Publishing, 1990, 1–162.

Tilly, Louise A., and Patricia Gurin, eds., *Women, Politics and Change*, New York: Russell Sage, 1990.

Toombs, Elizabeth O., "Politicians Take Notice! Columbus, Ohio Women Elected a Mayor." 70 *Good Housekeeping*, March 1920.

"Towns Run by Women." *The New York Times Magazine*, October 27, 1924, VII:17:2.

Trout, Grace Wilbur, "Sidelights on Illinois Woman Suffrage History," 13:2 *Illinois State Historical Society Journal*, July 1920, 145–79.

Tyer, Pearl, "Idaho's Twenty Years of Woman Suffrage," 114 *Outlook*, September 6, 1916, 35–39.

Tyler, Pamela, *Silk Stockings and Ballot Boxes: Women and Politics in New Orleans 1920–1963*, Athens: University of Georgia Press, 1996.

United States Bureau of the Census, *Education of the American Population*, by John K. Folger and Charles B. Nam, Washington, D.C.: Government Printing Office, 1967.

———, *Historical Statistics of the United States: Colonial Times to 1970*, Washington, D.C.: Government Printing Office, 1975.

Upton, Harriet Taylor, "Women as Citizens, An Interview." *The Woman Citizen*, May 31, 1924, 18–19.

———, *Random Recollections*, unpublished memoir presented to the Martha Kinney Cooper Ohioana Library Association by the Committee for Preservation of Ohio Woman Suffrage Records, n.d. (1926).

"Utah's Woman Alternate," 31 *The Woman's Journal*, June 30, 1900, 201.

Vaile, Anna Wolcott, and Ellis Meredith, "Woman's Contribution," Chapter XXI to *History of Colorado*, by Leroy Hafen and James H. Baker, Vol. 3, Denver: Lewis Historical, 1927, 1075–147.

VandeCreek, Drew E., "Unseen Influence: Lucretia Blankenburg and the Rise of Philadelphia Reform Politics in 1911," in Gustafson, Miller, and Perry, 1999, 33–44.

Varon, Elizabeth R., "Tippecanoe and the Ladies, Too: White Women and Party Politics in Antebellum Virginia," 82 *The Journal of American History*, September 1995, 494–521.

———, *We Mean to be Counted: White Women and Politics in Antebellum Virginia*, Chapel Hill: University of North Carolina Press, 1998.

Vernon, Mabel, *Speaker for Suffrage and Petitioner for Peace*, oral history interview by Amelia Fry, Suffragists Oral History Project, Regional Oral History Office, the Bancroft Library, University of California at Berkeley, November 1972, May 1973.

Villard, Oswald Garrison, "Women in the Municipal Campaign," 33 *The Woman's Journal*, March 8, 1902, 78–79.

———, "What the Blue Menace Means," 157 *Harper's Magazine*, October 1928, 529–40.

Vose, Clement, *Constitutional Change: Amendment Politics and Supreme Court Litigation Since 1900*, Lexington, Mass.: Lexington Books, 1972.

"Votes for Women: A Symposium by Leading Thinkers of Colored America," 10 *The Crisis*, August 1915, 176–92.

Wadsworth, James W., Jr., *The Reminiscences of James W. Wadsworth*, oral history interviews by Owen W. Bombard, Wendell H. Link, and Dean Albertson between 1950 and 1952; Oral History Research Office, Columbia University, 1952.

Wakefield, Dan, "Greenwich Village Challenges Tammany: Ethnic Politics and the New Reformers," *Commentary*, October 1959, 307–12.

Walsh, Justine, *The Centennial History of the General Assembly, 1916–1978*, Indianapolis: Select

Committee on the Centennial History of the Indiana General Assembly and the Indiana Historical Bureau, 1987.

Ware, Susan, *Beyond Suffrage: Women in the New Deal*, Cambridge: Harvard University Press, 1981.

———, *Holding Their Own: American Women in the 1930s*, Boston: Twayne Publishers, 1982.

———, "ER and Democratic Politics: Women in the Postsuffrage Era," in Hoff-Wilson, 1984, 46–60.

———, *Partner and I: Molly Dewson, Feminism, and the New Deal*, New Haven: Yale University Press, 1987.

———, *Modern American Women: A Documentary History*, Chicago: Dorsey Press, 1989.

———, "American Women in the 1950s: Nonpartisan Politics and Women's Politicization," in Tilly and Gurin, 1990, 281–99.

Watts, Arretta L., "Brought Society to Jungle Workers: Helen V. Boswell Organized Wives of Men Who Built Panama Canal," *Brooklyn Eagle Magazine*, Sept. 19, 1926, 11.

Weaver, Diane E., *Maryland Women and the Transformation of Politics, 1890s–1930*, Ph.D. Dissertation, University of Maryland, 1992.

Weis, Jessica, papers, microfilm, *Series 2, Women in National Politics: Part B: Republicans*, University Publications of America.

Wells, Mildred White, *Unity in Diversity: The History of the General Federation of Women's Clubs*, Washington. D.C.: GFWC, 1953.

Wendt, Lloyd, and Herman Kogan, *Bosses in Lusty Chicago: The Story of Bathhouse John and Hinky Dink*, Indiana: Bobbs-Merrill, 1943; reprinted by Indiana University Press, 1971.

Wertheimer, Barbara Mayer, *We Were There: The Story of Working Women in America*, New York: Pantheon Books, 1977.

Wesser, Robert F., *A Response to Progressivism: The Democratic Party and New York Politics, 1902–1918*, New York: NYU Press, 1986.

Whaley, Charlotte, *Nina Otero-Warren of Santa Fe*, Santa Fe: University of New Mexico Press, 1995.

What Republican Women are Doing, Brief Review of Republican Women's Activities Issued Bi-monthly by Harriet Taylor Upton, vice chairman, Republican National Executive Committee, 1920 Munsey Building, February 15, 1924; 4-page leaflet.

"What Women Do in Politics," *U.S. News and World Report*, December 12, 1958, 72–79.

"What Women Did in Gary," 68 *Ladies Home Journal*, October 1951, 51, 109–11.

Wheeler, Marjorie Spruill, *One Woman, One Vote: Rediscovering the Woman Suffrage Movement*, Troutdale, OR: NewSage Press, 1995.

Whelpley, J.D., "Female Suffrage in the United States," 44:2285 *Harper's Weekly*, Oct. 6, 1900, 949–50.

"When Lovely Woman Stoops to Politics: Her Methods Are So Up-to-date that the Male Graduate of the 'Practical' School Can Learn from Her," *New York Times Magazine*, February 21, 1904, III:1:4.

White, Deborah Gray, "The Cost of Club Work, the Price of Black Feminism," in Hewitt and Lebsock, 1993, 247–69.

White, Jean B., "Women's Place is in the Constitution: The Struggle for Equal Rights in Utah in 1895," 42 *Utah Historical Quarterly*, Fall 1974, 344–69.

White, Sue Shelton, "Women in the Democratic Party," *Democratic Bulletin*, July 1932, 39–40.

———, "Fifty–Fifty," *Democratic Bulletin*, February 1933, 20.

Whites, LeeAnn, "Rebecca Latimer Felton and the Problem of Protection in the New South," in Hewitt and Lebsock, 1993, 41–61.

Whitney, Richard Merrill, *Reds in America: the present status of the revolutionary movement in the U.S. based on documents seized by the authorities in the raid upon the convention of the Communist party at Bridgman, Mich., Aug. 22, 1922, together with descriptions of numerous connections and associations of the Communists among the Radicals, Progressives, and Pinks*, New York: Beckwith Press, 1924.

Whitney, Rosalie Loew, "Women on the State Committee," 4:12 *The Woman Republican*, December 1927, 2.

———, "Outline of the History of the Women's National Republican Club." 2:1 *The Guidon*, January 1928, 1, 4.

Wiebe, Robert H., *The Search for Order, 1877–1920*, New York: Hill and Wang, 1967.

Wiggins, Charles W., and William L. Turk, "State Party Chairmen: A Profile," *Western Political Quarterly*, June 1970, 321–32.

Williams, Brian, "Petticoats in Politics: Cincinnati Women and the 1920 Election," 35 *Cincinnati Historical Society Bulletin*, Spring 1977, 43–70.

Williams, Charl Ormond, "Advance of Democratic Women" 17:3 *Democratic Digest*, March 1940, 15, 38.

Williams, Clare B. (Assistant Chairman, RNC), *The History of the Founding and Development of the National Federation of Republican Women*, Washington, D.C.: Republican National Committee, 1962.

Williams, Katherine E. "The Alpha Suffrage Club," *The Half Century Magazine*, September 1916, 12.

Willard, Frances, *Glimpses of Fifty Years*, Chicago: H. J. Smith, 1889.

Willard, Frances, and Mary A. Livermore, eds., *Women of the Century: A Comprehensive Encyclopedia of the Lives and Achievements of American Women During the Nineteenth Century*, New York: Mast, Crowell & Kirkpatrick, 1897. Reprinted as *American Women*, Detroit: Gale, 1973.

Wilson, James Q., *The Amateur Democrat: Club Politics in Three Cities*, Chicago: University of Chicago Press, 1962, 1966.

Wilson, Margaret Woodrow, "Where Women in Politics Fail," 38 *Ladies Home Journal*, September 1921, 10, 70.

Wixson, Helen Marsh, "Equal Suffrage in Colorado," 10:4 *The Era*, October 1902, 408–16.

Wolfe, Carolyn, *Educating for Citizenship: A Career in Community Affairs and the Democratic Party, 1906–1976*, oral history interview by Miriam Feingold Stein, Regional Oral History Office, the Bancroft Library, University of California at Berkeley, 1978.

Wolfskill, George, *The Revolt of the Conservatives: A History of the American Liberty League, 1934–1940*, Boston: Houghton Mifflin, 1962.

"Woman's Hand in Maine," 66 *Literary Digest*, Sept. 25, 1920, 13–14.

"The Woman's Party and Mr. Hoover," 127:3300 *The Nation*, October 1928, 312.

"Woman Suffrage and Republican Platform," *The Woman's Journal*, June 30, 1900, 204.

"Woman Suffrage Declared a Failure," 81 *Literary Digest*, April 12, 1924, 12–13.

"Woman Suffrage in Colorado," 57 *The Outlook*, June 12, 1897, 405–6. Prepared "with the official approval of the Colorado Equal Suffrage Association and the Civic Federation of Denver."

"Women and Parties," *The Woman Citizen*, January 17, 1920, 722, 727.

"Women and Politics," *The Woman Citizen*, January 24, 1920, 752.

"Women as a Factor in the Political Campaign," *The New York Times*, September 1, 1912, part 5, p. 9.

"Women at the Republican Convention," 5:2 *The Woman Citizen*, June 12, 1920, 41.

"Women in National Politics," *Newsweek*, May 9, 1955, 30–32.

"Women in Politics" (in New York), *The Daily Picayune* of New Orleans, Nov. 2, 1880, p 6.

"Women in Politics," *The Woman's Journal*, August 6, 1888, 318.

"Women in the National Republican Convention," 35 *The Woman's Journal*, July 9, 1904, 224.

"Women to Help Run the G.O.P.," 78:1 *The Literary Digest*, July 14, 1923, 15.

Women's Committeee of the National Hughes Alliance, *Women in National Politics*, 1916; 38-page pamphlet. Unsigned, but author is probably Frances Kellor.

Women's Political Union, *Political Policy of the Women's Political Union*, New York: Women's Political Union, n.d. but about 1912; 15-page pamphlet in the Political Collections, Division of Social History, Smithsonian Institution.

Women's Trade Union League and its Principle Leaders, papers of Margaret Dreier Robins, microfilm, Research Publications, 1981.

Wood, Molly M., "Mapping a National Campaign Strategy: Partisan Women in the Presidential Election of 1916," in Gustafson, Miller, and Perry, 1999, 77–86.

Woodhouse, Chase Going, oral history interview by Betty G. Seaver, Sept. 1977 to June 1979, University of Connecticut, Center for Oral History, Storrs, Conn. Also in LoC.

Wyman, Rosalind Wiener, *"It's A Girl: Three Terms on the Los Angeles City Council, 1953–1965, Three Decades in the Democratic Party, 1948–1978,"* oral history interview by Malca Chall for the Regional Oral History Office, the Bancroft Library, University of Caifornia at Berkeley, 1977–78.

Yost, Lenna Lowe, "A Word from Republican National Headquarters" 8:7 *The Republican Woman of Illinois*, February 1931, 5.

———, "Feminine Stock-Taking in Politics," 6:1 *The Guidon*, October, 1931, 14, 19.

———, Mrs. Ellis A., "Republican Women contributing to Party Strength," *The Republican Woman* (of Pennsylvania), May 1934, 4.

Young, Louise M. *Understanding Politics: A Practical Guide for Women*, New York: Pellegrini & Cudahy, 1950.

———, *In the Public Interest: The League of Women Voters, 1920–1970*, Westport, Conn.: Greenwood Press, 1989.

Young, Nancy Beck, "'Me for Ma': Miriam Ferguson and Texas Politics in the 1920s and 1930s," in Gustafson, Miller, and Perry, 1999, 121–30.

Yount, Courtland M., "A Study of Nominating Methods, Election Machinery and Party Organization in Chicago," M.A. Thesis, Political Science, Northwestern University, 1916.

Zagarri, Rosemarie, "Gender and the First Party System," in *Federalists Reconsidered*, ed. Doron BenAtar and Barbara Oberg, Charlottesville: University Press of Virginia, 1999, 118–34.

Zelman, Patricia G., *Women, Work and National Policy: The Kennedy-Johnson Years*, Ann Arbor, Mich.: UMI Research Press, 1980.

Index

Note: Political parties are indexed by name except the Republican and Democratic Parties, because they are on too many pages.

About the Author

Jo Freeman holds a Ph.D. in political science from the University of Chicago (1973) and a J.D. from New York University School of Law (1982). She is the author of *The Politics of Women's Liberation*, winner of a prize given in 1975 by the American Political Science Association for the Best Scholarly Work on Women in Politics. SHe has edited three books: *Women: A Feminist Perspective* (1975, 1979, 1984, 1989, 1995), *Social Movements of the Sixties and Seventies* (1983), and (with Victoria Johnson) *Waves of Protest: Social Movements Since the Sixties* (1999). In addition she has published almost a hundred articles on women and politics, feminism, social movements, public policy and law, political parties, organizational theory, education, federal election law, and the national nominating conventions in *American Review of Politics, Political Science Quarterly, American Journal of Sociology Forum, Acta Sociologica, Prospects, Signs, Intellect, Pace Law Review, The Nation, Ms., Valparaiso Law Review, Trans-Action, School Review, Liberal Education, P.S.: Political Science and Politics, Law and Inequality: A Journal of Theory and Practice*, and numerous anthologies. She is on the editorial board of *Women and Politics*.